AA

THE TOURING BOOK OF

OF

BRITAIN

Published by the Automobile Association,
Fanum House, Basingstoke, Hampshire RG21 2EA

FRONT COVER *The photograph shows Castle Combe in Wiltshire, acclaimed as Britain's most beautiful village.*

BACK COVER *The photographs show:* a *The dovecot at Nymans* b *Polesden Lacey interior* c *Kit's Coty House* d *the Saxon church at Greensted* e *Skye, the Cuillins from Elgol.*

ENDPAPERS *The illustration shows part of an early 17th-century tapestry valance made in the workshops of William Sheldon.*

TITLE PAGE *The photograph shows Ross-on-Wye.*

PAGES FOUR & FIVE *(How to use this Book) The photograph shows part of a mosaic from Cirencester's Corinium Museum.*

Produced by the Publications Division of the Automobile Association
Editor **Barbara Littlewood**
Assistant Editor **Rebecca Snelling**
Art Editor **Dave Austin**
Assistant Art Editor **Bob Johnson**
Picture Research by **Sally Howard**
Editorial Contributors
    Special Features – **Dr Richard Muir**
    Gazetteer Entries – **Richard Garrett**
                Jennifer Gordon
                Jean Heselden
                Daphne Jolley
                Roger Prebble

Gazetteer information checked and touring information compiled by the Publications Research Unit of the Automobile Association

Maps produced by the Cartographic Department of the Automobile Association. Maps are based upon the Ordnance Survey Maps with the permission of the Controller of HM Stationery Office. Crown copyright reserved. The Ordnance Survey is not responsible for the accuracy of the National Grid in this production

ISBN 0 86145 202X

Filmset by Tradespools Ltd, Frome, Somerset, England
Printed and bound in the Netherlands by Royal Smeets Offset b.v., Weert.

Published by the Automobile Association
Fanum House, Basingstoke, Hampshire RG21 2EA

CHARLWOOD, SURREY

The beautifully carved angels (above) form part of the rood screen of the parish church in this charming old village set in lovely countryside on the borders of Surrey and Sussex. The screen was made in 1480 for one Richard Sanders; his initials and the letters 'IHS' (an abbreviation of the ancient Greek rendering of the name 'Jesus'), together with a crowned 'M' for the Virgin Mary, form part of the intricate design. The church itself dates back to the 11th century and also contains some interesting 13th-century wall-paintings.

Contents

London

Special Features

Motor tours (starting points)

Towns specially featured

The Gazetteer

The entries in the gazetteer cover the mainland of Britain – England, Scotland and Wales – and the offshore islands: Anglesey, the Isle of Man, the Isle of Wight, the Isles of Scilly, the Inner and Outer Hebrides, the Orkneys, the Shetlands, and several smaller islands, but not the Channel Islands or Ireland.

Places in the gazetteer are, with certain exceptions, listed alphabetically throughout. If a stately home, or other such place of interest open to the public, does not have a gazetteer entry under its own name, it will be found under the nearest town or village. Places on islands, or individual islands within a larger group, will be found under the entry for the appropriate group of islands: for example, **Lewis** and **Harris** will be found under **Outer Hebrides**; **Skye**, under **Inner Hebrides**; **Tresco** under **Isles of Scilly**. London has a special section of its own, which follows the end of the 'L' section of gazetteer. Some major towns and cities which are the subject of a special feature may be slightly out of correct alphabetical sequence, but never more than a page or two.

Each place name at the head of the entry is followed by the county name, then by a reference to the page of the atlas on which it can be found, and by its National Grid reference (see below for an explanation of the National Grid), to enable the reader to pinpoint locations accurately. A name in **bold** type in the text of the gazetteer entries indicates that the place in question has its own entry under the appropriate letter.

Motor tours

Within the gazetteer there are a number of suggested tours, each with a route map (see the legend on p. 6). A complete list is given on this page (above) and each tour is to be found on the page adjacent to the entry for the starting point of that tour. For example, the tour covering part of the Cotswolds starts at **Banbury** and will be found adjacent to **Banbury** in the gazetteer. The tour of Skye starts from **Kyle of Lochalsh**, and will therefore be found under 'K' in the

How to use this book

gazetteer. The exceptions are the tour of Dartmoor, which is under 'D', near to the entry for Dartmoor, and the tour of the Isle of Wight, which, similarly, will be found under 'I'.

Key places in the route directions for the tours have been emphasised in **bold** type, to help to make the directions easier to follow. The use of **bold** type in this instance does not necessarily mean that all these places have an entry elsewhere in the gazetteer, although they may. Route directions have been checked as carefully as possible, but road numbers sometimes change, new roads may be built and the line of existing roads altered within the lifetime of this book and the publishers cannot accept responsibility for errors.

Towns specially featured

A number of major towns (see the complete list on p. 4) are specially featured, with town plans (see the legend on p. 6). The town plans cover the town centres, but not the outskirts or the through routes. Places of interest mentioned in the text are shown on the plans, where possible, but places at some distance from the centre cannot be shown. We have made every effort to ensure that the plans are up to date, but changes may occur – for example the introduction of pedestrian precincts, one-way systems, etc, during the lifetime of this book and the publishers can accept no responsibility for errors.

Special features

Throughout the gazetteer there are a number of special features (see the complete list on the contents page). The fact that a number of places of interest are mentioned in the text of these features is not in itself an indication that there is public access to such places, and readers should check beforehand. A guide to the majority of places of interest, *Stately Homes, Museums, Castles and Gardens in Britain*, is published by the AA. Places mentioned in the Special Features are not cross-referenced to the gazetteer, but the more famous of them are likely to have an entry in any case.

Places open to the public

Places of interest, such as stately homes, castles, etc, that are open to the public, are indicated, where known, either by the letters 'OACT', meaning 'open at certain times'; or 'NT', standing for National Trust'; or 'AM', standing for Ancient Monument (i.e. one under the care of the Department of the Environment). Before a visit is made opening times should be checked in the AA's annual guide, *Stately Homes, Museums, Castles and Gardens in Britain*. Museums, zoos, wildlife parks, etc., which are, of their nature, open to the public, are not identified by any particular letters, but opening times should be checked, as above. The fact that a place is mentioned in the gazetteer should not necessarily be taken as indicating that it is open to the public. Every care has been taken to ensure accuracy, but places may open or close at short notice, and the publishers can accept no responsibility for errors.

The National Grid

This system of map reference divides the country into a series of 100km squares, each identified by two letters of the alphabet – for example, **SX**, **SY**, **NT**, **NU**, **TL**, **TM**. These large areas are shown on the maps by heavy blue lines and each square so formed contains the appropriate letters, printed in blue on the atlas pages at the end of this book. Each of these large squares is divided into 10 smaller squares of 10km, marked on the atlas by fainter blue lines and numbered 0–9 around the edges of the map. To find **Canterbury** for example, with a map reference **6 TR15**, turn to page **6** of the atlas, then find the large square (marked out by heavy blue lines) containing the letters '**TR**'. Next, look along the bottom edge of the map for the **number 1**, and along the side of the map for the **number 5**. Where these two lines cross is the bottom left-hand corner of the 10km square in which **Canterbury** will be found. The National Grid system is common to most modern atlases, of whatever scale, so that it is possible to find any place on any atlas by looking up the National Grid Number.

6　Legend to the town plans and motor tour maps

Examples of a town plan and a motor tour map are shown below. The town plans are based on aerial photography and local information. They show detail of the town centre, major places of interest, useful car parks, and pedestrian precincts or roads with restricted access. AA throughroutes are shown, wherever they cross the town centre, but the maps are not designed to be used as throughroute maps. See also the paragraph, 'Towns specially featured', on p.5. The motor tour maps take account of the most recent road information available to the AA. The main tour route is shown by a yellow road infill within a green band. Detours are also shown by a yellow line. Only roads relevant to the tour are shown on the maps. Starting points of each tour are printed in capital letters. See also the paragraph, 'Motor tours', on p.4.

TOWN PLANS

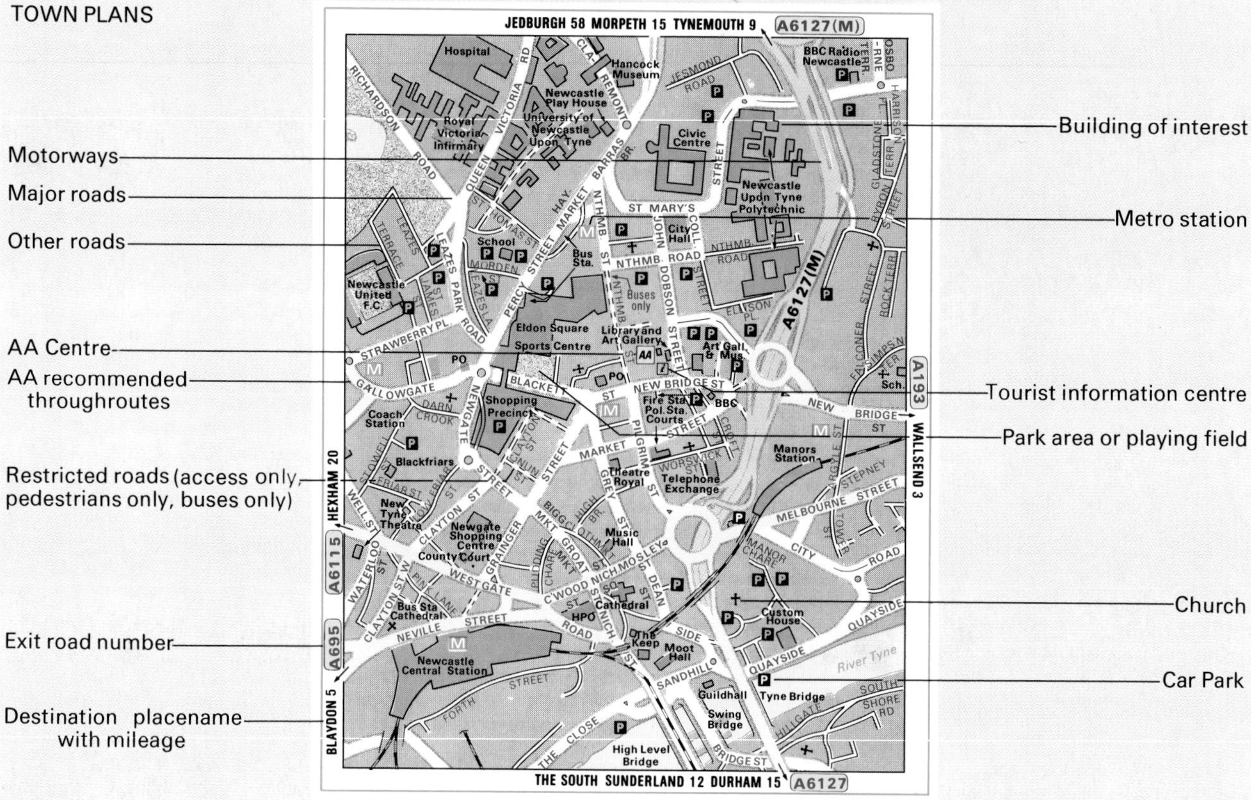

Motorways
Major roads
Other roads

AA Centre
AA recommended throughroutes

Restricted roads (access only, pedestrians only, buses only)

Exit road number

Destination placename with mileage

Building of interest
Metro station
Tourist information centre
Park area or playing field
Church
Car Park

MOTOR TOURS

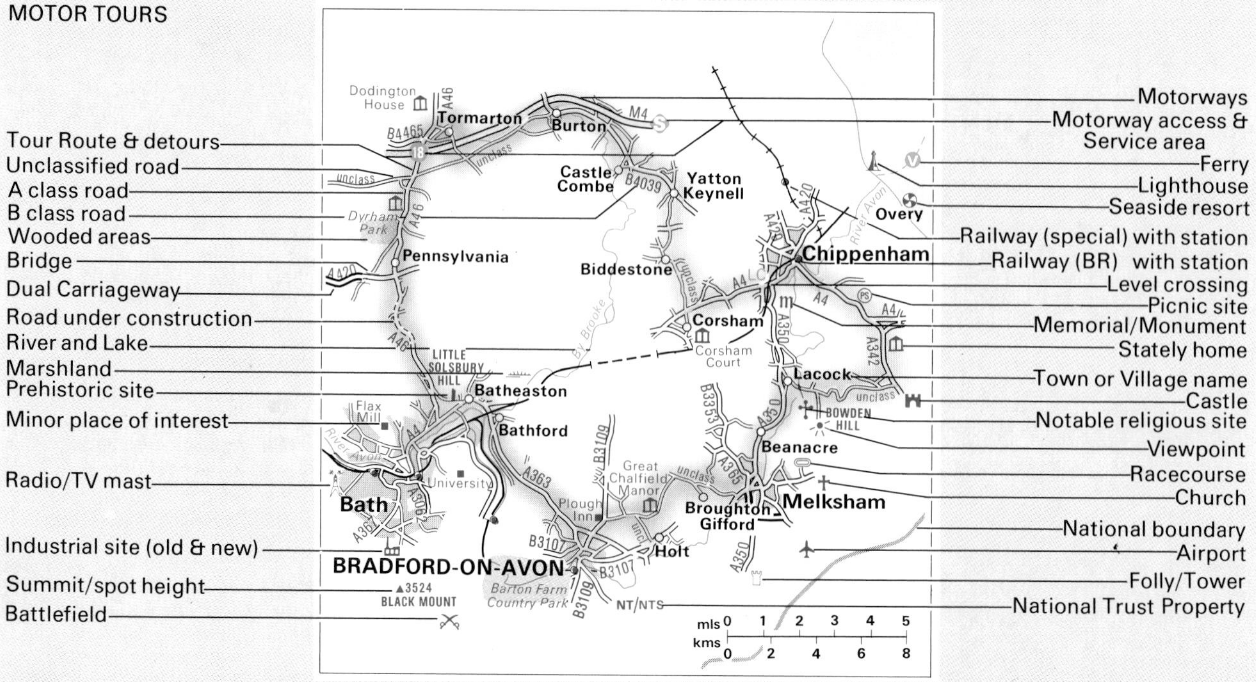

Tour Route & detours
Unclassified road
A class road
B class road
Wooded areas
Bridge
Dual Carriageway
Road under construction
River and Lake
Marshland
Prehistoric site
Minor place of interest
Radio/TV mast
Industrial site (old & new)
Summit/spot height
Battlefield

Motorways
Motorway access & Service area
Ferry
Lighthouse
Seaside resort
Railway (special) with station
Railway (BR) with station
Level crossing
Picnic site
Memorial/Monument
Stately home
Town or Village name
Castle
Notable religious site
Viewpoint
Racecourse
Church
National boundary
Airport
Folly/Tower
National Trust Property

FINE FEATHERS *make fine birds. The peacock's gorgeous plumage has made him a byword for vanity, but as an exotic ornament for formal gardens such as Abbotsbury the bird has no equal in splendour.*

ABBOT'S BROMLEY, Staffordshire
10 SK02
Abbot's Bromley is famous for the ancient Horn Dance performed there annually in September – traditionally to ensure good hunting. Hobby-horse, jester, maiden, archer, two musicians and six men wearing reindeer antlers dance for up to 12 hours. Near the church stands the school of St Mary and St Anne, a famous public school for girls founded in 1874.

A

ABBOTSBURY, Dorset   *3 SY58*
A narrow lagoon runs between Chesil Bank and the mainland, with Abbotsbury, a picturesque blend of thatched cottages and black and white houses, at its western end. Abbotsbury Gardens (OACT) specialises in subtropical plants, and the lagoon is a haven for wild birds, as well as for the famous swannery (OACT).

ABERDARON, Gwynedd   *13 SH12*
Steep lanes wind down to Aberdaron, a fishing village and resort at the tip of the Lleyn Peninsula with a fine view south over a wide bay dotted with tiny islands. Medieval pilgrims bound for the holy island of Bardsey awaited good crossing conditions in Y Gegin Fawr (The Big Kitchen), now a café.

Aberdeen, Grampian 28 NJ90

The Granite City

> *'Blyth Aberdeane thou berrial of all tounis*
> *The lamp of bewtie, bountie and blythness*
> *Unto the heaven (ascendit) thy renown is*
> *Off vertew, wisdome, and of worthines;'*
>
> WILLIAM DUNBAR, *To Aberdein*

Aberdeen received its first royal charter in the 12th century and was a thriving port by the 13th – but in 1336 much of it was burned to the ground by Edward III of England. The rebuilt areas of 'New Aberdeen' gradually merged with the remains of the old town, though the original cobbled streets and pink granite houses of the latter still exist as an easily identifiable nucleus.

The beginnings of modern Aberdeen came with the building of Union Street, opened in 1805, running broad and straight from the 17th-century Mercat Cross. Large numbers of neo-classical buildings were erected in the local, mica-flecked grey granite, and the city gradually assumed the face so often described as 'austere' – despite the many thousands of roses that bloom in its parks each year. Today it is a major commercial centre, involved in engineering, shipbuilding, papermaking and the production of granite and chemi-

cals; it is also the largest fishing port in Scotland, and has gained a new importance with the coming of the North Sea oil industry – its position and seafaring traditions making it an ideal base for the servicing of drilling rigs and production platforms. Oil has made a significant contribution to the life of the city. It is also an important university and cathedral city, however, with a wealth of fine old buildings that make its history a living part of the 20th century.

PLACES TO SEE

The Harbour has brought wealth to the city ever since the 13th century. Even today the trawling industry is important, and vast catches of fish are handled here – but in the 19th century the old docks also saw the launching of the famous clippers, the fast sailing ships that played such an important part in the expansion of trade with the Far East and Australia.

Shiprow runs up from the harbour and is possibly the oldest street in Aberdeen. It contains the 16th-century Provost Ross's House (NT), which, now restored, has been reopened and houses a Maritime Museum.

Castlegate, nearby, is the oldest part of New Aberdeen. The castle has long since disappeared, but the area has been regarded as the centre of the city for the past 600 years. The Mercat Cross (erected in 1686) is the finest burgh cross existing in Scotland today – a circular edifice of red sandstone with a pillar supporting a white unicorn.

King's College, dating back to 1494, is the old part of the university; its splendid tower is surmounted by a crown honouring James IV who aided the founding.

Marischal College was founded in 1593 as a Protestant alternative to King's College, but the two were merged into the University of Aberdeen in 1860. Attached to Marischal College is an anthropological museum with treasures from all over the world.

Provost Skene's House, a 16th-century building in Flourmill Lane, contains a folk museum on the top floor, and its chapel has interesting religious paintings on the ceiling.

James Dun's House holds a children's museum whose displays include Victorian toys and treasures from Scottish history; there are also opportunities for children to participate in various activities.

The Art Gallery, opposite James Dun's House, has paintings by Hogarth, Degas, Renoir and Augustus John. It also includes sculptures by Henry Moore and Dame Barbara Hepworth.

St Machar's Cathedral is one of three cathedrals in the city – the others being St Mary's (Roman Catholic) and St Andrew's (Episcopalian). It was founded in the 12th century but the present building dates mainly from the 15th. Partly castellated, it was fortified against attacks by the English on the seaward side and the Celtic Highlanders from the mountains.

St Nicholas' Kirk is one of the finest examples of ecclesiastical architecture in Scotland; it is also noted for having 48 bells – the largest carillon in Britain.

The Golf Links represent a bridge between the old and the new; the game has been played here since the 17th century, and the course – both literally and metaphorically – spans the distance between the city and the 'resort' on the wide beaches between the Rivers Don and Dee.

ABERDYFI, Dyfed   *7 SN69*
Shipbuilding and commercial seafaring
developed here at the mouth of the Dyfi in
the 17th century, but by the 1900s these
had died out and Aberdyfi became
fashionable as a genteel seaside resort.
Relatively unspoiled today, its attraction
lies in its pleasant sands, good golf course
and fine walks. Legend tells of an ancient
town lost beneath the sea.

ABERGAVENNY Gwent   *8 SO31*
Beyond this busy market town on the River
Usk stretches the splendour of the **Brecon
Beacons** National Park. The ruins of the
castle (AM) are thought to cover the
foundations of the Roman fort Gobannium,
and its grounds house a museum of local
bygones. St Mary's in Monk Street is the
original church of the 11th-century
Benedictine priory and has interesting altar
tombs. The buildings in Main Street
represent many periods; Old Court – a
house built into the town walls – dates from
1500.

ABERLADY, Lothian   *24 NT47*
The port of the former county town of
Haddington until its harbour silted up in
the 19th century, Aberlady has a safe,
sandy beach facing the Firth of Forth and
its 1439-acre Nature Reserve is well-known
to ornithologists. Myreton Motor Museum
has a comprehensive display of civilian
transport and is expanding its collection of
military vehicles.

ABERSOCH, Gwynedd   *13 SH32*
The tastefully restored cottages of
Abersoch and the sleek vessels lying at
anchor are a testimony to affluence – the
result of its sheltered position, mild climate
and safe bathing.

ABERYSTWYTH, Dyfed   *7 SN58*
Aberystwyth stands on a prehistoric town
site at the mouths of the Rheidol and
Ystwyth. Now the seat of local
administration and of some national
government departments, its importance
began in the 13th century with the building
of the castle – later destroyed by Cromwell
– whose ruins remain on the seafront, the
precincts laid out as public gardens.
Opposite stands a Victorian Gothic
building, the nucleus of the University of
Wales, whose campus on Penglais Hill
includes the National Library (housing
some rare early Welsh manuscripts).
Victorian workmanship also survives in the
funicular railway operating on Constitution
Hill.

ABINGDON, Oxfordshire   *4 SU49*
This attractive Thames-side town grew up
around its abbey, founded in 676. The
15th-century gatehouse survives, and St
Nicholas' Church adjoins it. The Guildhall
was originally an abbey outbuilding, whilst
buildings that were probably the granary
now house an Elizabethan theatre in which
public performances are given during the
summer. St Helen's Church contains a
medieval Lady Chapel, on the ceiling of
which is painted a 'Tree of Jesse'. The fine
County Hall (AM) in the Market Place
stands on tall pilasters with room for
market stalls beneath. It is attributed –
though without evidence – to Wren and one
of his masons, Kempster. Today it houses
the Town Museum.

Cardigan Bay and the Teifi Valley
75 miles

*The peaceful resorts and villages of Cardigan Bay, with their well-kept cottages
match the style of the gentle rolling hills around Lampeter, an agricultural landscape
of neat rectangular fields bounded by hedgerows. In contrast is the wilder scenery of
the Rheidol Valley, up which runs the Vale of Rheidol Light Railway, from
Aberystwyth to Devil's Bridge, where the river plunges into the awe-inspiring depths
of the Mynach Gorge, spanned by three bridges at different heights. Thickly wooded
and steep-sided, the Rheidol, Ystwyth and Teifi valleys are noted beauty spots.*

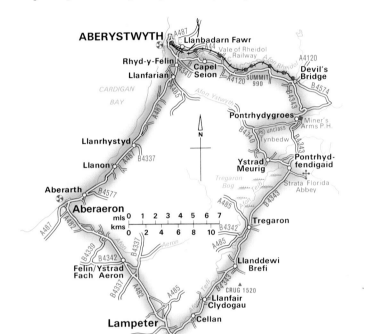

From **Aberystwyth** take
the A487 Aberaeron road,
crossing the Rheidol bridge. In
1¼ miles carry on to A4120
Devil's Bridge road. At **Devil's Bridge**
(the village lies straight ahead) turn right
onto the Tregaron road, B4343.
Descending into the Ystwyth valley, cross
the river into Pontrhydygroes, pass the
Miner's Arms and bear right SP
Trawscoed. Follow the river and pass
Tynbedw picnic site before turning left
onto the Pontrhydfendigaid road, B4340.
At **Pontrhydfendigaid** go forward onto the
Tregaron road, B4343, cross the River
Teifi and turn left to Strata Florida Abbey.
Return to the B4343, turn left for
Tregaron, where you turn left (SP
Llanddewi Brefi), cross the river and bear
right (SP Lampeter). At Llanddewi Brefi

turn right and pass through
Llanfair Clydogau and Cellan
before turning right at the junction
with A482 for Lampeter. At
Lampeter follow signs for A482
Aberaeron. Pass through pleasant hill
country before joining the Aeron Valley at
the combined villages of Felin Fach and
Ystrad Aeron, following the river valley
through attractive wooded scenery into
Aberaeron. Half a mile after crossing the
river turn right onto the A487
Aberystwyth road (for the main street and
harbour turn left). Follow the coast road
along Cardigan Bay, passing through
Aberarth, Llanon and Llanrhystyd where
the road goes inland and uphill before
descending to the Ystwyth Valley at
Llanfarian. Cross the River Rheidol for the
return to Aberystwyth.

PLACES TO SEE

Aberystwyth Ruined castle and gardens;
University and National Library of Wales
which has an outstanding collection of
early Welsh manuscripts, including the
famous *Black Book of Carmarthen*. Cere-
digion Museum; Vale of Rheidol Light
Railway, British Rail's only steam railway,
opened in 1902, which runs for twelve
miles through breathtaking scenery to
Devil's Bridge.

Devil's Bridge Spectacular waterfalls
plunge down the wooded Mynach Gorge,
spanned by three bridges: the lowest and
oldest was probably built by monks from
Strata Florida Abbey, though legend ascribes it to the devil.

Strata Florida Abbey Norman doorway
and ruined walls survive of this majestic
12th-century abbey set in a remote and
beautiful valley.

Tregaron Unspoilt little market town in
beautiful setting of Teifi Valley

Llanddewi Brefi Charming village with
associations with St David. Statue of him
by 13th-century church.

Lampeter Market and University town. St
David's College, founded 1822.

Aberaeron Quiet, pleasing seaside resort
with many Georgian houses.

Suffolk's Coast and Finest Castle
48 miles

The austere fishing villages of the windswept Suffolk coast have suffered much over the centuries from the ravages of the wild North Sea, and none more than Dunwich, once a thriving port, now reduced to a handful of lonely cottages and drowned churches. The unspoiled cliffs and fine shingle beaches offer magnificent seascapes and mile upon mile of wonderful walking country.
Inland, the towns and villages cluster around their ancient churches, rich in carving and medieval brasses, while at Framlingham the mighty castle built as an impregnable stronghold by the 1st Earl of Norfolk towers over the surrounding countryside.

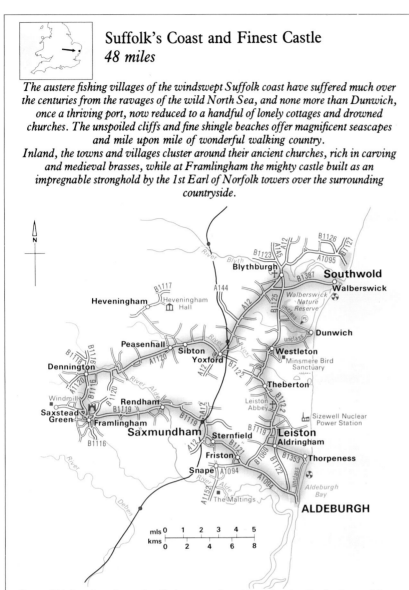

Leave **Aldeburgh** on the unclassified coast road to **Thorpeness** and take the B1353 to **Aldringham**, turning right there onto the B1122 to **Leiston**. Continue (SP Yoxford) to **Theberton** and beyond the village turn right onto the B1125 for **Westleton**. At the end of the village turn right for **Dunwich**. Leave on the Blythburgh road and turn right at the crossroads 1½ miles past Dunwich Forest picnic site onto the B1125 Southwold road. A short distance away is Walberswick Nature Reserve (detour right at next crossroads to Walberswick). In **Blythburgh**, turn left onto the A12

Ipswich road and at **Yoxford** turn right onto the A1120 SP Stowmarket) passing through Sibton and Peasenhall to **Dennington**. At Dennington church turn left onto the B1116 to **Framlingham** and here follow signs along B1119 for **Saxmundham**. On the town's outskirts, turn left and right, and right again at the T-junction onto A12 for town centre. Leave on the A12 Ipswich road and after 1 mile turn left onto the B1121 (SP Aldeburgh), passing through Sternfield and Friston. Shortly after Friston join the A1094 for the return journey to Aldeburgh.

PLACES TO SEE

Aldeburgh Famous for the annual music festival established in 1948 by the famous composer Benjamin Britten. Sixteenth-century Moot Hall; 15th-century church with interesting brasses.

Thorpeness Small coastal resort with House-in-the-Clouds, a water tower disguised as a mock Tudor House.

Leiston Abbey Ruins of 14th-century religious foundation and church.

Walberswick Picturesque village on Blyth estuary. Ferry to Southwold on the opposite bank of the river.

Blythburgh Outstanding 15th-century church with angel roof and carved bench ends of Seven Deadly Sins.

Yoxford An attractive village with many picturesque houses surrounded by parkland.

Dennington St Mary's Church with unique carved bench ends.

Framlingham Delightful old market town with massive ruined castle built by Hugh Bigod, 1st Earl of Norfolk. Lanman Museum of town's history. Fine Perpendicular church of St Michael.

ABOYNE, Grampian   *27 NO59*
Visitors flock to Aboyne each summer for its Highland Gathering, instituted in 1867. The village, set around the green where the traditional games and dances take place, has changed little since it was laid out by a Manchester banker in the 1880s. Before that time it was called Charlestown of Aboyne, after the first Earl of Aboyne who built a small settlement near his castle in 1670.

ACTON BURNELL, Shropshire
9 SJ50
Among the grey-stone Georgian houses and black and white cottages of this attractive village stand the remains of 13th-century Acton Burnell castle (AM), one of England's oldest fortified houses. To the east lie ruins believed to be those of its old barn, traditionally the meeting place (during a visit here by Edward I) of the first parliament to include commoners.

ACTON SCOTT, Shropshire   *9 SO48*
At Acton Scott Working Farm Museum, three miles south of Church Stretton, visitors can experience farming as it was before mechanisation and see some rare breeds of animals. Visitors can help with some of the work and at weekends craft demonstrations take place.

ALCESTER, Warwickshire   *10 SP05*
Alcester, pronounced 'Olster', stands on a Roman road and excavations confirm the likelihood of Roman settlement. The half-timbered, gabled Old Malt House is Alcester's oldest building (c.1500), the Town Hall dates from 1641, and 14th-century St Nicholas's Church houses the tomb of Fulke Greville, grandfather of the Elizabethan poet of the same name, and a benefactor of the town. Butter Street, Henley Street and Church Street all contain interesting old buildings.

ALDBURY, Hertfordshire   *11 SP91*
Since Aldbury was already dubbed 'old fort' by the Saxons, its history is obviously long. The manor house, church, thatched cottages and beamed almshouses overlook a village green where stocks and whipping post still stand near the pond. A monument to canal pioneer the third Duke of Bridgewater looks down over Ashridge Park (NT) designed by Capability Brown and Humphry Repton.

ALDEBURGH, Suffolk   *12 TM45*
Now perhaps best known in connection with Benjamin Britten and the Maltings at Snape, setting of the world-famous music festival each summer, Aldeburgh's history is one of shipbuilding and seafaring. Drake's ships *Pelican* and *Greyhound* were built here and local men sailed with him. The 16th-century Moot Hall (OACT), the striking building against which Britten set *Peter Grimes*, stands near the sea and at Slaughden stands the Martello Tower, modernised as holiday accommodation but originally a defence against Napoleonic invasion.

ALDERLEY EDGE, Cheshire   *14 SJ87*
A pleasant, busy little 19th-century village, Alderley Edge lies at the foot of the great sandstone bluff (NT) from which it takes its name. There are beautiful woodland walks on and around the Edge.

ALDERMASTON, Berkshire   *4 SU56*
The much-publicised home of the Atomic Weapons Research Establishment, Aldermaston is less well known as a picturesque old village in the wooded valley of the River Kennet. The pottery is famous for its beautiful glazes, and its wares are sold all over the country.

ALDERSHOT, Hampshire   *4 SU85*
Possibly the most famous military centre in Britain, Aldershot is very much an army town, with a number of service museums such as the Airborne Forces Museum and the Royal Corps of Transport Museum.

ALDWORTH, Berkshire   *4 SU57*
A remote village on the chalk downs above Goring, Aldworth has one of the country's deepest wells (372ft) and a yew said to be nearly 1000 years old – though it has only one living branch since the gales of 1976. The church contains nine 'giants' – huge effigies of the de la Beche family.

ALFRISTON, E Sussex   *5 TQ50*
Originally a Saxon settlement, Alfriston stands where a prehistoric travellers' route (now part of the South Downs Way) crossed the River Cuckmere, and the ruined market cross in the square is a reminder that today's village was once a market town. St Andrew's contains a marriage register dating from 1504 – probably the oldest in the country. The 14th-century Clergy House – the first building ever bought by the National Trust (in 1896) – overlooks the green.

ALLOWAY, Strathclyde   *22 NS31*
In Alloway stands Robert Burns' birthplace – a thatched cottage now incorporating the Burns Museum. The Burns Monument and the Land o' Burns Centre also ensure that the poet's memory is kept alive.

ALNWICK, Northumberland   *24 NU11*
Chief market town on the Aln and a developing yachting centre, Alnwick is historically the seat of the Earls of Northumberland, the Percy family, whose original Norman castle (OACT) was rebuilt

STONE GIANTS

The battered effigies of nine members of the de la Beche family in Aldworth church commemorate a knightly family whose male line died out in the 14th century. The seven knights were so tall that they have always been known as the 'Aldworth giants' and three of them were nicknamed 'John Strong', 'John Long' and 'John never-Afraid', for what reason is not clear.

to an Adam design in the 18th century. The Percy lion surmounts the Tenantry Column – erected in 1816 by 1000 grateful tenants whose rents were cut during a depression – and appears on the Hotspur Gate, the only remnant of the old town walls.

ALRESFORD, Hampshire   *4 SU53*
New and Old Alresford are joined by a causeway across a 12th-century reservoir. Much of New Alresford was rebuilt after fires in the 17th and 18th centuries, but it was originally a medieval wool town, belonging to the Bishops of Winchester before the Conquest. In its churchyard lie the graves of several Napoleonic prisoners of war, whilst the village church at Old Alresford is the burial place of Admiral Rodney. The area is famous for its watercress beds – hence the 'Watercress Line', the three-mile steam railway route between Alresford and Ropley.

ALTARNUN, Cornwall   *1 SX28*
Originally 'Altar of Nonna' (the 6th-century saint who was the mother of St David), this 15,018-acre village on the edge of Bodmin Moor is one of the country's largest parishes. The spacious church of St Nonna, known locally as 'the cathedral of the moor', has a fine Norman font and interesting 17th-century bench ends reflecting the life of the time. Plain slate-roofed granite cottages line the winding main street, and a medieval packhorse bridge crosses the stream. The head of John Wesley on the former Methodist chapel was carved by a local man, the 19th-century sculptor, Nevil Burnard.

ALTHORP, Northamptonshire
10 SP66
Althorp, situated six miles north-west of Northampton, is the home of the Spencer family. The house (OACT), basically Elizabethan but modified by later restoration, contains a fine collection of furniture, porcelain and pictures.

ACTON SCOTT is a working farm museum, where old breeds of animals are kept in a farmyard that preserves its traditional layout. Horses are used for transport, haulage and for ploughing.

In the Lee of the Cheviot Hills
55 miles

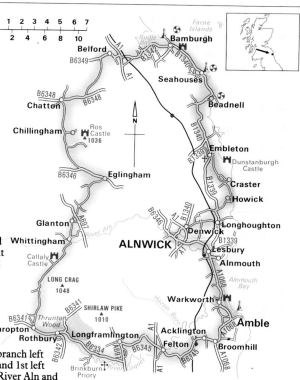

Centuries of ruthless warfare with marauding Scots caused no less than six grim fortresses to be erected in this remote and beautiful corner of Northumberland which lies between the Cheviots and the North Sea coast. Today their ruins overlook a largely unspoilt, little-visited landscape.

From Alnwick to Berwick, the coast has been designated an area of outstanding natural beauty. In the south, the River Coquet winds its way to the sea through one of Northumberland's most lovely valleys.

Follow signs Morpeth then Bamburgh to leave Alnwick by the B1340. Through **Denwick**, turn right SP Longhoughton. On reaching B1339 turn left to reach **Longhoughton**. One mile further turn right and in ½ mile go forward on unclassified road SP Howick. By Howick Hall entrance turn right and in ¼ mile keep on for Craster, later bearing left to reach coast. In 1½ miles, at crossroads, turn right and pass through an archway. At T-junction turn right for **Craster**. Return for ½ mile on same road, then follow SP Embleton. In ½ mile turn right and right again at T-junction. At Embleton keep left, then right at church onto B1339 SP Beadnell. In 1¼ miles go forward onto B1340 and in 1½ miles turn right. At crossroads turn right again to **Beadnell** and follow coast to **Seahouses**. Here turn right then left at war memorial for **Bamburgh**. Here branch right with B1342 SP Belford. In 2½ miles turn left at T-junction, cross level crossing and 1 mile

further turn right onto A1 for **Belford**. Here turn left onto unclassified road. In 3 miles turn right at T-junction onto B6348 SP Chatton. At end of village turn left SP Chillingham (and left at Post Office for castle). Return to road, joining B6346 to Eglingham. On village outskirts turn right SP Powburn, then branch left SP **Glanton**. Turn right and 1st left for **Whittingham**. Cross River Aln and turn right for Callaly Castle, skirting the grounds, and keeping left for Thropton and Rothbury. 2½ miles further turn left; outside **Thropton** turn left (SP Rothbury) at T-junction onto B6341. Keep on through town then bear right SP Morpeth onto B6334. In 3½ miles detour to Brinkburn Priory Church. 1½ miles further on, turn left SP Coldstream to join

A697. At Longframlington turn right onto B6354 to **Felton**. Here turn right SP Morpeth, cross the Coquet and in ¼ mile turn left for Acklington and **Broomhill**, then left onto A1068, SP Alnwick for **Amble**. Turn left and follow signs Alnwick. After 1½ miles turn right at T-junction into **Warkworth**. In 3½ miles at roundabout go forward for Alnwick.

PLACES TO SEE

Alnwick Castle (OACT) Dating from 12th and 14th centuries with 18th- and 19th-century additions, the castle has fine collections of painting and china. 15th-century St Michael's Church.

Howick Hall Gardens Fine gardens and grounds only are open.

Craster Small resort famous for traditional oak-smoked kippers. Cliff path leads to **Dunstanburgh Castle** (AM, NT) built by John of Gaunt.

Seahouses Boat trips from here to Farne Islands (NT) Bird Sanctuary.

Bamburgh Norman castle, formerly ancient seat of Kings of Northumbria. Grace Darling Museum contains pictures, documents and relics of the heroine who saved nine men from drowning in 1838.

Chillingham Park only is open. It contains famous herd of wild cattle, descended from prehistoric wild oxen that once roamed England.

Ros Castle Only mound remains, but superb viewpoint.

Callaly Castle 17th-century mansion with 15th-century pele tower.

Brinkburn Priory Church Fine, well-restored Augustinian priory, used occasionally for organ recitals.

Warkworth Notable 12th-century castle; Church of St Lawrence; 14th-century Hermitage.

ALTON TOWERS *The lovely terraced gardens at Alton were laid out by the 15th Earl of Shrewsbury*

ALTON TOWERS, Staffordshire
10 SK04
One of the most popular pleasure parks in Staffordshire, Alton Towers (OACT) offers amusements to please most tastes, ranging from planetarium and pottery studio to roller coaster and cable cars. For many, however, the attraction is still the 600-acres of trees and flowering shrubs, interspersed with lakes and fountains, that surround the ruined 19th-century Gothic-style mansion.

AMBLESIDE, Cumbria   *18 NY30*
A popular resort at the north end of Lake Windermere, Ambleside is a centre for walking and rock-climbing and is famous for its sheepdog trials. Each July a medieval ceremony is observed when children process through the streets to church bearing the rushes which would once have carpeted its floor. A stone summer house, set over a stream, houses the National

Trust Information Centre. A lane behind the Salutation Hotel leads to the 70ft-high Stock Gill Force.

AMERSHAM, Buckinghamshire
5 SU99
Although new residential areas are now developing, the fact that the Swan Inn was rebuilt in 1643 gives a fair idea of the character of this small country town, whose High Street is lined with cobbled courtyards leading to ancient inns and thatched cottages. Many of the town's larger houses are Georgian, as are the Market Hall and almshouses.

AMPLEFORTH, N Yorkshire   *15 SE57*
This stone-built village is set on the shelf of the Hambleton Hills, with Ampleforth College, the famous Roman Catholic public school founded by Benedictine monks in 1802, at the east end of its main street.

AMPTHILL, Bedfordshire   11 TL03
Many of the Georgian houses in Ampthill
owe their survival to Sir Albert Richardson,
a President of the Royal Academy who
lived in Avenue House – one of the best
examples of the period – and encouraged
extensive restoration. Earlier in its history
the town was much favoured by Henry
VIII, and Catherine of Aragon stayed here
while her divorce was brought about;
Catherine's Cross was erected in her
memory in 1773. Ampthill Park, built by
the first Lord Ashburnham, was formerly
a Cheshire Home.

ANDOVER, Hampshire   4 SU34
At first sight Andover seems a new town,
augmented in the 1960s by London
overspill housing and the introduction of
light industry – but it was, in fact, a
municipal borough under King John and
gained early prominence in the wool
trade. Sixteenth-century cottages still stand
in Chantry Street, the Guildhall is Georgian
and St Mary's Church Victorian Gothic,
whilst several of the old inns can boast royal
patronage over the centuries. The museum
contains items of geological and
archaeological interest.

**ANGLESEY, ISLE OF, Gwynedd
13 SH48**
Anglesey is a very popular holiday area,
offering in addition to its peace and natural
beauty such activities as golf, sailing,
offshore fishing and riding. The geology of
the island results in attractive contrasts of
scenery, the coastline, for instance, ranging
from cliffs with rocky bays to wide, smooth
beaches. 'Progress' has touched Anglesey
with the coming of the Irish Ferry
Terminal to Holyhead, the development of
an RAF base at Valley and – most recently
– the building of a nuclear power station at
Wylfa Head. On the other hand the visitor
can see many ancient monuments, such as
the passage grave of Bryn-Celli-Ddu (AM),
the best example of its kind in Britain.
Another fascinating site is Din Lligwy,
where the remains of a pre-Roman
settlement were discovered. Other places of
interest include Plas Newydd (NT), the
beautiful 18th-century house of the
Marquesses of Anglesey, and Beaumaris
Castle (AM) a magnificent fortress of
concentric design. The famous South Stack
lighthouse stands on a rocky islet off Holy
island, and that village with the long place
name, mercifully shortened to Llanfair
p.g., can be found in the south of the
island.

ANSTRUTHER, Fife   24 NO50
On either side of the harbour rises a 16th-
century church tower, the one belonging to
Anstruther Easter and the other to
Anstruther Wester – both Royal Burghs.
Anstruther Easter has a manse bearing the
date 1590, the oldest still inhabited in
Scotland, and St Ayles House (used at one
time by monks from Balmerino Abbey)
contains an interesting fisheries museum.
Six miles offshore lies the little island of
May, an important bird-watching station.

APPLEBY, Cumbria   18 NY62
Appleby lies at the foot of the Pennines in
the Eden valley, an area rich in both natural
beauty and historical interest. Each June
the country's largest horse-fair is held here,
when gypsies come from all over Britain to

PUFFIN ISLAND *Uninhabited save for the puffins, the island lies off the eastern coast of Anglesey. In early medieval times Augustinian monks had a settlement here, and a fragment of a tower remains.*

buy and sell horses. Still evident in the
town is the hand of Lady Anne Clifford,
Countess of Pembroke, who died in 1678
and is buried in St Lawrence's Church. At
each end of Boroughgate stands a cross
bearing her motto – 'Retain your loyalty,
preserve your rights'.

APPLEDORE, Devon   2 SS43
Steep cobbled streets of colour-washed
cottages, yachts on the horizon, lobster pots
and nets – all these make Appledore a
typically picturesque Devon fishing village.
The whole peninsula has gained a new
importance since the largest covered dock
in Europe was opened here in 1970. The
North Devon Maritime Museum is situated
in this former ship-building centre on the
Torridge estuary.

ARBROATH, Tayside   27 NO64
Famous worldwide for its 'smokies' –
haddock smoked over an oak fire –
Arbroath also attained a temporary
notoriety in 1951 when the Stone of Scone,
stolen from Westminster Abbey,
reappeared in the ruined abbey where
Robert the Bruce signed Scotland's
Declaration of Independence in 1320. The
abbey also contains the 'O of Arbroath', a
circular window traditionally lit as a beacon
for sailors, and the abbot's house is now a
folk museum.

**ARBURY HALL, Warwickshire
10 SP38**
Arbury Hall (OACT), set in 300 acres of
attractive parkland, is a unique blend of
Tudor and 18th-century Gothic, built on
the ruins of an Augustinian monastery. It is
the home of the Newdegate family, whose
collections of glass, china and furniture are
on display, together with documents of
family history. The plaster ceilings are
noteworthy, and the 17th-century stables
house a collection of old cycles. Mary Ann
Evans, later to write as George Eliot, was
born on one of the estate farms in 1819.

ARDINGLY, W Sussex   5 TQ32
The gardens of Wakehurst Place (NT), are
administered in conjunction with Kew by
the Royal Botanical Gardens. Though
primarily experimental they are open to the
public, and have a fine collection of rare
trees and flowering shrubs.

**ARDNAMURCHAN, Highland
25 NM56**
At the tip of the Ardnamurchan peninsula
is Ardnamurchan Point – Gaelic for 'the
point of the great ocean' – the most westerly
spot on the British mainland, where a
lonely 19th-century lighthouse overlooks
the islands of Muck, Eigg and Rum to the
north, Coll and Tiree to the west and Mull
to the south (see Inner Hebrides).

ARISAIG, Highland   25 NM68
At Arisaig the Road to the Isles meets the
sea, with Rum, Eigg and Muck clearly
visible across the bay and the mountains of
Skye beyond. To the north of the village
stretch smooth expanses of silver-white
sand and to its south lies Borrodale Beach,
scene of Bonnie Prince Charlie's landing in
1745 and his flight the following year; the
cave in which he hid before his escape is
near Arisaig House.

ARLINGTON COURT, Devon   2 SS64
Home of the Chichesters (family of
yachtsman Sir Francis) since the 14th
century, Arlington Court was left to the
National Trust in 1949. The present house
was built in 1820–3, and its plain façade
gives no hint of the rich interior. The last
owner, Miss Rosalie Chichester, was a
woman of wide interests, and her
collections – ranging through pewter
objects, model ships, snuffboxes and
seashells – are on display. The stables
contain a collection of vehicles, from pony-
drawn Bath chair to early motor car.
Visitors to the grounds can see Jacob sheep
and Shetland ponies, visit the heronry and
duck sanctuary, or follow the marked
nature trails.

ARRAN, ISLE OF, Strathclyde
21 NR93
Arran is famous for its association with
Robert the Bruce, who landed at Lochranza
('the loch of safe anchorage') in 1306 and
later sheltered in King's Caves near
Blackwater. The island is roughly 20 miles
long by 10 miles wide, and from Goat Fell
in the north (its highest point at 2,866ft)
there are magnificent views of the Clyde,
the Western Isles and the coast of Ireland.
The Isle of Arran Heritage Museum is at
Brodick, on the east coast, the most
important village. Its 15th-century castle
(NT) – traditional home of the Hamilton
family – overlooks Brodick Bay.

ARUNDEL, W Sussex   *5 TQ00*
Set where the Arun cuts through the Sussex
Downs, Arundel is dominated by its castle
(OACT) – largely rebuilt in the 18th
century after destruction by Cromwellian
troops but with a 13th-century barbican,
and containing 15th-century furniture, a
collection of armour, and pictures by
Gainsborough, Van Dyck and Reynolds.
From the castle one can enter the chancel of
the parish church – partitioned from its
main body when it was sold to the Fitzalan
family by Henry VIII. Nearby stands the
19th-century Roman Catholic Cathedral of
Our Lady and St Philip – designed by
Joseph Hansom, inventor of the Hansom
cab. In the Museum of Curiosity, Victorian
whimsy is displayed in such tableaux of
stuffed animals as the kittens' tea and
croquet party, arranged by the naturalist
and taxidermist Walter Potter, whilst the
town's history can be traced in Arundel
Museum and Heritage Centre.

ASHBOURNE, Derbyshire   *15 SK14*
Surrounded by hills rising to 600 feet,
Ashbourne is an attractive tourist centre on
the edge of the Peak District National Park.
It is famous for the free-for-all, no-holds-

VICTORIAN WHIMSY

Walter Potter, who lived from 1835
to 1918 was one of the great Victorian
eccentrics. His tableaux of stuffed
animals in the Museum of Curiosity
at Arundel may seem almost grotesque to modern taste, but they are
remarkable expressions of a unique
imagination. He is said to have been
inspired to start taxidermy when,
while still a child, he read that
famous poem, *The Death and Burial
of Cock Robin* in an old book of
rhymes belonging to his sister.

barred football match waged there over a
three-mile 'pitch' each Shrove Tuesday –
sometimes lasting well into Ash
Wednesday. Fine old buildings abound in
the town – Church Street has a 16th-
century grammar school, 17th-century
almshouses and a Georgian mansion visited
by Dr Johnson and Boswell. The church of
St Oswald – substantially 13th- and 14th-
century, with a 212ft spire – is one of the
finest in the country.

ROYALIST STRONGHOLD *Ashby-de-la-Zouch castle was built by the de la Souche family after the Conquest. Besieged for 15 months during the Civil War, it was later slighted by Cromwell.*

ASHBURTON, Devon   *2 SX76*
Ashburton stands within the Dartmoor
National Park, a small town whose steeply
rising streets still have a Regency flavour.
For centuries a stannary town for
Dartmoor's tin mines and the centre of the
local wool industry, it retains the ancient
offices of Portreeve, Bailiff and Court Leet,
though their significance today is purely
ceremonial. Buckfast Abbey occupies a site
believed to have been a Benedictine
monastery in the 6th century, the monks
today making stained glass windows, honey
and tonic wine.

ASHBURY, Oxfordshire   *4 SU28*
Ashbury is a village set against the chalk of
the Downs and largely fashioned from it.
Ashdown House (NT), south-east of the
village, contains paintings from the Craven
Collection. On the Downs, just off the
Berkshire Ridgeway, stands Wayland's
Smithy (*see* Compton Beauchamp).

ASHBY-DE-LA-ZOUCH,
Leicestershire   *10 SK31*
The La Souche family from Brittany
became Lords of the Manor of Ashby in the
12th century, and in the 15th century their
stone-built hall became the basis of the
castle whose ruins (AM) today stand behind
the main street. Near the castle lie the fields
in which Scott set the pageant and
tournament in *Ivanhoe*.

ASHWELL, Hertfordshire   *11 TL23*
Ash trees surround the springs at the source
of the Rhee, giving the village its name. It
owes its spacious planning to the Romans,
though the first settlement here was
probably an Iron-Age hill fort, the Arbury
Banks, controlling the ancient Icknield
Way. The tower of the mainly 14th-century
church of St Mary rises to 176ft, topped
with a small 'Hertfordshire spike', and on
the south wall beneath it is a carving of old
St Paul's. A Latin inscription in the tower
testifies to the plague, 14th-century killer of
a third of the village population, as do the
graves of victims outside. The restored
Town House (AM), probably once used for
tithe-gathering, contains a museum of
village history and rural life.

ATCHAM, Shropshire   *9 SJ50*
Two bridges, the arched 18th-century and
the modern road bridge, cross the Severn at
Atcham. Attingham Park (NT) is a late
18th-century mansion set in wooded
parkland, the elegance of its classical lodge
and gate dramatic among the surrounding
cottages.

AUCHMITHIE, Tayside   *27 NO64*
Set high above a sandy beach on red-
sandstone cliffs near Arbroath, Auchmithie
was once one of the most important herring
fishing villages on the Angus coast. The
fishermen's cottages are tastefully restored
now, but a rough pathway still runs steeply
down to the little harbour built at the end of
the 19th century – before that, the
womenfolk had to wade out to help the
boats launch and land. Nearby caves, under
the curious Pint Stoup rock stack, have
such curiosity-arousing names as
Dickmont's Den and Forbidden Cave. Sir
Walter Scott based 'Musselcrag' in *The
Antiquary* on Auchmithie, and artist
William Lamond spent 40 summers in the
village, painting local scenery.

AUDLEY END, Essex *11 TL53*
Standing over the foundations of a
Benedictine monastery, Audley End (AM)
was built by the first Earl of Suffolk in
1603. Today, only part of the original
mansion remains, but the Jacobean exterior
was carefully preserved in Robert Adam's
modernisation. Like the interior, the park
conforms to the 18th-century ideal of
elegance, with lakes, a temple, several
decorated lodges and a Palladian bridge
carrying a summerhouse.

AVEBURY, Wiltshire *3 SU06*
The 28 acres of the village of Avebury, but
not the fine Elizabethan Manor (OACT) lie
within a late Neolithic circle of vast
standing stones or sarsens – the largest
weighing some 60 tons – which is in turn
surrounded by earthworks. Inside the large
circle are two smaller, incomplete rings, the
stones in all three having been carefully
selected from the nearby Marlborough
Downs. It has been suggested that the tall,
narrow stones represent men and the more
diamond-shaped ones women, and that the
whole thing was an open air temple for
fertility rites, but we have no real
knowledge of its significance. Many of the
stones are missing, destroyed because of
medieval superstition or broken up for use
in local buildings. The Alexander Keiller
Museum, in what was formerly the manor
coach-house, contains objects excavated in
the village and also at Windmill Hill,
Silbury Hill and West Kennet Long
Barrow. The 50ft-wide avenue of megaliths
which apparently ran out past West Kennet
to Overbury Hill seems to indicate that the
Avebury circles were part of a larger
scheme, involving a number of these
ancient religious sites.

AVIEMORE, Highland *26 NH81*
Aviemore's position, on the edge of a 600-
acre nature reserve and at the heart of
Britain's winter sports area, was capitalised
in the 1960s by the building of a massive
leisure complex. Throughout the year the
energetic can swim, go-cart, dry-ski, skate
or curl before relaxing in theatre, concert
hall, restaurant and bar, whilst
accommodation ranges from luxury hotels
to chalets. Though the design of the
complex is modern the materials used were
wood and local granite, blending well with
its setting at the foot of the Rock of
Craigellachie, traditional gathering place of
Clan Grant.

AXMINSTER, Devon *3 SY29*
Built on high ground above the River Axe
and centred round a tree-shaded green, the
busy streets of this small market town are
still rich in Georgian and Victorian
buildings and it has several fine coaching
inns. Its name is synonymous with the
manufacture of fine carpets, though the
factory opened by Thomas Whitty in the
18th century – based on his close study of
Turkish methods – was in production for
only 80 years before being sold out to a
Wilton weaver, and the industry did not
return to the town until 1937.

AYLESBURY, Buckinghamshire
10 SP81
Aylesbury is now a busy modern town at
the junction of six main roads, but its
centre recalls more leisurely days. Narrow
Tudor alleys run between four squares – St
Mary's, Market, Temple and Kingsbury.
St Mary's square has old terraces of houses
on three sides and the ancient church, with
its distinctive 'Aylesbury' font, on the

fourth. The cattle market is still in use,
reached through the arches under the old
Town Hall, and in Market Square stands a
statue of John Hampden, famous for his
opposition to Charles I's demands for ship
money. The King's Head Hotel (NT) was
founded in 1386 and has a medieval
gateway and fine 15th-century stained
glass. The County Museum in Church
Street is set in dignified 18th-century
buildings that were originally a monastery
guest house.

AYLESFORD, Kent *6 TQ75*
A 14th-century bridge crosses the Medway
at Aylesford. On the outskirts of the village
stands The Friars (OACT) – a monastery
which was restored to its original use by the
Carmelites in 1949 (400 years after its
dissolution by Henry VIII). Despite
extensive restoration, much of the 14th–
15th-century fabric remains, with traces of
the original 13th-century building. Today's
monks manufacture pottery for sale to the
public, and their guesthouse is open to all,
regardless of denomination. On nearby
downland is Kit's Coty, a famous
Megalithic tomb.

AYNHO, Northamptonshire *10 SP53*
Apricot trees, thriving on the limestone
soil, climb the fronts of many of Aynho's
pale stone cottages – a relic of the days
when a toll of the fruit was paid to the
manor as rent. Aynho Park (OACT) is the
17th-century home of the Cartwright
family, beneficiaries of the apricot rent. St
Michael's Church, though substantially
altered in the 18th century, still has its
richly decorated 15th-century tower and
contains an interesting old carved chair
showing the Baptism.

STONE CIRCLES *keep their secrets well. Avebury, constructed between 3000 and 1500 BC, was certainly a temple, but its rituals are still mysterious.*

AYOT ST LAWRENCE, Hertfordshire
11 TL11

This attractive, tree-shaded village is quite near to Stevenage, but the high-banked lanes leading to it and its undisturbed old black-and-white cottages make it a place apart. At Shaw's Corner (NT) the playwright spent the last 44 years of his life, convinced that the area was healthy, it is said, by the epitaph to a 70-year-old woman which proclaimed 'Her Time was Short' – and, since he lived to be 94, his assumption was presumably correct! The house is virtually unchanged since Shaw's day, and the secluded summerhouse where he used to work has also been preserved.

AYR, Strathclyde *22 NS32*

The town is a fishing harbour and an attractive resort, but it is best known for its association with Robert Burns, who was born at nearby **Alloway** and baptised in the Auld Kirk of Ayr. The thatched Tam O'Shanter in the High Street now houses a Burns Museum. The MacLaurin Art Gallery includes sculpture by Henry Moore. The town still has its 'Twa Brigs': the modern one replacing an 18th-century structure, and the medieval Auld Brig – described by the poet as a 'poor narrow footpath of a street where two wheelbarrows tremble when they meet.'

AYSGARTH, N Yorkshire *19 SE08*

In woodland, near a 16th-century bridge across the River Ure, the spectacular set of falls known as Aysgarth Force extends over half a mile as the water plunges down three separate limestone terraces. Above the falls, slightly apart from the village it serves, stands St Andrew's Church, burned down and rebuilt in the 19th century. The National Park Centre displays maps, books and exhibits on the Aysgarth Force area. A collection of old carriages can be seen at the old Mill Museum, near the bridge.

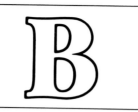

BAKEWELL, Derbyshire *15 SK26*

The rich brownstone of Bakewell is set against woodland at the foot of the Peak District hills. The church is on high ground, its spire a landmark for miles, and has a famous Saxon cross (AM) in the churchyard. One of the oldest packhorse bridges in the country crosses the Wye here. The early settlement grew up around 12 springs – their water now analysed as iron bearing and at a temperature of 15°C. Though most of them have run dry they are not forgotten, for their sites are decorated each July in the ancient ritual of well-dressing. Of interest are Old House Museum and Magpie Mine (OACT) a 19th-century lead mine, the town's oldest building and now a museum, and Bath House, still fed by warm springs. Lambton, the setting of Mr Darcy's residence in *Pride and Prejudice*, is said to be based on Bakewell; Jane Austen stayed at the Rutland Arms Hotel while writing it. The prototype Bakewell tart is said to have been made when an inept chef at the same hotel misunderstood a recipe!

BALA, Gwynedd *13 SH93*

Standing at the north end of Bala lake and the terminus for the Bala Lake Railway, Bala is surrounded by countryside of an impressive grandeur and is an excellent centre for sailing, fishing, golf, pony-trekking, walking or driving. The gwyniad, a white-scaled salmon, is a species peculiar to the lake.

BALA LAKE, in Welsh called Llyn Tegid, is the largest natural expanse of water in Wales. Less than a mile wide, it is nevertheless very deep – 150ft in places.

BALDOCK, Hertfordshire *11 TL23*

The main street of Baldock, attractively lined with trees and edged with grassy banks, has many fine Georgian buildings – and, more surprisingly, many more are to be found in the side streets.

BALERNO, Lothian *23 NT16*

In Balerno stands Malleny House (NT), built in the early 17th century and famous for its rose shrubberies and fine old 'doocot' – a pigeon house with 915 nesting boxes, originally designed to provide a supply of fresh meat during the winter.

BALLANTRAE, Strathclyde *17 NX08*

The village lies in Ballantrae Bay, near the estuary of the River Stinchar and looking out across the rocky island of Ailsa Craig. Robert Louis Stevenson has immortalised its name in the title of his novel, *The Master of Ballantrae*.

BALLATER, Grampian *27 NO39*

Ballater grew up in the 18th century to accommodate the many folk who came to 'take the waters' at the mineral wells of nearby Pannanich. It is now a popular holiday resort, set in an area of great beauty which also offers many sporting facilities – including the ski slopes at Abergeldie.

BALLOCH, Strathclyde *22 NS38*

The village of Balloch, popular with holidaymakers and yachtsmen, stands just south of Loch Lomond on the River Leven. On the eastern shore of the loch, Balloch Castle stands at the centre of Balloch Castle Park (OACT) with the ruins of Boturich Castle nearby. Cameron House (OACT) is owned by the Smollett family and has collections of porcelain and Staffordshire pottery, fine furniture, and an exhibition devoted to the 18th-century novelist, Tobias Smollett, author of *Humphry Clinker*; the Cameron Loch Lomond Wildlife Park numbers Britain's first bear park among its attractions.

BALMORAL, Grampian *27 NO29*

Queen Victoria first visited Balmoral Castle in 1848; she fell in love with it, and in 1852 Prince Albert purchased it (for £31,000) and began its transformation into a baronial-style mansion. It is still one of the Queen's private residences, used by the Royal Family as a summer holiday estate. The castle itself is not open to the public, but the gardens can sometimes be visited.

BAMBURGH, Northumberland
24 NU13

Bamburgh Castle (OACT), a border stronghold that was once the seat of the Kings of Northumbria, stands on a crag above the North Sea; objects of interest include its weapon collection, fine tapestries and paintings, and a cradle which belonged to Queen Anne. The Grace Darling Museum is opposite St Aidan's Church – her burial place – and the exhibits include the boat in which she and her father in 1838 rescued the survivors from the wrecked steamship *Forfarshire*. The **Farne Islands**, four and a half miles offshore, were the home of St Aidan and St Cuthbert in the 7th century. Now they are an important breeding ground for young seabirds, and have been designated as an area of outstanding natural beauty in order to preserve their unique character.

Daughter of the keeper of the Long-stone Lighthouse, on the Farne Islands, Grace Darling won everlasting fame in 1838 when, at the age of 23, she rowed out with her father at the height of a fierce storm to the wrecked steamer *Forfarshire* and rescued nine seamen. She is buried at Bamburgh and her boat is one of the exhibits in the museum.

BANBURY, Oxfordshire   10 SP44

The present Banbury Cross is a 19th-century replica of one destroyed by Puritans in 1602. The 'ride' of the nursery rhyme was probably a May Day ceremony and the 'fine lady' has been variously identified as Elizabeth I, Lady Godiva, and a member of the Fiennes family from nearby Broughton Castle. The making of Banbury cakes is no longer confined to Banbury, though they can still be bought here.

BANFF, Grampian   27 NJ66

Banff is an ancient town at the mouth of the River Deveron, created a Royal Burgh by Robert II in 1372. In the 18th century, when the harbour was built, it flourished as a port, but today it is a quiet holiday resort. The Biggar Fountain is built on the site of the old gallows where smuggler James Macpherson played his fiddle as he walked to his execution. Duff House (AM), a baroque-style house built by William Adam in the 1730s, was given to the townsfolk by the Duke of Fife, and the gardens are now a public park with a natural history museum.

BANGOR, Gwynedd   13 SH57

The town's bishopric – older than that of Canterbury – dates from the 6th century, and the *bangor* is the protective fence that would have surrounded the monastery founded at that time. Between the 12th-century Cathedral of St Deinol and the Tudor Town Hall lies the remarkable Biblical Garden, containing such of the trees, shrubs and flowers mentioned in the Bible as can survive the British climate. The Victorian mock-Norman walls of Penrhyn Castle (NT) house a large collection of dolls, stuffed animals and birds, and a slate bed weighing four tons; the grounds contain a wide range of exotic plants and a display of railway relics. The Old Canonry in the town centre has a Museum of Antiquities which includes traditional Welsh costume and furniture.

The Undiscovered Cotswolds
58 miles

This north-eastern section of the Cotswolds is comparatively little-known, yet has much to offer. Centred on Banbury lies a chain of delightful villages and the drive cuts across the corners of three shires: Oxfordshire, Northamptonshire and Warwickshire, passing through a secluded part of what may truly be called the heart of England.

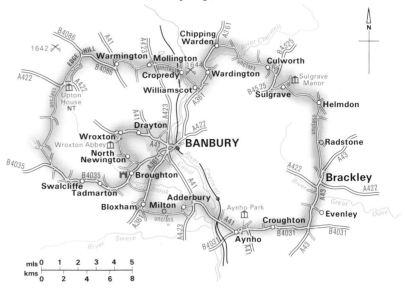

Take the A361 Swindon road from **Banbury** to **Bloxham**, turning left at the end of the village on to the Adderbury road, then left again into Milton road. Skirt Milton, and in a mile turn left for **Adderbury**, where turn left on to A423 and at traffic lights right onto A41 SP Aylesbury. Three-quarters of a mile beyond **Aynho** branch left on to B4031 SP Buckingham for **Croughton**, and 2 miles beyond the village turn left on to A43 **Brackley** road. Keep on through the town and in ¾ mile turn left SP Helmdon and **Sulgrave**. At Helmdon turn left for Sulgrave. Entrance to the manor house is on the right, but continue on the Culworth road and in 1 mile turn right on to B4525, then in ½ mile left SP Culworth. At T-junction turn left again to reach **Culworth**. In 1¾ miles turn right, cross a bridge, then in ½ mile turn left for **Chipping Warden**. Join the Banbury road, A361, to **Wardington** and 1 mile further turn right for **Cropredy**. At the Brasenose Arms turn

right and in ¼ mile turn left SP Mollington. Cross a staggered crossroads to reach **Mollington** and carry on to **Warmington**. Bear left to cross the green and on reaching the top of the hill, turn left on to A41, then sharp right past the church on to B4086 SP Kineton. After 2 miles turn left at T-junction SP Edge Hill. In 1¾ miles reach A422 and turn right SP Stratford (a short detour to the left on A422 leads to Upton House). Take the next left, SP Compton Wynyates, and after 3½ miles at crossroads turn left SP Banbury. One mile further turn left on to B4035 through Swalcliffe and Tadmarton to **Broughton**. Turn left SP North Newington and bear right to pass the entrance to Broughton Castle. Bear right again and in ½ mile turn left for **North Newington**. At the end of the village turn right SP Wroxton, then in 1¼ miles turn right on to A422 to skirt the village. Continue through Drayton for the return journey to Banbury.

PLACES TO SEE

Banbury The old cross was replaced in 1859, and nothing remains of that mentioned in the nursery rhyme. Banbury cakes can still be bought and the town has many charming old streets.

Aynho Idyllic little village famous for its apricot trees; 17th-century Anyhoe Park (OACT) is the home of the Cartwright family.

Croughton Medieval wall paintings in church

Sulgrave Manor Home (OACT) of the ancestors of American president George Washington, Sulgrave contains many family mementoes and period furniture.

Warmington Soldiers killed in the Civil War battle of Edgehill in 1642 are buried in the churchyard of this pretty little village.

Upton House (NT) Home of Lord Bearsted, whose fabulous art collection it houses, Upton is set in magnificent gardens, which feature terraces and a lake.

Broughton Castle (OACT) remodelled by the Fiennes family in the 16th century, contains period furniture and painting.

Wroxton Wroxton Abbey (OACT) is the showpiece of this charming village, a beautiful 17th-century house built on the foundations of an Augustinian priory.

BANHAM, Norfolk   *12 TM08*
The village is a pretty one, its green encircled by elms, but it is best known for its Zoo and Monkey Sanctuary. Here, in a 20-acre park, are collected all the usual animals, ranging from black panther to penguin – but the real attraction is the colony of woolly monkeys, one of only six in Europe. Here, too, is the International Motor Museum.

BANNOCKBURN, Central
22 NS89
The National Trust owns the 58-acre battlefield where, in 1314, Robert the Bruce triumphed over an English army that outnumbered his troops three to one. A rotunda encircles the Borestone in which the shaft of the Scottish standard is said to have rested, and in 1967 an information centre and a display entitled 'The Forging of a Nation' were opened.

BARCALDINE CASTLE, Strathclyde
25 NM94
This castle (OACT) was built in the 16th century by Duncan Campbell of Glenorchy; the family were forced to sell it in 1842, but by 1896 it had fallen into disrepair and they were able to repurchase it and begin restoration. On Loch Cleran is a fascinating Sea Life Centre.

BARDON MILL, Northumberland
19 NY76
At Vindolanda (Chesterholm) can be seen the remains of a Roman fort and settlement of the 3rd and 4th centuries AD. Museums contain the results of various excavations, and there are replicas of Hadrian's turf and stone walls. The only Roman milestone still to stand in its original position (AM) is situated at Chesterholm.

BARDSEY ISLAND, Gwynedd
13 SH12
Bardsey Island, off the Lleyn Peninsula, is now a bird observatory and a place where storm petrels, shearwaters and choughs can breed undisturbed (access being forbidden to the general public). Its history, however, is more eventful. Early Celts built a monastery, and the Island of Twenty-Thousand Saints (so called because of the many holy men who chose to end their days here) became a place of pilgrimage.

WEDGWOOD'S MASTERPIECE

The famous 'Portland' Vase, now in the British Museum, was copied by Wedgwood and became his most successful model. The technique took years to perfect; the vase is now the company symbol.

Durham's Dales and Woods
58 miles

The River Tees is famed for its spectacular waterfalls, and none so grand as High Force or Caldron Snout. No less beautiful are its tributary valleys of Deep Dale and the Lune, beloved of artists such as Turner. Between the Tees and Wear lies Hamsterley Forest, one of the finest countryside areas of the county. Beyond the woodland, to the north, Weardale winds through high moorland on the eastern approaches to the Pennines.

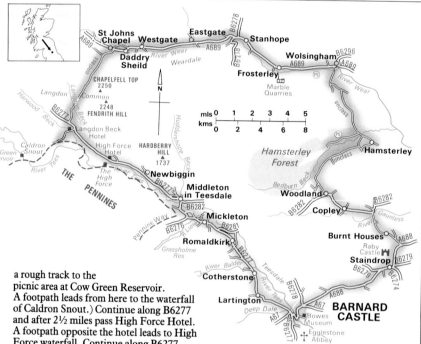

From **Barnard Castle** follow signs for Bishop Auckland, and at the end of the town turn left to follow A688 to **Staindrop**. Turn left by Staindrop church and in 1 mile pass the entrance to Raby Castle. Continue along A688 for ½ mile and turn left on to an unclassified road SP Cockfield. In ½ mile keep straight on SP Butterknowle, and in another 2¼ miles turn left on to B6282 for Copley and continue to Woodland. Meet a T-junction and turn left, then after 300yds turn right on to an unclassified road SP Hamsterley. After 3 miles turn right and left for **Hamsterley**. Here turn left for Bedburn and Wolsingham. Cross Bedburn Beck and after a short distance pass a left turn that leads into **Hamsterley Forest**, and drive through woodland before emerging into open countryside. Cross the River Wear and continue to the edge of Wolsingham. Turn left on to A689 SP Stanhope and continue through Frosterley and along A689 to **Stanhope**. Leave Stanhope on A689 SP Alston and continue to **Eastgate**. Leave Eastgate along A689 to reach Westgate. Continue through Daddry Shield to **St John's Chapel**. Turn left on to an unclassified road SP Middleton-in-Teesdale and climb to Langdon Common. Descend into Teesdale and at a T-junction turn left on to B6277. In ½ mile reach the Langdon Beck Hotel. (A short detour can be made here by turning right. Drive along

a rough track to the picnic area at Cow Green Reservoir. A footpath leads from here to the waterfall of Caldron Snout.) Continue along B6277 and after 2½ miles pass High Force Hotel. A footpath opposite the hotel leads to High Force waterfall. Continue along B6277 through Newbiggin to reach **Middleton-in-Teesdale**. Leave Middleton-in-Teesdale and turn right SP Scotch Corner. Cross the River Tees and in ½ mile keep left SP Barnard Castle. Continue for ¾ mile, rejoin B6277, and continue through Romaldkirk to Cotherstone and then turn left (A67). Recross the Tees and return to Barnard Castle.

PLACES TO SEE

Barnard Castle The castle ruins (AM) include the keep and Great Hall; on the edge of town, the Bowes Museum, containing one of the country's most important collections of painting, furniture, porcelain, etc is housed in a flamboyant Renaissance building.

Egglestone Abbey Ruins of 12th-century abbey (AM) in beautiful setting beside River Tees.

Raby Castle Towered, turretted and moated, this picture-book castle once belonged to the Nevilles; collections of furniture, paintings and ceramics.

Hamsterley Forest Woodland criss-crossed by footpaths; children's marked nature trail; red and fallow deer may sometimes be seen.

Stanhope Medieval church with many ancient relics, including fossilised prehistoric tree stump in churchyard.

Caldron Snout A tiered cascade falling over natural rock staircase below Cow Green Reservoir.

High Force Plunging dramatically over the menacing 70ft cliff of Great Whin Sill, High Force is one of England's most spectacular waterfalls.

BARLASTON, Staffordshire   14 SJ83

At Barlaston, in the Wedgwood Museum and Visitor Centre (OACT) which has been built on the site of the famous factory, is an exhibition of ceramics dating from the 18th century to the present day and including a comprehensive collection of the works of Josiah Wedgwood. Traditional skills are displayed in the demonstration area.

BARMOUTH, Gwynedd   13 SH61

Barmouth was a flourishing port until the 19th century, but today its little harbour shelters only sailing craft and lobster-fishing boats, for the town has become a popular resort. Visitors attracted by its fine beach and the beauty of the surrounding countryside will also find much of interest in the town itself – one of the most historic buildings being Ty Gwyn yn y Bermo on the quayside, said to have been built for Henry Tudor, later to become Henry VII. There are fine views of the estuary from the wooden bridge which spans it, or one can take the ferry to Penrhyn Point and admire it from the narrow-gauge steam train that runs two miles along the beach to Fairbourne.

BARNACK, Cambridgeshire   11 TF00

This area provided stone for the cathedrals at Ely and Peterborough and for Corpus Christi and other Cambridge colleges, but the supply was exhausted by the 18th century and the grassed-over quarries are now the Hills and Holes Nature Reserve. The stone is still much in evidence, however, in the village, which has attractive cottages, an old windmill and a church with a Saxon tower surmounted by a 13th-century spire.

BARNARD CASTLE, Co Durham   19 NZ01

On a cliff top 80ft above the Tees stand the ruins of Barnard (originally 'Bernard's') Castle (AM), built by Bernard Balliol in the 12th century on the site of an earlier family stronghold. The Balliols gained power in the 13th century, when John Balliol was crowned King of Scotland – and a member of the same family was later to found Balliol College in Oxford. Near the town stand the beautiful ruins of 12th-century Egglestone Abbey (AM). The Bowes Museum – built by a prominent local family in the 19th century – looks like a splendid Renaissance French château, set in its own parkland, and contains some 10,000 exhibits, including superb paintings.

BARNSLEY, S Yorkshire   15 SE30

We know from its inclusion in the *Domesday Book* that Barnsley existed in the 11th century; at that time the land belonged to the priories of Pontefract and Monk Bretton, and the ruins of the latter (AM) stand 1½ miles east of the town. Worsburgh Mill Museum, off the A61, is a 17th-century corn mill with an adjoining mill powered by a rare 1911 hot bulb oil engine.

BARNSTAPLE, Devon   2 SS53

Barnstaple is one of the most ancient boroughs in Britain, chronicled as minting its own coins in the 10th century and having a mayor by 1360. A regular market and many shows are held in the 19th-century covered Pannier Market. The North Devon Athenaeum and medieval St

THE BOWES MUSEUM *This statue of an ancient king guards the entrance to the museum.*

Anne's Chapel house interesting museums and a fine example of 18th-century architecture is Queen Anne's Walk, a colonnade where merchants and shipowners did business, their verbal bargains rendered binding when they were made at the Tome Stone.

BARNWELL, Northamptonshire   11 TL08

A stream runs the length of Barnwell, with a bridge and three fords linking the two halves – which were originally separate villages, each with its own church. Only the chancel of All Saints now stands, however, and it is St Andrews that the villagers use. The ruins of Old Barnwell Castle (built in 1266) stand in the grounds of the Elizabethan manor which is now known as Barnwell Castle.

BARRINGTON COURT, Somerset   3 ST31

Barrington Court (NT), three miles north-east of Ilminster, is a handsome Tudor mansion of yellow Ham stone with impressive spiral chimneys. The interior was restored in the 1920s, the National Trust tenant (Colonel A A Lyle, a member of the famous sugar-manufacturing family)

exercising enormous ingenuity and acquiring carved beams from Italy, linenfold panelling from demolished houses – and even a 16th-century Norfolk shop front from King's Lynn, which was converted into a screen. He also re-created an appropriate setting for the house – a beautiful garden (which contains an unusual 10-faced sundial) and a park ornamented with horse-chestnut trees. Colonel Lyle was also responsible for building the Tudor-Style accommodation for estate employees in the park.

BARROW-IN-FURNESS, Cumbria   18 SD26

Within 100 years, the population of Barrow-in-Furness has leapt from under 700 to over 64,000. It is an industrial town, manufacturing ships and nuclear submarines, but activities are centred on the docks and there is much unspoiled coastline. The ruins of 12th-century Furness Abbey (AM), which once wielded enormous administrative power, lie north-east of the town. The boundaries take in four islands – Foulney and Roa (both small), Walney and Piel. The Isle of Walney is a seaside resort, linked to the mainland by bridge, and the only building on Piel – apart from a reconstructed ruined castle – is an inn where the landlord is 'king' and can confer the title of 'Knight of Piel Island' on his customers. Furness Museum has displays of ship models as well as local history.

BARRY, S Glamorgan   8 ST16

Barry is an industrial town and an exporting centre for the area – its trade based mainly on coal at the turn of the century, but diversifying as early as the 1930s. It has a pebble beach, and 225-acre Porthkerry Country Park lies 2½ miles to the west. Barry Island is joined to the mainland by a causeway and has one of the largest amusement parks in the country.

THE GATE OF PARADISE *Bardsey Island, one of the sacred places of Celtic pilgrimage, bore this title in the Dark Ages, though it now seems merely a bleak hump of land.*

Bath, Avon 3 ST76

City of Georgian Elegance

> *'I really believe I shall always be talking of Bath . . . I do like it so very much. Oh! who can ever be tired of Bath?'*
>
> JANE AUSTEN, *Northanger Abbey*

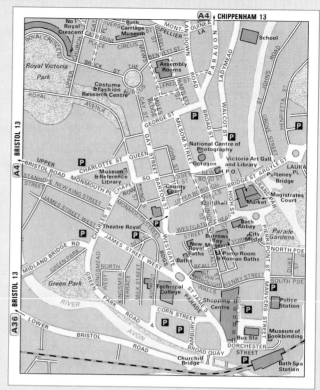

An elegant city of well-preserved Georgian buildings in the mellow local stone, Bath has its origins in the 1st-century Roman Spa of Aquae Sulis ('waters of Sul' – a Celtic goddess.) In fact its origins may be even older, and legend attributes the discovery of the springs to Bladud, a Celtic prince who is thought to have lived about 860 BC.

Since Roman times the value of the warm mineral springs has always been recognised, but the popularity of the place increased dramatically in the 18th century after Dr William Oliver – of Bath Oliver biscuit fame – opened a bath for the treatment of gout.

The building of Georgian Bath was largely due to the enterprise of a local postmaster, Ralph Allen, and the stone came from his quarries on Coombe Down. As the fine new buildings went up, the élite, led by the fashionable dandy Beau Nash, flocked to 'take the waters', and the social importance of being seen at the balls and assemblies of Bath is reflected in the pages of Smollett, Fielding, Jane Austen and Dickens. Although few people now come for health reasons, the Bath Festival of Music and Drama, held in May/June each year, attracts performers of international standing and thousands of visitors from all over the world.

PLACES TO SEE

No. 1, Royal Crescent has been restored by the Bath Preservation Society and furnished in period.

The Circus, Queen Square and Royal Crescent are fine examples of the replanned city's architecture. The formal pattern of squares, terraces and crescents and spacious thoroughfares lined with elegant houses, has never been bettered. The famous Circus and Queen Square were designed by John Wood the Elder, as was Prior Park on Coombe Down, the home of his patron, Ralph Allen. His son, John Wood the Younger, was responsible for the Palladian splendour of Royal Crescent, the first terrace ever built to this design, and one of the finest examples of its kind in Europe.

The Assembly Rooms, near The Circus, were completed in 1771 by John Wood the Younger. Badly damaged during World War II, these classically proportioned rooms have now been faithfully restored to their original elegance. In the basement is one of the world's finest museums of costume – based on the collection of Mrs Doris Langley Moore.

The Carriage Museum is housed in stables and coach-houses behind the Circus; the 30 carriages are displayed with all their accessories and trips can be taken in them during the summer.

THE KING'S BATH in the 18th century as seen (bottom) by Rowlandson. To house the fashionable, terraces like Royal Crescent (below) were built.

The Camden Works Museum preserves and displays a Victorian family business (J B Bowler) almost exactly as it would have been in its founder's day. Bowler's was a firm of engineers and brass founders, with a profitable sideline in bottled mineral waters.

The Octagon on Milsom Street, formerly a private chapel, houses the museum of the Royal Photographic Society.

The Guildhall contains a superb 18th-century banqueting hall (OACT) with three beautiful chandeliers.

The Roman Baths stand at the centre of the city, their remains shown to full advantage by means of skilful reconstruction; finds unearthed during the excavations are displayed in the adjoining museum.

The Pump Room still has two sedan chairs used by its 18th-century patrons. In these gracious surroundings modern visitors can partake of tea and coffee to the strains of music by the Pump Room Ensemble.

Bath Abbey is sometimes called the The Lantern of the West because of the enormous clear glass windows of the nave and choir. Bath owes its abbey to the energy of Oliver King, Bishop of Bath and Wells, who had a dream in which angels climbed up and down ladders to heaven and a voice exhorted a 'king to restore the church', which he did, between 1495 and 1503. His dream is carved in stone in the abbey.

Burrows Toy Museum contains exhibits covering 200 years of children's amusements.

Pulteney Bridge, based on the Ponte Vecchio ('old bridge') at Florence, is the only work of Robert Adam in Bath. The bridge, its three arches supporting a wide street lined on both sides by shops, is unique of its kind in Britain. At the western end, over the library, is the **Victoria Art Gallery** whose collections include one of antique watches.

The Holburne of Menstrie Museum in Sydney Gardens, has outstanding collections of porcelain and glass.

Claverton Manor, two and a half miles east of Bath, houses the American Museum in Britain which covers American life from the 17th–19th centuries.

BASILDON, Essex   *6 TQ78*
A village of about 200 souls until the
coming of the railway in the 19th century,
Basildon's growth was further accelerated
after the war when it was designated a
London overspill town; original plans were
for a population of 50,000, but projections
suggest 140,000. The cottages of the
original village clustered round the Holy
Cross Church, and this still stands. The
accent is on the new, however, epitomised
in the fountains and statuary of the
pedestrian concourse.

BASINGSTOKE, Hampshire
   4 SU65
London overspill has changed Basingstoke
from a pleasant country town to a complex
of shopping precincts surrounded by
industrial and housing estates. At the
centre, however, the Church of St Michael
survives, dating from Norman times and
containing some 16th-century stained glass
which came originally from the old Chapel
of the Holy Ghost, the ruins of which lie
near the station. The Willis Museum in
New Street – based on a 19th-century
collection of clocks – now also contains
items of archaeological and geological
interest.

BATTLE, E Sussex   *6 TQ71*
William the Conqueror swore that he would
build a church if he won the Battle of
Hastings, and he fulfilled that promise,
setting the high altar at the spot where
Harold fell. Nothing remains of that
original building now, and in 1903 Harold's
Stone was erected where the altar once
stood. Benedictine monks replaced this
church with St Martin's Abbey, the
remains of which (OACT) are now
incorporated into a school. Battle Historical
Society Museum in Langton House has
many relics of the Battle of Hastings,
including a half-size replica of the Bayeux
Tapestry.

BEACHY HEAD, E Sussex
   6 TV59
Beachy Head, at nearly 600ft above sea-
level, is one of the highest cliffs on the
south coast. There are magnificent views
from its top, ranging from the Isle of Wight
in the west to Dungeness in the east, and
the beam of the lighthouse at its foot sweeps
16 miles across the English Channel.

BEACONSFIELD, Buckinghamshire
   5 SU99
Beaconsfield is made up of two parts – the
old town with creeper-clad 17th-century
houses and timbered cottages, and, beyond
a strip of woodland, the new residential
area which has been developing since the
beginning of this century. The old town,
which grew up where the Oxford to
London and Aylesbury to Windsor roads
crossed, was a busy staging post and still
has several coaching inns. Highwaymen
abounded in the dense woods that fringed
the roads; cuts on the staircase of the
George Inn are said to have been made by
the sword of Claude Duval as he fought off
the Bow Street Runners. Bekonscot Model
Village (OACT) includes not only
miniature houses, but also working models
of funfair, airport, railway and docks.
Edmund Burke, the 18th-century politician
and writer, was born in Beaconsfield and
G K Chesterton lived here for many years.

LAST OF THE SAXON KINGS

This section of the Bayeux tapestry
shows the hill near Battle around
which the Battle of Hastings (so-
called) was fought on 14th October
1066. Harold's Saxon foot soldiers,
in a strategic position on top of the
hill, are under attack from the
Norman horsemen. They were defeated when William's troops lured
them from their stronghold and
killed them. The tapestry, made for
William's queen, is kept at Bayeux
in Normandy but there is a half-size
replica at the Battle Historical Society Museum.

BEAMINSTER, Dorset   *3 ST40*
The small town of Beaminster stands in an
area of outstanding natural beauty and was
much loved by Thomas Hardy, who made
it 'Emminster' in his novel, *Tess of the
D'Urbervilles*. The picturesque River Brit
runs along beside the main street, the little
square is edged by 18th-century houses of
golden Ham stone, and the church's richly
ornamented Tudor tower is one of the best
in Dorset. Rolling hills surround the town,
and 800ft-high Toller Down offers fine
views of the area. Two basically Tudor
houses stand near Beaminster – Mapperton
Manor House (gardens OACT) to the
south-east, and Parnham Manor (OACT) to
the south.

BEAMISH MUSEUM, Co Durham
   20 NZ25
The North of England Open Air Museum
was opened in 1971 on a 200-acre site that
was originally part of the Beamish Hall
Estate. It is concerned with Northern
people and their traditional way of life, and
demonstrations of such skills as bread-
baking and the making of proggy mats are
given in appropriate cottage settings. One
can go down an old pit to see the seams of
coal, or visit a farm, a Victorian
schoolroom, chemist's shop, public house
or teashop in the Hall. It is possible to
travel by tram or steam locomotive – and to
alight at Rowley Station as it was in 1876.

BEAULIEU, Hampshire   *4 SU30*
Beaulieu Abbey was founded in 1204, and
most of it has been demolished; of the parts
that remain, the refectory has been rebuilt
as the parish church, the lay dormitory is a
restaurant, and the Domus building
contains an exhibition on monastic life.
Palace House (OACT) was once the Abbey
gatehouse, but today, after being extended
and refurbished in the nineteenth-century,
it is the family home of Lord Montagu. The
National Motor Museum contains a large
library and over 250 veteran and vintage
cars, motor-cycles and bicycles. Exhibits
range from the first petrol-driven car of
1895 to Donald Campbell's 'Bluebird'.
Visitors can take monorail or veteran bus
rides in the grounds, and there is a model
railway. Steam fairs are sometimes held.

BEKONSCOT MODEL VILLAGE *The miniature village created at Beaconsfield never fails to fascinate
children with its meticulously accurate model railway and its streets of tiny houses.*

BRITAIN'S EARLIEST
TEMPLES
Stone Circles

The great stone circles of the late Stone Age and Bronze Age stand as silent witnesses to ancient ritual and beliefs long vanished. What forms of worship were practised is still a subject of debate.

CALLANISH *(left)* **on Lewis.**

STONE CIRCLES are amongst the most distinctly British of monuments, for while a few circle-like arrangments of boulders may be seen in Brittany, Britain and Ireland have a virtual monopoly of these ancient temples.

Most people will be aware of the existence of perhaps two or three British stone circles, but in addition to the major monuments there were scores of lesser stone circles containing stumpy little stones – which must have functioned as local temples for small communities. The circles are found in Scotland, Ireland, Wales and the western uplands of Britain, but they seem to have been absent in the English lowlands. This may simply reflect a lack of suitable, durable building stones in the eastern and southern plains.

Four thousand years or more after their construction, these stone rings remain uniquely fascinating and we are still groping to understand their original uses and meanings.

FANCIFUL NONSENSE has often been written about the function of the circles, in the process of academic speculation about their use. There can be little doubt that the circles were religious temples, since they can have been useful for few more mundane functions. The stones, or the outer ditches which are sometimes present seem to define a sacred area, within which rituals could be performed. Much has been written about the astronomical uses of circles, yet bulky boulders seem to be crude markers or sighting points. Such is the nature of the evidence that no astronomical claim can either be proved or disproved, while any random collection of stones will have alignments upon some heavenly event or other, for the heavens are criss-crossed with potential sighting lines. Even so, it is quite possible that some simple but significant alignments on events like the midwinter sunrise might have been included in a few monuments as secondary features. It is also possible that these temples could have served other more functional purposes as well – they could, for example have been market places for the exchange of goods like stone axes.

HENGE MONUMENTS, as the remains of ancient circular earthworks are known, tend to be a little older than stone circles, although some archaeologists believe that circles of stone were preceded in some places by timber circles. Being earthen constructions, henges have not always managed to withstand the ravages of time, and many are visible only in air photographs. Others are still imposing features of the landscape; the twin henges of King Arthur's Round Table and Mayburgh just south of Penrith are still impressive, while the Norman church at Knowlton in Dorset was built inside one of a group of henges. In some cases, circular henge earthworks surrounded the stone rings in 'henge circles' and the vast and beautiful Ring of Bordgar circle on Orkney is ringed in this way, while Stonehenge began its life as an unexceptional henge monument. The most remarkable henge earthworks surround the outer and two inner stone circles at Avebury in Wiltshire, where many visitors will find the gorge-like ditch even more staggering than the massive stones.

CIRCLES are difficult to date by archaeological means, but they seem to belong to the centuries before and around 2000 BC and can be of the later stages of the New Stone Age and of the earlier part of the Bronze Age. Their antecedents are uncertain and circles could have evolved from henges.

No two circles are exactly alike. Local geology has helped to determine some of the major differences, although the builders of Stonehenge were prepared to employ speckled bluestones which originally came from the Preselli Mountains in the south-west of Wales and to drag massive sarsen boulders across several miles of downland. The Orkney circles employ slabby sheets of the pinkish local sandstone, while the Callanish monument on Lewis is built of tough, angular blocks of the white-streaked grey gneiss which litters the barren setting. The glacial boulders of Castlerigg circle near Keswick are naturally smoothed and rounded, and the Avebury sarsens are naturally gnarled and pitted, while the sarsens of Stonehenge were pounded by hand to become smooth-faced. The Rollright Stones circle in Oxfordshire employs a local limestone and its members are pocked by weathering and dappled with lemon-coloured lichen. Other major circles include the lovely Long Meg and her daughters near Penrith, the Hurlers on Bodmin Moor and Arbor Low in Derbyshire, where the horizontal stones lie inside an impressive henge earthwork.

STONEHENGE *As twilight falls, the massive stones, stand cloaked in mystery.*

THE DEVIL'S ARROWS *(below)*.

AVEBURY *(above) Part of the village lies within the great circle which was once linked with other religious sites by avenues of stones.*

THE ROLLRIGHT STONES *(below) Pitted with holes and lichen-covered, this group, known as the King's Men, seems as old as time.*

STANDING STONES and monoliths are by no means always the remains of stone circles; some, like the enormous example in the churchyard at Rudston near Bridlington seem always to have been isolated 'monoliths' or 'menhirs'. Their functions are uncertain, but recent excavations around some western monoliths show that the solitary stone giant was sometimes surrounded by a large flock of little stones arranged in complex patterns. Occasionally, the standing stones are found in loose groups, the most impressive example being the Devil's Arrows near Boroughbridge in Yorkshire, three enormous blocks of millstone grit whose function remains completely mysterious. Other apparent stone circles are 'kerbs' of stone which originally surrounded tombs. Other circles seem rather to be henges embellished with a few standing stones, while some which the old antiquaries thought they had discovered were never temples, but the remains of the walls of ancient circular stone huts. At Merrivale on Dartmoor one can see the outlines of several such Bronze Age huts, along with one of the many puzzling stone rows, monoliths and circles, one of which surrounds a cairn.

Archaeology may never be able to provide a detailed explanation of the uses and designs of stone circles. But there is no doubt that with or without the answers to the riddles, the circles will continue to attract their scores of thousands of visitors.

As well as varying in their sizes and materials, the circles also differ in their shapes, the numbers of stones employed and their states of preservation. Many examples have been completely destroyed in the course of agricultural 'improvements', while others, like Avebury, were vandalised in the Christian era because of their associations with pagan worship. Many circles which now display just a few stones originally had many more, while some are the results of crude reconstructions so that not all the stones stand in their original places; some of the astronomical interpretations are based on such reconstructions and are therefore quite worthless. Several circles were designed in a perfectly circular form, but many others are not exactly circular, and it seems that the deviations sometimes represented attempts to create more sophisticated flattened-circle- and egg-shaped forms.

BECCLES, Suffolk *12 TM49*
Some of the ancient street names in Beccles – Saltgate and Ballygate, for example – date back to the 11th century. Newgate Museum has interesting displays about the printing trade, a prominent local industry. St Martin's Church survived fires in the 16th and 17th centuries as did Roos Hall (OACT), built in 1583 and the home of Sir John Suckling, an ancestor of Lord Nelson. The old Town Hall and St Peter's House are fine Georgian buildings.

BEDDGELERT, Gwynedd *13 SH54*
The long-held explanation of 'Beddgelert' – that it commemorates a favourite hound of Llewellyn the Great, Gelert, whom he killed in a rage, wrongly supposing the animal to have savaged his baby son when in fact the dog had killed a wolf that had attacked the child – has now been discredited. The name is more likely to have derived from 'Kelert', a St Kelert being associated with the priory that once flourished nearby. Even without the lure of the faithful hound, Beddgelert is an attractive place set where three valleys meet among the peaks of Snowdonia.

BEDFORD, Bedfordshire *11 TL04*
Bedford has existed since Saxon times and is now a thriving commercial and industrial centre on both banks of the River Great Ouse. On St Peter's Green stands a statue of John Bunyan, who lived in the town from 1655 until his death in 1688 and wrote *Pilgrim's Progress* while he was incarcerated in Bedford jail for his nonconformism. There is a John Bunyan Library in Harpur Street, and the nearby Bunyan Meeting House is now a museum.

BEDRUTHAN STEPS, Cornwall *1 SW86*
These huge, gnarled slaty rocks (NT), rising up to 200ft from an isolated beach, are held by legend to be the stepping stones of the giant Bedruthan.

BEER, Devon *3 ST28*
This seaside village was once the haunt of smugglers, attracted by the many caves in Beer Head – an isolated, 426ft chalk cliff. The Old Quarry dates back to Roman times and was worked until the 19th century. Bovey House Hotel is Tudor; its secret hiding places are a legacy of the time when it was a smugglers' lair. On the slopes behind the village the Beer Heights Light Railway runs through a Leisure Park with fine views of the bay to a full-size station, complete with refreshment room.

BEESTON CASTLE, Cheshire *14 SJ55*
Set in an almost inaccessible position on a steep rock, the ruins of Beeston Castle (AM), a former stronghold of the Earls of Chester overlook Peckforton Castle, a 19th-century mock-medieval stronghold in the Peckforton Hills near Tarporley.

BEKESBOURNE, Kent *6 TR15*
The collection of wild animals at Howletts Zoo Park includes a breeding group of gorillas. The visitor can also see snow leopards, smaller members of the cat family, tapirs and elephants. Deer and antelope run free.

BELTON, Lincolnshire *11 SK93*
Belton House (NT), built in 1685 and attributed to Wren, was the residence of the Brownlow family for almost 300 years. It has an extensive collection of paintings and porcelain, beautiful antique silver and tapestries. Lord Brownlow was Lord-in-Waiting to Edward VIII, and some personal souvenirs of the king are on display. The grounds offer nature trails and a riverside picnic area. The National Cycle, Carriage and Horse Museum is one of the many attractions of this historic property which was recently acquired by the National Trust.

BELVOIR CASTLE *Home of the Dukes of Rutland, Belvoir's towers look out on the lovely Vale of Belvoir, whose scenery is threatened by development of its coalfield.*

BELVOIR, Leicestershire *10 SK83*
Looking across the Vale of Belvoir (pronounced 'Beever') towards the Leicestershire wolds, the castle (OACT) stands on a ridge surrounded by dense woodland. In the 16th century the original 11th-century fortress was given to the Manners family, later to become Dukes of Rutland. It was rebuilt several times, and its present mock-medieval appearance is largely the work of James Wyatt in the early 19th century. The interior is famous for its Gobelin tapestries and for pictures by such artists as Van Dyck, Gainsborough and Holbein. It also houses the Regimental Museum of the 17th and 21st Lancers. The grounds – particularly the water-gardens – are splendid, and regular demonstrations of jousting and mock battles are held. This is prime fox-hunting country, and the famous Belvoir foxhound was bred here in the 18th century.

BEN NEVIS, Highland *26 NN17*
At 4406ft, Ben Nevis is Britain's highest mountain. The 2000ft-high vertical cliffs of its south-eastern face can be tackled only by skilled climbers, but the gentler south-western slope from the wooded valley of Glen Nevis offers a route to the summit that has actually been twice negotiated by car.

BEDRUTHAN STEPS *The sea has sculpted these rocks into shapes the locals have given names such as Queen Bess Rock.*

GLEN NEVIS *One of Scotland's loveliest glens, runs along the west and south flanks of Ben Nevis. The Water of Nevis, a swift-flowing mountain stream, courses between wooded banks along the valley.*

BENINGBROUGH, N Yorkshire
15 SE55
Beningbrough Hall (NT) is an attractive 18th-century red-brick house set in a wooded park. Purchased by the Earl and Countess of Chesterfield early in this century, it was forfeited in payment of death duties and passed from the Treasury to the National Trust in 1959. It contains some fine examples of wood-carving and beautiful Delft and oriental porcelain. Also on show are more than 100 pictures on loan from the National Portrait Gallery (dated 1688 to 1760).

BENINGTON, Hertfordshire
11 TL32
Benington is a very attractive village, the duckpond on the green fringed by willows and the green itself edged with 16th-century timber-and-plaster cottages and an old public house with overhanging gables. The church dates from the 13th century and has some faded medieval wallpaintings. Nearby stand the ruins of an old Norman castle on to which has been built a Georgian house, Benington Lordship, whose lovely gardens are open.

BENMORE, Strathclyde
22 NS18
The village of Benmore stands amid lochs and mountains – rising to the 2433ft peak of Beinn Mhor – with the forests of Glenbranter to the north and Glenfinart to the east. Benmore House now belongs to Edinburgh Corporation and is used as a Centre for Outdoor Pursuits; Benmore Younger Botanic Garden (OACT) specialises in conifers and shrubs.

BERKELEY, Gloucestershire
3 ST69
This small Georgian town stands at the centre of the Vale of Berkeley, a 15-mile stretch of flat land on the east bank of the Severn. It is dominated by its 12th-century castle (OACT), set in Elizabethan terraced gardens and deer park, the home of the

Berkeley family for 800 years. Here the barons gathered before they set out to witness the signing of Magna Carta in 1215, and here Edward II was murdered in 1327. The parish church has a fine rose window and its east window is dedicated to Edward Jenner, pioneer in the field of smallpox vaccination; there is also a Jenner Museum in the town, housed in the cottage that the doctor built for the first boy whom he vaccinated.

BERKHAMSTED, Hertfordshire
5 SP90
It was here that William the Conqueror accepted the throne of England from the Saxon leaders in 1066, and soon afterwards work started on the castle (AM) – of which only earthworks and a moat now remain. The Church of St Peter has a window dedicated to the 18th-century poet, William Cowper, whose father was its rector. Novelist Graham Greene was also born in Berkhamsted while his father was headmaster of the public school. The Grand Union Canal (built in the 19th century to link London and Birmingham) passes through the town, and Berkhamsted Common (NT) lies to the north.

BERKSWELL, W Midlands
10 SP27
The well of the village's name can still be seen, just outside the churchyard gate. The church dates from about 1150 and has a Norman chancel with the two original crypts beneath, one – the octagonal – being unique; the timbered and gabled 16th-century porch is unusual in having two storeys. Blind Hall and Ram Hall are interesting Tudor houses, while Berkswell Hall is noted for its rhododendrons. The 400-year-old Bear Inn has its original open fireplace and a cannon captured in the Crimean War. On the green stands a whipping post and a set of stocks with only five holes – an oddity which local legend ascribes to the village's once having a one-legged persistent wrongdoer!

BERRY POMEROY, Devon *2 SX86*
In a wooded valley to the north-east of the village stand the impressive ruins of Berry Pomeroy Castle (AM), founded by Ralph de Pomeroy in the late 13th century and destroyed during the Civil Wars of the 17th century. A wishing tree in the grounds is supposed to grant the requests of anyone walking round it backwards three times. The village itself is tiny, but it has a fine church of red Devon stone, built 500 years ago on Norman foundations by the Pomeroy family – whose coat of arms adorns the porch – and containing a 42ft long screen with fine tracings of saints.

BERWICK-UPON-TWEED, Northumberland *24 NU05*
Berwick-upon-Tweed, the most northerly town in the country, changed hands 13 times in the border struggles between England and Scotland before surrendering to the English Crown in 1482. The Elizabethan town walls (AM) – built as a defence against gunpowder – are ten feet thick in places, and the two-mile walk around their tops from Meg's Mound gives a fine view of the river, shipyards, salmon fisheries, quay and shore. Several of the houses on the quay are Georgian, as is the Town Hall, and the parish church (one of the few built during the period of the Commonwealth) dates from the 17th century, though it was extended in the 19th with stone from the castle ruins. The town has three bridges – the Royal Tweed road bridge of 1928, the 1850 Royal Border Bridge which carries the railway, and the 15-arch stone bridge built in 1611 on the orders of James I to link Berwick to Tweedmouth on the other side of the estuary. The Museum of the King's Own Scottish Borderers is housed in a barracks designed by Vanbrugh.

BETHESDA, Gwynedd *13 SH66*
Bethesda is named after its Nonconformist Chapel – a practice quite common in Wales, as witness Nebo, Carmel, Salem and Bethania. The town is surrounded by some of the most spectacular scenery in Snowdonia and has what is probably the world's largest slate quarry – covering 560 acres and over 1000ft deep – which is still producing slate of fine quality though it has been worked since 1765.

BETWYS-Y-COED, Gwynedd *13 SH75*
Three rivers, the Conwy, Llugwy and Lledr, foam over rocks between beautiful wooded slopes to meet in Betwys-y-Coed – a popular touring centre since Victorian times. Its most famous sight is the Swallow Falls, on the Llugwy two miles west of the town, where a railed footpath gives fine views of the spectacular series of cascades. The Conwy Falls and Fairy Glen Ravine are also well worth seeing. Near the town a picturesque 15th-century stone bridge, the Pont-y-Pair (or 'Bridge of the Cauldron'), crosses the Llugwy, with the strange Miners' Bridge – sloping from one bank to the other – further west; the Conwy is spanned by Thomas Telford's iron Waterloo Bridge (built in the year of the battle). Cyffty Lead Mine Trail in nearby Gwydyr Forest takes walkers round the old mine buildings. The Conwy Valley Railway Museum covers the whole railway scene, with special reference to North Wales.

BIBURY *The 19th-century artist and poet, William Morris, thought Bibury – its stone houses set beside the River Colne – the most beautiful village in England.*

BEVERLEY, Humberside   16 TA03
The prosperous market town of Beverley, its charter dating from 1129, was formerly the capital of Yorkshire's East Riding. The twin towers of the Minster are a landmark for miles, and it is generally recognised as one of the finest churches in Europe. St Mary's Church – also originally 14th-century – was largely rebuilt in the Tudor period, but the chancel ceiling, made up of 40 panels depicting the kings of England, is about 100 years older. Between the two churches are the Wednesday Market, a square surrounded by fine Georgian houses, and the Saturday market, with the Market Cross. Lairgate Hall – now used as municipal offices – has an interesting Chinese Room (OACT) with an Adam ceiling and hand-painted wallpaper, and the East Yorkshire Regiment Museum is housed at No. 11 Butcher Row. North Bar is the only one of the town's five medieval gates to have survived.

BEWDLEY, Hereford and Worcester   9 SO77
One of the stations on the Severn Valley Railway, Bewdley is an extremely attractive old town, the three-arched Telford bridge over the Severn leading into Load Street with its many fine Georgian houses. A museum in the Old Shambles illustrates traditional local trades, including the making of rope and charcoal-burning; occasional demonstrations are given by craftsmen. Not far away is the West Midlands Safari Park, on the A456 Kidderminster road, a popular local pleasure park with animal reserves and many other attractions.

BIBURY, Gloucestershire   10 SP10
Bibury is still charming despite its position on a busy main road. Arlington Row (NT) is now a terrace of gabled cottages; it began as a 14th-century sheep-house and was converted in the 17th-century to provide accommodation for workers at nearby Arlington Mill (now a museum). St Mary's Church is a blend of Saxon, Norman and Early English and has two interesting brasses depicting skeletons. Jacobean Bibury Court is now a hotel.

BICESTER, Oxfordshire   10 SP52
Bicester, on the edge of the Vale of Aylesbury, is a hunting centre so sensitive to the well-being of horses that its roadsides have wide grass verges to make the going easier for them. Sixteenth-century houses stand on the old Market Square – still the centre of the town – and there are other ancient buildings in Sheep Street and near the 12th-century church.

BICKLEIGH, Devon   2 SS90
Bickleigh is an attractive village of thatched, whitewashed cottages set where a five-arched bridge spans the Exe. Across the river stands Bickleigh Castle (OACT), also known as The Court. To the north of the village, Bickleigh Mill Craft Centre (OACT) – an old working watermill – has been given over to such traditional skills as woodturning, pottery and the making of corn dollies. There is a museum in adjacent Heritage Farm, which also has working shire-horses and many rare breeds of farm animals.

BIDDENDEN, Kent   6 TQ83
On the green at Biddenden stands a village sign depicting the Biddenden Maids – Siamese twins Eliza and Mary Chulkhurst, reputedly born joined at shoulder and hip some time in the 12th century. They lived for 34 years, and bequeathed 20 acres of land to provide an annual 'dole' for the poor; this, in the traditional form of bread and cheese, is still given to pensioners on Easter Monday, and commemorative biscuits showing the Maids are distributed to onlookers. Many of the half-timbered cottages of Biddenden have been converted into antique shops or eating-places to cater for visitors, and the weavers' houses and shops in High Street have now been declared Ancient Monuments. A fine medieval Cloth Hall survives, as do original pavements of Bethersden marble, which used to be quarried near here.

BIDEFORD, Devon   2 SS42
Sir Richard Grenville, famous for his fight against the Spaniards in the Azores in 1591, was a Bideford man, and his ship, *The Revenge*, was crewed by local men. He obtained a charter from Elizabeth I for the town, and its position on the River Torridge made it a prosperous port until trade declined in the 18th century. The bridge that spans the river here is famous; 677ft long, and with 24 arches, it still has some of the original 15th-century stonework. Offshore lies **Lundy Island** (NT), which can be reached by launch.

LUNDY STAMPS

By far the oldest and most 'genuine' local issues, Lundy stamps were first used in 1929 when the GPO closed the island post office. About 60,000 stamps are used each year, and they help defray the cost of transporting post to the mainland. The current issue is on sale in the island shop.

BIGGAR, Strathclyde   23 NT03
Each July, the 'Fleming Queen' is crowned here in a ceremony commemorating Mary Fleming, one of the 'four Marys' who were ladies-in-waiting to Mary Queen of Scots, the others being Mary Seton, Mary Beaton and Mary Livingstone. The Gladstone Court Museum – named after the family of the Victorian Prime Minister, who came from the area – contains, among other items of interest, a street of re-created 19th-century shops. Greenhill Covenanters' House (OACT) contains relics of covenanters.

BIGGLESWADE, Bedfordshire   11 TL14
The Shuttleworth Collection of Historic Aeroplanes and Cars (OACT), situated at Old Warden Aerodrome contains a wide range of methods of transport – and on certain days it is possible to take a plane trip. Swiss Garden (OACT), also at Old Warden has many rare plants.

BIGNOR, W Sussex *5 SU91*
The 4½-acre site of Bignor Roman Villa
(OACT) – first excavated in 1811, after a
section of floor depicting a dancing girl was
discovered during farm work – contains
some of the finest mosaics in the country.
The buildings, set round a large courtyard,
seem to have been the home of a rich man,
and they were probably occupied from the
2nd to 4th centuries AD. The results of
various digs are shown in the site museum.

BIRKENHEAD, Merseyside *14 SJ38*
Birkenhead, on the Mersey, gained
dramatically in importance with the
building of the shipyards in 1824 and the
docks in 1847. The coming of prosperity is
reflected in the impressive 19th-century
buildings, the Town Hall being a fine
example. The Williamson Art Gallery and
Museum has extensive collections of
English watercolours and ceramics.

BIRMINGHAM, W Midlands *10 SP08*
Birmingham, second only to London in
size, and a city since 1889, is traditionally
the home of small industries – anything
from coins and guns to steam locomotives
were made here. This rich industrial
heritage is admirably displayed in
Birmingham's excellent Museum of Science
and Industry.

Originally smiths of all kinds were
attracted by the availability of fuel from the
mines of north Warwickshire, and settled
in different parts of the city. Around St
Paul's Church, for example, was the old
silversmith's quarter. Nowadays the
principle industry is the supply of
components for the motor industry. The
university was founded in 1900, and in
1966 the College of Advanced Technology
in Aston also received university status.

There are two cathedrals – St Philip's
built as the parish church in 1711, which
has four superb pre-Raphaelite windows by
Sir Edward Burne-Jones, who was
christened here, and the Roman Catholic St
Chad's. The Victorian centre of
Birmingham was Victoria Square, where
the neo-classical Council House, with its
clock tower emulating Big Ben, dominates
the scene. The Town Hall, modelled on a
classical Roman temple, houses a fine organ
on which Mendelssohn gave several
concerts, and is the home of the
Birmingham Symphony Orchestra. Part of
the Council House is used for the Art
Gallery, which has an important collection
of modern sculpture and pre-Raphaelite
paintings, as well as the interesting Pinto
Gallery of wooden bygones.

Birmingham is said to have more miles of
waterway than Venice, though much of this
intricate network of canals is hidden and
neglected. Gas Street Basin and James
Brindley Walk, however, have been
restored and parts of the canals are now
lively once more.

The city is proud of its progressive
attitudes – symbolised perhaps by the
Rotunda in the Bull Ring, the Central
Library, an arrangement of ziggurat-like
buildings around a quadrangle, and the
road interchange system at Gravelly Hill,
popularly known as Spaghetti Junction.
Birmingham is now well established as an
international exhibition centre, with the
building of the massive new complex –
complete with its own railway station –
eight miles east of the city centre.

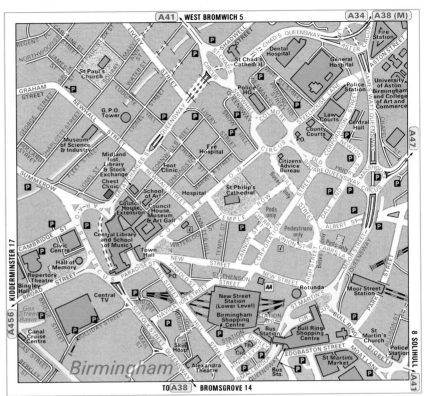

GAS STREET BASIN *Long neglected, Birmingham's canals are being renovated for pleasure craft.*

BIRNAM, Tayside *27 NO04*
Birnam Wood stands 12 miles south-west of
Dunsinane Hill – and the ironic prophecy
that Macbeth should not fall 'till Birnam
Wood remove to Dunsinane' was fulfilled
when his enemies camouflaged themselves
with branches before making their attack.
Today the wood consists mainly of silver
birch and scrub oak.

BISHOP AUCKLAND, Co Durham
20 NZ23
Bishop Auckland grew up round a market
at the gates of the Bishop of Durham's
palace, which began as a manor house in
the 12th century; it was extensively
improved in about 1300 and renovated in
the 18th century. The residents of today's
busy commercial town still have access to
the 800-acre Bishops Park, with its fine
lawns and trees and the small streams of the
Gaunless and Coundon Burn. The
impressive gatehouse is 18th-century, as is

a deer shelter inside the park, and a screen
of stone arches designed by James Wyatt in
about 1800 divides off the private palace
grounds. St Andrews's Church, to the
south of the town, is the largest parish
church in the county. It contains a 9th-
century Anglo-Saxon cross and a holy water
stoup made from a Roman altar.

BISHOP BURTON, Humberside
16 SE93
A large wayside pool reflects this attractive
black-and-white wold village, with
picturesque cottages set around its green.
For centuries it belonged to the
Archbishops of York, and one of their
palaces is said to have stood in a nearby
field called Knight Garth. Bishop Burton's
parish church contains a bust of John
Wesley, carved from an elm under which
he preached when he came to the village.
His visit is also commemorated by an open-
air service on the green each July.

THE FESTINIOG RAILWAY *was designed to a 2ft gauge and completed in 1836 to carry slate to Porthmadog from the vast quarries that ringed Blaenau Ffestiniog (left). Originally worked by horses it went over to steam in 1863. From the 1890s trade declined until the railway finally closed in 1946. Since 1951, however, the Festiniog Railway Society have worked to restore and re-open the line right through to Blaenau Ffestiniog – a goal they achieved in 1982. The trains now carry local traffic and Red Star parcels, performing a useful local service. 'Linda' was built in 1893 for the Penrhyn Railway.*

BISHOP'S CANNINGS, Wiltshire
3 SU06

Bishop's Cannings, a charming village of thatched and timbered cottages, lies in the shadow of St Mary's, which contains a rare meditation seat, painted with an enormous hand and inscribed with salutary Latin texts. From the 16th century to the 18th the village was the haunt of smugglers, and Wiltshire folk are called 'moonrakers' because of the story that the locals fooled the authorities into believing that they were trying to catch the moon's reflection when they were actually fishing for hidden casks.

BISHOP'S CASTLE, Shropshire
8 SO38

The original castle – now just a few stones – was built in 1127. The town stands on the edge of the Clun Forest, 500ft above sea level and surrounded by hills, the highest rising to 1500ft. It has three Tudor houses – the Old Hall, the Old Market Hall and the Old House on Crutches, with its overhanging upper storey supported on posts. The Town Hall is one of the smallest in England and contains two silver maces hallmarked 1697. The Three Tuns Inn dates from 1642 and is one of the few remaining public houses where the beer is made on the premises.

BISHOP'S STORTFORD,
Hertfordshire   *11 TL42*

For centuries the town has been the shopping and market centre for the area, but industrial interests began to develop when the River Stort was made navigable in the 19th century. The 15th-century church has some of its original woodcarving, and the old vicarage in South Road – where Cecil Rhodes, founder of Rhodesia, was born in 1853 – is now a museum.

BISHOP'S WALTHAM, Hampshire
4 SU51

The castle at Bishop's Waltham was the seat of the Bishops of Winchester, started in the 12th century. It was severely damaged by Cromwellian forces in the Civil War but the remains (AM) include parts of the great hall, cloister and tower.

BLACKBURN, Lancashire   *14 SD62*

The old and new merge in Blackburn – the old mills crowding round the canal locks and the clear-cut lines of the new multi-storey buildings rising above them. The town has been involved in the manufacture of textiles ever since Flemish weavers settled here in the 14th century (though it has now diversified into brewing, engineering and the making of electrical equipment) and the Lewis Textile Museum traces the development of the industry. It includes a model of the spinning jenny, for its inventor – James Hargreaves – was a Blackburn weaver.

BLACK COUNTRY, THE,
W Midlands   *10 SO99, SP18*

The name given to the once smoke-blackened industrial area between Birmingham and Wolverhampton.

BLACKNESS, Central   *23 NT08*

The ruined 15th-century castle (AM) – often called Ship Castle because of its shape – was one of the four left fortified in Scotland after it was merged with England by the Act of Union in 1707; it has been a prison for Covenanters in the 17th century, a powder magazine in the 19th – and a youth hostel in the 20th! The Binns (NTS) is a mansion built in 1478 and once linked to the castle by underground passage.

BLACKPOOL, Lancashire   *14 SD33*

Blackpool is perhaps best-known for its 'Golden Mile' of funfair attractions on the South Shore and the 518ft-high tower, with its ballroom, zoo, circus and aquarium. Trams, the last of their kind in England, run along the front, and the famous illuminated decorations attract many visitors each autumn. The beach stretches for six miles, and there are three piers with all the usual attractions – but the town also offers theatres, gardens, horse-trials, dog shows and dance festivals.

BLAENAU FFESTINIOG, Gwynedd
14 SH74

Blaenau Ffestiniog has been called 'a town of slate and rain', and certainly slate is very much in evidence – in the building of the houses, walls and paths, and in the towering tips of the background. The narrow-gauge Festiniog Railway – which originally used horses to pull its wagons – was built to carry the slate from here to Porthmadog, a thriving slate-exporting centre. However, at the turn of the century other roofing materials were introduced and the slate mines became unprofitable. Now they have taken on a new lease of life as a tourist attraction, for both the award-winning Llechwedd Slate Caverns and Gloddfa Ganol Slate Mine give a fascinating glimpse of the old days of slate mining. The Festiniog Railway has been re-opened, too; the final section of line was restored in 1982.

BLAIR ATHOLL, Tayside   *26 NN86*

The village of Blair Atholl stands on the River Garry where several glens meet – the situation chosen by the Duke of Atholl for his stronghold in 1269. The castle (OACT) is still the seat of the Duke of Atholl, head of Clan Murray – and the only British subject allowed to maintain a private army (the Atholl Highlanders). It contains a fine tapestry room and displays of china, weapons, armour and Jacobite relics.

BLAIR DRUMMOND, Central
22 NS79

The Safari Park at Blair Drummond (OACT) features a wide variety of animals in their natural surroundings. It includes a Pets' Corner and such attractions as Boat Safari and Astra Glide. There are picnic and amusement areas.

BLAIRGOWRIE, Tayside *27 NO14*
The little town of Blairgowrie lies at the centre of a prosperous soft-fruit-growing area, and it is also a resort – popular with anglers and with tourists exploring the area. The River Ericht is spanned here by the 19th-century Brig o'Blair which links the town to Rattray; two miles further north it flows through a steep gorge, above which stands 17th-century Craighall, the mansion which may be the original of Tully-Veolan in Scott's *Waverley*. Meikleour, four miles south-west of the town, is notable for a magnificent beech hedge – over 200 years old, 600 yds long and 90ft high – at modern Meikleour House.

BLAIRLOGIE, Central *22 NS89*
At one time Blairlogie was known as 'Goats' Milk Spa', for people in delicate health came from far and wide to drink the health-giving milk of the local animals. In 1820, however, mineral springs were discovered at nearby Bridge of Allan, and as its popularity waxed, Blairlogie's waned. The village was the first in Scotland to be conserved, and its jumble of cottages, backed by the 1375ft Dumyat, looks much as it did a hundred years ago. Two notable houses are The Blair, mainly 16th-century, and Powis House, built in 1750, which has some Adam characteristics.

BLAKENEY, Norfolk *12 TG04*
This village on the estuary of the River Glaven used to be a busy port and is now a popular boating centre. The church of St Nicholas reflects its preoccupation with things maritime, having a second tower which was used as a beacon to guide sailors at one time. The marshy flats which extend north-west towards Blakeney Point are rich in plant and insect life, and a ferry service sometimes runs to the 1000-acre Nature Reserve and bird sanctuary at the Point.

BLANCHLAND, Northumberland
19 NY95
The grey and yellow stone cottages of Blanchland were actually built in the 18th century to house workers at the nearby leadmines. Their arrangement, however, is based on the ground plan of a 12th-century monastic settlement, and the paved enclosure they surround was once an abbey courtyard. The church incorporates the remains of the original abbey, the Lord Crewe Arms includes part of its guesthouse, and a 15th-century gatehouse makes an impressive entrance to the village.

BLANTYRE, Strathclyde *22 NS65*
Blantyre is chiefly famous for its connection with explorer David Livingstone, born in 1813 in Shuttle Row. His birthplace has been restored and houses a museum, and there is a Livingstone Memorial Church which bears his statue on the tower.

BLANDFORD FORUM, Dorset
3 ST80
Blandford Forum (the suffix means 'market') was a very old settlement, but a fire in 1731 destroyed it almost completely, leaving a mere 50 or so houses standing. The rebuilt town has the classical proportions of Georgian architecture – the Corn Exchange being a fine example of the style. The only major buildings to survive were the Old House, Dale House and Ryves Almhouses, all 17th-century.

BLICKLING, Norfolk *12 TG12*
Early 17th-century Blickling Hall (NT) is a fine example of Jacobean architecture; it stands in formal gardens laid out by Repton and pleasant parkland where a crescent-shaped lake has been enlarged to stretch almost a mile. The pyramid-shaped mausoleum was designed by the Italian architect Bonomi in 1793 for the Earl and Countess of Buckingham. The State Rooms of the house have magnificent furniture and pictures, and the library contains the finest collection of pre-16th-century books in England. The estate was once owned by the Boleyn family, and Anne was born and spent her childhood in an earlier house on the same site. The Church of St Andrew (originally Early English, but much restored in the 19th century) has a typically East Anglian octagonal font and contains a memorial to Anne Boleyn.

BLISLAND, Cornwall *1 SX07*
Blisland – known in medieval times as Blisland-juxta-montem – is set against the western edge of Bodmin Moor. The little church is well-known for its carved screen, restored in the 19th century to the bright colours that the craftsmen of the Middle Ages would have used; it also has fine wagon roofs and a Jacobean pulpit. The dedication is to Sts Protus and Hyacinth, and in late September their feast is celebrated with a procession, followed next day by the traditional sheep fair. The village is set around a tree-bordered green – unusual in Cornwall.

BLYTH, Northumberland *20 NZ38*
A shipbuilding and coal-shipping centre in the 19th century, Blyth now serves as the industrial port for a large manufacturing area. Yachtsmen and fishermen also use the harbour, and a three-mile stretch of white sand attracts some holiday makers, although the town has never become a popular resort.

BLYTH, Nottinghamshire *15 SK68*
Blyth stands where an 18th-century bridge crosses the River Ryton on the old London to York highway. It was a staging point in Georgian days and still has three coaching inns, the Angel being the oldest. The Church of Sts Mary and Martin was part of an 11th-century Benedictine Priory and its nave is a particularly interesting example of early Norman work. Facing the elm-shaded village green is an ancient stone building with a 700-year-old doorway; now a private residence, it was founded in the 12th century as a leper hospital.

BLYTHBURGH, Suffolk *12 TM47*
Blythburgh's 15th-century church is one of the best-known in East Anglia; its size is indicative of the town's importance at that time – when it was a thriving port, with its own mint and two annual fairs – and the building rises magnificently above the marshy estuary of the River Blyth. The town's prosperity declined, however, as ships became bigger and could no longer use the river, and the church was neglected until restoration began in 1931. It has an angel roof and particularly fine carving – including vivid portrayals of the Seven Deadly Sins on the bench-ends. The wooden Jack-o'-the-Clock is one of the few examples now left in England.

BODIAM, E Sussex *6 TQ72*
At the edge of the village of Bodiam the romantic silhouette of its castle (NT) is reflected among the water-lilies of a moat designed to look like a lake. It was built in the 14th century, when the Rother was navigable as far as Bodiam and the French seemed set on hostilities. This attack did not materialise, and the castle also survived the Civil War, but soon afterwards it became uninhabited and fell into decay. The building remains a shell, but the exterior was restored early this century by Lord Curzon, who gave it to the nation.

BLICKLING HALL (NT) *is the Eastern Region Headquarters of the National Trust. Behind the house, Repton's formal gardens rise up the gentle slope of a hill.*

BODMIN, Cornwall *1 SX06*

Bodmin, set on the steep south-western edge of the moor, was once Cornwall's largest town and is the only one in the area mentioned in the Domesday Book. St Petroc is said to have founded a monastery here in the 6th century; he was the patron saint of the 12th-century Augustinian priory, and his name lives on in 15th-century St Petroc's – the largest parish church in the county. At one time the town was renowned for holy wells believed to cure eye complaints, and one, St Guron's, can be seen near the church. The Assizes are still held in Bodmin, though the 1974 local government changes diminished its importance as a borough.

BODMIN MOOR, Cornwall *1 SX17*

The rocky slopes of Bodmin Moor – designated an area of outstanding natural beauty – extend for about 12 square miles, and few roads cross their wild solitude. The plateau of the moor stands about 800ft high, and from this rise steep granite tors – the tallest being Brown Willy (1375ft) and Rough Tor (1312ft).

BOAT OF GARTEN, Highland
26 NH91

This village on the River Spey adopted its odd name from the ferry that served it before the bridge was built. The Strathspey Railway Association operates steam locomotives on five miles of line between

Boat of Garten and **Aviemore** (OACT). Ospreys – once believed extinct in Britain – now breed round Loch Garten; there is an RSPB observation point on the loch.

BOGNOR REGIS, W Sussex *5 SZ99*

Much of the architecture of Bognor Regis dates from the 18th century when it was a watering-place favoured by the aristocracy. It originated, however, as a Saxon, then medieval fishing village. Its attractions for today's visitor include good seafishing, five miles of sand and shingle beaches, bathing and a pier. Hotham House (OACT) is a Georgian mansion surrounded by woodland and gardens; its amenities include a children's zoo.

Coast and Tableland of South-east Cornwall
75 miles

Beneath the brooding heights of Bodmin Moor lies a high tableland stretching down to the coastal resorts of Looe and Polperro. Deep wooded valleys break up the surface of the plateau, and three of Cornwall's most historic towns lie within its bounds – St German's, a tiny village which was once the cathedral 'city' of the Duchy, and two of its four stannary towns, Liskeard and Lostwithiel.

Leave **Bodmin** on B3268 Lostwithiel road passing Lanhydrock Park on the left just after crossing the A30. At Sweetshouse, keep left and continue to **Lostwithiel**. From town centre turn right into Fore St, and at the end turn right to cross the Fowey. Cross a level crossing and in ¼ mile at crossroads turn right for **Lerryn**. At the post office keep left, then next left SP Polperro. In ¾ mile go forward at

crossroads and after 1½ miles at T-junction turn left. In 2 miles turn right to enter **Lanreath**. Keep left at church, then right on to B3359 for Pelynt. In 1½ miles turn right, SP Polperro, then again right on to A387 for **Polperro**. Return along A387 and keep with this road into Looe. From **Looe**, follow signs Plymouth via Torpoint and leave on A387, but in ½ mile, on the ascent, branch right on to B3253. In 3¾ miles rejoin A387 and at

Hessenford turn right on to B3247 SP Seaton. Continue to **Downderry**. Negotiate hairpin bend out of the village and in 1¼ miles bear right SP Crafthole. Continue on the Millbrook road for 2 miles, then turn right SP Whitsand Bay. The route leads to Cawsand and Kingsand, then bears left and in ½ mile turns right (SP Millbrook). At the top of the hill turn left on to B3247 (detour right to Mount Edgcumbe House) and at **Millbrook** turn left SP Torpoint, then bear right uphill. In 2¾ miles turn right for Antony where A374 Torpoint road leads to Antony House. The main drive turns left on to A374 SP Liskeard. At Polbathic turn right on to the B3249 SP St Germans and in 1 mile bear left SP Saltash to reach **St Germans**. On leaving village branch left SP Liskeard and then ¾ mile after crossroads turn right on to A374. At roundabout take 2nd exit to join A38. Follow the road for 5½ miles before branching left on to A390 for **Liskeard**. South of Liskeard on B3254 then SP by-road St Keyne is the Paul Corin Musical Collection. To leave Liskeard follow SP Bodmin and rejoin A38 for Dobwalls. Continue on A38 and A389 into Bodmin.

PLACES TO SEE

Bodmin St Petroc's church, the largest parish church in Cornwall.

Lanhydrock House (NT) Exquisite long gallery and two-storey gatehouse.

Restormel Castle (OACT) Ruined fortress of the Earls of Cornwall.

Lanreath Farm museum with old implements and demonstrations of rural crafts.

Polperro Picturesque old fishing village.

Looe Cornwall's chief centre for shark fishing has many old buildings and two museums – the Guildhall Museum and a Cornish folklore museum.

Woolly Monkey Sanctuary These rare South American monkeys and other animals can be seen at large in a free-roaming sanctuary.

Mount Edgcumbe House Restored Tudor mansion with good collection of furniture. Fine views across to Plymouth.

Antony House (NT) Queen Anne mansion, home of the Carew family.

St German's Former cathedral city of Cornwall. Fine Norman church.

Paul Corin Musical Collection Mechanical musical instruments from all over Europe are housed here in an old mill, including fairground organs, café and street organs and pianos. Exhibits are played every day.

Dobwalls Forest miniature railway based on American railroad in steam era.

Carnglaze Slate Caverns Slate caverns to explore where slate has been quarried here for six centuries.

BOLTON, Greater Manchester
14 SD70
Though engineering is Bolton's leading industry today, the town is traditionally connected with cotton, and two inventions that changed the course of the textile industry were made here in the 18th century. Arkwright's water frame and Crompton's spinning mule are among items displayed at Tonge Moor Textile Museum. Crompton's experiments were carried out while he was living at Hall i' th' Wood (OACT), a 15th-century half-timbered manor house which now contains a folk museum. Smithill's Hall (OACT), another fine half-timbered house, dates back to the previous century. The Old Man and Scythe Inn is housed in a building that has its origin in the 13th century; in 1641 Cromwell lodged Lord Derby there the night before he executed him. The Civic Centre is modern, with a museum and art gallery.

BOLTON ABBEY, N Yorkshire
15 SE05
The remains of 12th-century Bolton Abbey (in fact a priory) stand on the bank of the River Wharfe against a background of woods, meadows and waterfalls – the setting made famous by Landseer's painting of 'Bolton Abbey in Olden Time'. The nave still stands, having been used as a parish church since about 1170, and a gatehouse to the west has been incorporated into Bolton Hall, a 19th-century mansion. There are beautiful walks beside the river to the Strid, where the water surges under limestone ledges ('strid' being the Old English word for 'turmoil'), or on to 15th-century Barden Tower, which stands above a lovely humpbacked bridge.

BONAWE, Strathclyde *26 NN03*
The 18th-century ironworks of Bonawe stand on the south shore of Loch Etive, surrounded by mountains. Iron-smelting is now more associated with the Lowlands of Scotland, but the vast areas of woodland in the Highlands attracted the industry at a time when charcoal furnaces were used. A Lancashire firm began work here in 1762, employing hundreds of local people and setting up school, church, inn and quay. Towards the end of the 19th century the project was abandoned as being no longer profitable, and the buildings were left to rot. The Department of the Environment has now stepped in, however, and restored casting house, filling house and storage sheds. The furnace itself – built into the side of the hill so that it could be filled from above – still has lintels dated 1753.

BO'NESS, Central *23 NS98*
The Roman fortification known as the Antonine Wall had its eastern end at Bo'ness (Borrowstounness); a facsimile of a distance slab excavated in 1868 has been set up at the east end of the town, the original being on display in Edinburgh's National Museum of Antiquities. Bo'ness was an important port in the 19th century (until the development of Grangemouth a few miles away), but it is now involved in industry. Kinneil Museum, housed in the renovated 17th-century stable block of Kinneil House (AM), traces the growth of the town's industry and also has an extensive display of local pottery. Kinneil House itself has interesting 16th- and 17th-

BORTH-Y-GEST *Backed by wooded hills, this crescent-shaped village has changed little since Victorian times when many of its pleasant houses were built.*

century wall paintings, and in 1764 James Watt experimented with his steam engine in its park. The grounds are now open to the public, and Bo'ness car hill climb takes place here.

BORTH-Y-GEST, Gwynedd *13 SH53*
Borth-y-Gest, a neat Victorian village one mile from Porthmadog is a place of serene beauty, set against the magnificent backdrop of Moel-y-Gest. It has a sandy beach, and there is good bathing from sheltered coves. Tradition says that Prince Madog, son of Owain Gwynedd, left from its picturesque harbour when he set out to discover America 300 years before Columbus.

BOSBURY, Hereford & Worcester
9 SO64
Bosbury is notable for its free-standing church tower (one of seven in the county). The church itself was built in the 12th century as a refuge from the Welsh raiders whose depradations continued for the next hundred years. It contains two Elizabethan tombs of 1573, and a rare preaching cross survives in the churchyard. In the main street, the Crown Inn (with a panelled room dating from 1571) stands among attractive black-and-white cottages, whilst oast-houses are a reminder that this is the heart of an important hop-growing area.

BOSCASTLE, Cornwall *1 SX09*
Picturesque Boscastle is set in a glen where the Rivers Jordan and Valency converge before meeting the sea – which they do with dramatic effects when rivers are high and tides strong. The small harbour (NT) is protected by cliffs on either side, and behind it the long, broad road which forms the main part of the village rises through steep woodland. The Museum of Witchcraft and Black Magic has eerie but

fascinating displays from all parts of the south-west peninsula. One mile east of the village stands the isolated Church of St Juliot – its restoration in 1870 having been supervised by novelist Thomas Hardy – then still a practising architect.

BOSHAM, W Sussex *4 SU80*
Bosham, a popular yachting centre and the haunt of artists, occupies a small peninsula on Chichester harbour – and the high, stepped doors of houses near the quay are an eloquent reminder of the town's vulnerability to the tides. Legend claims that King Cnut tried to turn back the waves at Bosham, and also that his daughter is buried here; certainly a Saxon stone coffin containing the bones of a young child was found in the church about 100 years ago. The church is depicted in the Bayeux Tapestry, for Harold Godwin (later to become King Harold) attended mass here before sailing for France in 1064 to enter into the negotiations with William of Normandy that were to culminate in the Battle of Hastings.

BOSHERSTON, Dyfed *7 SR99*
Bosherston Pools – which in fact join to make a three-pronged lake – were formed when the mouths of three rivers were cut off from the sea by a sand bar. In summer the Pools are a magnificent sight, their surfaces transformed by a mass of white water-lilies. To the south, below Trevallen Downs, tiny St Govan's Chapel (measuring 20ft by 12ft) stands wedged into the cliffs and can be reached only by a steep flight of steps; it is mainly 13th-century. To the west along the cliffs stands Elegug Stack, a huge limestone stack which is covered with seabirds in the breeding season. Much of the area around Bosherston is part of the Castlemartin tank-firing range, and notices give details of times of restricted access.

Bournemouth, Dorset 3 SZ09

Queen of the South Coast

'Bournemouth where . . . the magic hand of enterprise has converted the silent and unfrequented vale into the gay resort of fashion and the favoured retreat of the invalid . . .'

Hampshire Advertiser (1842)

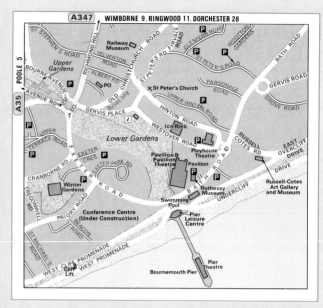

Bournemouth was 'discovered' by Victorian society in the mid-19th century when an eminent physician – one Dr Granville – recommended its mild, sunny climate to those in delicate health. Until 1811 the area had been completely undeveloped, a tract of wild commonland between Christchurch and Poole through which the stream of the Bourne wound its way to the sea. Then a local squire, Lewis Tregonwell, built himself a summer home where the Royal Exeter Hotel now stands, and in 1837 another local landowner, Sir George Tapps, saw the potential of the area and began to establish a resort to the east of Tregonwell's house. His investment was the beginning of a massive expansion; in the second 50 years of the last century the town's population grew from 695 to 59,000, as rich gentlemen built villas among the pines of the river valley and speculators erected hotels on the cliff tops.

The popularity of 'The Queen of the South' continues today, for few resorts can rival its six miles of sheltered sandy beaches, or the magnificence of the 100ft-high cliffs, split dramatically by wooded chines. The town does not rely solely on its natural advantages to tempt the holiday-maker, however: lifts and zig-zag walks connect the beaches with street-level, where, behind the promenades and gardens, is a modern town with excellent shops and a wide range of restaurants, cinemas and theatres. All sorts of sporting facilities are available – or, for those who prefer passive participation, there are league football, county cricket and tennis tournaments to watch.

Parks and gardens cover 2000 acres, one-sixth of the area of Bournemouth. The valley of the Bourne has been landscaped into Lower, Central and Upper Gardens, ablaze with flowering trees and shrubs in the early summer.

PLACES TO SEE

The Pavilion looks out over Lower Gardens; it was opened in 1929 and has restaurant, ballroom and theatre.

BOURNEMOUTH SANDS (below) in Victorian days – complete with bathing machines – and (left) the traditional bandstand audience in Pavilion Gardens.

The Winter Gardens has a more chequered history, for it was an indoor bowling green and it was also taken over by the RAF during World War II. After the war its resumed its original rôle of concert hall, providing a home for the Bournemouth Symphony Orchestra.

The Pier is the centre of traditional seaside entertainment, with amusement arcades and attractions for children.

The Big Four Railway Museum has over 1000 railway relics, including a large collection of nameplates and work plates.

The Russell-Cotes Museum and Art Gallery, set in 19th-century East Cliff House, is based on a display of Japanese and Burmese art given by Sir Merton Russell-Cotes, a former lord mayor. It includes the Henry Irving theatrical collection, period rooms and some good examples of Victorian art. It also has a freshwater aquarium and a geological terrace that contains specimens of stone from all the quarries in England.

The Rothesay Museum contains the Lucas collection of early Italian paintings and pottery, English china and furniture, a New Zealand room, an armoury room and a marine room with relics of Sir Cloudesley Shovell's flagship, HMS *Association*, sunk in 1707. Part of the first floor is occupied by the unique British Typewriter Museum, which has 300 vintage machines on display.

In **St Peter's Church** is buried the heart of the poet Shelley; his wife's tomb can be seen in the churchyard.

St Andrew's is the oldest church in the town, having a 12th-century tower and a 14th-century chancel, but 19th-century St Stephen's, with its spacious nave and its good screens and reredos, is the most beautiful.

BOSTON, Lincolnshire   *11 TF34*

Boston, on the River Witham, was once a very busy seaport, but its importance declined as the swing of trade to the New World favoured western ports – and this decline was accelerated by the partial silting up of its harbour. The name 'Boston' is said to be a corruption of 'Botolph's Town', St Botolph reputedly founding a monastery here in the 7th century. St Botolph's Church, largely built in the 15th century, has a 272ft-high tower nicknamed the 'Boston Stump'; the second highest in the county, and visible for miles across the Fens, it has long been a navigational aid to ships on The Wash. The Guildhall, built in 1450, has fine linenfold panelling which was restored earlier this century and houses the Borough Museum. The town has links with the early Pilgrim Fathers. Cells where they were imprisoned in 1607 can be seen in the Guildhall.

BOTHWELL, Strathclyde   *22 NS75*

Bothwell Castle (AM) is ruined now, but its remains are still impressive. It was the home of the Douglas family, built in the 13th and 15th centuries and one of the finest of Scottish strongholds. The Battle of the Brig, in which the Covenanters were defeated, was fought near here in 1679 and is commemorated by a monument. The Colliegiate Church dates back to the fourteenth century and has a magnificent pointed barrel vault. Sir Walter Scott wrote *Young Lochinvar* in the town.

BOUGHTON HOUSE,
Northamptonshire   *11 SP98*

Boughton House (OACT) was originally a 15th-century monastery; it was much enlarged in the next 200 years, finally being given a French-style addition in 1695 by the Duke of Montagu, who had been Ambassador to the Court of Louis XIV. It has beautiful painted ceilings and famous collections of furniture, carpets, tapestries, paintings and porcelain – many of the treasures having been brought back from France by the Duke. It is surrounded by attractive grounds containing some superb avenues of trees.

BOUGHTON MONCHELSEA,
Kent   *6 TQ74*

Boughton Monchelsea ragstone was probably worked by the Romans; certainly the quarries have been in more or less continuous operation for 700 years, and much of the village stands on filled-in workings. The stone was used to build the battlemented Boughton Monchelsea Place (OACT) and St Peter's Church, whose 15th-century lychgate is possibly the oldest in England.

BOURTON-ON-THE-WATER,
Gloucestershire   *10 SP12*

In a garden behind the New Inn, the picturesque village of Bourton-on-the-Water – its houses and church of mellow Cotswold stone, and the Windrush running under low-arched bridges to turn the wheel of the 18th-century watermill – can be admired in miniature, in a scale model one-ninth of the actual size. Other attractions are Birdland Zoo Gardens, with some 600 species of foreign birds, the medieval parish church, and the collection of old cars and motorcycles now housed in the watermill.

BOWNESS-ON-WINDERMERE,
Cumbria   *18 SD49*

Bowness stands on the east bank of Lake Windermere, thronged with people intent on hiring boats or participating in the water-sports for which the lake has become a popular centre. A ferry runs to Belle Island, where there is a completely round house (OACT), built in 1774 and the first of its kind in England. St Martin's Church is 15th-century and contains an ancient font, chained books, a Breeches Bible, old stained glass from Cartmel Priory and an unusual equestrian statue of the saint.

BOXFORD, Suffolk   *12 TL94*

The village of Boxford played an important role in the woollen industry, and the high latticed windows surviving in some of its buildings are those of former weavers' halls. Many of the quaint old houses are timber-framed; some in Butcher's Lane, with overhanging upper storeys and bowed roofs, date from the 15th century.

BOX HILL, Surrey   *5 TQ15*

Box Hill (NT) has been designated an area of outstanding natural beauty, and the summit is a popular viewpoint. Some of its box trees remain, but the majority were cut down in the 18th century when the wood was used for engraving.

BRADFORD, W Yorkshire   *15 SE13*

Bradford was an early centre for the wool trade, but the Industrial Revolution brought it real prosperity. In 1966 the Institute of Technology was given university status. The National Museum of Photography, Film and Television has superb examples of photographic art through the ages. The Cartwright Memorial Hall in Lister Park houses the Art Gallery and Museum, and there is another museum in Bolling Hall (OACT). At Eccleshill, is Moorside Mills industrial museum.

BRADFORD-ON-AVON, Wiltshire
3 ST86

The bridge at Bradford-on-Avon (AM) has two medieval arches and carries a chapel – originally provided for pilgrims travelling between Malmesbury and Glastonbury, but used as the town lock-up in the 17th century. The buildings in the steep winding streets, from medieval cottages to the Georgian mansions of the wealthy cloth-makers, are of Bath stone. The Saxon church in Church Street, lost for centuries among the surrounding buildings but rediscovered in the 19th century, was founded by St Adelin in the 8th century and is one of the finest remaining Saxon buildings in the country. A 14th-century Tithe Barn (AM) stands in Barton Farm Country Park, near the river.

BRADGATE PARK, Leicestershire
10 SK51

This 850-acre stretch of wood and heathland was given to Leicester for use as a public park in 1928. Information on the park can be obtained from Marion's Cottage near Newtown Linford. The ruins of Bradgate House lie within the park; it was built in 1500 by Thomas Grey, first Marquess of Dorset, and here Lady Jane Grey, his grand-daughter, was brought up. The highest point in the area, topped with a tower, is Old John – the name reputedly commemorating a local miller killed here.

BRAEMAR, Grampian   *27 NO19*

Of all the Highland Gatherings, that held at Braemar in September each year – with traditional music, dancing, and games culminating in the tossing of the caber – is possibly the most famous, perhaps because it is attended by the Royal Family. Nearby, Braemar Castle (OACT) overlooks the River Dee. Built by the 2nd Earl of Mar in 1628, it was burned down by the Farquharsons who then rebuilt it.

BOSTON *Tall cranes along the quay camouflage but do not obscure the view of the famous 'stump', as the tower of St Botolph's Church is known.*

On the Edge of the Cotswolds
54 miles

Mellow Cotswold stone has built many of the old wool towns such as Bradford-on-Avon or Chippenham, sturdy manor houses like Great Chalfield and Dyrham, and idyllic villages such as Lacock and Castle Combe which seem to grow from the peaceful landscape like natural features.

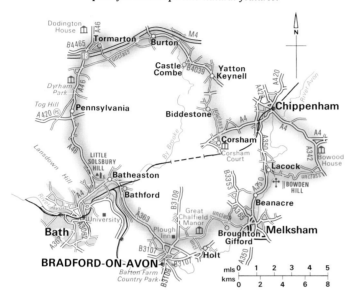

Leave **Bradford-on-Avon** by the Chippenham/Corsham Road, B3109 and after 1 mile turn right at the Plough Inn (SP Gt Chalfield and Holt). In another mile branch left (the right fork leads to The Courts), shortly passing the entrance to Gt Chalfield Manor. At T-junction turn right to reach Broughton Gifford. Beyond the village green, bear left on to the Melksham road. In 1¼ miles turn left on to B3107 and at the roundabout take 1st exit, A350 SP Chippenham, to skirt **Melksham**. 1½ miles after Beanacre turn right for **Lacock**. Entering the village turn right SP Bowden Hill and Calne to ascend Bowden Hill. At T-junction at the edge of Sandy Lane, turn left on to A342 then join A4 to **Chippenham**. Leave the town by A4 Bath road and in 3½ miles turn left at crossroads SP Corsham. In ½ mile at mini-roundabout turn left (SP Corsham Court) for **Corsham**. Leave village by following Chippenham signs and in ¼ mile turn

right at the T-junction, then in ½ mile go forward at crossroads SP Biddestone and Yatton Keynell. At **Biddestone** bear right for Yatton Keynell. Cross main road, SP Castle Combe and at Yatton turn left on to B4039, then left again. In 1¾ miles turn left into **Castle Combe**. Return to B4039 and turn left SP Acton Turville. At far side of Burton turn left on to Pucklechurch road. In 2¾ miles at crossroads turn right SP Tormarton. At **Tormarton** branch left past the Portcullis Inn and in ¼ mile at crossroads turn left SP Codrington. In ½ mile at next crossroads turn left opposite Dodington House on to A46 Bath road. Crossing the M4, take 2nd exit at roundabout and in 1¾ miles pass the entrance to Dyrham Park. Continue on A46 until it joins A4 on the outskirts of Bath, and here turn left onto A4 and drive through Batheaston, before branching right at roundabout on to A363 to Bradford-on-Avon.

PLACES TO SEE

Bradford-on-Avon Re-discovered Saxon church of St Lawrence; 17th century Avon bridge with lock-up; Barton Farm Park; weavers' cottages in Dutch Barton Street.

Holt The Courts (NT), an old 17th-century court house set in lovely gardens.

Gt Chalfield Manor (NT) 15th-century moated house.

Lacock (NT) Delightful little village filled with picturesque cottages; Abbey and manor house with Fox-Talbot museum of photography.

Bowood House House, and fine gardens designed by Humphry Repton and Capability Brown.

Chippenham An interesting old Cotswold market town.

Corsham 16th-century cottages and 17th-century almshouses. Corsham Court has a fine collection of furniture and paintings.

Biddestone Stone houses surround the charming green with its large duckpond.

Castle Combe Village with the well-earned title of 'most picturesque village in England'.

Dodington Park Palladian mansion designed by James Wyatt.

Dyrham Park 17th-century mansion with Dutch-style furnishings.

BRAINTREE, Essex *12 TL72*
Braintree and Bocking, now merged, are traditionally textile-producing towns. The woollen industry has thrived here since the 14th century but is now superseded by silk production, introduced by Courtaulds in 1880; the making of metal windowframes also dates from the 19th century. Modern buildings such as the Town Hall blend happily with centuries-old houses that reflect the town's long history. Excavations have indicated that there was a Roman settlement here, at the junction of two ancient cross-country routes.

BRAMBER W Sussex *5 TQ11*
A 76ft fragment is all that remains of Bramber's Norman castle (NT), destroyed during the Civil War. The House of Pipes (OACT) is a fascinating museum, with 35,000 exhibits covering 150 countries and 1500 years. It is believed to be the only exhibition of 'smokiana' in the world. The exhibition is set in a 19th-century shopping arcade.

BRAMHAM, W Yorkshire *15 SE44*
In the days when stagecoaches travelled the Great North Road, two inns stood on the village square – one, the Red Lion, still a public house today, and the other now identifiable by a bas-relief of a carthorse on its wall. Two miles south-west is Bramham Park (OACT), built in the classical style, and with gardens reminiscent of Versailles, by the first Lord Bingham in about 1700. It was damaged by fire in 1828 and restored early this century, but the exterior remains unaltered.

CRADLE OF CHAMPIONS

Brand's Hatch started life in 1928 as a grass-track circuit for motorcycle events. The short course – at first just under a mile, now 1.24 miles – with its many hazardous corners, made for spectacular racing. When the hard surface was laid in 1949, car-racing was introduced also and Brand's Hatch has come to be regarded as the best and most exciting circuit in the country. Above is one of the early 500cc car-racing events which took place in the early 1950s.

BRANDON and the BRECKLAND, Suffolk *12 TL78*

Brandon is largely built of the flint on which it stands; it seems that there has been a flint-knapping industry here since prehistoric times, for primitive tools have been excavated here and at **Grimes Graves** (AM), three miles north-east of the town. Breckland is a 300 square-mile stretch of rough heathland shared between Norfolk and Suffolk. 'Brecks' are pieces of land long ago broken up for cultivation but then allowed to become wild again.

BRAND'S HATCH, Kent *6 TQ56*

The famous motor-racing circuit at Brand's Hatch lies in a natural amphitheatre, with spectator stands on the slopes beside the track. Important events held here include the British Grand Prix.

BREAMORE, Hampshire *3 SU11*

The village of Breamore has a fine Saxon church and the brick-and-tile cottages typical of the New Forest. Breamore House (OACT), an Elizabethan manor with interesting tapestries, paintings and furniture, has a countryside museum in the grounds and a display of carriages in the stables. An intricate medieval miz-maze is cut into the turf of Breamore Down, north-east of the village; its original purpose is not known, but it is suggested that it might be the framework of a folk dance, or a route to be followed by a penitential monk.

BRECHIN, Tayside *27 NO66*

Red sandstone houses line streets that rise from the valley of the Esk against a background of hills culminating in the eastern Grampians. Brechin Cathedral (now the parish church) dates from 1170, though much restored early this century, and next to it is an unusual 87ft-high round tower which has served as watchtower and refuge in times of trouble.

BRECKLAND, THE *see* Brandon

BRECON, Powys *8 SO02*

Brecon, the old county town of Brecknockshire, is now the administrative centre for the **Brecon Beacons** National Park. Sheltered on all sides by hills, the town stands where the River Usk meets the Honddu. Some interesting old buildings survive in the narrow streets of the town, but the prevailing atmosphere is 18th- and 19th-century. Only the tower and a battlemented wall are left to show where the Norman castle stood. St John's, made a cathedral in 1923, was originally the church of an 11th-century Benedictine monastery; most of the present building is 13th- or 14th-century, but of the craft guild chapels that formerly filled the aisles only the corvisors' (shoemakers') remains. The objects of local interest in Brecknock Museum include a collection of love-spoons, and the South Wales Borderers house their Regimental Museum here.

BRECON BEACONS, Powys *8 SO02*

Bonfires once flared on the summits of the Beacons to alert people to important happenings in the days of less easy communications. This 500-square mile area of wild, hilly country was designated a National Park in 1957. The highest of the red sandstone peaks are Cribin (2608ft), Corn-Du (2863ft) and Pen-y-Fan.

PEN-Y-FAN *is the highest point (2907ft) of the Brecon Beacons. From its summit are views of the Malvern Hills, the Bristol Channel and the Black Mountains.*

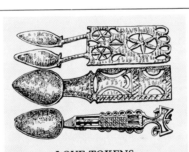

LOVE TOKENS
The tradition of young men making elaborately carved love spoons for their sweethearts lasted from the 17th to the early 20th century.

BREDON, Hereford & Worcester *9 SO93*

The 14th-century spire of St Giles' Church rises to 160ft, a landmark for miles, and the church contains the magnificent canopied tomb of Sir Giles Reed, whose family built the Reed almshouses in the main street. The Tithe Barn (NT), carefully restored after a fire in 1980, is 14th-century and one of the largest in England. Bredon Hill, three miles north-east, is reputed to offer views of 14 counties and is topped by ancient earthworks and a Gothic folly.

BREDWARDINE, Hereford & Worcester *9 SO93*

Bredwardine – 'the place on the slope of a hill' – stands where a fine, six-arched, 18th-century bridge crosses the Wye. The Norman church, extended – and curved slightly to the north – in the 14th century, has the original font, hewn from a single block of stone, and two medieval effigies of knights. This was the parish of the mid-Victorian diarist Francis Kilvert. Behind the village, on Merbach Hill, lies Arthur's Stone, the famous Neolithic long barrow.

BRESSINGHAM GARDENS, Norfolk *12 TM08*

Bressingham Gardens (OACT) contain five acres of alpine plants and hardy perennials. The arrangement of the grounds is informal and includes the Live Steam Museum – one of the most comprehensive collections of steam-powered engines in the country, ranging from carousel and organ to full-size locomotives, traction and road engines. There are also miniature steam engines on which visitors can ride around the gardens or along the Waveney Valley.

BRETFORTON, Hereford & Worcester *10 SP04*

Bretforton stands below a ridge of the Cotswolds, deep in the orchards of the Vale of Evesham. The Fleece Inn (NT), originally a 14th-century farmhouse, displays a priceless set of Stuart pewter-ware, and ancient 'witch-marks', presumably to protect patrons from evil spirits. Twelfth- and thirteenth-century carving survives in St Leonard's Church, once the property of Evesham Abbey, and the 17th-century manor house has the village stocks in its grounds. Bretforton Hall, with its battlemented tower, is 19th-century Gothic, and nearby stands a cottage incorporating one of several old dovecotes in the area. A footbridge near the ford probably gave the village its Saxon name – 'the ford with planks'.

BRIDGEND, Mid Glamorgan *8 SS97*

For centuries Bridgend, lying in the valley where the Rivers Ogmore, Garw and Llynfi meet, was the market town for this part of the Vale of Glamorgan; now it is also an industrial centre. Three castles dominate the area – a ruined Norman castle (AM) on the wooded hill above Bridgend, **Coity Castle** (AM) to the north-east, and **Ogmore Castle** (AM) to the south.

Brighton, E Sussex 5 TQ30

The Prince Regent's Town

'But have we any leisure for a description of Brighton? . . . for Brighton, that always looks brisk, gay and gaudy, like a harlequin's jacket . . . for Brighton, which used to be seven hours distant from London . . . which is now only a hundred minutes off.'

WILLIAM THACKERAY, *Vanity Fair.*

Most popular of all the seaside towns of the southeast, Brighton began life as Brighthelmstone – an unpretentious little fishing village. Its metamorphosis began in 1754 when Dr Richard Russell took up residence there and prescribed sea-air, sea-water and sea-bathing as the remedy for all ailments. In 1783 the Prince of Wales, later George IV, paid it a visit and decided to build himself a villa – designed by Henry Holland but later transformed into an Indian extravaganza by John Nash.

Fashionable London flocked to Brighton, and elegant squares and terraces were built – largely around the Steyne – to accommodate the new patrons. In Victorian times, the railways brought trippers in ever-increasing numbers – the famous Brighton Belle, which ran until the late 1960s, could do the journey from London in 55 minutes – and the town acquired a rather risqué reputation as an illicit weekend resort. Today, although the holiday trade may have fallen off somewhat, the town is a popular conference venue, and the vast modern marina, with moorings for more than 2000 craft, has given the seafront a new lease of life. The Kemp Town race-course was the setting of the climax of Graham Greene's novel of underworld life, *Brighton Rock*. The University of Sussex, designed by Sir Basil Spence in the 1960s, stands next to Stanmer Park on the Brighton Road, and the influx of students and of foreign visitors to the many language schools, has made its own contribution to this gay, cosmopolitan resort.

PLACES TO SEE

The Royal Pavilion dominates the town centre, a riot of gleaming white onion domes and minarets in the Indian Moghul style. Inside, the 18th-century 'chinoiserie' décor has been beautifully preserved. Particularly interesting are the kitchens.

The Dome is a splendid building, once the stables and riding school of the Prince Regent. It has now been divided into an art gallery, concert hall and exhibition centre.

The Lanes is an area bounded by North, West, East Streets and the sea, a charming enclave and all that remains of the 17th-century fishing village of Brighthelmstone. The attractive alleyways are full of antique shops.

THE ROYAL PAVILION *The Prince Regent's seaside home*

Palace Pier, a third of a mile long occupies a site near where England's first-ever pleasure pier, the Old Chain Pier once stood. This was swept away in a storm of 1896. The present pier boasts an elaborate gilded dome in the style of the Royal Pavilion, and all the usual seaside attractions. Brighton's other pier, West Pier, has an uncertain future.

Aquarium and Dolphinarium The aquarium dates back to 1869 and has more than 10,000 fish, from all over the world.

Volk's Railway, opened in 1883, was the first electric public railway in Britain. It runs in summer only to Black Rock.

Booth Museum of Natural History. About 1½ miles from the town centre, the museum has a comprehensive collection of British and other birds.

Preston Manor, stands off the A23, a Georgian house bequeathed to the Corporation in 1932. It contains a fine collection of period furniture and silver.

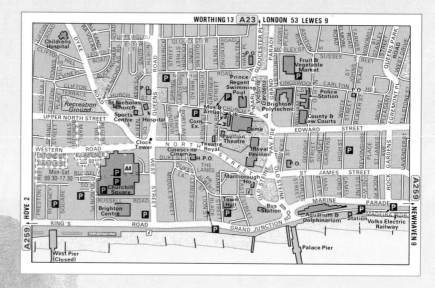

THE OLD CHAIN PIER, *the engineering marvel of its day, was originally built in 1823.*

BRIDGE OF ALLAN, Central
22 NS79

This small holiday resort, just north of the point where Allan Water joins the Forth, is a touring base for central Scotland and provides accommodation for many of those connected with nearby Stirling University. Early in the 19th century the efficacy of the local mineral waters was discovered, and the area enjoyed a period of popularity as a spa; the Baths and Pump Room still stand. Two miles away stands the 220ft-high Wallace Monument.

BRIDGNORTH, Shropshire   *9 SO79*

The old market town of Bridgnorth is divided into Low Town and High Town by a red sandstone cliff, the two parts linked by steps and by the Castle Hill Cliff Railway. Caves in the sandstone were used as dwellings until Victorian times, and one – the Hermitage (AM) – is said to have housed Ethelred, brother of King Athelstan, in the 10th century. The tower, sole remnant of the castle, leans 17 degrees from the perpendicular because it was undermined during the Civil War. The upper storey of the Town Hall incorporates parts of the old barn on whose site it stands. Bishop Percy's House (1580) is the most ancient building in Bridgnorth; it was the birthplace in the 18th century of Thomas Percy, who became Bishop of Dromore. St Mary Magdalene's Church, Italianate in style, was designed by the engineer Thomas Telford. The town is the headquarters of the Severn Valley Railway which, in the summer, runs steam trains between here and Bewdley. At nearby Stanmore Hall is the Midland Motor Museum.

BRIDGWATER, Somerset   *3 ST33*

Bridgwater, now an industrial centre, was a busy port until Bristol overshadowed it. A tidal bore comes up the River Parrett twice a day; the times are posted on the bridge. The 14th-century Church of St Mary is noted for its fine Jacobean screenwork, and from its tower the rebel Duke of Monmouth is said to have surveyed the field before the Battle of Sedgemoor in 1685. One of Cromwell's admirals, Robert Blake, was born here, and the house is a museum.

BRIDLINGTON, Humberside
16 TA16

Bridlington is a popular resort, its fine sandy beaches sheltered by Flamborough Head and offering good bathing, angling and sailing. The Bayle Gate (built 1388) – serving at various times as courtroom, school, sailors' prison and barracks, is now a museum. Sewerby Hall (OACT), a Georgian mansion north-east of the town, also has a museum (which includes relics of Amy Johnson) as well as an Art Gallery, and its grounds contain a small zoo.

BRIDPORT, Dorset   *3 SY49*

The wide pavements of the town (Thomas Hardy's Port Bredy) were once 'ropewalks' where the new ropes were laid out for twisting and drying. Ships' riggings are no longer in such great demand (nor, presumably, is the 'Bridport dagger' – the hangman's noose!) but the 750-year-old industry continues, supplying fishing nets, lines, and specialised ropes and twines to several countries. A museum is housed in a 16th-century house near the church.

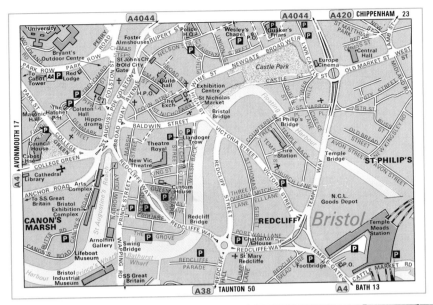

BRISTOL, Avon   *3 ST52*

Bristol grew up round a natural harbour on the River Avon, and for several centuries its wharfage continued to grow, originally involved in the export of wool, but diversifying its interests in the 16th century with the formation of the Society of Merchant Venturers. An earlier 'venturer' was John Cabot, whose explorations led him to the North American coast as early as 1497; his achievement is commemorated by the Cabot Tower (OACT) on Brandon Hill. In the 17th century the city became involved in the slave trade, and its abolition in the 19th century was a severe blow; the wine trade, however, continued to thrive and many of Britain's largest importers, such as Harvey's, are based at Bristol.

The engineer, Isambard Kingdom Brunel had a long association with the city, his name being perhaps most readily connected with the Clifton Suspension Bridge which spans the Avon Gorge. He also redesigned the docks and brought the Great Western Region's railway line from London as far as Bristol. His two great ships, the *Great Western* (1837) and the *Great Britain* (1843), were built here, and the latter (OACT) – the first screw-driven passenger ship to undertake Atlantic crossings – is now being restored in its original dock. The Bristol Industrial Museum and National Lifeboat Museum are at Prince's Wharf.

The city is rich in old buildings, and particularly in churches. The cathedral began life as the church of a 12th-century Augustinian abbey, becoming a cathedral in 1542. St Mary Redcliffe, the 'fairest, goodliest, and most famous parish church in England', as Queen Elizabeth I described it, is a graceful church which dates back to the 13th century. The interior is a magnificent achievement of the Perpendicular style and its 285ft spire is a noted landmark. The 18th-century Wesleyan chapel is the oldest Methodist chapel in the world. The 14th-century church of St John the Baptist, built over a vaulted medieval gateway, the ruined Temple Church, with its leaning tower, the Lord Mayor's Chapel, the only one to be owned by a City Corporation, and the ecclesiastical museum in St Nicholas' Church are also of interest. One of the most picturesque corners of the city is the

SS GREAT BRITAIN *The symbols on the bows and trail board are the unicorn from the national coat of arms; rope and scissors for the sailors and sailmakers; gear-wheel for the engine-room; dove showing peace not war; setsquare for the ship's designers and Mercury's winged staff for speed.*

quaintly named Christmas Steps, a narrow alley with many antique shops and antiquarian booksellers. Bristol boasts the oldest theatre – the Bristol Old Vic – in the country.

The University was opened in 1925 on the Clifton side of the city where the Regency crescents and Georgian terraces include Royal York Crescent, possibly the longest of its kind in Europe. Bristol Zoo is housed on Clifton Down.

The phrase 'paying on the nail', for prompt payment, originates in Bristol, the nails being four bronze pillars outside the 18th-century Exchange in Corn Street, the hub of the city's commercial life.

BRIXHAM, Devon   *2 SX95*

Brixham falls into two parts – the old village on the slopes of a hill, and the fishing village half a mile below. The sands at Mudstone Bay are popular with holidaymakers, and many artists have painted the picturesque harbour. Brixham Museum at Bolton Cross includes displays of shipbuilding. H. M. Coastguard National Museum is also here.

BROAD HAVEN, Dyfed   *7 SM81*

The little resort of Broad Haven stands on St Bride's Bay, where strangely-folded cliffs tower behind an expanse of silvery sand. The **Pembrokeshire Coast National Park** Information Centre is in the village.

ANCIENT BURIAL MOUNDS
BARROWS
Chambered Tombs & Passage Graves

Some of the oldest man-made monuments in the British landscape are tombs. Several are well restored and impressive, while others gradually surrender to agriculture and the elements. All are monuments to a lost religion, a particular vision of the afterlife and a respect for ancestors.

TOMB BURIALS became a customary means of dealing with the dead around 4300 BC, at a time when farming had become well-established in Britain, and it was at this time that interest in the construction of massive tombs erupted. The reasons for this sudden and unprecedented enthusiasm for monument-building are unexplained, but a change in religion was probably involved. Also, settled peasant families were better able to undertake great building works than their hunting and pioneer farming forebears had been.

The great tombs they built were surely more than just burial mounds and probably also represented attempts to stake claims over farming territories. Thus, by gathering the bones of important ancestors and placing them in a prominent tomb, communities were able to demonstrate a well-rooted claim over the surrounding lands.

Archaeology has also shown that the tombs were often the scenes of religious rituals in which the bones of dead ancestors featured. Some tombs were provided with forecourts in which such rituals would have been performed.

The tombs of the New Stone Age are associated with the rite of collective burial, with five, ten, thirty or more individuals being interred. Even so, it seems that the tombs housed the corpses of members of the local aristocracies and little is known about the burials of the common folk. From the bones retrieved from many such places, scientists have been able to reconstruct some aspects of ancient life. It seems that many people died in youth and childhood, while few could expect to reach the age of 40. Most people will have been fit and tough, but arthritis, deficiency diseases and dental troubles were common as a consequence of the arduous lifestyle.

TOMB INTERIOR *The well-preserved chambered tomb at Stoney Littleton dates from the Neolithic period.*

EARTHEN LONG BARROWS are the oldest tombs in England: elongated, often rather wedge-shaped mounds flanked by ditches from which the mound materials were dug. Although these appear today as rather featureless, many long barrows had complicated internal structures of timber. Some of these have been interpreted as 'mortuary houses' – in which bodies were gathered prior to the building of the covering mound.

Long barrows are very numerous in southern and midland England, with the most imposing examples being mainly concentrated in Wessex. Two accessible and quite well-preserved long barrows are the Pimperne long barrow near Blandford Forum in Dorset and the long barrow which is surrounded by several, more youthful, round-barrow neighbours at the Stonehenge crossroads on Salisbury Plain.

PASSAGE GRAVES, the most majestic of the British Stone Age tombs are found in Ireland, Wales and the Northern Isles. In these, the burial chamber lies at the end of an entrance passageway: Maes Howe on Orkney is the most imposing Scottish example, and Wales has good ones at Bryn Celli Ddu and Barclodiad y Gawres, both on Anglesey. Some of the passage graves have stones carved in the spirals and geometrical patterns of 'passage grave art', but whether the graves and their decorative motifs represent an ancient migration of peoples which carried their builders by sea to Wales, Orkney and Ireland, or whether it was simply the idea of the passage grave that travelled from one centre to another, we do not know for sure.

PENTRE IFAN *(left) these massive stones near Nevern in Dyfed are all that remain of a megalithic chambered tomb.*

WAYLAND'S SMITHY *(below) in Oxfordshire, named after the legendary Norse smith, is in fact a chambered tomb.*

ROUND BARROWS began to supersede the massive collective tombs in about 2500 BC, when new ideas concerning burial and the afterlife must have gradually emerged. These smaller round barrows covered one, two or three, though seldom more, bodies. Most of the burials made in the earlier of the round barrows were accompanied by a pottery drinking vessel or 'beaker', which is thought to have contained an alcoholic drink – perhaps to sustain the deceased on the journey to the afterlife. The name of 'Beaker People' has thus been given to these Bronze-Age folk. In most parts of Britain, these barrows have a simple bowl-shaped form, but in parts of Wessex, more elaborate variations in the form of bell-, disc-, pond- or saucer-shaped barrows were built, and a fine collection of different designs can be seen at the Bronze Age barrow cemetery at Lambourn in Berkshire. In the course of the Bronze Age, a variety of different burial rites were practised, but in the Iron Age the tradition of providing monumental tombs disappeared in almost every part of Britain.

Although stone circles (see pp 22–3) are the leading prehistoric tourist attractions, many of the older tombs are equally impressive – especially West Kennet, Maes Howe and Wayland's Smithy, where one can enter the dark recesses of the burial chamber. The Stoney Littleton tomb in Avon has a particularly tunnel-like and claustrophobic passageway. Many of the tombs, like Chun Quoit in Cornwall or Pentre Ifan in the Preseli Hills stand in areas of ruggedly beautiful scenery, while all are mysterious relics of a Stone Age religion which we may never be able to reconstruct with any real certainty.

CHAMBERED TOMBS soon began to replace the long barrows, whose interiors, sealed by the earth and rubble of the covering mounds, could not be re-entered for further burials. The chambered tombs, however, had stone-lined burial chambers which could be closed with a large blocking stone, but opened to allow new burials in the interior chambers. These tombs might have evolved from the earthen long barrows, but they were probably also partly influenced by continental chambered tombs – Brittany, in particular, having several fine and early examples of this new style.

Not surprisingly, the chambered tombs are mainly confined to Scotland, Ireland, Wales and the western parts of England, where suitable boulders of tough stone can be found. They come in many different sizes and variations. Amongst the most evocative are the 'portal

dolmens', often known as 'cromlechs' in Wales or 'quoits' in Cornwall. Examples like Trethevy Quoit and Chun Quoit in Cornwall or Din Lligwy on Anglesey display massive capstones supported by upright boulders, two of which seem to have served as entrance portals. Most of these tombs were originally covered by earthen mounds which have long since been eroded, exposing their angular stonework.

Other forms of chambered tomb were more elaborate. Famous examples include the West Kennet tomb near Avebury in Wiltshire and Wayland's Smithy, beside the Ridgeway in Oxfordshire. Both have imposing façades of massive upright boulders, entrance passages and side chambers. Belas Knap tomb in Gloucestershire may have been designed to thwart tomb robbers, for there is a false entrance to the mound.

THE GOLD CAPE OF MOLD

The majority of Britain's pre-historic burial mounds were looted centuries ago, but one magnificent survival dis-covered in a mound near Mold in Clwyd is this Bronze Age golden cape or corselet, now in the British Museum. Long before the excavation in 1930 revealed the treasure, the legend of a ghostly war-rior, clad in golden armour had formed part of local folk-lore tradition.

AN EARLY SCOUT CAMP

BE PREPARED As soon as Baden-Powell organised the first on Brownsea island in 1907, boy-scout camps became a regular event: in this photograph, taken in 1908, he is standing on the right. Gallant defender of Mafeking in the Boer War, Baden-Powell had first used boys to scout for him in Africa.

BROADHEMBURY, Devon 2 ST10
Almost all the houses in this charming Devon village are thatched, and the walls of some are made of 'cob' – the traditional mixture of clay, straw and animal hair. By the square stands the 13th-century Church of St Andrew, with a 100ft-high tower and a memorial to Augustus Toplady – vicar here for the last ten years of his life – who wrote the hymn, 'Rock of Ages'. Parts of nearby Church Gate Cottage may be even older than the church.

BROADSTAIRS, Kent 6 TR36
Several miles of sheltered, sandy bays made this resort popular in the Regency period, and it remains so today. To the north stand the chalk cliffs and lighthouse of the North Foreland, with wide views over the Thames Estuary. Bleak House is now a Dickens Museum: it contains early editions of his books, pictures, photographs and some personal items. Nearby Dickens House (which also contains a museum) was immortalised as the home of Betsy Trotwood in *David Copperfield*, written while the author was living in Broadstairs. In June each year a Dickens Festival is held, when the townsfolk throng the streets in appropriate dress.

BROADS, THE, Norfolk 12
In a roughly triangular area between Lowestoft, Sea Palling and Norwich, over 30 Broads of various sizes are joined by streams and rivers to create 200 miles of navigable waterway. Once thought to be the result of glacial action, the Broads are now accepted as the aftermath of centuries of widespread diggings for turf or peat. The five major ones are Wroxham, Barton, Hickling, Ormesby and Filby, and the chief rivers are the Bure, Yare and Waveney. Yachts and motor cruisers can be hired, and villages such as **Potter Heigham**, **Horning** and **Wroxham** cater for the needs of the holidaymakers.

BROADWAY, Hereford & Worcester 10 SP03
Its wealth of Tudor, Jacobean and Georgian buildings, blending every shade of the local stone, makes Broadway the best-known of the Cotswold villages. To the east, Fish

Hill, part of Broadway Tower Country Park, rises to over 1000ft, topped by a folly built by the Earl of Coventry in 1799. There are exhibitions on three floors, and a telescope giving views over 12 counties. The Fish Inn, 808ft above sea level, was a summerhouse on the estate. The park also offers nature trails and picnic areas. Three miles south, Snowshill Manor (NT) contains a unique collection of musical instruments.

HAND-MADE NAILS *Working on an anvil that his medieval forebears might have used, the blacksmith is one of several craftsmen who demonstrate at the Avoncroft Museum of Buildings near Bromsgrove.*

BROMSGROVE, Hereford & Worcester 9 SO97
Bromsgrove lies at the foot of the Lickey Hills, whose highest point, (1000ft Beacon Hill) gives a fine view of the surrounding countryside. Nearby Avoncroft Museum of Buildings contains a wide range of historic buildings – the oldest, 15th-century – dismantled and reassembled here when their existence was threatened by development. The Norton Collection Museum specialises in Victoriana.

BROWNSEA ISLAND, Dorset 3 SZ08
Brownsea Island (NT), one mile long and three-quarters of a mile wide, is the largest island in Poole Harbour. About half its area is taken up by a Nature Reserve, but even outside this the visitor can see red squirrels, peacocks, ducks and geese. The church was built in the 19th century by Colonel William Waugh, who bought the island because he was convinced – erroneously – that he could make a fortune from its china-clay deposits. The island was the site, in 1907, of the first Boy Scout Camp.

BRUTON, Somerset 3 ST63
Bruton is historically a textile town, and one of the first fulling mills in England was built nearby in 1290. The River Brue is crossed here by an ancient and exceptionally narrow packhorse bridge, known locally as Bruton Bow. Near the bridge stands a section of wall which, with the three-storey dovecote in a field above the town, is all that remains of the 12th-century priory. King's Grammar School dates from the 16th century and was attended by R D Blackmore, author of *Lorna Doone*. Hugh Sexey's Hospital, founded in 1638 by a former stableboy who rose to become auditor to Elizabeth I, has been converted into homes for old people. The mainly 16th-century church has a 12th-century chancel, two towers and a fine tie-beam roof.

BUCKDEN, Cambridgeshire 11 TL16
Buckden's High Street was once part of the road from London to the north, and it is still flanked by two old coaching inns, the 16th-century black-and-white Lion and the 17th-century red-brick George. The brick-and-timber cottages of the village are dominated by the remains of Buckden Palace (OACT), used by the Bishops of Lincoln from the 15th century until 1836. In the church which adjoins the Palace, Laurence Sterne, author of *Tristram Shandy*, was ordained in 1736.

BUCKFASTLEIGH, Devon 2 SX76
Buckfastleigh Station is the northern terminus of the Dart Valley Railway (OACT), a steam service operated by enthusiasts. It runs to Totnes and back, but passengers must do the round trip, and not disembark at Totnes. At the station locomotives in process of restoration are on show and there is a picnic area with a miniature railway. One mile north of the village is Buckfast Abbey, the work of a succession of teams of French Benedictine monks between 1906 and 1932. Built of limestone, with modern stained glass designed and made by the monks, the Abbey stands on the site of an original medieval monastery and incorporates the Gothic mansion that replaced it.

BUCKHAVEN & METHIL, Fife 24 NT39
Buckhaven and Methil were seaside villages that became mining towns in the 19th century. In 1891 they united to form Scotland's major coalport, and now, with the dwindling importance of the coal trade, the town is becoming increasingly involved in the production of North Sea oil. It still has many quaint corners, however, and the stepped streets typical of old Fife villages. Local fishermen brought the church in sections from St Andrews and re-erected it.

THE BEE MAN
Buckfast Abbey is famous for not only its tonic wine but also for honey. The monks have long studied the art of beekeeping, which dates from ancient times, and carry out careful experiments to breed new and more productive strains of bees.

BUCKINGHAM, Buckinghamshire
10 SP63
Buckingham, on the River Ouse, was declared the county town by Alfred the Great in 888 but yielded the distinction to Aylesbury in the 18th century. It has had frequent brushes with royalty – Catherine of Aragon stayed at Castle House (built in 1280) and Charles II held a council of war there; Elizabeth I dined at the 14th-century manor house which has a curious twisted chimney. The town is centred on its market place, which has an 18th-century gaol. The Town Hall and Parish Hall are also 18th-century in construction.

BUCKLAND ABBEY, Devon   *2 SX46*
A Cistercian abbey before the Dissolution and the home of Sir Francis Drake in the 16th century, Buckland Abbey (NT) is now a museum, with Drake relics and some fine model ships among its displays. Larger exhibits, such as farm wagons and fire engines, are housed next door in the 14th-century tithe barn. The abbey and the beautiful gardens, open at all reasonable times, are managed by Plymouth Corporation for the National Trust who own them.

BUCKLERS HARD, Hampshire
4 SU40
Today, pleasure-craft are the only boats at Bucklers Hard, but it was an important shipyard in the 18th and 19th centuries and built three of the ships that fought at Trafalgar – including Nelson's *Agamemnon*. Relics of the era are contained in the Maritime Museum, but to visit the village itself is to step back in time: the shipbuilders' cottages still face one another across the wide green that runs down to the River Beaulieu, while New Forest ponies graze with no fear of traffic, for there are no through roads and vehicles have to be left in a nearby car park. The hotel was once the house of Nelson's master-shipwright, and next to it stands an unusual chapel – a single consecrated room in a cottage.

BUDE, Cornwall   *1 SS20*
Bude was once notorious for shipwrecks, largely the result of its beaches facing the prevailing wind – but this condition is ideal for surfing, and the resort's popularity has grown with that of the sport. The large swimming pool on Summerleaze Beach, refilled each time the tide comes in, is popular with less hardy bathers. A three-mile cliff walk above the town offers exceptionally fine views.

BUDLEIGH SALTERTON, Devon
2 SY08
The sea-wall at Budleigh Salterton is the setting of *The Boyhood of Raleigh*, the famous picture by the Victorian artist Sir John Millais, for the Raleigh family lived just north of here when Sir Walter was born. Discreetly prosperous, the town has changed little since it was developed as a resort in the early 19th century; its chief attractions are the safe bathing and the magnificent views from its red cliffs. An 18th-century thatched house, complete with smugglers' cellar and lookout tower, holds the Fairlynch Arts Centre and Museum in Fore Street.

BUILTH WELLS, Powys   *8 SO05*
Builth Wells stands where the River Wye, crossed by a six-arched bridge, meets the River Irfon. Since the town was entirely destroyed by fire in 1691, its earliest buildings date from the subsequent rebuilding. The water of its wells – one containing salt, one sulphur – made it a popular spa in the 18th century. The Royal Welsh Show is held each July in the grounds of nearby Llanelwedd Hall.

BUNBURY, Cheshire   *14 SJ55*
Bunbury developed in three stages – the original church-centred settlement, Tudor growth around the common, and the incorporation of Bunbury Heath when commonland there was enclosed. In the village's winding streets, timbered cottages and black-and-white farmhouses stand beside buildings of Georgian red brick. St Boniface's Church dates back to the 14th century but has been much restored.

BUNGAY, Suffolk   *12 TM38*
It is an indication of Bungay's long history that its civic head still holds the office of Town Reeve. Originally it was a market town, but printing and leatherworking were introduced in the 18th century, and today its position on the River Waveney also makes it a popular yachting centre. Only the foundations of the castle – originally 12th-century – remain; they show an unfinished mineshaft that was intended to destroy the castle after Hugh Bigod's rebellion against Henry II. St Mary's Church had its bells melted by a fire that swept that part of the town in 1688, and the Bungay Stone (near the north porch) is said to be a Druid Cross 2000 years old. Earsham Otter Trust (OACT), 1½ miles out of the town has one of the largest collections of otters in the world.

BURFORD, Oxfordshire   *10 SP21*
Burford's narrow, three-arched bridge over the River Windrush is built of old Cotswold stone, as are the picturesque houses and inns that line its wide, climbing main street. The Church of St John the Baptist, with its impressive spire, is one of the largest in Oxfordshire. The Grammar School, the Crown Inn and the Bear Inn are virtually unchanged since the 15th century, and the Priory, though largely rebuilt in the early 19th century, still bears the arms of William Lenthel, who, as Speaker of the Long Parliament, defied Charles I. The Cotswold Wildlife Park (OACT) lies south of the town, in Bradwell Grove Estate.

BUCKLER'S HARD *was to have been, in the 1720s, the start of an ambitious scheme of the then Lord Montagu to build a port – Montagu Town – to rival Southampton. The scheme failed but in the Napoleonic era the place prospered as a shipbuilding centre because timber was readily available in the New Forest.*

BURGHCLERE, Hampshire   *4 SU46*

Two groups of almshouses and the Sandham Chapel (NT) were built at Burghclere in 1926 in memory of Henry William Sandham, a hero of the First World War. The walls of the chapel are completely covered with frescoes by another soldier, artist Stanley Spencer, and they depict his reaction to his experiences of that war.

BURNHAM BEECHES, Buckinghamshire   *5 SU98*

This 600-acre area of beech-woods is part of a huge forest which has spread across the Chilterns since prehistoric times. It was purchased by the City of London in 1879.

BURNHAM-ON-CROUCH, Essex   *6 TQ99*

Burnham-on-Crouch – set on the north bank of the river, six miles from the sea – has been described as 'the Cowes of the east coast', for it has five yacht clubs and at the height of summer as many as 2000 boats are moored here. The streets of the town climb up from the quay, Victorian and Georgian buildings interspersed with the weather-boarded cottages typical of the county. The area is famous for its oyster beds.

BURNHAM-ON-SEA, Somerset   *3 ST34*

A 19th-century curate built a lighthouse at Burnham-on-Sea and exacted tolls from passing ships to finance two wells which were to establish the town as a spa. The venture failed, but Burnham, with its seven miles of sandy beach and its fine views across Bridgwater Bay, became popular with holidaymakers – and the wooden 'lighthouse on legs' is still a tourist attraction. The medieval Church of St Andrew contains a 17th-century marble reredos designed by Inigo Jones and carved by Grinling Gibbons; originally made for the chapel of Whitehall palace, it passed to Hampton Court and Westminster Abbey before coming to rest here in the 19th century. The tower of the church tilts three feet from the vertical – the subsidence being due to its sandy foundations.

BURNHAM THORPE & BURNHAM MARKET, Norfolk   *12 TF84*

Lord Nelson was born in Burnham Thorpe in 1758, at Parsonage House (now demolished), son of the rector. The church contains the font at which he was christened and also a lectern made from the timbers of the *Victory*. The church at Burnham Market, an attractive little town, has unusual carvings of Biblical scenes on its battlemented tower.

BURNLEY, Lancashire   *14 SD83*

The gritstone buildings of Burnley were the hub of the cotton-weaving industry until the recession of the 1930s; now the town's chief involvement is in heavy industry. Townley Hall (OACT), to the south-east, contains a Museum and Art Gallery and offers battlements and dungeons to explore.

BURTON AGNES, Humberside   *16 TA16*

The sleepy village of Burton Agnes is one of the most attractive in the Wolds. The main attraction to visitors is Burton Agnes Hall (OACT), built by Sir Henry Griffith more than 380 years ago and still owned by his family. It stands among smooth lawns and clipped yews, its red brick mellowed by time, and its semi-octagonal plan echoed in the octagonal towers of the gatehouse (built slightly later). The interior is splendidly furnished and has a fine collection of Impressionist paintings, including works by Renoir, Pissarro, Manet, Gauguin and Sickert, as well as drawings by Augustus John and other 20th-century masters. The Norman church, containing a fine alabaster tomb, stands next to the hall, and nearby is a restored Norman manor house (AM).

BEER CAPITAL OF BRITAIN

Brewing started in a small way at Burton upon Trent in medieval times, but only developed commercially with the opening of the canal in 1777. In Victorian times there were 40 breweries here, including Bass, Worthington, Ind Coope and Marston. Many of the smaller independent breweries are now either defunct or part of Allied Breweries. The Bass Museum is housed in the old joinery at the brewery, and this Worthington Pale Ale Daimler truck is the pride of the collection.

BURTON-UPON-TRENT, Staffordshire   *10 SK22*

Legend has it that in the 13th century, at a time when Burton was involved in cloth-making, the Abbot realised the suitability of local water for brewing. Today the streets are permeated by its smell and the famous name of Bass is met at every turn, for the family gave the town some of its finest buildings, including the Town Hall. The Bass Museum traces the history of the brewing industry, and has many fascinating exhibits including a 1920's Daimler shaped like a bottle.

BURWASH, E Sussex   *6 TQ62*

Burwash was the centre of the iron industry 300 years ago, when most of the country's ore came from the Weald, and some of the old ironmasters' houses still stand. Rudyard Kipling lived in one of the finest of them, Bateman's (NT), which contains many relics of the author, and the countryside surrounding the village is described in his children's novel, *Puck of Pook's Hill*. St Bartholomew's Church has a Norman tower, a 15th-century octagonal font, and one of the oldest iron grave slabs in Sussex.

BURY, Lancashire   *14 SD81*

A statue of Sir Robert Peel, 19th-century prime minister and founder of the police force, stands in the market square of Bury, his birthplace. Two miles north of the town was born John Kay, who in 1733 invented the flying shuttle and thus revolutionised weaving methods. The Museum and Art Gallery has items of local interest reaching as far back as the Bronze Age and some fine paintings, whilst the Transport Museum specialises in the steam era of the railways. The town's traditional role in the manufacture of yarn has expanded to take in the printing of textiles, and its industries now also include engineering and papermaking.

SANDHAM MEMORIAL CHAPEL *Stanley Spencer's altarpiece,* **Resurrection of the Soldiers**, *is the culmination of the series of murals that cover the walls of the chapel at Burghclere. The scenes he depicted were inspired by his experiences in the RAMC in Macedonia during World War I.*

BURY ST EDMUNDS,
Suffolk   12 TL86
Bury St Edmunds, the county town of West Suffolk, is named after the last king of East Anglia, who died at the hands of the Danes in AD 870 and whose bones were interred in the monastery here some 30 years later. The town became a place of pilgrimage, and the remains of the Abbey founded in the 11th century show it to have been an imposing edifice. Both the parish church of St James, given cathedral status in 1914, and nearby St Mary's were originally 15th-century and the latter contains a magnificent hammerbeam roof and the grave of Mary Tudor, sister of Henry VIII. The Atheneum, the centre of social life in Regency times, stands on the town's spacious square; Dickens is known to have given readings here, and he used the Angel Hotel as the setting for *Pickwick Papers*. Moyses Hall – perhaps once the home of a Jewish merchant, is a 12th-century building of flint and stone with a vaulted ground floor. It houses a museum of local and natural history and of archaeological items. Angel Corner (NT), a Queen Anne mansion, contains the Gershom-Parkington collection of clocks and watches. The Norton Bird Gardens, on the A1088 (off A45) contain foreign birds and waterfowl.

BUTE, ISLE OF, Strathclyde
Bute is a 15-mile-long island divided from the Cowal Peninsula by the Kyles of Bute and from the larger island of Arran by the Sound of Bute. Before there were ferries to the mainland, cattle destined for market were made to swim across. The main town of the island is Rothesay, a resort in the less hilly, more fertile south. It has two ancient monuments – the deep-moated ruins of a 13th-century castle (AM) and of St Mary's Chapel – and a museum in which the history of the area is recorded.

BUXTON, Derbyshire   15 SK07
The waters of Buxton – charged with nitrogen and carbon dioxide, and bubbling up at a constant 28°C – were popular in Roman times, but it was the 5th Duke of Devonshire who established the spa in this small Pennine market town as a fashionable rival to Bath at the end of the 18th century, building the magnificent Crescent opposite St Anne's Well (OACT), which now houses a micrarium. The Devonshire Royal Hospital was opened in 1859, its 156ft dome among the largest in the world. Today one can swim in an indoor spa-water pool at the Pavilion, which is set in 23-acres of public gardens. The magnificent Edwardian opera house has recently been restored as a theatre. The 19th-century folly on Grin Low (1450ft) offers a splendid viewpoint and beneath it, Poole's Cavern in Buxton Country Park, is interesting to visit.

BYLAND ABBEY,
N Yorkshire   15 SE57
In 1177, after several false starts elsewhere, a colony of Cistercian monks settled here and established the community that was to last until the Dissolution. The site (AM) has been excavated, and the plan of the church and monastic buildings can be seen, as can well-preserved green and yellow glazed floor tiles. Most of the great west front of the Abbey stands, topped by a single turret and the broken circle of a rose window 26ft in diameter.

CADBURY CASTLE,
Somerset   3 ST62
The castle, of which only the earthworks survive, crowns a hill above the village of South Cadbury. Excavations have uncovered traces of cultures from Neolithic to Anglo-Saxon times. There is a powerful tradition that this was the site of Camelot, King Arthur's stronghold, but there is no positive proof. North-east of the village, Cadbury House is a fine example of Elizabethan architecture.

CADER IDRIS, Gwynedd   13 SH71
The Cader Idris range, with its highest point at 2927ft is dramatic to look at, and from the summits there are breath-taking views. Cader (or Cadair) means a seat, and attempts have been made to identify Idris with King Arthur although others say that he was a descendant of the Celtic chieftain Cunedda.

CADGWITH, Cornwall   1 SW71
The cottages in this pretty little fishing village near the Lizard have thatched roofs with chains on them – to prevent their being blown away when the gales storm in from the east. A footpath leads to the Devil's Fryingpan – a crater made when the roof of a cavern collapsed. The nearby lifeboat (also accessible only on foot) used to be kept unusually busy – rescuing the crews of ships impaled upon the rocks.

CAERLEON, Gwent   8 ST39
Four miles up river from Newport, Caerleon has associations with King Arthur, and is thought to be the 'Carlion' of Malory's romance, *Le Morte d'Arthur*, written in 1485. However, the town's Roman associations offer better possibilities for exploration. Caerleon was Isca Silurum, headquarters of the Second Augustan Legion from the 4th century BC until AD 75. The fort covered 51½ acres, and its ramparts can still be identified today. Finds from the site can be seen at the Legionary Museum. Exhibits include carved stone heads, coins, pottery, domestic items, glassware and a number of old weapons. You can also view the remains of one of the few Roman barrack blocks (AM) to survive in Britain. Until it was excavated, the Roman amphitheatre (AM) was popularly held to be King Arthur's Round Table. Tennyson stayed here, at the Hanbury Arms, while researching for his poetic work *Idylls of the King*.

CAERNARFON, Gwynedd   13 SH46
The name means 'Fort on the Shore'. The Romans were the first to build a fort here, and finds from the excavations can be seen at the site museum. The castle (AM) built by Edward I in the 13th–14th centuries is one of the most popular tourist attractions in Wales, especially since the Investiture of Charles, Prince of Wales in 1969. The first English-born Prince of Wales, the son of Edward I (the future Edward II) was proclaimed here, and he is said to have been born in the Eagle Tower in 1284. It was here, too, that Edward I issued the Statute of Wales, bringing the country under the sovereignty of the Kings of England. Opposite the castle balcony stands a statue of Lloyd George – apparently in full political cry.

CADGWITH *Some of the boats drawn up on the shingle beach of this attractive fishing village may be used for or by tourists, but fishing for shellfish is still a serious local business.*

CAERPHILLY,
Mid-Glamorgan *8 ST18*
Famous for its castle (the second largest in Britain after Windsor), Caerphilly was equally renowned for its cheese, which is still made, but not in any quantity in the town itself. Work began on the castle (AM) in 1268, under the direction of Gilbert de Clare, Lord of Glamorgan. It was only half-completed in 1270, when Llwelyn ap Gruffydd arrived in force and demolished it. Building had to start all over again, and on its completion, the castle, with its 320yd-long curtain wall and intricate system of defences, was virtually impregnable until Cromwellian times when it was slighted. As a result of Cromwell's destruction, it has a leaning tower, more steeply inclined than that of Pisa.

CAERWENT, Gwent *8 ST49*
The Roman walls survive as evidence that, 1800 years ago under the name of Venta Silurum, this was the second largest civilian settlement in South-west Britain (the biggest was Bath). The population of about 2000 enjoyed all modern Roman amenities – including an amphitheatre for their entertainment. Less enjoyable were the incursions of raiders from Ireland along the shores of the Severn. One of their victims was the future St Patrick, who was kidnapped from 'somewhere near to the sea', and quite possibly from Caerwent itself. The present town lies within the Roman walls, and in the porch of the 13th-century church is an interesting mosaic. The double lych-gate is a memorial to Thomas Walker – involved in the building of the Severn Tunnel and the Manchester Ship Canal.

CAISTER-ON-SEA, Norfolk *12 TG51*
In ancient times, before nature redesigned the coastline, Caister was a Roman port. Caister Castle (OACT) was built in 1432 by Sir John Fastolf, the model for Falstaff in Shakespeare's play *King Henry IV*. In real life he had command of the archers at Agincourt. In the castle grounds is a fascinating motor museum and the treewalk from Battersea fun-fair was re-erected here in the 1970s.

CAIRNGORMS,
Highland/Grampian *26/27*
The Cairngorms, which extend between Speyside and Braemar are the highest mountain massif in the British Isles. Several of its granite peaks are over 4000ft high and the tallest is exceeded only by Ben Nevis, Britain's highest mountain. In the 600-acre Cairngorm National Nature Reserve, golden eagles, capercaillzie (a large species of grouse), ptarmigan, wild cats and deer are all to be found. Access may be restricted in the grouse-shooting and deer-stalking seasons. **Aviemore**, Grantown-on-Spey and Carrbridge are the main ski resorts, and in the Glenmore Forest Park there are fine walks, particularly around Loch Morlich. Cairngorm stones, translucent, yellowish quartz crystals, are found in the granite, and are often sold as souvenirs.

CALDBECK, Cumbria *18 NY33*
The village, on the northern boundary of the Lake District National Park is famous as the burial place of John Peel, the huntsman who disturbed the morning silence with the sound of his horn and the cry of his hounds. He was born nearby at Greenrigg.

CALDER BRIDGE, Cumbria *18 NY00*
Just to the east of Calder Bridge on the A595, which forms the western boundary of the Lake District National Park, lie the ruins of Calder Abbey (AM). Founded in 1135 by the Savignac Order from Furness Abbey, only the nave, the church aisles and bits of the cloister survive in a lovely setting beside the River Calder.

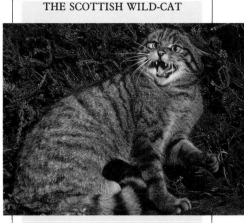

THE SCOTTISH WILD-CAT

Felis Sylvestris grampia, the Scottish wild-cat, is nowadays to be found only in the remote Highlands of Scotland, although it is no longer persecuted as it used to be. It bears a strong resemblance to a large domestic tabby, but it is not the ancestor of the household pet, which descended from related North-African and Asian species.

CALDY ISLAND, Dyfed *7 SR19*
Best reached from Tenby, Caldy Island still has the atmosphere of being a world apart; a storm-battered triumph of human settlement. The present occupants are a colony of Trappist Cistercian monks, but the island was first settled by the Benedictines. The church and parts of the monastery date from the 12th to 16th centuries. Whilst only men may visit the monastery itself, the other religious buildings are open to all members of the public. Perfume, made by the devout inhabitants from flowers and herbs, is on sale.

CAIRNGORM *Britain's highest mountain massif, the seemingly inhospitable Cairngorms provide a habitat for many rare birds and animals.*

CALEDONIAN CANAL
see Glen More.

CALLANDER, Central   *22 NN60*
Callander likes to describe itself as 'the natural gateway to the Highlands' and so, perhaps, it is – despite the fact that its appearance is more suggestive of a Lowland town. It is the Tannochbrae of the television series, 'Dr Finlay's Casebook', and there are some very pleasant houses built in the Regency style, especially in the main street and square. Several beauty spots are within walking distance – such as the Falls of Bracklinn and Ben Ledi. In the town is the interesting Kilmahog Woollen Mill (OACT), famous for its handwoven blankets and tweed.

CALSTOCK, Cornwall   *2 SX46*
This small village beside the Tamar is important as the place to make for when visiting Cotehele House (NT) – undoubtedly one of the finest Tudor manor houses in the country. The main part of the house was built between 1485 and 1539 by Richard Edgcumbe, a supporter of Henry VIII. The house and its gardens remained in the Edgcumbe family's possession until 1947, and the interior decoration and furnishings are superb. The great hall, with its collection of armour, its fantastic roof, the tapestries that hang from its walls, and its hunting trophies – including, of all things, the head of an albatross – exudes a fine sense of period. Cotehele Mill has been restored and can be visited, as can the picturesque quay with its small museum and Tamar sailing barge.

CAMBER, E Sussex   *6 TQ91*
The village is mostly composed of small holiday homes and a holiday camp, mercifully hidden from the beach. The seashore, where the English Channel retreats half a mile at low tide, is a splendid collection of dunes, marram grass, relics of World War II coastal defences, and acres and acres of sand, best walked late on a fine winter's afternoon, when the setting sun produces some stunning lighting effects. *Dunkirk* was one of several films made on location here. Camber Castle (AM), on the far side of Rye harbour, was built by Henry VIII as an artillery fort. With a little imagination one can discern that it is laid out in the shape of a Tudor rose. It stood originally on the shore, as a defence against the possibility of invasion from France, but the sea has gradually receded and it is now about a mile inland.

CAMBERLEY, Surrey   *4 SU86*
Camberley is deep in the heart of Sir John Betjeman's Joan Hunter-Dunn country – where, if the Poet Laureate is to be believed, love-sick subalterns once played tennis with girls named Pam and Joan. The Staff College was originated by the underrated Duke of York in 1799, and the Royal Military College at nearby Sandhurst was also his brainchild. Sandhurst used to be known as 'Hell-over-the-Hill' by the nearby public school at Wellington; and the cadets were once a wild bunch.

CAMBO, Northumberland   *20 NZ08*
Cambo itself is a pretty little village – indeed, it was built as a *model* village in 1740 and is an almost unspoiled example. The beautiful stately home of Wallington

Hall (NT) – a 17th-century mansion, about a mile away, was built by Sir William Blackett, a Newcastle merchant. Sir William's descendant, Sir Walter Blackett, dedicated 40 years of his life to improving the house and the 13,000 acres of land. A team of craftsmen from Italy carried out some magnificent plasterwork – notably on the ceilings of the hall and staircases. In the grounds, that master of the man-made landscape, Capability Brown, began his professional career. Nearly a century later, under the benevolent rule of Pauline, Lady Trevelyan, a picture gallery was created. The walls are decorated with pre-Raphaelite portrayals of the story of Northumberland, and the gallery contains works by Cranach, Reynolds and Gainsborough among others.

CAMBORNE-REDRUTH, Cornwall   *1 SW64*
It is hard to say where the one ends and the other begins. Pool acts as a hyphen between them, and here you can see a winding engine of 1887 and a pumping engine built in 1892, which have been preserved by the National Trust. As this may suggest, Camborne and Redruth were at the centre of Cornwall's tin and copper mining industries (in 1856, the country's output of copper ore amounted to 209,000 tons or £2 million of revenue). Nowadays, such employment as there is comes from light industries that have sprouted in the vicinity. Camborne was the birthplace in 1771 of the inventor Richard Trevithick, who in 1801 built the first passenger steam vehicle.

CORNWALL'S MINERAL WEALTH

Tin and copper, the essential metals of bronze, began to be mined in Cornwall in the Bronze Age. With the coming of the Celts the industry developed and tin was shipped from Cornwall all over Europe and, of course, to the rest of lowland Britain. Tin lodes are found within Cornwall's granite rocks, mostly in a belt stretching from near Land's End to Camborne and Redruth, and copper deposits are found in the nearby shale. From the medieval period right up until the middle of the Victorian era, tin was Cornwall's chief source of employment and prosperity. In the 1860s, though, many of the older mines were worked out, and competition from south-east Asia and South America crippled the industry. Thousands of out-of-work miners emigrated to the colonies, leaving gaunt ruins at places like Botallack, pictured below in its heyday, and Coranthony near Redruth (left), all over the area. Efforts to revive the industry have not been successful.

Riverside Towns of the Cam and Ouse
79 miles

Wide Fenland horizons, interrupted only by an occasional church spire, or the distinctive outline of a solitary windmill, lend a sense of exhilaration to the flat landscapes of the Cambridgeshire fens.
Old towns and villages hug the banks of the meandering River Great Ouse, and in Cambridge, punts drift by on inconsequential voyages under the willow trees along the River Cam.

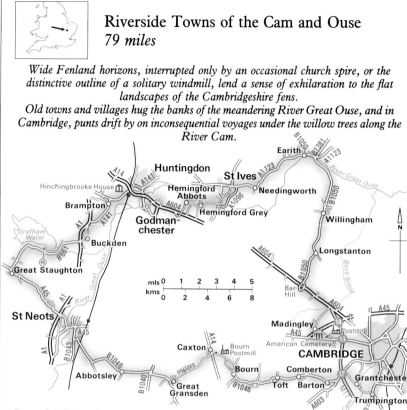

Leave **Cambridge** following A45 Bedford signs on A1303. In 2½ miles pass the American Cemetery, then at the roundabout take the 3rd exit to **Madingley**. Continue, turning left on to the A604 and in 2 miles branch left on to B1050 SP Chatteris. At the roundabout go right to stay with B1050 to **Longstanton**, where turn left for **Willingham**. Keep forward with B1050 and then turn left on to A1123 into **Earith**. Continue through Needingworth and in 1¼ miles follow town-centre signs into **St Ives**.

Follow Cambridge signs, cross the river and in ¼ mile turn right to **Hemingford Grey**. Turn left into Braggs Lane and right, drive to Hemingford Abbots and follow signs for Huntingdon to join A604. In 1 mile branch left, then turn right at a roundabout to reach **Godmanchester**. Branch right on to B1043 and cross the river to enter **Huntingdon**.

Follow signs Kettering (A604) from the ring road to leave on A141. Pass Hinchingbrooke House and continue on A141 turning left at the roundabout to

Brampton. Follow signs for London and in 2 miles join A1 and take the 2nd left turning to Buckden. At the roundabout take B661 (SP Kimbolton). Continue to **Great Staughton**, then turn left on to the A45. Continue into **St Neots**.

Leave the town by turning right (SP Little Barford) on to the B1043. At the roundabout take the 1st exit, B1046 (SP The Gransdens, then turn next right into Potton Rd, and in a mile bear left to **Abbotsley**. In 1½ miles turn right and left to **Great Gransden**, pass the Crown and Cushion PH and turn left (SP Industrial Estate). At the roundabout left again to **Caxton** and turn right then left (SP Toft, Bourn). Pass Bourn Postmill and in 1 mile turn right at a T-junction to drive through **Bourn**, then join B1046. Continue to Barton, then turn left on to A603. Cross M11 then take 3rd exit at the roundabout and continue through **Grantchester**, then cross the River Cam and drive to **Trumpington**. Here join A1309 and return to Cambridge.

PLACES TO SEE

Cambridge Ancient colleges of which most notable are Queens', with its unique Mathematical Bridge, King's College Chapel, St John's and Trinity. The Backs, immaculate green lawns stretching down to the Cam, are prettiest in Spring. Fitzwilliam Museum has outstanding collections of paintings and oriental art.

Willingham The 14th-century church has a magnificent angel roof.

St Ives An interesting market town with ancient bridge where a rare medieval chapel can be seen.

Godmanchester One of the most picturesque of the riverside towns on the Ouse.

Hinchingbrooke House (OACT), on the edge of Huntingdon is a Tudor mansion associated with the Cromwell family.

Brampton Pepys House (OACT), was the home of the diarist's parents.

Buckden Remains of the palace where Catherine of Aragon was imprisoned.

St Neots Attractive old market town.

Bourn Postmill (OACT) Dating from 1636, this is possibly the oldest working windmill in the country.

Grantchester A charming village immortalised by the poet Rupert Brooke.

GREAT ST MARY'S, *the university church, and Cambridge market.*

PLACES TO SEE

King's College Founded by Henry VI. Only the chapel, was completed in his lifetime.

Queens' College Founded at different times by two queens, Margaret, wife of Henry VI, and Elizabeth, wife of Edward IV. The 'Mathematical' bridge, built in 1749 without the aid of nails, and on geometric principles, was one of the curiosities of Cambridge. In 1867 it was dismantled, and could not be rebuilt in the old way.

Pembroke College The chapel is the first of Christopher Wren's designs ever to be completed. Not far from the college is **Hobson's Conduit**, named after a mayor of the city who had run a livery stable, and inspired the saying, 'Hobson's Choice' because he refused to allow his customers to choose their own horses.

Centre of Medieval Scholasticism

'We were walking the whole time – out of one College into another . . . I felt I could live and die in them and never wish to speak again.'
MARY LAMB, *Letters*

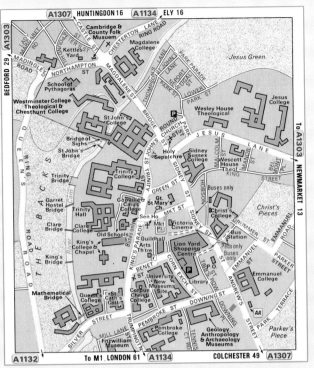

The unforgettable sight of Cambridge is the view across the River Cam and the Backs to the stately Gothic chapel of King's College. The town itself contains much new building, often at variance with the character of the old. Although overshadowed by the university, the town, too, is very ancient and has its origins in Celtic settlements around a ford on the Cam. The Romans built a bridge and established an outpost here, at the meeting point of a network of roads and navigable waterways. The town has always been a flourishing regional centre, and of recent years the university's scientific activities have encouraged the foundation in Cambridge of several research-based industries.

The university grew from small beginnings at the start of the 13th century, when a group of students, in trouble with the authorities at Oxford, came to Cambridge in 1209. There were no colleges as such at this period; the students were attached to the schools of cathedrals and monasteries, and lodged where they could in the town. The first college, Peterhouse, was founded in 1281 by the Bishop of Ely, and by 1284 was established in its own buildings. Over the next few hundred years, most of the other colleges were established – though there are a number of modern foundations, such as Churchill, Darwin and New Hall. New Hall (1954) is the most recent of the three women's colleges: Girton and Newnham date from the 19th century. Nowadays, after some debate, almost all the colleges have opted for co-education and admit both men and women as undergraduates.

Trinity College Three medieval colleges were incorporated into Trinity by Henry VIII. The Great Court has a magnificent Renaissance fountain, and the library, designed by Wren, has carvings by Grinling Gibbons.

Magdalene College Samuel Pepys was one of the famous alumni of Magdalene, and his diaries, together with his bookcases and the desk at which he worked are preserved in the Pepys Library.

St John's College Like Queens', St John's has a famous bridge, modelled on the Bridge of Sighs at Venice.

St Bene't's Church is the oldest building in the county, believed to date from the reign of King Cnut.

THE MATHEMATICAL BRIDGE (left), an 18th-century puzzle, spans the river behind Queens' College.

Holy Sepulchre One of only five round churches remaining in England, it was founded in 1130 by the Knights Templar on the model of the Church of the Holy Sepulchre at Jerusalem. Succeeding centuries have added to the original Romanesque structure.

Fitzwilliam Museum Egyptian, Greek and Roman antiquities, oriental porcelain and ceramics are among the objects bequeathed by the 7th Viscount Fitzwilliam as the nucleus of this outstanding collection of treasures.

The Cambridge and County Folk Museum displays local crafts, agriculture and industry.

Scott Polar Research Institute Arctic and Antarctic exhibitions with information on current scientific exploration.

University Botanic Gardens cover acres of grounds, filled with fine botanical specimens.

KING'S COLLEGE CHAPEL (below) in 1750, dominating the city skyline.

CAMPBELTOWN,
Strathclyde *21 NR72*

Kintyre is a long tongue of land reaching from the Highlands towards Northern Ireland, and protecting the Isle of Arran against the westerlies that rage in from the Atlantic. On the east coast of Kintyre, not far from the tip, is Campbeltown, its main centre. The excellent anchorage encouraged the growth of a herring fishing fleet; coal was discovered; other industries were established. At the end of the 19th century, about 650 fishing boats were based there, and the town had 30 distilleries producing the celebrated Campbeltown malt whisky. Now, alas, most of that has gone, and it is tourism that keeps the town alive. The museum is worth a visit; the facilities for sea angling, sailing, and so on are good, and the golf-course at nearby Machrihanish is famous. In a cave on Davaar Island at the mouth of Campbeltown Loch an artist named Archibald MacKinnon painted the Crucifixion. Lit by a shaft of daylight that pierces a hole in the rock, the effect is breathtakingly dramatic.

CANNOCK CHASE,
Staffordshire *9 SJ01*

Cannock Chase is one of those delightful surprises for which Staffordshire should be better known: an expanse of forest and heath which comes as a blessed interlude in a countryside dominated by mining and industry. It began as a royal forest – was sold by Richard I to the Bishop of Lichfield to raise money for a crusade, and was eventually abandoned by a later bishop. Much of it is now Forestry Commission land, and the rides offer excellent walking. The 258ft Post Office Tower, arrogant in its uncompromising concrete on Pye Green, has been described as 'a magnificent landmark'.

CANFORD CLIFFS, Dorset *3 SZ08*

This suburb of the busy resort of Poole is notable for a garden named Compton Acres (OACT) which was laid out in 1919. It contains seven sections – which include Japanese, Roman, and Italian – planted with appropriate blooms and adorned with imported statuary and buildings.

CANVEY ISLAND, Essex *6 TQ78*

This rather featureless bit of land in the Thames estuary not far from Southend is a mass of caravans and bungalows. Tragedy came to Canvey Island on the night of 31 January 1953 when the Thames broke in, destroyed countless homes, and caused 58 deaths by drowning.

CAPEL CURIG, Gwynedd *13 SH75*

A small, straggling village in the heart of Snowdonia, containing several hotels that cater for anglers and hill walkers. Nearby, two lakes joined by a channel provide good trout fishing. The settlement was founded by St Curig in the 6th century.

CAPESTHORNE, Cheshire *14 SJ87*

The old hall (OACT), home of an important Cheshire family, the Bromley-Davenports, was much altered and enlarged, first by Blore in 1837 and later, in 1867 by Salvin in a flamboyant Victorian style. Not far away, Redesmere is a charming wooded lake.

CAPE WRATH, Highland *29 NC27*

To reach Cape Wrath, the most north-westerly point of the British mainland, you must travel from Durness by ferry and then, in summer only, along a track by minibus. The cliffs, haunted by gannets, are 370ft high – the lighthouse, 400ft above the ocean at high tide. 'Wrath' does not refer to the temper of the sea but comes from the Norse *hvarf* – a turning point.

CARDIGAN, Dyfed *7 SN14*

Cardigan is a delightful and lively town that used to be a prosperous seaport until the River Teifi silted up. It is a town steeped in the culture – and, indeed, the blood – of Wales. The first national Eisteddfod was held here in 1177. Even the castle was not of Edward I's construction, but was built by Welshmen in an attempt to safeguard their independence. The fact that it is now in ruins is the price the town had to pay for its support of Charles I. In 1645, Parliament – determined to exact a penalty – turned its guns upon it. Nowadays the most imposing architectural feature is the bridge over the river, which dates from the 17th century. Even when Cardigan was the county town of Cardiganshire, it was too small to carry out its duties: the Assizes had to be held several miles away at Lampeter, and the Council sat at Aberystwyth. The Wildlife Park (OACT) near Gilgerran, specialises in European animals.

CARDINGTON,
Bedfordshire *11 TL04*

Cardington itself is an attractive little village that owes much to the brewing family of Whitbread (Samuel Whitbread, who founded the firm, was born there in 1720). On the edge of it, however, the giant airship sheds provide a grim reminder of Britain's last adventure into the construction of giant airships. One of them housed the R100, which might have been successful. The other, the R101 – the victim of muddled thinking and politics – crashed at Beauvais in France on her maiden flight. Only 6 of her 54 passengers and crew survived. Nowadays, the premises are occupied by the Royal Aircraft Establishment and are devoted to research. In St Mary's Church is a rare Wedgwood font, donated by Harriet Whitbread and several memorials to the family.

CARDINGTON *These huge hangars at Cardington were built to house the R101 airship developed here. It crashed in France in 1930 on its maiden flight.*

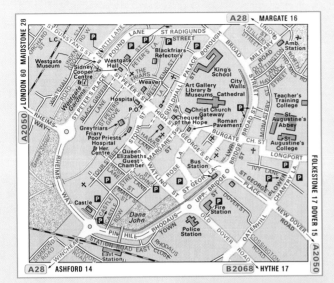

Mother City of England

'*Scarce any City is there in this Kingdom, which for antiquity of origins, or for the dignity of its fortune, can be compared to ours.*'
JOHN TWYNE (Mayor, 1553–4) in *The Official Guide*

Dominating the narrow streets and ancient buildings, the incomparable cathedral, setting for many dramatic events in past centuries, stands at the heart of a city that still retains its ancient character. Parts of Canterbury are still enclosed within the medieval city walls, about half of which, built on medieval foundations, remain, as does the keep of the castle, which has defied periodic attempts over the centuries to demolish it.

Settlements existed here at the time of the Roman invasion, and the Romans built their regional centre, Durovernum, on this site. A well-preserved Roman tessellated pavement of about 100 BC can be seen beneath one of the shops in the Longmarket shopping precinct.

When St Augustine arrived in 597, he founded his cathedral here in 602, and thus the city became the centre of the Anglican Church. The present cathedral was founded by the Normans in 1070, but the nave had to be rebuilt in the 14th century, and the central tower (called Bell Harry), which is such a feature of Canterbury, was added in 1500. The earliest Norman work is to be found in the splendid crypt, but the majority of the cathedral, in particular the nave, completed early in the 15th century, is a glorious expression of Gothic architecture. Despite the ravages of World War II, some magnificent stained-glass remains.

The most famous event that took place here was the murder of Archbishop Thomas Becket in 1170 by Henry II's knights. Becket was immediately proclaimed a martyr and his shrine drew innumerable pilgrims to Canterbury, such as those immortalised by Chaucer in *Canterbury Tales*, until the reign of Henry VIII when it was destroyed. Many former archbishops are interred here, some in tombs of great splendour, as is Edward, the Black Prince, and Henry IV and his queen.

Adjoining the cathedral was once a Benedictine monastery, the cloisters of which remain. Nearby, around Green Court, parts of the monastery are incorporated in the buildings of King's School, one of the oldest and foremost of English public schools.

Although the cathedral is the focal point of interest, there are several other historic churches, including St Martin's, said to be the oldest church in England still in use. It is believed to pre-date the arrival of St Augustine. A little way outside Canterbury, the new buildings of the University of Kent are also of interest.

PLACES TO SEE

CANTERBURY CATHEDRAL *looms large in the city's history.*

St Augustine's Abbey (AM) Founded in 602 by St Augustine, the abbey ruins are among the most important ecclesiastical remains anywhere in Europe. The foundations of a 7th-century church and of an 11th-century round church have also been uncovered on this site.

Greyfriars Picturesquely spanning the River Stour, this is the only remaining building of the first Franciscan settlement in England. Interior open by arrangement only.

Poor Priests' Hospital A museum of city history is housed in this medieval refuge for the poor and infirm. Here can be seen the *Invicta*, one of the world's oldest railway engines, built by George and Robert Stephenson for the Canterbury – Whitstable line, the oldest regular steam passenger service in the world.

Westgate Only remaining of the city's medieval gates, it now houses a small museum relating to the gatehouse and the medieval city walls.

Royal Museum (Beaney Institute) houses the Regimental Museum of the Buffs, and has collections of Roman, Saxon and medieval life.

Roman Pavement Canterbury's underground museum in Butchery Lane preserves the remains of a Roman town house.

St Thomas's Hospital (OACT) In this unassuming building are a superb Norman undercroft, a 12th-century refectory and a remarkable 14th-century chapel. Also known as Eastbridge, this is one of the city's oldest buildings.

Blean Bird Garden three miles north-west of the city has a fascinating collection of exotic tropical birds, kept in natural surroundings.

THE WEAVERS' HOUSE *where Huguenot weavers found refuge in Tudor times.*

Cardiff, S Glamorgan 8 ST17

Capital City of Wales

'We came in the evening to the ancient city of Llandaff and Caerdiff ... Llandaff is the seat of the episcopal see ... but Caerdiff ... is the port and town of trade ...'

DANIEL DEFOE, *A Tour through the Whole Island of Great Britain*

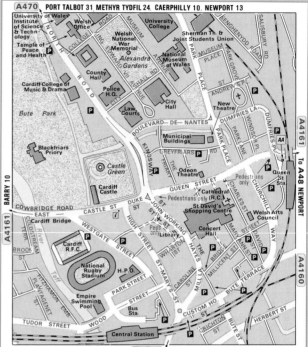

In 1955 Cardiff was created the official capital of Wales. The other contenders for the title, Machynlleth and Caernarfon had stronger historical claims, but Cardiff had better communications, was more accessible to London and, thanks to its docks, was a more flourishing centre of trade and industry.

Welsh speakers prefer to call the city Caerdydd, meaning 'seat of Dydd'. The identity of Dydd is uncertain, but he was probably a Roman commander, – the genesis of Cardiff was a Roman fort, built in what are now the castle grounds in AD 75. After the Norman conquest, Robert Fitz-hamon built a motte and bailey castle in 1093, and this was re-placed by a stone keep in the 12th century, the remains of which, restored in the 19th century by the 3rd Marquess of Bute, can be seen in the castle grounds.

In the Tudor period, the in-habitants of Cardiff were notori-ous pirates, preying on shipping in the Bristol Channel, with the connivance of city officials who grew rich on the proceeds. Seafar-ing continued to be an occupation even after piracy had been sup-pressed, but it did not become important to the city until the coal and iron ore of South Wales began to be exploited during the Industrial Revolution. It was the 2nd Marquess of Bute, whose family had acquired land in Car-diff, who saw the potential of this trade and in 1839 built the city's first dock – Bute West, later much extended.

This was the foundation of the city's prosperity and by the out-break of World War I Cardiff was the world's premier port for the export of coal. In 1898 the Bute family sold Cathays Park to the city corporation, and this became the site for an impressive complex of public buildings comprising the City Hall, the Law Courts, the National Museum of Wales, County Hall, the University of Wales Registry, the University of South Wales, the Welsh Office, the Temple of Peace and Health and the Welsh National War Memorial. All were built between 1905 and 1938. More recent land-marks are the National Rugby Stadium at Cardiff Arms Park, which, with seating for 50,000 people, is an expression of the Welsh passion for rugby, and the National Sports Centre.

PLACES TO SEE

Cardiff Castle A 'many-towered Camelot' of a castle, built for the wealthy and eccentric 3rd Mar-quess of Bute in the 1870s by the architect William Burges. The in-terior is a flamboyant expression of the Victorian imagination.

The National Museum of Wales Among the many famous works of art is a collection of Im-pressionist and post-Impression-ist paintings, Rodin's famous statue, *The Kiss* and an unrival-led collection of Ogham Stones.

City Hall (OACT) The Marble Hall, decorated with statues of Welsh heroes leads to the im-pressive Council Chamber with its display of city treasures.

Bute Park In this extensive park are the remains of a Dominican priory.

Welsh Industrial and Maritime Museum Traces the history of motive power in two centuries of Welsh industry.

VICTORIAN CARDIFF *and its busy docks (below) produced the wealth for the rebuilding of Cardiff Castle. (Left) the ceiling of the opulent Moorish Room.*

CAREW, Dyfed   7 SN00

Carew, which nestles in a creek about halfway between Tenby and Pembroke, is a remarkable village. The inn and the huddle of cottages are as picturesque as anyone could wish. The 14th-century church boasts an intricately carved 11th-century Celtic cross – 14ft high – that stands proudly outside. Carew Castle (AM) is early Norman, though its more important association is with Rhys ap Thomas, who was one of those who welcomed Henry Tudor when he landed – and fought on his side at the Battle of Bosworth. The name of the village comes from Thomas Carew who was born in Kent. For several generations, the Carews were keepers of the castle, and the family tombs can be seen in the church. Downstream, you can discover one of the few working tidal mills in Britain today. It was restored in 1972.

CARLISLE, Cumbria   18 NY45

In AD 80, Agricola founded a Roman settlement close to the Scottish border. He called it Luguvalium, and this was the origin of Carlisle. Protected to the north by Hadrian's Wall, it flourished during the Roman period. After the Romans left, the outpost fell to the Picts, later to the Vikings and the Scots. The Normans claimed it for England and work on the castle (AM) was begun by William II. King David of Scotland, who took it by storm in the 12th century, added to it, and Henry VIII carried out further improvements. It last witnessed shots fired in anger during the Jacobite uprising of 1745. Such were the comings and goings of warring factions from north and south of the border, that the citizens of Carlisle could scarcely have known whether they were English or Scottish.

In 1123, the more devout members of the community built a church – which, by 1133, had become a cathedral. Its east window is said to be 'the most lovely in Europe', but the church suffered much damage during the Dissolution and again under the Commonwealth. The Prior's Tower (OACT) in the grounds has a museum of Cathedral history and a room with unusual painted panels.

The town hall used to have two bells. One was used from 1584 until the mid 19th century to announce that the market was open. The other, known as the 'muckle town bell', was for sounding alarms. It could, so they said, be heard 11 miles away. Both are now in the city museum. Tullie House Museum, a Jacobean mansion, contains finds from Hadrian's Wall. Carlisle Cross dates from 1682 and it was here that Bonnie Prince Charlie made his proclamation in 1745.

The more military side of Carlisle is commemorated in Queen Mary's Tower (OACT) which now houses the museum of the former Border Regiment (regimental march: 'D'ye Ken John Peel'). Mary, Queen of Scots lodged in the castle on her constant and tragic wanderings from one prison to another, and the tower named after her, remains.

In the city centre, two round towers – near the railway station – mark the site of the citadel, an inner defence in case the castle was overwhelmed. They are a reconstruction of the original (built in 1541–3) – carried out in 1807 by Thomas Smirke, who designed the British Museum.

CAREW CASTLE *Overlooking the tidal estuary of the Carew River, the castle was largely rebuilt in the 15th century. The tide mill is one of the few such mills still in working order.*

CARLTON-IN-CLEVELAND, N Yorkshire   00 NZ50

Karl was the Norse word for a free man. Carlton, this fascinating village that broods over the Cleveland hills, began its life in Saxon times as a settlement of freed slaves. Among its more colourful inhabitants have been a couple of far from average vicars. One, George Sangar, rebuilt the church in 1879 – and, two years later, was suspected of burning it down. The reason, it was rumoured, was that his mind had become deranged by love for a local girl, who was about to bear his child. He was acquitted of arson, but the suspicions endured. The other, Canon John Kyle, might have been invented by Surtees. He rode to hounds, farmed, and ran a pub named the Fox and Hounds – which is now a private house. Canon Kyle died in 1943. The most impressive building is the 18th-century manor house, a nice essay in the Palladian style of architecture.

CARMARTHEN, Dyfed   7 SN42

Carmarthen can rightly claim to be one of the oldest towns in Wales. It probably began its life as a Celtic hill fort, but this was obliterated by the Romans who built a wooden fort here in AD75. This was the most westerly of their large forts, but few traces remain – though the discovery of an amphitheatre with a seating capacity of 5000 suggests that there must have been a fairly sizeable garrison. Later (inevitably, one might say), the Normans built a castle

here. The ruins (AM) can still be seen, but much of the site is now occupied by County Hall. Of the Augustinian Priory the Normans also founded little but the site remains. It was here that the oldest-known manuscript in Welsh was written – the *Black Book of Carmarthen*, now in the National Library of Wales in Aberystwyth. Among other legends, it tells the story of Merlin, King Arthur's wizard, who is said to have been born here. Anyone seeking evidence should recall that Carmarthen's Welsh name is *Caerfryddin*, 'the city of Merlin'. At the end of Priory Street, a carefully preserved stump of an oak tree stood until recently, bearing the prophecy 'When Merlin's oak shall tumble down, Then shall fall Carmarthen town'. The remains can now be seen in the foyer of St Peter's Civic Hall. On the River Tywi the ancient craft of coracle fishing is still practised.

CARNFORTH, Lancashire   18 SD47

The village owes much to the railway and is the home of the Steamtown Railway Museum where the famous *Flying Scotsman* is one of the most popular exhibits. Leighton Hall (OACT) three miles to the north, near the village of Yealand Conyers, was the home of the Gillow family, famous furniture makers from **Lancaster**. The house contains a fine collection of Richard Gillow's furniture. There is also a Birds of Prey museum, where eagles can sometimes be seen flying.

CARNOUSTIE, Tayside *27 NO53*

Carnoustie has two golf courses: the championship course and the Burnside. The former is thought to be the toughest in Britain: when the wind comes hurtling down the Firth of Tay from the North Sea, it can ruin even the most perfectly judged shot. Sandy beaches with lots of dunes, good bathing and an enviable record of sunshine make this a popular holiday resort.

CARRADALE, Strathclyde *21 NR83*

This small resort on Kintyre is the nearest point on the shore of Kilbrennan Sound to the Island of Arran, which stands grey and proud three miles away to the east. A harbour was constructed in 1959; but the fishing fleet, its intended user, has fallen upon hard times. An oval fort on Carradale Point seems, at first glance, to have been fashioned from glass. In fact, it has been vitrified by the effect of fire. Carradale House (OACT) has fine gardens, at their best from April to June.

CARTMEL, Cumbria *18 SD37*

Cartmel (AM), which stands on a stubby peninsula projecting into Morecambe Bay, used to be a powerhouse of faith and scholarship. The priory and its church of Sts Mary and Michael were established in the 12th century (the church in 1188). King Henry VIII dissolved the former: after it had fallen into disuse, local builders helped themselves to the stones until only the impressive gatehouse (NT) survived. The church remained, which is worth a prayer in itself. This wonderful, almost majestic, building has the atmosphere of a cathedral rather than that of a more modest place of worship. A number of people who failed to beat the tide on their journeys between Lancashire and the Lake District across the treacherous sands of Morecambe Bay – once a well-used thoroughfare – are buried in the graveyard.

CASTLE ACRE, Norfolk *12 TF81*

The word 'acre' is derived from the Saxon word *aecer* meaning a field. The castle, in this instance, was the work of William I's son-in-law, William de Warenne, who first built a huge mound and then constructed an enormous flint keep on top. It was well sited to command the point at which that ancient thoroughfare, the Peddars' Way, crosses the River Nar. Not a great deal of William de Warenne's work survives, though the gatehouse (AM) is still in good condition. Still impressive, however, are the ruins of the Cluniac priory, and the parish church is a noble achievement. Much of the village was contained within the outer defences of the castle; subsequent builders, with laudable sensitivity have conformed to the homogeneity of the brick-and-flint houses that characterise this compact settlement. During the 19th-century, Castle Acre was declared an open village. In other words, during the depressions, the homeless and unemployed could gather here to seek work – and, indeed, somewhere in which to live.

CASTLE COMBE, Wiltshire *3 ST87*

Picture a small village set in a wooded valley, with a stream ambling thoughtfully through the middle. The houses are of honey-coloured Cotswold stone: there is a medieval market cross; a three-arched bridge over the stream; and the church (its tower a gift from the 'clothiers of the district') has survived the ravages of well-meaning but ill-conceived Victorian restoration. Hardly any traffic passes along the street. Time seems to stand still in Castle Combe, held to be the prettiest village in England. (In 1962, the word 'probably' was deleted and the village became officially so). Drama came to Castle Combe in 1966, when the film makers turned it into what cinema audiences may have mistaken for a seaport for the filming of *Dr Doolittle*, starring Rex Harrison.

CASTLE DONINGTON, Leicestershire *10 SK42*

The 'castle' was Norman: built by Baron Haulton, hereditary Constable of Cheshire, in the 12th century. In 1595, it was virtually demolished, and another residence built in the park – two miles away. Nowadays, there are some charming houses in the town, including the Hall, which was designed by Wilkins – who also designed the National Gallery in London. When visiting the 13th–14th-century church, notice the pulpit: the inside of it is made from memorial slabs to children which were removed from the floor. Among the tombs is a fine brass to Robert de Staunton and his wife, and one commemorating a monk who died in 1320. Car enthusiasts will doubtless enjoy the Donington Collection of historic racing cars – though the nearby racing circuit and East Midlands airport make unfortunate contributions to the decibel level. Castle Donington Air Museum displays American, French and British aircraft.

CASTLE DOUGLAS, Dumfries & Galloway *17 NX76*

This pleasant market town was once an important commercial centre. Mons Meg, the famous cannon that is now in Edinburgh Castle, was probably forged by a local blacksmith. Going back even earlier, traces of prehistoric dwellings have been found on the shore of Carlingwark Loch. Threave House (NTS), one and half miles to the south, is a nice example of Scottish baronial architecture. Its gardens, run by the National Trust for Scotland's school of gardening, are open to the public. Interesting at all times of the year, they are especially fine in spring. Threave Castle (AM), built in the 14th century on an islet in the River Dee, is an evocative ruin. For many years, it was the stronghold of the Black Douglases. The town holds a civic week once a year. The highlight is a re-enactment of the ceremony in 1792, when it received its Charter.

CASTLE HEDINGHAM, Essex *12 TL73*

Miraculously the Tudor and, indeed, the medieval atmosphere of the village survives. Above it broods the massive keep, once a stronghold of the Earls of Oxford, who established a vineyard here in Norman times.

The castle (OACT) was admirably sited to control the trade route along the Colne valley. For the next 500 years, the de Veres were lords of the manor with only one setback. That was in 1215 when King John took the castle from Robert de Vere. However, the king later relented. Not long afterwards, he granted Castle Hedingham a Market Charter. Matilda, wife of King Stephen, died here in 1151. Queen Elizabeth I was the last sovereign to enjoy the de Veres' hospitality. Afterwards, and for no apparent reason, the 17th Earl of Oxford pulled part of the castle down. The stones were used to build a Georgian house by Robert Ashurst, who had bought the ruin from the 18th (and last) Earl of Oxford's widow.

The village, clustered round the Norman church, has some lovely houses and pretty little streets. The Colne Valley Railway and Museum, on the A604 Gt Yeldham road is worth visiting.

CASTLE ACRE *Attached to the ruins of the 11th-century priory founded by William de Warenne, 2nd Earl of Surrey, some of the old Norman buildings, including the Prior's House, survive.*

CASTLE HOWARD *The elaborate fountain, centrepiece of the gardens, was designed for the Great Exhibition of 1851.*

CASTLE HOWARD, N Yorkshire   16 SE77

To some people, this may be better known as 'Brideshead', for it was at Castle Howard (OACT) that much of the TV version of Evelyn Waugh's *Brideshead Revisited* was filmed. It is of course, tremendous. It was built for Charles Howard, 3rd Earl of Carlisle, to replace Henderskelfe Castle, which was burned down in 1693. Sir John Vanbrugh was chosen as architect; very much a Renaissance man, he was also a gifted playwright and as captain of marines, a man of action. With assistance fromNicholas Hawksmoor (Wren's clerk of works), he designed Castle Howard and then went on to conceive Blenheim.

It seems impossible that the interior of the house – which isn't really a castle at all – can match the exterior for sheer grandeur, but it does. In the 1000-acre grounds, there are two lakes, the Temple of the Four Winds and the Mausoleum, which is as big as a Wren church in London. Castle Howard cost £78,000 and took 37 years to complete (1700–1737). It is still owned by the Howard family.

CASTLE KENNEDY, Dumfries & Galloway   17 NX15

The name of the castle is Lochinch. It was built in 1867, and is the home of the Earl of Stair. Situated on a peninsula that juts out between White and Black Lochs, the present building replaced Castle Kennedy, which was destroyed by a fire in 1716, and *this* was the seat of the Kennedy family. The grounds (OACT) were laid out by the 2nd Earl of Stair – inspired by the gardens of Versailles.

CASTLE RISING, Norfolk   12 TF62

Castle Rising (AM) was built in 1150. The keep – 50ft high and of massive breadth was one of the largest in England. The Norman arcading of the walls can still be seen. Edward III confined his mother, Queen Isabella, in the castle as punishment for her role in the murder of her husband, Edward II, and it is said that her screams can still be heard. St Lawrence's Church has a superb west front of the Norman period. Trinity Almshouses (OACT), founded in the 17th-century by the Earl of Northampton, contain rooms with Jacobean furniture.

DERBYSHIRE'S RARE STONE

A translucent variety of fluospar, Blue John is found only in the Peak District of Derbyshire, in caverns under Treak Cliff Hill near Castleton. The stone may have bands of red, blue, purple or yellow, but blue is the predominant colour, hence the name. Blue John has been mined since Roman times to make jewellery and ornaments, and the two caves where it is found can be visited. In the Blue John Caverns, where the network of chambers and passages runs into the hillside for two miles, the mineral can be seen in its natural state. Both these and the Treak Cliff Caverns are noted for their stalactites and stalagmites.

CASTLETON, Derbyshire   15 SK18

Peveril Castle (AM, the scene of Sir Walter Scott's *Peveril of the Peak*), stands on high ground above the village, which was given to William Peverill by William I. The keep was added a century later by Henry II. Much of the castle has been capably restored: it's certainly worth the walk to see it. In Castleton itself and in the vicinity are some of the county's most famous caverns: the villagers used to seek sanctuary in them when raiders came. A secret passage connects one of them, Devil's Cavern with the castle. The Blue John Cavern, where the attractive blue stone is mined, Peak, Treak Cliff and Speedwell Caverns (OACT) are all fascinating to visit.

CAVENDISH, Suffolk   12 TL84

One of those lovely villages that seem to have been built with picture postcards or calendars in mind, Cavendish has thatched cottages, their walls washed with pink, which gather round a spot with the improbable name of Hyde Park Corner. The 14th-century church tower contains a room with a fireplace and a chimney. The name Cavendish comes from the Anglo-Saxon *Cafa's Edisc* ('Cafa's People'). However, the village also has associations with the Dukes of Devonshire (family name: Cavendish). Thomas Cavendish sailed round the world in the 1580s, and died at sea when making a second attempt. Sir John Cavendish was Chief Justice when Richard II put down the Peasants' Revolt and Wat Tyler was killed.

CAWDOR, Highland   26 NH85

Did Macbeth murder King Duncan at Cawdor Castle or, as some say, at Glamis? Or was it somewhere completely different? In fact, Macbeth (who was by no means so bad as Shakespeare painted him) probably slew him in battle near Elgin. However, Shakespeare has fixed the deed at Cawdor Castle (OACT). A high walled, medieval fortress it certainly looks a suitable setting for a dark deed. Still the home of the Earls of Cawdor, the family treasures include some exceptionally fine tapestries.

CEMAES BAY, Anglesey, Gwynedd 13 SH39

Cemaes Bay is a remarkable study in the survival of an attractive little seaside village against overwhelming odds. A nuclear power station is one mile away. Supertankers offload their cargoes at a buoy not far offshore, and nearby Point Lynas is where big ships pick up their pilots before entering the Mersey. Nevertheless, Cemaes Bay has weathered the storms of progress. Legend has it that St Patrick founded the church – after he'd been rescued from a ship that had gone aground on a reef.

CERNE ABBAS *Associated with ancient fertility rites, the giant is more than 1500 years old.*

CENARTH, Dyfed 7 SN24

As it approaches Cenarth, the River Teifi enters a wooded gorge. Constrained by these much more narrow walls, its pace quickens, and it thunders down a series of waterfalls towards the village's 18th-century bridge – which, interestingly, has circular holes in its arches to help against flooding. The river is rich with salmon, some of which are still caught from coracles. The fishing museum and salmon leap will be of interest to anglers. Cenarth's smithy has been restored. A sightly old mill stands amid the trees on the riverside.

CERES, Fife 24 NO41

Ceres has been described as 'the most attractive village in Scotland'. Certainly, it is one of the very few to have a village green, and its humpback bridge (for pedestrians only) dates back to the Middle Ages. Robert Bruce's men marched over it on their way to vanquish Edward II's troops at Bannockburn. When news of the victory reached Ceres, there were celebrations on the green – which is why the Bannockburn Games are held there every June. The Fife Folk Museum is housed in Weigh House cottages.

CERNE ABBAS, Dorset 3 ST60

The Cerne Abbas giant (NT) can be seen from afar, a 180ft-long figure, an unmistakeable symbol of virility, which was carved on the hillside during the Roman occupation, and probably represents Hercules, with elements of a local deity added. At the foot of Giant's Hill, the site of a Benedictine Abbey (987–1539) forms the heart of an unusually beautiful village in which thatched cottages happily co-exist with one or two Tudor buildings. Of the Abbey, only the gatehouse and the church survive. In the grounds of the latter (admirably restored in the 1960s) there is a wishing well named after St Augustine, who is said to have brought Christianity to the Dorset pagans.

CHADDESLEY CORBETT, Hereford & Worcester 9 SO87

A pleasant mixture of Georgian and Tudor architecture, among which the 17th-century Talbot Inn is outstanding. The church is Norman with an 18th-century tower, and is dedicated to St Cassian, an early-Christian school-teacher whose pupils, alas, were still pagans. In an episode that would outdo the worst excesses of present-day school anarchy, they stabbed poor Cassian to death.

CHALFONT ST GILES, Buckinghamshire 5 SU99

An attractive village to which Milton came in the year of the plague, 1665. Old, lonely and blind, he still managed to complete his masterpiece *Paradise Lost* and to write *Paradise Regained*. The former earned him £5. His cottage is now a museum. The Chiltern Open-Air Museum has old buildings and other artefacts relating to life in the Chilterns in days gone by. There is a nature trail in the 25-acre park.

CHARD, Somerset 3 ST30

Chard began its industrial life as a tanning centre in the 13th century. Two hundred years later, its inhabitants took up weaving and lace-making. At 400ft, it is the highest town in the county. The Guildhall, with its stately array of pillars should not be missed; nor should the Elizabethan manor opposite: The courtroom (OACT) on the first floor is well worth seeing. Forde Abbey (OACT) was the home of Cromwell's Attorney General. Its furnishings include a set of Mortlake tapestries.

CHARING, Kent 6 TQ94

If you look carefully, you can discern a few old houses (15th- and 16th-century) among the new. There used to be a palace for the Archbishop of Canterbury, but Henry VIII, having confiscated it, left it to decay: what was left of it was converted into a farmhouse. The Church of Sts Peter and Paul has a rare vamp horn, an instrument formerly played in church orchestras.

CHARLECOTE, Warwickshire 10 SP25

Charlecote Park (NT), four miles from Stratford-upon-Avon, has been the home of the Lucy family since the 13th century. The present Elizabethan house was built in 1558 and enlarged during the 19th century. The octagonal tower gatehouse, however, has remained unaltered, and is now used as a museum. Shakespeare is said to have been brought before Sir Thomas Lucy after he'd been caught poaching in the grounds, and satirised him as Justice Shallow in *Henry IV* (Part 2) and *The Merry Wives of Windsor*. Herds of fallow and red deer still roam the parkland. The house contains family portraits by Gainsborough and Kneller.

CHARMOUTH, Dorset 3 SY39

Jane Austen liked Charmouth for its peaceful atmosphere. The village, which used to be a fashionable stopping place for coaches, has many attractive old houses and enjoys fine views over Lyme Bay. Catherine of Aragon stayed at the Queen's Arms soon after arriving in England and in 1651, Charles II came here in disguise, seeking a boat that would take him to France. Black Ven, not far away, is where Mary Anning made the discovery of the fossilised ichthyosaurus, now in the Natural History Museum. Fossil-hunting is still a popular pastime on the attractive beach just south of the village, and the cliffs around Charmouth offer some excellent walks.

CHATHAM DOCKS *For more than 400 years ships of the British Navy, from the age of sail to the age of the nuclear submarine, have been built or refitted here.*

CHARNWOOD FOREST,
Leicestershire *10 SK41*

Like most of England's ancient woodlands, Charnwood Forest is only a shadow of its former self. Despite the depredations of mining, quarrying and building, about 212 acres of wood and moorland have been preserved. There are nature reserves at Bradgate Park and Swithland Wood (NT), and several pleasant walks.

CHARTWELL, Kent *5 TQ45*

Winston Churchill bought Chartwell (NT) in 1922, and lived here for 40 years. Never short of ideas for improving things, he made a number of alterations and added a new wing. The beauty of the place is that everything has been left just as it was, and every room is filled with family belongings and relics of the great man. Among the many paintings at Chartwell are Monet's famous study of *London Bridge* and works by Lavery, Sargent and William Nicholson. Churchill's own watercolours hang in the house and in his studio, a cottage in the gardens.

To celebrate their Golden Wedding, Sir Winston and Lady Churchill planted 32 species of yellow roses, and their family gave them an album of paintings of the roses, the illustrations by distinguished painters such as Ivon Hitchens and John Nash. The vegetable garden is of particular interest since the wall around it was built by Winston Churchill.

CHASTLETON, Oxfordshire *10 SP22*

Chastleton lies on a wooded ridge in the Cotswolds. Robert Catesby (later to take part in the Gunpowder Plot) lived here for a period but sold his property to an affluent wool merchant named Walter Jones. Mr Jones demolished Catesby's home, and built a Jacobean masterpiece (OACT) in its place, which has scarcely been altered since his day and contains much of its original

furnishings and woodwork. There is a secret room where a supporter of Charles I once hid and an interesting 17th-century topiary garden.

CHATHAM, Kent *6 TQ76*

Until Henry VIII decided to develop it as a naval base, Chatham was a small fishing village. Queen Elizabeth I followed by building a naval dockyard where several of the ships that defeated the Spanish Armada were constructed. The Stuarts quite rightly decided that the defences along the Medway needed to be improved, but by the time the forts were built, the Dutch Admiral de Ruyter had sailed up the river, bombarded the docks, and towed away in triumph the *Royal Charles* – pride of the fleet. Chatham's most famous product is HMS *Victory*. She was still fitting out in December 1771, when Nelson, then a young midshipman joined his first ship, HMS *Raisonnable*, which was moored nearby. Charles Dickens spent some of his boyhood in the town, where his father worked in the Navy Pay Office. In *Pickwick Papers*, he has quite a lot to say about it. Nowadays the future of the docks is uncertain.

CHATSWORTH, Derbyshire *15 SK27*

The principal seat of the Duke and Duchess of Devonshire in the lovely setting of Derbyshire's Peak District, Chatsworth (OACT), is one of the great houses of England, and its aspect is palatial. The estate was originally acquired by Sir William Cavendish, who married that indefatigable builder, Bess of Hardwick who later became Countess of Shrewsbury. Of this particular one of her houses nothing remains. The present Baroque mansion was begun by her great-great-grandson, the 1st Duke of Devonshire, and its construction was not quite completed when the 6th Duke inherited the title. Its stately rooms contain innumerable treasures, but the outstanding works of art are the paintings, which include works by Rembrandt, Frans Hals, Murillo, Veronese, Van Dyck and Lely. In 1760, Capability Brown was bought in to landscape the grounds, to splendid effect. Many of its most triumphant features, however, were wrought by Joseph Paxton – as, for example, the magnificent Emperor Fountain that throws its jets of water 260ft into the air.

CHAWTON, Hampshire *4 SU73*

Anyone passing through Chawton in a hurry might be forgiven if he failed to notice the modest brick house which stands on the village street. But this was Jane Austen's home for the last eight years of her life, and it was here that she wrote or completed her six great novels, working at a small fireside table in the living room. The house is, of course, a museum, but one of those that give the impression, despite the memorabilia, of still being a family home. Chawton House, which her brother inherited, still belongs to descendants of the family; it stands just outside the village, and is not open to the public.

CHEADLE, Staffordshire *9 SK04*

This market town is dominated by its redstone Roman Catholic church, built in 1846 and designed by Augustus Pugin who did much of the decoration of the Houses of

CHATSWORTH *The sea-horse fountain was designed for the 6th Duke by Joseph Paxton.*

Parliament. The 200ft spire is a local landmark. Three miles to the east of the town, the Hawksmoor Nature Reserve (NT) offers interesting possibilities for bird watchers. It was founded by J R B Masefield, a well-known naturalist and cousin of the poet John Masefield.

CHEDDAR, Somerset *3 ST45*

The Cheddar Gorge consists of nearly a mile of dramatic limestone cliffs that rise almost vertically to 450ft. The best view from the top is to be had by climbing 'Jacob's Ladder' at the north end. In the gorge itself, two caves, Cox's and Gough's, are profuse in stalagmites and stalactites. At the southern end, there's a car museum. The heavy hand of commerce has fallen upon an otherwise fascinating natural phenomenon, thereby doing damage to the overall effect. Cheddar chesse, once a local farm product, is these days mostly made on a commerical scale. The village of Cheddar has a fine market cross and an interesting church.

CHEDWORTH, Gloucestershire
10 SP01

Surrounded by superb countryside, Chedworth is a village set in the hills to the west of the Fosse Way. The houses are all built from stone; the church is a handsome mixture of the Norman and the Perpendicular. North of the village, you can find a Roman villa (NT) hiding modestly in 6½ acres of woodland. Discovered in 1864, it probably conveys the best impression, anywhere in Britain, of life as it was lived in Romano-British times. The mosaic pavements and the bathhouse have been excellently preserved.

CHELMSFORD, Essex 6 TL70

Chelmsford is the county town of Essex, and it must be admitted, has few old buildings. It is, however, an important communications link between London and the East coast, as well as being the centre of local government. There has been a livestock market here since about the year 1200. The 15th-century church of Sts Mary, Peter and Cedd was promoted to the status of cathedral in 1914. Its 15th-century tower is crowned by an 18th-century lantern and spire, and the south porch is a fine example of Perpendicular flush-work. Among the oddities is a figure of St Peter in the dress of a modern fisherman, and holding a Yale key in his hand.

In 1899, Guglielmo Marconi set up the world's first radio factory at Chelmsford and in February 1920, the first radio programmes (music, news, talks) were broadcast from the town. This was two years before the British Broadcasting Company (which, in 1927, became the British Broadcasting Corporation) was founded. In Oaklands Park, the Chelmsford and Essex Museum has much of local historical interest.

CHELTENHAM, Gloucestershire 9 SO92

Three hundred years ago, Cheltenham was just an ordinary Cotswold village. In 1715, however, somebody discovered a mineral spring, from having noticed (they say) the drinking habits of an unusually healthy flock of pigeons. The story may be apocryphal: nevertheless, Cheltenham has seen fit to include a pigeon on its crest. By the end of 1783, a retired privateer named Captain Henry Skillicorne had set up the first pump room, and 50 years later the town was established as a fashionable spa. George III, who had a great liking for these watering places, was a frequent visitor. When the Duke of Wellington came here for the cure in 1816, the spa's popularity increased dramatically, and the town was virtually rebuilt in a most pleasing blend of Regency and classical styles.

It soon became clear that the waters of Cheltenham were particularly salubrious for military officers and colonial administrators, whose livers had been ruined by excessively long service in the tropics and thus the town became a byword for its conservative attitudes. Nowadays, you can take the waters at the Town Hall as well as the Pump Room. Their beneficial effects are believed to be due to the presence of magnesium and sodium sulphates and sodium bicarbonate. The Pittville Pump Room (OACT, named after Sir Joseph Pitt, MP) was inspired by the colonnade of a temple in Athens and is a masterpiece of the Greek Revival style. The Promenade, Lansdown Place and Montpellier Parade are among the most impressive Regency achievements, and Montpellier Walk, ornamented with caryatids, is a most elegant shopping precinct. Gustav Holst, the composer, was born here, and the Holst Museum contains memorabilia. The Art Gallery and Museum has collections of ceramics, furniture and paintings.

Cheltenham College for Boys, on the Bath road was built between 1841 and 1843 as a public school for the sons of Indian Army Officers. The even more famous Cheltenham Ladies' College was founded by Miss Beale, a forceful Victorian champion of education for girls. The Festival of Music is held in July and the Festival of Literature in October.

Between the Rivers Wye and Severn
69 miles

On the borders of Wales, the Forest of Dean is a place of beauty and interest at all seasons of the year. Symond's Yat affords spectacular views of the Wye Valley, which is overlooked by three ancient castles: Chepstow, Goodrich and Monmouth, built originally as guardians against the Welsh. Occupying a beautiful site on the banks of the river, stand the ruins of the great Cistercian monastery, Tintern Abbey, the inspiration both of poetry and of painting.

Leave **Chepstow** on A48 (SP Gloucester), cross the River Wye, ascend, turning left on to B4228 (SP Coleford). Go on for 6¾ miles, then turn left, unclassified, to **St Briavels**. At the end of the village turn left to rejoin the Coleford road, B4228. In 2¾ miles turn right (unclassified, SP Parkend) into Sling. After another ¾ mile turn right on B4431 for **Parkend**. Continue on the Blakeney road, B4431, and in 1¼ miles turn left, SP Speech House, and enter the Forest of Dean. By Speech House Hotel turn right on to B4226 towards **Cinderford**. Skirt the town, ascend, then turn right to join A4151 to **Littledean**, where at the T-junction turn right, SP Newnham. Leave **Newnham** on A48 Gloucester road. Pass through Broadoak and turn left (SP Flaxley, Mitcheldean). Go through Flaxley, and in a mile bear right to enter **Mitcheldean**. At the church turn left for Drybrook, cross the crossroads then at the T-junction turn right on to B4277 to **Ruardean**, where follow SP Ross to join B4228, and continue to **Ross-on-Wye**. Follow SP Monmouth through Ross, cross the River Wye and at the next roundabout take 1st exit to Pencraig, then in ½ mile turn left to **Goodrich**. Here branch right, SP Symond's Yat, to join B4229. In ¾ mile turn left SP Symond's Yat East. Cross Huntsham Bridge, then in a mile keep left and ascend steep, narrow road to Yat Rock. Here join B4432 to **Christchurch** where the route turns right on to B4228, SP Coleford. In ¾ mile turn right on to A4136, SP Monmouth. Beyond **Staunton** in 4½ miles turn left on to A466, SP Chepstow (for Monmouth remain on A4136). Pass through Llandogo to **Tintern Abbey**. Continue past Chepstow racecourse and at the roundabout take 1st exit back to Chepstow.

Yat Rock Famous beauty spot overlooking the deep Wye Valley.

Monmouth Ruined castle; ancient bridge, 17th-century Great Castle House (all AM): east of town, fine viewpoint from Kymin Hill (NT).

Offa's Dyke Ancient earthworks, dating from reign of Mercian King Offa, can be seen near A466 between Redbrook and Bigsweir.

Tintern Abbey (AM) Remains of monastic buildings surround the roofless church of this once-great Cistercian Abbey.

PLACES TO SEE

Chepstow Massive castle (AM) guarding banks of River Wye. Quaint old town with many interesting streets.

Dean Forest Railway Collection of locomotives and railway equipment.

Forest of Dean Oldest of England's National Forest Parks.

Ross-on-Wye St Mary's Church, with 208ft spire; Market Hall (AM), dating from 17th century.

Goodrich Castle (AM) dates from the 12th century and occupies a beautiful site.

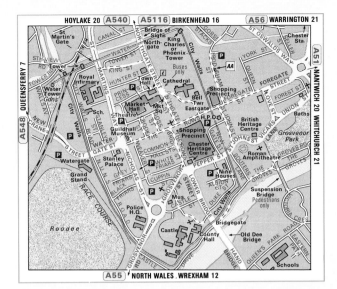

Walled City on the Dee

The tortuous wall . . . wanders in narrow file between parapets smoothed by peaceful generations . . . with rises and drops, steps up and steps down, views of cathedral tower and waterside fields, of huddled English town and ordered English country.

HENRY JAMES, *The Ambassadors*

One of the most important Roman military bases in the country, Chester was the headquarters of the famous 20th Legion, known as *Valeria Victrix.* Its Latin name, Deva, meaning 'holy place', honoured the goddess of the River Dee which, until it gradually silted up, was the source of Chester's wealth and importance throughout the medieval period, when the city conducted a flourishing trade with Ireland, Scotland and parts of Europe.

Architectually, Chester owes much to the Victorians, who greatly admired the black-and-white 'magpie' buildings which make the centre of Chester almost dazzling to look at, and so they built more of them, often in a more elaborate and exuberant style than the originals, and restored others. They also restored the Rows, a unique feature of the city. The Rows are raised, covered galleries, with shops at first-floor level and another tier of shops underneath at street level. They completely line Eastgate Street on both sides, and part of Bridge Street. Their origin is unknown, but the first mention of them is in the 13th-century documents, and they are peculiar to Chester, there being no record of anything similar in any other English town. Among the interesting buildings in the Rows are the 17th-century Bishop Lloyd's House, carved with heraldic beasts and panels depicting Biblical scenes. Also Biblical is the inscription on a neighbouring house, 'God's Providence is Mine Inheritance', which was a thanksgiving from the inhabitants for their escape from plague during a disastrous outbreak of the disease in the Civil War.

Another remarkable feature of Chester are its exceptionally well-preserved city walls, which completely enclose the old centre. A walkway along the top of them allows visitors to make the tour of the whole city. The Eastgate, surmounted by an ornate, gaily painted clock, erected to commemorate Queen Victoria's Jubilee, is still, as it was in medieval times, the main entrance to Chester. Tolls on trade passing through any of the four original gates helped, in the old days, to pay for repairs to the walls.

PLACES TO SEE

Roman Amphitheatre and Garden One of the largest yet excavated in Britain, the amphitheatre could seat 7000 spectators. In the Roman Garden are the remains of a hypocaust.

Grosvenor Museum Models illustrating life in a Roman fort and remains excavated in and around Chester are displayed here.

Chester Heritage Centre This was the first Heritage Centre in the country. A short film shows conservation work in the city.

British Heritage Exhibition Here can be seen a fascinating reconstruction of The Rows as they were in Victorian times.

St Werburgh's Cathedral Heavily restored in the 19th century, the cathedral has its origin in the Anglo-Saxon abbey of St Werburgh. The choir stalls are beautifully and intricately carved.

King Charles Tower From here, King Charles I watched the defeat of his troops at Rowton Moor. A small exhibition on Chester's part in the Civil War is housed here.

Cheshire Military Museum Housed in Chester Castle is the museum of the Cheshire regiments. The castle was entirely rebuilt in the 18th century as a barracks and administrative centre. It is regarded as a masterpiece of the Classical Revival.

Chester Zoo Just outside the city, the zoo has 110 acres of natural enclosures and parts can be toured by waterbus.

THE JUBILEE CLOCK

Edward Evans-Lloyd gave Chester its ornate clock, made by Joyce of Whitchurch to mark Queen Victoria's Jubilee of 1897.

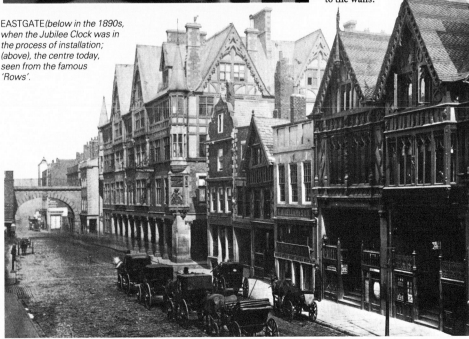

EASTGATE *(below in the 1890s, when the Jubilee Clock was in the process of installation; (above), the centre today, seen from the famous 'Rows'.*

Chichester, W Sussex *4 SU80*

County Capital and Seaside Haven

'From hence to . . . Chichester are 12 miles, and the most pleasant beautiful country in England . . . The cathedral here is not the finest, but is far from being the most ordinary.'
DANIEL DEFOE, *A Tour through the Whole Island of Great Britain.*

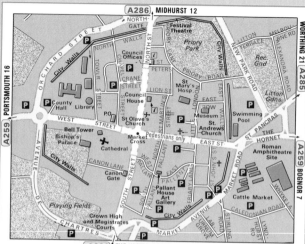

A Roman fort existed here before Chichester became a capital of the South Saxons, given by their King Aella to his son Cissa, whence Cissa's Ceaster, the origin of its name. It has always been a peaceful place, the city centre still more or less confined within the lines of the Roman walls, parts of which have been incorporated into the gardens of the Bishop's Palace.

Four main roads, North, South, East and West Streets divide the centre into tidy quadrants, and meet at the market cross, which is Chichester's most prominent landmark, built by Bishop Story in 1501. It is an octagonal stone structure, its central tower supported on open arcades. The carvings, which have recently been restored, are superb.

The south-east quadrant is also divided into four segments, by charming streets known as the Pallants – again called north, south, east and west – which form a complete Georgian townscape in miniature. Pallant House, at the crossroads, is an elegant Queen Anne Mansion which has now been restored and opened as an art gallery.

Although many of Chichester's finest buildings are 18th-century, the period when the city prospered from shipping and the corn trade, some more ancient houses survive around the cathedral, and near St Martin's Square, a unique almshouse, founded in the 13th century as a hospital. It is England's only example of such a building still in use. Originally, hospital and chapel, divided by a beautiful carved screen, were housed in the same building, so that the sick could benefit from religious services. The infirmary

CHEPSTOW, Gwent *3 ST59*

Although the name Chepstow is derived from the Anglo-Saxon *ceap* (meaning 'market') and *stow* (meaning 'town'), its importance was as a fortress town on the historically unquiet border of Wales and England. The Normans built a great stone castle (AM) in 1067–1071, on a limestone cliff above the River Wye, which was thought to be impregnable until Cromwell's guns breached its walls in the Civil War. Marten's Tower, which was added in the 13th century, is named after its most celebrated resident – Henry Marten, one of those who signed Charles I's death warrant. He was later held captive in it for 12 years until his death in 1680. The castle is still very evidently a castle, although after the 17th century it gradually fell into ruins, and it does not require much imagination to recall its past. The town, which is cradled in an elbow of the River Wye, is all the more picturesque for that.

LYNCHETS IN THE CHEVIOTS *Traces of ridge and furrow ploughing are clearly visible on the high fells even though cultivation has been abandoned for centuries. In the medieval period or even earlier, farmers colonised the uplands, only to retreat when the climate deteriorated or in times of unrest.*

has now been converted to flats for eight old ladies, but the character of the ancient building is still unchanged.

Chichester Cathedral, founded in the 11th century, was largely rebuilt after a fire at the end of the 12th-century, and its spire collapsed in 1861 in a violent storm, but was rebuilt by Sir Gilbert Scott. Inside, treasures range from 12th-century stone carvings to John Piper's vividly coloured altar tapestry and windows by Marc Chagall.

The Festival Theatre, one of the most prestigious provincial theatres in the country, opened in 1962 under the direction of Sir Laurence (now Lord) Olivier.

JOHN PIPER'S *tapestry (right) hangs in Chichester Cathedral.*

PUBLIC PENANCE
Petty criminals could be wheeled all over town on this mobile whipping post cum stocks (District Museum).

PLACES TO SEE

Bishop's Palace Gardens (OACT summer) Delightful enclosed gardens bounded on two sides by the city walls.

District Museum Housed in an 18th-century corn store, the displays are concerned with local history. The Royal Sussex Regimental Museum is also here.

Guildhall Museum The beautiful church of the Greyfriars has been converted to house archaeological finds from the region.

Vicar's Close Four 15th-century cottages, which inspired some of the descriptions in Keats' poem *The Eve of St Agnes*.

ST RICHARD'S WALK *(right) leads from the cathedral cloisters past the gardens of the Bishop's Palace.*

CHEQUERS, Buckinghamshire *4 SP80*
Chequers Court was originally a 13th-century manor house, which was rebuilt in the 15th century. The sister of Lady Jane Grey was put under house arrest here by Elizabeth I, after she had married without obtaining the Queen's consent: her husband died in prison. In 1917, it was presented to the nation by Lord Lee of Fareham – as a country retreat for Prime Ministers. Understandably, it is not open to the public.

CHESIL BANK, Dorset *3 SY58*
This 18-mile natural breakwater, which separates the English Channel from the Fleet (An elongated lake) between Portland and Abbotsbury, is the product of thousands of years of labour by the sea, the tides, and the storms – which threw up masses and masses of pebbles. The process of time has succeeded in grading them: at the Portland end, they average 3½ inches in diameter, declining little by little until, at Abbotsbury, they are just under one inch in diameter. Many and most various things have been washed up on the bank, but the merman, reported in the 18th century, should not be taken too seriously. The 95-

ton sloop, thrown over Chesil Bank by a gale in 1824, and dumped in the Fleet, is a fact.

CHESSINGTON ZOO, Greater London *5 TQ16*
Zoos have to be commercial to survive, but Chessington, which was established in 1931, has the welfare of its animal occupants as its first consideration. Set in spacious surroundings, the enclosures give them as much freedom as is compatible with public safety.

CHESTERFIELD, Derbyshire *15 SK37*
Chesterfield is mostly known for its church of St Mary and All Saints, which has a crooked octagonal spire. The fault is believed to have been caused by changing temperatures distorting the lead that covers its wooden frame. The church was built in the 14th century and is a nice example of ecclesiastical architecture of that period. Among many fine monuments are those of the Foljambe family. Apart from the church, most of Chesterfield's interesting buildings are modern, but a Heritage Centre has been set up in the medieval timber-framed Peacock Inn.

CHEVIOTS, Borders *24 NT71*
The Cheviots, an impressive range of bleak, rounded hills, extend for 35 miles, occupying 200 square miles of Northumberland (including the northern part of the Northumberland National Park) and, in Scotland, 100 square miles of the Borders. The density of population is estimated at one person per 350 acres; there are rather more sheep. The walking is superb – though the country is wild, recalling the centuries of Border raids between Scotland and England, and visitors should take care to be adequately equipped.

CHEW MAGNA, Avon *3 ST56*
In medieval times, this used to be a prosperous centre of the wool industry. The church contains a monument to Sir John Hantville – a man reputed to have been endowed with 'super-human strength'. Just outside the church gates is the 14th-century Church Ale House – so called because beer was brewed there for the benefit of the parish funds. Hidden behind a tall stone wall are the remains of Chew House – or 'The Palace of Chew' as it was called when, in the 14th century, it was owned by the Bishop of Bath and Wells. On Dundry Hill stands a folly, Chew Tower.

CHICHELEY,
Buckinghamshire   *11 SP94*
Chicheley Hall (OACT) was built between
1719 and 1723 for Sir John Chester. With
its fine Georgian craftsmanship exemplified
in the brickwork, the stone and the wood-
carving, it is one of the most perfect and
pristine 18th-century houses in the
country. A naval museum and an
impressive collection of English sea
paintings add to the attractions.

CHICHESTER see pp. 58–9

CHIDDINGSTONE, Kent   *5 TQ54*
Sometimes used for location sequences in
films set in Tudor times, the whole village
is administered by the National Trust. A
row of 16th- and 17th-century houses
occupies one side of the street, facing the
church, rebuilt in the 17th century after a
fire. The name may, just possibly, come
from a large rock behind the school –
known as 'the Chiding Stone'. Scolding
wives were brought here to be nagged in
retribution. The so-called 'Castle' (OACT)
is a manor house re-built in mock-Gothic
style and contains oriental art treasures.

CHILHAM, Kent   *6 TR05*
When you can see Chilham through the
crowds of people that go there, you can
only stand and marvel; so much beauty,
and so unspoiled. The village is built
around a square, with the church at one
end. Behind it, the Queen-Anne rectory
makes a nice contrast with the half-
timbered Tudor and Jacobean houses
nearby. Chilham Castle grounds (OACT)
contain a Battle of Britain Museum, and a
falconer gives demonstrations at certain
times in summer.

OAST HOUSES

Characteristic of the Kentish landscape, oast houses like these near
Chiddingstone, are used for drying
hops, which were introduced from
Europe in the 15th century to improve the flavour of the beer.

CHILLINGHAM,
Northumberland   *24 NU02*
Chillingham Castle, which was fortified in
1344, is the home of the Earl of
Tankerville. The grounds only are open to
the public. Chillingham is famous for its
herd of white cattle, the last remaining
descendants of the prehistoric wild oxen
which once roamed freely in Britain. This
herd is believed to have survived extinction
by being trapped in 1220 when the park
was walled in.

Cotswold Towns and Villages
71 miles

*Honey-coloured buildings of local stone cluster together in picturesque villages and
bustling market towns such as Chipping Norton, Stow-on-the-Wold, Bourton-on-the-
Water and Burford; little streams, old stone bridges and tree-clad hills typify the
attraction of the Cotswolds, once one of the greatest wool-producing regions in all
England, for today's tourist.*

From **Chipping Norton** take B4450 Stow
road to **Churchill** and continue to
Bledington. Leave Bledington on A436 to
Stow-on-the-Wold. From Stow-on-the-
Wold follow (SP Tewkesbury) to join
B4077 for **Upper Swell**. Remain on B4077
to Stanway. At the crossroads turn right on
to unclassified road to Stanton. In 1¼
miles turn right to reach **Stanton**. Bear
left, SP Broadway, then in ¾ mile turn left
on to the Cheltenham road, A46, and
continue to Toddington roundabout. At
the roundabout keep forward and in 1 mile
turn left up a narrow by-road to Hailes
Abbey. Return for 200 yards and turn left.
At the T-junction turn left then right to
Guiting Power. In ½ mile at the T-
junction turn right (SP Andoversford),
then turn left (SP Stow), pass a left turn to
Cotswold Farm Park and continue to
Lower Swell. Turn right on to B4068,
then left (SP The Slaughters) on to an
unclassified road to **Upper Slaughter**. At
the end of the village turn left to **Lower
Slaughter**. Cross a bridge and turn right.
Later turn right on to A429. In ½ mile
turn left on to B4068 to **Bourton-on-the-
Water**. In Bourton-on-the-Water turn
right at the Post Office and at the
crossroads take the unclassified Sherborne
road. In 4 miles turn left for **Sherborne**.
Continue to **Windrush**, bear left and in ¾
mile at the T-junction turn left to **Great
Barrington**. At the war memorial bear
right for Taynton. Follow Burford signs
and later join A424, then turn right on to
A361 for **Burford**. Leave on the
unclassified Swinbrook road. In 1 mile
turn left and continue to the edge of
Asthall. At the T-junction turn right (SP
Witney). Later turn left on to B4047. In
1¾ miles turn left by the White Hart PH
on to the unclassified Leafield road. Cross
the River Windrush and pass Minster
Lovell village, then continue to Leafield.
At the war memorial turn left (SP Shipton)
then at the Fox Inn bear right. Continue to
Shipton-under-Wychwood and here turn
right on to A361 for the return journey to
Chipping Norton.

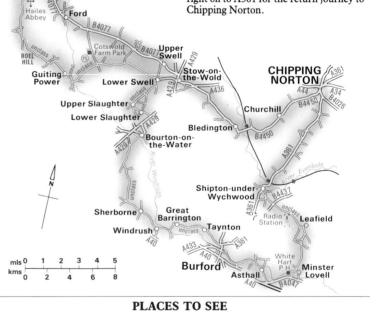

PLACES TO SEE

Cotswold Farm Park Rare breeds of farm
animals in a farm setting. Young animals,
pets' corner and rides on pony-drawn trap.

Tithe Barn Situated in the village of
Stanway, part of Stanway House, and
mentioned in the *Domesday Book*.

Hailes Abbey Interesting 13th-century
ruins and small museum of relics.

Upper Slaughter A beautiful village, with
a fine Elizabethan mansion. Neighbouring
Lower Slaughter is also charming.

Bourton-on-the-Water One of the most
picturesque of the Cotswold villages,
Bourton is reproduced at one-ninth its real
size in the garden of the Old New Inn.

Birdland Zoo Gardens Over 600 exotic
species in 3½ acres of grounds.

Sherborne A cottage on the Windrush
road, once an old chapel and still retains a
Norman doorway.

Burford The main street of this old wool
town is lined with fine buildings.

CHILTERNS, THE,
Buckinghamshire 4
Rightly described as an Area of
Outstanding Natural Beauty, the Chilterns
run in an arc from **Goring** in the Thames
Valley to a point near **Hitchin** in
Hertfordshire. Although the woodlands are
not as extensive as they once were, the hills
are noted for their beech trees. The name of
the county may well be derived from the
old word for beech tree, *buccan*. One of the
highest points is Coombe Hill (853ft). The
North Bucks Way, a stretch of 30 miles
from Wolverton to **Chequers**, provides
admirable walks. Around the **High
Wycombe** area, the old rural craft of chair-
making once flourished. Traditional
Windsor chairs are made of beechwood,
with ash and elm used for the bow and seat.

CHIPPENHAM, Wiltshire 3 ST97
King Alfred used to hunt in the forests not
far away from Chippenham, but industry
has recently intruded – mostly food
processing and the manufacture of railway
signals – on this historic market town. A
few old houses remain, including the Town
Hall and Hungerford Chapel. Sheldon
Manor (OACT) has lovely terraced
gardens.

CHIPPING CAMDEN,
Gloucestershire 10 SP13
The word 'chipping' keeps on recurring in
the Cotswolds. It is Old English for
'market' or 'trading centre'. Chipping
Campden's speciality in the 15th and 16th
centuries was wool. The fleece was brought
to the 14th-century Woolstapler's Hall,
which is now a museum. Many prosperous-
looking stone houses have survived to lend
character to this attractive old market town,
and the Market Hall (NT) is a fine Jacobean
building. Old sports cars can be seen in the
Campden Car Collection Museum.

CHIPPING NORTON,
Oxfordshire 10 SP32
Another former Cotswold wool-trading
town, where, indeed, tweed was
manufactured as recently as 1980; the
Victorian mill is Chipping Norton's largest
building. The ample market place remains
the centre of community life. The White
Hotel in the High Street was an 18th-
century staging post – and has relics of the
period.

CHIRK, Clwyd 14 SJ23
Chirk is mainly notable for its castle (NT)
and its aqueduct. The latter, built by
Thomas Telford, carries the Shropshire
Union Canal high above the Ceiriog Valley
supported by a ten-arch span. The castle
was built in the reign of Edward I on land
given to a local baron for his part in
overthrowing Llywelyn the Last (the last
Welsh Prince of Wales). It is a fine example
of a border stronghold, with four massive
drum towers at the corners of the
courtyard, but it is also the family home of
the Myddletons, who since 1595 have made
many alterations and improvements. There
is a notable collection of Restoration
furniture and portraits. The intricate
tracery of the elegant wrought-iron
entrance gate was the work of Robert and
John Davies of Wrexham in the 18th
century.

CHOLMONDELEY CASTLE,
Cheshire 14 SJ55
The Castle (pronounced Chumley) is early
19th-century, and is the home of the
marquess of Cholmondeley. The grounds
(OACT) feature ornamental gardens and
rare breeds of animals.

CHORLEY, Lancashire 14 SD51
At first glance, Chorley seems to have little
to commend it to the historian. If its mills

CHILTERN CRAFTS

In the Chilterns are to be found the
most extensive beechwoods in Britain
and it was here that chair-making
developed in the 18th century. Several craftsmen worked on different
parts of a Windsor chair: bottomers
made the seat of elm; benders shaped
the back bow of ash; bodgers made
the legs of beech. This workshop
is in High Wycombe Museum.

are no longer dark and satanic, it is,
nevertheless, an industrial town. However,
among its most illustrious sons was Henry
Tate, who was born there in 1819. Having
made his fortune from sugar, he used some
of his wealth to endow the Tate Gallery in
London. Ten minutes' walk from the town
centre Astley Hall (OACT) an exquisite
Renaissance structure stands beside a lake
and has collections of furniture, pottery and
paintings.

CHIRK CASTLE *The red hand of the Myddleton family crest surmounts the elegant wrought iron gates which mark the entrance to the castle.*

CIRENCESTER *The tower of the parish church affords an excellent view over the rooftops of the town to Cirencester House and its noble park with the five-mile long avenue of chestnut trees.*

CHRISTCHURCH, Dorset *3 SZ19*

The River Stour which forms a boundary between the two, has, perhaps, saved Christchurch from being engulfed by its neighbour, **Bournemouth**. Both the Avon and Stour meet here – hence the town's original name of Twynham. The name Christchurch emanates from the building of the church. The townspeople had decided on St Catherine's Hill for the site, but every night their building materials were removed and when a beam that had been cut too short was mysteriously lengthened, they decided that Christ himself had intervened, built their church on the new site and renamed their town. The priory church has a magnificent Norman turret on the north transept. The Red House Museum contains interesting exhibits from the excavations at Hengistbury Head. Between Christchurch and Bournemouth is Tucktonia (OACT), which has scale models of famous buildings.

CHYSAUSTER, Cornwall *1 SW43*

Chysauster (AM) is one of the few Iron-Age settlements where not only the outlines of the houses but also a clearly identifiable village street can be seen. The village, set high on a hillside, seems to have been inhabited between 100 BC and AD 300. The village was not fortified, but the house walls were massive, probably as a defence against the weather. Each of the houses opened on to a central courtyard, and each had its own terraced garden. A short distance away were tin-mines, suggesting that the inhabitants were miners.

CILGERRAN, Dyfed *7 SN14*

This small hamlet is set in beautiful surroundings beside the River Teifi. The romantic site of the castle (AM), perched high on a crag, has inspired paintings by Turner and de Wint. Cilgerran Wildlife Park specialises in European animals.

CILYCWM, Dyfed *8 SN74*

North of Cilycwm, there is great natural beauty – thankfully not spoiled too much by the recent building of a reservoir. This region is one of the last strongholds in Britain of the Red Kite. The village, encircled by hills, was an early stronghold of Methodism and its chapel is said to be the first Methodist meeting place in Wales.

ROMAN MOSAICS

Many fascinating relics of the Roman way of life have been discovered in Cirencester, which was one of the most important of the south-western regional capitals. The Hare Mosaic was excavated in Beeches Road in 1971 and is currently the symbol of the re-developed Corinium Museum. It probably came from one of the villas built by well-to-do Roman settlers whose large agricultural estates flourished in the 3rd and 4th centuries AD. These were the forerunners of the medieval manors, and it is likely that when the Romans left, the Saxon invaders took them over, but may not have lived in the houses.

CIRENCESTER, Gloucestershire *3 SP00*

In Roman times Cirencester was the second most important city in Britain, after London, and the many relics of its Romano-British heritage are displayed in the Corinium Museum – Corinium Dobunnorum was the town's Roman name. There is also an amphitheatre just outside the town. Cirencester's fortunes declined in the Anglo-Saxon period, but in the Middle Ages it became wealthy again when the wool trade came to the Cotswolds, and as one of England's largest wool markets, justified its claim to be the 'Capital of the Cotswolds'. Its magnificent parish church, much enlarged in the 15th and 16th centuries, is nearly as big as a cathedral. From the market place, the three-storey porch, with its superb fan-vaulting, and the soaring tower, are an uplifting spectacle. Inside, as is fitting, are many monuments and brasses to the wool merchants. The peal of 12 bells is the oldest in the country, and there is a valuable collection of silver, and beautiful stained glass in the east and west windows. Cirencester House is not open, but the park, with its great avenue of chestnut trees, is.

CISSBURY, W Sussex *5 TQ10*

An Iron-Age fort, on the downs just to the north of Worthing, Cissbury (AM) was occupied from the 5th century BC until the middle of the 1st century AD. It is an enormous fortress, and it has been estimated that 60,000 tons of chalk were needed to construct the ramparts.

CLACTON-ON-SEA, Essex *6 TM11*

In the 1870s, with the spread of the railways, and the fashion for such things, Clacton was suddenly transformed from a quiet little village into 'the seaside', from which period the building of such hotels as the Royal (1872) and the Grand (1897) dates. The pier, which has been rebuilt several times, was erected in 1873; seven years later, the Pavilion was added.

CLAYDON HOUSE, Buckinghamshire *10 SP72*

All the four Claydons: Botoph Claydon, East Claydon, Middle Claydon and Steeple Claydon are attractive, but at Middle Claydon is one of the great houses of Buckinghamshire, Claydon House (NT), the home of the earls of Verney. It was the 2nd earl who transformed this house in the mid 1700s into a classical mansion, decorated inside with superb rococo carvings – at their most imaginative in the fantastic Chinese Room. One suite of rooms is devoted to relics of Florence Nightingale whose sister, Parthenope, married Sir Harry Verney in 1858.

CLEOBURY MORTIMER, Shropshire *9 SO67*

Locals claim this attractive old place to be the birthplace of William Langland, one of the great English medieval poets, who wrote his masterpiece, *Vision of William concerning Piers the Ploughman* in the 14th century. No evidence has been found, but one of the east windows in the church is dedicated to the poet. Appropriately it shows Piers dreaming his dreams. The wooden church spire has an interesting twist to it, and has defied all efforts to straighten it.

CLEVEDON, Avon *3 ST47*
A delightful little resort that provides Bristol residents with an opportunity to get away from it all, the atmosphere still reflects the town's Victorian origins: though the pier – built in 1869 and once said to be the finest in Britain – has collapsed. Clevedon Court (NT) formerly the home of a wealthy Bristol merchant named Sir Arthur Elton, dates back to the 12th century, with later additions. St Andrew's Church, on the headland to the south-west of the town is where Arthur Hallam, whose death inspired Tennyson's *In Memoriam*, lies buried.

CLITHEROE, Lancashire *14 SD74*
The second oldest borough in Lancashire, Clitheroe retains much of its charm, despite industrialisation, and there are some delightful walks in the vicinity. The Norman castle is interesting as it has one of the the smallest keeps in England, all that remains since the Civil War. The adjoining museum contains fossils and many items of interest. Tudor Browsholme Hall (OACT), north-west of the town, belongs to the Parker family, hereditary Bowbearers of the Forest of Bowland.

CLIVEDEN, Buckinghamshire *5 SU98*
Cliveden House (NT) is flanked on one side by the Thames, on the other three by woodland. Built in 1851, it is the third house of its name to be erected on the site. Home of the Astor family, it was famous (or infamous, depending on your point of view) for 'the Cliveden Set', which – aided by Dawson of *The Times* – thought it knew what was best for Britain in the 1930s. Nancy, Lady Astor, was a political hostess of great influence, and Britain's first woman MP, representing Plymouth from 1919 until after World War II. The house is now let to an American University and only two rooms are open, but the grounds can be visited.

CLOUDS HILL, Dorset *3 SY89*
This cottage (NT) a mile north of Bovington Camp in Dorset, was rebuilt by T E Lawrence (of Arabia) in 1923, who lived in it when he was serving with the Royal Tank Corps. In a letter, he described it as 'very quiet, very lonely, very bare' and listed the contents as 'a bed, a bicycle, three chairs, 100 books'. He seldom slept here, but used it as a retreat. It was from Clouds Hill that, at 11.30am on 13 May 1935, he set off on his motorbike for the village of Moreton, swerved to avoid two errand boys, was thrown off, and died at eight o'clock on the following Sunday.

CLOVELLY, Devon *1 SS32*
Possibly the prettiest coastal village in Britain, it occupies one cobbled street that runs down a steep, wooded slope to the shore. Sleds towed by donkeys were used for carrying loads, as the motor car has not been allowed to intrude. Clovelly was restored by Christine Hamlyn (the Hamlyns were lords of the manor) in the early 1920s.

CLUMBER PARK, Nottinghamshire *15 SK67*
Clumber Park (NT) covers 3800 acres of Sherwood Forest. The house, which was built in 1770, was considerably improved in Victorian times by the Duke of Newcastle,

CLIVEDEN *The cockleshell fountain, sculpted in Sienna marble and ornamented with classical statues, overlooks the lake at one end of the Long Avenue in the magnificent park.*

who then owned it and employed Sir Charles Barry, designer of the House of Commons, as his architect. It was demolished in the 1930s, but the park, with its many beautiful trees, is open. This estate, together with those of three other dukes: Norfolk, Kingston and Portland, jointly made up an area of the county, for obvious reasons nicknamed '*The Dukeries*'.

CLUN, Shropshire *8 SO38*
Despite its peaceful air, Clun has had a tempestuous history: Caractacus, one of the Romano-British chiefs, made a determined stand against the Romans here. Edric the Wild, an English earl, harried the Norman invaders, despite the castle they built overlooking the River Clun. On at least four occasions between 1195 and 1400, the Welsh stormed the castle and burned the town (making light of Offa's Dyke, which is not far away). An excellent museum displays relics of this eventful past.

CLYDEBANK, Strathclyde *22 NS56*
In 1871, Clydebank amounted to no more than a farm. Late that year, James and George Thomas moved in and began to establish a shipyard. In 1882, the American firm of Singers built a sewing-machine factory and the last traces of rural life were swept away. In 1899, John Brown and Co. from Sheffield acquired the shipyard. Among the famous vessels built there were the *Lusitania*, *Queen Mary*, *Queen Elizabeth*, and the *QE2*.

CLYRO, Powys *8 SO24*
Clyro was once the site of a Roman camp large enough to provide quarters for a legion. Like the Norman castle that came later, its purpose was to guard the main route into south-west Wales. Clyro's curate from 1865 until 1872 was the Reverend Francis Kilvert, the well-known diarist.

COALBROOKDALE, Shropshire *9 SJ60*
The Industrial Revolution owes much to the Ironmasters of Coalbrookdale, Abraham Darby and his successors. It was here that they discovered how to smelt iron with coke instead of charcoal. The first steam-engine cylinder was cast here in 1761, the first iron bridge built (1779), and the first cast-iron aqueduct (1791). The blast furnace where Abraham Darby perfected his technique for smelting is part of a fascinating Museum of Iron. See also under **Ironbridge**.

COBHAM, Kent *6 TQ66*
Cobham Hall, (OACT holidays), now a girls' school, is one of the largest historic houses in Kent. The village is chiefly famous for its church, which contains an unrivalled collection of memorial brasses to members of the Cobham family. Owletts (NT), is a charming Jacobean house nearby, and the Leather Bottle, an interesting old public house, was featured by Dickens in his comic masterpiece, *The Pickwick Papers*.

COCKERMOUTH, Cumbria *18 NY13*
A fine 18th-century house on Main Street was the birthplace (NT) of the poet William Wordsworth in 1770, and is now a museum devoted to his life and works. The town is a very old one, and an excellent centre for touring the Lake District.

COCKLEY CLEY, Norfolk *12 TF70*
Here can be seen a full-scale reconstruction (OACT) of an Iceni encampment – showing how the tribe of that vengeful and bloodthirsty queen, Boudicca, lived 2000-odd years ago. A museum set up in one of the old cottages fills in some of the details.

COGGESHALL, Essex *12 TL82*
The interesting thing about Coggeshall is Paycocke's House (NT). Built in the 15th century, it has been lovingly preserved and gives us an admirable insight into the residence of a prosperous Tudor merchant. The secluded garden is most attractive.

COITY, Mid Glamorgan *8 SS98*
The 12th-century castle (AM, now in ruins) was, if the story is true, the scene of an interesting transaction. After the Norman Conquest, Morgan, the last Welsh ruler of Coity, was besieged by Norman soldiers led by one Payn de Turberville, who was seeking to conquer his lands. The Welsh prince came before them – holding his daughter by one hand and carrying a sword in the other. Payn could choose, he said, either to marry the girl – or else he, Morgan, would fight to the last drop of his and his warriors' blood. Wisely, perhaps, de Turberville chose marriage.

COLONSAY, Isle of;
  Strathclyde *21 NR39*
Colonsay, eight miles long and two and a half miles wide, is linked to **Oban** by a car ferry. Colonsay House has a subtropical garden, which may seem remarkable until one remembers that the Gulf Stream makes possible so many improbabilities. At low tide, you can walk across to the neighbouring island of Oronsay, but be careful not to be cut off from Colonsay by the incoming tide.

COLWYN BAY, Clwyd *13 SH87*
As with many seaside resorts, Colwyn Bay owes its existence to the railway line, built in the 1840s. It is a most attractive resort with parks, substantial houses, and fine shopping arcades. It has sandy beaches, three miles of promenades, and, on a nearby hillside, the Welsh Mountain Zoo.

COMPTON, Surrey *5 SU94*
The Pilgrims' Way crosses the high ground to the north of the village. In the centre of the houses that straggle along Compton's main street stands the church of St Nicholas, perhaps one of the most impressive in Surrey. The Norman pillars and arches, carved from the chalk of the Hog's Back, make the interior a study in white. The Watts Gallery was endowed by the widow of the Victorian painter and sculptor George Frederick Watts, and contains about 200 of his works.

COMPTON ACRES, see Canford Cliffs

COMPTON BEAUCHAMP, Oxfordshire *4 SU28*
A mile or two to the south of the village lies a megalithic long barrow named Wayland's Smithy (AM). In Norse legend, Wayland was the blacksmith of the gods, and manufactured swords and armour that rendered their users invincible. Using coins left for the purpose he also, according to local legend, shod horses that were left there overnight.

CONGLETON, Cheshire *14 SJ86*
Signs suggest that there were Stone- and Bronze-Age settlements in the Congleton neighbourhood, though it became a town only with the arrival of the Normans. The parish church of St Peter has a splendid Georgian interior. Students of canals will find the bridge, of the type known as a 'snake', interesting: it enabled the horse to cross over to the towpath on the far side without having to be unhitched from the barge. Four miles south-west of the town is Little Moreton Hall (NT), much photographed as one of the finest examples of a black and white half-timbered house in the country.

CONISBROUGH, S Yorkshire *15 SK59*
The Norman castle's huge circular keep (AM), 90ft high and 52ft in diameter, lords it over the village which nestles beneath it. It is one of the finest examples in Britain, dating from the late 12th century and founded by the powerful de Warenne family. In Sir Walter Scott's novel, *Ivanhoe*, Conisbrough was the home of the Saxon prince, Athelstane. St Peter's Church contains a rare Norman tomb-chest, decorated with scenes of chivalry.

CONISTON, Cumbria *18 SD39*
The village, which lies beside Coniston Water, is dominated by the summit of the Old Man of Coniston, 2627ft above sea level. John Ruskin, that eloquent 19th-century scholar, lived on the east side of the lake in a house called Brantwood (OACT) which contains many relics and pictures. Coniston Water has been used for attempts to break the World Water Speed Record – sometimes with tragic results. Donald Campbell was killed here in 1967, when his jet-powered boat *Bluebird* went out of control at over 300mph.

CONISTON WATER *This view from Brantwood, the house on the east side of the lake, that Ruskin bought in 1871, must have inspired him in his later years.*

Capital of South-east England

'Colchester is . . . large, very populous; the streets fair and beautiful; there are abundance of very good and well-built homes.'
DANIEL DEFOE, *A Tour through the Whole Island*

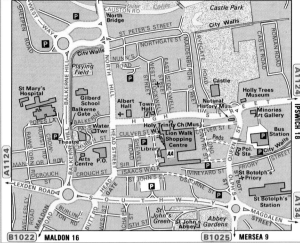

and many Flemish refugees settled here in the 17th and 18th centuries, in the area around West Stockwell Street known as the Dutch Quarter. This has been restored, but much of the town centre is now a modern shopping precinct. After the decline of the wool trade, Colchester developed an engineering industry. In the 1960s the University of Essex was established in Wivenhoe Park, its four stark concrete towers already a local landmark. As a fishing and trading port, Colchester is no longer significant, but its oysters were famous even in the Roman period.

OYSTERS *(left) are as much a part of Colchester's heritage as Roman remains. St Botolph's Priory (below) was built with Roman bricks.*

When the emperor Claudius received the surrender of the British kings here in AD 43, Colchester had been an inhabited site for something like 1000 years. It was at that period named Camulodunum, and was the capital of Cunobelin (Shakespeare's Cymbeline), ruler of south-east England.

The Roman city, the first they founded in Britain, was sacked by Boudicca and the Iceni, but after her defeat, it was eventually rebuilt as a walled city and became one of the most important centres of Roman administration. Parts of the walls may still be seen, and the arch of the Balkerne gate remains, which marked the entrance of the Roman road from London. The many Roman remains are the nucleus of the museum contained in the massive keep of the Norman castle, built in about 1085 on the vaults of the Roman Temple of Claudius. In the medieval period, Colchester was a centre of the cloth industry

PLACES TO SEE

The Castle Now a museum of Roman life, the castle keep is the largest in Britain, measuring 151 by 110ft. Some of the stone used to build it was imported from Normandy, but part of it was built on Roman foundations.

Hollytrees is a museum in a fine Georgian house containing exhibitions of costume, old doll's houses and other bygones.

All Saints Church has been converted into a natural history museum with dioramas depicting the flora and fauna of Essex.

Holy Trinity Church The only Saxon building in Colchester, the church now houses a museum of social history.

St Botolph's Priory More than 900 years old, the priory is built of Roman bricks.

The Minories This attractive house was rebuilt in 1776 from original Tudor buildings. It is an art gallery and centre for the visual arts, with a changing programme of exhibitions.

Bourne Mill (NT), a mile south of the city, dates from 1591.

Colchester Zoo Three miles west of the city, housed in the 40-acre park of Stanway Hall.

Beth Chatto Gardens, White Barn House Plants for many different types of conditions are displayed here. Particularly interesting are the Dry and Shade Gardens, and the exotic marsh plants around the five fishpools.

Perspective View of Colchester, in the County of Essex

Conwy Bay and Snowdon's Foothills
52 miles

Green valleys, wild passes, and coastal areas are the elements that make up this attractive North Wales countryside. Small, mountain-girt villages, a cathedral city and ancient castles are the landmarks on a route that travels through the Vale of Conwy, Nant Ffrancon Valley and finishes on the coast at Conwy Bay.

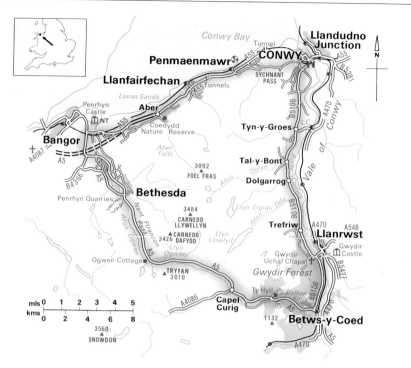

Leave **Conwy** by the Castle, on B5106 (SP Betws-y-Coed). Continue along the west side of the Conwy Valley and go through Tyn-y-Groes, Tal-y-Bont and Dolgarrog to **Trefriw**. In 1¾ miles turn right, still with B5106, SP Betws-y-Coed). Leave on the Bangor road, A5. After 2 miles, pass on the right Swallow Falls, and in ¼ mile pass on the left a picnic site and arboretum. After another ½ mile pass Ty Hyll. Continue to **Capel Gurig** and stay on A5 to **Bethesda**. From Bethesda, continue on A5 towards Bangor. At the roundabout keep forward and in ¾ mile turn right and pass the entrance to Penrhyn Castle. Continue and join the Conwy road, A55 to **Llanfairfechan**. From Llanfairfechan the tour follows the coast road alongside Conwy Bay to **Penmaenmawr**. At the traffic signals in the town keep forward then bear right (SP Sychnant). Cross Sychnant Pass to return to Conwy.

PLACES TO SEE

Conwy Castle: Between Telford's Bridge and Stephenson's Bridge. With medieval walls 30ft high and 21 towers.

Gwydyr Uchaf Chapel: Dates from 1673 with rare, painted roof. Former private chapel of Gwydyr Castle.

Gwydyr Castle: Magnificently furnished Tudor residence. Contains an unusual carved bed, illustrating scenes from the Bible. Beautiful grounds with peacocks.

Swallow Falls: Famous waterfalls in deep, wooded valley. Ty Hyll 'The Ugly House', constructed of huge rocks of different sizes is ½ mile away.

Penrhyn Castle: A striking building with crenellated towers and great walls. A fascinating doll collection and a curious 4-poster bed made entirely out of slate are among the many exhibits.

Penrhyn Quarries: Gouged out of the slopes of Brion Llywyd, a total area of 560 acres, the biggest open-cast slate quarry in the world.

Coedydd Nature Reserve: A conservation area in a beautiful setting.

CONWY, Gwynedd *13 SH77*
This was the third of Edward I's great castles (AM), built on a rocky site defended by both river and sea. With its massive battlemented walls and eight commanding drum towers, it is one of the best-preserved of all the medieval castles. The old town, situated at the mouth of the Afon, is still surrounded by medieval walls. Among the few ancient houses that survive are Aberconwy (NT) a 14th-century house used for exhibitions of the life of the town, and Plas Mawr, one of the finest extant examples of an Elizabethan town house. The Afon estuary is spanned by three bridges, the most impressive being Telford's great suspension bridge, built in 1826. On the picturesque quayside is Britain's 'smallest house' (OACT), a Victorian fisherman's cottage.

COOKHAM, Berkshire *4 SU88*
This very pretty Thames-side village has been immortalised in the works of Stanley Spencer, one of the greatest modern British painters. Some of the best of his works can be seen in the small art gallery. The old ceremony of swan-upping takes place near Cookham and swan-upping on the Thames is the theme of one of the best-known of Spencer's paintings.

CORBRIDGE, Northumberland *19 NY96*
Half a mile away lies the Roman camp at Corstopitum, the ancestor, perhaps, of this very pleasant, stone-built market town, where the road still crosses the Tyne on a bridge built in 1674 (the only bridge to survive the great Tyne flood of 1771). The Roman camp (AM) was initially a cavalry depot, then in AD140 it was modified to serve as a base for operations against Scotland; there is an excellent museum on the site. Of the old buildings in the town, the pele tower of Low House and the fortified vicarage, reminders of fierce border raids, are particularly interesting. At nearby Newton, the Hunday National Tractor and Farm Museum has, among other items, more than 250 tractors and engines.

CORBY, Northamptonshire *10 SP88*
Until 1932, Corby was just a village. Then the steel industry arrived, and if its fortunes pick up, then so may Corby's. If not, the extraordinary, almost surrealist monstrosity of a steel works should be classified as an historic monument.

CORFE CASTLE, Dorset *3 SY98*
One of the most impressive ruins in southern England, Corfe Castle (NT) was the work of William I. Earlier, at a hunting lodge on the site, the Saxon King Edward ('The Martyr') was murdered in 978. His step-mother wished to seize the throne for her 11-year-old son Ethelred (the Unready). King John added to the saga of villainy when he used the Norman castle as his treasure-house and prison. The final infamy came in the Civil War – when, after the Roundhead forces had failed to reduce the castle, a member of the garrison turned traitor and let them in. Corfe Castle Museum contains many items of local interest.

CORRIS, Gwynedd *13 SH70*
In fact, there are two Corrises: Upper Corris and Corris – which is the older. When one realizes that the name is simply 'quarries' given a Welsh pronunciation, much becomes clear. As one might expect, both villages are constructed almost entirely from slate – even to fences and a bridge. Now they have a rather sad look, and the rusting railway lines, the spoil-stacks, and the decaying work shacks do little to remove the impression. The Railway Museum, housed in a Victorian building, is devoted to the narrow-gauge Corris Railway.

CORSHAM, Wiltshire *3 ST86*
Corsham has grown in recent years, but fortunately, the mellow, stone buildings in the centre have escaped the claws of progress. Corsham Court (OACT) was an estate that belonged to the Royal Family until it was sold in 1582 – to a Customs official. The handsome Cotswold-stone house was subsequently sold to Paul Methuen in 1777, and the alterations he made include a picture gallery, destined to house the collection of Old Masters he inherited from his cousin.

CORSTORPHINE, Lothian *23 NT17*
Now part of western Edinburgh,
Corstorphine still manages to be a village.
On top of Corstorphine Hill stands the
Clermiston Tower, erected to celebrate the
centenary of Sir Walter Scott. The Scottish
National Zoological Park has been built
beneath it. The church is 15th-century.

CORWEN, Clwyd *13 SJ04*
The wooded scenery of the beautiful Dee
valley surrounds this small town
overlooked by the Berwyn Mountains. It
was here that the foundations of the first
Welsh National Eisteddfod were cemented,
in 1789, when the first public event was
held at the Owain Glyndwr Hotel. This is
the heart of Glyndwr country. His estates
were nearby, and a groove in the lintel of
the church door was supposedly made by a
dagger flung by him in a fit of rage.

COSFORD, Shropshire *9 SJ70*
Cosford Airfield has a fascinating
Aerospace Museum. The array of aircraft
includes nearly all the stars of World War II
– Spitfire, Mosquito, Messerschmitt, etc. –
plus those two sinister agents of mass
death, the VI and V2 rockets. The British
Airways collection and a Moon Buggy
reflect the less bloodthirsty achievements.

COTSWOLDS, Gloucestershire *3, 10*
The Cotswold hills extend from near Bath
in Avon across to north Oxfordshire and
part of Northamptonshire. At first, their
wooded slopes descend steeply to the
Severn Vale. Later, however, they seem to
shake off the trees as they roll towards the
Midland plain. Near Cheltenham Spa, and,
again, on the high ground above Broadway,
they reach heights of nearly 1000ft.

COTSWOLD SHEEP

Ever since the Middle Ages the
Cotswolds have been noted for
their sheep. The export of wool
to Europe and the manufacture
of woollen cloth formed the
basis of England's economy
from the days of the monasteries to the start of the Industrial Revolution in the 18th century. Sheep from Britain made
the fortunes of Australia, and in
the 19th century several flocks
of English sheep were shipped
to America, including this
famous one from Northleach
painted by Richard Whitford.

Drystone walls, towns and villages built
exclusively either from silver-grey or
yellowish limestone (all of it quarried
locally), characterise the Cotswolds.
Although the wool industry has gone into a
decline – largely due to the introduction of
machinery – sheep continue to roam the
hills, and the manufacture of cloth has
survived in the area around Stroud.

COTTESMORE, Leicestershire
10 SK91
Deep in the heart of huntin' country,
Cottesmore, stone-built and surrounded by
trees (were it not for an airfield and
quarries) is all that one expects of a village
in the Shires. The Cottesmore hounds
were, in fact, established at Exton in 1732,
and moved here in 1788, since when this
has been one of the most famous hunts.

COUGHTON COURT, Warwickshire
10 SP06
Built in the 16th century and approached
by way of a majestic stone gatehouse,
Coughton Court (NT) was, for many years,
the home of the Throckmorton family. One
of the most anxious moments in the history
of this formidable house occurred on 5
November 1605, when the wives of several
gunpowder-plot conspirators awaited
anxiously for news of their husbands.
Before the year was over, most of them had
become widows. But the dramas, so far as
Coughton Court was concerned, were not
yet ended. During the Civil War, it was
occupied by Roundhead forces, bombarded
by the Royalists, and finally abandoned in
flames. When James II left the country, the
poor old house was pillaged. In the 18th
and 19th centuries it was remodelled.

CORFE CASTLE *Purbeck's quarries furnished the stone for the Norman castle, and after Cromwell's men slighted it, the villagers used much of it for their cottages.*

CRAIL *A haven for holiday makers, Crail is Fife's most easterly port. On the coast near here Mary of Guise, who became the mother of Mary Queen of Scots, landed from France to marry James V.*

COVENTRY, Warwickshire *10 SP37*
Coventry began in the 7th century, when an Anglo-Saxon convent was erected somewhere near the present city centre. Four centuries later, Leofric, Earl of Mercia, built a Benedictine Abbey, and the town began to grow. The story of his wife, Lady Godiva riding naked through the streets, with only her long hair to preserve her modesty, first came into circulation in 1235.

The 19th century, that great age of innovation, brought the manufacture of sewing machines and cycles to the city – and then came the motor car. In 1898, the Daimler Company produced Britain's first horseless carriage in Coventry. From then onward, Coventry was a strong magnet, attracting labour from all over Britain. The Museum of British Road Transport tells Coventry's part in the history of transport. The Herbert Art Gallery and Museum has collections of social history, art and archaeology.

On a terrible night in November 1940, German bombers blew the heart out of the city. The Church of St Michael – which, in 1918, had been promoted to the status of cathedral – was almost totally destroyed. Only the medieval tower and the spire survived. Work on building the new cathedral began in 1951, when Basil Spence (later Sir Basil) won an open architectural competition for his striking modern design which incorporates the ruin of the old. Perhaps the best-known feature is the altar tapestry by Graham Sutherland, but there is much else about the building that is equally distinguished, in particular the beautiful modern stained glass.

The phrase 'sent to Coventry' originated in 1647. It referred to a group of Royalists who had been captured by Parliamentary forces in the Midlands, and were imprisoned in Coventry's Church of St John. They had, to put it another way, been banned from society.

COVERACK, Cornwall *1 SW71*
Driving to Coverack, you pass the space-age creations on the top of Goonhilly Downs and feel that you have been swept through time into the far future. But then reason is restored by this entirely delightful fishing village, with its thatched cottages (they're sheltered from the westerlies) and the kind of harbour you feel that all such places ought to have.

COXWOLD, N Yorkshire *15 SE57*
One of the most idyllic villages in this part of Yorkshire, Coxwold's broad main street is lined by warm-toned, stone cottages, set back behind the wide green verges so often found in rural Yorkshire. In the 18th century, the village was fortunate to have as its clergyman the eccentric and writer Laurence Sterne, whose comic masterpiece, *The Life and Opinions of Tristram Shandy* had been published just before his appointment to Coxwold. He named his house Shandy Hall (OACT) and it now belongs to the Sterne Trust who have preserved and renovated both it and the garden.

CRAIGELLACHIE, Grampian *27 NJ24*
Confidently considering itself to be one of the most beautiful villages in the region (and who shall deny it?), Craigellachie stands at the junction of the rivers Fiddich and Spey – looking across meadows to a wooded island and so to Craigellachie Rock. The rock marks the boundary between Strathspey and the lands of the Grants (war cry: 'Stand fast, Craigellachie!') Telford's bridge over the Spey is a gem of civil engineering on the smaller scale.

CRAIGIEVAR CASTLE, Grampian *27 NJ51*
With its profusion of turrets and conical roofs, Craigievar (NTS) is the perfect example of Scottish Baronial. It is a tower-house, six storeys high and its internal decoration has changed as little as its exterior since 1626 when the building was finished. All the rooms are decorated in the Renaissance manner and the ceiling of the Great Hall is particularly magnificent. The inscription 'Doe not vaiken sleeping dogs' should perhaps be heeded.

CRAIGMILLAR, Lothian *23 NT27*
The ruins of Craigmillar Castle are dark with tales of terrible deeds. In 1477, the Earl of Mar (youngest son of James II of Scotland) bled to death here. In 1544, the castle was burned down. Mary Queen of Scots was a frequent visitor and she may have plotted Darnley's murder here (assuming that she was involved in it at all).

CRAIL, Fife *24 NO60*
A picturesque fishing port of crow-stepped red-tiled houses that used to be the haunt of smugglers, Crail is now more popular with artists and tourists. The town was exporting salt fish to Europe as early as the 9th century, and Robert the Bruce gave it a royal charter in 1310 – conceding that its inhabitants might trade on the Sabbath. Two hundreds years later, John Knox made plain his views on the matter, when he preached one of his more violent promises of hell-fire from the pulpit of the parish church. A large blue stone at the gateway to the church is said to have been thrown by the devil from the Isle of May, five miles away. The church was founded in the 12th century and contains one of the town's two ancient Pictish crosses.

CRAMOND, Lothian 23 NT17

Cramond, which has become almost a suburb of Edinburgh, has long been a retreat for citizens who wanted to get away without going too far. Situated on the lovely Almond estuary, it is popular with yachtsmen. An interesting tradition persists in the Howison family, who were given the land round Braehead by James V. The condition of their ownership is that they should always be ready to present their sovereign with a basin and ewer of water. This ceremony was last observed at the coronation of Queen Elizabeth II.

CRANBORNE CHASE, Dorset & Wiltshire 3 ST91

The Chase, which covers 100 square miles, used to be a hunting forest, often visited by King John, who loved to hunt the fallow deer here. In time, the forest laws, instead of keeping poachers out, allowed the Chase to become an unsavoury haven for all kinds of miscreants, until in 1830 Parliament passed a special Act to bring it under the control of the law. Cranborne itself, once the centre of the Chase Court, is now a picturesque village, its attractive houses grouped around a village green. The gardens (OACT) of Cranborne House were laid out in the 17th century by the 1st Earl of Salisbury.

CRASTER, Northumberland 24 NU22

A small fishing village famous for its oak-smoked kippers – though, nowadays, the herring are fished from South Shields. However, the local fisherman still catch lobsters and crabs. Craster Tower is the home of the Craster family, who built the town's harbour in memory of a brother who'd been killed in Tibet.

CRATHES CASTLE, Grampian 27 NO79

Crathes Castle (NTS) is an L-shaped tower house with an early 18th-century formal garden. It used to be the home of the Burnetts of Leys. Alexander Burnet built it in the 16th century, and much of the interior decoration is his work, particularly the painted ceilings of such rooms as the Chamber of the Nine Nobles the Chamber of the Nine Muses, and The Green Lady's Room. The family's most prized possession is the 'Horn of Leys' a bejewelled horn of fluted ivory, given to a 14th-century Burnet by King Robert I as a symbol of his authority over the Forest of Doum.

CRAWLEY, W Sussex 5 TQ23

Crawley New Town, the only one of that generation of post-war new towns to be built south of London, has been grafted on to old Crawley, which has many ancient buildings. Particularly worthy of note is the church, which dates back to the 14th and 15th centuries. The new town has its own fine examples of modern architecture, which make their own contribution to an urban environment which was designed to take account of the best ideas in town planning.

KIPPERED HERRINGS

For more than 100 years, a small factory at Craster has produced excellent kippers by the traditional method of smoking over a fire of green oak chips. This gives the fish the best flavour and keeps the flesh moist and succulent, say connoisseurs of this breakfast delicacy.

CREDITON, Devon 2 SS80

Crediton used to be the cathedral city of Devon in Saxon times until Exeter usurped its position. Tradition says that St Boniface, who brought Christianity to the Germans, was born here in the 7th century.

CREETOWN, Dumfries & Galloway 17 NX45

Creetown used to be called Ferrytown of Cree – the ferry was across the River Cree's estuary. The name was changed in 1785 on the instructions of the local laird, McCulloch of Barholm. In Scott's *Guy Mannering*, it appears as 'Porton Ferry'. Granite from the vicinity was used in the building of Liverpool's docks. The Creetown Gem Rock Museum and Art Gallery has the largest private collection of such specimens in Britain. There is also a craft shop and workshops.

CREWE & NANTWICH, Cheshire 14 SJ75

The railway town of Crewe has joined forces with its neighbour, Nantwich. The latter is famous for its handsome parish church and old timbered buildings.

CREWKERNE, Somerset 3 ST40

A pleasant little town with traditions stretching back to Anglo-Saxon times, when it had the right of minting coins. In later centuries, it became associated with the flax-weaving and sail-making industries. The sails for HMS *Victory* were made here – and those for several Americas Cup contenders. The 15th-century church has fine stained glass. Clapton Court Gardens (OACT) are three miles south.

CRICCIETH, Gwynedd 13 SH53

A very pleasant and unspoiled little resort, with the Lleyn peninsula providing shelter from north-westerlies, and Snowdonia supplying a dramatic backdrop to the north. The Welsh royal line of Llywelyn had already built a castle (AM) before the arrival of Edward I: the English king merely had to strengthen it, but over the centuries it crumbled peacefully into ruins.

CREETOWN *The rivers of Dumfries and Galloway are famous for their salmon, and the Cree estuary is no exception. Here a man is preparing the tall salmon nets.*

CRICH, Derbyshire   *15 SK35*

People interested in tramcars probably know all about Crich. There are more than 40 old trams in the Tramway Society's Museum. Set in a disused quarry, several lines have been laid down and these fascinating vehicles make small journeys along the Derwent Valley. To enhance the period feeling, a number of historic buildings are being re-erected along the route. The Peak District Mines Historical Society has an exhibition of the Derbyshire lead-mining industry.

CRICKET ST THOMAS,
Somerset   *3 ST30*

A Ham-stone house, built in 1804, is surrounded by 1000 acres of parkland (OACT) running gently down to a river that has been dammed to make waterfalls and lakes. A zoo occupies one corner – though you may come across camels, llamas, bison, and wallabies wandering contentedly in the wild. The National Heavy Horse Centre is also housed here.

CRICKHOWELL, Powys   *8 SO21*

Crickhowell is a pleasant little town lying in the Usk valley in the shade of the Black Mountains. In the churchyard is the grave of Sir George Everest, the military engineer who gave his name to Mount Everest.

CRICKLADE, Wiltshire   *3 SU09*

Cricklade's name means 'the passage over the river by the hill' and is indeed the only Thames-side town in Wiltshire – though, admittedly, the river at this point is not impressive. Pleasant 17th and 18th-century houses abound, but the most lovely building is the church of St Sampson, with its elaborate Tudor tower.

CRIEFF, Tayside   *22 NN82*

Crieff is yet another 'gateway to the Highlands' and none the worse for that. Its original name was Drummond; but, after the Drummond estates had been forfeited to the Crown in 1745, somebody thought that a change might be politic. The Industrial Revolution resulted in its manufacturing interests being spirited away to the Lowlands. To compensate, Crieff became a spa in the 19th century. A 17th-century tollbooth and two crosses are attractive features of the town. Glenturret is Scotland's oldest distillery.

CROFT CASTLE, Hereford &
Worcester   *9 SO46*

Until the National Trust acquired it in 1957, the castle had been owned by the Croft family almost continuously (with a break between 1750 and 1923) since the Norman invasion. Standing in 1636 acres of parkland, its still retains its 14th-century appearance. The little church, close by the house, has a splendid tomb containing the remains of Sir Richard Croft and his wife.

CROMARTY, Highland   *30 NH76*

Cromarty is a small seaport on the Black Isle – serving Easter Ross and guarding the entrance to the Firth of Cromarty. Much of the town is now devoted to the cause of North-Sea oil. However, it still celebrates the birth of geologist Hugh Miller in 1802. The cottage (NTS) in which he was born contains a collection of geological specimens.

CROMER, Norfolk   *12 TG24*

Like so many resorts, Cromer was a small fishing village until the 19th century, when the railways brought sea fever to Britain. You can still see the original cottages clustered around the church of Sts Peter and Paul – the tower of which, 160ft high, is the tallest in the county, and there are several fine Victorian hotels, a pier, and a small zoo. A former Cromer lifeboat coxswain, Henry Blogg, saved so many lives, that the lifeboat is named after him. Crabs are a popular local delicacy.

CRICH TRAMWAY MUSEUM

The one-mile tramway route follows part of that laid down for the quarry railway by George Stephenson. Exhibits range from mid Victorian horse-drawn trams and Edwardian opentop trams to Sheffield's last tram, which ran in 1960.

CROMFORD, Derbyshire   *15 SK25*

It was here, in this stone-built Derbyshire village, that Richard Arkwright built, in 1771, the world's first mechanised textile factory. The original mill (OACT) survives, a rather grim-looking place that appears to have been designed along the lines of a fortress – presumably to fend off attacks from angry and jobless weavers. The Arkwright Society is undertaking renovations of the mill, warehouses and watercourses. The church and some of the cottages were built for his workers.

CROSSRAGUEL ABBEY,
Strathclyde   *22 NS20*

Duncan, Earl of Carrick founded this Cluniac (a body of Benedictines) monastery (AM) in 1244. Since it was far enough from the border to escape the ravages of English raiders, the ruins are in remarkably good order. Much of the work is 15th-century and very distinguished, too. The gatehouse and the Abbot's Tower are especially well preserved. The dovecot contains 240 nesting boxes.

CROSTON, Lancashire   *14 SD41*

Croston is the home of the Royal Umpire Museum and Carriage Exhibition which, as its name implies, is a collection of coaches, carriages and vintage cars. It is considered to be one of the best in the country. Other attractions include rare birds and animals – and a haunted room. The church has some interesting brasses.

CROWLAND, Lincolnshire   *11 TF20*

St Guthlac came to Crowland to live the life of a hermit. After his death in 714, his relative, King Ethelbald of Mercia, established a Benedictine abbey in his memory. The ruins remain, and are magnificent. A triangular bridge, built in the 14th century, stands in the centre of the village, the main streets of which used to be waterways for tributaries of the River Welland. In 1720, it was embellished with a figure of Christ which is believed to have come from the ruined abbey.

CRICKET ST THOMAS *The National Heavy Horse Centre exists to breed the kinds of horses that were once the mainstay of British agriculture, being used for all the heavy work on the land.*

CRUDEN BAY, Grampian *28 NK13*
Before World War II, Cruden Bay was
notable for its huge hotel and its
championship golf course. The hotel has
gone; the golf course remains. Nowadays,
the resort is perhaps better known as the
place where the pipeline from the Forties
North Sea oil field comes ashore. If you are
not interested in pipelines, you can admire
the 1697 Bishop's Bridge spanning Cruden
Water – and the ruins of Slains Castle 'built
upon the margin of the sea, so that the walls
of one of the towers seem only a
continuation of a perpendicular rock, the
foot of which is beaten by the waves'. So
wrote Dr Johnson, who was much
impressed by the castle, which was given by
Robert the Bruce to the Earl of Errol in the
early 14th century. Dr Johnson was equally
impressed by the Buller of Buchan, a vast
amphitheatre, gouged out by the sea,
'which no men can see with indifference
who has either sense of danger or delight in
rarity'.

CULLEN, Grampian *27 NJ56*
The old town, known as Invercullen, was
demolished in 1822, and a new one, built to
the instructions of the Earl of Seafield,
erected in its place. The Mercat Cross
should be seen – also Cullen House. The
latter is a 16th-century fortified mansion
much extended in 1861.

CULLODEN, Highland *26 NH74*
A sad place this: a windswept ridge of
moorland (NTS) with a plantation of trees
where cairns commemorate 1200
Highlanders who were slain in 40 minutes
by the Duke of Cumberland's forces at the
Battle of Culloden on 16 April 1746.

CULROSS, Fife *23 NS98*
A beautifully restored 16th- and 17th-
century small Scottish town, once famous
for its baking plates ('girdles') and its trade
in coal and salt. Culross Palace (AM) is
small as palaces go, but it was large enough

to merit a visit from James VI (James I of
England). The Study (home of the national
Trust for Scotland's representative), the
Nunnery, Parley Hill House and the Manse
are among other buildings that should be
seen. The delightful snuffmaker's house
bears the inscription: 'Who would have
thocht it, noses would have bocht it'. The
choir of the old Abbey (AM) is used as the
parish church.

CULZEAN CASTLE, Strathclyde
22 NS21
Robert Adam designed this fine castle
(NTS) in 1777, building it around an
ancient tower that had belonged to the
Kennedy family. The interior, with its
elegant central staircase and its round
drawing-room, is just as fine as the exterior.
The grounds, Scotland's first countryside
park, include an aviary, a swan pond, a
camellia house and a home farm. The so-
called National Guest Flat was put at
Eisenhower's disposal in 1946 to afford him
a residence in Scotland.

CUMBERNAULD,
   Strathclyde *22 NS77*
In 1956, Cumbernauld Development
Corporation planned a new town to house
Glasgow's 'overspill' population. This
attempt to create a new environment has
since served as a source of ideas to town
planners all over the world. The shops,
offices, hotels and places of entertainment
are all grouped together in a many-storey
complex, but the most interesting and
successful idea was to divide the town up
into 'villages' – each of them virtually self-
sufficient.

CUPAR, Fife *24 NO31*
At Cupar, the market place for Fife's
agricultural produce, the Thanes built a
stronghold on Castlehill. Here, too, in
1559, the Queen Regent (Mary of Guise –
mother of Mary, Queen of Scots) signed a
treaty with the Lords of the Congregation –

with the result that all French troops quit
Fife. Nearby is Hill of Tarvit Mansion
(NTS), containing a notable collection of
paintings and furnishings, and set in fine
gardens.

CYFARTHA, Mid Glamorgan *8 SO00*
Cyfartha iron works was founded in 1765.
Thirty years later, the management was
taken over by an iron master named Robert
Thompson Crawshay. Crawshay was a
remarkable man. He built a church with an
impossibly Gothic tower, and then carried
Victorian Gothic to the wildest extremes in
the creation of his home, Cyfartha Castle
(OACT). He was also an excellent
photographer, who summoned his
daughters with the blast of a whistle
whenever he needed models. You can see
his work in the castle's museum. The
epitaph on his gravestone, 'God Forgive
Me', suggests that he was not above self-
criticism.

CYNWYL ELFED, Dyfed *7 SN32*
Set in a lovely wooded valley where the
Rivers Duad and Nant Coch (it means 'red
stream') meet, the village is a sheer delight
– very neat and trim and artlessly pleasing
to the eye. A number of Roman relics have
been dug up in the vicintiy – including a
golden figure of the goddess Diana. In a
farmhouse about a mile away, the Rev. D H
Elved Lewis was born. This grand old man
lived to be 94 and became one of the most
famous writers of Welsh hymns. A museum
in the house honours his memory.

CYNONVILLE, W Glamorgan *8 SS89*
Just outside this small mining settlement, a
large stretch of the wooded Afan Valley has
been designated a Countryside Park.
Waymarked trails and picnic areas cater for
visitors, and by the information centre is
the small but fascinating Welsh Miners'
Museum which vividly illustrates the harsh
conditions in which miners and their
children had to work.

CROMER *One of the most Victorian of all the seaside resorts on the North Norfolk coast, Cromer still has many of its 19th-century hotels, and has kept its pier.*

THE EARLIEST 'CASTLES'
HILLFORTS
Strongholds of the Iron Age

THE OLDEST HILLFORTS date back to the years before 1000 BC, but most examples date from the turbulent centuries of the Iron Age and were built between about 750 BC and AD 43.

The fortresses tell of a long and unsettled chapter in the British past; they are the most imposing features to survive from their age and some archaeologists think that the term 'Hillfort Age' is a more apt description of the period than the traditional 'Iron Age'. The hillforts appeared at a time when British farming had existed for up to 4000 years and when most lands had a long history of agricultural use. This was also a time of quite high population levels, creating problems of land shortage which were made more severe by climatic changes. As the climate became cooler and damper, many areas of upland farming were abandoned as sour blankets of peat spread across the slopes and plateaux, intensifying the competition to control workable lands below.

Walk to the top of any dominating hill in Wessex and, more likely than not, you will find the summit ringed by a girdle of prehistoric ramparts. From the Scottish Highlands to Cornwall and from Snowdonia to Northamptonshire, these ancient strongholds are a characteristic feature of the British landscape.

MASSIVE RAMPARTS, ditches and entrance defences tell us that the hillforts are clearly military monuments, but they were also much else besides. A series of quite recent excavations have shown that the forts frequently contained settlements. Some of these were small and temporary affairs, some were village-sized while some were the size of small towns and occasionally show the neat arrangements of buildings that are generally associated with organised planning. While one can quite understand how a threatened population in an unstable society would construct a well-defended hilltop bolt-hole, it is less easy to see how villages and larger settlements should have been built in such windswept and inaccessible settings.

RAMPART *and ditch defences of an Iron-Age hillfort crown the Herefordshire Beacon in the Malvern Hills. Elgar used it as the setting for Caractacus.*

THE SITES of some of the hillforts are so lofty that the rambler faces a stiff and tiring climb to reach the ancient ramparts – and is left with considerable respect for the toughness of the Iron Age people who lived in such places or made the ascent regularly in the course of day-to-day living. Hillforts are found in such places as the strange tabular summit of the great Pennine massif of Ingleborough in Yorkshire, while the swelling bulk of Mam Tor in the Peak District, was also defended, and within the ramparts are hollows which represent former huts thought to date from a pre-hillfort phase of settlement. While conditions on the top of Mam Tor or Ingleborough can seldom have been very hospitable, a far more forbidding situation was tolerated by the community who constructed their fort on Mither Tap of Bennachie, a 1698ft summit in the severely cold and exposed mountains of north-east Scotland. Many of the lofty peaks of Snowdonia were capped by hillforts, but probably the most worthwhile fort to visit in North Wales is Tre'r Ceiri overlooking the Lleyn Peninsula, and here, ramblers who make the stiff ascent can see the drystone walling of the ramparts and the remains of many stone-walled huts, some dating from the end of the Iron Age and some from the Romano-British period.

COMMANDING HILLS and ridges were not always available in places where people felt the need for defence and some 'hillforts' consist of ramparts and ditches constructed in lowland settings or on gentle ridges like the one near Cambridge which accommodates Wandlebury fort. Coastal headlands and peninsulas were often defended by ramparts to form 'promontory forts' like Hengistbury Head in Dorset. The hillforts also varied enormously in size, from the ditch-guarded farmsteads or 'raths' which are sprinkled across the Irish countryside in thousands to massively defended 'capitals' like Maiden Castle in Dorset. This is one of the most striking and fascinating hillfort sites in Britain, with massive ramparts which were built in several different stages enclosing a central area of some 47 acres. Hambledon Hill and its neighbour Hod Hill, also in Dorset, are other imposing examples.

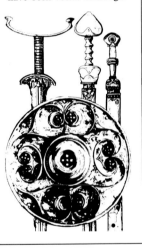

IRON-AGE WEAPONS
Shields (detail shown) and swords like these were found in rivers and lakes and may have been votive offerings.

EARTH, TIMBER, AND STONE were the materials used, as the hillforts also varied in the nature of their construction. In some cases the ramparts of earth and rubble were reinforced by timber frameworks of varying types, while in mountainous areas where earth was not available and the rocks were too hard to permit the construction of deep ditches, the ramparts were built of great thicknesses of drystone walling. Far more mysterious are the 'vitrified forts' of Scotland. These forts were built with stone rubble ramparts reinforced by a framework of lacing timbers, but the ramparts have been 'vitrified' or turned to a glassy stone substance by burning at very high temperatures. Such vitrification did not enhance the military qualities of the ramparts and one cannot imagine how defenders would stand idly by while an attacking force heaped the necessary masses of inflammable brushwood around their defences. Nevertheless, the vitrified forts are quite common in Scotland and include examples like Craig Phadrig just west of Inverness or Inverfarigaig fort overlooking Loch Ness.

THE ROMAN CONQUEST and pacification of England and Wales brought the Age of the hillfort almost to its close. Wherever the great forts presented a challenge to Roman rule they were evacuated, as at Maiden Castle, where the survivors of the storming of the fort were eventually resettled in Roman Dorchester. In some of the more remote upland areas life in hillforts was still tolerated, as at Tre'r Ceiri. The days of the hillfort were not entirely over

however, and several English examples were refurbished and briefly occupied during the rough and tumble of Dark Age warfare; South Cadbury Castle has long been associated with the Arthurian legends and a modern excavation of the hillfort did produce evidence of its re-fortification in Arthurian times.

EXAMPLES OF HILLFORTS can be found almost everywhere in Britain, although they are thinly distributed over the eastern counties of England, but elsewhere hillforts are thickly scattered across the landscape. Where the ramparts are well-preserved, the visitor is sure to be impressed by the prodigious amount of toil expended in the construction of the sinuous stretches of banks and ditches and left to wonder whether more was involved than just the communal need for defence? Archaeology is not yet able to provide a complete explanation, but it seems that the hillforts were often more than refuges or defended settlements. Many excavated sites were found to be packed with grain-storage pits and some revealed structures which have been interpreted as granaries. And so the hillforts could have been regional centres from which the Iron Age chieftains supervised the redistribution of grain grown in the area dominated by the citadel. Whatever new details of hillfort functions and design may emerge from large scale excavations like the one recently mounted at Danebury fort in Hampshire, the hillforts provide a striking testimony to the turbulence and insecurity of Iron Age life.

LLANMELIN, GWENT (left) This artist's impression by the renowned painter of historical reconstructions, Alan Sorrell, clearly shows how the entrance to a Welsh hillfort, occupied by the Silures, may have looked in about 250 BC. Inset (above) an aerial photograph reveals the outlines of the defences around the site.

MAIDEN CASTLE (right) One of the greatest Iron-Age forts in the south country, Maiden Castle in Dorset, covered a hill-top area 100 acres in extent.

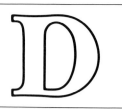

DALKEITH, Lothian *24 NT36*
An old mill and market town on the banks
of the River Esk, Dalkeith has a modern
centre that serves the mining and
agricultural districts south-east of
Edinburgh. Dalkeith Palace – now
occupied by a computer firm – originally a
12th-century building, was remodelled in
about 1700 by Vanbrugh for Anne,
Duchess of Buccleuch. Widow of the rebel
Duke of Monmouth, she was the Duchess
of Scott's *Lay of the last Minstrel*. The
grounds (OACT) of the palace contain a
beautiful Adam Bridge and an orangery.
The ruins of 12th-century Newbattle
Abbey are just south of the town.

DANBY, N Yorkshire *20 NZ70*
A stone village at the head of Danby Dale in
the lovely Esk Valley, Danby's main street
leads from the wooded river up on to
Danby Low Moor. Danby Lodge National
Park, a former shooting lodge, is the
information centre for the North York
Moors National Park. The Eskdale railway
runs between the village and the restored
Saxon church of St Hilda where Canon
Atkinson, author of the classic *Forty Years
in a Moorland Parish* was buried in 1900.

DARLINGTON, Co Durham *20 NZ21*
This busy industrial town on the River
Skerne, cooling towers on the skyline, was
first a Saxon settlement, growing into a
market and later a textile town. Then came
the Stockton and Darlington railway. The
world's first public passenger train was
Stephenson's *Locomotion No.1* (1825),
financed by the Quaker businessman,
Edward Pease. You can see this and six
other locomotives at the Darlington
Railway Museum which is housed in North
Road Station.

DARTINGTON HALL, Devon
2 SX76
The fine 14th-century quadrangular manor
house by the River Dart has been, since
1925, an innovative centre for education
and the arts. It has a progressive school, a
college of arts and music, and units for
adult education and young people. It is also
a centre for practical research into, and the
scientific development of, rural industries.
The Trust which controls the hall runs
farms and forests, a textile mill, shops, and
civil-engineering, horticultural, and glass-
making companies.

DARTMOUTH, Devon *2 SX85*
It is the turquoise River Dart that gives this
attractive Elizabethan town its character.
Dartmouth is about a mile from the mouth
of the river, on its steep, wooded west
bank, sheltered by prosperous countryside.
But you cannot help seeing the new houses
on the hills, nor the bulk of the Britannia
Royal Naval College (1905).
On the waterfront, at Bayards Cove, is
one of Henry VIII's defensive castles

DARTMOOR, Devon *2 SX58*
The 'moor' often conveys a feeling of ill-
omen, of high moorland, broken by jagged
granite tors; of mist-shrouded blanket bog
where unwary travellers are sucked to
oblivion. Whether this impression comes
from the landscape itself, from the grim
prison at Princetown, from the Sherlock
Holmes adventure related in *The Hound of
the Baskervilles*, or from all three is hard to
tell. In 1951 Dartmoor was made a National
Park, covering 365 square miles. Its
boundaries are, roughly speaking,
Okehampton in the north, Ivybridge in the
south, Tavistock in the west and Bovey
Tracey in the east. Most of the land is over
1000ft above sea level and the highest
points are High Willhays (2038ft) and Yes
Tor (2030ft). Fourteen rivers rise on
Dartmoor, among them the Teign, the
Bovey and the Dart. Some of the most
beautiful scenery is to be found in the
wooded river valleys – for example around
Dartmeet, where the waters of the East and
West Dart join. Here and at Postbridge are
fine examples of the ancient clapper bridges
– rough slabs of granite supported on
boulders, many of which date back to
medieval times and beyond, when tin was
extensively mined here. Human settlement
dates back to the Bronze Age, and the area
is rich in prehistoric monuments and
remains; probably the best-known village
site is at Grimspound. Tin-mining
flourished throughout the medieval and
Tudor periods, when the tinners virtually
ruled the moor, with stannary towns at
Plympton, Tavistock, Ashburton and
Chagford, and their own 'parliament', held
in the open on Crockern Tor for more than
400 years – from 1305 to 1749. Nowadays,
apart from the tourists and the 'wild' ponies
(which in fact all have owners and are
rounded up in the autumn 'pony drift'), the
only business is that carried on by the army
who use large parts of the moor as a firing
range. Among the most famous beauty
spots are Lydford Gorge (NT), the ancient
Wistman's Wood, where gnarled oak trees
shelter a nature reserve; Yarner Wood, also
a nature reserve in oak woodland;
Dunsford Nature Reserve on the River
Teign, and, finally, that famous village
Widecombe-in-the-Moor.

GRIMSPOUND *(above)* on Dartmoor was a
Bronze-Age village, consisting of 24 huts
within a defensive wall. Remains of ancient tin-
workings suggest the inhabitants were miners.

HAYTOR ROCKS *(Left)* on the east side of
Dartmoor are one of the most evocative of the
moor's granite outcrops, weathered by time
into fantastic, often menacing outlines.

DARTMOUTH *The ceiling of No 12, the Butterwalk, depicts a 'Tree of Jesse'.*

(OACT); and a stone recording the sailing of the *Mayflower*. The arcaded Butterwalk, which houses a maritime museum (AM) is among the best of Dartmouth's 17th-century buildings. By the river, too, you can see the first effective steam engine, invented by the Dartmouth-born inventor Thomas Newcomen (1663–1729). The Dart-side road to the harbour mouth takes you to Dartmouth Castle (OACT) that was built in the 15th century to guard the approaches to the town.

DAWLISH, Devon   2 SX97

This seaside town, between the Exe and Teign estuaries, is like Lyme Regis but in a lower key. Jane Austen liked both; Dickens made Dawlish the birth-place of Nicholas Nickleby, hero of his novel of the same name. The town is set slightly back from the sea, and the elegant Regency houses on the Strand were built, unusually, facing inland. Also unusual is the fact that the main railway line runs between the town and sands on its lovely route between Exeter and Newton Abbott. It was here that Brunel tried out his experimental atmospheric trains.

Dawlish's deep-red cliffs, sandy beaches and colourful, luxurious vegetation attract as many visitors as anywhere in Devon. The town's main feature is the Lawn, landscaped gardens created in 1803 round Dawlish Water.

The South Devon Railway Museum and a model railway are on the sand-dune peninsula of Dawlish Warren; so is a national wildfowl reserve, but so too are holiday camps and caravan sites.

DEAL, Kent   6 TR35

Now a seaside resort, with fishing boats beached on the pebbles, a 1000ft pier built only in 1957, and many Georgian houses, Deal has received a new lease of life as a holiday resort. The narrow streets of the old part of town, source of smugglers' tales, run down to the seafront, where a plaque marks the spot where Julius Caesar is said to have come and seen, in 55 BC, not yet ready to conquer.

Ships pass close inshore to avoid the Goodwin Sands, recalling Deal's last importance as a Channel port. The Time Ball Tower on the seafront told Greenwich Mean Time to shipping from 1854–1927, by dropping its black ball down the shaft at 1pm precisely.

Deal Castle (AM, 1540), one of a chain built by Henry VIII to guard against Catholic invasion, was designed like a Tudor rose to give it maximum defensive power. Walmer Castle (AM), Deal's twin, also dates from the 16th century and is the official residence of the Warden of the Cinque Ports.

Dartmoor's Eastern Edge
48 miles

Dartmoor is a unique place, a land of mystery and legend, of extremes of scenery and extremes of weather. The route from Ashburton, skirts the edge of the Dartmoor National Park.

Leave **Ashburton** on an unclassified road (SP Buckland). From **Buckland-in-the-Moor** follow signs to Widecombe. Cross the river and at the T-junction turn right. In 1 mile enter **Widecombe-in-the-Moor**. Take the Bovey Tracey road, bearing right past the green. Descend the Bovey Valley and in 3 miles at cross-roads by Edgemoor Hotel turn left and in ½ mile left again on to B3344, SP Manaton. Continue to **Manaton**. Pass the church and in ¾mile at a T-junction, turn right on to North Bovey road and in 1½miles cross the river into **North Bovey**. Turn left to leave the village and in ¼mile bear right (SP Princetown). Recross the river, climb sharply and bear right. In 1¼miles at T-junction turn left on to B3212 SP Princetown. Continue, passing the Grimspound/Hameldown Tor road, to **Postbridge**. Stay on B3212 to reach the edge of **Two Bridges** and turn left on to B3357 Ashburton road and after 4¼miles descend sharply to Dartmeet bridge, then climb steeply to Sharp Tor and continue to **Poundsgate**. Descend to cross the river at New Bridge and enter Holne Chase woods. In ½mile turn right on to unclassified road to **Holne**. From Holne follow signs for Buckfastleigh and in ½mile descend to the bottom of the hill and keep left. In 1½miles, at the crossroads, turn left (SP Buckfast and Totnes). In ¼mile bear right then left, and in ¾mile enter **Buckfast**. In ½mile at the T-junction turn left (right leads to Buckfastleigh). Cross the River Dart, turn left again and after 1¾miles at T-junction turn left on to B3357, then right to return to Ashburton.

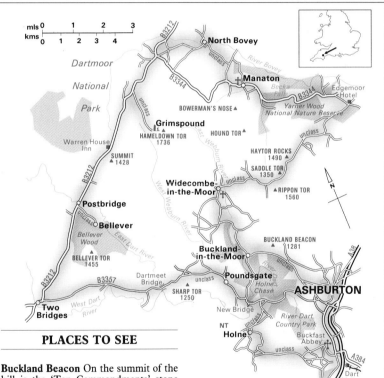

PLACES TO SEE

Buckland Beacon On the summit of the hill is the 'Ten Commandments' stone carved by a local stonemason.

Buckland-in-the-Moor   Stone-built, thatched cottages make this one of the showplaces of the moor.

Widecombe-in-the-Moor   The fair, famed in song, is held in early September.

Haytor Rocks Spectacular crags, accessible by car. Fine viewpoint.

Yarner Wood National Nature Reserve Unspoilt woodland haven with nature trails.

Becka Falls Becka Brook cascades 70ft over a series of boulders.

North Bovey Enchanting village set in delightful countryside.

Grimspound Bronze-Age shepherds' settlement with 24 hut circles in a walled enclosure.

Postbridge Fine old clapper bridge built of massive granite slabs.

Dartmeet Bridge A popular National Park beauty spot with many walks.

Buckfast Abbey The famous abbey dates from the 10th century. Nearby is a fascinating shell museum.

Dart Valley Railway Visitors can take a 14-mile round trip on this old steam railway built in 1872.

DEAN, FOREST OF, Gloucestershire
9 SO61
These 27,000 acres of largely wild
woodland, lying between the Severn and
the Wye, are a reminder of the days when
England was largely afforested. Since
Roman times, the area has housed a wide
variety of rural industries and many survive
today – iron-making, charcoal-burning,
stone-quarrying, and coal-mining. Traces
of the Roman occupation of the area
abound; there are temple ruins at Camp
Hill and remains of paved Roman roads at
Blakeney and Little Dean.

Ancient rights peculiar to the area still
remain, bearing testimony to its
independent nature. They range from the
Foresters' right to graze sheep, to 'pannage'
– the right for pigs to forage for acorns from
the many mature oaks which, with birch,
beech and holly, (some holly trees in
Speech House Wood are over 300 years
old), form the backbone of the forest.

DEDHAM, Essex *12 TM03*
Dedham Vale, designated an Area of
Outstanding Natural Beauty in 1970, is
interpreted for us in the paintings of John
Constable (1776–1837), and nowadays
there is a Countryside Centre in the village.
The key to the landscape is the River Stour,
the natural boundary between the chalk
lowlands of Essex and Suffolk, running
past mill wheels, locks and sluices, willows,
elms, poplars, water meadows and drainage
channels. Among the interesting buildings
in the village is the Master Weaver's House,
dating back to the 15th century.
Constable's father's watermill has been
replaced by a Victorian one, but the old
grammar school he attended still stands.
Castle House (OACT), the home of Sir
Alfred Munnings (1878–1959), President
of the Royal Academy, contains several
examples of his work.

DEENE, Northamptonshire *11 SP99*
The 7th Earl of Cardigan set out from
Deene Park (OACT), home of the
Brudenells, to lead the ill-fated Charge of
the Light Brigade. It is a largely 16th-
century house of Weldon stone with
Jacobean and Georgian additions.

Kirby Hall (AM), 1½ miles west, dates
from 1572 but was altered in the mid 17th
century for Sir Christopher Hatton, the
Lord Chancellor. The interior, sadly, was
gutted by fire some years ago and only the
shell remains.

DELABOLE, Cornwall *1 SX08*
The biggest man-made hole in England –
500ft deep and just under two miles round
– is here, product of years of slate
quarrying. Delabole's museum chronicles
the history of this local industry which
dates back to Henry VII's time and which
happily still survives.

DENBIGH, Clwyd *13 SJ06*
The ruins of Denbigh Castle (AM) are a
reminder of the particularly fierce
resistance which successive English rulers
met in this part of Wales. The ancient
market town itself was originally walled but
after being burnt down twice in the 15th
century, it was rebuilt outside the walls,
traces of which still remain. The town's
landmark is the 16th-century ruin known as
Leicester's Folly (AM), meant to be a
cathedral but never completed.

DEVIZES LOCKS *The 29 locks on the Kennet and Avon Canal were completed on 28th December 1810.
Although long disused, the canal is now being cleared and re-opened for holiday traffic.*

DENT, Cumbria *18 SD78*
This village of twisting, cobbled streets and
grey-stone and colour-washed cottages, lies
in Dentdale, one of the smallest dales in the
Yorkshire Dales National Park. The village
was once a centre for cheese-making, hand-
knitting and marble-quarrying. The
railway could not save Dent's declining
rural industries but the station, although
officially closed by British Rail, re-opens
for special trains for the benefit of tourists
and enthusiasts each summer.

DERBY, Derbyshire *10 SK43*
This ancient county town on the River
Derwent retains much of its past, despite
rapid expansion over the last century and
being created England's newest city by
Queen Elizabeth on her Silver Jubilee visit
in 1977. Its cathedral, built in Henry VIII's
reign, was rebuilt, except for its 178ft
pinnacled tower, in 1725 by James Gibb.
Inside you can see the tomb of Bess of
Hardwick, Countess of Shrewsbury, who
died in 1607.

Porcelain was first made here in 1756 by
William Duesbury to whom George III
gave the right to use the Crown insignia,
and Queen Victoria the right to call it
Royal. But it was the coming of the
Midland Railway works in the 19th century
that marked Derby's industrial revolution
and in 1908 Rolls-Royce opened its car-
manufacturing works. There is a
monument to Sir Henry Royce in the
Arboretum – the largest of many urban
parks, which also has a plaque stone. Rolls-
Royce aero engines are among the many
exhibits in the Industrial Museum, housed
in an 18th-century silk mill.

'THE BEST CAR IN THE
WORLD'

It was a 1909-model Silver Ghost that
earned the Rolls-Royce this accolade,
but a pair of chassis had already
aroused interest at Olympia in December 1906. The luxurious car
below was the first 40/50 HP Silver
Ghost to be given coachwork and was
one of the chassis from Olympia. In
1908 Rolls-Royce moved to their new
factory at Nightingale Road, Derby,
where they celebrated their 75th anniversary in 1983.

DEVIL'S BRIDGE, Dyfed *8 SN77*
This 12th-century stone bridge is the lowest and oldest of three built over the gorge of the River Mynach. Later bridges were built at higher levels, of stone and iron respectively, in 1753 and 1901. Here the Mynach Falls cascade in a spectacular 300ft-drop to meet the Rheidol in a landscape of woods, valleys and rocks.

The Narrow Gauge Railway which runs from Devil's Bridge down the Vale of Rheidol to Aberystwyth is the last outpost of steam on British Rail.

DEVIZES, Wiltshire *3 SU06*
An old market town on the edge of Salisbury Plain, set in rich agricultural country near the source of the Wiltshire Avon, Devizes had a Norman Castle, built by the Bishop of Salisbury on the boundary between manors, so giving the town its name. The original castle was destroyed by Cromwell: the present one is 19th-century.

The town has some fine old houses and inns, including the Bear Hotel which enjoyed such a high reputation in the 18th century that the landlord put posts across the Plain from Salisbury to guide fashionable travellers such as Mrs Siddons and Fanny Burney.

From Devizes, the Kennet and Avon Canal climbs 230ft up Caen Hill, by means of 29 of Rennie's locks – the longest flight in Britain.

DIDCOT, Oxfordshire *4 SU59*
The Great Western Railway put Didcot, until then a quiet, thatched village with a handsome 15th-century church, on the map. Today the Great Western Society (OACT) is a poignant reminder of the glories of 'God's Wonderful Railway'. Its painstakingly restored collection of steam locomotives, rolling stock and other railway memorabilia is overlooked by the 20th-century power station, a landmark from all over the Berkshire Downs.

DINAS-MAWDDWY, Gwynedd
13 SH81
Dinas lies at the junction of the Rivers Dovey and Cerist in a natural amphitheatre formed by the surrounding steep, smooth and rock-crested mountains. It is a well-tended, stone-built village, off the main tourist routes, but nevertheless a popular holiday and fishing centre.

The old slate workings in the village are disappearing beneath fast-growing conifers. Meirion Mill (OACT) on the banks of the Dovey, is a working woollen mill.

DINGWALL, Highland *26 NH55*
Macbeth, in real life, is said to have ruled Ross-shire from here before he captured the Scottish throne from King Duncan in 1040. Of the castle, ruined since 1700, only traces remain. Once a Royal Burgh and the county town of Ross and Cromarty, Dingwall lies near the mouth of the River Conon and is a popular Highland holiday centre. The harbour was built by Thomas Telford.

DIRLETON, Lothian *24 NT58*
One of Scotland's most beautiful villages, Dirleton lies in the prosperous farming land on the east Lothian coast. Its large tree-framed green is bordered by handsome 17th- and 18th-century houses, and is dominated by the ruined castle (AM). The

village boasts a 17th-century bowling green, still used, and an early 17th-century church, now restored. The Yellowcraig Nature Trail follows the unspoiled shoreline off which lies Fidra, a small island housing a bird sanctuary.

DISLEY, Greater Manchester *15 SJ98*
Lyme Park (NT), former ancestral home of the Leghs, an influential family of Cheshire landowners, lies in 1300 acres of deer park high on the edge of the Derbyshire moors. The quadrangular Elizabethan mansion, with its 18th-century Palladian front, is one of the finest in England. Many of the rooms have elaborate decorations and carvings in the Jacobean style.

The Peak Forest Canal passes through delightful countryside near Disley.

DISS, Norfolk *12 TM17*
A small, attractive town set around its impressive mere. Narrow, twisting streets lead enticingly off the triangular market place, at the top of which stands the 15th- and 16th-century St Mary's Church, where John Skelton, poet and tutor to Henry VIII, was once rector. The town has an attractive Victorian Shambles, and a wealth of Georgian and earlier buildings. The 18th-century Lacon's Maltings and the ancient timbered Dolphin and Greyhound Inns represent both ends of the brewing process.

DITCHLEY PARK, Oxfordshire
10 SP32
A classical 18th-century mansion (OACT) designed for the 2nd Earl of Lichfield by James Gibbs, architect of Oxford's Radcliffe Camera. The interior design is

mainly by William Kent; the park outside landscaped by Capability Brown.

In wartime it was Sir Winston Churchill's weekend headquarters; in peacetime it is now an Anglo-American conference centre.

DOBWALLS, Cornwall *1 SX26*
You can enjoy a taste of America here: at the Forest Railroad Park you can ride on a miniature railway modelled on the Denver and Rio Grande's Cumbres Pass route and on the Union Pacific's Sherman Hill route. The miniature-scale locomotives climb the steepest gradients on the English miniature railway system.

The Thorburn museum and gallery displays the work of the great local bird-painter who lived from 1860 to 1935.

DODDINGTON, Lincolnshire
16 SK97
In 1770, Sir John Delaval, then owner of Doddington Hall, rebuilt St Peter's Church in remembrance of his dead daughter. The hall itself (OACT), now the home of the Jarvis family, a mellow brick-built Elizabethan mansion with a largely 18th-century interior, is set in attractive walled rose gardens and houses an impressive collection of tapestries and china.

DODINGTON, Avon *3 ST78*
Dodington House (OACT) home of the Codrington family, was built between 1796 and 1813 by James Wyatt. The formal Palladian design of the house – almost perfectly square, with a façade of six Corinthian columns – is complemented by the handsome Park, which was laid out by Capability Brown.

DIDCOT POWER STATION *dominates the landscape of the flat Thames Valley, its immense grey cooling towers overshadowing the spring fruit blossom of Harwell's orchards.*

WELSH GOLD
Although the Celts and Romans were the first to mine for gold in Wales, the Gwynfynydd Mine near Dolgellau was opened only in the 19th century – this print is dated 1895.

DOLAUCOTHI, Dyfed 8 SN64
The Romans mined for gold here, in the 2577 acres of the Dolaucothi Estate (NT), exploiting the Ogofau goldmines, originally worked by the Celts. Water for the mines was brought from the Cothi and Annell rivers by a seven-mile-long aqueduct, channelled along the hillsides. The Romans had departed by the middle of the 2nd century AD but the mines were re-worked as recently as 1939.

DOLGELLAU, Gwynedd 13 SH71
A compact, slate-built market town in the Mawddach Valley, Dolgellau lies at the foot of the impressive Cader Idris (2927ft). There is a handsome seven-arched 17th-century bridge across the River Wnion and Maesgwm Visitor Centre recounts the story of the local goldmines, worked from 1844 until the middle of the 20th century, and which provided the gold for the wedding rings of both Queen Elizabeth II and the present Princess of Wales. Dolgellau is a well-positioned base from which to explore the Snowdonia National Park.

DOLLAR, Central 23 NS99
The character of the 'classic burgh' is preserved by strict local government control. Dollar is known for its Academy, designed in 1818 by William Playfair, architect of the Royal Scottish Academy and the National Gallery.

The beautiful Dollar Glen (NTS) runs between the Burn of Sorrow, flowing through Windy Pass, and the Burn of Care, on the slopes of the 2111ft King's Seat. Of ruined Castle Campbell (AM), on a crag in Dollar Glen, you can still see a 14th-century tower and a 16th-century wing.

DONCASTER, S Yorkshire 15 SE50
In 1875, Charles Dickens watched the 110th St Leger from the 18th-century Italianate grandstand at the Town Moor racecourse. Today's racegoers probably think of Doncaster only as a mining and railway town. Yet it has Roman origins; is a thriving farming centre for the neighbouring rural lowlands; and possesses fine Georgian architecture, particularly James Paine's 18th-century Mansion House, now used for civic occasions.

JUDGE JEFFREYS *sentenced 74 men at the Dorchester Assize of 1685 to be hanged and quartered for taking part in the Duke of Monmouth's rebellion. The house where he lodged is now used as a restaurant.*

DORCHESTER, Dorset 3 SY69
Dorchester is still the busy county market town in which Thomas Hardy set *The Mayor of Casterbridge*, full of farmers buying and selling livestock and food, between times drinking the beer brewed here since the Middle Ages. Hardy, born at nearby Higher Bockhampton (cottage, NT, OACT), lived his last years just outside Dorchester at Max Gate, designed by himself: he had trained as an architect, assisting in the restoration of St Peter's Church, a mainly 15th-century building, one of the few to survive a series of fires in the 17th and 18th centuries that left Dorchester a little disappointing to look at. The main street, however, with many buildings of Portland stone, is a handsome thoroughfare.

We are reminded of the Bloody Assize of 1685 by a restaurant named after Judge Jeffreys, and by his supposed courtroom in the Antelope Hotel. The Shire Hall, scene in 1834 of the trial of the Tolpuddle Martyrs, is now a TUC memorial.

DORCHESTER, Oxfordshire 4 SU59
Dorchester is a lovely English village on the River Thame, near its junction with the Thames. The Romans made Dorchester a walled town on the road between Silchester and Alchester. Nothing survives, except a few fragments of wall, but the cobble-paved High Street, now bypassed by the main road from Henley to Oxford, follows the line of the Roman road. Many handsome buildings line the street, and in the old lanes are enchanting, thatched cottages.

Dorchester Abbey, among the willows by the Thame, was built by the Normans, and enlarged in medieval times. Its fine glass includes the famous Tree-of-Jesse window.

DORKING, Surrey 4 TQ14
Canterbury-bound pilgrims must have paused in this town, settled by the Anglo-Saxons, and lying on the old crossroads of the Pilgrim's Way and the Roman Stane Street. Later famous visitors included Dickens, a guest at the 15th-century White Horse Inn.

Dorking is nicely placed on the River Mole, between Box Hill and the Downs. Although on the Southern Region, and therefore a commuter town, much of the old market town, with its attractive bow-fronted shops, survives.

DORNIE, Highland 25 NG82
A crofting village in a beautiful mountain setting where Lochs Long and Duich meet. A path inland leads to the impressive Falls of Glomach (NTS).

Eilean Donan Castle (OACT), veteran of many a chocolate-box cover, is strikingly situated just south of the village on a small island where the two lochs meet a third – Loch Alsh. A 13th-century fortress of the Mackenzies, the castle was destroyed in 1719 by the English warship *Worcester* in its assault on the occupying Spanish Jacobites.

DORNOCH, Highland 30 NH78
This Royal Burgh and former county town of Sutherland, enjoys the dubious distinction of being the site of Britain's last recorded judical execution for witchcraft. The town's cathedral is a notable landmark, built originally in 1224. The first anguished cries of golfers missing putts rang out on the famous seaside course as far back as the early 17th century.

DOUNE, Central 22 NN70
An argument over a ferry crossing led to the construction of Doune's first bridge over the River Teith. Robert Spittal – reputedly tailor to James IV – built it in 1535 as an act of retaliation towards the hapless ferryman who had refused him passage. Bridge and river are dominated by the well-preserved 14th-century castle (OACT) A royal residence, following confiscation by James I, it later passed to the Earls of Moray.

DOVEDALE, Derbyshire & Staffordshire 15 SK15
The Twelve Apostles, Jacob's Ladder, Lion Rock, Dovedale Castle, Lover's Leap, Viator's Bridge, Tissington Spires: Dovedale's rocks have weathered into strange shapes. There are caves, too, notably Dove Holes and Reynard's Cavern. Dovedale itself is a lovely, twisting limestone gorge in the gentler south of the Peak District National Park, beloved of fishermen since Izaak Walton's day.

DOVER CASTLE *commands a hilltop first fortified by the Ancient Britons. The ruined tower in the foreground was a lighthouse built by the Romans.*

DOVER, Kent 6 TR34
Dover's famous white cliffs, the seaward tip of the North Downs, have for centuries been Britain's first line of defence against, invaders, from the Vikings to the Luftwaffe. One of the original Cinque Ports in the 12th century it is now the main gateway to and from the Continent – a huge passenger port with one of the world's largest artificial harbours shared by ferry and hovercraft men and Dover-sole fishermen alike.

Dover Castle (OACT) was first fortified by the Romans, whose lighthouse is a survivor of their walled city. The castle is largely Norman in style – Peverell's Tower, its oldest part, was built after the Conquest and the keep about 100 years later.

Under the castle is a tunnel system, dug during the Napoleonic Wars, used as air raid shelters in the last war. A relic from earlier wars is a brass cannon in the castle grounds nicknamed 'Queen Elizabeth's pocket pistol'.

Near the castle is the restored Saxon Church of St Mary in Castra, and Dover boasts a rare surviving wayside chapel, St Edmunds. The Roman Painted House (OACT), is famous for its wall paintings.

Clifftop memorials celebrate the heroism of the Dover Patrol and the first cross-channel swim by Captain Matthew Webb in 1875. North Fall Meadow contains Bleriot's Memorial, marking the famous flight in 1909.

DOWNHAM MARKET, Norfolk
12 TF60
Pottery finds tell us that Downham Market belongs to the lonely, compelling Breckland. The Great Ouse Flood Protection Scheme, finished in 1964, is succeeding where the orginal, started by Charles I's engineer Vermuyden, failed.

DOWNSIDE, Somerset 3 ST65
In 1844 the Benedictines came to the eastern foothills of the Mendips and founded the monastery that became the Abbey in 1899. The huge Abbey Church, white stonework contrasting with its black-clad priests, reached its present form in 1935. Largely the work of the prolific Sir Giles Gilbert Scott and, latterly, Thomas Garner, its next-door neighbour is the famous Roman Catholic boys' school.

DOWNTON, Wiltshire 3 SU12
The bar of the 17th-century Bull Hotel resounds to the fishy tales of the anglers who flock to the Wiltshire Avon. The river bisects this pleasant market town, once an Anglo-Saxon settlement. The Borough – a wide, handsome street of mainly brick and thatch houses, with a central grass strip – was laid out by the Bishop of Winchester in 1205. Trafalgar House (1733) was a present from the nation to Nelson's brother after the Battle of Trafalgar.

DRAYTON MANOR PARK,
Staffordshire *10 SK10*
The 160 acres of park which form this well-known Midlands playground offer all kinds of attractions from real Big Cats in the 15-acre zoo, to realistic imitation dinosaurs in the 'Lost World'. The house, home of the 19th-century statesman Sir Robert Peel, no longer exists.

DREWSTEIGNTON, Devon 2 SX79
Drewsteignton sits on a ridge above the Teign gorge and on the edge of the Dartmoor National Park. The yellow-lichened, 15th-century tower of Holy Trinity Church overlooks the granite and thatch houses clustered round the attractive village square.

One mile south-west of the village is

Castle Drogo (NT). Completed in 1930 and designed by Sir Edwin Lutyens, this extravagantly towered and battlemented building is built on a 900ft-high granite rock with extensive views of Dartmoor.

DROITWICH, Hereford & Worcester
9 SO96
Salt made Droitwich. The town stands on an agricultural plain by the River Severn, sheltered by the Malvern and Lickey Hills. The Romans were the first to become aware of this underlying commodity, and salt mines were worked in Saxon and Norman times. Later the market town was developed into an elegant spa by the 19th-century businessman, John Corbett.

Capitalising on the popular Victorian fashion of 'taking the waters' he built the original St Andrews Brine Baths, and re-modelled the 16th-century timbered Raven Hotel. More flamboyantly, he built at Dodderhill a château in the style of François I, now the Château Impney Hotel.

DRUMLANRIG CASTLE, Dumfries &
Galloway *22 NX89*
This 17th-century Lowland castle (OACT), was designed by Sir William Bruce for the 1st Duke of Queensbury who was so horrified at the expense incurred, he only spent one night there. It is, indeed, a princely achievement, lavishly decorated and displaying a remarkable collection of paintings by European masters.

DRUMNADROCHIT, Highland
26 NH52
On the west bank of Loch Ness, the village is a centre for monster-spotting. Here you can see the official Loch Ness Monster Exhibition. Urquhart Castle (AM), one of Scotland's grandest ruins, overlooks Loch Ness from Strone Point.

DRYBURGH ABBEY, Borders
24 NT53
The ruins of this 12th-century abbey
church (AM) stand quietly now amid lawns
and trees beside the River Tweed. It was
not always so: three times in the 14th
century and again in the 16th the abbey was
plundered and burned, victim of the
constant Border raids and skirmishes
between England and Scotland. The
cloisters have survived well, but except for
the transept, little remains of the church
itself. Here are the graves of Sir Walter
Scott and Earl Haig.

DUDLEY, W Midlands   *9 SO99*
Countryside and industry co-exist in
Dudley, former capital of the Black
Country, and an iron town since the Middle
Ages. The solid ruins of the castle (AM),
built largely in the 13th and 14th centuries,
with walls 8ft thick in places, stand on a
wooded hill. Dudley Zoo lies in the castle
grounds and below are the remains of a
Norman priory.
 Underneath Castle Hill runs the Dudley
Canal, its one-and-three-quarter mile
tunnel recently re-opened and now offering
trips on the *Electra*, the world's first electric
narrow boat. At the Tipton end of the
tunnel is the Black Country Museum, an
open-air village.

DUFFTOWN, Grampian   *27 NJ33*
Set in a bowl of the coastal plain as it rises
towards the foothills of the Cairngorms, the
town was planned in the shape of a cross by
the Earl of Fife in 1817. It is in the heart of
Speyside malt country, near the junction of
the River Fiddich with Dullan Water.
Nearby, by the peat water of the Robbie
Dubh, is the Glenfiddich Distillery
(OACT), founded in 1866 by William
Grant.

DUMBARTON, Strathclyde   *22 NS37*
Formerly Dunbreaton – Fort of the Britons
– the centre of the ancient kingdom of
Strathclyde, and now a Royal Burgh, the

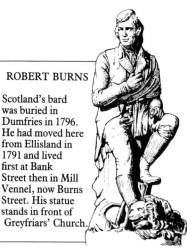

ROBERT BURNS

Scotland's bard
was buried in
Dumfries in 1796.
He had moved here
from Ellisland in
1791 and lived
first at Bank
Street then in Mill
Vennel, now Burns
Street. His statue
stands in front of
Greyfriars' Church.

town is commanded by one of Britain's
oldest strongholds, Dumbarton Rock,
rising 240ft above the Rivers Clyde and
Leven. The remains of the castle (AM)
perched on the Rock include the Wallace
Tower (he was imprisoned here in 1305).

DUMFRIES, Dumfries & Galloway
18 NX97
Sir Walter Scott's 'Queen of the South' is a
prosperous and handsome county town and
market centre; with old sandstone
buildings and large parks.
 The town's focal point is the Midsteeple,
the municipal building dating from about
1707. On its walls are an ell measurement
and a table of distances that includes
Huntingdon – for the 18th-century cattle
drovers made long journeys. Dumfries
Burgh Museum and Camera Obscura
(1835–6) occupy an old windmill. The
stone Old Bridge replaced the wooden one
erected by the Lady Devorgilla, wife of
John of Balliol, founder of Balliol College,
Oxford. Here you can see the Old Bridge
House Museum, and downstream, the
Caul, an 18th-century weir where salmon
leap. The remains of the collegiate church
of Lincluden College (AM) stand on the
west side of the river.
 Burns House (OACT) is where the poet
lived until his death in 1796. His
Mausoleum is in St Michael's Churchyard.

DUNBAR, Lothian   *24 NT67*
An ancient town and royal burgh with an
attractive harbour, cobbled quays, and
fisherman's houses, Dunbar now has only a
small fishing fleet, being mainly a tourist
and agricultural centre for the Borders and
the east Lothian coast.
 Ruined Dunbar Castle (AM) stands on a
rocky promontory above the harbour.

DUNBLANE, Central   *22 NN70*
An ancient town at the south-west tip of
Strath Allan, which became a Victorian
spa, Dunblane is now residential and a
tourist centre for the Ochil Hills and the
Perthshire Highlands. The town has lovely
views over Allan Water.
 Dunblane Cathedral (AM) has a Norman
tower and some fine 13th-century Gothic
architecture: Ruskin thought its west front
a masterpiece. Leighton Library houses the
17th-century collection of the Bishop of
Dunblane, later Archbishop of Glasgow;
and the Dean's house is a museum.

DUNDONALD, Strathclyde   *22 NS33*
An attractive village on the Firth of Clyde.
Robert II, the first Stuart king, built the
now-ruined hill-top castle (AM). He died
there in 1390 as, in 1406, did his successor,
Robert III. Dr Johnson visited the castle in
1773, when he was staying with the
Countess of Eglinton at Auchars House.

DUNDONNELL, Highland   *29 NH18*
Near the head of Little Loch Broom, in the
green valley of Strath Beg, Dundonnell sits
beneath 3484ft An Teallach – 'the forge' –
so named from the mists around its peaks.
Dundonnell House (OACT) is a fine 18th-
century mansion with oriental gardens.
Destitution Road, going north, is one of
several that Scottish navvies built simply in
return for food after they had been reduced
to the extremes of poverty during the
1846–7 potato famine.

DUNDRENNAN, Dumfries &
Galloway   *17 NX74*
Defeated at the Battle of Langside in 1568,
and destined shortly after to be imprisoned
in England, Mary Queen of Scots spent her
last night on Scottish soil at Dundrennan
Abbey (AM). This Cistercian foundation is
now a ruin, thanks to the resourceful local
villagers who used much of the Abbey stone
to build their own homes.

DUNFERMLINE, Fife   *23 NT08*
A royal burgh and ancient capital of
Scotland, in the Kingdom of Fife,
Dumfermline was the home of Scotland's
kings from Malcolm III in the 11th century
until the Union of the Crowns in 1603.
 Dunfermline Abbey (AM), in
Pittencrieff Park, was founded in 1072 by
Queen Margaret, wife of Malcolm
Canmore. Robert Bruce is buried here and
there is a shrine to Margaret, who was
canonised in the 13th century. Pends
Archway links the abbey to ruined
Dunfermline Palace (AM). Malcolm
Canmore's Tower, built in the 11th
century, stands in the grounds of
Pittencrieff House, now a museum.
 Pittencrieff Glen, which has fine views of
the Abbey and the Forth Estuary, was
given to Dunfermline by Andrew Carnegie,
the millionaire philanthropist born here in
1835. The first of nearly 3000 Carnegie
libraries was founded here.

DUMBARTON CASTLE *Standing high on its basalt rock, the castle, now a museum, was for centuries a
royal stronghold. The medieval building has vanished but the 17th- and 18th-century fortifications remain.*

On the Banks of the 'Silvery Tay'

'Beautiful railway bridge of the Silvery Tay,
Alas I am very sorry to say,
That 90 lives have been taken away,
On the last Sabbath day of 1879.'

WILLIAM MCGONAGALL, *Tay Bridge Disaster*

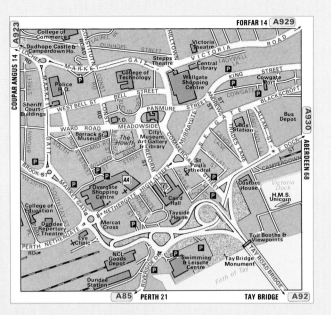

Scotland's fourth largest city stands on the banks of the Tay, backed by the Sidlaw Hills. Dundee has been known since the 19th century for its jams – in fact, Mrs Keiller began making marmalade in 1797; for jute – its carpet industry still flourishes; and journalism – the ever-popular comics, *Beano* and *Dandy* are published here. Since 1881 it has been a university city, and its royal charter dates back to the 12th century, at which time it had a castle and a monastery. A plaque on Castlehill marks the site of the castle, and commemorates William Wallace, who began his rebellion against the English by killing the son of Dundee's constable. Of the old town walls, all that remains is Cowgate Port (Wishart Ark). The Old Steeple, sole relic of St Mary's Church, typifies the fate of many of the city's old buildings: since Dundee was a strategic point in the defence of Central Scotland, it was fought over by English and Scots for more than 300 years. Much of what survived the many battles was in its turn pulled down to make way for industrial expansion.

A natural deep-water harbour on the Firth of Tay has made Dundee an all-cargo port, and an expanding base for the off-shore oil industry. Its shipyards built the *Terra Nova* for Shackleton and the *Discovery* for Scott; they still do work on ships destined for voyages in polar regions.

The toll bridge across the Tay, opened in 1966, is one of the longest (1½miles) river bridges in Britain, and links Dundee with Fife and southern Scotland. The railway bridge, on the main line between Edinburgh and Aberdeen was opened in 1887 to replace the one that collapsed in the 1879 disaster, made notorious by Dundee's self-styled poet, William McGonagall.

Dunhope Castle, now used as offices, was the home of the hereditary constable of Dundee, and was rebuilt in the 16th century when this office passed to the Graham family, by John Graham of Claverhouse, the 'Bonnie Dundee' made famous by Sir Walter Scott. On the opposite side of the city, the ruined Mains of Fintry Castle was also a Graham stronghold.

DUNDEE DOCKS *Like many ports on the east coast of Scotland, Dundee's harbour has enjoyed a new period of prosperity thanks to the exploitation of North Sea Oil.*

THE HARBOUR *(below) in 1840, full of sailing ships.*

PLACES TO SEE

The Albert Institute houses the Central Museum and Art Gallery; among the exhibits to do with the city's maritime traditions is a rare astrolabe of 1555.

Barrack Street Museum is also devoted to the city's seafaring history.

Camperdown House Formerly the residence of the Duncans, this now contains a fascinating and unusual museum of Scotland's national game, golf.

HMS Unicorn Lying in the Victoria Dock, this early 19th-century wooden warship has been renovated as a floating museum.

Broughty Castle (OACT) Four miles east of the city, the castle, a 19th-century estuary fort, has displays relating to the whaling industry, arms and armour, and natural history.

Durham, Co Durham

Medieval Stronghold on the Wear

'Grey Towers of Durham, yet well I loved thy mixed and massive piles. Half church of God, Half castle 'gainst the Scot'

SIR WALTER SCOTT, *Poems*

Built on a wooded rock, lapped on three sides by the River Wear, Durham is one of the most splendidly-sited of English cities. Dominating the sandstone outcrop, the dramatic outlines of cathedral and castle stand as a reminder of the great medieval strongholds of the Norman invaders. Durham was the only English city to be ruled as a County Palatinate by a Prince-Bishop, with his own army and privileges. The bishops retained this status, in name at least, until it was revoked by Act of Parliament in 1836.

The cathedral's defensive position, with the border country to the north as a second line of defence, was originally colonised by Saxon monks, particularly those driven from Holy Island by the war-mongering Vikings. Their monastery grew into a cultural and religious centre and was the shrine of the two great Saxon saints of the North: Cuthbert, whose coffin, the story goes, rooted itself to this spot; and the Venerable Bede, whose bones were stolen from Jarrow by Durham's Sacrist. These ecclesiastical treasures ensured that Durham prospered on pilgrims' money.

The Saxon monastery has long vanished, but the tombs of St Cuthbert and Bede were housed by the Normans in the cathedral they built. It is a magnificent building, uniting strength and size with grace. The whole of its main structure was built between 1093 and 1133; its great central tower being rebuilt in 1470. Particularly striking are the huge decorated pillars; the first successful execution on a grand scale of ribbed vaulting; and the evoca-

tive 12th-century sanctuary knocker which gave fugitives the right of sanctuary once they had seized hold of it. Sadly, all the ancient woodwork, save for Prior Castell's four-faced 15th-century clock, was destroyed by the 3000 Scotsmen that Cromwell imprisoned here after the Battle of Dunbar. The Normans set Durham Castle (OACT) beside the cathedral and it proved to be the only northern castle never to fall to the Scots. Inhabited ever since the Prince-Bishops made it their palace over 900 years ago, the castle today, with its 19th-century keep, is part of the university. The challenge of expanding the university from its fortified setting, enhanced by the 18th-century houses in North and South Bailey, has exercised the minds of such modern architects as Ove Arup, who designed one of the bridges.

The city itself grew compactly around the fortified rock. Its downhill streets and the steep,

THE BLACK STAIRCASE *(above)*, was installed by Bishop Cosin; THE SANCTUARY KNOCKER *(below)* dates from the 12th century.

winding alleys known as vennels, form one of the best townscapes in Britain, running past the 17th-century Bishop Cosin's House and the old grammar school, to the three old bridges across the Wear – Elvet, Prebends and Framwellgate. The 19th-century town hall was designed by the same architect who was responsible for the late-lamented Great Hall at Euston Station in London, and contains the relics of 'Lord' Tom Thumb, a tiny Polish violinist, just one metre tall, who died in 1837 aged 98.

PLACES TO SEE

Durham Cathedral Tomb of the Venerable Bede, the great early-English historian whose remains were brought from Jarrow in 1020. In the Monks' Dormitory Museum is the coffin of St Cuthbert and other cathedral treasures. In College Green, the cathedral close, are the Norman stables and monks' prison.

Durham Castle (OACT) Two chapels, one 11th-century, and the other 16th-century with beautifully carved choir stalls. The outstanding features of the castle are Bishop Cosin's magnificent three-storey Black Staircase and the 15th-century kitchens. Bishop Cosin's Library, in Palace Green, contains portraits and original furnishings.

Durham Heritage Centre The 17th-century church of St Mary-le-Bow now houses displays of the history and conservation of the city.

Saddler Street Nos. 43–4 have restored their original 18th-century frontage, thought to have been a theatre box-office.

Archaeology Museum Reached by a riverside path, the museum is housed in an old fulling mill.

Gulbenkian Museum of Oriental Art Collections of Egyptian, Chinese, Japanese and Tibetan art, including jade, ceramics and sculpture.

Durham Light Infantry Museum and Arts Centre As well as the history of the famous regiment, the building houses an Arts Centre.

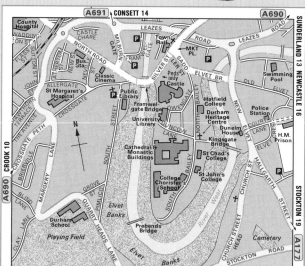

DUNGENESS, Kent   *6 TR01*
What the sea erodes elsewhere, it gives to Dungeness. It is still building up this isolated, flat, shingle headland at the tip of the Romney and Denge marshes. The area's unique atmosphere has not quite been destroyed by the untidy seaside chalets and the massive nuclear power station (OACT by arrangement). The 1200-acre nature and bird reserve has played host to over 200 local and migratory species of bird in the last ten years.

DUNKELD, Tayside   *27 NO04*
Choose from four separate vantage points for views of Dunkeld: Birnam Hill (1324ft), Craig Vinean (1247ft), the wooded Craigiebarns (1106ft) and Newtyle (996ft) – each offer differing aspects of this attractive cathedral town set in the wooded Tay Valley. The lawn-surrounded cathedral ruins (AM) date from the 14th and 15th centuries. The cathedral was despoiled in 1689 at the Battle of Dunkeld. The National Trust for Scotland's Visitor Centre is in the converted 'Little Houses' which were rebuilt after the battle. At the Loch of Lowes Nature Reserve, a variety of wildlife can be observed.

DUNOON, Strathclyde   *22 NS17*
For over 130 years Glasgow's holidaymakers have enjoyed the short boat trip from Gourock across the Firth of Clyde to this popular unspoilt resort. Behind the town is the wild country of the Cowal Peninsula in which lie the woods and waterfalls of Morag's Fairy Glen.
   In the grounds of Castle House is a statue of 'Highland Mary', sweetheart of Scotland's premier poet, Robert Burns.

DUNSTABLE, Bedfordshire   *11 TL02*
Dunstable Cross stands on one of England's earliest crossroads. Here, where Watling Street crossed the old Icknield Way, the Romans built the posting station which later grew into a market town and then into today's modern motor-manufacturing centre.
   Few old buildings remain. Of the priory, founded *circa* 1132, only the Norman nave and west front survived the Dissolution.
   On Dunstable Downs (NT), is Five Knolls, the county's best-known ancient burial site, a group of round barrows where a Bronze-Age skeleton was found.

DUNSTER, Somerset   *2 SS94*
This medieval, timbered Exmoor village boasts more to see than many a large town. The Norman castle (NT) sits on a wooded, pyramid-shaped hill at one end of the village, and at the other end is Conygar Hill Tower (1775), a noted landmark for Bristol Channel shipping. The former Priory Dovecote (OACT), the distinctive eight-sided yarn market and the packhorse bridge (AM) across the River Avill provide an interesting cross-section of English architectural styles between the 12th and 18th centuries.

DUNWICH, Suffolk   *12 TM47*
Dunwich has all but lost its battle with the sea. Looking today at the single street of this lonely fishing village, it is hard to visualise the once-prosperous port. The local museum records the savage storm in 1326 which swept away three of the town's nine churches and some 400 houses. Dunwich never recovered: gradually more of the town slipped into the sea. The shell of the 13th-century Greyfriars Monastery and ruined chapel of the 12th-century Leper hospital give an inkling of the town's architectural heritage.
   Dunwich Heath (NT) gives views of the Minsmere bird reserve and, beyond, Sizewell Gap Atomic Power Station.

DURDLE DOOR, Dorset   *3 SY88*
West of the famous Lulworth Cove lie two bays, divided by a limestone headland in which the sea has cut an arch – Durdle Door. This is one of the most beautiful parts of the Dorset coast. There is sheltered bathing and a 5-mile footpath – happily free of the military restrictions which bedevil this part of the county – along the high chalk cliffs.

DYMCHURCH, Kent   *6 TR12*
This old smuggling port on the edge of Romney Marsh is now a holiday village with miles of beach, chalets and caravans. The famous Romney Hythe and Dymchurch miniature steam railway passes through here en route to **Dungeness**.
   It was for centuries the headquarters of the 'Lords of the Level', local governors of this part of Romney Marsh, who met in New Hall. A restored Martello Tower (AM) is now a museum.

DYRHAM PARK, Avon   *3 ST77*
A 17th-century mansion (NT) originally built for William Blathwayt, Secretary of State to William III. The west front was designed in 1692 by the Huguenot Hautduroy; the east in 1698 by William Talman. Since Blathwayt had spent many years at The Hague, he developed a taste for Dutch paintings, Delftware and Dutch furniture.

DYSART, Fife   *24 NT39*
This Royal Burgh, with its old houses and rocky foreshore has now joined forces with **Kirkcaldy**. It was once an important harbour, trading with Holland, and nail-making was its major industry in the 18th century. In the old town notable buildings are a tolbooth damaged by Cromwell in 1576 and the ruined 16th-century St Serf's Church with its fortress-like tower.

DURDLE DOOR *The action of the sea has worn a great arch in the headland which divides two of Dorset's most unspoiled bays.*

ROMAN BRITAIN
The Advance of Civilisation

JULIUS CAESAR mounted a reconnaisance in force of southern England in 55 BC but it had few lasting consequences. An invasion was planned during the reign of Caligula (AD 37–41) but it did not materialise and it was not until the reign of Claudius that a large and successful invasion was mounted in AD 43, landing at Richborough in Kent and at two other as yet unidentified places. The Roman motives were varied. In part they were attracted by the agricultural and mineral resources of the islands and in part by the continuing drive to advance the frontiers of the Empire. Matters of politics and prestige were also important. Britain had long been a focus for Celtic religion and unrest, encouraging rebellion amongst the Celts in Gaul. Also, in order to maintain the trust of the native puppet rulers in the Empire, Rome had to be seen to support the king of the Atrebates tribe of southern England who had been expelled and had appealed to the Romans for help, while at the same time, the reputation of any Emperor who had achieved a conquest of Britain would be greatly enhanced.

More than 1500 years have passed since the collapse of Roman rule in Britain, yet many fascinating relics of the different facets of Roman life remain: evidence of their efficient network of roads is still apparent; solid remains of many of their forts and town walls have lasted for more than 1500 years and their great country estates may have formed the basis of today's field patterns.

UNREST AND UPRISINGS followed swiftly on the heels of the Roman advances. The Celts in southern England were swiftly defeated or offered submission and in the years that followed, the legions advanced northwards, establishing bases at Lincoln and York. A major rebellion led by Queen Boudicca of the Iceni tribe took place in AD 60, Colchester was sacked and refugees fled from London. But thereafter, the conquest of England and Wales was achieved and the Roman

forces pressed on into Scotland. The incorporation of the whole of Scotland into the Roman Empire was probably intended, but in the event, unrest amongst the Brigantes of northern England and the withdrawal of a legion for use on the continent led to the decision to build a defensible frontier between the Solway and the Tyne. Hadrian's Wall was the result, and its construction seems to have been decided during a visit to Britain by Emperor Hadrian in AD 122.

HARD KNOTT FORT *(above), which covered over two acres, guarded lonely Hard Knott Pass.*

MOSAIC *flooring (left) of outstanding quality at Lullingstone Roman Villa in Kent which dates from the 1st to the 5th century AD.*

THE ROMAN RULE of Britain showed up a distinction between the English lowlands, which, as Roman power consolidated) functioned as a civil zone with prosperous towns, productive farmlands and numerous extensive estates which were managed from villas occupied by Romans or by Romanised Britons, and the highland zone of the west and north. This latter area continued to be a military zone, penetrated by military roads, policed from camps and forts, producing valuable minerals such as lead, but never securely at peace.

The Roman contribution to the development of Britain came in many forms. Celtic Britain had reached the verge of civilisation, for its sprawling native capitals might almost have been regarded as towns and many of them contained mints which produced tribal coinages. The country however was fragmented between abandoned when Hadrian's Wall was built, then reoccupied as a small garrison town and later developed during the 3rd century as a supply town for the garrison of the wall, when it attracted a substantial civilian population. In addition to the military towns and splendid provincial foci, the new economic prosperity which resulted from Imperial rule encouraged the development of many other forms of town, ranging from unplanned, industrial, boom towns to roadside townlets and small rural service centres.

OWNERS OF VILLAS, which were both farms and elegant country houses, soon took control of the land in a number of agriculturally-productive areas in England. A number of fine examples have been excavated and opened to the public,

including Lullingstone villa in Kent and Chedworth villa in Gloucestershire, while Fishbourne in W Sussex seems to be much more than a villa and was most probably the palace of a native king. Even in the areas which were dominated by the villas, native farming practices seem to have continued, while in the north and west the indigenous lifestyle was little disrupted by the political changes. The remains of villages occupied at the time of Roman rule can be seen at Chysauster and Carn Euny in Cornwall, Din Lligwy on Anglesey and, less obviously, above Grassington in Yorkshire. Most dwellings in such native settlements continued to be built in the traditional circular manner, although Roman influences did gradually come to inspire the adoption of rectangular dwellings.

ROMAN MILITARY ARCHITECTURE in Britain was based on a range of designs tried and tested in continental campaigns. The simplest and most commonplace of Roman fortifications were the camps with earthen ramparts, like playing cards with rounded corners and usually with four entrances, one at the midpoint of each side. Some of the larger and more permanent fortifications had palisades of stout timber posts and the section of reconstructed palisade and gatehouse at the Lunt fort near Coventry revives the appearance of such defences. A number of formidable stone fortresses were integrated in the Hadrian's Wall system; Housesteads Fort is probably the most impressively restored example, preserving the typical rectangular plan and the remains of many of the internal buildings, while the most imposing remains at Chester Fort, a few miles away, are those of the bath-house. Other stone forts were strategically located to house garrisons and protect routeways in the more isolated upland areas and the most striking remains are those of Hard Knott Fort, which controlled Hard Knott Pass on the route traversing the Lake District. Some long sections of Hadrian's Wall survive and some of the finest views of the wall and its bleakly beautiful setting are obtained from Hotbank Crags just west of Housesteads and Peel Crags, about 3 miles further west. Hadrian's Wall was scarcely complete when the legions re-advanced into Scotland and constructed a new frontier work – the Antonine Wall – between the Forth and the Clyde. Most of the troops returned to garrison Hadrian's Wall in AD 163 and, being built of turf rather than stone, the Antonine Wall only survives in a much-eroded state. Perhaps the most dramatic of the military works surviving today are the Saxon shore forts built in the closing phases of Imperial rule when Britain was threatened by coastal barbarians; Burgh Castle in Suffolk, Richborough in Kent, Pevensey in E Sussex and Portchester in Hampshire all preserve fine stretches of wall.

LLANTWIT MAJOR *This painting by Alan Sorrell (1949) shows the Roman villa as it might have looked in the 4th century.*

a series of mutually hostile tribes and one of Rome's greatest achievements was that of offering a vision of a united and integrated territory. A keystone in the realisation of this goal was the provision of a 'national' system of roads, many of which survive as important thoroughfares.

THE TOWNS which the Roman established were of several different types. Many developed from military camps while the most prestigious of the provincial capitals displayed the neatly-planned lay-outs, imposing civic amenities, fine masonry and elegant accommodation evident in their continental prototypes. Although never one of the most important towns in Roman Britain, Corstopitum on the outskirts of modern Corbridge now displays some of the most impressive remains. It was established as a fort guarding a river crossing on the Tyne, in the 1st century,

HOUSESTEADS *was one of the largest of the 17 major forts built along Hadrian's Wall as quarters for the Roman troops.*

BARBARIAN ASSAULTS on Roman Britain increased during the latter part of the occupation and a particularly destructive invasion by Picts, Scots and Saxons took place in AD 367. The Romans were never completely vanquished in Britain and the collapse of Roman rule was caused by barbarian threats to the heart of the Empire. The British connection with Rome was largely severed around AD 410 following a period in which the Roman institutions and civilising influences had fallen into decline. Only in the closing decades of the Saxon period was centralised rule restored.

EARDISLAND, Hereford & Worcester 9 SO45

This beautiful village, a medley of brick, timbered and colour-washed houses is set in an equally lovely setting in the meadows of the River Arrow. Beside the old Bridge is a 13th-century yeoman's hall, and in the grounds of the manor house is an interesting gabled dovecot.

EASBY, N Yorkshire 19 NZ01

Situated on the banks of the River Swale, just a mile away from Richmond, the haunting ruins of 12th-century Easby Abbey (AM), founded for the Premonstratensians, are a silent testimony to the ravages of medieval warfare. St Agatha's Church, nearby, has ancient wall paintings, including an illustrated calendar of the labours of the months.

EASDALE, Strathclyde 21 NM71

Off the far west coast of Argyll, on the island of Seil, looking out across the Firth of Lorn to Mull, Easdale is a remote outpost in wild country, and it is a surprise to find An Cala Garden (OACT) where cherry trees, azaleas and roses blossom round rock and water gardens.

EAST BERGHOLT, Suffolk 12 TM03

John Constable, son of a local miller, was born here in 1776, and the landscape of Dedham Vale and the Stour Valley inspired this most English of English landscape painters. The birthplace has vanished, but his parents are buried in the churchyard, as is Willy Lott, whose little white cottage near Flatford Mill (NT) he often painted.

EASTBOURNE, E Sussex 5 TV69

Held to be one of the sunniest resorts in England, Eastbourne owes much to the Victorians who laid out many parks and gardens and built the pier. In the early 19th century, fortifications against the French included the Redoubt, transformed into a model village, aquarium, grotto and Services museum. The Museum of the RNLI is housed in the Wish Tower, which incorporates a Martello tower. In the Towner Gallery are works of 19th- and 20th-century British painters and sculptors.

EAST CLANDON, Surrey 5 TQ05

The village sits pleasantly around its 13th-century church, but the visitors come to see Hatchlands (NT), the 18th-century house, thought to be Robert Adam's first commission in England, built for Admiral Boscawen. **Clandon Park** stands near the sister-village of West Clandon.

EAST COKER, Somerset 3 ST51

An attractive village in its own right, with houses and church of golden Ham stone, East Coker was made famous by the poet T S Eliot, whose ashes lie in the place from which his forebears emigrated to America. 'East Coker' is the second of his cycle of poems, *Four Quartets*.

Wealden Towns and Villages
77 miles

The Sussex and Kentish Weald is the name given to the tract of hilly, wooded country that lies between the North and South Downs. Once the great primeval forest of Anderida clothed the Weald in dense woodland, isolating its scattered towns and villages, but now only small belts of trees remain.
From Eastbourne and Beachy Head, the route runs north across the Weald to Tunbridge Wells, returning south to cross the Pevensey Level and back to the coast.

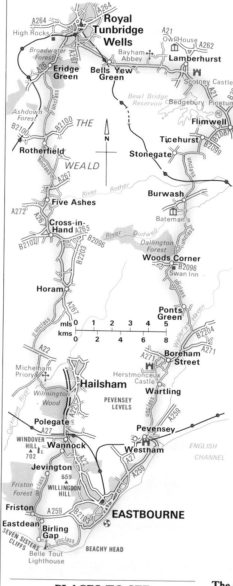

Leave **Eastbourne** by B2103. After the ascent turn left (unclassified) to Beachy Head. Continue to Birling Gap and **Eastdean**. Turn left on to A259: ascend and turn right, unclassified, for Jevington and **Polegate**. Turn left on to A22 and in 2¾ miles turn left (unclassified) to Michelham Priory. In ½ mile turn right then left (SP Golden Cross). On reaching A22 turn left, then take next right, unclassified (SP Horam). Later join A267 into **Horam** and continue to **Five Ashes**. In ½ mile turn left, unclassified (SP Rotherfield). In 2 miles turn right for **Rotherfield**. Keep forward with the Eridge road then in 4 miles turn right on to A26 and continue to **Tunbridge Wells**. Take A267 Eastbourne road and in almost ¾ mile turn left on to B2169 (SP Lamberhurst). Pass through Bells Yew Green and later pass a left turn to Bayham Abbey, then another left turn to the Owl House. In 1¼ miles go over crossroads (SP Hastings), then turn right to join A21, passing the entrance to Scotney Castle. In 4 miles, at **Flimwell**, turn right on to B2087 (SP Ticehurst) and later turn right again, B2099, into **Ticehurst**. Here turn left, unclassified, (SP Burwash). In 1 mile bear right, then in ¾ mile turn left and continue to **Burwash**. Turn right on to A265 then left (unclassified), SP Wood's Corner. In ½ mile pass a right turn to Bateman's, and 1 mile further turn right and drive to **Wood's Corner**. Here turn right and left (SP Bodle Street) and follow signs for Pont's Green, then Ninfield. Later turn right on to B2204 (SP Boreham Street), and in 1 mile right again, A271, to Boreham Street. In ½ mile turn left, unclassified, for **Wartling**, where bear right and continue to **Pevensey**. Turn right on to A259, then left to **Pevensey Bay**. Here turn right and return to Eastbourne.

PLACES TO SEE

Beachy Head The famous chalk promontory where the South Downs plunge down to the sea.

Michelham Priory Attractive ruins of a 13th-century Augustinian priory.

Tunbridge Wells In the Jacobean period this was a fashionable spa, much visited by Queen Anne and members of the court. The charming Pantiles is a street of this era.

Bayham Abbey (AM) Extensive ruins of one of the most impressive groups of buildings in Sussex.

The Owl House Gardens famed for spring flowers and shrubs surround this 16th-century smugglers' hideout.

Scotney Castle (NT) partly ruined 14th-century castle and 17th-century manor house.

Batemans (NT) Rudyard Kipling's home, this 17th-century stone manor house has many relics of the writer.

Herstmonceux Castle Home of the Royal Greenwich Observatory, the 15th-century castle has been restored.

Pevensey Impressive remains of the Norman castle, built on the site of a Roman fort.

EAST DEREHAM, Norfolk *12 TF91*
Now that the main A47 bypasses Dereham, its pleasant old character can be enjoyed. The market place has several handsome buildings in one of which the tragic poet William Cowper, spent his last four years. St Nicholas's Church contains a memorial to him and a noteworthy 15th-century font with carved panels. In the churchyard is St Withburga's Well, dedicated to the saint who founded a nunnery here in 654. Bishop Bonner's Cottages, 1502, house the museum, and at the nearby village of Gressenhall is the Norfolk Rural Life Museum, housed in an old workhouse.

EAST FORTUNE, Lothian *24 NT57*
The Museum of Flight is situated at East Fortune Airfield, part of the Royal Scotttish Museum. Exhibits, some of which can be operated by visitors, include a Spitfire, a de Havilland Sea Venom and Hawker Sea Hawk.

EAST GRINSTEAD, W Sussex *5 TQ33*
Sackville College (OACT), an early Jacobean almshouse founded by the 2nd Earl of Dorset in 1609, is still in use as an old people's home, but despite necessary modernisation, retains its character and some fine oak furniture. Although much built around, the old centre is basically that of a small market town, and several Tudor buildings can be found in the main street. The Queen Victoria Hospital was noted for its skill in plastic surgery during World War II. Standen (NT), off the B2110 south of the town is a late Victorian house with decorations by William Morris.

EAST LINTON, Lothian *24 NT57*
Preston Mill (NTS), with its attractive pantiled roof, is the oldest working water-driven meal mill in Scotland, and dates from the 18th century. Also of interest is Phantassie Doo'cot (NTS) which once housed 500 birds. Originally, it stood in the grounds of Phantassie mansion where the engineer John Rennie was born. Ruined Hailes Castle (AM), where Bothwell fled with Mary Queen of Scots, lies a mile away, and south of it rises Traprain Law, where a famous hoard of Roman silver was found.

EASTLEACH, Gloucestershire *3 SP10*
Eastleach Martin and Eastleach Turville, two enchanting hamlets on the banks of the River Leach, are linked by an old stone clapper bridge, called Keble bridge in memory of the founder of Keble College, Oxford, whose family owned Turville Manor. Eastleach Martin church has five old sundials; its neighbour has a beautifully carved Norman doorway.

EAST MEON, Hampshire *4 SU62*
The valley of the River Meon is the unspoiled setting for the pretty villages of East and West Meon. Peaceful East Meon, where a little stream runs alongside the main street, has a majestic Norman church, thought to be the work of Bishop Walkelyn of Winchester; like Winchester, it has a beautifully carved black Tournai marble font. The historic 15th-century Court House of the Bishops of Winchester, almost opposite, has been converted into a private house. At West Meon Thomas Lord after whom Lord's Cricket Ground in London, home of the MCC, is named, is buried.

THE ARMOURY *at Eastnor Castle contains such fine pieces as this resplendent 17th-century set of tourney armour.*

EASTNOR CASTLE, Hereford & Worcester *9 SO73*
Sir Robert Smirke designed this massive neo-Gothic castle (OACT) in 1812 for the 1st Earl Somers, whose son brought in Augustus Pugin to ornament the family home with lavish gilding and plasterwork.

EASTONS, THE, Essex *12 TL62*
In St Mary's Church at Little Easton are a series of superb paintings, the oldest dating back to the 12th century. There are also fine brasses and monuments to members of the Bourchier and Maynard families. Great Easton has the remains of an ancient castle.

EASTON FARM PARK, Suffolk *12 TM25*
Rare breeds of farm animals can be seen here, and in a reconstructed Victorian dairy visitors can see cows being milked by hand.

EBBW VALE, Gwent *8 SO10*
First coal-mining, then the steel industry have been the mainstays of Ebbw Vale. The town made the rails for the historic Stockton to Darlington railway, and was one of the first places to use the Bessemer process of converting iron to steel. Its name is forever linked with that of the great labour politician Aneurin Bevan who was its MP for 31 years, from 1929 to 1960.

ECCLEFECHAN, Dumfries & Galloway *18 NY17*
Arched House (NTS), so called because it was built over a pond, was the birthplace in 1795 of the scholar Thomas Carlyle. His statue is a prominent sight in the village, and he is buried in the churchyard.

EDALE, Derbyshire *15 SK18*
Dale and village are among the quieter parts of the Peak District, and offer superb walking country. The valley itself is sheltered, but the Kinder Hills can be bleak and forbidding. Mam Tor is the most famous local peak, its summit crowned by an Iron-Age fort. Kinder Scout, at 2088ft, is the highest plateau in the Peak District.

EDENHAM, Lincolnshire *11 TF02*
Impressive monuments to the family of the Earls of Ancaster, steadfast supporters of the Royalist cause in the Civil War, fill the lofty parish church of this stone-built village. Dominating the scene, Grimsthorpe Castle, a Tudor building, partly remodelled by Sir John Vanbrugh, stands amid fine parkland.

EDENSOR, Derbyshire *15 SK26*
Finding that the village spoiled the view from Chatsworth, the 6th Duke of Devonshire had it pulled down and rebuilt on its present site in 1839; his architect, giving reign to Gothic fantasy, created this charming model village in a variety of 'antique' styles.

PRESTON MILL *at East Linton dates from the 18th century but there has been a mill here since the 12th. Rank Hovis McDougall have done much to restore it and to find experienced millers to act as custodians.*

Edinburgh, Lothian 23 NT27

The Athens of the North

'Edinburgh . . . a lyric, brief, bright, clear and vital as a flash of lightning.'

CHARLOTTE BRONTË, *Letters*

Before the border between England and Scotland was finally settled, Edinburgh was part of Northumbria. Edwin, King of Northumbria, built the earliest fortress, which gives the city its name – 'Edwin's Burgh' – in the 6th century. The English King Edward I later took the castle and fortified it, and Robert the Bruce destroyed all but St Margaret's Chapel in 1313. Edward I captured it again, but the Scots finally retook it in 1341. Edinburgh, however, as a capital, is not as old as Dunfermline and Perth.

The old town, clustered in narrow, winding streets around the base of Castle Rock, was confined within the boundaries of the defensive King's Wall, built in 1450 by James II, and, unable to spread outwards, the buildings grew upwards in a maze of tenements, sometimes as much as 14 storeys high. Characteristic old buildings of this period may still be seen on the Royal Mile and around the Grassmarket. Eventually, the city outgrew these limits and extended towards Greyfriars Church and the area where the university now stands, but the threat of conflict with the English still kept the city within narrow limits until the 17th century. By the mid 18th century however, when life had become more settled, the loch, which lay at the foot of the castle where the railway stations and Princes Street Gardens are today, was drained, and increased shipping trade on the Firth of Forth brought the prosperity that resulted in the building of the New Town.

The contrast between the regular lay-out of the wide streets, crescents, squares and gardens of the Georgian development, and the winding, erratic streets of the old city can be seen simply by looking at a map, and the difference is equally striking as one crosses from the old to the new. James Craig was the principal architect of new Edinburgh, but Robert Adam, Thomas Hamilton and Charles Cockerell were also instrumental, at various times, in giving a new look to the city. Princes Street, named after the sons of George III, is the main east-west thoroughfare, with buildings on one side only, and open on the south to Princes Street Gardens with their famous floral clock, installed in 1903. Its parallel in the old city is the Royal Mile, which runs from Castle Hill down to the royal palace of Holyroodhouse, built in the 16th century by James IV.

Edinburgh won its nickname of the 'Athens of the North' in the 18th and early 19th centuries, when it was the home of many distinguished men of letters such as James Boswell, the philosopher David Hume, Sir Walter Scott and Thomas Carlyle. The university, founded in 1582, also expanded greatly in the 18th century and established the distinguished reputation which it enjoys today. Since 1947, the Edinburgh International Festival, held in August/September every year, contributes to the city's cultural life with an excellent range of theatrical productions, concerts, exhibitions and a host of avant-garde 'Fringe' activities.

In addition to its historical and cultural importance Edinburgh is naturally also the legal and administrative centre of Scotland. Here are housed the Supreme Courts of Justice, the Scottish Office, and, if devolutionists have their way, the Scottish Assembly. The Palace of Holyroodhouse is the monarch's official residence in Scotland.

FAITHFUL TO THE DEATH
Greyfriars Bobby, who watched over his master's grave for 14 years.

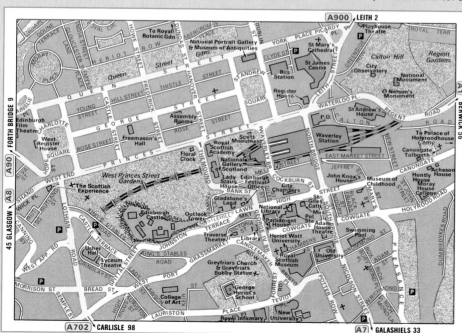

HOLYROODHOUSE *The palace (above), built by the Stuart kings, stands beside the ruins of an abbey founded by King David I.* THE MUSEUM OF CHILDHOOD *(left) has a rich collection of toys.*

John Knox's House A 15th-century house with many relics of the famous preacher.

The Museum of Childhood A rich collection of toys, books and games of all periods.

Canongate Tolbooth Once a prison, it is now used for exhibitions and a permanent display of Highland dress.

Huntly House A reconstructed 16th-century town house, with period rooms and workshops.

Palace of Holyroodhouse Charles II did most of the building, though there are older apartments associated with Mary Queen of Scots. The ruined Abbey of Holyrood stands beside the palace.

PLACES TO SEE: Old City

Edinburgh Castle Built on the commanding heights of a volcanic rock, the castle is a magnificent spectacle. The oldest part is St Margaret's Chapel, dedicated to the saintly queen of Scotland, sister of the Atheling, who married Malcolm III in 1109. The Great Hall dates from the reign of James IV and has a fine collection of armoury. In the Old Royal Palace are displayed the Scottish crown jewels. Mons Meg, the massive cannon forged in the 15th century, stands at the chapel door. The Military Tattoo is held every year on Castle Esplanade and marks the end of the festival.

Greyfriars Church Built in the 17th century, the church has many memorials to Covenanters. Nearby is the statue of Greyfriars Bobby.

Outlook Tower Fine views of the city from the top of this tower and a fascinating Camera Obscura.

Gladstone's Land Restored 17th-century merchant's house.

Lady Stair's House In a close off Lawnmarket, the house (1662) has exhibitions about Burns, Scott and Stevenson.

St Giles Cathedral Outside the west door is the 'Heart of Midlothian', marking the site of the Old Tolbooth prison, and outside the east door, the old Mercat Cross. St Giles has a beautiful 15th-century crown steeple, and its showpiece is the Thistle Chapel.

PLACES TO SEE: New City

National Gallery of Scotland Paintings by Scottish artists and the great European masters.

National Museum of Antiquities of Scotland and the **National & Portrait Gallery** are both to be found in Queen Street.

Scott Memorial Characters from his works fill 64 niches on this elaborate memorial erected by George Kemp in 1844.

Charlotte Square No 7 in this gem of Georgian architecture was designed by Robert Adam. The rooms have been furnished in period and in the basement is a display about the building of the New Town.

Royal Botanic Garden Situated some distance from the city centre, and noted for displays of rhododendrons. **The Scottish National Gallery of Modern Art** is also here.

Edinburgh Zoo Animals are housed in 80 acres of grounds. This is one of Europe's finest zoos.

EDNASTON, Derbyshire   *15 SK24*
The Manor House was designed by Sir Edwin Lutyens, one of the last of the builders of grand-scale country houses. The garden (OACT) has a large collection of flowering shrubs and plants of botanical interest.

EGHAM, Surrey   *5 TQ07*
At nearby Runnymede, King John was obliged to sign Magna Carta in 1215. Curiously enough, the monument that marks what is thought to be the historic site was erected by the American Bar Association, not the British. A plot of land opposite Magna Carta Island was given to the United States in 1963 and here stands the John F Kennedy memorial.

ELAN VALLEY, Powys   *8 SN96*
The picturesque scenery of this miniature Lake District is partly man-made, for the four lakes are reservoirs for the city of Birmingham. Garreg Ddu reservoir is separated from Caban Coch by a unique submerged dam. The other two lakes are Pen-y-Garreg and Craig Coch.

PEN-Y-GARREG, *one of four man-made lakes in the remote Elan Valley, is framed by wild moorland scenery.*

ELGIN, Grampian   *27 NJ26*
Even in ruins, Elgin Cathedral (AM), the 'Lantern of the North' is an impressive sight. The devastation caused in 1390 by the notorious 'Wolf of Badenoch' is the most famous incident, but the cathedral suffered several attacks, until the central tower finally collapsed in 1711.
    Elgin Museum contains a famous collection of fossils.
    Six miles away stands Pluscarden Abbey (OACT), founded in 1230 and restored by Benedictine monks.

ELLESMERE, Shropshire   *9 SJ33*
This pleasant little market town lies at the heart of Shropshire's lake district, a tranquil region of nine lakes in the northwest of the county. Some, such as Cole, Blake and Kettle Meres are small, wooded and more or less untouched by the 20th century; others, such as White Mere and The Mere, are used for sailing and other leisure activities; Crose Mere and Sweet Mere are well known for their bird life.

ELLISLAND FARM, Dumfries & Galloway   *18 NX98*
Robert Burns, Scotland's national poet, lived in this Nithdale farmhouse (OACT) from 1788 to 1791. It was here that he composed many of his poems, including the famous 'Tam O'Shanter'.

ELVASTON, Derbyshire   *15 SK43*
Elvaston Castle belonged to the Stanhope
family for centuries until the County
Council took it over in 1969 for use as a
country park. In addition to the
magnificent parkland and nature trails
there are beautiful formal gardens, a riding
centre and a countryside museum.

ELY, Cambridgeshire   *11 TL58*
The great mass of the cathedral, with its
soaring octagonal lantern and lofty west
tower, seems to dwarf the little fenland
market town that surrounds it. Until the
fens were drained in the 17th and 18th
centuries, Ely was isolated by water, which
makes the size and splendour of its
cathedral the more remarkable. The lantern
tower is a triumph, not only of medieval
craftsmanship, but also of engineering skill,
when one thinks of the great weight
supported on the ancient timbers. In the
North Triforium is an exhibition of stained
glass from redundant churches and other
buildings. Ely also has much fine carving,
particularly in the choir stalls and chapels,
but during the Reformation, many of the
statues were damaged – especially in the
Lady Chapel where vandalism was at its
worst. Oliver Cromwell lived in what is
now the vicarage to St Mary's Church when
he was a collector of cathedral tithes.

EMBLETON, Northumberland
24 NU22
A path leads from the village to the ruins of
Dunstanburgh Castle (AM, NT) which
stands high on the cliffs, looking out over
the North Sea. It dates from the 14th
century and parts of it were built by John of
Gaunt, Duke of Lancaster.

EMPINGHAM, Leicestershire
11 SK90
Among the many delightful towns and
villages Leicestershire gained when
Rutland was absorbed are Empingham,
where the 13th-century parish church
contains a fine sedilia and piscina, and its
neighbouring villages. Rutland Water, a
large reservoir near Empingham, has
become a favourite local beauty spot.

EPPING FOREST, Essex   *6 TL40*
For east Londoners, Epping Forest is a
welcome and extensive 6000-acre tract of
beautiful woodland, and it is hard to
imagine the original area of the forest which
must have been in the region of 100,000
acres. The woodland is particularly famous
for its hornbeams: there is a conservation
centre at High Beech.
   Queen Elizabeth's hunting lodge at
Chingford has displays explaining the
history of the forest.

EPSOM, Surrey   *5 TQ26*
Horse-racing has been an established sport
on Epsom Downs since the 18th century. It
is here that the Derby is run, that most
famous of English flat races, named after
the Earl of Derby in 1780; the Oaks, named
after his country seat, had been instituted
in 1779. The town was, in the past, well
known for medicinal springs; Epsom Salts
can still be purchased.

EPWORTH, Humberside   *16 SE70*
The Old Rectory (OACT) birthplace and
home of the founding fathers of
Methodism, John and Charles Wesley, was
burnt down by a mob who objected to their
father's politics in 1709, two years after the

birth of Charles. It was rebuilt and still
contains family furniture and other
memorabilia.

ESHER, Surrey   *5 TQ16*
Claremont Woods (NT), near Esher, form
part of the grounds of Claremont House.
Three of England's foremost landscape
artists, Sir John Vanbrugh, William Kent
and Capability Brown were employed at
different times to design this lovely park.

ETON, Berkshire   *5 SU97*
Linked to **Windsor** by the old bridge over
the Thames, the ancient town of Eton has
become synonymous with England's
second oldest public school, round which
the life of the town revolves. The college
(parts OACT) founded by Henry VI in
1440, stands at the end of the long main
street. Lower School, dating from 1443,
and still in use, and the chapel, similar to
that of King's College, Cambridge, also
founded by Henry VI, are the original
buildings, though the school has grown
enormously over the years. Other parts of
the college, such as Lupton's Tower, the
cloisters and Upper School, where various
scholars, among them Shelley and
Gladstone, have carved their names on the
desks and the panelling, can also be visited
when not being used by the school.

EUSTON, Suffolk   *12 TL87*
Stuart portraits by Van Dyck and Lely are
the chief attractions in a remarkable
collection of paintings on show at Euston
Hall (OACT), home of the Duke of
Grafton. The house was originally built in
the 1770s and rebuilt after a fire in 1902.

EVESHAM, Hereford & Worcester
9 SP04
The town lies on the River Avon, at the
centre of the fertile Vale named after it, a
region of orchards. Evesham has many
interesting old buildings, including the
Round House, also known as Booth Hall, a
charming half-timbered structure that
stands in the market place and was formerly
an inn. In the Abbey Gardens are, besides
the ruined abbey, two churches, St
Nicholas and All Saints, and a lovely 16th-
century bell tower. The Almonry (OACT),
a 14th-century building connected with the
abbey, houses a museum of local history.

EWELL, Surrey   *5 TQ26*
Finds from Nonsuch Palace, the great
house begun by Henry VIII are displayed
in the interesting museum of local interest
which forms part of Bourne Hall Cultural
Centre. In the same building are an art
gallery, library and theatre. Of Nonsuch
Palace, nothing but the park remains.

EWENNY, Mid Glamorgan   *8 SS97*
Ewenny Priory (AM), on the outskirts of
Bridgend, was founded in 1141 for the
Benedictines. Although largely ruined, the
buildings are still surrounded by their
defensive walls. The nave of the priory
church is still in use.

EWLOE CASTLE, Clwyd   *14 SJ26*
Unlike many other so-called Welsh castles,
Ewloe (AM) was built by the Welsh, not
the invading English. Llewelyn the Great is
thought to have founded it, and Llewlyn ap
Gruffydd extended and fortified it in the
13th century.

NORMANTON CHURCH *near Empingham is the survivor of a village destroyed by 18th-century magnate,
Sir Gilbert Heathcote. His memorial calls him: 'A great Instrument in founding . . . the Bank of England'.*

South-Western Sentinel

'Excester is a large rich, beautiful, populous, and was once a very strong city, but as to the last, as the castle, the walls and all the old works are demolished . . .'

DANIEL DEFOE, *A Tour through the Whole Island of Great Britain*

Founded in about AD 50 by the Romans, Exeter has a long history, though much of the physical evidence was destroyed by the Germans in 1942. Parts of the Roman walls, much strengthened in the Norman period, still stand, and can best be seen around Southernhay and Paul Street. In Anglo-Saxon times Exeter flourished, but was several times sacked by the Danes, and eventually, in 1068, captured by the Normans. William I promptly built a castle, of the distinctive local sandstone, and the ruins of the walls, gatehouse and Athelstan's tower now form part of the aptly named Rougemont ('red hill') Gardens.

Thereafter Exeter flourished from the proceeds of the cloth trade and from continental trade through its port, until the Countess of Devon in 1290 built a weir across the river to spite the citizens. In 1563, however, predating the canal era by two centuries, the Exeter ship canal opened and trade was restored, so that Daniel Defoe could write, around 1724; 'The city derives a very great correspondence with Holland, as also directly Portugal, Spain and Italy; shipping off vast quantities of woollen-manufactures. . . .' Nowadays other industries have superseded shipping and the docks are largely disused.

Exeter cathedral dates from the early medieval period, apart from the two towers, which are Norman. Its magnificent west front has tiers of figures of kings, queens and angels. Around the cathedral precinct, some of Exeter's old buildings survived both the air-raids and modern development. The best-known is Mol's Coffee House, now an art shop, where, it is said, Drake and Hawkins used to meet. St Martin's Church, consecrated in 1065, has a fine wagon roof and 17th-century gallery. Other interesting churches are the Norman St Mary Arches and St Mary Steps which has a 17th-century clock with moving figures which strike the hour and the quarters. Alone of all England's medieval cities Exeter had a man-made pure water supply. The underground passages built as conduits can be seen in Princesshay. Exeter University occupies an attractive campus just outside the city.

THE MARITIME MUSEUM *Hundreds of craft from all over the world can be seen at the museum, many of them afloat.*

PLACES TO SEE

Exeter Cathedral The 300ft-long nave is the longest span of unbroken Gothic rib-vaulting in the world, and is also noted for the beautifully carved roof bosses. Much fine wood-carving, including the earliest set of misericords in England, an elaborate Bishop's throne and an exquisite minstrel's gallery. The Cathedral Library has priceless old manuscripts.

MOL'S COFFEE HOUSE *where Drake and others used to meet.*

Maritime Museum More than 100 craft from all over the world are housed in the docks and canal basin. Some are afloat and can be boarded. A river ferry links the two parts of the museum.

Rougemount House Museum contains local archaeological discoveries.

Royal Albert Memorial Museum houses collections of local interest, including natural history, Honiton lace, china and glass.

St Nicholas Priory Restored remains of Benedictine Priory with Norman undercroft.

Tuckers' Hall The old hall of weavers, fullers and shearmen, dating from the 15th century.

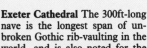

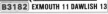

EXMOOR, Somerset/Devon   2

From the coast at Combe Martin to the Brendon Hills, 265 square miles of moorland have been designated a National Park, and should thus be safe from development, though the whole of Exmoor is remarkably unspoiled. The underlying sandstone has created less dramatic scenery than the granite of **Dartmoor**, but the gentle contours are no less beautiful, with their hidden network of valleys and belts of woodland. Dunkery Beacon (1705ft) is the highest point.

Red deer, as well as ponies, still roam the moor and are sometimes hunted – Exford is the centre – and Bampton in Devon holds a famous pony fair in October.

Of the many rivers crossing Exmoor, the Barle and the Exe are the most important. The famous ancient clapper bridge, 'Tarr Steps' (AM, NT) crosses the Barle south-west of Winsford Hill. Other well-known tourist attractions are Doone Valley, setting of R D Blackmore's *Lorna Doone*; Brendon, a show-piece village, as is Dunster, with its famous ancient castle (NT); and, of course, the seaside resorts – Minehead and Lynmouth are the most popular. The whole coastline, with its towering cliffs, is superb.

THE BEACON VAULTS *This Exmouth inn sign recalls the days of signal fires.*

EXMOUTH, Devon   2 SY08

Although not an especially attractive town, Exmouth is the oldest of Devon's seaside resorts. The Country Life Museum at Sandy Bay has hundreds of exhibits and many farm animals. A La Ronde (OACT) two miles from the town is a unique 16-sided house designed by the Misses Parminster in 1798 and contains many curiosities, including a shell gallery.

EYAM, Derbyshire   15 SK27

This is the plague village, whose rector, William Mompesson, persuaded his parishioners to isolate themselves when plague struck in 1665 and so prevent the disease reaching other communities. More than 80 per cent of the villagers died. A memorial service is held at the end of August every year in a nearby dell called Cucklet Church where Mompesson held open-air services in the plague year. In the churchyard, where his wife, a plague-victim, is buried, there is an unusual 18th-century sundial which tells world-time. Eyam is one of several Derbyshire villages which take part in well-dressing ceremonies (second to last Sunday in August).

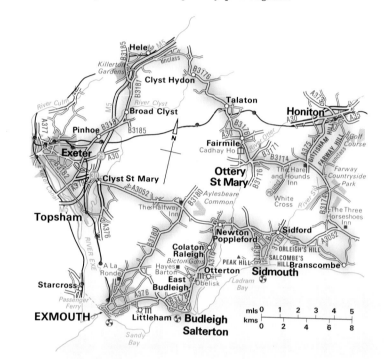

East Devon Hills and Rivers
73 miles

The attractive coastal resorts of East Devon lie amid hilly country in the shadow of the great city of Exeter, Devon's capital. The Rivers Clyst and Otter occupy pleasant valleys, peopled by quiet towns and sleepy villages of great charm. At Honiton lace, the traditional industry of the town, is still hand-made, and Sidmouth, on the coast, preserves an atmosphere of quiet elegance.

Leave **Exmouth** on A376, and drive through **Budleigh Salterton**. Two miles beyond it, turn left for **East Budleigh**. Turn right by East Budleigh church and shortly rejoin A376. Pass Bicton Gardens and in 1½miles turn right on to A3052 into **Newton Poppleford**. Later turn right on to B3176 for Sidmouth.

Leave Sidmouth by B3175 (SP Honiton) and drive to **Sidford**. Turn right on to A3052, climb Orleigh Hill and, ½mile beyond the top, turn right for Branscombe. From **Branscombe** follow signs for Beer as far as the top of a hill, then turn left (SP Honiton). In 1 mile turn left on to A3052. After ¾mile pass the Three Horshoes Inn and turn right on to B3174. After 2½miles bear right on to an unclassified road and cross Farway Hill. In ¾mile keep forward for Honiton, and turn left by a golf course to descend into **Honiton**. Turn left into the High St (the Exeter road), and in ¾mile turn left on to A375 (SP Sidmouth). Climb Gittisham Hill and continue to the Hare and Hounds

Inn. Turn right on to B3174 into **Ottery St Mary**. Leave along Hind St (B3176) and cross the river to Cadhay House, then cross A30 at Fairmile and follow signs for Cullompton. Continue to **Clyst Hydon** and, at the end of the village, turn right. In ¾mile turn left, then in 2miles, at B3185 junction, turn left and right for **Hele**.

Pass under M5, cross the River Culm and turn left. After 1½miles keep forward on B3185, recross the Culm and in ¾mile turn right for Killerton Gardens. Return to B3185, and at the junction with B3181 turn right. Pass through **Broad Clyst** and go forward on B3212 Exeter road. On the outskirts of Exeter, turn left for the ring road. Join A3052 and at the roundabout with B3182, take 1st exit SP Topsham. Continue from **Topsham** to a T-junction in Clyst St George. Turn left here and, at the roundabout at **Clyst St Mary**, take the third exit (SP Lyme Regis, A3052). In 4¾miles, at the Halfway Inn, turn right on to B3180 to complete the return journey to Exmouth.

PLACES TO SEE

A la Ronde A unique 16-sided house, built in 1789, with a curious shell gallery.

Bicton Gardens A pinetum and countryside museum are among the attractions of these gardens, parts of which can be seen by miniature railway.

Sidmouth Unspoiled Regency town, its bay ringed by dramatic sandstone cliffs.

Honiton Famous for lace-making, displays of which are given at Allhallows Museum.

Ottery St Mary Beautiful church and, just outside the village, off B3176, 16th-century Cadhay House.

Killerton House & Gardens (NT) The 18th-century house contains a costume museum and is set in lovely grounds.

EYE, Suffolk *12 TM17*
This little brick- and flint-built town on the
Suffolk-Norfolk border is famed for its
beautiful church tower, a soaring, slender
edifice of characteristic Suffolk flushwork.
The timber-framed Guildhall dates back to
the 16th century.

EYE, Hereford & Worcester *9 SO54*
The Manor House, which was built in 1680
for a West Indian sugar planter,
Ferdinando Gorges, is famous for its
elaborately moulded plaster ceilings,
decorated with swathes of foliage, fruit and
flowers. The house has recently changed
hands and future plans are uncertain.

EYNSFORD, Kent *6 TQ56*
Around this little village is grouped a trio of
interesting ancient buildings. The oldest is
Lullingstone Roman Villa (AM), which has
a fine tessellated pavement. Twelfth-
century Eynsford Castle (AM) is ruined,
but Lullingstone Castle (OACT) is still
inhabited by descendants of the Peche
family who owned the estate in the 14th
century. There is a fine Tudor gatehouse,
and the 'castle', actually a Tudor manor
house remodelled in the 18th century, has
impressive State Rooms.

FAIRFORD CHURCH *Ancient stained glass
windows tell the story of the Christian faith from
the Creation onwards.*

FAIRFORD, Gloucestershire *4 SP10*
Fairford is one of the most attractive and
least spoiled of the Cotswold towns. Lying
on the gentle River Coln, its chief glory is
its late 15th-century church built,
unusually for England, to one uniform
design by John Tame, a wealthy cloth
merchant. Twenty-eight impressive stained
glass windows dating from the 15th and
16th centuries depict the entire Christian
faith from the Creation to the Last
Judgment in fascinating detail.
    John Keble, poet and cleric, author of
the classic work *The Christian Year*, was
born here in 1792. Keble College, Oxford
was founded in his memory.

FALKLAND, *a royal burgh, was the site of the former hunting palace of the Stuart kings. Its distinctive
round towers can be seen at the end of the attractive town square.*

FAIR ISLE, Orkney & Shetland
28 HZ27
This, the most remote inhabited island in
Britain, only three miles long and under
two miles wide, lies mid-way between the
Orkney and Shetland Isles.
    Its bird observatory, (which offers
limited accommodation to ornithologists)
has recorded over 300 species of wild birds
ranging from the alpine swift to the osprey
and is noted for its contribution towards
bird-migration research. The island is
perhaps most famous for its unmistakable
knitted wear.

FAIRLIE, Strathclyde *22 NS25*
A small resort, on the Firth of Clyde,
Fairlie has a sandy beach and a pier; an
anchorage protected by the island of Great
Cumbrae opposite; a well-known yacht-
builders; and a ferry service to Arran
(though cars must go from **Largs**), whose
mountains rise to the south-west. St
Margaret's Church contains the ancient
Fairlie Stone.
    The ruins of Fairlie Castle grace the top
of a pretty glen. Kelburn Castle nearby
(OACT), a mansion built in about 1700
onto an ancient tower, is the seat of the
Earls of Glasgow, and is set in lovely
grounds, where there are nature trails and
craft workshops.

FALKIRK, Central *22 NS88*
Falkirk, situated on the Firth of Forth, is a
centre for coal-mining and for the great
Carron Ironworks, which began making
'carronades', as the cannon were known,
for Nelson's navy in 1760. Falkirk Museum
has some interesting local exhibits and just
west of the town is Rough Castle (AM), one
of the 19 Roman forts which guarded the
Antonine Wall. On the east of the town, in
the grounds of Callendar House is one of
the best-preserved sections of the wall (AM).

FALKLAND, Fife *23 NO20*
On the fringe of the fertile Howe of Fife,
Falkland is a small and ancient royal burgh,
its cobbled streets bordered by picturesque
old houses and weavers' cottages. The town
is sited below the Lomond Hills. Falkland
Palace and Gardens (NTS), the old hunting

palace of the Stuarts until 1625, was built in
the mid 16th century in Renaissance style.
Its tennis court is the oldest in Britain –
1539. Sir Walter Scott used the Palace in
The Fair Maid of Perth.

FALLS OF GLOMACH, Highland
26 NH02
The Falls (NTS), among the highest in
Britain, cascade from a height of 370ft
above wild Glen Elchaig. They are hard to
reach, off the road between the Kyle of
Lochalsh and Cluanie, north of the Five
Sisters of Kintail.

FALMOUTH, Cornwall *1 SW83*
Sir Walter Raleigh can claim some of the
credit for putting Falmouth on the map: it
was he who saw the commercial
possibilities of this large natural harbour. It
became the first station for the Royal Mail
Packet Service in 1688, reaching its heyday
in 1827 when 39 packet steamers operated
from the port. Nowadays its dry dock is
home to huge modern oil tankers. The
town with its lovely setting on the Cornish
Riviera developed as a holiday resort in the
19th century following the arrival of the
Great Western Railway. Pendennis Castle
(AM) was one of Henry VIII's coastal forts
and was the last Royalist stronghold in
England to surrender to Cromwell.
Together with St Mawes Castle (AM) on
the opposite side of Carrick Roads, it
guards the harbour. The Church of St
Charles the Martyr was built in the 17th
century and dedicated to Charles I. Among
the 18th- and 19th-century buildings near
the harbour is 'King's Pipe' – a chimney
where tobacco-smugglers' dreams literally
went up in smoke – burnt by Excise men.

FARNBOROUGH, Hampshire *4 SU85*
To most people, Farnborough means the
Royal Aircraft Establishment and the
biennial International Airshow. The town
itself is unexceptional but nearby is St
Michael's Abbey, built in 1881 in
flamboyant French Gothic style by the
Empress Eugénie, wife of Napoleon III,
who lived in exile in nearby Farnborough
Hall, now a convent. St Peter's Church has
a Norman nave and a 17th-century tower.

FINCHINGFIELD *The green, ancient bridge and duckpond combine to make this much photographed Essex village a tourist magnet.*

FARNE ISLANDS, Northumberland
24 NU23
A collection of 15 or so islands of bare volcanic rock lying between two and five miles off the Northumberland coast, the Farne Islands form a noted wild-life sanctuary. Boat trips from Bamburgh or Seahouses give visitors exciting close-ups of grey seals and seabirds.

Largest, and nearest to the mainland, is Farne Island , its 16th-century tower built by Prior Castell of Durham, now converted into the headquarters of the Farne Islands Bird Observatory.

FARNHAM, Surrey   *4 SU84*
A small, red-brick country town, happily unspoilt despite its position in prime commuter country, Farnham has a wealth of handsome Georgian and earlier buildings, including gabled 17th-century almshouses and half-timbered Tudor buildings. A wide street lined with attractive shops and houses leads up to Farnham Castle. It has a Norman keep (OACT), and the remainder (not open) was built between the 15th and 17th centuries. The William Cobbett Inn, formerly the Jolly Farmer was the birthplace in 1763 of William Cobbett, the radical politician and author of *Rural Rides*.

FAVERSHAM, Kent   *6 TR06*
There is evidence of a Saxon village here in King's Field and the Romans were also later settlers. Once a flourishing port, it has now settled into being a market town whose main claim to fame is the wealth of Tudor, Stuart and Georgian buildings, of which over 50 are listed for preservation. In the former Queen's Arms James II was held prisoner after his capture when he tried to flee the country in 1688. The Church of St Mary of Charity is partly Norman, partly Early English, in style with particularly fine misericords. The Chart Gunpowder Mills (OACT) date from the late 18th century and are a reminder of the town's importance as a centre of the gunpowder industry.

FELBRIGG, Norfolk   *12 TG23*
Felbrigg Hall (NT) is a beautiful example of Jacobean architecture with surrounding gardens laid out in the 19th century by Humphry Repton.

The present village lies one mile east of the original Danish settlement, whose position in the hall grounds is marked by the surviving Perpendicular church with its rare 14th-century brasses commemorating Simon de Felbrigg.

FELIXSTOWE, Suffolk   *12 TN33*
A busy but unpretentious seaside resort since the late 19th century, Felixstowe is now perhaps better known as a roll-on, roll-off cargo and container port serving Rotterdam and Zeebrugge, and as an oil-tanker terminal. An elegant promenade arcs round the two-mile long Felixstowe Bay, its Victorian and Edwardian houses with well-tended gardens and lawns, overlooking the shingle beach. The Dooley, one of the town's oldest inns, has numerous doors – allegedly to allow customers plenty of choice in escaping from Press Gangs and Revenue Men.

FETTERCAIRN, Grampian   *27 NO67*
This mid 18th-century village sits on the edge of the Howe of Mearns, near the Cairn o' Mount Pass over the Grampians. Queen Victoria and the Prince Consort once visited it and the great Gothic memorial arch is hard to miss. Fasque (OACT), home of the Gladstone family since 1829 has mementoes of the Prime Minister, and displays of domestic life in a 19th-century mansion.

FILEY, N Yorkshire   *16 TA18*
Charlotte Brontë was a frequent visitor to this clifftop holiday resort, with its sandy beach and elegant hotels. The Romans established a signal station on Carr Naze headland, below which lies Filey Brigg, a mile-long jagged reef forming a natural breakwater, and now part of a nature trail. A few surviving fishing cobles (a type of boat) on the beach are a reminder of more prosperous fishing days for the town.

St Oswald's Church, mainly Early English in style, has a fine south doorway and massive tower adorned by a fish-shaped weather vane.

The town lies on the Cleveland Way, a 90-mile, long-distance footpath which runs from Saltburn-on-Sea to Helmsley, inland on the North Yorkshire Moors.

FINCHAMPSTEAD, Berkshire
4 SU76
Finchampstead, with Easthampstead, is one of the oldest villages of the Great Windsor Forest, which, in the early 19th century, covered 59,000 acres.

Its church, with early Norman font and 18th-century brick tower, sits on a platform enclosed by earthworks. Finchampstead Ridges (NT) one mile north-east, offer fine views over heath, heather, and woodland stretching over three counties. Nine-Mile Ride follows the line of the former Roman Road and a splendid double avenue of Sequoia Pines borders Crowthorne Road.

FINCHINGFIELD, Essex   *12 TL63*
Duck pond, stream, green, church on the hill and a pleasant jumble of variously shaped and sized houses all combine to make this one of the most photogenic and photographed villages in Britain. The church of St John the Baptist has a Norman tower with an 18th-century bell turret and there is a handsome 15th-century timber-framed Guildhall which now houses the local museum.

FIRLE, E Sussex   *5 TQ40*
Firle Place (OACT) is a charming Georgian stately home with a Tudor core, home of the Gage family for 500 years. It contains a connoisseur's collection of Old Masters, porcelain and furniture. From the nearby village of West Firle a track leads up to Firle Beacon with commanding views of the Weald and the English Channel.

FISHBOURNE, W Sussex   *4 SU80*
Fishbourne's Roman Palace (OACT) was a splendid and skilful example of Roman architecture and, extending over six acres, the biggest site discovered in Britain. Just west of the important settlement at Chichester, it was inhabited during the 2nd and 3rd centuries AD, the height of Roman occupation. Archaeologists did not discover the Palace until 1960 although in medieval times a ploughman is known to have cut a furrow across one of its mosaic pavements. For these pavements Fishbourne is famous, especially the centre-piece of the boy on the dolphin. The museum gives a good idea of life in the Palace, and a formal garden has been re-created along Roman lines in the courtyard formed by the four wings.

FISHGUARD, Dyfed   *7 SM93*
Fishguard, with its attractive old harbour, quay, cottage rows and bridge over the River Guann made a fitting setting for the 1971-film-version of Dylan Thomas' *Under Milk Wood*. The town enjoyed the unlikely honour of being the venue of the last invasion of Britain: in 1797, the Black Legion, a French force commanded by the Irish-American William Tate, landed below Carregwasted Point intending to raise a rebellion against George III. They allegedly mistook the local women's red cloaks for British uniforms and surrendered.

Across the North Downs
69 miles

The rolling North Downs of Kent halt abruptly at the white cliffs of Dover, chief of the ancient Cinque Ports whose castles guard the English Channel. Inland, Canterbury, metropolitan city of the Anglican Church, preserves its 2000 years of English history.

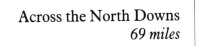

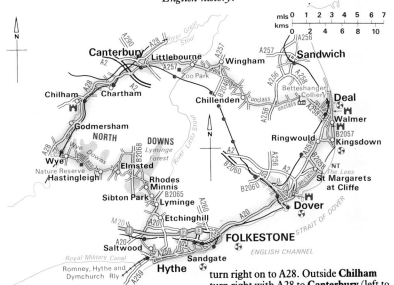

Leave **Folkestone** by A259 (SP Hythe) and follow the coast through Sandgate to **Hythe**. Approaching the town, turn left at the roundabout (SP Hastings), follow the one-way system, at the end of which turn right (SP Ashford A261). Past the station, keep left, then turn right for Saltwood. Ascend, shortly turning left, then bear right with Bartholomew Lane. At **Saltwood**, turn left on to the Sandling road (detour right for the castle), and in 1¼miles at the junction with A20 turn right (SP Folkestone) crossing over M20. In about ½mile branch left (SP Lyminge) and in 1½miles join B2065. On the far side of **Lyminge** turn left (SP Rhodes Minnis) passing through the village where at the Gate Inn turn left (SP Stone Street). At the junction with B2068 turn right (SP Canterbury) then in 1½miles turn left (SP Hastingleigh, Wye). In 2 miles bear right then keep left for **Hastingleigh**. Follow the Wye road through **Wye**, then Ashford signs to a T-junction where the route turns right, crosses the river and a level crossing, then right again (SP Canterbury). In a mile

turn right on to A28. Outside **Chilham** turn right with A28 to **Canterbury** (left to visit village). Follow Dover then Sandwich signs to leave Canterbury on A257, passing through **Littlebourne** (for a detour to Bekesbourne Zoo Park turn right) to **Wingham**. Turn right on to B2046 (SP Folkestone), left (SP Goodnestone) then right again to reach a T-junction where the route turns right to **Chillenden**. Go over the crossroads (SP Eyethorne), then turn left (SP Northbourne, Deal). Follow Deal signs, cross the main road, then in 1½miles at a T-junction turn right and left, then at the main road right on to A258 for **Deal**. At the roundabout on the front turn right (SP Walmer, Dover) then branch left on to B2057 (SP Kingsdown). At **Kingsdown** bear right, then turn right for **Ringwould** where the route turns left on to A258 (SP Dover). In 1¾miles turn left on to B2058 for **St Margaret's-at-Cliffe**. Pass the church and turn right into Reach Road (or keep forward for the bay), then continue towards Dover, at the main road turning left with A258. At the foot of the hill turn left again to enter **Dover**. Follow the Folkestone signs and leave on A20 to return to Folkestone.

PLACES TO SEE

Folkestone Channel port and home (OACT) of the writer H G Wells.

Hythe Cinque Port and terminus of the Romney, Hythe and Dymchurch narrow-gauge railway.

Saltwood Castle (OACT) from which murderers of Thomas Becket set out for Canterbury.

Wye Nature Reserve on the Downs nearby.

Chilham One of the prettiest villages in Kent. Gardens (OACT) of Chilham Castle.

Canterbury Magnificent Norman cathedral and shrine of Thomas Becket. Many other ancient and interesting buildings are to be found in the old streets of this historic city.

Littlebourne Bekesbourne Zoo Park.

Deal Castle (AM) built by Henry VIII, and delightful old town.

Walmer Castle (AM) and official residence of the Lord Warden of the Cinque Ports.

Dover Castle (AM), Town Hall Museum, Roman Painted House.

FLADBURY, Hereford & Worcester
9 SO94
An attractive village on the River Avon, Fladbury has a restored Norman church containing notable 15th-century brasses. Delamere Bird Gardens (OACT) offer a wide range of attractions from animals to model railways.

FLAMBOROUGH, Humberside
16 TA27
A sea-faring village with whitewashed stone cottages high on the chalk cliffs, Flamborough is exposed on three sides to the often-fierce, North-Sea winds. St Oswald's Church, probably Norman in origin, was largely rebuilt some 300 years later and has a rare 15th-century rood screen and loft. It contains a bizarre monument to Sir Marmaduke Constable (d. 1520) – his heart being swallowed by a toad.

The famous lighthouse (AM) looks out over the North Sea from Flamborough Head which is almost severed from the mainland by Danes' Dyke, an Iron-Age earthwork. A mile of the Dyke is now a nature trail. Nearby Bempton, on the cliffs, is the most important mainland breeding ground for seabirds in England. It is partly owned by the RSPB who provide visitor's observation posts.

FLEETWOOD, Lancashire   18 SD34
Four miles of beach with distant views of the Lake District mountains make this peninsular port on the Wyre estuary an attractive holiday resort, but Fleetwood's prosperity previously depended upon its famous deep-sea trawler fleet, and efforts to save it are being made.

The town was founded in 1836 by Sir Peter Fleetwood-Hesketh of Rossall Hall and was once a busy ferry and rail link with Ireland, Scotland and the **Isle of Man**.

FLINT, Clwyd   14 SJ27
Edward I built the first of his Welsh castles (AM) here on the banks of the Dee in 1277. Largely destroyed by the Puritans in the 17th century, the ruins still look out over three empty miles across the sands of the Dee to the Wirral Peninsula. The plan of the castle is unique in Britain: square, with three corner towers and a detached keep. Richard II was held here after his capture by Bolingbroke, later Henry IV. Once the port for Chester, the town is perhaps better known now for its proximity to the huge Shotton Steelworks.

FOLKESTONE, Kent   6 TR23
To many, Folkestone is simply another gateway to the Continent with its enormous cross-channel ferry passenger terminal. However, it has much to offer in its own right. A holiday town since the coming of the railway, it has a picturesque harbour with a small but active fleet, narrow cobbled streets, and a splendid seafront with a grassy promenade along the clifftop. The oddly-named Church of St Mary and Eanswith was built between the 13th and 15th centuries, its second name being that of the grand-daughter of Ethelbert, the first Christian King of Kent who established the first nunnery in England in AD 630.

To the east of the town is the Warren, a landslip basin between high cliffs and the sea which contains contains rare plants, fossils, and the remains of two Roman villas. A cliff path leads to Dover.

FORD, Northumberland *20 NT93*
The present model village was rebuilt in
1859 by the Marchioness of Waterford in
remembrance of the Marquis who died in a
horse-riding accident.

The ruins of Ford Castle date from the
13th and 14th centuries. James IV of
Scotland stayed here before his defeat and
death at the Battle of Flodden Field in
1513. Nearby are the 19th-century
Heatherslaw Mill (OACT) and the Lady
Waterford Hall (OACT). This building,
once the village school, contains murals
painted by a previous Marchioness of
Waterford in the pre-Raphaelite-style and
depict children from the village and the
estate in Biblical scenes.

FORDWICH, Kent *6 TR15*
Once medieval Canterbury's port, on the
no-longer navigable River Stour, Fordwich
keeps its status as a town but its character is
that of a village. Its brick-faced, tiled
cottages and humped-backed bridge date
from the 18th century. St Mary's Church,
with Saxon, Norman and early 13th-
century work, contains a tomb once
supposedly that of St Augustine. The old
Town Hall (AM) is a small, 16th-century,
timber-framed building overlooking the
river. Medieval justice is recalled by the
ducking stool in the museum and the stocks
outside it.

FOREST ROW, East Sussex *5 TQ43*
This ancient Ashdown-Forest village lies on
the hillside above the River Medway.
Spring Hill Wildfowl Park (OACT) is home
to nearly 1000 species of exotic birds.

FORFAR, Tayside *27 NO45*
Set between the little Lochs Forfar and
Fithie, this quiet and industrious former
county town offers tourists golf, sailing,
trout fishing and, at Glenshee, skiing.
Round about, the area is well known for
soft-fruit and nursery gardening, and
Forfar manufactures agricultural
machinery as well as jute.

On the shores of Loch Fithie, ruined
Restenneth Priory dates from the 12th
century. The son of Robert the Bruce is
buried here. Five miles south-west of
Forfar, at Kirkwynd Cottages, is the
fascinating Angus Folk Collection.

FORRES, Grampian *27 NJ05*
This royal burgh has a lovely setting, near
the estuary of the River Findhorn.
According to Shakespeare, this was the site
of King Duncan's court, and the 'blasted
heath' – now wooded and cultivated –
where Macbeth and Banquo met the weird
sisters is named Macbeth's Hill.

The Falconer Museum concentrates on
fossils found locally, among other items of
interest. Here is kept the key to Nelson's
Tower (OACT), built in 1806 by survivors
of Trafalgar, and a magnificent viewpoint.
Sueno's Stone (AM) is a monument
thought to commemorate a victory by the
Danes over King Malcolm in 1008. On one
side of the stone is carved a cross; on the
other a group of warriors.

FORT AUGUSTUS, Highland
26 NH30
One link in the Hanoverian chain of
defences in the Great Glen (**Glen More**),
Fort Augustus was built after the 1715
Jacobite Rising and named after the Duke
of Cumberland. Its remains now share the
site with a 19th-century Benedictine abbey
and a Roman Catholic school. General
Wade extended Fort Augustus in 1730 and
built his famous network of roads to open
up the Highlands and control the clans: the
present main road partly follows the line of
the one he built through the Great Glen
connecting **Fort William** and **Inverness**.
The village of Fort Augustus, in wooded
hill country at the south-west end of Loch
Ness, near the entry of the Caledonian
Canal, is an angling and tourist centre. The
Great Glen Exhibition (OACT), in addition
to its historical displays, gives the latest
information on the search for the Loch
Ness Monster.

FORT GEORGE, Highland *26 NH75*
The stern bulk of Fort George (AM) was
built in 1773 by the Adam brothers to
replace General Wade's original fort, 12
miles west, at Inverness, which had been
blown up by the Jacobites in 1746. An
irregular polygon with six bastions, it is one
of the best examples of 18th-century
military architecture in the country.

The fort stands on a narrow spit of land
between the Moray and Inverness Firths
and is maintained and garrisoned by the
Queen's Own Highlanders, whose
regimental museum it houses.

FORTINGALL, Tayside *26 NN74*
This pretty village of thatched cottages,
lying in a narrow valley at the entrance of
Glen Lyon was renovated in the late 19th
century by Sir Donald Currie, a wealthy
shipowner and resident of Glen Lyon
House. The way into the beautiful glen lies
over the Pass of Lyon.

In the churchyard is a huge yew tree,
which is said to be 3000 years old and is
probably the most ancient tree in Britain.
The surrounding countryside is full of
prehistoric remains: ring forts, stone
circles, disc barrows and standing stones.
However, the local tradition that Pontius
Pilate was born here while his father was on
an embassy from the Emperor Augustus,
has been dismissed by archaeologists.

FORT WILLIAM, Highland *26 NN17*
The stone fort built in Williams III's reign
to help control the clans withstood Jacobite
assaults during the 1715 and 1745 Risings,
but met its match when, save for a gateway,
it was demolished to make way for the
railway. Inverlochy Castle (AM) is
currently (1983) under repair and not
accessible. The town, known variously in
the past as Gordonsburgh, Duncansburgh,
and Maryburgh, and squeezed between
loch and mountain, is now a well-known
tourist centre for the West Highlands. The
West Highland Museum dates from the
18th century and is famous for its secret
portrait of Bonnie Prince Charlie, reflected
on a cylinder.

FOTHERINGHAY, Northamptonshire
11 TL09
Wild Scotch thistles, reputedly planted by
Mary, Queen of Scots, grow on the
earthworks which are the only remains of
the 14th-century castle where Mary was
executed in 1587. Earlier, the castle was the
birthplace of Richard III.

The village itself, with its solid limestone
cottages and 18th-century bridge over the
River Nene, lies on the edge of what
remains of Rockingham Forest. Its chief
glory is the Church of St Mary and All
Saints, an imposing building of cathedral-
like proportions. Its unusual octagonal
lantern tower, rising in stages and topped
by a gilt falcon badge of the House of York,
is a landmark all over the Nene Valley.

FOULNESS, Essex *6 TR09*
Ten thousand Brent Geese can't be wrong!
Every year that number of long-distance
migrants winter on the lonely mudflats,
creeks and saltings of this typical Thames
estuary island – now apparently safe from
being turned into London's third airport.

PONTCYSYLLTE AQUEDUCT *in the Vale of Llangollen ranks with the Menai Suspension Bridge as one of Thomas Telford's major feats of engineering. Telford wanted to avoid a stairway of locks to carry the Shropshire Union Canal across the ravine of the River Dee, so built an aqueduct 1007ft long which carries the canal in a cast-iron trough supported on 18 stone piers.*

FOWEY, Cornwall *1 SX15*

Two ruined forts at either side of the Fowey estuary still guard this charming Cornish coastal town. The harbour, and the quaint narrow streets climbing steeply from it, attract holiday makers but the town is also an important commercial port exporting large cargoes of china clay. The wide variety of old buildings include the ruins of St Catherine's Castle (AM) the Church of St Finbarres, 14th-century in origin and with a fine 16th-century tower, and the impressive town hall built in 1792 but incorporating several 14th-century windows. Noah's Ark, a 14th-century house, houses a museum of Cornish domestic life.

Nearby, there is safe bathing at sandy Readymoney Cove. Between Polridmouth and Polkerris Coves lies 'Menabilly'. The house, built in 1600 and added to in the 18th and 19th centuries, was formally the home of the Rashleigh family and, more recently, of Daphne du Maurier.

FOYERS, Highland *26 NH42*

This riverside village on a steep hillside overlooking Loch Ness was opened up to Victorian tourists by General Wade's road from Fort Augustus to Inverness. They came to see the spectacular Falls of Foyers and the magnificent scenery of Loch Ness.

Foyers was the site of the first hydro-electric scheme in Britain: to feed the British Aluminium Company works, two lochs were joined to make the Loch Mhor reservoir. The company closed in 1967, but there is a massive electricity power station, completed in 1974, which supplies the national grid.

FRAMLINGHAM, Suffolk *12 TM26*

A handsome market town amid the open Suffolk farmlands, Framlingham has a splendid ruined castle (AM), built in about 1190 by Roger Bigod, 2nd Earl of Norfolk and extensively rebuilt in the 16th century. You can walk around the castle walls between the towers. The almshouses within the walls are built partly from fragments of the Great Hall.

After the sequestration of the castle as a consequence of the Bigods' treachery, it became the seat of some of the great families of East Anglia: principally the Howards, created Dukes of Norfolk after the Battle of Flodden. The church of St Michael, in fine late Perpendicular style, is known for the splendid tombs of the Howard family.

FRASERBURGH, Grampian *28 NJ96*

A trim, embayed town built in the mid-16th century by Alexander Fraser, Laird of Philorth, Fraserburgh is both a port, landing mostly white fish since the decline of the herring, and a resort on the sandy Buchan coast. Town and harbour lie in the protection of Kinnaird Head, a promontory known to Ptolemy and of Fraserburgh Castle that was built on the headland in 1569; only its central tower survives, adapted as a lighthouse in 1787. At the rocky foot of the castle, the Wine Tower – in fact probably a watchtower – stands unchanged since its construction, which was probably during the 15th century.

FRENSHAM, Surrey *4 SU84*

Frensham has an extensive common (NT), famous for its wild life, and ancient prehistoric barrows line its crest; over 200 species of birds can be seen here. Frensham Ponds are ideal for fishing and sailing: Great Pond – one of the biggest in southern England – and Little Pond – where water lilies flourish – together stretch over 100 acres. The River Wey runs nearby and the three curious-looking hills are called the Devil's Jumps: the largest is Stony Jump (NT), which gives a fine view over Surrey.

Frensham's church, although restored, still retains 14th- and 15th-century characteristics. It has a Norman font and a medieval witch's cauldron, said to belong to Mother Ludlam, denizen of the local caves.

FRINTON, Essex *12 TM21*

A quiet, sober resort that has cultivated its genteel trimness since the 1890s. Visitors came here for the golf-course, tennis clubs, sea fishing and bathing from the fine sandy beach – not for amusement arcades or pubs.

FROME, Somerset *3 ST74*

Frome is a busy market town – too busy in the holiday season. A key contribution to its prosperity now comes from light industries such as carpet-making and printing. The town, bisected by its river, preserves its attractive old heart around the market place. Its steep, narrow streets – such as Cheap Street with its central, open water-course – are fine with medieval, Tudor, and especially 18th-century buildings. By the bridge you can see The Blue House, an 18th-century almshouse and its contemporary Bluecoat School.

FRONCYSYLLTE, Clwyd *14 SJ24*

Here, in the Vale of Llangollen, is Telford's 'Stream in the Sky' – the Pontcysyllte Aqueduct. Built between 1795 and 1805, its 18 piers carry the Shropshire Union Canal 120ft high above the River Dee. A pioneering piece of iron-engineering, it connected the Llangollen Canal with the English canal system – cause and result of the development of the coalfields and iron foundries on the Welsh Marches.

FYLINGDALES, N Yorkshire *20 SE99*

'The geometry of the Space Age at its most alluring and frightening' wrote Pevsner of the three giant pearly-white balls which form part of the Ministry of Defence's Ballistic Missile Early Warning Station and which dominate this high moor inland from Robin Hood's Bay. The heather-covered moor is part of the North York Moor's National Park and is traversed by the famous Lyke Wake Walk.

FYLINGDALES MOOR, *a wild Yorkshire heath lying between Pickering and Whitby, is the site of a missile early-warning station. The space-age 'golf balls' seen in the distance are a local landmark.*

THE EARLIEST ROADS
TRADE ROUTES
Ancestors of the Modern Highway

*The British network of roads has developed over thousands of years
and some originally humble trackways have become important
highways, while once-important roads have sometimes passed
completely out of use. The origins of a road are not always clear, but
winding, deeply hollowed roads are invariably old.*

THE OLDEST TRACKS in Britain must have been game trails which were followed by Old Stone Age and Middle Stone Age hunters in the millennia before about 5000 BC. Such roads will have been dirt tracks, unsurfaced and unimproved, but anyone who wants to tread in the steps of the really ancient Britons can make the ascents to cave dwellings like the Victoria Cave near Settle or the Thor's Cave group in Derbyshire. The prehistoric hunters will frequently have followed river and stream courses and will have crossed the more accessible cols and passes in hill and mountain ranges to get from one valley to another. The oldest routeways which can be roughly dated belong to the New Stone Age, between around 5000 and 2500 BC. Very little is known about the swarms of local roads and little trackways which must have existed at this period, but two other types of routeway are known. Firstly, there are the wooden trackways currently being excavated in the Somerset Levels and of which some date back to the New Stone Age. These were built of brushwood mats and lattices of poles and provided a local system of communication to link the firmer areas in the marshland. Secondly, there were the long distance routeways like the Icknield Way, which ran from Norfolk to Wessex, and the Ridgeway which followed the chalk scarps westward through Wessex.

Routeways such as these will have been used by traders dealing in products like stone axes or pottery. They were not surfaced and did not consist of a single deeply-worn line of highway, but rather, they were broader 'zones of movement', containing numbers of weaving, branching tracks. Sea transport was probably quite important at this time, and the use of sea-going ships would explain the fact that axes made from stone quarried in the Lake District are commonly found in the vicinity of the Humber and Thames estuaries.

The number of local and regional routeways will have increased during the Bronze and Iron Ages, and since the British countryside of around 1000 BC was quite heavily populated and productive, there is no reason to suppose that many of our hollowed and winding country lanes should not date from such a time. There is a reason for every little kink and twist in a country

FOSSE WAY *Roman engineers built this remarkable road between Lincoln and Exeter as a means of linking their forts. Here (left) it can be seen to the north-east of Malmesbury.*

road, even if these deviations can seldom be explained today. Originally the lanes or tracks may have avoided ground that was once marshy, but in areas where the roads or lanes developed after the surrounding field systems, many of the kinks can be explained by the fact that the road had to weave around the peripheries of the fields.

Much has been written about 'old straight tracks' or 'leylines' which are described as dead-straight ancient trackways which ran for tens or hundreds of miles without deviation. The whole topic is quite easily dealt with, for such routeways never existed and are no more than a figment of the imagination of lunatic-fringe 'archaeology'. Wherever a proposed 'leyline' has been subjected to serious scrutiny, it has been swiftly debunked.

THE ROMANS did tend to build straight routeways wherever possible, but they were always ready to concede to terrain by deviating to a good bridging point or by curving a road around a hill. In difficult and thinly populated areas the Romans tended to make use of existing trackways, some of which were already ancient by the time of the Roman Conquest. The main highways of Roman Britain began as military highways built by legionaries. They were skilfully engineered and continued to provide the skeleton of the English communication network long after the collapse of Roman rule. Many Roman alignments are still in use, but in general modern roads will tend to follow a Roman route for a few, noticeably straight, miles, then depart from the old route at a slight bend, but often return to the Roman alignment a few miles later. The deviations from the Roman route tend to reflect the way in which Roman road systems were modified to take account of the needs of later generations of travellers.

One of the most famous stretches of Roman routeway, crossing Blackstone Edge on the Yorkshire-Lancashire border, is currently a source of dispute, as some commentators regard it as being a much later construction. An uncontroversial stretch of Roman road can be seen on Wheeldale Moor in the North York Moors above Pickering. Although the surface, which was probably of beaten gravel, has been eroded, the rubble foundations of this road are well displayed.

IN THE DARK AGES, after the Roman collapse, the maintenance of the old network was neglected, although long sections of Roman routeway remained in constant use. Little is known about the roads of this period, but it seems that some new, long-distance trackways were developed by traders, particularly those dealing in salt. Road names like Saltgate, Saltway or Salter's often allow such tracks to be identified. Although many medieval achievements are underrated, most of the communications of the period fell in the range between 'difficult' and 'dreadful'. No medieval ruler was able to create a network of roads to equal those of Roman Britain, and the roads that existed were poorly maintained under an ineffective parochial

TOLLHOUSES *(above) were built to finance road repairs.*
CLAPPER BRIDGES *(below) as at Postbridge in Devon, were in use until the last century.*

system of organisation. The wheeled transport of the period also tended to be inefficient and long-distance transport relied heavily on small river boats and packhorses. Packhorses continued to ply difficult routes across hill country until well into the 19th century and the packhorse trade has left a delightful legacy of trackways and small stone bridges. The majority of packhorse bridges date from the 18th century, but there are a few medieval examples, like the one at Moulton (Suffolk) near Newmarket.

Despite the inadequacies of the medieval roads, they offered the opportunity for the creation of lucrative markets to the fortunate owners of the villages which lay along their routes. It seems that the village of Caxton in Cambridgeshire, for example, was relocated to lie alongside the Old North Road when the local lord gained his market charter in 1247.

TURNPIKE TRUSTS brought about the long-awaited improvement of the road network, and their formation can be traced back to 1663 when the Justices in three counties were empowered to levy tolls for the purpose of road building. Only seven Turnpike Trusts had been created by 1700, but the movement gained momentum during the 18th century and gradually petered out in the course of the 19th century. The Trusts were responsible for the sections of routeway which lay within their jurisdictions and financed the improvement of old roads and the building of new alignments by levying tolls on road-users. In addition to the numerous legacy of surviving roads, the turnpike era is still reflected in the landscape by the many converted toll houses which exist, and which can sometimes be recognised by a three-sided façade which faces the road and which once contained a ticket window.

THE MOTORWAY ERA will probably be regarded by historians as being no less revolutionary than the turnpike age. Although the construction of motorways has resulted in losses of agricultural land and the destruction of a substantial part of the archaeological heritage, it has also had an important conservational effect by removing heavy, destructive traffic from the hearts of scores of delightful old towns. More urban by-passes are still desperately needed, while the exploration of the countryside on foot would be greatly encouraged if more small parking places were created within walking distance of places of historic interest.

GAINFORD, Co Durham *20 NZ11*

This attractive village on the River Tees was made a Conservation Area in 1971. It was once a popular retreat for the wealthy merchants of Darlington, eight miles east, whose comfortable Georgian and Regency houses cluster around the village green. On a corner of the green is the 13th-century parish church, overlooking the river. High Row, a terrace of picturesque cottages, curves towards restored 17th-century Gainford Hall (not open), the focus of the village. The house is remarkable for its eleven tall chimney stacks; nearby stands a commodious stone dovecot.

GAINSBOROUGH, Lincolnshire *16 SK88*

Gainsborough, on the River Trent, is a market town and industrial centre and also a busy port whose quayside is lined by 18th-century warehouses. Of particular interest, in a town of largely 17th-century and later red-brick buildings, is the 15th- and 16th-century Old Hall (AM), one of the largest medieval buildings open to the public in England. Richard III, Henry VIII and Katherine Howard all stayed here.

GAIRLOCH, Highland *29 NG87*

Superbly situated on Loch Gairloch, with its sandy beaches and good fishing, the village has become a holiday resort. It has a golf course, rare in this part of Scotland, and a fascinating sight for visitors is the returning fishing fleet, bringing salmon in the morning and prawns, lobsters and crabs in the evening. The history of this typical West Highland parish is traced in the range of interesting exhibits of the Gairloch Heritage Museum.

The Lochs of Wester Ross
108 miles

Remote and lonely, the north-west of Scotland is a primeval landscape of sombre lochs and harsh, snow-scoured mountains. Scattered hamlets cling to the shelter of the valleys and to the sea-shore, where sandy bays are the haunt of sea-birds, and the sheltered gardens of Inverewe provide an unexpected contrast to the grim Torridons.

From **Gairloch** take A832, the Kinlochewe road and follow the River Kerry to Gairloch Dam. Just before the dam the road becomes single-track through Slatterdale Forest as far as **Loch Maree**. Follow the loch shore to **Kinlochewe** and from here take the single-track Achnasheen road through Glen Docherty, along the shore of Loch a' Chroisg, to **Achnasheen**. From here continue along Strath Bran to Loch Luichart (end of the single-track section) and at **Gorstan** turn left on to A835 (SP Ullapool). Follow the Black Water and Glascarnoch River, then cross Dirrie More to **Braemore Junction**, where the route turns left on to A832. Follow Dundonnell River to **Dundonnell**, and continue, skirting the shore of Little Loch Broom to **Gruinard**. The route follows the coast to Laide, then crosses inland to **Aultbea**. From here follow the shore to **Poolewe**, then cross high ground for the return to Gairloch.

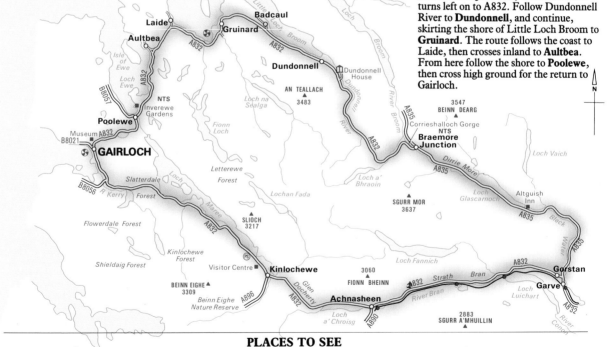

PLACES TO SEE

Loch Maree This beautiful inland loch in Scotland, has many wooded islands, among them the Isle of Maree, associated with the Druids and Celtic Christianity.

Corrieshalloch Gorge (NTS) A spectacular canyon with the 150ft Falls of Measach.

Dundonnell A good climbing centre lying at the head of Little Loch Broom.

Gruinard Bay Sandy beaches backed by mountain scenery. Views of Gruinard Island, now uninhabitable and contaminated by anthrax.

Inverewe Garden (NTS) Magnificent sub-tropical gardens, which have been established here since 1865.

Poolewe An excellent centre for trout and salmon fishing, beautifully situated at the head of Loch Ewe.

GAIRLOCH *The village lies in a sheltered, sandy bay of this great sea-loch, with view out to sea to the Outer Hebrides. Inland rise the Torridons and the peaks of Flowerdale.*

GALASHIELS, Borders   24 NT43
An annual pageant, the Braw Lad's Gathering, illustrates the history of this busy border town, noted for its tweed and wool, and celebrates the granting of its charter in 1599. The Scottish Woollen Technical College is the centre of wool studies in Scotland. An exhibition of textile artist Bernat Klein's work can be seen at Waukrigg Mill.

GATESHEAD, Tyne & Wear
20 NZ26
Stretching for almost 13 miles along the River Tyne, Gateshead was well-known as a centre for ship-building and repair. The town is a modern one, rebuilt since a fire destroyed much of it in 1854. Six notable bridges link it with Newcastle upon Tyne.

GATWICK, W Sussex   5 TQ24
The site of London's second airport, Gatwick provides visitors with a spectators' enclosure and car parking facilities. There is access from the M23 London to Brighton motorway. By 1988 the second terminal should be finished, which will increase the number of passengers from the present annual figure to 12.5 million.

GAWSWORTH, Cheshire   14 SJ86
Mary Fitton, one of the Fitton family who owned Gawsworth Hall for four centuries, may have been the 'Dark Lady' of Shakespeare's sonnets. The fine black-and-white Tudor manor house (OACT) has a beamed interior and outside can be seen a rare tilting ground. The carriage museum is also worth visiting. The mainly 15th-century village church contains a notable range of monuments to the Fittons, including Mary. Many local people, past vicars of the church among them, claim that her ghost haunts the church.

Surrounded by woodland, pools, and parkland, the village itself is a delight. In addition to the Fitton manor house, there are two old vicarages and another Elizabethan hall, used as a Cheshire Home. Maggoty Johnson's Wood (NT) is named after England's last professional jester who lived in the village in the 18th century and is buried in the wood that bears his name.

GIRVAN *Mending fishing nets is an age-old occupation in this old port.*

GEDDINGTON,
Northamptonshire   10 SP88
In 1290 Eleanor of Castile, wife of Edward I, died near Lincoln and her coffin was taken south for burial at Westminster Abbey. At each of the 12 resting places on the journey memorials were built. Only three now remain, and the best-preserved of the Eleanor Crosses is the one erected in this attractive stone-built village in 1298.

Originally a 15th-century monastery, Boughton House (OACT) half a mile east, was enlarged to such an extent between 1530 and 1695 that it has been called the English Versailles. Surrounded by water-gardens, the mansion contains many treasures and has a magnificent park with picnic area, nature trail and woodland adventure playground.

GIFFORD, Lothian   24 NT56
This delightful village on Gifford Water dates from the 18th century. It replaced an earlier village demolished by the 2nd Marquis of Tweeddale to make way for the parkland surrounding Yester House. To the south of the village are the sheep-grazed Lammermuir Hills, ideal for walking and pony-trekking.

GIGGLESWICK,
N Yorkshire   15 SD86
The pale limestone cottages of this peaceful Pennine village on the River Ribble have mullioned windows and date mainly from the 17th and early 18th centuries. Outside the Perpendicular church, which contains an effigy of Sir Richard Tempest, buried with the head of his favourite horse in 1488, is an ancient market cross, stocks and tithe barn. To the north are the heights of Ingleborough and Pen-y-Ghent (2,273ft).

GIGHA, ISLE OF,
Strathclyde   21 NR65
Only six miles long, this flat little island with a rocky shoreline can be reached by ferry from the west coast of Kintyre, three miles away. The ferry crosses the Sound of Gigha, from Tayinloan to Ardminish. Here there is a unique 50-acre garden (OACT) of azaleas and rhododendrons. A steamer also sails to the island from West Loch Tarbert.

GILLING EAST,
N Yorkshire   15 SE67
The main attraction in this village situated between the Hambleton and Howardian Hills is the castle, dating from the 14th century. Although it now houses a preparatory school for Ampleforth College, the magnificent Elizabethan great chamber can be seen and there are fine gardens.

GILLINGHAM, Kent   6 TQ76
An industrial town on the Medway estuary, Gillingham is the largest of the Medway towns, sharing with its neighbour, Chatham, the Royal Naval Dockyard, founded by Henry VIII. Exhibits in the Royal Engineers Museum in the suburb of Brompton include relics of General Gordon, killed in Khartoum in 1885.

GIRVAN, Strathclyde   22 NX19
Now a seaside resort with sandy beaches, this town at the mouth of the River Girvan, looking out across the Firth of Clyde, grew up round a small fishing port. A well-known whisky distillery in the town can be visited, and boat trips can be arranged to see the lonely 1114ft-high rock of Ailsa Craig. Lying to the west, ten miles out to sea, it is home only to lighthouse keepers and thousands of seabirds. South of the town a beautiful coastal road to Ballantrae negotiates the dramatic Kennedy's Pass.

GLAMIS, Tayside   28 NO34
Birthplace of Princess Margaret in 1930, baronial, much-haunted Glamis Castle (OACT) was also the childhood home of the Queen Mother. The tower has 15ft-thick walls and dates from the 14th century, but most of the turreted castle was rebuilt during the late 17th century in the style of a French château. Items of interest include tapestries, furniture, paintings and weapons, and the fine grounds were laid out by 18th-century landscape gardener Capability Brown. From the battlements there are fine views of the Vale of Strathmore, the eastern Grampians and the Sidlaw Hills. The Angus Folk Museum (NTS) in the village is housed in a row of 19th-century cottages.

GLANDFORD, Norfolk *12 TG04*
This village of flint and red-brick houses is worth visiting for its unusual Shell Museum containing Sir Alfred Jodrell's collection of seashells and curios from all over the world. Sir Alfred was also responsible for the restoration of the village church at the beginning of this century, incorporating features typical of Norfolk.

GLASGOW, Strathclyde *22 NS56*
Scotland's largest city, and the third most populous city in Britain, Glasgow owes its rapid development during the Industrial Revolution to its situation on the Clyde, only 20 miles from the sea, and surrounded by coalfields. Its prosperity had begun earlier, in the 17th century, when Port Glasgow, on the Clyde estuary, began to handle a flood of goods from the New World. Heavy industry and ship-building developed in the 19th century, requiring the massive work-force whose cheap housing became the notorious slums of this century.

In recent years there has been a switch to lighter engineering, and an extensive programme of slum-clearance has replaced much of the old city by new flats and road

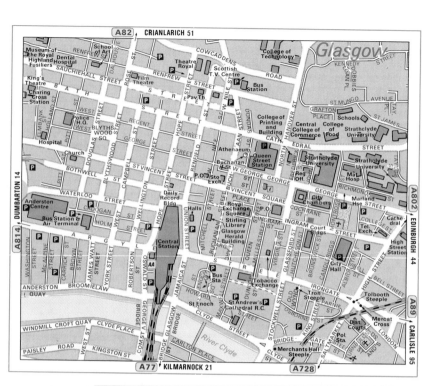

RENNIE MACKINTOSH *developed the 'Glasgow Style' (above) and built the Glasgow School of Art.*

THE ORIENTAL SPLENDOUR *of the Templeton carpet factory (above) enlivens Glasgow's streets.*

GREAT WESTERN ROAD *in about 1896. The busy trams are still horse-drawn, but conversion to electricity was soon to come.*

networks. The city's underground, re-opened by the Queen in 1979, is now one of the most modern in the world, and its airport lies seven miles to the west. Smoke-begrimed Glasgow is fortunate in its large number of parks and other open spaces, covering in all 6000 acres. In Pollok Park, three miles outside the centre, the fabulous Burrell Collection of paintings, sculpture and other works of art is housed in an award-winning building.

Glasgow Cathedral, begun in the 12th century and completed at the end of the 15th, is considered the finest example of pre-Reformation Gothic in Europe. The city's university was established as early as 1451 and treasures in its Hunterian Art Gallery include paintings by Rembrandt, Rubens and Whistler. The Hunterian Museum is based on the wide-ranging collections of an 18th-century surgeon. Glasgow has several other outstanding museums and art galleries, including: the Glasgow Art Gallery and Museum; Haggs Castle, a museum for children; People's Palace, containing a visual record of the history and life of the city, and the Transport Museum.

GLASTONBURY, Somerset *3 ST53*
A busy market town with sheepskin and
leather industries, Glastonbury, 'Cradle of
Christianity', draws visitors to the ruins of
its once-powerful, legend-steeped abbey
(AM). The abbey is said to have been
founded in AD 700 on the site of a chapel
built by Joseph of Arimathea after he
arrived from the Holy Land to convert the
British. The last abbey to be built on the
site was begun in the early 13th century and
only completed just before being dissolved
by Henry VIII: only fragments now
remain. The abbey barn and farmhouse
contain the fascinating Somerset Rural Life
Museum, while the Abbey Tribunal, or
courthouse, contains finds from prehistoric
lake dwellings near Glastonbury Tor. The
Holy Grail, the chalice used at the Last
Supper, and reputedly brought to England
by Joseph of Arimathea, is said to lie
beneath Chalice Spring on this steep hill
which dominates Glastonbury, and many
have identified the town with Avalon where
King Arthur was buried.

GLENCOE, Highland *26 NN15*
Savage peaks and ridges overlook the little
white-washed houses along the straight
main street of Glencoe village. It is not the
present village which Scotsmen think of
when they hear the name however, but the
starkly beautiful glen, a mountain
wilderness ascending 1100ft in ten miles to
the vast expanse of Rannoch Moor. Known
as 'the Glen of Weeping', it was the scene of
the infamous massacre of 38 MacDonalds
in 1692, when Campbell troops billeted in
the glen turned on their hosts because of
their failure to forswear the Jacobite cause.
The heather-thatched Glencoe and North
Lorn Folk Museum in the village houses
among other items MacDonald and
Jacobite relics, and the Glen Coe Visitor
Centre at the north end of the glen is close
to the site of the massacre. Red deer,
ptarmigan, golden eagles and wildcats
inhabit the glen, which offers the hill-
walker a splendid choice of routes.

GLENEAGLES HOTEL,
  Tayside *22 NN91*
On moorland near Auchterader, palatial
Gleneagles Hotel has a 700-acre estate
containing a number of golf courses,
making it one of Scotland's best known golf
resorts. The £1,500,000 Indoor and
Country Club complex recently opened has
made Gleneagles even more popular.

GLENELG, Highland *25 NG81*
In summer a car ferry crosses the Sound of
Sleat from this scattered village to the Isle
of Skye. To the north are the gaunt ruins of
Bernera Barracks, where soldiers were
quartered for 70 years following the
Jacobite rebellion of 1715. Two miles
south-east, in narrow Glen Beag, reached
by the steep and winding Mam Rattachan
Pass, are the well-preserved Glenelg
Brochs, Dun Telve and Dun Trodden.
These 30ft-high defensive towers were
probably built by the Picts 2000 years ago.

GLENFINNAN, Highland *25 NM88*
This hamlet was the rallying point for
Bonnie Prince Charlie's clans after he
landed from France. A statue of a kilted
highlander tops a monument (NTS) at the
head of Loch Shiel, marking the spot where
the prince unfurled his father's standard in

THE GLEN OF WEEPING *The savage massacre of the MacDonald Clan in 1692 has earned Glencoe its
name. Nevertheless, the glen has some of the most beautiful mountain scenery in Scotland.*

1745 at the beginning of his doomed
campaign to regain the throne for his
father, the Old Pretender. There is also a
Visitor's Centre near the Monument. The
Road to the Isles runs through Glenfinnan.

GLENGOULANDIE DEER PARK,
  Tayside *25 NN75*
Pets must be kept in cars when visiting this
park where red deer, Highland cattle and
other animals and birds are kept in
surroundings as much like their natural
environment as possible.

GLENLUCE,
  Dumfries & Galloway *17 NX15*
The castellated 16th-century Castle of Park
overlooks this large village from the brow of
a hill across the Water of Luce. Situated a
little to the west of the river, the village is
near its estuary in Luce Bay. Two miles
north-west are the beautiful ruins of
Cistercian Glenluce Abbey, founded in
1192 (AM).

GLEN MORE, Highland *26 NH30*
Overlooked by lofty hills, culminating in
4406ft Ben Nevis to the west, the highest
mountain in the British Isles, this
remarkable natural feature is better known
as the Great Glen, short for the Great Glen
of Albin. Great it certainly is, for it divides
the mainland of Scotland in two, stretching
from Inverness down to Fort William. The
chain of lochs along the glen, including
Loch Ness, and Telford's Caledonian
Canal, enable boats to pass between the
North Sea and Atlantic Ocean. East of
Aviemore, is the beautiful 12,500-acre Glen
More Forest Park.

GLYNDEBOURNE,
  E Sussex *5 TQ40*
The name Glyndebourne conjures up
visions of opera-lovers in evening dress,
partaking of elegant picnics on balmy
summer evenings, in an idyllic Sussex
setting. Glyndebourne's unique traditions

and atmosphere developed after 1934 when
opera-lover John Christie built an opera
house in the grounds of his Tudor manor
house, one mile north of Glynde village.

GOATHLAND,
  N Yorkshire *20 NZ80*
Sturdy grey-stone houses surround the
large sheep-grazed greens of this scattered
and attractive moorland village, a popular
starting point for walks on the North York
moors. Moorland streams cascade over
rocks in several spectacular waterfalls, the
best known being 70ft-high Mallyan Spout.

GODALMING, Surrey *5 SU94*
An important staging point on the London
to Portsmouth road in stagecoach days, this
attractive North Downs town retains
several old coaching inns as well as many
other 16th- to 18th-century buildings.
Local antiquities can be found in the
Borough Museum.

GODOLPHIN CROSS,
  Cornwall *1 SW63*
Near this quiet hamlet, in a secluded
woodland setting, is one of Cornwall's most
interesting historic houses, Godolphin
House (OACT). Former home of the
enterprising Earls of Godolphin, it dates
mainly from the 16th century. Of particular
interest to horse-lovers is the painting by
John Wooton of 'Godolphin Arabian'. This
stallion owned by the 2nd Earl was one of
the three imported Arab stallions from
which all British thoroughbred horses
descend.

GOLSPIE, Highland *30 NC80*
This old fishing town has become a tourist
resort, and is also an administrative centre
for the Highland Region. Dunrobin Castle
(OACT), one mile north-east, is the ancient
seat of the Earls and Dukes of Sutherland.
It contain much fine furniture and there are
interesting paintings. The castle is
surrounded by magnificent gardens.

Gloucester, Gloucestershire 9 S081

Cathedral City of the Cotswolds

❛Gloucester town lyes all along on the bancks of the Severn . . . here are the fine Lamprys taken in great quantitys in their season . . . here are very good Cloysters finely adorn'd with fretwork . . .❜

The Journeys of Celia Fiennes

THE CLOISTERS *of Gloucester Cathedral (above). In an alley off the Close (left), Beatrix Potter set 'The Tailor of Gloucester'.*

County capital and an important inland port on the River Severn, Gloucester is linked by a canal, completed in 1827, to docks at Sharpness on the Bristol Channel 16 miles away. The canal can accommodate ships of nearly 1000 tons, making the city an important commercial centre with a port that now stretches for miles and handles the output of local engineering industries. A fortified harbour existed here as long ago as Roman times. Built for the invasion of Wales during the 1st century AD, the fort of Glevum guarded the lowest Severn crossing and the legions' routes into Wales. The city's main thoroughfares, Northgate, Southgate, Westgate and Eastgate still follow the pattern of the original Roman roads.

Gloucester is known for the

Three-Choirs music festival which takes place every third year: in the two intervening years it is held in turn at Hereford and Worcester. Gloucester's main attraction for visitors is the beautiful cathedral containing the tomb of Edward II.

A splendid example of Norman architecture, the main part of the cathedral, built between 1089 and 1260 contains a massive 174ft-long nave lined with piers, and a Norman crypt. Later the building was partly transformed by Edward III, and the transepts and choir, remodelled in the mid 14th century, mark the birth of the Perpendicular style in England. These were re-designed to hold the splendid tomb of Edward II, murdered at Berkeley Castle in 1327. The apse was replaced by Britain's second largest stained-glass window, measuring 72ft by 38ft. Made in about 1350, it is a glorious memorial to those who died at the Battle of Crécy in 1346, and depicts the Coronation of the Virgin.

Originally an abbey, the building did not become a cathedral until the reign of Henry VIII. The lovely 14th-century cloisters,

THE OLD PORT *Looking across a sea of masts to the cathedral.*

enclosing a delightful monastic garden with a well, have exquisite fan vaulting. The fine, 225ft pinnacled central tower contains a three-ton medieval bell, Great Peter.

In the close, entered by two old gateways, is a cross to the memory of Bishop Hooper, a protestant who was martyred in 1555 during the reign of Mary I. In one of the alleys leading into the close is the quaint old shop immortalised by Beatrix Potter in *The Tailor of Gloucester*; it is a bookshop and contains a small museum to this ever-popular children's writer.

PLACES TO SEE

Bishop Hooper's Lodging In 1555 Bishop Hooper spent the night before his martyrdom in this 15th–16th-century timber-framed building. It is now a fascinating folk-life museum, illustrating ancient crafts.

Blackfriars Abbey The remains of church and cloister date from the 13th century.

City Museum and Art Gallery The museum contains many finds relating to the Roman origins of the town, including mosaics, and sculptures. Recent excavation has revealed the site of a two-acre Roman forum, and this would appear to confirm the theory that the city was occupied twice by the Romans. Apart from archaeological finds, the museum has many other items of interest.

City East Gate Here, on Eastgate Street, the Roman and medieval city defences can be seen in an underground chamber.

Church of St Mary de Crypt The grave of Robert Raikes, founder of the Sunday School Movement and for many years editor of a local newspaper, can be found in this Norman church which stands near to his house (now the Golden Fleece Inn) in Southgate Street.

New Inn Northgate Street. A half-timbered 15th-century pilgrim's hostel whose courtyard has well-preserved surrounding balconies.

The Old Custom House Built in the 19th century on the quayside, the building houses the Museum of the Gloucestershire Regiment.

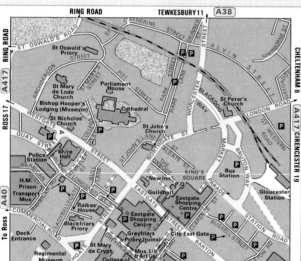

GOODWOOD, W Sussex *4 SU81*
Formerly part of the Goodwood estate, the racecourse here is famous for the 'Glorious Goodwood' meeting in July. Goodwood House (OACT) built by James Wyatt, is a treasure-house of fine pictures, furniture, tapestries and Sèvres porcelain.

GOOLE, Humberside *16 SE72*
Some 50 miles from the North Sea, at the confluence of the Rivers Ouse and Don, this low-lying red-brick town is a port, one of the furthest inland in Britain. Since docks were built and a canal in 1826 the town has become a large industrial and commercial centre.

GOOSNARGH, Lancashire *14 SD53*
Moated 13th-century Chingle Hall (OACT) near Goosnargh has the reputation of being the most haunted house in Britain. It is a sturdy, white-walled cruciform structure, surrounded by a moat and, as well as a chapel, has four priest holes.

GORDON, Borders *24 NT64*
This village one mile west of the Eden Water is associated with the 'Gay Gordons', who moved to old Aberdeenshire in the 14th century. Mellerstain House (OACT), three miles south, is an Adam house with fine plaster ceilings, period furniture and pictures.

GORING-ON-THAMES,
  Oxfordshire *4 SU68*
Here the Thames flows lazily through the gentle gorge of Goring Gap, between the beech-clad Chilterns and the high Berkshire Downs. In prehistoric times an important ford over the river linked the Ridge Way and Icknield Way; today the attractive town is a popular stopping point for holiday cruisers.

GORLESTON-ON-SEA,
  Norfolk *12 TG5204*
Good cliff-backed sands and a small harbour for fishermen and sailors make this suburb of Great Yarmouth a popular holiday resort in its own right. Separated from its more boisterous neighbour by the River Yare, Gorleston has its own 19th-century pavilion and lighthouse.

GOSFIELD, Essex *12 TL73*
Some of the houses in this tidy village were built by the Courtauld family, who established a silk factory in nearby Halstead in 1826. For a while they also owned Gosfield Hall (OACT), a Tudor and later mansion with a fine gallery. A large lake built on part of the estate in the 18th century is now a recreation centre with paddling and water-skiing areas, and rowing boats available for hire.

GOSPORT, Hampshire *4 SZ69*
Badly damaged during World War II, this naval town on the Solent has many new buildings lining the seashore. From its humble origins as a fishing hamlet it has become a victualling station and submarine base for the Navy. HMS *Alliance*, a World War II submarine, has been restored and houses a museum, showing the history and development of submarines up to the present nuclear age. The town is also a holiday centre, with shingle beaches at Stokes Bay, and is linked to Portsmouth by passenger ferry.

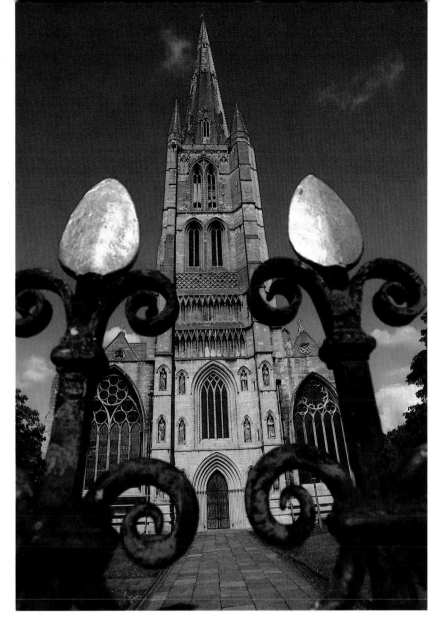

GRANTHAM CHURCH *The magnificent church is largely the legacy of the 14th century. Once an important staging post, Grantham is now famous as the birthplace of Mrs Thatcher.*

GOUDHURST, Kent *6 TQ73*
The old houses in this attractive Wealden village have fine views of orchards and hopfields from their hilltop setting. At the bottom of the hill is a duck pond, and at the top a fine, mainly 15th-century church, whose treasures include the life-size 16th-century painted wooden figures of Sir Alexander Culpeper and his wife. Finchcocks (OACT), a little distance south-west, a magnificent early 18th-century house set in beautiful parkland, contains an antique keyboard instrument museum. Two miles south, at Bedgebury, is the 75-acre National Pinetum (OACT), an offshoot of Kew Gardens.

GRAMPIANS, THE, Grampians/
  Highland *26/7*
Britain's largest and highest land-mass, the Grampians incorporate the **Cairngorm** range. Many of the summits exceed 3000ft, and some, in the Caringorms, top 4000ft. The mountain range stretches from the old county of Argyll in the west to old Aberdeenshire in the north east. Ski-ing is possible in some parts in winter, particularly around Glenshee.

GRANGEMOUTH, Central *23 NS98*
This busy port on the Forth estuary has important docks and is the site of Scotland's largest complex of oil installations, refineries and ancillary works.

GRANGE-OVER-SANDS,
  Cumbria *18 SD47*
A place of retirement in Victorian days, Grange-over-Sands is a quiet resort overlooking Morecambe Bay. It has a sand and shingle foreshore, and mile-long promenade, backed by gardens, parks and wooded fells. Bathing is unsafe but the open-air swimming pool is available during summer months. The Kent estuary is protected as an Area of Outstanding Natural Beauty.

GRANTCHESTER,
  Cambridgeshire *11 TL45*
Poet Rupert Brooke lived here before World War I. Travelling in Germany, and homesick for the tranquil little village set in meadows beside the River Cam, he immortalised it in his poem *The Old Vicarage, Grantchester*.

GRANTHAM, Lincolnshire *11 SK93*
The beautiful 14th-century spire of St Wulfram's Church is a landmark for miles around this ancient farming and hunting town. The church has a chained library, left to it in 1598. Mrs Margaret Thatcher, Britain's first woman prime minister, was born and educated in the town, where her father owned a grocer's shop. Sir Isaac Newton, discoverer in 1685 of the law of gravity, was educated at the 15th-century grammar school.

GRASMERE, Cumbria *18 NY30*

In its idyllic setting below Helm Crag and Nab Scar, to the north of Grasmere lake, this little stone village was pronounced by 18th-century poet William Wordsworth 'the loveliest spot that man hath ever found'. Wooded slopes sweep down to the lake and the River Rothay flows near the village. Wordsworth spent 14 years here.

From 1799 to 1808 he lived in Dove Cottage (OACT) at Town End, a simple limewashed, slate-roofed stone cottage, originally an inn called the Dove and Olive Bough. From 1808 the writer Thomas de Quincey lived in the cottage, which contains many items of Wordsworth's furniture. Opposite is the Wordsworth museum containing some of his personal possessions, portraits and newly-discovered manuscripts. The poet later lived at Allan Bank, and at the Rectory, opposite the church where he is buried with his wife, three of their young children and his sister.

The popular Grasmere Sports, held in late August, feature such traditional events as lakeland wrestling, hound-trailing and races to the summit of Butter Crag and back which really test the fitness of the hardiest competitors.

GRASSINGTON, N Yorkshire *15 SE06*

A popular touring centre for Wharfedale and the surrounding dales, Grassington's houses crowd round the small cobbled market-place. The village contains a National Park Centre for the Yorkshire Dales.

GRAVESEND, Kent *6 TQ67*

Here the Thames estuary narrows and the many ships coming up-river exchange coastal for river pilots. The town is a busy residential, commercial and industrial centre, connected to Tilbury on the north bank of the river by passenger ferry. Opposite St George's Church, where she is buried, is the statue of the famous Red Indian princess, Pocahontas, who married one of the first American settlers in Virgina, an Englishman named John Smith, and died in the town in 1617.

GREAT BADMINTON, Avon *3 ST88*

Badminton House (open only occasionally), a magnificent Palladian mansion in a 52,000-acre estate, was originally built in 1682 and remodelled by William Kent in the 18th century. The house, home of the Dukes of Beaufort, contains priceless paintings, works of art and Grinling Gibbons carving. The famous Badminton Three Day Event Horse Trials are held in the park each April, usually attended by the Royal family. On the edge of the estate lies the neat stone-built village.

GREAT BEDWYN, Wiltshire *3 SU26*

This peaceful village lies on the Kennet and Avon Canal, on the edge of Savernake Forest. The tomb of Sir John Seymour, father of Jane Seymour and grandfather of Edward VI, can be seen in the church. The Bedwyn Stone Museum has open-air exhibitions explaining the ancient history of the freemason. To the south-west, the fascinating 19th-century Crofton Beam Engines, including the oldest working steam engine in the world, pump water 40ft to the top level of the canal, and can be seen in steam on certain weekends.

GREAT BOOKHAM, Surrey *5 TQ15*

King George VI and Queen Elizabeth spent part of their honeymoon at Polesden Lacey (NT), one mile south of the village. This early 19th-century house, containing the Greville collection of pictures, tapestries and furnishings, is set in 140 acres of beautiful grounds, including a superb rose garden.

GREAT BUDWORTH, Cheshire *14 SJ67*

Dominating this extraordinarily pretty village from its hill-top site is the red-sandstone Tudor church. Among other items of interest, the church contains the private chapel of the locally important Warburton family, a massive medieval oak chest, and fine carvings in the nave.

GREAT COXWELL, Oxfordshire *4 SU29*

William Morris described the well-preserved stone 13th-century barn (NT) here as being as 'noble as a cathedral'. Built by the Cistercian monks of Beaulieu Abbey, it is 152ft long, 44ft wide and 50ft high. From the limestone village there are wide views of farmland rising to the White Horse Hills and the Iron Age fort of Uffington.

GREAT DUNMOW, Essex *11 TL62*

A unique custom, imported from Brittany in the 13th century, takes place here every four years. A flitch of bacon is presented to any married couple who have not quarrelled or regretted their marriage for at least a year and a day – recipients being tried by a bewigged amateur judge and counsel. The town itself is a bustling little place, with many attractive buildings.

GREAT BOOKHAM *Exhibits at Polesden Lacey (above) include this 'famille verte' Chinese figure.*

A SAXON SHRINE

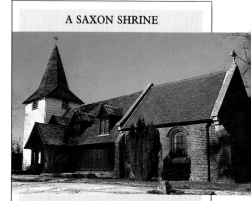

The Saxon King Edmund was an early Christian martyr, killed by the Danes in 1013. His body was brought to this log-walled church and rested here on its way to Bury St Edmunds. There is a legend that when the martyr's severed head was found, it was guarded by a wolf. A carving in the church illustrates the story.

GRASMERE one of the loveliest of the smaller lakes, Grasmere and its tree-sheltered village are irrevocably associated with William Wordsworth and his poetry, much of it written at Dove Cottage.

GREAT TEW, Oxfordshire *10 SP32*
Declared a village of 'outstanding interest'
by the Department of the Environment in
1978, Great Tew is a lovely, mellow
Cotswold village of 17th-, 18th- and 19th-
century honey-coloured, thatched or slate-
roofed cottages, surrounded by woods. It
was designed as part of an improvement
scheme by J C Loudon in 1808.

GREAT YARMOUTH,
Norfolk *12 TG50*
Now one of Britain's most popular seaside
resorts, the town was for centuries a centre
for the herring-fishing industry. These days
the harbour is used mainly by cargo ships
and vessels servicing North Sea gas and oil
rigs. Five miles of sandy beach provide safe
bathing, and the numerous entertainment
facilities include two piers with theatres, a
leisure centre and a vast pleasure beach
with 'all the fun of the fair'. Anna Sewell,
author of *Black Beauty*, lived near the vast
parish church, and her house is now a
museum. The Elizabethan Houses, the
Tollhouse and the Old Merchant's House
are also interesting historical museums.
Other attractions include the House of
Wax; the Maritime Museum for East
Anglia; and the Merrivale Model Village.

GREENOCK, Strathclyde *22 NS27*
Situated on the Clyde estuary, Greenock
was an important industrial and ship
building town, suffering severe bomb
damage in World War II. Among other
exhibits in the McLean Museum and Art
Gallery are those connected with shipping,
and relics of James Watt, inventor of steam,
who was born here in 1736.

GREENSTED-JUXTA-ONGAR,
Essex *6 TL50*
The lovely village church is a rare survival
from Saxon times, being founded possibly
as early as 850, or 1013 to commemorate St
Edmund, who was martyred by the Danes:
opinions differ. The split oak logs originally
used to construct the nave can still be seen,
and are the only surviving log walls in
Britain.

GRETNA GREEN, Dumfries &
Galloway *18 NY36*
For over a century this border village was a
favourite destination for runaway English
lovers wishing to marry without their
parents' consent. After a law of 1754,
clandestine marriages were banned in
England, but in Scotland all that was
required was for a couple to declare that
they wished to become man and wife in
front of witnesses. In Gretna Green this
took place over the anvil, which can still be
seen. In 1856 a new law required one of the
couple to live in Scotland for three weeks,
but it was not until another law was passed
in 1940 that the village smith was banned
from performing the ceremony altogether.

GRIMES GRAVES, Norfolk *12 TL88*
Not graves at all, the 350 holes in the
ground and the labyrinth of tunnels that
bear this name are in fact the largest
prehistoric flint mines (AM) in Europe.
Using tools made from deers' antlers,
Neolithic man extracted flints and exported
them throughout the south of England to
be used for arrowheads and axes. One of
the shafts can be explored; although it is lit,
a torch may still be useful.

The Wooded Surrey Downs
57 miles

*The wooded hills and heaths of Surrey spread out beneath the dramatic chalk ridge of
the Hog's Back, where Guildford occupies a strategic gap in the North Downs. This
is a country of winding lanes, pretty villages and famous beauty spots.*

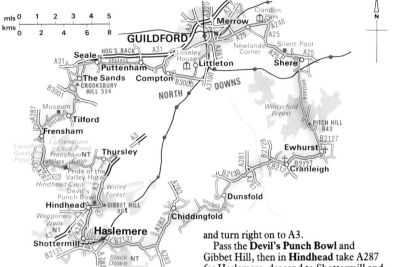

From **Guildford** follow Godalming A3100
signs as far as the Ship PH and turn right
into Sandy Lane. After 1 mile keep left for
Littleton, drive through the village, pass
the entrance to Loseley House, and at the
T-junction turn right on to B3000. Drive
through **Compton**, then turn left on to A3,
then right on to B3000 (SP Farnham).
Drive to **Puttenham** and turn left on to an
unclassified road that leads along the
southern slopes of the Hog's Back to
Seale. Turn left beyond Seale church and
in ½mile, at a crossroads, turn left for The
Sands. Cross a main road (SP Tilford),
then at a crossroads turn left (SP Elstead).
Soon turn left on to B3001 and take the
next right turn for **Tilford**.
    Cross the River Wey twice (SP
Frensham) and in ¼mile turn left. After
1½miles turn left on to the A287 (SP
Hindhead). Pass **Frensham Great Pond**,
then in ¾mile turn left (SP Thursley). In
1½miles, cross a main road by the Pride of
the Valley Hotel and after 1¾miles turn
right for **Thursley**. Continue for ½mile

and turn right on to A3.
    Pass the **Devil's Punch Bowl** and
Gibbet Hill, then in **Hindhead** take A287
for Haslemere, descend to Shottermill and
keep forward on B2131 for **Haslemere**.
Leave Haslemere on B2131 (SP Petworth)
and in 2½miles bear left (SP
Chiddingfold). In ¾mile, turn left at a T-
junction on to A283 for **Chiddingfold**.
Turn right by the Crown Inn (SP
Dunsfold), bear right on the far side of the
green then in 1 mile turn left and go
through **Dunsfold**. After 1 mile turn right
on to B2130 (SP Cranleigh). In 1 mile bear
left, and ¼mile later turn right. Drive over
a staggered crossroads and in 1¼miles
turn right on to B2128 for **Cranleigh**.
Turn left at the end of the village on to
B2127 and in 2¼miles turn left again into
Ewhurst. Keep forward on to the Shere
road. In ¾mile bear left and drive to
Shere. At a T-junction turn left (SP
Guildford), and at the next T-junction
turn left again on to A25. Pass the Silent
Pool, and at the crossroads 1 mile beyond
Newlands Corner turn left on to A246.
(By keeping forward here a detour can be
made to Clandon Park.) Continue along
A246 to Guildford.

PLACES TO SEE

Guildford Archbishop Abbott's Hospital
(OACT); the Guildhall, with its famous
clock; St Mary's Church; Castle Keep
Museum; Striking modern cathedral.

Loseley House (OACT) Tudor Mansion
with original panelling and furnishings.

Compton Memorial Gallery and Chapel to
the Victorian artist G F Watts.

Tilford Near the village is the Old Kiln
Agricultural Museum.

Frensham The Great and Little Ponds,
with surrounding Common (NT).

Hindhead Near Hindhead is the spectacular Devil's Punchbowl (NT) and the viewpoint of Gibbet Hill.

Haslemere Attractive town, with the Dolmetsch musical instrument workshops and
associated museum and also the Haslemere
Educational Museum.

Chiddingfold Picturesque village with
green, duck-pond and ancient thorn-tree.

Shere Pretty, much-visited village on the
River Tillingbourne.

Silent Pool The lake, in beautiful woodland, has associations with King John,
according to local legend.

Newlands Corner Famous beauty spot
and viewpoint on the crest of the Downs.

Clandon Park A Palladian mansion (NT)
set in landscaped grounds.

GRIMSBY, Humberside *16 TA20*
Long famous as one of the world's great fishing ports, Grimsby, originally in Lincolnshire, is still Britain's major centre for seine-net fishing, and the docks handle a variety of cargoes, although the fleet has drastically declined. Exhibits in the Welholme Galleries include Napoleonic and 19th-century ship models, and marine paintings.

GROOMBRIDGE,
Kent/E Sussex *5 TQ53*
The Kent Water, a tributary of the River Medway, divides the village and also marks the boundary between Kent and East Sussex. The latter contains the larger, modern part of the village while the triangular village green overlooked by attractive brick, tile-hung and weather-boarded cottages lies in Kent.

GROSMONT, Gwent *9 SO42*
Set in lovely scenery by the River Monnow, Grosmont is a favourite centre for anglers. Its ruined castle (AM) was one of three built by the Norman Lords of Abergavenny to protect their territory. In 1410 it was seized by Owain Glyndwr, but he was soon afterwards defeated by Henry Monmouth, who later became Henry V.

GUILDFORD, Surrey *5 TQ04*
Guildford's impressive modern Anglican cathedral, consecrated in 1961, looks down on the county town of Surrey from its hilltop setting on the outskirts. Close to the cathedral are the modern buildings of the University of Surrey, and the Yvonne Arnaud Theatre was opened in 1958 on the banks of the River Wey.

Despite being a busy modern shopping centre the town retains many old buildings, and its steep High Street has an unchanging Georgian character, with a very ornate 17th-century Guildhall. All that remains of

the castle is the 12th-century keep (OACT), but also of interest are the 17th-century Guildford House Gallery, Guildford Museum and the Tudor Hospital of the Blessed Trinity (OACT). Loseley House (OACT) is a stone-built Elizabethan manor with fine period furnishings. It stands two and a half miles south-west.

GUILSBOROUGH,
Northamptonshire *10 SP67*
In the beautiful grounds of a 19th-century house is Guilsborough Grange Wildlife Park, a collection of over 500 birds, waterfowl and animals in natural surroundings.

GUISBOROUGH, Cleveland *20 NZ61*
This busy market town, a touring centre for the nearby Cleveland Hills, and North Yorkshire Moors, contains an architectural gem in the remains of a 12th-century priory (AM). They include a gatehouse and dovecote, and the magnificent 14th-century east end of the building. The work of artists and craftsmen can be seen at the Chapel Beck gallery.

GUITING POWER,
Gloucestershire *10 SP02*
Through the far-sighted action of a local landowner, the rural character of this village of Cotswold stone buildings clustered round a triangular green should be preserved. Rare breeds of farm animals can be seen at the Cotswold Farm Park (OACT), three miles north-east of the village.

GWEEK, Cornwall *1 SW72*
At the head of the Helford River, this quiet village has become a popular destination for tourists, who come to visit the fascinating Seal Sanctuary. Here sick and injured seals rescued from Cornish beaches are cared for in the well-run hospital and five pools.

GUILDFORD HIGH STREET *This delightful street with its many historic buildings, has maintained its distinctive Georgian character. The gilded Guildhall clock dates from the 17th century.*

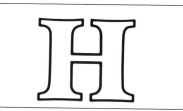

HADDENHAM,
Buckinghamshire *10 SP70*
This charming little village of thatched cottages and timber-framed houses has unusual boundary walls, giving it a distinctive, almost Mediterranean atmosphere. At the centre of the village is the green, with a duck pond overlooked by the 13th-century parish church.

HADDINGTON, Lothian *24 NT57*
In the 12th century the town was laid out in a narrow triangle, whose boundaries can be traced following High Street, Market Street and Hardgate. Today this gracious town of wide streets is one of Scotland's best preserved, with 129 buildings scheduled as of special architectural or historic interest. The splendid Town House, with its slender spire, was built by William Adam, father of Robert Adam, in 1748. The medieval red sandstone St Mary's Church, where John Knox worshipped as a boy, has in recent years been extensively restored.

HADDON HALL, Derbyshire *15 SK26*
A splendid example of a well-preserved 12th- to 15th-century medieval and manorial house, Haddon Hall (OACT) has belonged to the Manners family since 1567 and probably looks much the same as it did 300 years ago. Beautifully situated on the River Wye, its battlemented towers and turrets of warm-coloured Derbyshire stone, never used in self-defence, blend serenely with their peaceful surroundings. Of particular interest are the chapel; the long gallery, panelled in oak and walnut and the Mortlake Tapestries.

HADLEIGH, Essex *6 TQ88*
Impressive ruins remain of a 13th-century castle (AM), rebuilt by Edward III in the 14th century, but destroyed during a landslide. A painting of the ruins by John Constable can be seen in the Tate Gallery. From the castle there are views of the Thames estuary and the Kent coast.

HADLEIGH, Suffolk *12 TM04*
Fine houses in the long High Street of this former wool town on a tributary of the River Stour represent an unusually wide variety of architectural styles: timber-framed, brick, plaster-work with and without the decoration known as pargeting. The 14th- to 15th-century church contains an unusual 14th-century bench-end depicting a wolf holding the decapitated head of St Edmund, illustrating an old legend. The nearby 15th-century Deanery Tower is all that remains of the palace of Archdeacon Pykenham, while the fine 15th-century timbered Guildhall (OACT) has two overhanging storeys.

HADRIAN'S WALL (See Housesteads.)
Building of this great wall began in AD 122 after the Emperor's visit to Britain. The 15 ft wall was 7½ ft thick and ran from Wallsend to the Solway Firth.

HAILES ABBEY,
Gloucestershire   9 SP03
Only ruined walls in a secluded wooded setting remain of the once-impressive Cistercian abbey (NT, AM), founded in 1246. Pilgrims once came to see the sacred phial said to contain the blood of Christ. A museum now houses relics such as roof bosses and tiles found during excavations.

HAILSHAM, E Sussex   6 TQ50
Two miles west of this pleasant market town situated below the Sussex Downs is Michelham Priory (OACT). The nucleus of this Tudor manor was an Augustinian priory, founded in 1229 and partially destroyed during the Dissolution of Monasteries in 1536. Approached by an ancient bridge over the wide moat, the priory is entered through a splendid 14th-century gathouse. The interior contains 17th-century furniture, and other items of interest include Sussex ironwork. The seven-acre grounds contain a Tudor great barn, old wagons and ploughs, and a Sussex craft shop.

MICHELHAM PRIORY *To form the 6½-acre moat, the monks diverted the River Cuckmere near Hailsham.*

HALIFAX, W Yorkshire   15 SE02
Old and new blend in this ancient cloth-manufacturing town, rising on steep hills from the Hebble Brook in the Pennine foothills. New flats and office blocks contrast with solid stone-built mills and their tall chimneys; old cobbled streets, with glimpses of the surrounding green hills lead to modern pedestrian precincts.

The cloth trade was important to the town as long ago as the 13th century. Carpets and yarns are still manufactured in the town, but evidence of the past importance of cloth can be seen in the splendidly restored 18th-century Piece Hall (OACT). Here 315 rooms open off colonnaded galleries round a large quadrangle. The cottage weavers once exhibited and sold their 'pieces' or lengths of cloth in the rooms. Today they are occupied by an industrial museum, exhibitions and a wide range of crafts, antique and souvenir shops, while three times a week there is also a busy open-air market. Bankfield Museum and Art Gallery also has a comprehensive collection of costumes and textiles among many other items of interest. On the edge of the town 15th-century Shibden Hall (OACT).

HALLAND, E Sussex   5 TQ51
Over 1000 wildfowl, swans, geese, ducks, flamingoes, cranes and peacocks can be seen here at the Bentley Wildfowl Reserve in the 100-acre grounds of a country house.

FINE ENGLISH WINES

English vineyards, introduced by the Romans and later cultivated by the monks, disappeared after the 16th century. The revival started at Hambledon, home of cricket, where Major General Sir Guy Salisbury-Jones planted a vineyard in 1952. The bat and ball motif on his labels is a reminder of the role of this Hampshire village in the history of England's traditional game.

HALLATON, Leicestershire   10 SP79
Pleasantly situated in hilly country, this old village has two unusual customs which take place on Easter Monday. A huge hare pie – once token rent for a field – is distributed to residents by the rector, and then the villagers compete to elect the Hallaton Bottle King, by pushing two small casks of beer over a local stream to Hare Pie Hill.

HAM HOUSE, Gtr London   5 TQ17
The house (NT) was built in the 17th century for Sir Thomas Vavasour, but it was the later owners, the Duke and Duchess of Lauderdale who transformed the interior, decorating it in a rich Baroque style. The original furnishings of the Stuart era have been preserved and the house is now used as an annexe by London's Victoria and Albert Museum.

HAMBLEDON, Hampshire   4 SU61
A predominantly Georgian village, Hambledon is well-known to cricket enthusiasts. The Hambledon Club, playing at Broadhalfpenny Down, two miles north-east, was particularly important between about 1772 and 1787, when it formed proper rules for the game and helped found the MCC. On the slopes of Windmill Down is a vineyard and press house (OACT by arrangement).

HAMILTON, Strathclyde   22 NS75
A Clyde Valley industrial town, Hamilton's surroundings remain relatively unspoilt. The extravagant 19th-century Hamilton Mausoleum still stands near the racecourse, although the palace of the Dukes of Hamilton was demolished in 1927 because of subsidence. There is an interesting district museum housed in a late 17th-century inn.

HANBURY,
Hereford & Worcester   9 SO96
Views from the hilltop church in this scattered village take in the Malverns and Bredon Hill. Built in 1701, Hanbury Hall (NT), set in 13 acres of parkland, is a red-brick Queen Anne period house with a contemporary orangery. The Long Room has particularly good plaster decoration, and the house contains the Watney collection of porcelain.

HANDCROSS, W Sussex   5 TQ22
Nymans Gardens (NT), one mile north-east of the village, contain beautiful trees, shrubs and plants from all over the world.

HAPPISBURGH, Norfolk   12 TG33
The red and white lighthouse in this little fishing village was built in 1791 to warn shipping of treacherous sands seven miles offshore. The village, pronounced 'Hazeborough', has a long sandy beach.

HAPPISBURGH LIGHTHOUSE *A vital landmark for shipping, the lighthouse makes the 100ft tower of St Mary's Church insignificant. The toll of the sea is evidenced by many seamen's graves in the churchyard.*

HARDWICK HALL, Derbyshire 15 SK46

A striking feature of this Elizabethan mansion, built in 1597 for the Dowager Countess of Shrewsbury ('Bess of Hardwick'), is the large number and size of windows. A symmetrical, stone building, it has a huge tower at each corner topped with decorative open stonework incorporating the letters ES for Elizabeth Shrewsbury. Of particular interest inside are fine tapestries and needlework.

HAREWOOD, W Yorkshire 15 SE34

Rebuilt in the 18th century at the same time as Harewood House (OACT), the long terraces of the village extend from the main gates of this opulent yellow-stone mansion. Planned by John Carr, the exquisite interior of the house, home of the Earl and Countess of Harewood, was largely decorated by Robert Adam. The park, created by Capability Brown, has a four-acre lake, and a fascinating bird garden.

HARLECH, Gwynedd 13 SH53

Harlech's sturdy fortress, 13th-century Harlech Castle (AM) dominates the town from its rocky crag, once protected by the sea on one side and wide moat on the other. Built by Edward I, the castle has survived repeated attacks. There are marvellous views from the battlements of Snowdonia and the Lleyn peninsula. This town of steep narrow streets and granite-built houses on Tremadog Bay is popular with tourists. To the north is a National Nature Reserve, Morfa Harlech.

HARLOW, Essex 6 TL41

Harlow New Town was conceived in 1947 and was planned to develop alongside the old market town. It was the first town to have a pedestrian precinct and now has a population of 80,000. Passmores House is an early Georgian building converted to a museum, and the Mark Hall Cycle Museum displays more than 50 machines, the earliest dating back to 1819.

HARROGATE, N Yorkshire 15 SE35

An attractive, spacious town of dignified Victorian stone buildings, lightened by flower-beds and open spaces, Harrogate stands 400–600ft above sea level, within easy reach of the dales.

In 1804 the Royal Pump Room was erected on a sulphur-well, and the town

---

Leave **Hastings** on A21 following 'London' signs and in 1½miles at the traffic lights join B2159 (SP Battle). After 2 miles, at the junction with A2100, bear left for **Battle**, pass the square, then turn right on an unclassified road to **Whatlington**. Beyond the village join A21 (SP Hurst Green). In ½mile turn right on to B2090 (SP Tenterden, Northiam), then right again on to B2089. At **Cripp's Corner** turn left on to B2165 (SP Staplecross). Here go forward on to the unclassified Bodiam road. Leave **Bodiam** by the Hawkhurst road and in about 1 mile turn right on to A229. At **Hawkhurst** traffic lights turn left on to A268 and drive to **Flimwell**, then turn right on to A21 London road and in about ¾mile turn right again on to B2079 to **Goudhurst**. From here follow A262 Ashford road for 1¾miles, then turn right on to B2085 (SP Hawkhurst) and in another 1¾miles turn left (SP Cranbrook). Reach the main road and turn left and right for the town centre. Drive through **Cranbrook** and join A229 for ¼mile, then turn right on to A262 (SP Ashford) and drive to **Sissinghurst**, then **Biddenden**. At the end of the village turn right and in ¾mile branch right for **Benenden** and **Iden Green**. Two miles past Iden Green turn left on to A268 for **Sandhurst**, then **Newenden** where the route joins A28. After the level crossing bear right (SP Hastings), drive to **Northiam**, then branch left for **Beckley** and then turn right on to B1268 for Rye. Leave **Rye** by A259 Hastings road and in 2 miles bear right then turn left for **Winchelsea**. Return through the town's Strandgate and turn right on to A259 and right again for **Winchelsea Beach**. Follow the coast road to **Fairlight**, and past the turning for Fire Hills Country Park rejoin A259 to return to Hastings.

PLACES TO SEE

Hastings Castle ruins and old houses in historic Cinque Port. Near the Net Huts on the beach is a Fishermen's Museum. Local History Museum in the Town Hall.

Battle Site of the Battle of Hastings. Battle and District Historical Museum; ruined St Martin's Abbey (OACT).

Bodiam Moated 14th-century castle (NT).

Bedgebury National Pinetum All types of conifers can be seen in this horticultural station.

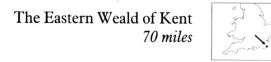

The Eastern Weald of Kent
70 miles

Kent is justly called the 'Garden of England' and this gentle, wooded countryside, scattered with orchards, is the apt setting for many lovely villages, windmills and romantic castles. On the coast, three ancient Cinque Ports dream of forgotten glory and the battle that shaped England's history.

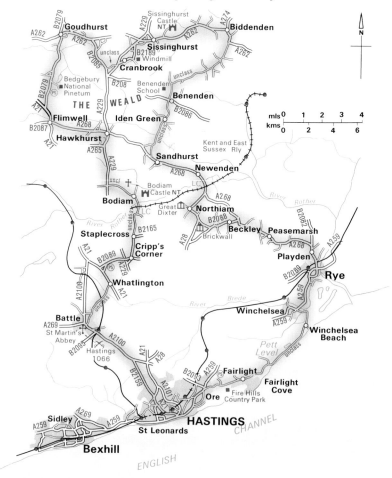

Sissinghurst Castle (NT) Home of the late Harold Nicolson, and his wife Vita Sackville-West who created the magnificent gardens.

Biddenden Picturesque village, famous for the legend of the Maids.

Rye Charming old town and former Cinque Port. Ypres Tower Museum and Lamb House (NT), home of the novelist Henry James.

Winchelsea Former Cinque Port. Museum in 14th-century Court Hall.

HARROGATE PUMP ROOM

This Victorian panel of the angel troubling the waters commemorates the discovery of the Old Sulphur Well around which the Royal Pump Room, now a museum of costume, was built in 1842.

became a popular spa resort. The Royal Baths, opened in 1897, became one of the largest hydrotheraphy establishments in the world.

On the south side of the town is a 200-acre common known as the Stray. A path joins Valley Gardens where there is an attractive sun pavilion, and the 60-acre Harlow Car Gardens, with its comprehensive collection of plants, shrubs and trees, and trial grounds for experimental agriculture. With its location and many attractions it is not surprising that the town has now become a busy conference centre.

HARTINGTON, Derbyshire   *15 SK16*
Overlooked by the red sandstone church, this grey limestone village on the River Dove is built round a spacious square and set in the beautiful moorland scenery of the Peak District. This is one of the few villages outside Leicestershire where Stilton cheese is permitted to be made.

HARTLAND, Devon   *2 SS22*
Three miles inland from the lighthouse and spectacular sheer cliffs of Hartland Point, this little town is situated in bleak, flat and sparsely populated farming country. There is an interesting 14th-century church one and a half miles west, and one mile farther are the savage cliffs of Hartland Quay. The dangers of this coast are portrayed in Hartland Quay Museum's shipwreck exhibits.

HARTLEBURY,
  Hereford & Worcester   *9 SO87*
A 17th-century wing of 13th to 18th-century Hartlebury Castle now contains a fascinating folk museum, the Hereford and Worcester County Museum, with a varied collection of exhibits.

HARTLEPOOL, Cleveland   *20 NZ53*
Although there are some remains of the medieval walls of this ancient seaport on Hartlepool Bay, most of the town is thoroughly modern, with busy docks, modern marina and fish quay, nuclear

power-station and diverse industries. The Maritime Museum features the maritime history of the town, and its shipbuilding industry which came to an end in 1962 when the last shipyard was closed. Gray Art Gallery and Museum is of interest.

HARWICH, Essex   *12 TM23*
The ancient walled town and port of Harwich grew up on a small peninsula, and this area of narrow streets still retains its medieval atmosphere. The 180ft-diameter fort known as the Redoubt was built in 1808 to defend the port against Napoleonic invasion. Round the bay is Parkestone Quay, departure point for continental ferries. Dovercourt, on the south side, has a sandy beach and has developed into a busy seaside resort.

HASCOMBE, Surrey   *5 TQ03*
From 100-acre Winkworth Arboretum, one mile north of Hascombe, there are fine views of the North Downs. This hillside arboretum with two lakes is especially worth visiting in May for bluebells and October for autumn foliage.

HASLEMERE, Surrey   *5 SU93*
Situated in hilly, wooded country, much of it designated an area of outstanding natural beauty and ideal for walking, this small town is well-known for its Dolmetsch Musical Instrument Workshops where there is a museum of musical instruments. An annual festival held in July is devoted to early music. The town also boasts a unique Educational Museum, founded in 1888 by a Victorian surgeon called Sir Jonathan Hutchinson, who was an avid collector.

HASTINGS, E Sussex   *6 TQ80*
Now a popular seaside resort, whose three-mile promenade is reached by narrow streets though the old half-timbered town, Hastings was one of the Cinque Ports. The

harbour silted up centuries ago, but fishing boats are still winched up on the shingle beach, their nets hung up in unusual three-storey huts. The Fishermen's Museum contains the last lugger built in the town in 1909. Hastings Museum and the Museum of Local History are also of interest. The remains of a Norman castle (OACT) on the cliffs are a reminder that here William the Conqueror prepared for his decisive battle in 1066, actually fought six miles inland at **Battle**. Near the castle are the extensive St Clements' Caves (OACT).

HATFIELD, Hertfordshire   *5 TL20*
Hatfield New Town, begun in 1946, lies adjacent to the ancient market town. Imposing E-shaped Hatfield House (OACT) was built in the early 17th century for the influential Cecil family, and has a large park. Its fine contents include portraits of Queen Elizabeth I, who spent much of her childhood in the nearby Old Palace, of which one wing only remains.

HATHERSAGE, Derbyshire   *15 SK28*
Beautifully situated above the River Derwent, this sturdy Peak District village was the inspiration for 'Morton' in Charlotte Brontë's *Jane Eyre*. She stayed at the 18th-century vicarage and must have taken her heroine's name from the Eyre family monuments in the church. Robin Hood's friend 'Little John' is said to be buried in a 14ft grave in the churchyard.

HAVERFORDWEST, Dyfed   *7 SM91*
Dominated by the hill-top ruins of a Norman castle 'slighted' by Cromwell during the Civil War, the houses of this important market town crowd the slopes of two hills. There are splendid views from the castle (OACT), which now houses the town's museum, art gallery and record office. St Mary's Church dates from the 13th to 15th centuries.

HATFIELD HOUSE *A tribute to the wealth and influence of the Cecil family in the 17th century, this great mansion replaced an earlier house where Elizabeth I spent her childhood.*

The Northern Dales
71 miles

Widdale, Wensleydale, Swaledale, Dentdale, Barbondale: these lonely valleys on the borders of Yorkshire and Cumbria are ringed by high fells and rugged summits, a country of isolated hill farms and grey-stone towns and villages.

Leave **Hawes** on an unclassified road (SP Hardrow, Muker) and at the T-junction turn left, then next right, following the Muker signs to ascend the Buttertubs Pass (alternatively, keep on to Hardrow for access to Hardrow Force). Descend to Swaledale and at the junction with B6270 turn left and drive through **Thwaite** to **Keld** (follow signs for a detour to Kisdon Force) and continue to **Nateby**. Here turn right on to B6259 for **Kirkby Stephen** and leave by A685 Kendal road. After 2 miles turn left on to A683 (SP Kirkby Lonsdale, Sedbergh) and drive to **Sedbergh**, then take the unclassified road to **Dent**. Return on this road for ¾mile then turn left (SP Barbon). At **Gawthrop** turn left again and drive through Barbondale, branching right

into **Barbon**. Follow the Sedbergh signs for ¼mile, then turn left on to A683 (SP Kirkby Lonsdale). At the junction with A65 turn left (SP Skipton; alternatively right to visit Kirkby Lonsdale), drive to **Ingleton** and here turn left on to B6255 for the return to Hawes.

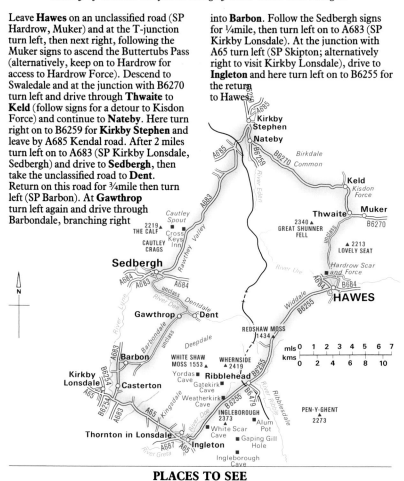

PLACES TO SEE

Hawes Famous for the making of Wensleydale Cheese. Yorkshire Dales National Park Centre.

Hardrow Force Path to 100ft waterfall from the Green Dragon PH at Hardrow.

Buttertubs Pass The 1726ft Pass links Wensleydale and Swaledale. The 'buttertubs' are deep limestone shafts of uncertain origin.

Keld Nearby is the spectacular Kisdon Force waterfall.

Kirkby Stephen Pretty old town with a fine church.

Cross Keys Inn (NT) From the 17th-century inn a path leads to Cautley Spout waterfall.

Sedbergh National Park Centre.

Dent Picturesque old stone village in lovely countryside.

Ingleton Centre of the Craven District, with many caves to explore.

HAWES, N Yorkshire   *19 SD88*
Situated in the heart of the Yorkshire Dales National Park, this scattered little village of grey stone cottages on the River Ure is an ideal starting point for exploring the high moors of Wensleydale. There is a National Park Centre and a Folk Museum of the Upper Dales. A 100ft-high waterfall, Hardraw Force, can be reached by a footpath behind the Green Dragon Inn.

HAWICK, Borders   *24 NT51*
Some of the fascinating exhibits in the local museum and art gallery reflect the importance of the wool trade in the history

of this large Border town, world-famous for knitwear, and situated in Teviotdale. The Horse Monument in the High Street commemorates the defeat of the English by local youths in 1514, evoked annually in an event known as the Common Riding.

HAWKSHEAD, Cumbria   *18 SD39*
Near the head of Esthwaite Water, the stone cottages of this delightful Lake District village are clustered round little courtyards and narrow alleys. William Wordsworth attended the grammar school here from 1778 to 1787. The school was built in 1585 and is now a museum

containing the poet's desk, on which he carved his name. Nearby is Anne Tyson's cottage where he lodged. The pre-Reformation Courthouse (NT) dating from the 15th century is of great interest.

HAWORTH, W Yorkshire   *15 SE03*
A small Pennine manufacturing town of slate-roofed, grey-stone houses, Haworth lies on the edge of sombre moors made famous by Emily Brontë's *Wuthering Heights*. The steep, paved little main street is now flanked by shops designed to appeal to the tourists who flock here from all over the world. At the top a lane winds past the churchyard to the parsonage (OACT) where the Brontë sisters lived from 1820 to 1861. Inside, the house contains items of furniture and personal possessions belonging to this gifted family. The Keighley and Worth Valley Railway, connecting Keighley and Oxenhope, has a station, workshops and museum.

HAXEY, Humberside   *16 SK79*
Remnants of the ancient strip system of field division can still be found in this old farming centre. A custom known as Throwing the Hood takes place here every January 6th, Twelfth Night. The game, which resembles a boisterous Rugby match, consists of a competition to get several 'hoods' to various village inns, while costumed 'boggins' try to intercept them. The custom is said to have originated in medieval times when the lady of the manor lost her hood while out riding, and a group of peasants competed to return it.

HAYLE, Cornwall   *1 SW53*
On the estuary of the Hayle River, in St Ives Bay, this port and market town has fine, dune-backed sands. Holidaymakers will find plenty of interest at Bird Paradise (OACT). In addition to a collection of colourful and exotic birds, rare breeds of domestic animals can be found in Paradise Farm, and there is also a miniature steam railway for enthusiasts.

THE HAXEY HOOD

The place of Lady de Mowbray's hood is now taken by several heavy leather rolls which are tossed into the crowd to be fought for and borne off in triumph. The King Boggin and his 11 strangely garbed attendants try to capture the hoods.

HAYLING ISLAND,
Hampshire   *4 SU70*
Joined to the mainland by a road bridge, this flat island, approximately ten square miles in area, between Langstone and Chichester Harbours has a three-mile-long seafront on the southern side, backing the main sandy beach. Grassy dunes lie between the road and shore and part of this area has become a popular holiday centre.

HAY-ON-WYE, Powys   *8 SO24*
Booklovers come to this market town, beautifully situated on the River Wye at the north-east corner of the Brecon Beacons National Park, to visit the 'largest second-hand bookshop in the world', housed in an old cinema. The older part of the town, with its narrow, winding streets and little shops is particularly attractive.

HEACHAM, Norfolk   *12 TF63*
Pocahontas, the Indian Princess who married a local man, John Rolfe, a settler in Virginia, in 1614, is commemorated in the sign of this village, just inland from the Wash. Norfolk Lavender (OACT) the largest growers and distillers of lavender in Britain, with fields covering 100 acres, can be found at nearby Caley Mill. There is a herb garden and shop.

HELMINGHAM, Suffolk   *12 TM15*
The magnificent parkland (OACT) of Helmingham Hall, a moated half-timbered house where the two drawbridges are still raised at night, contains red and fallow deer and Highland cattle.

HELMSLEY, N Yorkshire   *15 SE68*
Starting point of the Cleveland Way, this attractive market town of red-roofed greystone houses lies in a hollow of the River Rye at the edge of the moors. Only gaunt ruins remain of the 12th- to 13th-century castle (AM).

HELSTON, Cornwall   *1 SW62*
A busy market town, Helston is particularly worth visiting on Floral Day, on or near May 8th. This is the day of the ancient Furry Dance, with dancing up and down the hilly streets, just as described in the popular song. Nearby is the fascinating Cornwall Aero Park with collections of historic aircraft and motor vehicles. An added attraction are the reproduction old-world cobbled streets of Flambards Village. The story of Cornish tin-mining is re-created at Poldark Mine and Wendron Forge, three miles north of Helston.

HEMEL HEMPSTEAD,
Hertfordshire   *5 TL00*
Since 1947 a sprawling new town has been added to the original attractive market town on the River Gade in the Chilterns. Several shops in the delightful High Street, which is lined with 18th-century buildings, have charming bow-fronted windows. To the south is the Grand Union Canal.

HENLEY-ON-THAMES,
Oxfordshire   *4 SU78*
Henley Royal Regatta, held each year at the beginning of July, has made the pleasant Thames-side town internationally famous. This rowing regatta along a straight stretch of the river has been part of the high-society season since late Victorian days. The town is well provided with old coaching inns, and many of the houses in the main streets have Georgian frontages. Altogether over 300 buildings in the town are listed as 'of special architectural or historic interest'. Particularly interesting is the Chantry House (OACT) which dates back to the 15th century. Gabled Elizabethan Greys Court (NT) two miles west, retains part of a medieval castle. Four miles north-west of Henley, Stonor Park (OACT) contains examples of some of the earliest domestic architecture in the county. In July and August, Fawley Court (OACT), designed by Sir Christopher Wren and now the Divine Mercy College can be visited. There are furnishings by Grinling Gibbons and a museum devoted to the Polish Army.

THE ROYAL REGATTA

The course of Henley's Royal Regatta runs between Temple Island and the town's bridge. The regatta developed from the first Oxford–Cambridge boat race held here in 1829.

HEREFORD, see p. 114.

HERMITAGE CASTLE,
Borders   *24 NY59*
In 1566 Mary Queen of Scots came to this sturdy 14th-century castle (AM) to visit the wounded Earl of Bothwell. A year later she married the earl, after the murder of her husband Lord Darnley.

HERSTMONCEUX,
E Sussex   *6 TQ61*
This small village is the setting for an attractive mid 15th-century moated castle. Restored in the 1930s, the fine fortified brick manor house contains the Royal Greenwich Observatory which moved here when Greenwich became too polluted. Only the grounds are open.

THE YORKSHIRE DALES *Illuminated by a sudden ray of sunlight, the fence along the Oughtershaw road out of Hawes stands out sharply against the sombre tones of the high moorland landscape.*

Hereford, Hereford & Worcester 9 SO53

West Mercia's Ancient Capital

'Closely beneath us lay the dark rich flats of hedgey Worcestershire and the copse-chequered slopes of rolling Hereford, white with the blossom of apples.'

HENRY JAMES, *A Passionate Pilgrim*

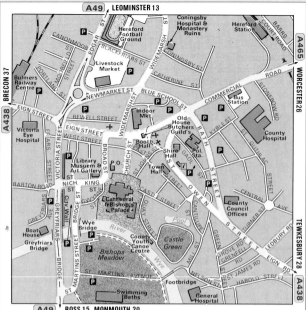

LEAFY HEREFORD *seen from the banks of the River Wye.*

ANCIENT BOOKS *The cathedral's chained libraries are treasurehouses of rare manuscripts.*

On the banks of the River Wye, to the east of the Welsh mountains, Hereford was founded about AD 700 and became the Saxon capital of West Mercia. There has been a cathedral here since then, the present building dating from the 12th century. Situated among orchards and rich grazing pastures, Hereford is famous for its cider, having the world's biggest cider-making plant, and for the beef of its red-and-white Hereford Cattle. To the west is the beautiful Golden Valley, and to the south spectacular stretches of the Wye Valley and the dramatic gorge of Symonds Yat. Despite modern development, the streets in the centre of this busy market town and administrative centre are lined with attractive 17th- and 18th-century houses. High Town and the Buttermarket, now a spacious pedestrian precinct, was the original market place in Saxon times. Gwynne Street is named after a famous, if not particularly respectable lady who was born

here: Nell Gwynne, the orange-girl who became the favourite mistress of Charles II.

In one of the most attractive areas of the town a 15th-century six-arched stone bridge spans the River Wye, overlooked by the cathedral. The massive red sandstone tower was built in the early 14th century, but sadly the Norman building was partly destroyed in the 18th century when the west tower collapsed. The beautiful Early English Lady Chapel dates from the 16th century, and the impressive north transept dates from the 13th century. Of particular interest are the fine brasses, and the chained library with over 1600 books. Another great treasure in the Cathedral is a unique late 13th-century *Mappa Mundi*, a map of the world, which shows the world as being flat, with Jerusalem at its centre. Every third year the Three Choirs Festival is held here, an event shared with Worcester and Gloucester. Adjoining the cathedral, the Bishop's Cloisters and the delightful College of the Vicars Choral are well worth visiting.

JACOBEAN SPLENDOUR *is preserved in the Old House which stands in High Town, once the old market place.*

PLACES TO SEE

The Bishop's Palace This basically Norman hall has a fine Georgian façade. It is connected to the cathedral by a 15th-century gallery.

Bulmers Railway Centre On the premises of H P Bulmer Ltd, a cider-makers founded in 1887, this railway centre is operated by the 6000 Locomotive Association. One Sunday a month and at Easter and on Spring Bank Holidays the engines can be seen in steam, and the museum is open at other times in the summer months.

Churchill Gardens Museum and Brian Hatton Art Gallery A Regency house in fine grounds contains a Victorian nursery, butler's pantry and parlour. The art gallery mainly has works by local artist Brian Hatton.

Museum of Cider A fascinating museum illustrating the history of British and European cidermaking from the 16th century onwards.

Hereford Museum and Art Gallery Exhibitions in the art gallery are changed every month and exhibits in the museum include Roman tessellated pavements.

The Old House (OACT) Jacobean furniture is displayed in the rooms of this beautifully restored 17th-century house in High Town.

St John's and Coningsby Museum Armour and other items connected with the Order and Chapel of Knights of St John are displayed in an early 13th-century hall. Adjoining almshouses were added in 1614.

All Saints Church Like the cathedral, this church too has a chained library, including a 15th-century book on the Seven Deadly Sins.

HERTFORD, Hertfordshire *5 TL31*
Three rivers, the Lea, Beane and Rib meet at the centre of this ancient and picturesque county town. Only a modernised 16th-century gatehouse remains of the castle where Elizabeth I spent much of her childhood, but there is a genuine secret passage. The riverside grounds are open.

HEVER, Kent *5 TQ44*
Wealthy American William Waldorf Astor bought Hever Castle (OACT) a small crenellated 15th-century moated manor house in 1903, and spent a small fortune on sympathic restoration. A miniature Tudor-style village was built to provide extra accommodation, a 35-acre lake excavated, and Italian garden, maze and Tudor-style flowerbeds created. Hever has recently changed hands, but house and gardens remain open.

HEXHAM, Northumberland *19 NY96*
A busy shopping and market centre, beautifully situated on the River Tyne, Hexham is a convenient base for visiting the Northumberland Dales and Hadrian's Wall. From the Seal, a public park originally a monastic enclosure, there are views of the town below. Of particular interest is the abbey dating from the 12th century, with a fine Anglo-Saxon crypt remaining from the original church completed in 678. The many treasures in the church include an Anglo-Saxon frith stool, font bowl and cross, a Roman monument and altars, and medieval misericords.

HIGH FORCE WATERFALL,
  Co Durham *19 NY82*
High Force is reached by a short wooded path opposite the High Force Hotel on the B6277. One of England's most spectacular waterfalls, it is particularly impressive when, swollen by rain, the Tees cascades over the cliff of the Great Whin Sill to plunge to a deep glen-enclosed pool 70ft below.

HIGH WYCOMBE,
  Buckinghamshire *4 SU89*
Situated in a gap of the Chiltern Hills, this large town is well-known for its furniture industry, although other industries today include paper-manufacture and engineering. The town's furniture industry developed from the simple manufacture of chairs using wood from the beautiful Chiltern beeches, and this is shown in the Wycombe Chair and Local History Museum. The Guildhall dates from 1757 and there are Elizabethan almshouses.

HINGHAM, Norfolk *12 TG00*
Elegant Georgian houses cluster round the two squares of Hingham, evidence of its former prosperity as a market town. In 1637 one of President Abraham Lincoln's ancestors emigrated from here to Hingham, Massachusetts, a settlement founded by a local rector. The president's bust can be seen in the splendid 14th-century church.

HITCHIN, Hertfordshire *11 TL12*
This old market town on the River Hiz has many buildings of architectural interest, including the 17th-century Biggin Almshouses, moated 18th-century Hitchin Priory and perpendicular St Mary's Church containing fine 15th-century screens.

HODNET HALL GARDENS *Ornamental ponds and well-stocked trout lakes, surrounded by attractive woodland are a feature of these lovely Midland gardens, at their best in spring and autumn.*

HODNET, Shropshire *9 SJ62*
A rare chained 15th-century Nuremberg Bible can be found in the 14th-century church of this small hill town, which has black-and-white timbered houses typical of north-west England. The beautiful 60-acre landscaped gardens (OACT) of Victorian Hodnet Hall are well worth a visit.

HOGHTON, Lancashire *14 SD62*
Hoghton Tower (OACT) contains a magnificent banqueting hall and several state rooms. There is also a collection of antique dolls and dolls' houses. Hoghton lays claim, as do several other mansions, to be the place where James I knighted the loin of beef, hence 'sirloin'.

HOLBEACH, Lincolnshire *11 TF32*
At the centre of Lincolnshire's bulb-growing district, rightly called 'Parts of Holland', this ancient market town is full of sightseers in tulip season.

HOLKER, Cumbria *18 SD37*
Magnificent red-sandstone 16th-century Holker Hall (OACT) lies in a 122-acre park containing a large herd of deer as well as formal and woodland gardens and children's adventure playground. Additional attractions include the large motor museum, countryside museum, aquarium, and large-gauge model railway.

HOLKHAM, Norfolk *12 TF84*
Built by William Kent in 1734 for the 1st Earl of Leicester, this vast Palladian mansion is set amid magnificent landscaped parkland. The house has a marble hall and the magnificent state rooms with their fine furnishings contain works by Rubens and Van Dyck. The 1st Earl's nephew, Thomas Coke, carried out his pioneering agricultural experiments on the estate and his reforms played a significant part in the Agricultural Revolution.

HOLT, Norfolk *12 TG03*
Four miles inland from Cley-next-the-Sea, this pleasant old market town is the site of famous Gresham's School. Founded by Sir Thomas Gresham in 1555, the school moved to the Cromer road in 1900. To the south-east are the ruins of the late 15th-century moated Baconsthorpe Castle (AM).

HONITON, Devon *2 ST10*
Allhallows Museum has displays of the lace for which this attractive small town, at the heart of dairy-farming country, was famous from the 16th to 19th century. The craft just about survives locally, and lacemaking demonstrations are given at the museum. The museum also contains locally-excavated prehistoric animal bones.

HORNSEA, Humberside *16 TA24*
Lying between the 487-acre freshwater lake of Hornsea Mere, and the sea and sandy beach three-quarters of a mile away, this Holderness town has become a popular holiday resort. An additional attraction is Hornsea Pottery (OACT), where there are factory tours, a country crafts centre, a mini-zoo and a model village.

HORRINGER, Suffolk *12 TL86*
The 104ft-high domed rotunda is the central feature of the village's Ickworth House (NT), built between 1794 and 1830. Standing in a park landscaped by Capability Brown, the house contains 18th-century and Regency French furniture, silver and pictures.

HORSHAM, W Sussex *5 TQ13*
Despite extensive modern development, this busy town retains many interesting old buildings, particularly in a cul-de-sac known as the Causeway, leading to the 12th-century and later church. A 16th-century black-and-white timbered house here contains the local museum.

THE HOUSE OF GOD
CHURCHES
From Saxon to Victorian Times

At some periods during the Roman occupation of Britain, Christianity was tolerated or encouraged, but at others, Christians were persecuted. During the Dark Ages Christianity in England would have been almost submerged by pagan cults, but for the Celtic monastic communities in Ireland, Wales and parts of Scotland who have kept the faith alive until the conversion, or re-conversion, of England was achieved in the course of the nine decades following the landing of St Augustine in 597.

THE PARISH CHURCH is, almost invariably, the oldest building in a village. Very rarely is this church the product of a single building phase or fashion and most churches display the evidence of several stages of rebuilding, enlargement and repair. Only in the small number of cases where a medieval church has been completely excavated have all the different phases been recognised, and sometimes ten or more episodes of rebuilding and adaptation are revealed. Little is known about the earliest English Christian churches, which were probably simple timber buildings, perhaps resembling the Saxon log-walled church which survives at Greensted-juxta-Ongar in Essex. Most Saxon churches seem to have been provided by members of the local landowning nobility and until a church was built, peasants would have worshipped in the open air under a preaching cross, with the service being conducted by a priest dispatched from a nearby 'minster' church.

THE SAXON CHURCHES that were built during the closing centuries of Saxon rule in England have, for the vast majority, disappeared completely in the course of successive rebuilding operations, but a number of very attractive examples survive, normally as

components in churches incorporating the work of many different ages. One of the most appealing is at Earls Barton in Northamptonshire. Here, the original church was dominated by its massive tower, as was also the case at Barton-on-Humber in Humberside, where another Saxon tower survives and where the church has recently undergone an extensive programme of excavation and restoration. Both these towers display the characteristic 'flat band' form of decoration. A Saxon church which is virtually complete can be seen at Bradford-on-Avon in Wiltshire, while the churches at Wing in Buckinghamshire, Escomb in Co Durham and Brixworth in Northamptonshire are among others which have substantial legacies of Saxon masonry.

Both the Saxons and their Norman successors employed a 'Romanesque' form of architecture which was distantly inherited from the Roman world. This style is associated with the use of rounded arches, which restricted the size of buildings, and the provision of window

FARLEIGH (above), although modified, suggests the simple form of a Norman village church.

ST PETER'S CHURCH (left) at Barton-upon-Humber preserves a rare Saxon tower.

openings. Norman church architecture was variable in terms of its quality and stability, splendour and decoration. In its most austere form, Norman architecture is evident in scores of rather gloomy little parish churches, while monumental, impressive and dignified expressions of the Norman style can be seen in the cathedrals at Durham, St Albans and St David's. Most Norman churches contain at least a morsel of decorative carving, often in the form of bands of geometrical lozenge or chevron patterns.

THE 'EARLY ENGLISH' style, a new system of architecture based on the pointed arch, was developed towards the end of the 12th century and offered many new possibilities. It is often associated with graceful but restrained interiors with high, vaulted roofs and narrow, pointed 'lancet' windows which are often provided in groups of twos or threes. Such groups of lancets represented the early stages in the development of the ornate window tracery which was to become such a highlight of church architecture in the centuries that followed. In its most imposing forms, Early English architecture can be admired at some of the great northern Cistercian monasteries like Fountains Abbey or in cathedrals such as Salisbury. It is displayed in some stately churches, like the one at Skelton near York, but it was also the style that was in fashion during one of the most vigorous periods in parish church building and was used in scores of inexpensive and unadorned little churches, like the pure and simple building at Up Marden in West Sussex.

Further experiments with the pointed Gothic arch and increasing proficiency in the use of buttresses to relieve the stresses placed on walls allowed windows to become larger and more ornate. At the same time, the Decorated style, which emerged around 1275, emphasised not only the geometrical or flowing patterns of window tracery, but also the embellishment of capitals with exuberant foliate carvings, sacrificing the purity and serenity of the Early English style for displays of lively, detailed carving. The Decorated style may perhaps be seen at its best at Wells cathedral, but it also found expression in some remarkable parish churches.

THE PERPENDICULAR style began to be adopted around 1350. It had less in common with the architectural styles of the continent than its predecessors and was associated with a strong emphasis upon the vertical line as expressed in narrow window mullions and soaring towers. In terms of detail and decoration,

BRADFORD-ON-AVON (above) This Saxon church was remarkably well built for the period.

KILPECK (right) The elaborate carving, not typical of Norman churches, was a result of local patronage and unusual local skill.

WINDOW TRACERY (right) evolved in the Early English period when two or more windows were combined under one arch and the space beneath the point was pierced.

PATRINGTON CHURCH (left) with its large, mullioned windows, pinnacles and delicate stonework, is a fine example of the Decorated style which spanned a century.

CIRCULAR WINDOWS are sometimes seen in Norman and Decorated churches. The one in St Mary's Cheltenham appears, somewhat unusually, in a side-chapel.

LAVENHAM parish church (below) is one of many splendid English churches employing the Perpendicular style.

the spotlight shifted from stone carving to woodwork and the painted glass in the vast window spaces. The Perpendicular style never really passed out of fashion, and although a few Classical churches were built during the 18th century, Perpendicular designs were still being used in the English backwaters when the 19th-century Gothic Revival made each and every medieval Gothic style fashionable. As a result of its longevity and the periodic rebuilding and enlargement of many older medieval churches, the Perpendicular style is the one that is most frequently displayed in parish churches, and most have at least some Perpendicular work. Since it appeared after the completion of most great cathedral-building operations it tends to be associated more with parish churches than with the greater buildings. The churches at Lavenham and Long Melford in Suffolk, Titchmarsh in Northamptonshire and Batcombe and North Petherton in Somerset are among many fine examples of the Perpendicular style.

LOCAL MATERIALS and stylistic preferences also found expression in the building of parish churches. This brought regional variety to the Romanesque and Gothic styles, which influenced church design throughout the whole of Britain, and to the continental Flamboyant style of the 14th and 15th centuries which had some impact in Scotland and Ireland. Only when a wealthy and willing patron was available could top-quality stone be imported from a prestigious quarry like Barnack in Cambridgeshire or Doulton in Somerset. Otherwise, the church builders used the products of local quarries, while in the chalklands, where the local stone was usually too soft for external work, a good 'freestone' was imported for use in the corners and details while walls were built of flints or river cobbles. The local regional differences which were due to geological circumstances are easily explained, but it is much harder to know why other architectural features should have become the hallmarks of some areas, but be ignored in others. In the East Midlands, for example, broach spires were extremely popular during the earlier centuries of the Gothic era yet they only became numerous in other areas during the Gothic Revival. In Yorkshire the regional taste tended to favour a long, low building with an imposing tower that was tipped with tiny pinnacles, while in Hertfordshire the tower was often capped by a small leaded spirelet. In these and many other ways, the development of local building traditions prevented the national building styles from becoming repetitive and monotonous.

HORTON-IN-RIBBLESDALE,
N Yorkshire *18 SD87*
The Pennine Way passes through his little moorland village in the heart of the Yorkshire Dales, a convenient centre for fell-walkers and potholers. Beneath the huge stone terraces of 2273ft Pen-y-Ghent lie Hunt Pot and Hull Pot.

HOUGHTON, Norfolk *12 TF72*
Eighteenth-century Houghton Hall (OACT), approached from the village by a long avenue through beautiful parkland where a herd of white deer roam, was designed for Sir Robert Walpole, England's first prime minister by Colin Campbell and Thomas Ripley, and is one of the finest examples of Palladian architecture in England. Staterooms contain interior decorations and furniture by William Kent and there are many family portraits and exquisite porcelain. Traditional heavy horses and Shetland ponies can be seen in the stables.

HADRIAN'S WALL *The view from Housesteads, one of the 17 Roman forts along the wall.*

HOUSESTEADS,
Northumberland *19 NY76*
Perhaps the finest of the Roman forts on Hadrian's Wall, 'Vircovicium' (AM, NT) would have accommodated 1000 infantrymen in its five acres: ramparts, gateways, granaries, latrines, headquarters and barracks are still clearly visible. There is a museum, and from the fort, with its cliff-top setting, there are fine views of the wall snaking over the bleak hills of the Border country. To the west is the substantial ruin of a Roman mile-castle.

HUDDERSFIELD,
W Yorkshire *15 SE11*
Occupying a hilly site in the Colne Valley on the edge of the Pennines, Huddersfield has been a centre for textile production since the 18th century, tall mill chimneys still being a feature of the town's landscape. There is an unusual Museum of Hand Tools, while exhibits in the Tolson Memorial Museum include those relating to the development of the cloth industry. Famous artists represented in the art gallery include L S Lowry, Turner and Constable.

HUGHENDEN,
Buckinghamshire *4 SU89*
Prime Minister Benjamin Disraeli lived at Hughenden Manor (NT), a large mansion he had remodelled in 1862. It stands in a 169-acre estate which includes the church where he is buried. The statesman's study contains letters from Queen Victoria and remains as it was at the time of his death.

The North-West Norfolk Coast
76 miles

Open countryside and wide horizons are characteristic of this corner of Norfolk. On the coast, miles of flat sandy and shingle beaches are backed by salt marshes where samphire grows.

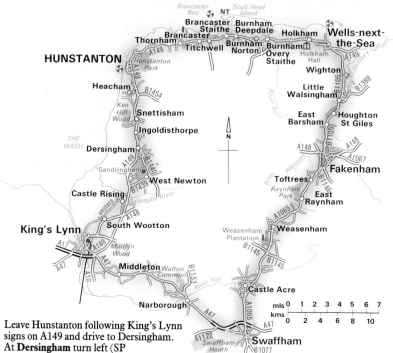

Leave Hunstanton following King's Lynn signs on A149 and drive to Dersingham. At **Dersingham** turn left (SP Sandringham) on to B1440. Pass the gates of Sandringham Park and in 1 mile turn right (no sign) into **West Newton**. At the main road turn left to rejoin A149 for a mile, then turn right to **Castle Rising**. Drive on to **South Wootton**, go forward at the traffic lights, and at the T-junction turn right (A1076) into King's Lynn. Leave **King's Lynn** by the Swaffham road (A47) and drive through Middleton and Narborough then in 4 miles branch left into **Swaffham**. Take the Cromer road, A1065 and in 2¾ miles turn left to visit **Castle Acre**. In the village turn right (SP Newton) then rejoin A1065. Continue through Weasenham and East Raynham then in 2½ miles turn right for **Fakenham**. From the town centre follow King's Lynn signs and join A148, then in ½ mile turn right (SP Walsingham) on to B1105. Drive through **Little Walsingham** and continue on B1105 towards Wells. In 4½ miles turn left, joining A149, then turn right (SP The Beach) to enter **Wells-next-the-Sea**. At the end of the town, join A149 again (SP Hunstanton) and drive through **Holkham** and several north-coast villages and resorts to Old Hunstanton. Beyond the village turn right (SP Front) for **Hunstanton**.

PLACES TO SEE

Hunstanton A popular seaside resort with good bathing.

Sandringham Park The grounds and the house are open regularly in summer.

Castle Rising (AM) A fine, restored Norman keep with impressive earthworks. Trinity Hospital Almshouses (OACT) date from the 17th century.

King's Lynn The old centre has many attractive and historic buildings; of the two market places Tuesday Market is the most handsome. St George's Guildhall (NT) is now a theatre; two museums of local history are the Lynn Museum and St George's Guildhall. Notable buildings include the Custom House, the Hanseatic Warehouse, Hampton Court and Thoresby College. St Margaret's and St Nicholas' church are also of interest.

Swaffham A most attractive 18th-century town with a lively market on Saturdays.

Castle Acre Impressive earthworks of the castle and a ruined priory are of interest in this delightful little village.

Houghton St Giles The Slipper Chapel is the last in a chain of chapels on the pilgrim's way to Walsingham.

Little Walsingham A picturesque village with the remains of a priory and the modern Anglican shrine of Our Lady. The Shirehall Museum is housed in an 18th-century courtroom.

Holkham Hall Magnificent mansion (OACT) where the 18th-century agriculturalist, Thomas Coke, lived and made his experiments which had a far-reaching influence on English agriculture.

SUMMER RECREATION *The game of bowls, played on this well-tended green at Hunstanton, the largest resort in north-west Norfolk, is ideally suited to the Victorian atmosphere of the old town.*

HULL, Humberside   15 TA02

The Humber Bridge, opened in 1981, spans the River Humber and is (or was when it was completed) the largest single-span suspension bridge in the world. Previously, the easiest way to reach the city from the south was by ferry from New Holland. Officially named Kingston-upon-Hull, the city was badly damaged in World War II and so contains much modern development: several of the new office blocks are architecturally very striking. Among the parts of the old city that survive is the curiously-named 'Land of Green Ginger', a narrow street that recalls Hull's former importance as a trading centre. Hull's dockland stretches for seven miles, handling a wide variety of cargoes and also serving continental ferries, although in recent years the fishing industry has drastically declined.

Displays in the Town Docks Museum illustrate the past importance of fishing, whaling and shipping to the town. Other places to visit include the Transport and Archaeological Museum; Ferens Art Gallery; and 17th-century Wilberforce House (OACT) where the anti-slavery campaigner William Wilberforce was born.

HUNGERFORD, Berkshire   4 SU36

Situated on the Kennet and Avon Canal and also the River Kennet, this pleasant town with a wide High Street and many antique shops, was granted fishing rights by John of Gaunt in the 14th century. This is celebrated at Hocktide (after Easter) by a picturesque ceremony that involves 'tutti-men' (tithe men) who carry decorated poles. The revelry lasts all day, and there is much kissing of pretty girls and distributing of oranges. Tudor Littlecote House (OACT) two miles west, has a unique collection of Cromwellian armour, interesting Roman remains, and beautiful gardens laid out around a trout stream.

HUNSTANTON, Norfolk   12 TF64

Pronounced 'Hun'ston', this town has a long sandy beach facing west towards the Wash, backed by unusual striated cliffs. The town was developed in Victorian times into the seaside resort it is today, and is divided into 'old' and 'new' towns.

HUNTINGDON, Cambridgeshire   11 TL27

At the centre of a rich agricultural area, this attractive town with fine Georgian buildings was the birthplace of Oliver Cromwell. The building where Cromwell and, later, Samuel Pepys went to school is now a museum of Cromwellian relics. Hinchingbrooke House, a Tudor manor half-a-mile west, was once the home of the Cromwells and subsequently the Earls of Sandwich. Although used as a school, it can be visited.

HUNTLY, Grampian   27 NJ54

Situated at the meeting point of two rivers, this attractive market town is popular with anglers. In a beautiful wooded park are the ruins of Huntly Castle (AM), which dates from 1602. The local history museum has a regular programme of special exhibitions and the interesting Agricultural Museum has a collection of more than 500 bygones.

HURSTBOURNE TARRANT, Hampshire   4 SU35

A little stream, tributary of the River Test, runs through this pretty village with thatched cottages, lying in a deep valley. The church contains some remarkable 14th-century murals, and there is an exhibition of crafts in the Bladon Gallery.

HUTTON-LE-HOLE, N Yorkshire   20 SE79

One of the prettiest villages in the Yorkshire Moors, its neat red-roofed houses are scattered round a green through which flows a little stream. Ryedale Folk Museum is a fascinating museum featuring reconstructed buildings such as cruck-framed houses and an Elizabethan glass furnace.

HYTHE, Kent   6 TR13

A mellow seaside town, Hythe is one of the Cinque Ports and stands on the Royal Military Canal, built for defence in Napoleonic times. The Romney, Hythe and Dymchurch Light Railway has its terminus here and half a mile north is Saltwood Castle (OACT). This was the stronghold from which Henry II's knights set out to murder Thomas Becket.

ICKLETON, Cambridgeshire   17 TL44

The Hovells is the oldest house in Ickleton and once belonged to the Cistercians. In fact, a great deal of the parish property was held by the monasteries until the Dissolution of the 1530s under Henry VIII. Caldrees manor, Mowbrays and Durhams are all legacies of medieval monastic connections. Earlier still, the Romans had a military outpost at nearby Great Chesterford, and a villa in Ickleton itself was excavated in 1842. The pre-Roman Icknield Way (see below) passes close by and probably takes its name from the Iceni tribe. Today all is quiet and the only vestiges of a once-thriving wool trade are the foundations of a mill near to Frogge Hall, a 16th-century house.

ICKNIELD WAY

One of the great pre-Roman routes, the Icknield Way is now largely only negotiable by walkers. It starts near Marlborough in Wiltshire, crosses the Thames at Goring, intersects with the old Roman road known as Watling Street at Dunstable, then passes by Letchworth and on to the Wash.

ICKWORTH HOUSE, see Horringer

IGHTHAM MOTE *Succeeding centuries have built onto the medieval foundations of this old manor.*

IGHTHAM, Kent   6 TQ55

Brick-and-tile cottages are interspersed with half-timbered houses in and around the village square. Ightham is a corruption of Etheham (or Etha's Ham) which was its original name until Norman times. The Fenpond Road church, which was largely rebuilt during the 14th and 15th centuries, boasts several brasses and sculptures. Also inside is a plaque commemorating one Benjamin Harrison, a local grocer who earned himself national recognition as an archaeologist. His nearby excavations included those of the Iron-Age settlement at Oldbury Hill, an ancient camp located across the busy bypass at the end of Sevenoaks Road. The 120-acre site is roughly in the shape of a diamond. Some two and a half miles to the south is Ightham Mote (OACT), a delightfully preserved medieval country house built partly of stone, partly of timber.

ILAM, Staffordshire 15 SK15

The River Manifold meanders past this ancient village, which was given a substantial face-lift by Jesse Watts-Russell in the last century, transforming it into a 'model' village. The Hall (NT but not open), also part of Russell's programme, has some 50 wooded acres (OACT) and houses, in part, a youth hostel. Parts of the local church date back to the 13th century. Among several items of interest is a shrine to St Bertram, supposedly the bringer of Christianity to this region. Still earlier left-overs from the past are the two Anglo-Saxon crosses in the churchyard.

ILCHESTER, Somerset 3 ST52

Although now a quiet little town, Ilchester was an important military station on the Fosse Way in Roman times. Roger Bacon, the remarkable scholar-churchman of the 13th century, was born here. A 700-year-old octagonal mace (the oldest of its kind in England) is housed in the town-hall. Some three miles north-east of the town is Lytes Cary (NT) an interesting medieval manor which preserves its 14th-century chapel and original Great Hall.

ILFRACOMBE, Devon 2 SS54

A popular holiday resort situated on Devon's lovely north coast, Ifracombe was originally just a sleepy fishing harbour, but has since evolved, thanks to 19th-century enterprise, as a thriving seaside centre. The many large Victorian houses and hotels are necessarily built in terraces, because of the steeply shelving hills that meet the shore-line. Ilfracombe's numerous coves are sand-cum-shingle and offer ample scope for rock-pool exploration. Many small craft are still to be found dotted around the picturesque harbour during the summer months, as this is the main departure point for **Lundy Island**, the bird-watchers' Mecca. Public gardens in this area are particularly well kept and there is a zoo – Bicclescombe Park Tropical Wildlife Park – south of the town at Comyn Hill. Chambercombe Manor (OACT), situated one-and-half miles south-east of Ilfracombe, is a mansion which although largely Elizabethan, has parts which are much more ancient. It is one of the oldest inhabited houses in England. A haunted room and a 12th-century cider-press are among its interesting relics and furnishings. A mile to the east, Hele Mill (OACT) has been restored to working condition and produces wholemeal flour. Watermouth Castle, three miles north-east of the town, offers varied amusements.

ILKLEY, W Yorkshire 15 SE14

Although situated in the River Wharfe valley, this inland health resort is over 700ft above sea level. At first glance the town appears comparatively modern, but tucked away here and there are some much earlier buildings: Box Tree Cottage and Manor House (OACT), which is built on the site of a Roman fort, are two prime examples. Much earlier, though, is All Saints, a 13th-century church with a fine old tower and some rare wood-carvings. Three Saxon crosses are to be seen in the churchyard. Several Bronze-Age carvings have been found in this area and examples are on display within the garden opposite the church. Nearby Heber's Ghyll is the site of the Swastika Stone, a unique carved relic believed to have been instrumental in ritual fire-worship. The surrounding Ilkley Moor remains the bleak but beautiful setting immortalised in the Yorkshire anthem *On Ilkla Moor baht 'at*.

ILKESTON, Derbyshire 10 SK44

Lace and iron are the sources of livelihood for many of the town's 35,000 inhabitants. Ilkeston is tucked just inside Derbyshire's eastern boundary and was built mainly during the 19th century on high ground above the Erewash Valley. The oldest building hereabouts is St Mary's, a parish church with some of the original Norman parts intact. A rare 14th-century stone screen and a Crusader's tomb are to be found inside. One of the community's more tangible links with the past is the three-day fair held in the market-place every October.

ILMINGTON, Warwickshire 10 SP24

A pleasant Cotswold village, this has all the 'olde-worlde' features such as mossy stone roofs and mullioned windows. Some half-a-dozen buildings in the parish are over 200 years old and include the Rectory, Crab Mill, the Manor House and Foxcote, an impressive Georgian house. The Ilmington Morris Dancers keep alive one of several annual rural events that take place in and around the region. The highest point of the hills (854ft) commands fine views of Warwickshire.

ILMINSTER, Somerset 3 ST31

A bustling market town on the A303 at the foot of the Blackdown Hills. The rows of thatched cottages just off the main road are reminiscent of those in Devon and the focal pillared market house is pleasantly surrounded by a Ham-stone square. The local high school dates back to 1586, while the church is over a century earlier still. Sir William Wadham, founder of the Oxford college named after him, was the church's main benefactor. Jordans, a house on Taunton road, was the residence of John Speke, discoverer of the definitive source of the Nile. Some three-and-a-half miles north-east of Ilminster is Barrington Court (NT), an early 16th-century Ham-stone Tudor house with eye-catching spiral chimneys. The nearby stable block dates back to the 1670s and near to it stands a decahedral sun-dial.

IMMINGHAM, Humberside 15 TA11

This dockland port acts as a sister to Grimsby, which is five miles further down towards the open sea. In recent years new deep-sea oil and coal terminals have been established here, and a large refinery is at nearby Killingholme. At South Killingholme there is a monument commemorating the Pilgrim Fathers' point of departure for Holland, prior to their departure for the New World.

INCHNADAMPH, Highland 29 NC22

Underground streams and caves are the striking features of the area surrounding this village stop-over in Scotland's wild north-western corner. Fishing is the main activity here and the local Assynt Church is on the south-eastern shore of the loch named after it. To the north are the stark ruins of Ardvreck Castle, a one-time Macleod fortress. Lovers of non-dangerous climbing will find the peaks of Quinag a delight. The hills are situated some seven miles north-west of Inchnadamph and afford superb views, including that of Glas Bheinn, a 2541ft peak and source of Eas Coul Aulin, Britain's highest waterfall. The sheer 658ft-drop can be reached by boat or on foot from Glasven.

ARDVRECK CASTLE *Ruined stronghold of the MacLeods, Ardvreck stands sentinel over Loch Assynt. Here Montrose was captured in 1650, some say by the treachery of MacLeod, and sent to his death.*

BAROQUE MASTERPIECE *The plasterwork at Ingestre church exemplifies 17th-century craftsmanship.*

INGESTRE, Staffordshire   9 SJ92
Although not fully authenticated, it is believed that the village's 1677 church was designed by Sir Christopher Wren. Inside there is an oak chancel screen and a plasterwork ceiling. The Hall suffered much fire damage in 1822 but the present building, now functioning as an arts centre, has been cleverly styled as the original hall.

INGLETON, N Yorkshire   18 SD67
A busy little town, Ingleton acts as a useful base from which to visit the abundant caves and waterfalls in the region. Some three-and-a-half-miles east is Ingleborough Hill, an impressive 2373ft peak with the remains of an Iron Age settlement at its summit. This, with Whernside and Pen-y-Ghent, forms the gruelling course of the Three Peaks race. Beneath Ingleborough is a maze of limestone and millstone-grit caves, within which is Gaping Gill, the largest limestone chamber in Britain.

INKBERROW, Hereford & Worcester   9 SP05
Half-timbered and red-brick houses and hotels are clustered round the village green. One of these, the Old Bull, is a local pub with two famous connections. Shakespeare stayed at the inn *en route* to Stratford in 1582, while much nearer to the present day, the Bull served as model for the Archers' local in radio's most popular village, Ambridge. St Peter's was built in the 12th century, but much of the church has been reconstructed over the years. Inside is the impressive canopied tomb of John Savage (a high sheriff) and some rare maps once belonging to Charles I.

INKPEN, Berkshire   4 SU36
Le Nôtre, the man who masterminded the gardens at Versailles, stayed for a spell at the village's 17th-century rectory, while the 13th-century church has connections with the Knights Templars. The summits of Inkpen Beacon and Walbury Hill, at 954ft and 974ft respectively, are the highest chalk downs in England. On Inkpen Beacon stands Combe Gibbet, a macabre reminder of the fate of pre-Victorian malefactors.

INNER HEBRIDES, Highland
The Inner Hebrides comprise Skye, Mull, Jura and Islay, plus a host of smaller islands; some well known, such as Iona, Eigg, Rhum, Tyree and Colonsay; some little visited, such as Canna, Raasay and Coll. Easily the most visited isle is Skye. This oddly-shaped piece of land is only about 50 miles long and 15 miles across, yet has over 1000 miles of craggy coastline, and

some of Scotland's wildest mountain scenery in the Cuillins. Most of the peaks in this forbidding range should only be attempted by experienced walkers and climbers. Portree is Skye's main town (if town is the right word – there are only around 8000 inhabitants). The local Royal Hotel is where Bonnie Prince Charlie bade his final farewell to Flora Macdonald before fleeing to France. The episcopal church of St Columba also has connections with Scotland's best-loved heroine: it has a special Flora Macdonald memorial window. A high percentage of Portree's work-force earn their living at the combined tweed and wool mill, but perhaps not surprisingly the expanding venture here nowadays is the tourist trade: August sees the community's own mini-Highland Games.

Further north is the oddly-named Uig (an Old Norse word for 'bay'). From here passengers can travel, with cars if they wish, to Harris and North Uist in the Outer Hebrides. Fishing is popular from Uig pier, which is the longest in Scotland. Back at the southern end of the island Kyleakin is likely to be your first port of call if you are visiting Skye by car or at the end of a rail journey. Just out from Kyleakin pier are the ruins of Castle Moil, a 600-year-old stronghold, only accessible at low tide.

Broadford, Skye's only other community of any size, is a handy base from which to explore the island. Places of interest on Skye include the Clan Donald Centre (OACT) at Armadale Castle; Dunvegan Castle (OACT), ancestral home of the Chief of the Macleod; the Skye Black House Folk Museum, a restored crofter's house; the Skye Watermill (OACT) of Glendale; and the Skye Cottage Museum at Kilmuir.

Both Eigg and Rhum, humorously known as the 'cocktail islands', tend to be somewhat bleak but draw tourists by their sheer natural beauty. Many weirdly-formed caverns punctuate Eigg's coastline and one such, the cave of St Francis, was where a vengeful 16th-century MacLeod clan was reputed to have killed 200 hapless victims by starting a fire and blocking the cave

entrance. Charred remains since found tend to bear out the macabre tale. On Rhum, the village of Kinloch and the few fertile acres around it are now readily accessible, thanks to the Nature Conservancy Council's 1957 acquisition of this land for the purpose of observing red deer.

Much further south is Mull, the second largest of the Inner Hebrides. The isle's biggest burgh is Tobermory, a fishing port as busy in the 1980s as it was in Dr Johnson's day. Places of interest include Duart Castle (OACT), home of the Macleans, and the Victorian Torosay Castle (OACT), set in magnificent gardens: both castles are near Craignure. At Dervaig, the Old Byre Heritage Centre illustrates crofting life at the time of the Clearances.

Iona lies across the water from Mull's most westerly community, Fionphort. This bleak isle is where St Columba chose to found a monastery in the 6th century. Today, the oldest building on Iona is St Oran's Chapel. Although largely restored the church has a carved Norman doorway among its 11th-century remains.

DRAMBUIE
Prince Charles Edwards
LIQUEUR

THE ISLE OF SKYE LIQUEUR

DRAMBUIE

It means 'the drink that satisfies'. The recipe came to a Mackinnon of Skye from Bonnie Prince Charlie when he arrived there in 1745.

THE ISLE OF MIST *Skye, with its spectacular landscape, seen from the coast of Rhum.*

INNERLEITHEN, Borders   *23 NT33*

The town is situated on Leithen Water near its junction with the River Tweed. Innerleithen has been long known for its woollens – the first tweed mill was opened here back in 1790. To the south of the town on the other side of the Tweed is Traquair House (OACT) which is thought to be the model for 'Tullyveolan', the house in Scott's *Waverley*.

INVERARAY, Strathclyde   *22 NN00*

This picturesque white-walled burgh on the eastern end of Loch Shira was virtually rebuilt in the late 18th century. Inveraray Castle (OACT) is the home of the Campbell clan chiefs and houses fine displays of Scottish armoury.

INVERNESS, Highland   *26 NH64*

Long dubbed the 'capital of the Highlands', Inverness is a historic burgh on the River Ness just inland from the Moray Firth. Scotland's King David built the first castle here in the 12th century, but of this and of subsequent castles built on this site, little evidence remains today, and the present castle dates from 1834. Another interesting fortress to see nowadays is

INVERNESS MUSEUM *This silver-mounted sporran and 'sgian dubh' were locally made.*

Castle Stuart, six miles east, on the A96. Also of interest is Aldourie Castle, to the south-west on the northernmost tip of Loch Ness. Inverness was the terminal point for the system of metalled military roads built by the engineer and soldier George Wade during the period 1726–1737, following on the Rebellion of 1715. Fort George, the old town barracks named after Wade, was blown up by Prince Charles Edward's forces in 1746 but a new-style Fort George was subsequently built a few miles outside town. Abertarff House (OACT) is on Church Street and dates from the mid-16th century; inside is a rare, early spiral staircase. Its present-day function is as the headquarters of *An Comunn Gaidhealach*, the Gaelic Preservation Society. The Town House in Castle Street was the scene of the first Cabinet meeting to be held outside London: Lloyd-George, holidaying in Scotland in 1921, called an emergency meeting here to discuss a letter on the question of Irish independence from Eamon de Valera, the Irish politician who became the first President of Eire. Across the river is St Andrew's Cathedral, a mid Victorian edifice with notable carved pillars. Other interesting buildings include the library, museum and art gallery.

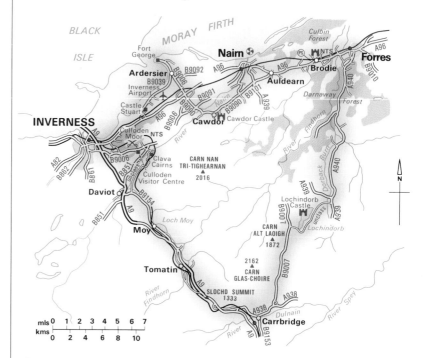

Inverness and the Moray Firth
89 miles

Inverness, capital of the Highlands, lies at the southern end of the Moray Firth, close to the tragic battlefield Culloden Moor. South and east lie the mountains of the Cairngorm range; to the north-east, Cawdor Castle and the country of Shakespeare's tragic hero Macbeth.

Leave **Inverness** on the Perth road (A9) and in 1½ miles at the roundabout take the 3rd exit on to B9006 (SP Croy) to reach Culloden Moor. Shortly after the Information Centre turn right (SP Clava Cairns), go over the next crossroads, cross the River Nairn and turn right. One mile after the Cairns turn right (SP Daviot) and in 3¼ miles turn left on to B9154 for **Moy**. Drive on past Loch Moy and later turn left on to A9. In 9 miles turn left on to A938 for **Carrbridge**. Leave by the Grantown road and in 1¾ miles turn left on to B9007 (SP Forres). Drive across the moors for 6¾ miles then turn right (SP Lochindorb) to reach the shore of the loch, with its ruined castle on an island. Carry on to the junction with A939, then turn left (SP Forres) then right on to A940 and continue to **Forres**. Leave by the Inverness road (A96) and drive through **Brodie** to **Auldearn** and then to **Nairn**. Leave by B9090 (SP Cawdor) and continue to **Cawdor**. Beyond the village, in 1¼ miles turn right then cross the River Nairn, go over the next crossroads (SP Ardersier) and keep on with B9006 and cross the main road to reach **Ardersier**. From here, B9096 leads to Fort George. From Ardersier turn left with B9039 to follow the Moray Firth coast. On reaching the junction with A96 turn right to return to Inverness.

PLACES TO SEE

Inverness The castle, built in 1834 is now used for administration; there is an information centre here. Abertarff House (OACT) contains an exhibition on the Gaels and their history. St Andrew's Cathedral has fine carved columns.

Culloden Moor (NTS) Bonnie Prince Charlie's troops were finally defeated by those of the Duke of Cumberland in 1746. Old Leanach Cottage contains information and exhibits about the battle.

Clava Cairns (AM) Three concentric rings of great stones, Clava Cairns dates from the Neolithic or early Bronze Age.

Carrbridge The landmark visitor centre has exhibitions and film shows about the Highlands.

Forres Sueno's stone (AM) commemorates a Danish victory in 1008; Nelson Tower (OACT) was built by survivors of Trafalgar.

Brodie Castle (NTS) Contains beautiful furniture, porcelain and paintings.

Auldearn The magnificent 17th-century doocot (NTS) marks the spot where Montrose raised his standard against the Covenanters for Charles I in 1645.

Cawdor Castle (OACT) This is where, according to Shakespeare, Macbeth murdered King Duncan.

Fort George (OACT) Contains the Regimental Museum of the Queen's Own Highlanders.

INVERURIE, Grampian   27 NJ72

A royal burgh, located near the confluence of the Don and the Urie, Inverurie has many features and connections of historical interest, including the visit of Mary Queen of Scots in 1562. Brandsbutt Stone (AM) is two-and-half miles north-west of Inverurie and bears ancient inscriptions, while the Easter Aquahorthies Stone Circle is some two-and-a-half miles to the west. Another early Christian monument in the area is the Maiden Stone (AM), four-and-a-half miles north-west of Inverurie.

IPSWICH, Suffolk   12 TM14

The county town of Suffolk acquired its name from an Anglo-Saxon settlement called Gippeswic. The town was eventually granted a charter by King John in 1200 and steadily grew in importance, reaching a peak as a flourishing cloth port in the 16th century. Its development then tailed off until the mid 19th century when a second upturn in fortune resulted in its present significance as a port, market town and East Anglian seat of administration. The docks now handle over 2,500,000 tons of cargo a year, being ideally placed for European trading.

Architecturally, Ipswich has many places of interest including the Ancient House in Butter Market, built in 1567 (also known as Sparrowe's House after a onetime occupant). The front of the house features the intricate decorative plasterwork known as pargeting, an art characteristic of East Anglia. Beneath the front windows are thematic panels depicting the then known continents of the world. Cardinal Wolsey was born in Ipswich and later founded the Cardinal College of St Mary. All that is left of the building today, though, is the red-brick gateway in College Street. Old Ipswich had medieval walls and Northgate Street, Westgate Street and Tower

Rampart are all reminders, along with Priory Street which once had houses built by Augustinians, Franciscans, Dominicans and Carmelites.

At the junction of Tavern and Northgate Streets is the Great White Horse Hotel. Murals on the dining-room walls record the activities here of Charles Dickens' Samuel Pickwick, hero of the *Pickwick Papers*. Christchurch Mansion (OACT), in Christchurch Park, has a fine art gallery which includes works by both Gainsborough and Constable.

COALPORT CHINA

Much prized by collectors, Coalport china was made in these old works beside the Severn from 1790 to 1926. The traditional, bottle-shaped kiln and warehouse have been restored as a museum of china and form part of the Ironbridge Gorge complex.

IRONBRIDGE, Shropshire   9 SJ60

The town is situated in the deep, wooded gorge of the River Severn and developed, like many others in this region, during the Industrial Revolution. The community takes its name from the world's first iron bridge, built here in 1778–81. It was designed by the ironmaster Abraham Darby III as an example of the quality of his cast iron and was cast at his foundry in **Coalbrookdale**. The bridge is 196ft long, weighs 380 tons and, seen from a distance, as it spans the wooded Severn Gorge, presents a romantic and inspiring picture. Nowadays access is restricted to pedestrians. Scattered along Ironbridge Gorge is a unique series of museums of industrial history, under the general title of the Ironbridge Gorge Museum. These include: Blists Hill Open Air Museum, which covers 42 acres, re-creating the iron, coal and clay industries; Coalbrookdale Museum and Furnace Site, Abraham Darby's original blast furnace; the Coalport China Works Museum; and the Severn Warehouse. To the north-west of the town are Buildwas Abbey ruins (AM), and about two miles south-west is Benthall Hall (NT), an interesting 16th-century house.

IRVINE, Strathclyde   22 NS33

A royal burgh located where the River Irvine joins Annick Water, Irvine and nearby Kilwinning have been paired to form a 'seaside new town', the first in Great Britain. In Kilwinning are the ruins and gardens of Eglinton Castle.

Robert Burns lived here between 1781 and 1783, working briefly as a flax-dresser in the Glasgow Vennel area. The Burns Club was inaugurated in 1826 and has since been converted into a museum. On the north-west perimeter of Irvine is the Ardeer explosives factory, one of Britain's major production centres for high explosives.

IRONBRIDGE *Spanning the deep gorge of the River Severn, the world's first iron bridge was made by Abraham Darby III and completed in 1781.*

Peter Davies 'jumps' the famous Ballaugh Bridge during a 1980 Formula 1 Race over the Isle of Man's famous Snaefell mountain course. These races, which started in 1907, take place on mountain roads, rising to a height of over 1300ft. Each lap is 37¾ miles and takes in more than 200 testing bends.

ISLE OF MAN, 17 SC18

Douglas Bay and Promenade provide an unrivalled first glimpse of the Isle of Man. Nowadays, all passenger vessels arrive at Douglas, which is justifiably dubbed the 'gateway to Man'. Perhaps Douglas' most famous amenity is Summerland. Alas, a disastrous fire gutted a large section of the complex and claimed many lives in 1973, but now the area is largely reconstructed. The Manx Museum and National Library provide visitors to Douglas with a glimpse of early folk life in the form of tableaux. At Laxey, the 'Lady Isabella' (OACT) can be seen, a giant wheel constructed to keep the lead mines free of water.

To the north, Ramsey lies in a 10-mile L-shaped bay. Here, the Grove Rural Life Museum has many interesting exhibits. The town makes a good base from which to go walking on the many hills to the south, which include 2034ft Snaefell.

Peel is on the west of the isle and has old twisting streets leading down to a busy fishing quay. Across the harbour from Peel is St Patrick's Isle, or Holmpatrick as the Vikings called it. The isle has many Irish connections, the most unusual of which is Peel Castle. The structure dates back to the 10th century and is 50ft high.

Back at the southern end of Man is Castletown, a strongly individualistic community situated at the mouth of Silver Burn. The 600-year-old Castle Rushen (OACT) dominates the harbour area and is remarkably well preserved. The Nautical Museum contains among its exhibits an 18th-century Manx yacht. Ronaldsway, the Isle of Man's airport, is two miles north-east of Castletown. West of Castletown are Port Erin and Port St Mary, two harbours only a mile and a half apart but with markedly different weather conditions. Port Erin is subject to persistently strong winds, while Port St Mary is a quiet haven for pleasure craft. About one mile south-west of Port St Mary is Cregneash, a village steeped in Manx customs. The Manx Open Air Folk Museum is housed in a group of traditional cottages. The Calf of Man has been designated a bird sanctuary.

ISLE OF WIGHT, Hampshire 4 SZ37

The Garden Isle was once described as a miniature England cast adrift in the English Channel. Its coastal perimeter extends some 60 miles, varying from pleasant sands, to chines (as the deep coastal ravines are called), grottoes and eye-catching rock formations. Inland, the picturesque landscape is punctuated with stone cottages, thatched farmhouses and secluded villages. The seaboard townships provide excellent facilities for holidaymakers, especially those keen on yachting and fishing. The island can be reached from four main ports: Lymington, Southampton, Southsea and Portsmouth. Assuming a Portsmouth departure, visitors arrive at Ryde, whose tourist attractions include a pavilion, canoe lake, Appley Gardens and Puckpool Park; it is the home of the Royal Victoria Yacht Club.

Leaving Ryde and moving clockwise round the island, Bembridge is the home of yet another yacht club. The nearby small public school has a library of John Ruskin's works. The last windmill on the island (NT) stands near the B3390. The Maritime Museum has an interesting collection of model ships.

The south-east side of the island is dominated by Sandown Bay. The town of Sandown is at the centre of the bay and accordingly makes an ideal base for holidaymakers. Battery Gardens are in the grounds of an old fort, while the Museum of Isle of Wight Geology houses, among other exhibits, over 5000 fossils found on the island. A pleasant six-mile cliff walk leads around the edge of the bay to Shanklin, which has a split personality with its hurley-burly pier end contrasting with secluded Hope Beach. The old village has thatched cottages festooned by roses, and gardens with exotic trees. Six miles south of Shanklin is Ventnor. Predominantly Victorian, the town has imposing hotels with verandas, an abundance of parks and gardens and, because of its sheltered beach, is known as the Madeira of England. Places of interest include ruined Appuldurcombe House (AM) at Wroxall, and the Museum of the History of Smuggling which traces this fascinating occupation back over 700 years. Just west of the isle's southernmost tip, St Catherine's Point, lies Blackgang Chine, one of the best known of these deep rocky clefts, which has a large amusement complex to add to its natural attractions. Moving inland from Blackgang, Newport lies some nine miles to the north. This centrally-positioned community serves as capital of the island. South-west of Newport is Carisbrooke Castle (OACT) where Charles I was imprisoned for a year (1647–1648) before his eventual execution in London. Other places of interest include the Roman Villa (OACT) and the Albany Steam Museum. Freshwater is eight miles west of Newport and one of its buildings, Farringford House, though now a hotel, was once the home of Alfred, Lord Tennyson. The Museum of Clocks, with more than 200 exhibits, stands in beautiful countryside. Beyond Freshwater, at the most westerly point of the island lies Alum Bay, surrounded by cliffs whose strata are many-coloured, and offshore are the Needles, three huge chalk pillars jutting from the sea. At their end is Needles Lighthouse, built in 1858.

Yarmouth stands at the mouth of the Yar opposite mainland Lymington. The harbour is a delight, full of craft of all sizes. Yarmouth Castle (AM) was built by Henry VIII, and Fort Victoria, to protect the

COWES WEEK Cannon fire and a puff of smoke and they're off. Yacht racing during this week in August is the high spot of the yachtsman's year.

THE NEEDLES Treacherous to shipping, the gleaming white chalk pinnacles of the Needles are the most westerly point of the Isle of Wight.

A Tour of the Isle of Wight
76 miles

Separated from Hampshire by the Solent, the Isle of Wight is a self-contained community. Its delightful landscape, cliff-sheltered beaches and dramatic coastal ravines have ensured its continuing popularity.

Leave **Cowes** by Park Rd (B3325) and follow signs for Gurnard. Pass Gurnard Hotel, descend Church Rd and turn right into Lower Church Rd. At the T-junction turn left into Marsh Rd (SP Yarmouth). In 1½ miles turn right at the T-junction then bear right, and in 1½ miles turn right for **Porchfield**. In another 1½ miles turn right (SP Newtown). Continue to Newtown Old Town Hall, turn right at the T-junction (no sign) and at the next junction right on to A3054 (SP Yarmouth). Drive through Shalfleet to **Yarmouth**. Leave by the Freshwater road and follow Totland signs to **Totland**, and join B3322 to **Alum Bay**. On the return branch right to **Freshwater Bay**. Leave on the Ventnor road, A3055, and follow the coast to **Chale**, after which branch right for **Blackgang**. Return to the

main road, turn right and continue to **Ventnor**. On leaving, follow Shanklin signs and continue through **Shanklin** to **Sandown**. From the town centre follow signs Bembridge (B3395), along the sea front. Later pass Yaverland Church and at the T-junction turn right. Beyond Bembridge Airport turn left at the crossroads and continue into **Bembridge**. Follow the one-way system and take B3395

Ryde road. In 1½ miles at the T-junction turn right on to B3330 to enter **St Helen's**, then turn left (SP Ryde) for **Nettlestone**, here branching right (SP Seaview) on to B3340, then follow Sea Front signs for the village. Descend and turn right along the coast road. Pass through a toll gate then veer inland and later turn right on to B3330. In ½ mile join A3054 to Ryde. From **Ryde** follow Newport signs to leave on A3054 and drive through **Wootton Bridge** to the roundabout and turn right (SP East Cowes) on to A3021, then turn right again. In a mile turn left for Whippingham Church. A mile past the church at the T-junction turn left into Victoria Grove, and at the end of Adelaide Grove turn left on to A3021 for **East Cowes**. Return along A3021 Ryde road, passing the entrances to Osborne House and Barton Manor. At the roundabout turn right on to A3054 and drive to **Newport**. Here follow Cowes signs to leave on A3020. At **Northwood** branch left on to B3325, and after a mile turn right to drive back into Cowes.

PLACES TO SEE

Cowes England's foremost yachting centre. Cowes is famous for its regatta.

Yarmouth Fort Victoria, built in 1853 is now a Country Park; Yarmouth Castle (AM) was built by Henry VIII.

Alum Bay Famous for its stratified chalk cliffs of many colours, Alum Bay looks out towards the Needles.

Blackgang Chine One of the most spectacular of the chines, this one also contains a model village.

Bembridge Windmill (NT) The only windmill left on the island, it dates from 1700 and is in working order.

Bembridge In the Ruskin Art Gallery and Museum there are drawings and manuscripts by this 19th-century artist and scholar.

Whippingham Prince Albert had a hand in the design of this ornate church which Queen Victoria and her family attended.

Newport The capital of the island, Newport lies in the shadow of Carisbrooke Castle (AM) now the home of the Isle of Wight Museum.

western approaches to Portsmouth, in 1853; it is now a country park (OACT).

Last, but certainly not least, is Cowes, facing the Solent. West Cowes is the headquarters of the Royal Yacht Squadron and Cowes Week, held during the first week in August, is *the* fashionable event of the yachting calendar. On the outskirts of Cowes, Osborne House (AM), a favourite residence of Queen Victoria, stands in a superb park and is a fine example of Victorian architecture.

Among the many other places of interest on the island are Arreton Manor on the Newport–Sandown road; Gatcombe House, off the Newport–Shanklin road; the Isle of Wight Steam Railway at Haven Street, south-west of Ryde, and the Flamingo Park at Seaview, a village just along the coast from Ryde. Brading, inland from Sandown, has a Lilliput Doll and Toy Museum, Osborn-Smith's Wax Museum and Animal World, and not far from the town are the remains of a Roman villa and 17th-century Morton Manor.

RYDE PIERHEAD STATION IN 1964

On the left is one of the old trams that used to run along the pier at Ryde. Transport nowadays is provided by retired London tube trains. Steam trains like No. 22 'Brading' (right), were in use on the Isle of Wight until 1966. A similar locomotive, No. 24 'Calbourne' can be seen at Haven Street where the Isle of Wight Steam Railway Museum runs old engines and rolling stock.

ISLES OF SCILLY, Cornwall

Twenty-eight perilous miles south-west of Land's End lie the Scillies, separated from Cornwall by some of the most dangerous waters around the British coast. Only five islands are inhabited – St Mary's, Tresco, St Martin's, Bryher and St Agnes – many of the others being little more than stumps of rock: in total, the archipelago covers about 3000 acres. Once privately owned, they are now part of the Duchy of Cornwall. St

VICTIMS OF THE SEA

Ship's figureheads from some of the many wrecks around the Scilly's treacherous reefs are displayed in Tresco's Maritime Museum.

Mary's is the largest island in the group and can be reached from Penzance by helicopter or boat. In the 'capital', Hugh Town, sits the council of the isles, supervisors of the islands' administration. The main square of Hugh Town has a little park where the rites of May are celebrated every year. High above the town on the Hugh Peninsula is Star Castle, an Elizabethan fort-turned-hotel encompassed by 18th-century granite walls. The whole area around here has consequently become known as The Garrison.

St Martin's Island has excellent white sandy beaches; the three small communities here are prosaically named Higher Town, Middle Town and Lower Town. Tresco is an island of contrasts and is the home of the former Lords Proprietors of the island, the Dorrien-Smith family. The house built by their ancestor Augustus Smith in 1841, Tresco Abbey, is world-famous for the sub-tropical gardens he planted.

Because the Isles of Scilly enjoy a very mild, virtually frost-free winter a flourishing flower-growing economy has been developed. The season starts in November and reaches its peak in mid March when large quantities of daffodils are exported to mainland Cornwall. These are followed by irises and tulips in April.

ST MARY'S *The Isles of Scilly enjoy a mild climate that enables them to support a sub-tropical vegetation. St Mary's (below) is the largest of the islands. Beyond the trees can be seen Hugh Town, the islands' capital.*

IXWORTH, Suffolk   *12 TL97*

Ixworth has several Roman connections and in nearby Stow Lane are the remnants of a building believed to have been part of an Iceni camp. Ixworth Abbey (OACT) dates, in part, to 1170 when an Augustinian priory was built here; the remains are incorporated into a 17th-century house. The church of St Mary contains a

decorative tomb in memory of Richard Coddington and his wife, and portrait brasses of other members of the Coddington family.

Close by is the village of Ixworth Thorpe, where All Saints Church has a thatched roof. The church door is only 5ft high and the pews have carved ends depicting animals, birds and humans.

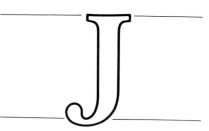

JARROW, Tyne & Wear   *20 NZ36*

The town became the centre of attention in the 1930s when unemployed shipyard workers marched to the Houses of Parliament and demanded work. Their plight illustrated the danger of a community having its prosperity directly linked to a single industry. Today the town supports a greater diversification of industry with factories producing furniture, metal goods and chemical products.

Deeper historical roots can be traced through St Paul's Church (OACT), an important Christian shrine that was once part of the monastery where the Venerable Bede wrote many of his 79 books, including the *Ecclesiastical History of the English People*.

The Saxon church has seen many architectural changes since its original foundation in 682 by Benedict Biscop. After being sacked by the Danes and then subsequently razed to the ground by William the Conqueror, the church was rebuilt in 1074. The Bede Monastery Museum in Jarrow Hall contains archaeological finds from St Paul's Monastery.

JEDBURGH, Borders   *24 NT62*

During the Middle Ages Jedburgh was at the centre of the Border Wars between the Scots and the English. Today the town quietly pursues its material industries of rayon, tweeds and woollens. The county prison, known as 'the Castle', was built in 1823 on the former site of Jedburgh Castle, casualty of a 1409 foray.

Jedburgh Abbey (AM, OACT) was founded in 1118 and consistently suffered at the hands of English invaders until 1523 when the Earl of Surrey finally ordered it to be burnt down. The Norman tower has been reconstructed and now overlooks a roofless nave. Queen Mary's House (OACT) is a Museum displaying artefacts associated with the Queen's stay in the town in 1566.

JERVAULX ABBEY, N Yorkshire   *15 SE18*

Jervaulx Abbey ruins are located four miles north-west of the village of Masham. Founded in 1156, the monastery housed Cistercian monks until 1537, when the last abbot was hanged for having taken part in the ill-fated 'Pilgrimage of Grace'. The remains are few, but the ground plan can be easily identified and the site, partly overgrown by trees, is in lovely countryside.

JODRELL BANK, Cheshire   *14 SJ77*

The Mark 1A radio telescope at Jodrell Bank, where the Nuffield Radio Astronomy Laboratories are situated, measures 250ft and is one of the largest steerable radio telescopes in the world. The site is open to the public at specified times. Display material and working models are shown, and there is also a planetarium and arboretum.

JOHN O'GROATS,
Highlands   *30 ND37*

The village of John O'Groats takes its name from a Dutchman, Jan de Groot who arrived in Scotland in the early 16th century, with his two brothers. Eventually there were eight families and an argument developed concerning precedence, but Jan supplied an answer by building an octagonal house with a door in each side. Although the house no longer exists, the site is marked by a mound and a flagstaff. John O'Groats looks out to the waters of Pentland Firth and the fine views include those of the Orkney Islands Stroma and South Ronaldsay. To the east is Duncansby Head with the three Stacks of Duncansby jutting out of the sea. For the record, Land's End, at the tip of the Cornish peninsula, is 877 miles away by road.

JORDANS, Buckinghamshire   *5 SU99*

Located two miles west of Chalfont St Giles, the village of Jordans is well known for its Quaker connections. Just outside the village is the brick-built Friends' Meeting House which was erected in 1687, shortly after James II issued the Declaration of Indulgence. William Penn, founder of Pennsylvania, USA, is buried in the local churchyard along with his two wives. The other notable Friends interred here include Joseph Rule and the Peningtons.

KEDLESTON HALL, Derbyshire
10 SK34

Kedleston Hall (OACT), an 18th-century mansion in a 500-acre park, was created by Robert Adam and is considered to be one of his greatest achievements. It has a magnificent marble hall, state rooms and a fine collection of pictures; additional attractions are an Indian Museum and a colony of Canada geese in the park. Members of the Curzon family have lived in houses on this site since 1100

KEELE, Staffordshire   *14 SJ84*

Keele, three miles west of Newcastle-under-Lyme, was once an administrative centre of the Knights Templars. The University of Keele, founded in 1962, is well-known for its broadly-based courses which combine Arts and Social Sciences; the modern buildings are grouped around old Keele Hall to form an American-style campus.

DUNCANSBY STACKS *The jagged pinnacles of these three 'stack' rocks are a dramatic outpost of land off Duncansby Head near John O'Groats. These are the most impressive of the group of five.*

KELLIE CASTLE, Fife   *24 NO50*

Kellie Castle (NTS) dates mainly from the 16th and 17th centuries and contains notable plasterwork, and is painted with idealised landscapes.

KELLING, Norfolk   *12 TG04*

At Kelling Park Aviaries (OACT) a colourful collection of European and tropical birds – including flamingoes, macaws, cockatoos and ornamental pheasants – is displayed in four acres of beautiful gardens.

KELMSCOT, Oxfordshire   *3 SU29*

William Morris, the poet, designer and printer, lived here from 1871 until his death in 1896. His home was the gabled Elizabethan Kelmscott Manor, and a woodcut depicting it formed the frontispiece of his book, *News from Nowhere*. The house was restored in 1968 as a Morris Museum; it can be seen on the first Wednesday of the month (April–September) or by arrangment with the owners, the Society of Antiquaries.

KELSO, Borders   *24 NT73*

Kelso, a little market town overlooking the Tweed and centred on a cobbled square, was described by Scott as 'the most beautiful, if not the most romantic village in Scotland'. The 12th-century abbey (AM) was the greatest of the Border abbeys until its destruction in the 16th century, and the little that remains gives evidence of fine Norman and early Gothic workmanship. Floors Castle (OACT) is an imposing 18th-century building, the home of the Duke and Duchess of Roxburgh; it contains superb English and French furniture, tapestries and paintings.

KEMNAY, Grampian   *NJ 7316*

Granite from the quarries at Kemnay was used in the building of the Forth Bridge and of the Thames Embankment. Castle Fraser (NTS), two and a half miles to the south-west, is an impressive example of the Scottish Baronial style built between 1575 and 1636 and incorporating an earlier stronghold; it contains an exhibition telling the story of 'The Castles of Mar'.

KENDAL, Cumbria   *18 SD59*

Kendal is the largest town in South Lakeland and its administrative capital. It developed into a centre of commerce with the establishment of the woollen industry in the 14th century, and its traditional mint cake and snuff are well-known. The River Kent meanders through pleasant fell countryside on the edge of the Lake District National Park, overlooked by the remains of the castle (AM), which dates back to the 12th century and was the birthplace in 1512 of Catherine Parr, the last of Henry VIII's wives. Three miles to the south lies Sizergh Castle (NT), with its ancient pele tower. The centre of the 'Auld Grey Town' is made up of picturesque yards and narrow streets. The Abbot Hall Art Gallery is a fine 18th-century house, appropriately decorated and furnished, with a Museum of Lakeland Life and Industry housed in its stable block. Kendal Museum, in Station Road, specialises in natural history and archaeology. George Romney, the portrait painter, was born in the town in 1734, and a collection of his work hangs in the mayor's parlour.

KERSEY *One of Suffolk's most attractive villages, Kersey was an important centre of the woollen industry, weaving a cloth to which it gave its name; its sister village, Lindsey, wove a lighter cloth.*

KENILWORTH,
Warwickshire   *10 SP27*

Kenilworth, a pleasant residential town with some half-timbered houses dating back to the 15th century, stands in the heart of England, between Warwick and Coventry. Near the parish church of St Nicholas (which has a fine Norman doorway) lie the remains of an Augustinian abbey. The town's most famous building, however, is its 12th-century castle (AM) – immortalised by Scott in his novel, *Kenilworth* – which has been described as the grandest fortress ruin in the country. John of Gaunt added a great hall in the 14th century, and Robert Dudley, Earl of Leicester, built on a gatehouse in the 16th. Today's visitor can see the original keep (its massive walls giving an indication of the fortress's strength), parts of the banqueting hall and the gatehouse, now known as Lord Leicester's Buildings.

KENMORE, Tayside   *22 NN74*

Today Kenmore is a popular salmon fishing resort, but at the beginning of the 16th century only a ferryman's cottage stood here beside the River Tay; the introduction of market fairs instigated the development of the village, and it was furthered by the building of the bridge across the Tay in 1744. In the mid 19th century Kenmore was 'restored' in a Victorian mock-rustic style by the second Marquis of Breadalbane, and since this is a conservation area the village looks much the same today. The home of the Breadalbanes was 16th-century Balloch Castle (now ruined); Taymouth Castle was built as a replacement for Balloch, but since the death of the third marquis in 1922 it has been used as hotel, military hospital and school. To the east is Croft Moraig, the site of a prehistoric double circle of standing stones, 185ft in diameter, and set on a platform built for the purpose.

KERSEY, Suffolk   *12 TL94*

At one time most of the working men of England were clad in tough Kersey cloth, while their womenfolk wore the softer fabric made in neighbouring Lindsey. The fine Perpendicular church of this charming village reflects the early prosperity that the wool trade brought; the roof of its south porch is particularly notable, being made up of 16 magnificently carved 15th-century panels. The colour-washed houses lining the main street as it runs steeply down to a watersplash are dark-timbered with age and include a group of pre-Reformation weavers' cottages.

KESWICK, Cumbria   *18 NY22*

Keswick, an old market town with narrow streets and greystone buildings, stands on the River Greta between Skiddaw and Derwentwater. Set in magnificent scenery, it is a popular centre for exploring the Lake District. Hugh Walpole and the poet Southey had connections with the area and manuscripts and personal relics relating to them are included in the Fitz Park Museum. Lingholm (OACT), on the west shore of Derwentwater, has both formal and woodland gardens, with a large collection of rhododendrons, azaleas and other shrubs. Castlerigg Stone Circle (AM, NT), just outside the town, is a most impressive prehistoric circle of 38 stones, four of which form a rectangle within the ring; it is also known as the Druids' Circle.

KIDDERMINSTER,
Hereford & Worcester   *9 SO87*

Flemish weavers brought prosperity to Kidderminster in the 13th and 14th centuries, and the carpet-manufacture for which the town is famous began during the 18th; a working model of an old carpet loom can be seen in the Museum in Exchange Street. The success of the industry was reinforced during the second half of the century by the building of the Staffordshire and Worcestershire Canal, designed by James Brindley. Nineteenth-century mills dominate the town, and little remains of medieval Kidderminster except the Church of St Mary and All Saints, which has a 13th-century chancel, a 15th-century Lady Chapel, and interesting brasses and monuments. Sir Roland Hill, who introduced the penny post, was born here in 1795. Harvington Hall (OACT) stands a mile to the north-east; the 16th-century brick house is built around a late medieval original and contains a warren of secret passages and priests' holes.

KIDWELLY, Dyfed   *7 SN40*

Kidwelly Castle (AM) was built in a good strategic position above the River Gwendraeth by a 12th-century Bishop of Salisbury and was subsequently much involved in the struggles of the Welsh rebels against the English crown. Additions were made to the castle in the 13th and 14th centuries – notably a three-storeyed gatehouse and an outer ward; the vast ovens also built at that time can still be seen in the extensive ruins.

KILBARCHAN, Strathclyde   *22 NS46*

The Weaver's Cottage (NTS) is an early 18th-century house of cruck construction; it dates from the days when cloth-making was a cottage industry and contains looms and other weaving equipment. A local weaver-poet, Robert Allan, is commemorated by a fountain nearby.

KILCHRENAN, Strathclyde   *21 NN02*

Ardanaiseig Gardens, three miles north-east of Kilchrenan, offer wonderful views across Loch Awe and are well-known for their azaleas, rhododendrons and rare shrubs.

KILDRUMMY CASTLE,
Grampian   *27 NJ41*

The ruins of 13th-century Kildrummy Castle (AM) overlook the valley of the Don from a height of 800ft, the original choice of site obviously influenced by the ravine that guards it on two sides. Bravely defended by Sir Nigel Bruce in 1306, it survived until the Jacobite Rising of 1715, after which is was dismantled. The grounds include an attractive water garden, and the quarry which provided the stone for the castle has been planted with alpines and shrubs.

KILLERTON HOUSE, Devon   *2 SS90*

Eighteenth-century Killerton House (NT) is set in 15-acre gardens, with hillsides of trees and shrubs (many of them rare) sloping down to the smooth lawns that surround it. The Paulise de Bush collection of costumes, is shown in room-settings of the appropriate period.

KILLIECRANKIE, Tayside   *26 NN96*

Killiecrankie is best known for the battle which took place at the head of the Pass in 1689, when Viscount Dundee – the 'Bonnie Dundee' of Scott's ballad – won a decisive victory for the Jacobite cause, though he was killed in his moment of triumph. The National Trust for Scotland owns much of the Pass, and its Visitor Centre stands close to the site of the battle. A steep path runs down to the narrow opening of the gorge known as 'Soldier's Leap' because a trooper fleeing from the Highlanders jumped across the River Garry here.

KILMARNOCK, Strathclyde   22 NS43

It was in Kilmarnock that Scotland's national poet, Robert Burns, published his first collection, *Poems Chiefly in the Scottish Dialect*; his intention was to raise enough money to emigrate to Jamaica, but the success of the book persuaded him to remain. A copy of this first edition and an extensive collection of original manuscripts are contained in the Burns Museum, a Victorian tower built to commemorate the poet. The Dick Institute includes displays of archaeological and geological interest, a collection of small arms, a children's museum and an art gallery. Dean Castle (OACT) contains exhibitions of European arms and early musical instruments, and there is a nature trail in the extensive park. A famous name connected with Kilmarnock is that of Johnnie Walker, a grocer in King Street until he began to blend whisky in 1820.

KILMARTIN, Strathclyde   21 NR89

Dunadd Fort (AM), three miles to the south of Kilmartin, is a prehistoric hillfort which was once the capital of the ancient Scots kingdom of Dalriada. Other prehistoric remains include the Temple Wood circle and cist and several cairns and groups of cup-and-ring marked rocks. Carnasserie Castle (OACT) overlooks the valley from a high point about a mile from Kilmartin, and the ruins of another castle stand on the outskirts of the village.

KILPECK,
Hereford & Worcester   9 SO43

This is an ancient village, listed in the Domesday Book and existing much earlier. Its name, from the Celtic 'Kilpedric', means 'cell of St Pedric'. The original Celtic church was replaced by a Saxon one in the 6th or 7th century and the existing building dates mainly from the 12th. It is one of the finest Norman churches in Britain and has an outstandingly well-preserved south doorway with elaborate carvings of mythical monsters.

KILVERSTONE, Norfolk   12 TL88

Kilverstone 'Latin-American' Wildlife Park (OACT) is set in the grounds of 17th-century Kilverstone Hall, the home of Lord and Lady Fisher; they have brought together a varied collection of South-American mammals and birds, and hope to breed from some of the rarer species. The miniature horse stud and the English walled garden are also of interest.

KIMBOLTON,
Cambridgeshire   11 TL06

Kimbolton, lies among pleasant fields, the River Kym flowing along its north-eastern edge. A broad main street of mainly Georgian houses leads to St Andrew's Church, parts of which are 700 years old. The castle (OACT) also dates back to the 13th century; it was greatly extended in the 17th, and later alterations were made by Vanbrugh and Robert Adam.

KIMMERIDGE, Dorset   3 SY97

Low cliffs of black shale overlook the small bay where thatched cottages stand beside the derelict quay of Kimmeridge. Smedmore House (OACT) to the south-east is originally Jacobean, with Queen Anne and Georgian additions, and contains an exhibition of antique dolls and marquetry furniture. Ruined Clavel coastguard tower on the cliffs was once a summer house belonging to Smedmore.

KINCARDINE-ON-FORTH,
Fife   23 NS98

The port of Kincardine lies on the east bank of the Forth, its bridge the last to span the estuary before it widens. A 17th-century mercat cross stands in the market place and many old houses survive. Ruined Tulliallan Castle, a 15th-century building with ground-floor vaulting, is of great architectural interest.

KIMMERIDGE BAY *Looking down on the bay from Smedmore tower. The low, dark-coloured cliffs are made of soft rock known as Kimmeridge Clay, famous for its fossils and its oil-rich shale.*

KINCRAIG, Highland   26 NH80

Kincraig stands on the north side of Loch Insh, through which the River Spey flows to join the Feshie. Nearby is the Highland Wildlife Park, which displays native animals of Scotland including species no longer found in the wild.

KINGSBRIDGE, Devon   2 SX74

This little market town is situated in the South Hams, at the head of the Kingsbridge estuary. It was the birthplace in 1705 of William Cookworthy, who discovered china clay in Cornwall and made the first porcelain in England. An exhibition commemorating his achievement is contained in one of the galleries of the Cookworthy Museum. Kingsbridge has a late 16th-century arcade, The Shambles, and two interesting churches – St Edmund's, with its 13th-century tower, and 16th-century Dodbrooke.

KINGSDON, Somerset   3 ST52

Lytes Cary (NT), for 500 years the home of the Lyte family, has a 15th-century great hall and a chapel which dates back to the 14th century. The house has an interesting collection of furniture.

THE NODDING DONKEY

The Nodding Donkey on the cliffs above Kimmeridge marks the site of the productive oil-well sunk in 1959.

KING'S LYNN, Norfolk   *11 TF62*
Until the 16th century the town was
Bishop's Lynn, the area belonging to the
See of Norwich, but it was appropriated by
Henry VIII at the Dissolution of the
Monasteries. By that time it was not only a
flourishing market town, for the Tuesday
and Saturday markets – the former ringed
by distinguished buildings – have been
thronging round the churches of St
Margaret and St Nicholas since the 12th
century, but was also fast becoming one of
the busiest ports in England; the elegant
17th-century Customs House indicates the
status that the town had achieved by then.
Prosperity really came, however, with the
corn-shipping trade of the 18th century,
and the substantial Corn Exchange and
elaborate merchants' houses date from this
period. The town's historic buildings
include St George's Guildhall (NT), the
largest surviving medieval guildhall in the
country, now used as a theatre; the
Hanseatic Warehouses, dating from 1428;
Thoresby College, founded in 1500; and
timber-framed Hampton Court. Lynn
Museum has interesting exhibits of local
and natural history and the Museum of
Social History concentrates on domestic
bygones.

KINGSWEAR, Devon   *2 SX85*
Kingswear lies on the River Dart, and car
ferries run from here to Dartmouth. It is
also the terminus of the Dart Valley steam-
operated branch line from Paignton. The
castle is Tudor in origin.

KINGSWINFORD,
   W Midlands   *9 SO88*
Kingswinford, on the western edge of the
Black Country, lies just north of
Stourbridge, whose early importance was
due to its glass-making industry. Many fine
examples of its craftsmanship are included
among the exhibits on show at Broadfield
House Glass Museum, which covers both
English and Continental glass from the late
17th century until the present day. Visitors
can also see glass-making tools and an
engraving studio.

KINGTON,
   Hereford & Worcester   *8 SO35*
Kington is a small market town on the
River Arrow, famous for its autumn sales of
Clun Forest and Kerry Sheep. It lies in
pleasant hill country, sheltered by Hergest
Ridge and Rushock Hill – the latter being
crossed by Offa's Dyke, the old Mercian
defence against the Welsh. Hergest Croft
Gardens display a variety of trees, shrubs
and flowers, together with an old-fashioned
kitchen garden and a woodland valley filled
with rhododendrons, some 30ft high.

KINGUSSIE, Highland   *26 NH70*
Kingussie, the so-called 'Capital of
Badenoch', stands on the wooded slopes of
Strath Spey with clear views across to the
Cairngorms. The district of Badenoch is
sometimes called 'the drowned land'
because the Spey floods so often, in spite of
its banks having been heightened and
reinforced. The Highland Folk Museum,
which was originally founded in Iona and
maintained by four Scottish universities,
covers 200 years of farming and local
craftsmanship and includes an old cottage,
a reconstructed Hebridean mill and a
primitive 'black house'.

THE OLD CUSTOMS HOUSE *at King's Lynn dates from 1683 and was designed by a local architect,
Henry Bell. At that period, Lynn was already a thriving port, trading with several European countries.*

KINLOCHEWE, Highland   *29 NH06*
The small village of Kinlochewe is scattered
round the head of Loch Maree, amid
magnificent scenery dominated by the
3217ft 'spear', Slioch. It is a base for
climbing and hillwalking and offers
excellent fishing for sea trout, brown trout
and salmon. To the west stretches the
Beinn Eighe National Nature Reserve, the
first of its kind in Britain; it covers over
10,000 acres, preserving the remains of
ancient Scottish pine forests and protecting
such species as deer, wild cats, pine
martens and golden eagles. Beinn Eighe
itself is of interest geologically, being
formed of 750-million-year-old red
sandstone topped with 600-million-year-old
white quartzite.

KIRKBY LONSDALE,
   Cumbria   *18 SD67*
Kirkby Lonsdale is a little market town
attractively set on a hill above the River
Lune. John Ruskin, the 19th-century
writer, considered his favourite view from
the town to be 'one of the loveliest scenes in
England and therefore in the world';
Ruskin Walks are signposted near the
churchyard. The ancient, three-arched
Devil's Bridge (AM) which spans the Lune
just outside Kirkby is now closed to traffic.
The great pool beneath it is popular with
salmon fishermen and aqualung divers. The
town has an old market cross and the
church, St Mary's, is Norman. The Brontë
sisters attended the Clergy Daughters'
School at Cowan Bridge, near here, and
Kirkby is the model for Lowton in *Jane
Eyre*.

KIRKCALDY, Fife   *23 NT29*
Now an important coal port and industrial
centre, Kirkcaldy is an ancient town which
has been a Royal Burgh since 1450.
Fifteenth-century houses stand near the
harbour, and Sailors' Walk contains some
from the 17th century which have been

restored (NTS). The 'Lang Toun', so
called because of the mile-long main street
that stretches along the Firth of Forth, was
the birthplace in 1723 of Adam Smith, the
economist and author of *The Wealth of
Nations*; five years later Robert Adam was
born here, and Thomas Carlyle, the famous
historian, once taught at the Burgh School.
Kircaldy has three interesting museums –
the John MacDouall Stuart Museum
(which is a memorial to the 19th-century
Scottish explorer), the Town Museum and
Art Gallery (with a section on local pottery,
including the famous Wemyss Ware) and
the Industrial Museum. Ravenscraig Castle
(AM) is an impressive ruin on a rocky
headland at the eastern end of the town.

KIRKCUDBRIGHT,
   Dumfries & Galloway   *17 NX65*
Kirkcudbright, an ancient Royal Burgh on
the Dee estuary, is the most important
town in the area, with a small harbour at
the head of Kirkcudbright Bay. Its name
means 'Church of Cuthbert', and part of
the old gateway to the town is incorporated
in the entrance to the churchyard. Buried
here is Billy Marshall, the 18th-century
tinker 'king' who lived to be 120 – having
reputedly fathered four children after the
age of 100. At the Selkirk Arms Hotel in
the High Street, Burns wrote the famous
Selkirk Grace:

   Some hae meat and canna eat
   And some wad eat that want it,
   But we hae meat and we can eat
   And sae the Lord be thankit.'

The Stewartry (or 'county') Museum
includes firearms, domestic and
agricultural equipment and a natural
history section, while 18th-century
Broughton House (OACT) has an
interesting library and an attractive garden.
McLellan's Castle (AM) is an impressive
castellated mansion overlooking the
harbour, built in 1582 by Sir Thomas
McLellan who was Provost at that time.

Dumfries and Galloway
88 miles

Among the wooded hills of south-west Scotland the rich pastures are grazed by small but fierce black Galloway cattle. Around Wigtown Bay the high hills sweep down to the shore, with far-reaching views across the bay to the wild Machars Peninsula.

Leave **Kirkcudbright** on A755 via Bridge Street, and cross the River Dee, following signs for Gatehouse of Fleet. In 4½ miles turn left on to A75 (SP Stranraer) Continue through **Gatehouse of Fleet** and past Cardoness Castle. Continue on A75 passing Carsluith Castle on the left, and enter **Creetown**. Leave on A75 and in 3½ miles reach Palnure. (On the right, the dead-end road leads to Bargaly Glen and part of Galloway Forest Park). Drive on for 3 miles, and at the roundabout, take the third exit, A714, to enter **Newton Stewart**. Leave Newton Stewart following signs for New Galloway, cross the Cree Bridge, and enter **Minnigaff**. Drive for 1 mile beyond the village and turn left on to A712 (SP New Galloway). Continue for 6 miles and pass Murray's Monument and in

4½ miles pass Clatteringshaws Loch, then in 6 miles turn right on to A762 into **New Galloway**. Continue on A762 (SP Kirkcudbright) pass Loch Ken and continue through Laurieston to Ringford. At **Ringford** turn left on to A75 (SP Dumfries). In 3½ miles, cross the River Dee, and a mile further, pass a track that leads left to Threave Castle. In another ½ mile a detour can be made by taking an unclassified right turn to Threave Gardens. On the main route, continue to **Castle Douglas**. Leave on A745 (SP Dalbeattie), and in 5 miles join the Auchencairn road, A711. To the left is the market town of **Dalbeattie**. Continue along A711 passing through Palnackie, Auchencairn and Dundrennan to complete the return journey to Kirkcudbright.

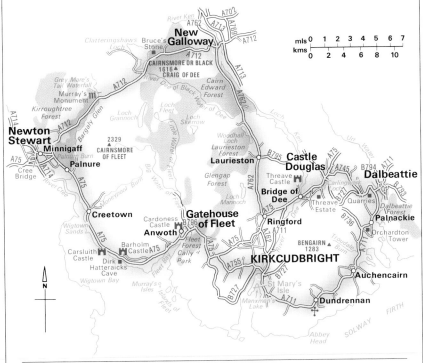

PLACES TO SEE

Kirkcudbright An attractive old fishing port on the Dee estuary, with two museums: Broughton House, with paintings and a library; and the Stewartry Museum of local history. Ruined MacLellan's Castle (AM) dates from 1583.

Cardoness Castle (AM) A ruined 15th-century stronghold on high ground overlooking the Water of Fleet.

Newton Stewart A historic old market town on the edge of Galloway Forest Park.

Murray Monument An obelisk on Cairnsmore of Fleet (2329ft) commemorates a local shepherd boy who became Professor of Oriental Languages at Edinburgh. The Grey Mare's Tail Waterfall is nearby.

New Galloway Formerly Scotland's smallest Royal Burgh and a noted angling centre.

Threave Castle (AM) Beautifully situated on an island in the River Dee; access is by rowing boat.

Threave Gardens (NTS) These exceptionally interesting gardens are run by the National Trust for Scotland's School of Gardening.

Castle Douglas A pleasant old town with a flourishing cattle market.

Dundrennan Ruins of the 12th century abbey where Mary, Queen of Scots, spent her last night on Scottish soil.

KIRKOSWALD, Strathclyde   *22 NS20*
Souter Johnnie's Cottage (NTS), a thatched 18th-century house, was once the home of John Davidson, the village cobbler (or 'souter') of Burns's poem *Tam O'Shanter*. Tam O'Shanter himself lived here: he was Douglas Graham of Shanter, who made his living by supplying malted grain to a brewhouse in Ayr. Life-size stone figures of the two and their friends stand in the garden of the cottage.

KIRKSTALL ABBEY, W Yorkshire   *15 SE23*
The ruins of Kirkstall Abbey (AM), lying beside the River Aire, are mainly late Norman. It was founded in 1152 by Cistercian monks from Fountains Abbey, who pioneered the exploitation of the iron-ore in the area as well as being involved in the more traditional pursuits of farming, spinning, weaving and pottery-making. The original gatehouse now contains an interesting museum in which three Victorian streets have been re-created.

J M BARRIE'S BIRTHPLACE MUSEUM at Kirriemuir is a tribute to the author of 'Peter Pan'.

KIRRIEMUIR, Tayside   *27 NO35*
Sir James Barrie (1860–1937), the author of *Peter Pan*, was born in Kirriemuir; his birthplace in Brechin Road and the wash-house which he used as a theatre now form the Barrie Museum. The town appears in his novels as 'Thrums', the cottage he called 'A Window in Thrums' standing in Southmuir, a suburb where the weavers lived. The textile industry is still important here, the other local industry being the milling of oatmeal.

KNARESBOROUGH, N Yorkshire   *15 SE35*
Knaresborough is an attractive town with narrow streets of Georgian houses, steep steps and alleyways. The area is full of caves, the most famous being that named after Mother Shipton, the 15th-century seer; she is said to have predicted trains and aircraft, but most of the prophecies attributed to her were in fact written in the 19th century. The most interesting phenomenon is the Dropping Well, where drips of water containing a lime deposit are gradually petrifying a curious assortment of objects placed beneath them by the owners of the cave and others. On a cliff-top high above the river stand the remains of the 14th-century castle (OACT), including the keep, two baileys and gatehouse; the Court House Museum is situated in the castle grounds. The Zoological Gardens at Conyngham Hall contain sea-lions and llamas as well as their 'big cats'.

KNEBWORTH HOUSE *Lord Lytton's study, with mementoes of the author.*

KNEBWORTH,
Hertfordshire   11 TL22

Knebworth House (OACT) has been the home of the Lyttons since it was first built in 1492 and contains many portraits and personal mementoes of the family. It was largely rebuilt in 1843 by the Lord Lytton who wrote *The Last Days of Pompeii*, and some of his manuscripts are on display. The magnificent Tudor banqueting hall, with fine 17th-century plasterwork and panelling, was preserved in the reconstruction. The vast park has now been turned into a Country Park, offering such attractions as a crazy-golf course, skate park, Astroglide, narrow-gauge railway and adventure playground in addition to the more traditional deer park.

KNIGHTSHAYE'S COURT,
Devon   2 SS91

Nineteenth-century Knightshaye's Court was the home of the Heathcote Amory family and contains Sir Julian Amory's collection of Old Masters. Both outside and inside, the house retains a typically Victorian atmosphere of elaborate opulence. The gardens, overlooking the Exe Valley, are large and wooded, with fine azaleas, rhododendrons and other flowering shrubs; the topiary is unique.

KNIGHTON, Powys   8 SO27

This greystone market town in the sheep-rearing countryside of the Teme valley has clung tenaciously to its hillside for at least 1000 years. The first settlers were Saxons, followed in the 11th century by the Welsh and then the Normans. A wooden Norman castle stood on the mound which is still called Bryn y Castell, and a hilltop on the other side of the town retains traces of a 12th-century stone stronghold. The old Welsh name for Knighton was Trefyclawdd, 'the town of the dyke', for Offa's Dyke (built by an 8th-century King of Mercia to keep Welsh predators out of his domain) runs through it. The Central Wales Railway line still operates, and the station is a charming example of Victorian Gothic, for Sir Richard Price-Green, who first releasd the land to the railway company, insisted on personally approving all their structures.

KNOCKANDO, Grampian   27 NJ22

At the Tamdhu Distillery (OACT) visitors to Knockando can see the whole process of whisky-making. The Cheeryble brothers in Charles Dicken's *Nicholas Nickleby* are said to be based on the Grant brothers, who lived here. There are some ancient carved stones in the churchyard, and the church has an internal gallery.

KNOLE, Kent   5 TQ55

Knole (NT), one of the largest private houses in England, was the birthplace of Vita Sackville-West in 1892 and is still the home of the Sackville family. Built of Kentish stone, it stands on a rounded hill or 'knoll' (whence the name) just outside

---

A Tour of Skye
104 miles

The black peaks of the Cuillins cut a six-mile arc across the south-west of Skye; the island's most dramatic natural feature, they are often wreathed in the mists that have made Skye an island of mystery.

Take the car ferry from **Kyle of Lochalsh** on the mainland to **Kyleakin** on the Isle of Skye. Follow A850 to **Broadford** (from here a detour left on A881 leads along a single-track road to Elgol on Loch Scavaig) and continue along the coast and the shore of Loch Ainort, then inland to Sconser. Drive along the shore of Loch Sligachan, and follow Glen Varragill to the shore of Loch Portree. (To visit Portree turn right on to A855). From Loch Portree, follow A850 Dunvegan road across the island, in about 4 miles keeping left past an inlet of Loch Snizort Beag. The road becomes single-track as far as **Edinbane**, then after crossing the Red Burn, double-track to **Dunvegan**. Leave on A863 Sligachan road (in 1¼ miles, the Glendale road, B884, right, offers a detour to the Skye Black House Folk Museum at Colbost and the Watermill at Glendale) and follow it through **Struan** and round Loch Beag (at the junction with B8009, the Carbost road, a detour can be made to the distillery and the weavers' village of Port-na-Long). Continue on A863 to **Sligachan**, then turn right on to A850 to Kyleakin for the car ferry back to Kyle of Lochalsh.

PLACES TO SEE

Sligachan A well known walking centre for the Cuillins.

Portree 'Capital' of Skye and a fine touring centre with ferries to the Isle of Raasay.

Dunvegan Massive moated castle (OACT) home of the Chief of Macleod. Its chief treasure is the famous 'fairy flag' which dates back to the 7th century.

Colbost Skye Black House Folk Museum is a restored Hebridean black house with typical furnishings.

Glendale Skye Watermill. A restored 200 year old grain mill and kiln.

Dun Beag Extensive remains of a 2000 year old Pictish Broch.

Carbost The famous Talisker whisky distillery stands on the shore of Loch Harport.

Port-na-Long Harris tweed is woven in this tiny village.

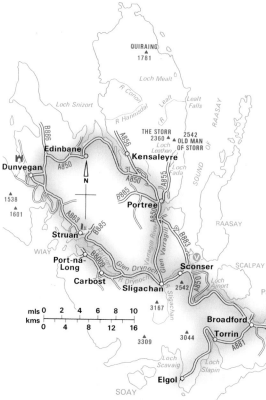

Sevenoaks, spreading over some four acres. The building was begun by Thomas Bourchier, the Archbishop of Canterbury, in the 15th century and was extended in the 17th; the 365 rooms, 52 staircases and 7 courtyards represent the number of days in a year, weeks in a year and days in a week. The state apartments, with their fine plastered ceilings, retain much of the original Jacobean and Caroline furniture, and the house contains priceless collections of pictures, silver, carpets and tapestries. The 26-acre garden, enclosed by an Elizabethan wall, has changed little since the 17th century, and herds of fallow and Japanese deer roam in the 1000-acre park.

KNOWSLEY, Merseyside   14 SJ49
Knowsley Hall, the home of the Earls of Derby, is an impressive 17th–19th-century mansion surrounded by 2500 acres of parkland – part of which has been given over to a Safari Park. The drive-through reserves contain elephants, giraffes, rhinos, monkeys, lions, tigers and many other animals. There are a children's amusement park and pets' corner, and, during the summer months, a dolphinarium.

KNUTSFORD, Cheshire   14 SJ77
The town derives its name from the reputed fording of a local stream by King Canute. An attractive town, with narrow streets and a number of black and white houses, it is the original of Mrs Gaskell's 'Cranford'; the authoress was married in the parish church and is buried behind the Unitarian chapel. Tatton Hall (NT) is set in 1000 acres of wooded parkland to the north of the town; built in 1800, it was the home of the Egerton family and contains fine collections of furniture, pictures, china, silver and glass. Its grounds include a Japanese Garden and an ornamental lake.

KYLE OF LOCHALSH,
Highland   25 NG72
Kyle of Lochalsh, the culmination of one branch of the romantic 'Road to the Isles', is a busy fishing and shipping village at the western end of Loch Alsh. It is the traditional 'Gateway to Skye', which lies only a short distance away across the waters of Kyle Akin. The railway line from Inverness terminates here, and steamers ply to Mallaig (passenger) and Skye (vehicle).

KYLESKU, Highland   29 NC23
Kylesku is one of the most remote places in Britain – and also one of the most beautiful. It stands on an inlet of Eddrachilly Bay in an area of coastline often compared with the Norwegian fjords. Eas-coul-Aulin is the highest waterfall in Britain, with a sheer drop of 658ft.

KYNANCE COVE, Cornwall   1 SW61
This cove, in an area of coast owned by the National Trust, is possibly the most spectacular on the Lizard Peninsula. The remarkable cliffs of serpentine rock are streaked with red, purple, and green, and round the beach there are numerous caves with names like 'Devils Letter Box' and 'Ladies' Bathing Pool'. To the north-west stand the magnificent cliffs known as Pigeon Hugo and The Horse. Just offshore is Asparagus Island (so called because the plant grows there in abundance), where the sea spouts dramatically through a rock known as the Devil's Bellows.

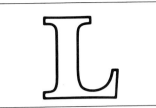

LACOCK, Wiltshire   3 ST96
Lacock is owned almost entirely by the National Trust; the oldest buildings in its twisting streets date back to medieval times and none is later than the 18th century, the village as a whole presenting an attractive blend of grey stone, red-brick, whitewashed and half-timbered constructions. There are a 14th-century church and tithe barn, ancient inns and weavers' houses, a King John hunting lodge, an old lockup, a stepped cross and a packhorse bridge. The most impressive building, however, is the riverside Abbey, founded by the Countess of Salisbury in the 13th century and converted into a house by Sir William Sharington shortly after suppression of the monastery in 1539. The original sacristy, chapter house and cloisters were preserved and a large courtyard, octagonal tower and twisted chimney stacks were added. A Gothic-style entrance hall and great hall were built on in the 18th-century by the Talbot family, into whose hands the Abbey had then passed; a museum housed at the entrance to the abbey traces the work of W H Fox-Talbot, the pioneer of photography who produced the first photographic prints in 1838 and was awarded the Royal Society Medal for his achievement.

LAIRG, Highland   30 NC50
Lairg is traditionally a market village where important lamb sales are held, but its beautiful setting in wild countryside at the end of Loch Shin makes it popular with anglers and holidaymakers, whilst archaeologists are drawn to the area by the presence of prehistoric circles and tumuli. In woodland about three miles south of the village are the spectacular waterfalls of the River Shin, where salmon can be seen leaping at certain times of year.

LAKE DISTRICT, see entries on
individual places.

LAKENHEATH, Suffolk   12 TL78
There has been a United States Air Force station at Lakenheath since 1941, and it is still one of the largest of such bases in the country. St Mary's Church is particularly fine, with a Norman chancel arch and a 16th-century wooden roof embellished with angels; the bench-ends in the nave and the 15th-century pulpit also have beautifully carved motifs

LAMBERHURST, Kent   6 TQ63
Lamberhurst, its long main street crossing the River Teise, looks substantially as it has for hundreds of years. Today's small village was once a centre for iron but it is now better known for its flourishing vineyard. The ruins of Bayham Abbey (OACT), founded in the 13th century, are situated in the grounds of a modern house two miles to the west, and those of moated Scotney Castle (NT), set in beautiful landscaped grounds lie to the south-east. Owl House, the one-time haunt of smugglers, is a small half-timbered house set in large gardens (OACT).

LAMBERHURST *To reach the ruins and gardens of Scotney Old Castle, visitors cross the moat, whose waters in early summer are thickly carpeted with waterlilies.*

MONASTERIES
Convents, Priories and Abbeys

RIEVAULX ABBEY *Spectacular ruins (above) indicate the foundation's former grandeur.*
ROMSEY PSALTER *Detail (left) of the 15th-century manuscript.*

MONASTICISM did not begin in Britain and the first Christian monks lived isolated, hermit-like existences in remote parts of the Roman Empire. In the early years of the 4th century, such recluses began to gather together to form monastic communities. The Benedictine order emerged in the early years of the 6th century, uniting numerous communities under the Benedictine Rule, which regarded the monk as a member of a closely integrated community, led by an abbot or 'father' and dedicated to prayer and the service of God. Until the 10th century this was virtually the only continental Order and the initial stages in the conversion of Saxon England were achieved by Benedictine monks led by St Augustine. In Ireland, Wales and parts of France however, Celtic monasticism flourished and placed more emphasis on prayer, scholarship and fasting. Irish monasteries made an enormous contribution to learning and some of the ancient Irish monastic sites are fascinating.

In many parts of the continent, monasteries that were founded during the Middle Ages are still living communities. In England and Wales, however, the great majority of abbeys and priories exist only as romantic ruins and have been deserted since they were dissolved in the years 1536–40.

By 700, paganism had been almost completely conquered in Britain and both Celtic and continental monks had contributed to the Christian victory. In 634, King Oswald of Northumbria invited the Celtic monks to Iona to send an evangelist to his people, and as a result, a community was established under St Aidan on the island of Lindisfarne. At a time when the hold of Christianity in England was still fragile, a split between Celtic traditions and the Roman influences which were rooted in Canterbury would have proved disastrous – but the doctrinal differences were resolved at the Synod of Whitby in 663. The Roman success owed much to the arguments of Wilfrid, a monk who had studied in Italy and Gaul. He became a very influential churchman in Northumbria, founding an abbey at Hexham. However, he incurred the wrath of King Ecgfrith when he encouraged the Queen to become a nun at Coldingham, and was expelled from Northumbria in 677. In due course, he founded several monasteries in the Midlands kingdom of Mercia and introduced the Rule of St Benedict to the English communities. In later years, English monks played a vital role in the conversion of German and Scandinavian lands.

THE BENEDICTINES established their communities throughout Britain during the remaining centuries of the Saxon era, and built cathedrals and mother churches or 'minsters'. The Danish invasions which followed the sacking of Lindisfarne in 793 caused terrible destruction, but a revival took place in the 10th century. By the

of the cruel harrying of the North by William I. As these northern abbeys acquired vast estates which were profitably worked as sheep ranges, several populated areas were cleared to create new grazings and preserve the monks from contact with the laity.

THE CARTHUSIAN ORDER, and others that were established later had a less dramatic impact. The Carthusians, founded in 1084, sought to recreate the stark austerity of the lifestyle followed by the early Christian hermits. The first Carthusian priory in Britain was founded at Witham in Somerset in 1178 as part of the penance of Henry II for his role in the murder of Archbishop Thomas Becket. However, it was only in the late 14th century, when the main era of monastic foundation was long passed, that the Carthusian Order gained a vigorous new lease of life in Britain and it seems that patrons respected the simple devotion of the Carthusian communities in times when some of the houses of the greater Orders had become lax or corrupted.

The Canons of St Augustine or the 'Black Canons' were members of an older Order, with less severe regulations but a deep involvement in the management of parish churches. Their first English house seems to have been St Botolph's Priory at Colchester, dating from 1103. Although the Order established 13 abbeys in Britain, the emphasis was on the foundation of smaller priories closely associated with churches, and about 200 examples were created, of which Bolton Priory in Wharfedale is one of the most attractive. In addition, medieval England contained a spectrum of other religious movements, including inspiring preachers like the Franciscan, Dominican and Carmelite friars, crusading military Orders such as the

Hospitallers and Templars and smaller monastic Orders like the Gilbertine Canons, whose houses were largely concentrated in Lincolnshire, where they provided numerous hospitals and orphanages, and the Premonstratensians, who held the abbey at Bayham in East Sussex.

MONASTIC WEALTH grew as monastic fervour waned during the latter part of the Middle Ages. Many abbeys contained only half their full complement of monks and there were fewer recruits to the Orders. Even so, on the eve of the Dissolution, England and Wales had around 10,000 monks, canons, nuns and friars dispersed in around 800 foundations. All these houses were eliminated by 1540. Although some communities had become corrupt, and while the issue of the marriage of Henry VIII to Anne Boleyn had damaged relations

FOUNTAINS ABBEY *Like Rievaulx, one of the great Cistercian houses.*

BOLTON PRIORY *(below) was founded on the banks of the Wharfe in 1151. The nave is now used as the parish church.*

between Church and State, the main reason for the Dissolution seems to have been royal greed directed towards the fantastic resources in money and land which the monastic Orders controlled. In the aftermath of the Dissolution, monastic sites were frequently sold to private owners and the religious buildings were robbed of stones which were used to build opulent new mansions.

MOST ABBEYS were built on sites which offered the copious supply of water which was essential to sustain a sizeable community. These sites, usually along with surrounding estates, were donated by royal or noble benefactors who favoured particular Orders and, once established and successful, a monastic house might be invited to create daughter houses in widely dispersed parts of the country and could expect to receive generous endowments of land. Most of the abbeys were built to a plan which demanded a very imposing church, while the domestic buildings were grouped around a rectangular courtyard or cloister which lay on the south side of the east-west church orientation. In looking at monastic ruins it is interesting to compare the splendour of a richly-endowed foundation like Fountains or Rievaulx with the humbler buildings at one of the smaller, less affluent and more typical houses like Buckfast Abbey in Devon. It is also interesting to see how the priorities of the different Orders were expressed in their buildings, with Cluniac splendour being evident in the remains at Castle Acre, while the surviving buildings at Mount Grace Priory near Northallerton reveal the Carthusian principle that each monk should devote several hours each day to solitary prayers in a tiny private cell.

middle of the 11th century, England contained about 50 surviving, revived or new monasteries and 12 nunneries.

After the Norman Conquest in 1066, most of the English church leaders were replaced by Normans and the Norman kings favoured continental monastic models, particularly the Cluniac form, with its emphasis on liturgy and ceremonial splendour and new Cluniac houses were established at Lewes, Bermondsey and Castle Acre in Norfolk. By the middle of the 12th century, however, Cluniac influence was in decline and the baton passed to the Cistercians, whose tightly-organised Order stressed the simple, ascetic life. The first Cistercian foundation was at Waverley in Surrey in 1128, while Rievaulx in Yorkshire was founded in 1132 and Fountains appeared shortly after. The Cistercians sought seclusion from the lay world and were attracted to several remote areas in the North of England which still lay desolate as a result

Lancaster, Lancashire 18 SD46

'Time-honour'd Lancaster'

'Lancaster . . . lies, as it were, in its own ruins . . . locked in between the hills on one side, high as the clouds and the sea on the other, and the sea itself seemed desolate and cold . . .'

DANIEL DEFOE, *A Tour through the Whole Island*

The name of the city indicates its origin: the Roman *castrum*, or camp, beside the River Lune. Flint tools found around the rock of Castle Hill indicate that prehistoric man had also settled here. After the Romans left, the Saxons took over the site, and after the Conquest, the town passed to Roger de Poitou, who built the first Norman castle. The keep dates from about 1100 and both King John and John of Gaunt, first Duke of Lancaster, and ancestor of the Royal House of Lancaster (the Duchy of Lancaster still belongs to the Crown) added to the fortifications.

For many hundreds of years Lancaster was an important port and in the 18th century was England's chief port for trade with America; much of this trade involved a triangular route via Africa to pick up a cargo of slaves on the outward journey, and then tobacco and cotton on the return.

The handsome Customs House on St George's Quay dates from this prosperous period and was designed by Richard Gillow, one of the famous family of furniture-makers whose workshops were in Lancaster. Also dating from this era are the many handsome Georgian houses that can be found in the principal streets. As the River Lune silted up, and Liverpool, further south, expanded, Lancaster's maritime trade declined, but in the 19th century many cotton mills were built in the southern part of the town. Most of these have now closed or been converted to other uses, but several of the buildings still stand near the canal.

As the county town of Lancashire, Lancaster is an important administrative centre and in the 1960s was selected as the site for a new university, designed in 1963–4, and built at Bailrigg, three miles south.

THE SHIRE HALL *with its striking 18th-century ceiling.*

HENRY IV'S ARMS
The arms of the first Lancastrian king, are part of the Shire Hall display.

PLACES TO SEE

Castle and Shire Hall Dominating the city from the heights of Castle Hill, Lancaster Castle still looks medieval, though, of course, much restored. It was and is still used as a gaol, and among its famous prisoners were the so-called 'Lancashire Witches' in 1612, and George Fox, founder of the Society of Friends. The law courts are also housed here, but subject to court requirements, parts of the castle and Shire Hall, with its collection of more than 600 coats of arms, including those of all the sovereigns since Richard I, can be visited.

The Priory Church of St Mary stands near the castle and occupies the site of a 2nd-century Roman church. Most of the present building dates from the 15th century when the church belonged to the convent of Syon, but there are traces of older Saxon and Norman buildings. The choir stalls, with their exquisitely carved canopies, date from the 14th century and came originally from Cockersand or Furness Abbey.

Judge's Lodgings Visiting judges were lodged in this elegant Georgian house, now a fascinating museum decorated in period, with furniture made by Gillows. The Barry Elder Doll Collection is here, with an interesting collection of other toys and children's games displayed in the old nurseries.

Hornsea Pottery Guided factory tours and 42 acres of landscaped parkland are available to visitors to the famous pottery.

The Music Room In fact this is a tall, narrow house, which takes its name from the first-floor music room, famous for its elaborate plaster ceiling cast in about 1730 by Italian craftsmen. The Landmark Trust owns the building, and the room can be seen sometimes.

The City Museum Housed in the dignified Old Town Hall, the museum contains interesting archaeological finds and displays of local crafts, such as Gillow's furniture, and the history of the area. The museum of the King's Own Royal (Lancaster) Regiment is also here.

St Peter's Cathedral This Roman Catholic cathedral dates from 1859. Ornate and highly gilded, it looks back in style to the 1300s.

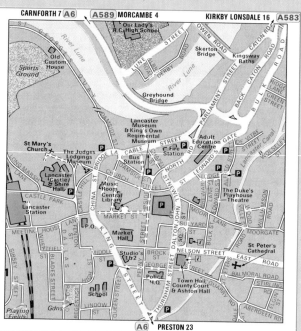

LAMPETER, Dyfed   7 SN54

Lampeter, once famous for its horsefair, has had a market since 1284 and is still an important centre for the sale of the disease-resistant cattle bred in the area. It has a Victorian town hall and a parish church which was completely rebuilt in the 19th century, though some 17th-century memorials are preserved in the porch. St David's College (now part of the University of Wales) is noted for its library containing some 80,000 books, ancient manuscripts and first editions. The 19th-century building is an unspoiled example of early Gothic revival, and a nearby mound marks the site of a medieval castle.

LAMPORT, Northamptonshire
10 SP77

Lamport Hall (OACT), dating chiefly from the 17th and 18th centuries, stands in pleasant parkland about eight miles from Northampton. The south-west front was designed by John Webb, the son-in-law and pupil of Inigo Jones. The house, now the property of the Lamport-Hale Trust, was for 400 years the home of the Isham family, and a fine collection of their portraits is on display, together with other works by well-known artists and displays of china and furniture.

LANARK, Strathclyde   22 NS84

The market town of Lanark, set high above the Clyde, is an ancient Royal Burgh, its importance established in the 12th century when King David I built a castle here. New Lanark began as an 18th-century sociological experiment by philanthropist David Dale, who built houses and operated welfare schemes for the workers in his cotton mills. It looks over Cora Linn, which has the most spectacular of the Clyde Falls, a magnificent 90ft plunge. To the west of the town, Cartland Crags rise to 400ft over a chasm nearly a mile long by Mouse Water. Two time-honoured rituals are still observed in the town – Whippity Scoorie at the beginning of March (believed to originate in a pagan festival to drive away winter) and pageants to celebrate the Beating of the Bounds in June.

LAND'S END, Cornwall   1 SW32

Land's End, England's most westerly point, has predictably become a Mecca for tourists. Beyond the snack bars and souvenir shops, however, the brownish-granite cliffs plunge dramatically into the sea, and this stretch of coast has been designated an area of outstanding natural beauty. On a clear day there are good views of the Longship and Wolf lighthouses, respectively one and a half miles and eight miles offshore.

LANHYDROCK HOUSE, Cornwall
1 SX06

Lanhydrock House (NT) is approached by a half-mile avenue of ancient beeches and sycamores, running through flowering trees and shrubs to the formal gardens of lawns, rose beds and clipped cypresses around the house. The brown stone building is simple in design and dates back to the 17th century, though much of it was rebuilt after a fire in 1881. Inside, the atmosphere is informal, the house very obviously lived in. The daily routines of earlier days are illustrated by the collection of curios in the kitchen and buttery. Lanhydrock's

LANHYDROCK HOUSE *Neatly clipped cypress trees give shape to the trim lawns and formal rose beds that form the attractive gardens surrounding the old stone manor house.*

showpiece, however, is the original 17th-century plaster ceiling of the long gallery in the north wing, which local craftsmen decorated with early Old Testament scenes.

LARGS, Strathclyde   22 NS25

This popular yachting resort on the Firth of Clyde is sheltered by hills rising to more than 1700ft. It is the starting point for steamer excursions to the islands in the Firth and to the Kyles of Bute and there is a vehicle ferry to Great Cumbrae. Of the church of St Columba which once stood here, only Skelmorlie Aisle (AM) remains, but the saint is commemorated each year in early summer by the Colm's Day Festival.

LAUDER, Borders   24 NT54

Lauder, the only Royal Burgh in old Berwickshire, claims to have been granted this distinction during the reign of William the Lion, and it has certainly held its charter since 1502. The church is 16th-century, with an octagonal spire, and magnificent Thirlestane Castle (OACT), just outside the town, also dates back to this period though with later additions; it now houses the Border Country Life Museum. Old Lauder Bridge set the scene for the hanging of several favourites of James III by the Earl of Angus in 1482, and the days of the old street fairs are recalled by the curious little stepped tollbooth where stallholders used to pay their dues. Lauder Common Riding, a horse-riding festival held here each June, is one of the oldest in the country, and the Leader Water offers excellent fishing.

LAUGHARNE, Dyfed   7 SN31

Laugharne, a 'timeless, mild, beguiling island of a town', is famous as the home of Dylan Thomas, who lived for 16 years in The Boathouse on Cliff Walk and is buried in the churchyard. The poet himself denied that the characters of *Under Milk Wood*

were based on local people, but they seem happy with the association, and the play is performed regularly here. The town has an attractive old harbour and a church which dates back to the 13th century, though much restored; the ruined castle once guarded an important strategic position, but it was converted to use as a residence by Sir John Perrot, an illegitimate son of Henry VIII. The town charter, granted by the Normans in 1307, is kept in the Town Hall, and under its provisions a Portreeve still presides over sessions of Court Leet and Court Baron.

LAUNCESTON, Cornwall   1 SX38

Launceston once guarded the main route into Cornwall from Devon, and it was the county capital until 1838. A primitive motte-and-bailey stronghold was built here in the 11th century, but the present castle (AM) dates from the 13th. When it fell into disrepair after the Civil War, one tower continued to be used as a prison, and public executions were carried out below its walls until 1821. Lawrence House (NT) is one of the many interesting Georgian buildings in the old streets around the Square; it now houses a local history museum, but during the Napoleonic Wars it was a favourite rendezvous with French prisoners on parole. St Thomas's Church is notable for its large Norman font, and St Mary Magdelene's has fine woodwork inside and remarkable 16th century carving on the granite of the exterior.

LAURISTON CASTLE, Lothian
24 NT57

Lauriston Castle (OACT), a late 16th-century mansion, stands on the north-west outskirts of Edinburgh. Antiques and furniture on display represent both English and French styles. The house is associated with the 18th-century broker John Law and owned by Edinburgh Corporation.

LAVENHAM GUILDHALL *was built in the mid 16th century, soon after the Guild of Corpus Christi had been founded by the Earl of Oxford, whose figure is carved on the corner post of the building.*

LAVENHAM, Suffolk   *12 TL94*

Lavenham is a village of exceptionally beautiful timbered houses and inns; it has an old Wool Hall (now incorporated into the Swan Hotel), an ancient market cross, a fine Guildhall (NT) and an attractive church with a massive tower. Its early prosperity sprang from the Suffolk wool trade, for which it was a centre, Lavenham blue cloth being famous from the 15th century. Little Hall (OACT) contains the Gayer-Anderson Collection of antique furniture, ceramics and paintings.

LAWERS, Tayside   *26 NN63*

Lawers, on Loch Tay, lies at the foot of Ben Lawers, at 3984ft, the area's highest mountain, famous with naturalists because of the varieties of Alpine flowers and species of birds found there. On its slopes stands the Mountain Visitors Centre, which contains an exhibition and is the starting point for guided and self-guided tours.

LAXTON, Nottinghamshire   *16 SK76*

The village of Laxton somehow evaded the Enclosure Acts of the 18th century, and its arable land is still divided into three enormous tracts (West, South and Mill Fields) which are farmed on the three-year rotation basis, one being left fallow each year. The fields are overseen by the Court of the Manor, acting for the Lord of the Manor (now the Ministry of Agriculture). A foreman and jurors apportion strips of land to local farmers on a yearly basis and see that boundaries are respected and ditches cleared – a system of administration practised since medieval times and an almost unique survival of strip-farming.

LEAMINGTON SPA, Warwickshire
10 SP36

Leamington is an inland spa situated on the River Leam; it gained the prefix 'Royal' when Queen Victoria made a visit in 1838 and has been a fashionable health resort ever since. The baths in the Pump Room, where about 50,000 people are treated for rheumatic complaints every year, are fed by saline waters flowing underground from natural springs in the area; the waters can be tasted at a fountain in the Pump Room Annexe. The town is attractively spacious, with fine Georgian, Regency and early Victorian houses arranged in squares and terraces. The Warwick District Art Gallery and Museum contains interesting paintings.

LEATHERHEAD, Surrey   *5 TQ15*

Leatherhead's name comes from Saxon words meaning 'public ford', for the original settlement grew up at a crossing place on the River Mole where it cuts through the North Downs. Though the town is rapidly being modernised, with an up-to-date shopping centre and new theatre, it still has attractive narrow streets with gabled houses, and fine inns that are a reminder of its importance in coaching days. There was a church here in Anglo-Saxon times, and part of the present building dates back to the 12th century; Anthony Hope, the author of *The Prisoner of Zenda*, is buried in the churchyard.

LECHLADE, Gloucestershire   *3 SU29*

Today only pleasure craft cluster round Lechlade's old wharves, but in the 17th century they were used by barges carrying stone for the building of St Paul's Cathedral. Halfpenny Bridge spans the Thames here, its name a reminder of the toll once payable. St John's Bridge stands half a mile to the east, where the Leach meets the Thames and the borders of Gloucestershire, Wiltshire and Oxfordshire come together. Outside the town the Thames, flowing through a pleasant park, is referred to locally as the Isis, just as at Oxford. The poet Shelley stayed at a local inn and was inspired by the serenity of the riverside scene to write *Stanzas in a Summer Evening Churchyard*.

LEDBURY, Hereford & Worcester
9 SO73

Ledbury stands in rich pasture-land intersected by slow-moving streams, an unspoiled small town in hop-growing country not far from the Malvern Hills. John Masefield, Poet Laureate, was born here and always remembered the 'fair and half-timbered houses black and white'. The 17th-century Market House (AM) is particularly striking, raised on pillars of oak and timbered in a herringbone pattern, whilst there is an excellent example of 16th-century building in the Feathers Hotel. The illusion of being transported back in time is strongest, however, in a nearby lane – narrow, cobbled, and overhung by the projecting upper storeys of ancient houses. At the end of the lane stands the impressive church of St Michael and All Angels, basically Norman, but containing memorials dating back to the Middle Ages. Eastnor Castle (OACT), two miles to the east, is a 19th-century edifice in the baronial style, set in a deer park and containing fine furnishings, pictures and an extensive collection of weaponry and suits of armour.

LEEDS, Kent   *6 TQ85*

Leeds Castle (OACT) was named after Led, chief minister of a 9th century King of Kent, Ethelbert IV. It stands on two islands in a lake formed by the River Len and was described by Lord Conway as 'the loveliest castle in the world' – though the 12th-century architects of the present structure were more concerned with its effectiveness as an impregnable stronghold. It became known as 'Lady's Castle' because of the number of Queens of England who occupied it: Eleanor and Margaret (the two wives of Edward I), Philippa of Hainault (wife of Edward III), Catherine de Valois (Henry V's queen) and Catherine of Aragon all lived here at various times, and Elizabeth I was held prisoner here before she was crowned. King Henry VIII made it an official Royal Residence, and it remained so for over 300 years. It now belongs to the Leeds Castle Foundation and is used for top level conferences, though it is open to the public most afternoons during the summer. It houses a unique museum of medieval dog collars and the parkland surrounding it contains rare swans, geese and ducks.

LEEDS, W Yorkshire   *15 SE33*

Originally a wool town, Leeds has developed into a world centre for ready-made clothing; it is also involved in the manufacture of a large variety of commodities ranging from footwear to ferro-concrete constructions. Despite this concern with progress, however, the old town has not been completely obliterated. The Grammar School was founded in 1552 and both Corn Exchange and Town Hall are 19th-century. St John's Church has interesting 17th-century woodwork, while St Peter's preserves a restored pre-Conquest cross. Three miles to the north-west of the town stand the extensive remains of Kirkstall Abbey, whose Cistercian monks came from Fountains Abbey in the 12th century. It is now a museum of folk studies and houses three reconstructed Victorian streets. To the south-east lies Temple Newsam (OACT), a splendid house which was the birthplace of Lord Darnley. Middleton Colliery Railway (OACT), dating from 1758 and the oldest in existence, is still in operation, manned by a group of enthusiasts. The town is represented by a well-known football team and is also prominent in Rugby League circles; Headingley County Cricket Ground is a traditional Test Match venue.

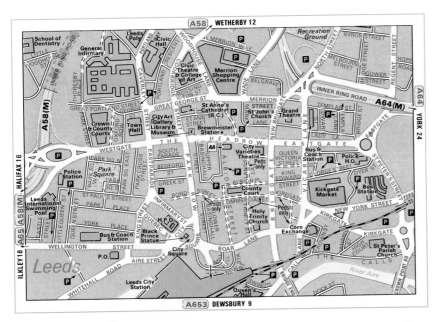

THE IVANHOE CLOCK *in Thornton's Arcade, Leeds, depicts a scene from Scott's* Ivanhoe.

LEEK, Staffordshire   15 SJ95
In the mid 18th century, canal pioneer James Brindley designed a local mill (OACT) which was used for grinding corn until the 1940s and has now been restored. St Edward's Church has a fine pinnacled tower, and an ancient pillar (either Saxon or Danish) stands in the churchyard. Although an industrial centre, with important silk mills, Leek is a true moorland town and lies not far from the spectacular millstone-grit formations of Hen Cloud and Staffordshire Roaches.

LEICESTER, Leicestershire   10 SK50
Leicester's development from a small county town to the sprawling industrial city of today was prompted by the coming of the railway in the 19th century, for this provided easy access to the coalfields. There was a settlement here in Roman times: the Jewry Wall is believed to date from AD 130, and excavations have also revealed a public bath and shops. Of the Norman castle only motte and great hall remain, the latter used as a law court. St Mary de Castro, the church of the castle, is also basically Norman, and St Martin's Cathedral has its origin in a 13th-century church. The richness of the city's history is

reflected in its many museums: Newarke House Museum concentrates on the period from 1500 to the present day, while the Leicestershire Museum and Art Gallery includes exhibitions on ceramics, natural history and Egyptology, together with a notable collection of German Expressionist paintings. The Museum of the Royal Leicestershire Regiment is housed in the 15th-century Magazine Gateway, and the Wygston's House Museum of English Costume in a building which is basically late medieval. Giant beam engines are displayed in the Leicester Museum of Technology, and the results of various digs in the Jewry Wall Museum. The medieval Guildhall (OACT) survives, as does the 18th-century mansion of Belgrave Hall (OACT). Leicester University founded the country's only School of English Local History.

LEIGHTON BUZZARD, Bedfordshire
11 SP92
The centre of the old market town of Leighton Buzzard is the scene of a strange ceremony each May, when a choirboy stands on his head while portions of the founder's will are read aloud at Wilks Almshouses. Nearby is an elegant five-sided market cross, its two tiers of arches holding carved figures, which was erected in 1400. The Leighton Buzzard Light Railway leaves from Pages Park Station to travel through almost four miles of beautifully wooded country.

LEIGHTON HALL, Lancashire
18 SD47
Standing in extensive grounds, Leighton Hall (OACT) is a fine stone mansion to which an attractive neo-Gothic facade was added in the early 19th century; sheltered by Warton Crag, it looks north towards the Lake District. In 1822 it was bought by Richard Gillow, a member of the famous furniture-making family, and a superb collection of their early work is on display. Many birds of prey are kept in the grounds, where they are flown, weather permitting.

LEITH, Lothian   23 NT27
Leith, which has officially been a part of Edinburgh since 1920, stands where the Water of Leith enters the Firth of Forth. It is a seaport with a busy modern dock and container quay; shipyards, sawmills and chemical works are the other major employers of labour in the area. The town was twice sacked by the English, in 1544 and 1547. When Mary, Queen of Scots returned from France (where she had spent her childhood) in 1561, she landed here and stayed at the home of a local merchant – Lamb's House (NT), which still stands, used now as an old people's home. St Mary's Church is restored 15th-century, and Trinity House has an interesting collection of paintings.

THE ROACHES *Favourite training ground of aspiring rock-climbers, this ridge of strangely weathered rocks near Leek supports a small herd of wallabies which run wild on the Staffordshire moors.*

On the Marches of Wales
63 miles

Mighty Ludlow Castle dominates the mild green hills of Hereford and Worcester, where nowadays there is no threat from Wales. A country of abundant rivers and fertile valleys, this is one of the few remaining truly pastoral regions of England.

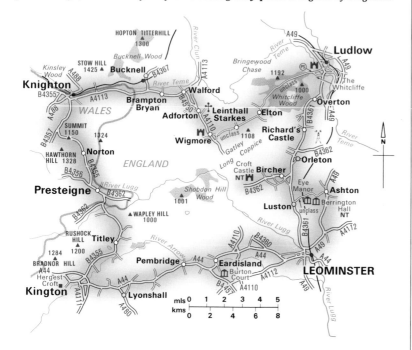

From **Leominster** take A44 Rhayader road and drive through Eardisland and Pembridge to **Kington**. At the first roundabout turn right, and at the next again right for Presteigne (B4355). Pass through Titley and shortly after crossing the Welsh border turn left into **Presteigne**. Stay on B4355, following Knighton signs, to the outskirts of **Knighton**, where the main route turns right on to A4113 for Ludlow (for Knighton turn left here). Drive through Brampton Bryan to **Walford**, turn right (SP Hereford) then in 1 mile right again on to A4110. Drive to **Wigmore**, and at Ye Olde Oak (PH) turn left (SP Ludlow) and drive along an

unclassified road to the edge of **Ludlow**. The main route turns right (no sign) on to B4361 (but for Ludlow town-centre turn left). After 1 mile turn right with B4361 Presteigne road and pass through Overton and Richard's Castle. Skirt Orleton and in 1 mile bear left (SP Leominster). Alternatively, turn right (SP Presteigne) on to B4362, then right again into **Bircher**. One mile further on is the entrance (right) to Croft Castle. Return through Bircher and turn right on to B4361. Just outside **Luston** turn left (SP Ashton) for Eye Manor and continue past Berrington Hall to the main road. Turn right on to A49 to return to Leominster.

PLACES TO SEE

Leominster A town of narrow medieval streets and timber-framed houses. The beautiful priory church dates from the 12th to the 15th centuries.

Eardisland One of the prettiest old villages in the county, situated on the River Arrow.

Pembridge Almost the equal of Eardisland, Pembridge too is a place of great charm.

Knighton To the west of this border town are the earthworks of Offa's Dyke, the ancient frontier between England and Wales. The Dyke is, since 1971, a long-distance footpath.

Ludlow The castle (OACT) was built by the Earl of Shrewsbury in 1085. This was the home of Catherine of Aragon for the

short period of her marriage to Henry's elder brother, Arthur, Prince of Wales. St Lawrence's Church dates from the 15th century: it has a beautiful east window and superbly carved misericords. The old Butter Cross is now the town's museum.

Croft Castle (NT) Set in stately parkland, the castle dates back to the 14th century, but the interior is an outstanding example of the 18th-and 19th-century craftsmanship.

Eye Manor (OACT) Famous for the elaborate decoration of its fine plaster ceilings, Eye once belonged to a Barbados sugar-planter and slave-trader.

Berrington Hall (NT) A neo-classical building designed by Henry Holland and set in a park landscaped by Capability Brown.

LELANT, Cornwall *1 SW53*
Lelant is a delightful village and golfing resort set on the estuary of the River Hayle; its church, Norman and Perpendicular, has an interesting 18th-century sundial. The greatest attraction to visitors, however, is Lelant Model Village (OACT), where scale models of many of the county's notable buildings are displayed in landscaped grounds. A museum illustrates Cornish crafts and history (with particular emphasis on shipwrecks, smugglers and tin-mining), and the work of local artists is on sale. The grounds also include water gardens, a junior assault course and children's playground and a model railway exhibition.

LEOMINSTER, Hereford & Worcester *9 SO45*
Leominster stands at the juncture of the Rivers Pinsley and Lugg, in countryside chequered with cider-apple orchards and hop-fields. Today the famous Herefordshire cattle are exported all over the world from here, but the town's traditional involvement is with sheep, for 13th-century monks bred the sturdy Ryelands whose wool – the fine-textured 'Lemster Ore' – was in great demand until the 18th century. The greystone, three-naved priory (founded, according to tradition, by Earl Leofric, husband of Lady Godiva, in the 11th century) has some fine windows and contains an old ducking stool once used for the punishment of nagging wives. Grange Court, a 17th-century brick and timber house, originally served as the Town Hall and stood at the central crossroads, but it was moved to its present site in 1855. Leominster's architecture spans many centuries – there are medieval buildings in the High Street, Tudor in Draper's Row, Jacobean in Pinsley Road and Georgian in Broad Street and Etnam Street. The Leominster and District Folk Museum has displays of smocks, corn dollies and many agricultural implements. Berrington Hall (NT), built by Henry Holland in 1778, lies four miles to the north-east of the town.

LEUCHARS, Fife *24 NO42*
The Norman church at Leuchars, built by the de Quincy family, is one of the finest in Scotland. The bell turret was added in the 17th century, but the original chancel and apse have survived and the building is elaborately carved, both inside and out; the Earlshall stones date from 1584 and 1635. On the edge of Tentsmuir, an area of great beauty encompassing forestry plantations and a nature reserve, stands the late 16th-century mansion of Earlshall.

LEVENS, Cumbria *18 SD48*
Levens Hall (OACT) stands in 100 acres of parkland through which flows the River Kent; its topiary gardens are probably the best of their kind in the country and were designed in about 1700 by a Frenchman called Beaumont, who also remodelled the gardens of Hampton Court for James II. The house itself is a fine Elizabethan mansion incorporating part of a 14th-century pele tower (built to protect the border against the Scots). The richly-carved panels and moulded ceilings were added by James Bellingham, who bought the house in 1580. The former brewhouse now houses a unique collection of steam-driven traction engines.

Dr Johnson's Birthplace

'I lately took my friend and showed him genuine civilized life in an English provincial town. I turned him loose at Lichfield that he might see for once real civility.'

SAMUEL JOHNSON

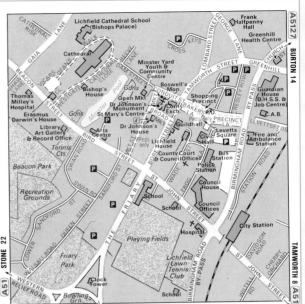

Lichfield lives in the shadow of its beautiful cathedral, a small masterpiece in red sandstone, whose three graceful spires deserve their nickname of 'the Ladies of the Vale'. They are best seen reflected in the waters of Minster Pool, or from a distance from across Stowe Pool, the two artificial lakes created by Bishop Clinton, who laid out the medieval plan of the city; Dam Street is built on the medieval dam which separated the two, and is lined with charming Georgian houses – nothing much older because the whole street was reduced to rubble when Lichfield was besieged in the Civil War and the Parliamentary commander, Lord Brooke, was shot down here by the son of the Royalist commander, stationed in one of the cathedral spires.

Almost the whole of the compact town centre is Georgian red brick and stucco and, despite the city's involvement in the industrial life of the Midlands, is remarkably well preserved. The 18th century was the 'Golden Age', when learning and literature flourished. This was the home (the house still stands on the main street) of Erasmus Darwin, grandfather of Charles, and a noted botanist and inventor in his own right. Together with his friends, Josiah Wedgwood and the inventors Matthew Boulton and James Watt, he founded the Lunar Society, so-called because the 'lunatics' met on nights of full moon so that they had light to travel by. Another of his

friends was the then famous but now forgotten poetess, Anna Seward, called the 'Swan of Lichfield.' The actor David Garrick also lived here and was for a time a pupil of Samuel Johnson who taught at the Grammar School. Johnson, whose father was the local bookseller, is by far the town's most distinguished son. His statue, and that of his friend and biographer James Boswell, stand outside his birthplace, which is now a museum. Every year on the Saturday nearest the anniversary of his birth, 18th September, a memorial service is held and a wreath is laid on his statue.

DR JOHNSON'S STATUE, *by RC Lucas, stands outside his house.*

LICHFIELD CATHEDRAL'S *graceful spires dominate the city.*

PLACES TO SEE

Cathedral of St Mary and St Chad The present building, begun in 1195, was completed in 1338, but the intricate carvings of the west front are mostly 19th-century work. Inside, the windows of the Lady Chapel, all except two, are of 16th-century Flemish glass, and notable, and there is an exquisite sculpture by Sir Francis Chantrey of two sleeping children. In complete contrast, is the bronze head of Bishop Woods by Epstein.

Vicar's Close Entered through an archway off the gracious 18th-century Close, the lodgings of the vicars' choral, who used to be attached to the cathedral, are delightful half-timbered houses.

Samuel Johnson Birthplace Museum The eight rooms of this attractive 18th-century house built by his father, Michael Johnson, are devoted to relics of Samuel Johnson and his work.

St Chad's Church Memorials to Dr Johnson's step-daughter, Lucy Porter, and an old family servant, Catherine Chambers, can be seen in this restored medieval church, said to be built on the site of the monastery founded by St Chad, Lichfield's first bishop and the 'apostle of the Midlands' in 669. In the churchyard is a well on the site of the spring where the saint used to pray.

Hanch Hall Three miles north-west of the city, the mansion (OACT) is a blend of Tudor and later architecture.

The Staffordshire Vale
63 miles

*The level expanses of the plain are speckled with pretty villages and bustling towns.
The Trent and Mersey Canal runs across the centre of the Vale and north of the
ancient woodlands of Cannock Chase: where once it carried industry to Staffordshire
it now brings pleasure-craft and narrow boats.*

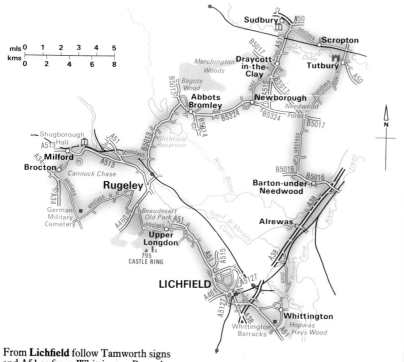

From **Lichfield** follow Tamworth signs
and A51 as far as Whittington Barracks,
then turn left (SP Whittington). Drive
through the village and join the Alrewas
road and in 3 miles turn right on to A38.
Pass the edge of **Alrewas**, and in 2¾ miles
turn left (SP Barton-under-Needwood)
then right on to B5016. Continue through
Barton on the Yoxall road, then after a
mile, at the Bell PH turn right on to an
unclassified road to reach **Tutbury**. Leave
by the High Street, A50, and after the
level-crossing turn left (SP Scropton). Pass
the village and in 2 miles turn left on to
A515 Lichfield road (or turn right to visit
Sudbury). After **Draycott-in-the-Clay**
ascend, then turn right (unclassified) for
Newborough, then turn right again on to
B5324 and drive to **Abbots Bromley**. Turn
right on to the Uttoxeter road, B5014, then
in a mile turn left on to B5013 (SP
Rugeley). Two miles after the reservoir
turn right and follow Leisure Drive signs,
turning left at the crossroads then left
again to join A51, before turning right (SP
Stafford) on to A513. Shortly before
reaching **Milford**, pass the entrance to
Shugborough Hall. At **Milford** turn left
for Brocton, then follow Stafford signs to
reach A34 and turn left (SP Cannock),
then take the next turning left (unclassified
SP Hednesford). Drive through Cannock
Chase, pass the German Military
Cemetery, then at the next crossroads turn
left (SP Rugeley) and in 3¼ miles right
into Post Office Lane. At the Horn PH
turn right. Later turn left on to A460, then
in ¾ mile turn right (SP Upper Longdon).
After the ascent, join Startley Road to
reach Upper Longdon. Beyond the village
turn right on to A51 and stay on this road
for the return to Lichfield.

PLACES TO SEE

Lichfield The cathedral, with its three
distinctive spires, has an ornate west front
with many statues and rich interior furn-
ishing; Dr Johnson's House (OACT) in
the market place was his birth-place and is
now a museum of his life and work.

Tutbury An attractive old town on the
River Dove, dominated by the ruins of its
castle (OACT).

Sudbury Hall (NT) A 17th-century house
with fine carvings by Grinling Gibbons; it
contains a Museum of Childhood.

Abbots Bromley Famous for the Horn
Dance that takes place early in September,
the town has many interesting old buildings and a famous girls' public school.

Shugborough Hall (NT) The Staffordshire County Museum is housed in this
17th-century mansion set in beautifully
landscaped grounds.

Cannock Chase Twenty-six square miles
of ancient royal forest are now designated
as an area of outstanding natural beauty.
Castle Ring, at 795ft, is the highest point.

LEWES, E Sussex *5 TQ41*
The site of Lewes, on the River Ouse and in
a hollow of the downs, was chosen by the
Normans as the ideal place for a defensive
stronghold, and a castle stood here until the
17th century, when much of the fabric was
sold as building material. The only parts to
survive were a stone keep (AM) and a
gatehouse, now known as Barbican House
and containing a museum of Sussex
archaeology. Most of the old buildings in
Lewes, including the market tower which
holds the town bell, are 18th-century, and
many are attractively tile-hung. One house
in Southover, however, dates from 1559; it
was given to Anne of Cleves by Henry VIII
and it now holds a museum of local history.
The history of the British army is traced in
the Military Heritage Museum at Regency
House. St Michael's Church has a curious
round tower, and St Anne's and St John's
are both partly Norman – the former
having a Norman font and the latter a
carved stone covering the grave of one of
William the Conqueror's daughters. The
famous 17th-century diarist John Evelyn
went to school in Lewes and spent periods
of his life at Southover Grange. Each Guy
Fawkes night huge torch-lit processions
parade through the steep streets of the
attractive, old town.

LEWES *This corner of the attractive High Street
shows a medley of styles of building, from tile-
hung and timbered to brick and flint.*

LEYBURN, N Yorkshire *20 SE19*
The old market town of Leyburn is set
above the River Ure in Wensleydale. The
area is popular with walkers, one of its most
interesting features being a two-mile-long
limestone scar known as The Shawl. To the
east of the town stands 18th-century Constable Burton Hall, whose large, informal
gardens (OACT) have fine displays
of roses and alpine plants.

LILFORD PARK, Northamptonshire
11 TL08
Herds of deer roam freely in the 240 acres
of Lilford Park (OACT), once the home of
the fourth Baron of Lilford, who first
created its impressive aviaries and gardens.
Seventeenth-century Lilford Hall is opened
to the public only for certain events, but the
aviaries have been rebuilt and stocked with
hundreds of birds – including the Lilford
Crane and the Little Owl, the latter first
established in Britain through birds
released from here. The Park offers
pleasant riverside walks and picnic spots,
a children's farm with pony rides, craft and
antique centres and a museum. It is the
venue of the East of England Motor Show.

City of the Eastern Plains

'By this to Lincoln come, upon whose lofty scite
Whilst wistly Witham looks with wonderful delight,
Enamour'd of the state and beauty of the place ...'

MICHAEL DRAYTON *Poly-Olbion*

When the Romans invaded Britain they found at Lincoln a Celtic hillfort named Lindon, the 'fort by the pool'. They took over the name, changing it to the Latin form, Lindum Colonia, from which we get Lincoln. In time, a sizeable town grew up around the Roman fort, and a remarkable relic of these days can be seen in Bailgate, where the Roman north gate is partly preserved in Newport Arch, the only Roman gateway in Britain that is still open to traffic; fragments of the east gate can be seen in the courtyard of the hotel of that name. Modern Lincoln

owes much to engineering industries, but the historic centre of this ancient city is remarkably untouched: narrow medieval streets such as the Strait, Steep Hill and Bailgate contain many interesting and historic buildings. Some are half-timbered, like the quaintly named Cardinal's Hat, which is thought to be named after Cardinal Wolsey who was Bishop of Lincoln for one year (1514–15); and some are of stone, like the two remarkable Norman houses, the Jew's House, and the House of Aaron the Jew. These buildings both date from the 12th century, when the Normans were encouraging Jews to settle in prosperous towns so that they could help to finance trade, and Aaron's House is probably the oldest inhabited house in England. Before it turned to engineering, Lincoln was an important centre of the cloth industry, and was particularly famous for a type of cloth devotees of the Robin Hood story will remember as Lincoln Green. Lincoln is dominated by its majestic three-towered cathedral, crowning the steep hill that rises so dramatically from the Lincolnshire plain. Complementing the cathedral in size if not in grandeur is the great limestone castle, built in 1080 to control this eastern corner of the kingdom.

STEEP HILL is one of Lincoln's fascinating old streets.

PLACES TO SEE

Lincoln Cathedral The impressive west front, decorated with many statues, is all that remains of the first cathedral the Normans built. Most of the rest of this majestic building dates from the 13th century when St Hugh of Avalon was bishop. St Hugh's Choir, with its lovely choir stalls, and the Angel Choir, so-called from the 28 carved angels supporting the roof, are particularly fine. Among the carvings in the Angel Choir is the figure of the legendary Lincoln Imp, turned to stone for his misdeeds. Ancient stained glass has survived in some windows, particularly the two rose windows of the transepts, known as the Dean's Eye and the Bishop's Eye. Among the cathedral treasures is one of the four extant original copies of Magna Carta.

Lincoln Castle Although alterations have been made over the years, the basic plan of this great walled fortress with its two massive towers is unchanged. In Cobb Hall prisoners were kept chained to iron rings, and until 1859 the town gallows stood on its roof. The prison chapel is of interest for the narrow enclosed cubicles which were so partitioned as to allow prisoners to see only the preacher and not each other.

Greyfriars City and County Museum Housed in part of an old Franciscan friary, the museum contains archaeological finds and collections of arms and armour.

Usher Gallery Founded in 1927, the gallery contains many paintings by Peter de Wint, who drew his inspiration mostly from the Lincolnshire countryside, and there is a room devoted to Lincolnshire's most famous poet, Alfred, Lord Tennyson.

The Museum of Lincolnshire Life Exhibits range from Elizabethan to modern times.

Museum of the 10th Foot Royal Lincolnshire Regiment Housed in Sobraon Barracks, exhibits cover regimental history from the 18th century to the present day.

LINCOLN CATHEDRAL, seen from the south in this late Victorian engraving (above) crowns the hill overlooking the city: (left), the superb west front.

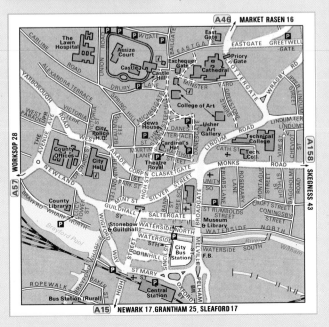

LINDISFARNE, Northumberland
24 NU14

Lindisfarne, or Holy Island, is accessible from the mainland by a causeway which is covered at high tide. The island has been designated an area of outstanding natural beauty and part of it is a National Nature Reserve; the limestone cliffs and sand dunes of the north shore teem with birdlife, and seals are often seen offshore. Missionaries from Iona who settled here in the 7th century, led by St Aidan, who founded the first monastery on the island, and later St Cuthbert, brought Christianity to Northumbria. The monks were driven out by the Danes in 875, but a Benedictine Priory was established in the 11th century, and its remains (OACT) incorporate a museum. A small, 16th-century castle (NT), restored by Sir Edwin Lutyens, stands on a rocky point.

HOLY ISLAND *Lindisfarne is so named for its associations with St Aidan and St Cuthbert.*

LINLITHGOW, Lothian   *23 NS97*
In 1424 James I instigated the building of a new palace on the site of an earlier one destroyed by fire; this was later the birthplace of Mary Queen of Scots – and was itself burned in the 18th century. The ruins (AM) look down on the ancient town of Linlithgow from a knoll on the south shore of the town loch, and within their precincts stands the Church of St Michael, dating from the 13th century but much restored after the 15th-century fire. The original crown steeple of the tower was removed for safety in the 1820s, and a symbolic crown of thorns has replaced it since 1964. The oldest bell is almost 500 years old and was tolled in 1513 after the Scots' defeat at Flodden. The town has many old buildings, some late 16th-century houses (NTS, not open) in the High Street being of particular interest. Blackness Castle ruins (AM), stand four miles to the south-east, and to the east is the House of Binns (NTS), a magnificent 17th-century house, with beautifully moulded plaster ceilings a feature of the interior.

LINTON, Cambridgeshire   *11 TL54*
Linton, an attractive town with timber-and-plaster houses and a half-timbered Guildhall, stands on the River Granta. The church, which dates back to the 13th century, has some interesting brasses and monuments. Linton Zoological Gardens stress the importance of conservation of threatened species, and snakes, insects and spiders are on display as well as the more usual animals and birds. The zoo's ten acres are laid out with flower-beds, shrubberies and exotic trees, and its enclosures are attractively landscaped – each being made as similar as possible to the natural environment of the native country of its occupants.

LIPHOOK, Hampshire   *4 SU83*
Liphook's Royal Anchor Hotel is a well-known 17th-century coaching inn whose famous patrons have included Queen Victoria and General Blücher. Bohunt Manor Gardens (OACT), the property of the World Wildlife Fund, offer woodland and lakeside walks, fine roses and herbaceous borders and a water-garden; there is also a collection of over a hundred ornamental ducks, geese and crane. At Hollycombe House Gardens (OACT) a remarkable array of steam-driven fair machinery and a 2ft gauge railway are displayed against a woodland setting, and there are occasional demonstrations of ploughing, threshing or steam-rolling. Nearby lie the beauty spot known as Waggoners Wells (a string of ponds first constructed for the iron industry), and 40 acres of Bramshott Chase belonging to the National Trust.

LITTLE GADDESDEN,
  Hertfordshire   *5 SP91*
Little Gaddesden is a beautiful old village set against a magnificent backcloth of beechwoods and bracken-covered commons. Its Perpendicular church has several interesting monuments. The manor house is Elizabethan, and John o'Gaddesden's House – timber-framed, with an overhanging upper floor and a timber roof – was built in the 15th century. Ashridge Management College occupies Ashridge House (OACT), a large neo-Gothic mansion rebuilt by James Wyatt in 1808 on the site of a 13th-century original. It stands amid wooded parkland laid out by Capability Brown and gardens designed by Humphry Repton, the National Trust owning the majority of the estate.

LITTLEHAMPTON, W Sussex
  5 TQ00
This ancient small town was once a prominent port on the River Arun, used by passengers to Normandy and involved in the export of timber and the import of Caen stone. Today it is a popular yachting centre and holiday resort, with a huge expanse of sand, safe bathing and good fishing. Attractive river trips are available, an 18-hole golf course is easily reached by ferry, and there is a funfair. The local museum concentrates on sailing and marine subjects. **Arundel** and the South Downs are within easy reach.

LIVERPOOL, Merseyside   *14 SJ49*
There was a settlement here, on the north bank of the River Mersey, as early as the first century AD, and this had grown into a sizeable fishing village by the time King John granted its charter in 1207. Trade with the West Indies encouraged the port's development, but the emergence of modern Liverpool really began with the introduction of steamships in the middle of the 19th century, and today the seven-mile-long dock is one of the finest in the world, although trade has sadly declined over recent years. The city has two cathedrals, both built this century – the Gothic-style Anglican, begun in 1904, and the strikingly different Roman Catholic one, with its stained glass tower and central altar, which was consecrated in 1967. The Walker Art gallery has an outstanding collection of European paintings and the Sudley Art Gallery concentrates on British paintings.

THE LIVERPOOL SOUND

John, Paul, George and Pete Best, not Ringo, at the Cavern in 1961. Beatlemania is still strong, and there is an information centre, Cavern Mecca, in Mathew Street for Beatles fans.

Housed in restored 19th-century quays on the waterfront is the Merseyside Maritime Museum, which has a fine collection of full-size craft. The City Library is one of the country's largest reference libraries, with over 2,000,000 books. The university is growing in both size and reputation, and the Royal Liverpool Philharmonic orchestra is famous. Aintree Racecourse is the scene of the Grand National each spring, and both Everton and Liverpool are football teams of note. Two tunnels beneath the Mersey join Liverpool with Birkenhead, which stands on the opposite bank. Some of the buildings and landscaping carried out for the 1984 International Gardens Festival have been used as part of the programme of urban renewal now being undertaken.

THE LIVER BUILDING (below), seen from across the waters of Liverpool's dockland.

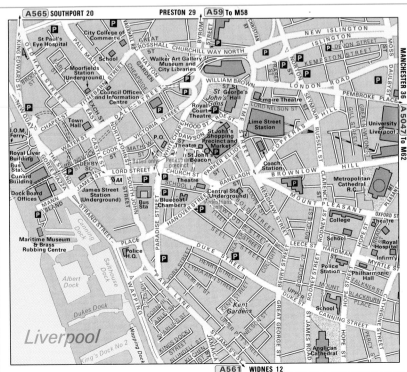

LIZARD, Cornwall 1 SW71
Lizard Point, the tip of the Lizard Peninsula, is the southernmost point in England. The name comes from the Cornish words 'lis' (place) and 'ard' (high). The famous veined serpentine rock is found only here. The scenery is dramatic, as towering walls of cliff and magnificent rock pinnacles stretch down to turbulent seas on a stretch of coast notorious for shipwrecks. There are sandy beaches to the east at Housel Bay, and Kynance Cove (see separate entry) lies west of the Point. A few miles inland, on Goonhilly Downs, stands the Post Office's satellite tracking station.

LLANARMON DYFFRYN CEIRIOG, Clwyd 14 SJ13
The remote village of Llanarmon Dyffryn Ceiriog is set below the Berwyn Mountains at the head of the beautiful Ceiriog valley; it is an excellent centre for walking, riding, fishing or shooting holidays. John Ceiriog Hughes, the great Welsh lyric poet, was born nearby. He left the area to become first a railway clerk in Manchester and then a station master in mid-Wales, but his poems hark back to the countryside of his boyhood.

DINORWIC QUARRIES at Llanberis were once the largest slate quarries in the world.

LLANBERIS, Gwynedd 13 SH56
This little town is the starting point for the easiest walk to Snowdon's summit and also the terminus of the Snowdon Mountain Railway – established in 1896 to carry tourists to the top of the mountain, and the only rack and pinion steam railway in Britain. Llanberis Lake Railway, by contrast, uses the old line from Dinorwic Quarries to Port Dinorwic, following the valley along Llyn Padarn. The huge Dinorwic slate quarries were once the world's greatest, but they were closed in 1969 because of the decline in demand for the material. The Welsh Slate Museum contains much of the original machinery used in the workshops, together with the 54-foot waterwheel that provided the power to operate it. Just outside the town the ruins of Dolbadarn Castle (AM), a native Welsh fortress with a three-storeyed, 13th-century round tower, overlook the valley.

LLANDAFF, S Glamorgan *8 ST17*

The little city of Llandaff officially became part of Cardiff in 1922, but it still retains a sense of identity, clustered closely round its ancient cathedral. The present building, begun in the 12th century, stands on the site of a church founded by St Teilo in the 6th; it has survived several periods of ill-treatment and neglect – and even a German landmine. The interior is dominated by Epstein's soaring aluminium figure of Christ in Majesty, whilst, by contrast, a 10th-century Celtic cross stands outside. The cathedral grounds contain the remains of a 13th-century bell tower, and a public garden has been made inside the ruins of a former bishop's palace (sacked by Owain Glyndwr in 1402).

LLANDDEWI BREFI, Dyfed *8 SN65*

The village, its huddle of colour-washed cottages a reassuring sight against the wild beauty of the hills that surround it on three sides, is set well off the main road in the Teifi valley. The mound on which the 13th-century church stands is said to have risen miraculously beneath the feet of St David as he spoke against the Heresy of Pelagius in the 6th century. A modern sculpture by Mancini shows the saint as a barefooted traveller with a stout staff and the dove of peace on his shoulder; St David's Staff is one of five carved Celtic stone crosses which survive. The 'dewi' of the village's name is the Welsh form of 'David' and the 'Brefi' refers to a little stream which flows through it to join the Teifi.

LLANDEILO, Dyfed *7 SN62*

Llandeilo, set amid rich agricultural land on the north bank of the River Tywi, is both a market town and a centre for touring and fishing. The Church of St Teilo, originally 13th-century, was virtually rebuilt in the 19th; two Celtic cross heads from the 10th or 11th century are preserved inside. On a cliff above the river stand the ruins of the old castle, which also dates back to the 11th century.

LLANDINAM, Powys *8 SO08*

Llandinam is best known as the birthplace of David Davies, the great Victorian industrialist who changed Barry, in South Wales, from a fishing village of 85 people to an important coal port with a population of 13,000. His career reputedly began with the purchase for £5 of an oak tree which he sold as planks for £80; this same business acumen led to his successful involvement in road and bridge building, railways and coal-mining. He is commemorated by a statue which stands at the end of the 19th-century iron bridge over the River Severn.

LLANDOVERY, Dyfed *8 SN73*

Llandovery, its name meaning 'the church amidst the waters', stands where the Rivers Bran and Gwydderig run into the Tywi. The church is St Mary's on the Hill, with fine tie-beam roof and barrel-vaulted chancel; it is built within the walls of the Roman fort that once stood here, and its fabric includes some Roman tiles. The town is the traditional market centre of the upper Tywi valley, and the Victorian and Georgian houses in the streets round the cobbled square are interspersed with a surprising number of old inns, for at one time Llandovery was the only town in the area permitted to keep taverns.

LLANDRINDOD WELLS, Powys *8 SO06*

The waters of Llandrindod Wells first became famous in the reign of Charles II, and by the 1850s it was the largest and most popular of the Welsh spas, with some 80,000 visitors a year. The original hamlet quickly expanded to provide all the attractions of a fashionable watering place; parks and gardens were laid out, surrounded by wide streets lined with extravagant hotels, ballrooms, eating-houses and gaming rooms. Today the town, its broad streets and 19th-century architecture substantially unchanged, is the administrative capital of the newly-formed county of Powys and is developing as a conference centre; it is also popular as an inland resort, offering an excellent base for touring as well as facilities for golf, bowls, angling and boating. Visitors can glimpse the glories of Llandrindod's fashionable era in the Victorian Spa Gallery of the War Memorial Gardens Museum, which also contains the Paterson Doll Collection and an exhibition of finds from Castell Collen, a Roman camp to the north of the town.

LLANDUDNO, Gwynedd *13 SH78*

The resort of Llandudno, the largest in Wales, lies on a crescent of sandy bay dominated by the huge limestone headland of Great Orme. There are panoramic views from the 678ft-high cliff-top, which can be reached by Edwardian tramway, funicular railway or modern cabin-lift, and a five-mile Marine Drive has been cut into the side of the cliff. St Tudno's Church, on the north slope of the Orme, dates back to the 12th century (though St Tudno's mission here probably began some 600 years earlier); the font is medieval, and the roof above the altar bears the stigmata – the marks of Christ's wounds. On the lower slopes, overlooking town and bay, are the Happy Valley Rock Gardens and the terraced Hauffre Gardens. Llandudno has two museums: the Rapallo House Museum and Art Gallery displays a traditional Welsh kitchen, weaponry and Roman relics, as well as collections of porcelain, sculpture and pictures; the Dolls Museum has over a

LLANDUDNO *The sheltered, sandy beach of this pleasant resort is protected by Great Orme Head.*

PUNCH AND JUDY

Llandudno's Punch and Judy theatre is a family heirloom – handed down from father to son ever since the 19th century. The puppeteers all call themselves by the professional name of 'Professor Codman'.

thousand dolls, representing various eras of fashion, and the same building houses a large model railway. A stone on the promenade depicts the White Rabbit consulting his watch – for Lewis Carroll was here, staying with the Liddells and their daughter Alice, when he decided to write his famous book.

LLANELLI, Dyfed *7 SN50*

Llanelli is the largest town in south-east Dyfed. Originally a market centre, its rapid growth began with the 19th-century introduction of ironworks and continued with the exploitation of its coal resources, which in turn gave way to the modern steelworks. An industrial museum is contained in the Trostre Works of the British Steel Corporation, and the Parc Howard Art Gallery and Museum contains interesting paintings and Llanelli pottery.

LLANFAIR CAEREINION, Powys
8 SJ10

This quiet little town, dating largely from
the 18th century, stands on the site of an
old Roman fort above the River Einion
(also known as the Banwy). Its church was
rebuilt in the 19th century but still has a
stone effigy of a knight which possibly dates
from the 14th, and a doorway of 13th-
century origin. An ideal centre from which
to explore north Powys, it is also the
terminus of the Welshpool and Llanfair
Light (Steam) Railway, which was restored
by a preservation society formed in the
1960s after British Rail had closed the line.

LLANFAIRFECHAN, Gwynedd
13 SH67

Modern Llanfairfechan is a resort with
sandy beaches and the usual seaside
attractions, offering fine coastal walks with
superb views and good sailing. The older
part of the town stands on the banks of the
River Llanfairfechan where it flattens out
after dropping 2000ft in a distance of three
miles on its journey to the sea.

LLANFAIR PG see Anglesey.

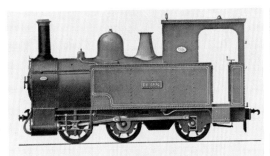

WELSHPOOL LLANFAIR CAEREINION

Work on the narrow-gauge railway that was to
transport goods from Welshpool to Llanfair
Caereinion was completed in 1903 and goods trains
ran along this hilly and remarkably scenic route
until 1956. A preservation society was soon formed,
which has re-opened the eight mile line as far as
Raven Square station outside Welshpool. 'The
Earl', above is one of the original locomotives and
the 'Sir Drefalwyn', opposite, (meaning County
of Montgomeryshire), a German-designed tank
engine, came from Austria.

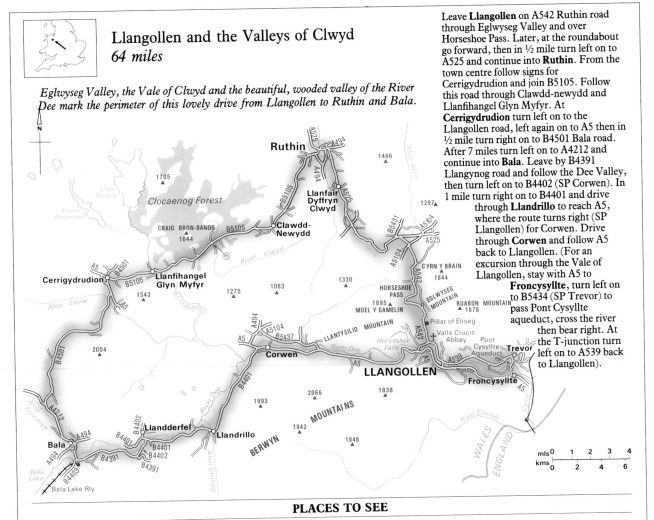

Llangollen and the Valleys of Clwyd
64 miles

*Eglwyseg Valley, the Vale of Clwyd and the beautiful, wooded valley of the River
Dee mark the perimeter of this lovely drive from Llangollen to Ruthin and Bala.*

Leave **Llangollen** on A542 Ruthin road
through Eglwyseg Valley and over
Horseshoe Pass. Later, at the roundabout
go forward, then in ½ mile turn left on to
A525 and continue into **Ruthin**. From the
town centre follow signs for
Cerrigydrudion and join B5105. Follow
this road through Clawdd-newydd and
Llanfihangel Glyn Myfyr. At
Cerrigydrudion turn left on to the
Llangollen road, left again on to A5 then in
½ mile turn right on to B4501 Bala road.
After 7 miles turn left on to A4212 and
continue into **Bala**. Leave by B4391
Llangynog road and follow the Dee Valley,
then turn left on to B4402 (SP Corwen). In
1 mile turn right on to B4401 and drive
through **Llandrillo** to reach A5,
where the route turns right (SP
Llangollen) for Corwen. Drive
through **Corwen** and follow A5
back to Llangollen. (For an
excursion through the Vale of
Llangollen, stay with A5 to
Froncysyllte, turn left on
to B5434 (SP Trevor) to
pass Pont Cysyllte
aqueduct, cross the river
then bear right. At
the T-junction turn
left on to A539 back
to Llangollen).

PLACES TO SEE

Llangollen The 12th-century bridge is
reckoned to be one of the 'Seven Wonders
of Wales'; west of the town are the Horseshoe Falls. Plas Newydd (OACT) is the
fascinating home of the famous 'Ladies of
Llangollen'. In the restored railway station
are historic locomotives and rolling stock;
on the wharf, the Canal Exhibition Centre.

Valle Crucis Abbey (AM) Ruins of this
splendid 13th-century abbey stand in a
tranquil valley north of Llangollen.

Ruthin In the square of this pretty old
town is the Maen Huail Stone: according
to legend King Arthur slew his rival Huail
here for love of a woman.

Bala At nearby Parc is Cyffdy Farm, the
North Wales Farm Park and Rare Breed
Centre, with more than 100 species of
animals to see. Bala Lake is the terminus
of the Bala Lake Railway.

Pont Cysyllte Telford's famous aqueduct
carries the canal 127ft above the River.

PLAS NEWYDD *won fame in the 18th century as the home of the well-born Irish eccentrics Lady Eleanor Butler and Miss Sarah Ponsonby who fled conventional society to set up house in Llangollen.*

LLANFIHANGEL-Y-PENNANT, Gwynedd   *13 SH60*

This remote village, in lovely countryside on the south side of Cader Idris, is the starting point of the easiest route to the summit of the 2927ft-high mountain. A memorial marks the ruined cottage that was once the home of Mary Jones, whose determination to have her own Bible inspired the founding of the British and Foreign Bible Society. As a 16-year-old girl, after several years of hard saving, she walked to **Bala** and back – a round trip of 50 miles – to buy the book.

LLANGOLLEN, Clwyd   *14 SJ24*

Llangollen, a small town on the River Dee, was once a slate-quarrying centre, but the beautiful vale has been scarcely touched by industrial development and is famous as the setting of the International Music Eisteddfod, held here each summer since 1947. The 14th-century stone bridge that spans the river is acclaimed as one of the Seven Wonders of Wales. The famous 18th-century 'Ladies of Llangollen' were two eccentric and masculine women who set up house together at Plas Newydd (OACT), a fine black-and-white house which became a fashionable meeting place of society. Valle Crucis Abbey (AM) was founded in 1201 by Madog ap Gruffydd, Prince of Powys, and most of the remains date from that period. Llangollen Station (OACT), in the town centre, is a restored Great Western station complete with locomotives and rolling stock; trains run to Fford Junction during the summer months. The Canal Exhibition Centre uses models, murals and films to tell the story of Britain's great canal era, and it is possible to take a trip on a horse-drawn passenger boat at certain times.

LLANGURIG, Powys   *8 SN97*

The village, flanked by towering wooded hills, lies in the remote upper valley of the River Wye. Its church was founded by 6th-century St Curig, but the oldest parts of the existing building are 600 years later, and it was radically restored in the 19th century.

LLANIDLOES, Powys   *8 SN98*

At the heart of the little town of Llanidloes is its unique Market House, a half-timbered building standing on pillars, the open space beneath once having been used for traders' stalls. The upper storey now houses a museum, but over the centuries it has been a meeting house for Quakers, a chapel for Wesleyan Baptists, a public library, a working men's institute and a court house.

LLANRUG, Gwynedd   *13 SH56*

On a wooded hillside overlooking the quarryman's village of Llanrug towers early Victorian Bryn Bras Castle (OACT), built in Romanesque style on the basis of an 18th-century structure and still lived in.

LLANRWST, Gwynedd   *13 SH86*

Llanrwst is a pleasant old market town in the Conwy valley. Gwydyr Castle (OACT), a magnificently furnished Tudor palace, stands in beautiful grounds where peacocks and tropical birds are kept. Gwydyr Uchaf Chapel (AM), once the private chapel of the castle but now used as an exhibition centre, has a rare Welsh painted roof dating from 1673. The North Wales Museum of Wildlife is aptly named Encounter.

LLANSTEPHAN, Dyfed   *7 SN31*

The village of Llanstephan stands on a peninsula formed by the estuaries of the rivers Taf and Tywi. The 12th-century church with its lofty tower overlooks a square where the former village pound is now used as a shop, and the main street, lined with unpretentious Victorian and Georgian houses, runs down to the attractive area of waterfront known as The Green. The remains of the castle (OACT), dating back to the eleventh century, are set on a wooded headland high above the beach.

LLANTHONY, Gwent   *8 SO22*

The ruins of 13th-century Llanthony Priory (AM) stand in the beautiful, unspoiled valley of the River Honddu, with the Black Mountains on the west and 1748ft Hatteral Hill rising to the east. This is border country (the English boundary a mile away also defining the limit of the Brecon Beacons National Park and following the path of Offa's Dyke), and the Priory was founded by a Marcher Lord of Hereford, Hugh de Lacy. The original 12th-century community numbered 40, but the remoteness of the spot made for a primitive existence which many monks shunned, and by the time of the Dissolution only five remained. What was the Prior's house is now an hotel, and a church contemporary with the priory still stands, retaining some Norman features, though restored.

THRI THLWS CYMRU *Acclaimed as being one of the 'three beauties of Wales', Llangollen Bridge also features in a traditional rhyme as one of the 'Seven Wonders of Wales'.*

LLANTRISANT, Mid Glamorgan
8 ST08

The remains of an Iron Age fort to the east of Llantrisant indicate that the potential of this site – an easily-defended ridge overlooking the Ely valley and the Vale of Glamorgan – was recognised many centuries ago. There were native Welsh rulers here long before they were ousted by the Normans whose ruined castle keep can be seen today, overlooking an attractive little town with steep streets running down the hillside. The church, though much restored in the 19th century, is Norman; it has a 13th-century font, and an ancient slab of stone bearing three crosses is set into the outside of the north wall. The coming of the Royal Mint in 1967 led to the development of a virtually separate new town to the south of the old. The legality of cremation was established in a trial involving an inhabitant of Llantrisant: Dr William Price, a famous 19th-century eccentric who tried to live according to what he imagined would have been the teaching of the Druids, defended successfully his right to burn the body of his dead child, instead of having it buried as was customary at the time. When he himself died ten yers later, he too was cremated. A plaque commemorates this extraordinary figure.

LLANVAPLEY, Gwent *8 SO31*

At Llanvapley, four miles to the east of Abergavenny, the Gwent Rural Life Museum exhibits some 500 'bygones' of country life. These include the tools of such craftsmen as blacksmith and cooper, animal traps, farm machinery and domestic items.

LLANUWCHLLYN, Gwynedd
13 SH83

Llanuwchllyn lies at the end of Bala Lake, with the Arennig Mountains to the north. The town is the terminus of the Bala Lake Railway (OACT) – a narrow-gauge railway that runs four-and-a-half miles beside the lake, using ex-Dinorwic Quarry steam engines and diesel locomotives.

DAVID LLOYD GEORGE

The great Welsh Prime Minister, was brought up and buried in Llanystumdwy. His portrait by Orpen is in the National Portrait Gallery.

LLANVIHANGEL CRUCORNEY, Gwent *8 SO32*

Set beside the River Monnow, this village has old stone houses and an ancient inn. The church porch contains a carved stone commemorating an 18th-century blacksmith. Llanvihangel Court (OACT) is a Tudor house standing in attractive gardens; it has a fine yew staircase and a number of interesting portraits and furnishings.

LLANYSTUMDWY, Gwynedd
13 SH43

Llanystumdwy is the burial place of David Lloyd-George, one of Britain's most remarkable statesmen and a social reformer who took the first steps towards the Welfare State. He spent the early years of his life here, brought up at a year old to live with his uncle, the village cobbler, after his father died. The cottage where he was brought up (OACT) stands, marked by a plaque, on the Criccieth to Pwllheli road. In later life he returned to live at Ty Newydd, a Jacobean mansion near the village, and it was at his own wish that he was buried on a wooded bank above the River Dwyfor, his monument a boulder carved only with the initials DLG and the dates of his life.

LOCH ASSYNT, Highland *29 NC22*

Botanists are lured to the wild and mountainous countryside around Loch Assynt by the rare plants and ferns that grow on its lonely shores. Ben More Assynt rises to 3273ft near the eastern end of the loch, and on the north shore stand the shell of 16th-century Ardvreck Castle and the remains of Calda House, the ancient home of the Mackenzies.

LOCH AWE, Strathclyde *21 NN01*

Loch Awe is long and narrow, 22 miles long and only about a mile wide in most places. A ruined castle stands at each end – Fincharn in the south and Kilchurn to the north – and there is another on the island of Fraoch Eilean, whilst the Isle of Inishail has an ancient chapel and burial ground. To the north towers 3689ft Ben Cruachan, where the world's second-largest hydro-electric power station pumps water from the loch to a reservoir 1315ft up the mountain.

LOCH CARRON, Highland *25 NG83*

Island-strewn Loch Carron is no more than half a mile wide at its narrowest point, Stromeferry. Nearby stand the ruins of Strome Castle (NTS), a MacDonald stronghold devastated by the Mackenzies in 1602, with fine views across the Inner Sound to Skye. The loch was much fished for herring until the beginning of this century, and the village of Lochcarron, near its head, has an area round the harbour known as 'Slumbay' (meaning 'safe bay') which used to shelter hundreds of boats.

LOCH ETIVE, Strathclyde *26 NN03*

This is a sea loch, its waters meeting with those of the Firth of Lorn at the Connel Narrows. At the loch head lies remote Glen Etive, amid towering peaks of well over 3000ft.

LOCH FYNE, Strathclyde *21 NR99*

Loch Fyne, one of the longest sea lochs in Scotland, stretches 40 miles from the Sound of Bute. It is famed for the spectacular scenery at its mountainous head, and – more mundanely – for its herring catch, a large proportion of which is smoked to make kippers.

LOCH LEVEN, Tayside *24 NO10*

Well-known for its catches of salmon trout, Loch Leven is the site of international trout angling competitions each year; in winter it is also a centre for the sport of curling. The ruins of 15th-century Loch Leven Castle, (AM) from which Mary Queen of Scots escaped in 1568, stand on an island which can be visited by boat during the summer months. On the west shore of the loch 17th-century Kinross House (built by the architect of the Palace of Holyroodhouse in Edinburgh) is set in beautiful grounds (gardens OACT) between the town of Kinross and the waterside.

LOCH LOCHY, Highland *26 NN29*

Loch Lochy is the second largest of the chain of inland lakes that runs along the Great Glen, forming part of the Caledonian Canal. The hilly shores, wooded in many places, reach their greatest height in Glengarry Forest to the north-east. The Laggan Locks, at the north end, allow vessels using the Canal to be raised from the level of Loch Lochy to that of its highest section, Loch Oich.

LOCH LOMOND, Strathclyde & Central *22 NS39*

Loch Lomond, the 'Queen of Scottish Lakes' and the largest in Great Britain, runs from Ardlui in the north to Balloch in the south – a distance of some 23 miles – and varies in width between five miles and three-quarters of a mile. There are 30 islands in its length, the most significant being Inchmurrin (with the ruins of Lennox Castle) and Inchcaillach (where the remains of a former nunnery lie near the burial ground of the McGregor clan). There is good fishing for trout, pike and powan (a white freshwater herring found in Scottish lochs and Welsh lakes). A National Nature Reserve covers the south-west corner of the loch and five of its islands. A prisoner of Prince Charles Edward is said to have composed the song 'Loch Lomond' on the eve of his execution – the 'low road' being the path that his spirit would take back to its native land when released by death.

RURAL SETTLEMENTS

VILLAGES

Traditional Communities

CONTRARY TO POPULAR OPINION, the village is not one of the oldest features of the rural landscape. Prehistoric people generally tended to live in dispersed farmsteads or in small, hamlet-sized hut groups. Some villages certainly seem to have existed in the New Stone, Bronze and Iron Ages, but they were exceptions to the rule. At Skara Brae on Orkney, the visitor can see well-preserved remains of a small village of squarish stone-walled huts which are connected by little alleyways and which date from the later part of the New Stone Age. At various places on Dartmoor one can see the doughnut-shaped arrangements of stones which were once the walls of round huts with conical thatched roofs. These settlements belonged to the Bronze Age and Grimspound, Kestor and Merrivale are amongst the best examples. Similar hut settlements were built in the Iron Age and the Pimperne House at Butser Hill near Petersfield in Hampshire is a remarkable reconstruction of a large Iron-Age dwelling. Several village-sized settlements were occupied during the Roman period and Din Lligwy on Anglesey displays the remains of several round and rectangular buildings which lie inside a protective stone wall or rampart. The Saxon settlers of the 5th and 6th centuries AD, like all previous tenants of the British landscape, were more typically adjusted to life in dispersed settlements, but also built some villages, and a remarkable reconstruction of one can be seen at West Stow in Suffolk.

THE FIRST VILLAGES seem to have appeared in the latter part of the Saxon era, the 8th, 9th and 10th centuries AD. In this period, a village-building revolution seems to have spread across the country, although the contemporary documents have little or nothing to tell us about it. However, the villages seem to have been mushrooming at about the same time that 'open field' farming was being established, and so they seem to have been an essential component in the reorganisation of agriculture on new and more productive lines. Throughout the medieval period and for several centuries afterwards, the village was in essence the home of a community of peasant farmers who worked in the surrounding fields: a sort of agricultural dormitory for the feudal tenants of the local landowners. It is widely thought that many villages preserve their medieval appearances, but the

CHYSAUSTER (left) in Cornwall. The drystone walls of the courtyard houses are Romano-British. At Lower Slaughter (inset) limestone cottages have gradually encroached on the village green.

When most townspeople think of the English countryside, the village features as prominently as the fields and hedgerows in their perceptions. In the past, the village was closely bonded to its surrounding fields and the village and its lands were inseparable. Today, links are far weaker than ever before, but the village has secured such an important niche in our perception of the countryside that it is hard to imagine that it will not survive and discover new roles to play.

MIDDLETON *in Yorkshire. Note how some of the house-backing plots or 'tofts' and some field strips have survived.*

vast majority of buildings in any medieval village were squalid, insubstantial peasant dwellings which were unlikely to survive for even a century. Again, in contrast to popular belief, the village was not stable and rooted to a particular place and form. Most villages underwent several centuries of growth, reorganisation and experimentation before they began to stabilise according to a particular form. Village plans began to appear in the closing years of the Middle Ages – but most frustratingly, by this period, villages tended to have settled on the lay-outs which they still preserve, and so their formative developments remain puzzling, and the origins of the close patterns of tightly clustered, or 'nucleated' dwellings which make up village England are still partly mysterious.

THE GREEN was an area of common or public land usually in the heart of the village. It seems that greens have a variety of origins and they were not always an original village feature. Some were created as medieval market places which were inserted into older villages which had been fortunate enough to gain market charters. Others seem to result from peasant settlement around useful areas of common pasture, and others still were elements in the design of planned villages. The village is often regarded as a completely spontaneous sort of settlement, but in fact a great many villages were developments completely or partly planned during the Middle Ages.

EVIDENCE OF PLANNED VILLAGES is often preserved in the forms of rectangular or triangular market places and 'grid-iron' lay-outs in which the streets intersect each other at right angles. This type of planning is very common in villages like Castleton in Derbyshire and Castle Rising in Norfolk which were closely linked to medieval castles, but it is also frequently seen in other villages like Appleton-le-Moors in Yorkshire. The planned villages have the simplest lay-outs, but most other villages are very complicated. Some consist of both planned and unplanned components, many have drifted from their original sites or are shrunken, with bumps and hollows in the surrounding fields marking the places of lost streets and dwellings. Many other villages have resulted from the merging of two or more formerly separate components. Anyone seeking to reconstruct the history of a village should study all the old maps which depict the village lay-out at different periods in time, search the surrounding lands for the traces of earthworks which may mark a former street or boundary and look very closely at the surviving road pattern, for every little kink or abandoned lane will have a story to reveal.

THE SIZE OF A VILLAGE may reflect former glories, as at places like Long Melford in Suffolk or Finchingfield in Essex, which were important centres in the medieval textile industry. Villages also vary widely from one part of the country to another:

many East Anglian villages are so large that they would be regarded as small towns in parts of Wessex. In areas that were lacking in good farmland, the villages tend to be small and fewer in number. In the uplands and damper or more thinly-soiled places, livestock farming was more important than crop-growing and the farmsteads were scattered across the countryside or grouped together in little hamlets. Only the larger of these hamlets could support churches and so as one moves from the lowland plains and vales into the hills and plateaux, so the settlement landscape of plump villages with churches, pubs and shops changes to one of scattered farmsteads and small roadside clusters. In Scotland, Ireland and Wales, villages tend to be confined to the more favourable farming localities, while many Scottish and Irish villages result from the deliberate village plantation policies of landowners.

FISHING AND INDUSTRIAL VILLAGES have existed at all times since the early medieval period and the early decades of the Industrial Revolution tended to spawn compact new industrial villages rather than sprawling conurbations. Often, these villages were tied to a particular industry like coal-mining or were built by the owners of a particular factory. There are many examples, some squalid and deprived, others embodying amenities which the people of nearby agricultural villages must have envied. Perhaps the most attractive example is Saltaire near Bingley, the creation of the cotton magnate, Titus Salt.

FOLLOWING THE ENCLOSURE of many open fields and commons in the 18th and early 19th centuries, and the mechanisation of farming which decimated agricultural employment, the prospects for the village seemed bleak, but commuting and the introduction of small-scale industries have revived many shrinking settlements. Currently, the axing of rural bus services, the closing of village schools and the competition which village shops face from their big city rivals produce severe problems for many rural communities and for those who would like to see the village surviving as much more than just a dormitory settlement for commuters. A select handful of villages, like Lower Slaughter in Gloucestershire, Broadway in Worcestershire, Castle Acre in Norfolk and Thaxted in Essex now flourish as 'showpiece' villages and attract scores of visitors. However, every village has its own particular story, and some of the villages which today seem most nondescript have the most interesting histories.

LOCH NESS MONSTER

Ruined Urquhart Castle (above) looks out over the dark waters of the loch, where the great mystery of the monster is still unsolved despite hours of systematic observation, submarine searches, sonar probes, and all the aids of advanced technology. St Columba was reputedly the first to see a water beast – but in the River Ness, not the loch.

LOCHMABEN, Dumfries & Galloway
18 NY08

The small Annandale town of Lochmaben has Castle Loch to the south-east, Kirk and Mill Lochs to the north-west and Brumel Loch to the east. The vendace, a rare fish with a heart-shaped mark on its head, is found in Castle and Mill Lochs. Castle Loch is also a nature reserve, and at its south end stand the ruins of Lochmaben Castle. Rammerscales (OACT) is a house with many Jacobite relics; it has associations with Flora Macdonald.

LOCH MAREE, Highland *29 NG97*

Loch Maree is probably Scotland's most beautiful inland loch, its south-east shore dominated by the huge mass of Slioch and the south-west lying within the Ben Eighe National Nature Reserve. Tiny Isle Maree still bears oaks – the sacred trees of the Druids who once worshipped here; there are traces of a very early chapel, superseded by the 7th-century hermitage of St Maelrubha. All the islets on the loch are controlled by the Nature Conservancy authorities, from whom permission must be obtained before landing, for the area affords a valuable refuge for threatened wildlife.

LOCH NESS, Highland *26 NH52*

Loch Ness is the largest of the Great Glen lochs (see Loch Lochy). Its waters, dark with peaty soil washed down by the rivers and streams that feed it, are over 900ft deep in places and have never been known to freeze. The view to the west is particularly beautiful, with the ruins of Urquhart Castle (AM) guarding the entrance to Glen Urquart. The loch's legendary monster is world-famous, and tales of sightings go back to the 7th century. Many modern sightings seem well authenticated, and it is now being suggested that unknown fish, giant slug-like creatures, or even fish-eating dinosaurs could exist in the depths.

LOCH SHIEL, Highland *25 NM87*

Loch Shiel is one of the finest freshwater lochs in the Highlands, with wonderful mountain scenery at its north end and 2895ft Bheinn Odhar Bheag rising from its west shore. No more than a mile wide at any point, it stretches from Acharacle to Glenfinnan Monument (NTS), the tribute raised to the Highlanders who died for Bonnie Prince Charlie in the '45 Rising. The loch is touched by public roads only at its head and its foot; none run along its shores.

LOCKERBIE, Dumfries & Galloway
18 NY18

The market town of Lockerbie is famous for its August·Lamb Fair, which has taken place ever since the 17th century. In 1593 one of the last of the Border family feuds ended here, when Lord Maxwell and 700 of his men were slaughtered by the Johnstones. The victors chopped off the ears of many of their victims – a method of mutilation subsequently known as the 'Lockerbie Nick'.

LODE, Cambridgeshire *11 TL56*

Anglesey Abbey (NT) stands in 100-acre grounds, laid out this century with long avenues of trees, statuary and flower displays. Although almost completely remodelled in the 16th century, the house incorporates the 13th-century monastic undercroft, that once formed part of the Augustinian Abbey originally founded on this site in the 12th century.

LONG CRENDON, Buckinghamshire
39 SP60

Long Crendon is an attractive village with straggling thatched cottages, set where a four-arched bridge spans the River Thames. Needle-making was introduced here in the 16th century and continued until the work was taken over by factories in the 1830s. Long Crendon Manor, part stone and part timber-framed, dates from the thirteenth century and has a courtyard guarded by a stone gatehouse. The Court House (NT) is a late 14th-century building which was probably first used as a wool staple hall or store, but manorial courts were held here in the 15th century by the stewards of Catherine, wife of Henry V, who owned the manor at that time. The tall-towered greystone church was begun in the 13th century and is an indication of the village's prosperity at that time.

LONGLEAT, Wiltshire *3 ST84*

The building of Longleat House (OACT), one of the most-visited stately homes in the country, was undertaken in 1568 for Sir John Thynne, an ancestor of the Marquess of Bath who owns it today. As a result of 19th-century renovations, the house has exquisite Venetian ceilings and Italian decor, and it contains fine paintings, tapestries and leatherwork. The family's state robes are on show, together with their state coach and a waistcoat said to have been worn by King Charles I at his execution. There are fully-equipped Victorian kitchens, with a shop selling culinary goods and gifts in the former scullery. The real attraction of Longleat, however, is the Safari Park, famous for its lions but also including elephants, tigers, buffaloes and antelope. It is open in summer and visitors can also take a Safari Boat, cruising through groups of sea-lions and hippos and passing the ape islands. Additional attractions for children are Leisureland (an exciting adventure playground), donkey and camel rides, and Pets' Corner with its chimps' tea-party.

THE LIONS OF LONGLEAT

The lions in the 'Safari Park' have all but eclipsed the splendours of Longleat House and the trend has been taken up by other Stately Homes. Lions are the most famous residents of the park, but there are also tigers, rhinos, hippos and elephants, among other exotic fauna.

LONG MELFORD *The 15th-century Church of the Holy Trinity at Long Melford is considered to be the finest of all Suffolk's wool churches.*

LONG MELFORD, Suffolk *12 TL84*
Long Melford, with its attractive main
street, almost two miles long, of fine old
shops and houses, is one of the most
impressive villages in Suffolk. At the upper
end of its triangular green stands Melford
Hall (NT), a turreted, red-brick Tudor
house containing collections of fine
paintings, furniture and porcelain. It was
built in the 16th century by Sir William
Cordell, Speaker of the House of Commons
and Master of the Rolls during the reign of
Queen Elizabeth I. He died in 1580 and is
commemorated by a fine monument in the
church. Kentwell Hall (OACT) lies to the
north of the village, surrounded by a moat
and beautiful gardens and approached by a
300-year-old avenue of lime trees. Holy
Trinity Church is a huge 15th-century
building occupying the site of a Roman
temple; its exterior is decorated with
flushwork and the interior has notable
stained glass and beautiful worked pillars.
The Bull Inn also dates from the 15th
century.

LOOE, Cornwall *1 SX25*
Although a 15th-century bridge had
spanned the river here, East and West Looe
were separate entities until the building of
the Victorian bridge in 1883. After this date
the two towns merged, still much involved
in fishing but also developing as a holiday
resort. Today Looe is England's foremost
shark-fishing centre and the venue each
autumn of the British Sea Angling Festival,
but it is also an ideal place for a family
holiday, offering fine surfing conditions and
excellent bathing from large sandy beaches.
West Looe is centred round its picturesque
quay and the Church of St Nicholas – built
mainly from the timbers of wrecked ships,
and containing in its tower a Scold's Cage
for the incarceration of nagging wives. In
East Looe stands the 16th-century
Guildhall, its upper floor now housing a
museum; the building was once used as a
gaol, and the old stocks and pillory can be
seen downstairs. Looe Aquarium displays
examples of fish caught locally and includes
a shark museum, whilst at Murrayton there
is a woolly monkey sanctuary.

LOSSIEMOUTH, Grampian *27 NJ27*
This popular resort, at the mouth of the
River Lossie on Spey Bay, is a major RAF
base. It also has an active fishing industry,
and Branderburgh harbour, at the west end
of the town, serves as a port for Elgin.
Nearby caves display unusual rock
formations. Ramsay MacDonald, Britain's
first Labour Prime Minister, was born in
Lossiemouth in 1866.

LOSTWITHIEL, Cornwall *1 SX15*
A medieval bridge (AM) crosses the River
Fowey at Lostwithiel, now a popular
touring centre but once the capital of
Cornwall and a centre for the tin trade.
Fourteenth-century Duchy House in Quay
Street includes the remains of an old
Stannary Court where the regulations of the
local tin mines were administered. The
remains of Restormel Castle (OACT),
dating back to the 12th or 13th centuries
overlook the valley about a mile away; from
here the Duke of Cornwall once ruled the
area.

LOTHERTON HALL, N Yorkshire
15 SE43
Eighteenth-century Lotherton Hall
(OACT) is now a country house museum,
containing fine furniture, silver and
ceramics from the Gascoigne Collection
(the Gascoignes being the former occupants
of the house); English works of art are also
on display and there are fashion galleries
and exhibitions of contemporary crafts.
The small chapel nearby has a noteworthy
beamed roof and an elaborately carved
pulpit. The grounds include Edwardian
and Bird Gardens.

LOUGHBOROUGH, Leicestershire
10 SK51
Today Loughborough is involved in
hosiery manufacture and engineering
industries, but it is internationally famous
for its bell foundry, brought here from
Oxford by John Taylor in 1858 and
responsible for casting Great Paul for St
Paul's Cathedral. All Saints Church (dating
from the 14th century, but restored by Sir
Gilbert Scott in the 19th) has memorials to

the Taylor family – and, appropriately, a
peal of ten bells. A Victory Peal of 5,041
changes was rung here in 1919, and the
War Memorial built in Queen's Park in
1923 took the form of a tower containing a
carillon of 47 bells. The University of
Technology is recognised as a major
teaching and research centre; covering 140
acres, it incorporates a specially designed
student village. The Main Line Steam
Trust, based on Central Station, runs the
Great Central Railway, and steam
locomotives journey from here to Rothley.
Loughborough Central contains a museum
and locomotive depot.

LOUTH, Lincolnshire *16 TF38*
The architecture of Louth is predominately
Georgian, but the fine Church of St James,
soaring to almost 300ft and providing a
landmark for miles across the flat fen
countryside, is 15th-century. Louth Park
contains the remains of a Cistercian abbey
which was founded to the east of the town
in 1139 and destroyed at the Dissolution.
Tennyson attended the Grammar School
and his work was first published in Louth.
The Greenwich meridian passes through
the town and is marked by a plaque.

LOWESTOFT, Suffolk *12 TM59*
The great fishing fleets are now a thing of
the past, but Lowestoft is still a busy port,
with trawlers docking and unloading. The
lifeboat is famous, and the station was
founded in 1801, twenty years before the
RNLI came into being. The Maritime
Museum contains model ships and fishing
gear. The 'Scores' are a reminder of the old
town: these narrow alleyways descend
steeply from the level of the High Street
until they reach the shore where the fish
houses for curing herrings used to stand.
South town is developing a 'seaside'
atmosphere and offers attractions for
children – notably a boating lake and a
miniature steam railway. Nearby Oulton
Broad is popular for water-sports and is
used for yacht, dinghy and motor boat
racing. The East Anglia Transport
Museum, with all types of old cars and
commercial vehicles is an added attraction.

LOWTHER, Cumbria *18 NY52*
A Wildlife Adventure Park is set in the 130 acres of parkland that surround the ruins of 19th-century Lowther Castle (not open). It specialises in European species of animals and birds and keeps rare breeds of cattle and sheep. The castle was once the home of the Earls of Lonsdale, and their mausoleum stands outside the nearby Church.

LULWORTH, Dorset *3 SY87*
Lulworth Cove, deep in Hardy country, is an exquisite small bay backed by magnificent chalk cliffs, its waters almost totally enclosed by two arms of Portland and Purbeck stone. Stair Hole, with its strangely twisted rock strata, is of considerable geological interest. **Durdle Door**, the natural rock arch that juts out into the sea just west of the cove, is a spectacular sight on stormy days, when huge waves crash through it. Lulworth Castle, gutted by fire in 1929, stands in 600 acres of woodland. The adjoining Rotunda (built in 1786) is the first Roman Catholic church for which Royal permission was given after the Reformation, George III agreeing to it on condition that it did not *look* like a church.

LULWORTH COVE *The cliffs of East Dorset (right) are formed of hard limestone. Where the sea has managed to breach this barrier, the softer rocks behind have been easily eroded to form deep, sheltered bays, as here at Lulworth, which is still almost completely encircled by promontories.*

STAIR HOLE *(above) A natural phenomenon, the acute folding and steep dip of the Portland and Purbeck limestone beds in this chasm near Lulworth Cove are of outstanding interest to geologists as an example of early erosion.*

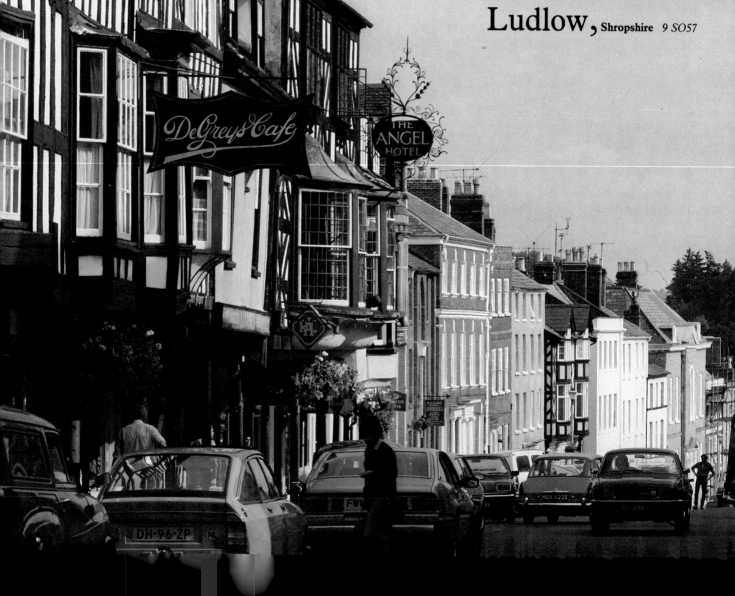

Ludlow, Shropshire *9 SO57*

LUNDY, Devon   1 SS14

This tiny granite island stands in the Bristol Channel, about 12 miles off Hartland Point and easily accessible by steamer from Ilfracombe; since 1969 it has been owned by the National Trust, which leases it to the Landmark Trust. The scanty ruins of Marisco Castle, the stronghold of a piratical family who once ruled the island, lie near the quay. The Shutter Rock will be familiar to readers of Kingsley's *Westward Ho!* Puffins and other seabirds breed on the rocky coastline, which also offers some of the finest sea cliff climbing in England. The word 'Lundy' is derived from the old Norse word for puffin (see also Bideford).

LUTON, Bedfordshire   11 TL02

Light engineering and operation of an international airport have superseded the manufacture of pillow-lace and straw hats as Luton's industries, though these crafts of a bygone era are illustrated in the museum in Wardown Park. Luton Hoo (OACT) is a palatial mansion, originally designed by Robert Adam and set in a 1500-acre park. It houses the magnificent Wernher collection of pictures, tapestries, porcelain and Russian Fabergé jewels.

Watchtower of the Marches

*❛Oh, come you home of Sunday
When Ludlow streets are still
And Ludlow bells are calling
To farm and lane and mill❜*

A E HOUSMAN, *A Shropshire Lad*

In Ludlow, wide Georgian streets contrast with narrow medieval alleys, and elegant 18th-century brick and stucco rubs shoulders with half-timbered Tudor buildings with leaning walls and steep-pitched roofs. In the 12th century Ludlow was a 'planned town', its streets designed on the usual grid-iron, pattern that can still be traced today. The most famous of all the

GROTESQUE FACES *(above) and carvings ornament the timbered facade of the Feathers Hotel.*

BROAD STREET *(left), has some of Ludlow's handsomest 17th- and 18th-century buildings.*

timbered buildings, the Feathers Hotel, its exterior ornamented with heads and other carvings, has stood in the Bull Ring, where bulls used to be penned before market, since 1603. Even older is the Bull Inn, and another attractive old tavern is the Angel, its overhanging upper storeys supported on slender columns. More ancient than the inns and overlooking the church of St Laurence is the Reader's House, a medieval stone building with an attractive three-storey timbered porch, dating from the Tudor period. It is not usually open.

Ludlow, built on a steep hill washed on two sides by the rivers Corve and Teme, has, since earliest times been recognised as a strategic site, and the Normans were quick to take advantage of this. The castle, now an impressive ruin, crowns the hilltop, looking out over the Welsh Marches, as it has done since it was built in 1085 by Roger de Lacy, the henchman of the Earl of Shrewsbury, Roger Montgomery. Apart from a period of just under 100 years, from 1461 to 1552, when it was a royal castle, Ludlow retained its connection with the earls, and it was for the children of the Countess of Bridgewater that Milton wrote his masque, *Comus*, which the children first performed at the castle in 1634. One of Shakespeare's plays is always performed here during the annual Ludlow Festival. If the castle forms one focus of attention in Ludlow, the other is provided by St Laurence's Church, cathedral-like in the nobility of its design, and dating from the 15th century. It soaring crossing tower stands, at 135ft, higher even than the castle.

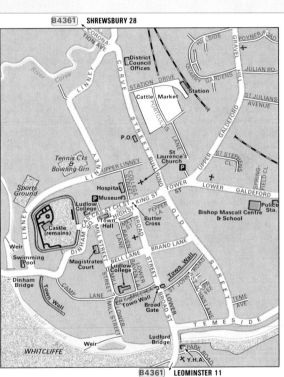

PLACES TO SEE

Ludlow Castle (OACT) Although now ruined, the castle is still impressive. As a royal residence, however, its history is sad, for it was from here that Edward IV's elder son, one of the 'princes in the Tower', set out on his last, ill-omened journey, to meet his death either at the hands of Richard III or of Henry VII, according to your point of view. Henry's own eldest son, Prince Arthur, brought his young bride, Catherine of Aragon, to live at Ludlow for a short period, before his untimely death. Their apart-

ments and the terraced gardens he had made for her, can still be seen. There is also a rare example of a Norman round chapel.

Ludlow Museum The classical stone Butter Cross, built in 1746, houses the town's museum on its first floor, which was once a school.

St Laurence's Church The interior is lit by a magnificent east window, depicting the life and miracles of the saint, and there is a famous set of misericords in the choir. In the churchyard, the ashes of the poet A E Housman were buried in 1936.

LYDFORD CHURCH *The old wheelwright's stone lies outside the church where miners were buried.*

LYME REGIS *The Cobb, as the old harbour is known, dates from the 14th century. Dramatic episodes from Jane Austen's 'Persuasion' and 'The French Lieutenant's Woman' take place here.*

LUTTERWORTH, Leicestershire
10 SP58

John Wycliffe, the reformer who attacked the wrongful use of papal power in politics, was rector at the parish church of Lutterworth in the 14th century and is commemorated by an obelisk. The church itself was much restored in the 19th century, a massive tower replacing the original spire, but it still contains some 15th-century wall paintings. A three-arched bridge crosses the River Swift here, and the town has some well-preserved half-timbered houses.

LUXULYAN, Cornwall   *1 SX05*

Luxulyan is a small, pretty village on the side of an exceptionally beautiful Cornish valley which runs deep between wooded hillsides. The church, a plain building of large granite blocks, is basically 15th-century. Granite was also used for the viaduct which spans the road outside the village; it still carries a water supply for the china clay industry, though the railway that once transported stone from local quarries no longer exists.

LYBSTER, Highland   *30 ND23*

The village of Lybster stands on Lybster Bay, on the wild and rugged coastline south-west of Clyth Ness, and has a small fishing industry. The church has a west door and chancel entrance of ancient local design and is built of locally dressed flagstones. The Grey Cairns of Camster (AM), two megolithic chambered cairns almost 5000 years old, lie about five miles north of the village.

LYDD, Kent   *6 TR02*

This busy little town, once on the coast but now standing three miles inland, is said to have the lowest rainfall in England, it also has the distinction of having given its name to the explosive lyddite, tested near here in the late 19th century. The fine 130ft tower of 'the Cathedral of Romney Marsh' still stands, despite bomb damage during the last war, and inside the church are 16th-

century brasses and a 15th-century screen. A Nuclear Power Station (OACT) lies four miles to the south-east.

LYDFORD, Devon   *2 SX58*

In the days of tin-mining Lydford was an important centre, and one of Devon's four 'stannary' towns, with the right of assaying metal and minting coins. Although now no more than a moorland village, it remains one of England's largest civil parishes, covering the greater part of Dartmoor. Today's village is dominated by the remains of the 12th-century castle (AM); at one time the upper floor served as a Stannary Court, administering the mining laws, and the lower floor was used as a prison. Lydford Gorge (NT) is a deep, wooded ravine about

a mile long from which the River Lyd emerges to be joined by a stream at the 90ft-high White Lady waterfall.

LYDIARD, Wiltshire   *3 SU18*

Lydiard Park (OACT) is a pleasant, mainly Georgian manor house, for generations the home of the St John family but now the property of Thamesdown Borough. It has fine rococo ceilings and there is a small agricultural museum in the stable block. In the park stands St Mary's, the parish church of Lydiard Tregoze, dating back to the 14th century and rich in memorials to the St Johns. Particularly striking are the Golden Cavalier, a gilded life-size figure of Edward St John, killed in the Civil War, and the vast canopied tomb of St John, his

FOSSIL-RICH CLIFFS

The cliffs all along Lyme Bay are rich in fossil remains, and ammonities such as the one pictured here, *Parkinsonia Parkinsonii* are especially easy to find. The local people used to add to the family income by selling the fossils they found as curios to visitors, and the most spectacular find along the whole coast was made in the early 19th century by a 12-year-old girl, Mary Anning. She found the fossil of an ichthyosaurus, a prehistoric marine reptile, in the cliffs at Black Ven near Lyme Regis. Thereafter fossil-hunting became something of a local obsession.

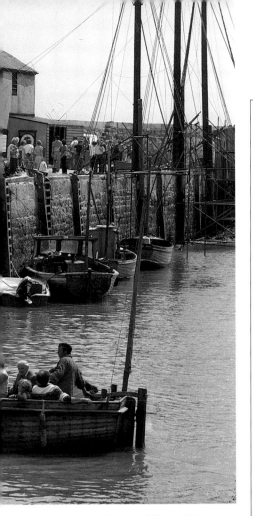

two wives and thirteen children. The church also has ancient stained glass and a tryptych in a cabinet.

LYME PARK, Cheshire, *see* Disley

LYME REGIS, Dorset *3 SY39*
In the 18th century Lyme Regis was one of the first towns on the south-west coast to gain popularity as a seaside resort. Jane Austen loved the town and used the Cobb, as the old harbour, west of the town centre, is known, as the setting for part of her novel *Persuasion*, in which one of her characters has a severe fall from a precipitous flight of steps in the old harbour, popularly known as 'grandmother's teeth'. The area is rich in fossils, many of which can be seen in the town museum, and 12-year-old Mary Anning became famous when she found the skeleton of an ichthyosaurus in the Blue Lias rock (see Charmouth). The town is substantially unchanged today, with Georgian houses lining the steep main street that runs down to the harbour and the shingle beach. The cliff area is unspoiled, much of it having been designated a nature reserve, and is dramatically beautiful – Golden Cap, at 617ft, being the highest cliff on the south coast of England.

LYMINGTON, Hampshire *4 SZ39*
The ancient town of Lymington has become a sailing centre and busy resort, its tidal harbour usually packed with yachts and Pier Station the departure point for car ferries to the Isle of Wight. The church and many of the houses reflect the prosperity of the area in the 18th century. Part of Pressgang Cottage, a former inn, was the headquarters of an 18th-century pressgang, and the old Harbour Master's office was once a bath house. Historian Edward Gibbon represented the town as a Member of Parliament.

On the Edge of Exmoor
31 miles

The Doone country, immortalised in R D Blackmore's novel Lorna Doone, *is a region of deep, wooded ravines and moorland ablaze with gorse, caught between the edge of Exmoor and the coasts of North Devon and Somerset.*

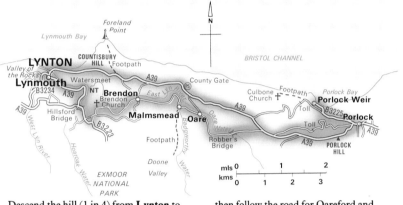

Descend the hill (1 in 4) from **Lynton** to **Lynmouth** and from there follow A39 Barnstaple road along the East Lyn Valley to **Watersmeet**. Continue alongside Hoaroak Water for ½ mile then turn left on to B3223 (SP Simonsbath). Cross Hillsford Bridge and in ¾ mile go round a hairpin bend and keep forward on to an unclassified road (SP Brendon Valley).

In another ½ mile turn right, then descend to **Rockford** and **Brendon**, then continue alongside the East Lyn River to **Malmsmead**. (From here there is a diversion, on foot or by pony, through the valley of Badgeworthy Water into the heart of the so-called 'Doone Country'). Cross the river bridge here and continue to **Oare** then follow the road for Oareford and Robber's Bridge for 1½ miles. Cross the bridge and continue climbing then turn right to join A39. Go down Porlock Hill into **Porlock**, and from here there is an excursion to Porlock Wier on B3225. From **Porlock Weir**, either return to Porlock, or take the toll road (Lynton via Worthy Combe) and join the main route (A39) at Culbone Stables Inn. The main route leaves Porlock on the Lynmouth Road, then branches right on to an unclassified road (SP 'Alternative Route via Toll Road') turn right after 4 miles on to A39 and continue to Countisbury Hill which leads steeply downhill back into Lynmouth, and uphill to Lynton.

PLACES TO SEE

Lynton Perched on the hillside 500ft above **Lynmouth**, the two resorts are linked by cliff railway. A footpath leads to the spectacular Valley of the Rocks.

Lynmouth The old lower town is picturesque and bright with gardens. Strong walls have been built as a protection against flooding after the 1952 disaster.

Watersmeet (NT) A noted beauty spot, with tumbling cascades, in the East Lyn Valley.

Malmsmead Foot and bridle-paths lead alongside Badgeworthy Water, into the legendary Doone Valley, Hoccombe Combe.

Oare In the novel, Lorna Doone was married in the old church of this hamlet.

Porlock This enchanting village lies at the foot of the notoriously steep Porlock Hill. Porlock Weir, nearby, is also a gem of a village. A short walk leads to Norman Culbone Church, the smallest church in use in England.

Countisbury Hill At the summit are an old inn and ancient earthworks (NT) of a prehistoric fort. Beyond the church there are superb cliff walks.

WATERSMEET

Brendon Water and Hoaroak Water meet, in this aptly named beauty spot in one of Exmoor's prettiest valleys, to form the East Lyn River. The area now belongs to the National Trust.

LYNTON AND LYNMOUTH *From Countisbury Head there are magnificent views of the coastline. Lynton clings to the top of the hill and Lynmouth is almost hidden in the bay beneath.*

LYMPNE, Kent *6 TR13*

Lympne was a coastal village until the sea receded, and the Romans built a fort here as part of their defences. Its ruins, known as Studfall Castle, stand about 300 yds from Lympne Castle (OACT), a fortified manor house which still retains its Norman appearance despite extensive restoration. The grounds offer wide views over Romney Marsh and across the channel to France. Port Lympne Zoo Park and Gardens lie just west of the village; the animals on view include Indian elephants, Siberian and Indian tigers, leopards, monkeys, wolves, rhino and bison. At the centre of the fifteen acres of spectacular garden stands the mansion (OACT) in whose library the Treaty of Paris was signed after World War I. Among several interesting rooms is the Rex Whistler 'tent' room.

LYNDHURST, Hampshire *4 SU20*

A typical New Forest village, set in attractive woodland scenery and roamed by untamed ponies, Lyndhurst is popular with tourists. The huge old Knightswood oak, with a girth of more than 21 feet is thought to be about 600 years old. The church is nineteenth-century, with work by Leighton, Burne-Jones and Millais; a Mrs Hargreaves buried in the churchyard was formerly Alice Liddell, the original of Lewis Carroll's heroine. Six times a year the ancient Verderers' Court still sits in 17th-century Queen's House to administer the forest laws.

LYNMOUTH, Devon *2 SS74*

Lynmouth is an attractive little resort at the mouth of the East and West Lyn Rivers; it has a small shingle beach, and charming thatched cottages line the narrow street by the harbour. Countisbury Hill, rising over 1000ft to the east, includes some of the steepest cliffs in England (NT) and nearby the East Lyn converges with Hoar Oak Waters in wooded Watersmeet Valley (NT). The lighthouse at Foreland Point (NT) is also surrounded by exceptionally beautiful scenery. Lynmouth will always be remembered, however, for the floods caused by a freak storm over Exmoor in 1952, when 28 bridges were swept away, 100 houses damaged or destroyed and 31 lives lost.

LYNTON, Devon *2 SS74*

Lynton is set high on the cliffs above Lynmouth (see separate entry), to which it is connected by a 19th-century cliff railway. To the west lies the spectacular Valley of the Rocks, leading to a wooded stretch of coast with fine cliff scenery. Lee Abbey, an imposing mock-Gothic Victorian mansion, is now used as a Church of England centre for study courses and holidays. Old St Vincent's Cottage has been turned into the Lyn and Exmoor Museum.

LYTHAM ST ANNE'S, Lancashire *14 SD32*

This popular northern resort at the mouth of the Ribble estuary is quite different in character from its neighbour, Blackpool. Floral displays abound, particularly on the promenade, and there are beautifully set-out public gardens. The town's extensive golden sands are the site of the British Sand Yacht Racing Championships each May. The area also boasts four championship golf courses, including the Royal Lytham and St Anne's, home of several major tournaments. Overlooking the estuary is the Motive Power Museum and Lytham Creek Railway, its exhibits ranging from industrial steam locomotives to modern aero-engines. A 19th-century windmill near the shore forms a well-known local landmark.

VALLEY OF THE ROCKS *One-and-a-half miles west of Lynton, this wilderness of rocky pinnacles, grazed by half-wild goats looks down a sheer drop of 800ft.*

THE NATION'S CAPITAL

LONDON

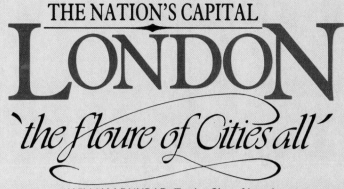

'the floure of Cities all'

WILLIAM DUNBAR, *To the City of London*

THE VISSCHER MAP OF LONDON

(detail) Drawn in 1650, the panorama shows London as it was in the Commonwealth era, before the great fire of 1666. In the foreground is the old, medieval London Bridge, at this period almost completely covered with tall houses and shops. On the fortified gateway at the Southwark end the severed heads of criminals are displayed. The buildings were torn down in the mid 18th century because of the danger of fire, but the bridge itself lasted until 1832, when it was replaced by Rennie's bridge. This 19th-century 'London Bridge' was sold to Lake Havasu City in the USA in 1968, and a new one has been built. Recent excavations have shown that the site of the first 'London Bridge' – the one built by the Romans – was only a short distance down river from the present bridge.

London History and London Landmarks

LONDON'S HISTORY begins in the middle of the 1st century AD when the invading troops of the Roman Emperor Claudius swept across south-east Britain to the Thames. The area was uninhabited marshland, and the Romans had to bridge the river to get to Colchester, then the most important town in the south-east. In time, they built roads converging on the bridge, river traffic increased, and a settlement grew up which they named Londinium. Its position ensured its prosperity and by the 3rd century it had become the centre of Roman administration and a prosperous walled city with a fort, a large temple, a basilica and a governor's palace. Recent excavations have shown that the present London Bridge is sited only a few hundred yards from the Roman one. Until the 17th century, London Bridge, lined on both sides with shops and houses, was the only access to the city from the south, and until the 16th century, London stayed more or less confined within the limits of the Roman walls. Southwark, on the south side of the bridge, was outside the jurisdiction of the city authorities, and by medieval times had become a refuge for criminals and the quarter where playhouses such as the Globe, forbidden within the City, could flourish.

Until after the reign of Edward the Confessor, English kings were not crowned at London. However, Edward had completed the rebuilding of Westminster Abbey just before his death, and Harold, his successor, was crowned there, as was William the Conqueror, who made Westminster his capital, at the same time conferring on London the status and privileges of a city, but also building the Tower as a symbol of his

authority. London thus became truly the capital of England – but for centuries there were two centres of authority – Westminster where the monarch had his palace and where eventually parliament met, and the City where the powerful merchant guilds were supreme. Gradually wealthy landowners built themselves residences along the Strand, which linked the two centres, and the legal profession set themselves up on the site of the Temple of the Knights of St John.

From the 17th century onwards, London grew at an amazing rate, spreading far beyond the Roman and medieval walls. Even the Great Fire of 1666, to which we owe the creation of St Paul's Cathedral and many other churches designed by Wren, did not halt expansion, and surrounding villages like Chelsea, Marylebone, Islington, Kensington, Hampstead and Highgate were gradually swallowed up. The Victorian era, especially after the building of the railways, saw a phenomenal growth in size and population as trade with the Empire boomed and by 1901 the population of the capital stood at 4½ million, more than four times the number there had been in 1801.

The devastation of World War II has resulted in massive new office blocks, and whole areas of houses have been demolished to make way for high-rise or high-density flats, which have, say many, brought more problems than they have solved. Other post-war developments, such as the Barbican and the South Bank Arts Centre, have been widely acclaimed. Despite the drift of people from the centre, where housing is scarce and expensive, to the suburbs, London continues to grow and efforts are being made to attract industry back to the centre.

SURVIVOR OF THE BLITZ *St Paul's Cathedral, built after the Great Fire of 1666 as a symbol of the rebirth of the City, emerges defiantly from the smoke of a World War II bombing raid.*

Buckingham Palace see p. 165
The Houses of Parliament, p. 162
St Paul's Cathedral, p. 162
The Tower of London, p. 163

WESTMINSTER'S LANDMARKS

WESTMINSTER ABBEY Since the consecration of the abbey on 28 December 1065, the coronation of every English monarch has been held here, with the exception of the two uncrowned kings, Edward V and Edward VIII. It is also the burial place of all English monarchs from the time of Henry III, to whom we owe the rebuilding in Early English style of most of the abbey, to the reign of George III.

THE ABBEY *showing the delicacy of the fan-vaulting.*

Their tombs, particularly that of Edward the Confessor and that of Henry VII, housed in the beautiful, fan-vaulted chapel he had built in the early 16th century, are magnificent, but outnumbered by the thousand or so monuments to the great and famous. Poets' Corner is the best-known section, where many distinguished writers are remembered. Statesmen honoured include Disraeli and Gladstone, Churchill and Attlee.

WHITEHALL The old palace of Whitehall, burned down in 1698, was made the official residence of the sovereign by Henry VIII. The site is now occupied by government departments and by the Banqueting Hall, a Palladian masterpiece by Inigo Jones, which was planned as the start of a new royal palace. The ceiling of the main hall was painted for Charles I by Rubens. In the centre of the road is the Cenotaph, designed by Sir Edwin Lutyens and unveiled in 1920. Memorial services are held here every year in November. Leading off Whitehall is Downing Street, home of the Prime Minister and the Chancellor of the Exchequer.

WEST-END LANDMARKS

LEICESTER SQUARE
Devoted almost entirely to the cinema and other entertainments, the square was laid out in the 17th century on land belonging to the earls of Leicester. The streets between the square and Shaftesbury Avenue form the nucleus of London's Chinatown.

PICCADILLY CIRCUS AND SOHO
The centre of London's West End and theatreland, Piccadilly Circus was once known as the hub of the Empire. At its centre is the famous statue of Eros, London's first aluminium monument, erected in 1893 to commemorate the social reformer, the 7th Earl of Shaftesbury. It represents, not Eros, but the Spirit of Christian Charity. Between Shaftesbury Avenue and its theatres and Oxford Street lies Soho, famous for its many restaurants and now notorious for sex shops and stripshows.

MARBLE ARCH
Made redundant as a gateway almost as soon as it was built, Nash's imposing archway had to be moved from Buckingham Palace because it was too narrow to admit Victoria's State Coach, and was re-erected as the entrance to Hyde Park. By 1908, however, the traffic was too much for it, and it was removed to its present site, islanded by traffic on all sides, at the west end of Oxford Street, on the spot where the notorious Tyburn gallows used to stand.

POST OFFICE TOWER
Completed in 1964 and opened in 1966, the Post Office Tower, 580ft high and surmounted by a 40ft mast, is one of London's tallest buildings. At the top is a viewing platform and there used to be a revolving restaurant, but this has been closed for some years now.

ROYAL ALBERT HALL AND ALBERT MEMORIAL
Much loved as the home of the Proms, the Royal Albert Hall, an immense, domed, circular structure opened in 1871, commemorates the Prince Consort, as does the elaborate Gothic memorial opposite, showing the Prince seated under a canopy and reading a catalogue of the Great Exhibition.

TRAFALGAR SQUARE
Famous for its flocks of pigeons and as a rallying point for demonstrations of all kinds, Trafalgar Square, on the site of the old Royal Mews, commemorates Lord Nelson's victory over the French in 1805. It was laid out between 1829 and 1841, but Landseer's lions, flanking Nelson's Column, were added in 1867 and the fountains, in which late-night revellers sometimes bathe, in 1948.

PICCADILLY CIRCUS *and the statue of Eros are the most famous and recognisable landmarks in London.*

CITY LANDMARKS

FLEET STREET AND THE STRAND
Although many newspapers, including *The Times*, now have their offices elsewhere in London, Fleet Street is still synonymous with the power of the Press. Many of its pubs are the haunt of journalists and some, such as the Cheshire Cheese, have a long and distinguished history. The great Dr Johnson had his house in Gough Square, one of the many courts leading off the street. Fleet Street, which takes its name from the old Fleet River, runs from Ludgate to Temple Bar, the old boundary of the City with Westminster. The archway was removed in 1878, but a memorial plinth remains. St Bride's Church, designed by Wren, is known as the Parish Church of the Press, and its spire is said to have been the inspiration for the traditional three-tier wedding cake. The Strand is the continuation of Fleet Street towards Trafalgar Square. As the name suggests, this was the river bank until the building of the Embankment. Between the Strand and the river lie two of London's four Inns of Court, the Inner and Middle

HOME OF THE PROMS *The Royal Albert Hall seats more than 5000 people in its huge, circular auditorium.*

Temple, a peaceful enclave of mostly 17th-century courts, linked by steps and alleys. The Temple Round Church, one of only five in England, dates back to the time of the Knights Templar who originally occupied this site in the 12th century. Two other famous churches, both on islands in the Strand, are St Clement Danes of nursery-rhyme fame and, since its rebuilding after the war, the RAF church, and St Mary-le-Strand, designed by James Gibbs in 1714–19.

THE BANK OF ENGLAND
This massive, windowless stone fortress stands rock-solid (whatever the state of the pound) in Threadneedle Street. Sir John Soane's original designs for the building can be seen in the Soane Museum (p. 170), but much of his structure was rebuilt by Sir Herbert Baker in the 1920s. Nearby are the Stock Exchange in Throgmorton Street, and Lloyds of London in Lime Street.

THE MONUMENT *offers a magnificent City panorama.*

THE MONUMENT
Despite the towering office blocks, the Monument is still one of the City's most visible landmarks. Erected in 1677, it commemorates the Great Fire of 1666. From the top (202ft – the distance from its base to the place in Pudding Lane where the fire started) there are splendid views of the City.

OLD BAILEY
Properly called the Central Criminal Court, the Old Bailey, crowned by the traditional figure of Justice, takes its popular name from the street where it is sited, near St Paul's. It was built where the old Newgate Prison, scene of public executions until 1868, used to stand.

THE BARBICAN
London's most ambitious scheme for making the City a place to live as well as to work, the Barbican is a massive, self-contained complex west of Moorgate. Flats and tower-blocks look out on to a series of courtyards, gardens and a lake. At one end is the Museum of London (p. 170), at the other, an arts centre incorporating exhibition halls, a concert hall and a theatre, now the home of the Royal Shakespeare Company.

The River: Westminster to Greenwich

London owes its existence to the Thames and to the bridge the Romans built in the 1st century AD. Until less than a hundred years ago the river was busy with shipping of all kinds but nowadays even the distinctive flat-bottomed lighters have all but disappeared and the sailing barges are museum pieces.

To travel down the Thames from Westminster Pier to Greenwich in one of the many pleasure launches is to voyage past a fascinating panorama. After the splendours of Westminster, the City and the Tower of London, the scene changes to the warehouses and docks of the Pool of London and Limehouse, ending in the open spaces of Greenwich, and the Royal Naval College.

WESTMINSTER PIER AND BRIDGE Westminster Pier, just north of the bridge, is the embarkation point for many of the trips up and down the river. The bridge itself, built in the 19th century, seems to blend in with the Houses of Parliament.

THE HOUSES OF PARLIAMENT Kings from Edward the Confessor to Henry VIII lived here, but the Court had to move to St James in 1515, after a fire, and Henry VIII then built himself a new palace at Whitehall. Westminster Palace became the Houses of Parliament. In 1834 most of the old palace burnt down. Charles Barry designed the present Gothic building, and much of its intricate decoration was entrusted to Augustus Pugin. The buildings are 940ft long and include 1100 apartments and two miles of corridors. The clock tower at the north end, although smaller than the imposing Victoria Tower at the south end, is affectionately known the world over as Big Ben, although properly speaking this is the name of the 13½ ton bell that strikes the hours. Westminster Hall, 240ft long, may well be the largest Norman hall in Europe. Its magnificent hammer-beam roof dates from the reign of Richard II.

COUNTY HALL A modern building with 750 ft of river frontage, it is the administrative headquarters of the Greater London Council.

CLEOPATRA'S NEEDLE This 69½ft-tall obelisk was given to this country in 1819 by the Viceroy of Egypt. It had been erected at Heliopolis in about 1500BC – but it has no real connection with Cleopatra.

THE SOUTH BANK COMPLEX This complex includes the Festival Hall, National Theatre and National Film Theatre, the Purcell Room, the Hayward Gallery and the Queen Elizabeth Hall.

WATERLOO BRIDGE By the 1920s John Rennie's 19th-century Waterloo Bridge was showing signs of structural weakness, and work began on this elegant replacement, designed by Sir Giles Gilbert Scott, in 1939.

SOMERSET HOUSE Elizabeth I lived in the palace that once stood on this site, and Oliver Cromwell lay in state here before his funeral. The present building dates from 1776 and a large part of it is occupied by the Registrar General's staff.

ST PAUL'S CATHEDRAL Sir Christopher Wren's magnificent Baroque cathedral replaced Old St Paul's, destroyed in the Great

WESTMINSTER *The familiar shape of the Houses of Parliament and Westminster Bridge.*

THE TOWER OF LONDON *The massive keep or 'White Tower' built by William I dominates the riverside.*

Fire of 1666. Seen from the river, it retains its majesty despite surrounding office blocks. The height to the top of its cross is 365ft, and the dome is 112ft in diameter, with three galleries – the famous Whispering Gallery, the Stone Gallery and the Golden Gallery, the two latter giving fine views over London and the Thames. In the crypt are the tombs of Lord Nelson and the Duke of Wellington.

LONDON BRIDGE The medieval London Bridge was a remarkable structure, its 950ft length supported on 19 piers and bearing shops, houses and a chapel. The buildings were demolished in 1760 because of the danger of fire, and in 1831 the bridge itself was replaced by a five-arched granite bridge designed by John Rennie, and this was again replaced in 1968.

HMS BELFAST Almost opposite the Custom House is moored HMS *Belfast*, a World War II cruiser – the largest and most powerful ever built for the Royal Navy – now a museum.

THE TOWER OF LONDON In its time the Tower has been royal residence, prison, stronghold and place of execution – but it is now occupied by the Yeomen Warders, who wear picturesque Tudor costumes, the ravens, whose continued presence there is believed to guarantee its safety, and thousands of tourists who file through to see the Crown Jewels and a comprehensive collection of weapons and armour. William the Conqueror built the keep, known as the White Tower, between about 1078 and 1098, an outstanding example of Norman military architecture. Succeeding kings built and extended the defensive walls and added more towers. Many prisoners met their deaths here, including two of Henry VIII's wives, Anne Boleyn and Catherine Howard.

TOWER BRIDGE This, the most spectacular of London's bridges, was designed in the late 19th century by Sir John Wolfe-Barry. The roadway between the Gothic towers is carried on twin bascules which are raised to allow ships to enter the Pool of London; the original machinery is still in working order, though the steam engines have been replaced by electric motors for reasons of economy. A pedestrian high-level walkway has now been opened between the towers, and the original machinery can be inspected.

ST KATHARINE'S DOCK The buildings have now been adapted to a variety of uses and the docks themselves converted to marinas. The Maritime Trust's Historic Ship Collection illustrates the evolution from sail to steam and also includes the RRS *Discovery*, Captain Scott's vessel.

EXECUTION DOCK Pirates and sailors found guilty of serious crime on the high seas were hanged in chains here until three tides had washed over them. Nearby is the famous Prospect of Whitby public house.

THE GRAPES This picturesque old Limehouse pub stands near Regent's Canal Dock. Regent's Canal and the Grand Union Canal enabled goods to be shipped by barge from the Midlands to the Thames.

THE ISLE OF DOGS Charles II had his royal kennels here and this gave the island its name. Brunel's steamship *Great Eastern* was launched from a site near Millwall Docks.

GREENWICH The river gives the best view of Wren's superb Royal Naval College (p. 170, originally a naval hospital). Behind them and behind the Queen's House (now part of the National Maritime Museum, p. 170) rise the landscaped acres of Greenwich Park and at the top of the rise stands the Old Royal Observatory (p. 170). Moored near the pier are two historic ships, *Cutty Sark*, and *Gypsy Moth IV* (p. 170).

STEAM BARGES *(left) still common around Tower Bridge in the 1950s.*

THE PROSPECT OF WHITBY *is possibly the oldest of London's riverside pubs. In the foreground, the river police.*

CUTTY SARK *The only surviving example of the swift tea clippers lies in dry dock.*

GREEN PARK Charles II purchased this extension to St James's Park, from which it is divided only by The Mall, in 1667. He was fond of walking, and Constitution Hill, which runs alongside, is thought to have been the route of his favourite 'constitutional'. Green Park differs from the other Royal Parks in having no flowerbeds and no water.

GREENWICH PARK Greenwich Park was enclosed in 1433 to form a setting for Bella Court Palace, built there a few years earlier by the Duke of Gloucester. In Tudor times it was popular as a hunting chase, and it was not until the reign of Charles II (who had a palace there) that the present, semi-formal layout was achieved. Wide expanses of lawn, broken by avenues of trees and an ornamental pond, sweep up towards Blackheath from the Maritime Museum and the Queen's House on the riverside. Fallow deer roam in a 13-acre tract of bracken and wild flowers known as The Wilderness, and there are three bird sanctuaries. The Old Royal Observatory (now a museum) stands in the park, as does a stone bearing a strip of brass marking the Meridian – zero degrees Longitude – to which measurements made all round the world are referred.

HYDE PARK Henry VIII designed Hyde Park specifically for the purpose of hunting when the land, previously the property of the Abbey of Westminster, came into his possession at the Dissolution. In Stuart times the park was used for horse-racing, and the one-and-a-half miles of Rotten Row (a corruption of 'Route du Roi') is still popular with riders. The Serpentine Lake was formed at the instigation of Queen Caroline by damming the underground River Westbourne; it provides facilities for rowing and sailing – or even year-round bathing for the intrepid few! At the north-east corner of the park, nearest to Marble Arch, is Speaker's Corner, where anyone prepared to face the heckling of bystanders can have his say.

KENSINGTON GARDENS Kensington Gardens were once part of Hyde Park, but when William III came to the throne in 1689 he feared the effect of Whitehall Palace's damp atmosphere on his asthma and so acquired Nottingham House, at the west end of the park. This became Kensington Palace, its grounds Kensington Gardens – more formal than Hyde Park, though now divided from it only by a road and sharing the same stretch of water. Generations of children have flocked here to see the statue of Sir James Barrie's Peter Pan, the fantastically-carved Elphin Oak and the craft of model boat enthusiasts on the Round Pond.

Parks and Palaces

London is well-blessed with open spaces; they range from the compact green squares of residential districts to great open spaces like Hampstead Heath. Best-known, however, are the royal parks, tracts of land still owned by the Crown though the public is privileged to use them. London is also rich in royal palaces, as some past monarchs, such as Henry VIII, were keen builders. Today 'the Palace' denotes Buckingham Palace – but this has only been so for a comparatively short time, Queen Victoria being the first monarch to make her home there. The English Court remains 'the Court of St James', and it is to this that foreign ambassadors are still appointed.

REGENT'S PARK Marylebone Park was renamed after the Prince Regent, later to become George IV, who was responsible for the elegant Nash residences built round its fringe; these were part of a huge neo-Classical development that would have covered the park itself had it been completed. Fortunately this was not feasible, and Nash laid out the area more or less as we know it today, with Inner and Outer Circles, artificial lake and Regent's Canal. Today there is boating on the lake, and pleasure cruises on the canal pass through London Zoo at the north end of the park. The Inner Circle encloses the rose-beds of Queen Mary's Garden, together with the Open-Air Theatre where performances of Shakespearian plays are given during the summer months.

RICHMOND PARK This, the largest of the royal parks, was originally an area of wild countryside enclosed by Charles I and used for hunting by his successors; King Henry VIII's Mound was constructed as a vantage point from which the monarch might survey the killing of his deer. The park is still fairly wild, the deer roaming freely through its coppices, but exotic shrubs have been introduced and

the 18-acre Pen Ponds have been developed for fishing. Londoners owe their continued right to use the park to an 18th-century brewer called John Lewis, who opposed the Crown's attempts to bar the public.

ST JAMES'S PARK Until the reign of Henry VIII a 12th-century hospice for lepers, dedicated to St James the Less, stood here; Henry replaced it with St James's Palace, stocking the grounds with deer for the royal hunt. James I used the park to house a menagerie of animals from all over the world, many of them the gift of foreign royalty. The park remained swampy grassland, however, till the reign of Charles II, when it was redesigned in the formal French style. One of its attractions was an aviary (along the road still known as Birdcage Walk), and the islands of the ornamental lake were stocked with a collection of wildfowl.

LONDON'S ROYAL PARKS *are displayed clearly from the air as the 'lungs' of the capital.*

GREENWICH PARK *(right) and* ST JAMES'S PARK *(left) show the contrasting seasons: spring colours at Greenwich; mellow tones of autumn in St James's.*

HAMPTON COURT *The great Tudor gatehouse dates from Henry VIII's time, but the heraldic 'king's beasts' are modern.*

THE VICTORIA MEMORIAL *was erected outside the Palace at the head of the Mall in 1911.*

II, and afterwards the palace, after extensive restoration, was opened to the public. There are priceless paintings to be seen, and fine tapestries and furniture – but perhaps most impressive of all is the magnificent hammerbeam roof in the Great Hall.

KENSINGTON PALACE, *Kensington Gardens, W8* Nottingham House, the London home of the Earl of Nottingham, was purchased by William III in 1683 and was remodelled as Kensington Palace by Sir Christopher Wren. It remained the home of the reigning monarch until George II died here in 1760; it was also the birthplace of Queen Victoria, who lived here until her accession to the throne. It is now the home of Princess Margaret, but the State Apartments, where there is fine work by Wren, Grinling Gibbons and William Kent, are open.

BUCKINGHAM PALACE, *The Mall, SW1* Buckingham Palace – formerly Buckingham House, built in 1703 for the Duke of Buckingham and Chandos – has been the principal home of the sovereign since Queen Victoria came to the throne in 1837. The original brick building was bought by George III in 1761 as a dower house for Queen Charlotte, and in the reign of George IV it was remodelled and clad in Bath Stone by John Nash. Victoria put on a new frontage, however, having Marble Arch (Nash's grand entrance) moved to Hyde Park because it was too narrow for the state coach. In 1912 the east front of the building was refaced again, being given a classical façade of Portland stone to blend with the Victoria Memorial which stands opposite the top of the Mall. Buckingham Palace is open to the public only on such occasions as investitures, though it is possible to visit the Royal Mews and the Queen's Gallery (see p. 171).

HAMPTON COURT PALACE, *Hampton Court Road, Kingston-upon-Thames* When Cardinal Wolsey began work on Hampton Court in 1514 he intended to become the owner of one of the most magnificent palaces in Europe; later, however, he gave it to Henry VIII in a vain attempt to curry favour. Hampton Court, in its fine riverside park, was one of the king's favourite residences. He was often there, playing Royal Tennis (today's 'real' tennis) in the enclosed court and jousting in the area where the Tiltyard Gardens are now. Five of his wives lived there, and the ghosts of two (Jane Seymour and Catherine Howard) apparently haunt it. Anne Boleyn's Gateway, a fine example of Tudor brickwork, dates from this time, surmounted by Henry's fine astronomical clock. The intricate gardens, with their famous maze, were added by Charles II and are reminiscent of Versailles. The last monarch to live there was George

ST JAMES'S PALACE, *St James's St., SW1* This rambling, rectangular brick mansion was built for Henry VIII. It remained the official residence of the sovereign until the time of Victoria and was the birthplace of Charles II, James II, Mary II, Queen Anne and George IV. Charles I spent his last night in its guardroom before going to the scaffold in Whitehall. All that remains of the original structure is a fine Tudor gatehouse, in front of which the Brigade of Guards parade each day. The Chapel Royal has been much altered over the centuries, but it has the original Holbein ceiling; William III, Mary II, Queen Anne, George IV, Victoria and George V were married there, and it is the setting for the annual Royal Epiphany Gifts Service (see p. 166). The Chapel is open to the public for services from October to Palm Sunday, though the Palace itself is not, being occupied by various Court officials.

ROYAL CEREMONIES

THE STATE OPENING OF PARLIAMENT (*Late October or early November*) After the summer recess, the new session of Parliament is opened by a speech from the monarch. The Monarch, accompanied by other members of the royal family, rides from Buckingham Palace in the Irish State Coach, a gun salute heralding their arrival at Westminster. After changing into royal robes and crown in the Robing Room, the Monarch is escorted to the Upper Chamber, where the Lords in their ceremonial robes are already assembled. The official known as Black Rod summons the Speaker and Members of the House of Commons, having first knocked three times on the door with his staff, and the Monarch then outlines the proposed government legislation for the coming session.

TROOPING THE COLOUR (*Second Saturday in June*) This ceremony takes place on Horse Guards Parade on the occasion of the sovereign's official birthday. Wearing the uniform of one of the regiments of which he or she is Colonel-in-Chief, the sovereign rides out from Buckingham Palace and takes the salute of the Brigade of Guards and the Household Cavalry. This is followed by a display of marching and the 'trooping' (display) of the 'colour' (or flag) of one of the five regiments of foot guards.

THE DISTRIBUTION OF THE ROYAL MAUNDY MONEY (*March*) Each Maundy Thursday the sovereign personally distributes alms (now purses of money, representing the original gifts of food and clothing) and, since the reign of Charles II, a purse of specially minted Maundy money, to old folk chosen from various parts of London.

London's Pageantry

Pageantry and ceremonial are colourful parts of London life, observed not only in the panoply of state and civic occasions but also in the meticulous observance of minor rituals so old that their origins have in some cases become obscured by time.

CHANGING THE GUARD *at Buckingham Palace. This daily ceremony is one of London's best-loved tourist attractions.*

DAILY CEREMONIES

THE CEREMONY OF THE KEYS (*10 pm*) Each evening the gates of the Tower of London are locked by the Chief Warder of the Yeoman Warders who is ceremonially challenged by a sentry as he nears the Bloody Tower. At 10 pm the Last Post is sounded and the Chief Warder hands over his keys to the Resident Governor and Major in the Queen's House. Applications to attend the ceremony can be made at the constable's office in the Tower.

THE CHANGING OF THE GUARD AT BUCKINGHAM PALACE (*11.30 am*) The guard, usually formed from one of the regiments of Foot Guards (the Scots, Irish, Welsh, Coldstream and Grenadier) is changed each morning. A band leads the new guard to the palace and the old one back to its barracks.

THE MOUNTING OF THE GUARD (*11 am weekdays, 10 am Sundays*) The Mounting of the Guard takes place at the Horse Guards, opposite Whitehall. The guard is formed from two units of the Household Cavalry – the Blues (identified by the red plumes on their helmets) and the Life Guards (white plumed).

CIVIC CEREMONIES

ELECTION OF THE LORD MAYOR AND LORD MAYOR'S SHOW A new Lord Mayor of London is elected every year on 29th September, Michaelmas Day. The retiring holder of the office and his aldermen attend a service at St Lawrence Jewry and then process to the Guildhall, where they make the final choice from the candidates put forward by the livery companies; the City bells ring as the old and new Lord Mayors ride to the Mansion

House together in the state coach. On 8th November, after attending a luncheon at the Mansion House, together with liverymen of their companies, they go in procession to the Guildhall, where the insignia of office are finally transferred; bells ring in all the City churches as they return to the Mansion House. The new Lord Mayor publicly assumes office on the second Saturday in November, in the 600-year-old ritual of the Lord Mayor's Show. He is flanked by a bodyguard of pikemen and musketeers as he rides to the Royal Courts of Justice in the ceremonial coach, behind a procession of colourful floats depicting some aspect of London's history. The Lord Mayor's Banquet takes place at the Guildhall on the following Monday.

PROCESSIONS In early January the Lord Mayor and his officers lead processions to the opening session of the Central Criminal Court (Old Bailey); to the first sitting of the newly-elected Court of Common Council (January) and the Church of St Lawrence Jewry for the Spital Sermon, preached by a bishop on an Easter theme (second Wednesday after Easter).

OTHER CEREMONIES

JOHN STOW'S QUILL CEREMONY (*Around 5th April*) During the memorial service for John Stow, 16th-century author of *The Survey of London*, at the Church of St Andrew Undershaft, the Lord Mayor places a new quill in the hand of Stow's statue.

ROYAL EPIPHANY GIFTS SERVICE (*6th January*) Officers of the Household offer up gold, frankincense and myrrh – the currency equivalent of the gold then being distributed to old people – at a service in St James's Chapel.

THE LORD MAYOR'S SHOW *is a tradition dating back more than 600 years.*

TROOPING THE COLOUR.

CHARLES I COMMEMORATION CEREMONY (30th January)

Each year, members of the Society of King Charles the Martyr and the Royal Stuart Society process from St Martin-in-the-Fields to the king's statue in Trafalgar Square to commemorate his execution on that day in 1649.

THE BLESSING OF THE THROATS (3rd February, St Blaise's Day)

Throat sufferers commemorate St Blaise, who, on his way to a martyr's death, saved a child who was choking on a fishbone, in a service at St Ethelreda's Church in Holborn.

CAKES AND ALE SERMON (Ash Wednesday)

Members of the Stationers' Company walk to St Paul's Cathedral to hear a sermon preached in accordance with the wishes of John Norton, a member of their Company who died during the reign of James I. Cakes and ale are distributed.

ORANGES AND LEMONS CHILDREN'S SERVICE (End March)

The children from the local primary school attend a service to commemorate the restoration of the famous bells at St Clement Danes Church in the Strand, and each receives an orange and a lemon.

HOT-CROSS BUNS SERVICE (Good Friday)

Morning service at St Bartholomew-the-Great, Smithfield ends with the distribution of hot-cross buns and money (provided by an ancient charity) to 21 local widows.

OAK APPLE DAY (29th May)

Chelsea Pensioners celebrate the escape of the founder of the Royal Hospital, Charles II, after the Battle of Worcester, decorating his statue with oak leaves in memory of the oak tree in which he hid.

PEARLY KING at Battersea.

CEREMONY OF THE LILIES AND ROSES (21st May)

Eton College and King's College, Cambridge, join in placing flowers on the spot where Henry VI, their founder, was killed in 1471.

THE KNOLLYS RED ROSE RENT (24th June)

In the 14th century Sir Robert Knollys was fined for building a footbridge over Seething Lane to join two of his properties. The fine was a nominal one – a red rose to be delivered to the Lord Mayor on Midsummer Day – and payment is still made by the Churchwardens of All Hallows-by-the-Tower, who carry the flower to the Mansion House.

SWAN UPPING (Around the last Monday in July)

The swans on the Thames between London Bridge and Henley belong to the Monarch and the Companies of Vintners and Dyers. The Monarch's Swan Keeper and the Swan Wardens and Swan Markers of the two Companies inspect the swans and mark the cygnets.

DOGGETT'S COAT AND BADGE RACE (Late July/early August)

Six Thames watermen row against the tide from London Bridge to Chelsea Bridge, and the winner is presented with a scarlet coat with silver buttons and badge. This is the oldest rowing event in the world, instituted in 1715.

QUIT RENTS CEREMONY (Late October)

In this, one of the oldest public ceremonies carried out in London, the City Solicitor makes token payment for two properties. The rents, accepted by the Queen's Remembrancer at the Royal Courts of Justice, comprise two faggots of wood, a billhook and a hatchet (for land in Shropshire) and six horseshoes and sixty-one nails (for a forge which once stood in the Strand).

WEMBLEY Football fans.

HAMPTON COURT Henry VIII's astronomical clock.

Calendar of Events

For Royal and Civic Occasions, see 'London's Pageantry'. Precise dates for most events may vary from year to year.

JANUARY
International Boat Show
(Earl's Court)

FEBRUARY
Cruft's Dog Show
(Earl's Court)

MARCH
Daily Mail Ideal Home Exhibition
(Earl's Court)
Druid Observance of Spring Equinox
(Tower Hill) around 21st
Harness Horse Parade
(Regent's Park) Easter Monday
Easter Parade
(Battersea) Easter Sunday
Oxford and Cambridge Boat Race
(Putney to Mortlake) end Mar/Apr

APRIL
London Marathon
Milk Cup Football Final
(Wembley Stadium)

MAY
May Day Procession
(Hyde Park) 1st May
Rugby League Cup Final*
(Wembley Stadium)
Summer Exhibition Opens
(Royal Academy)
London to Brighton Walk
(From Westminster Bridge)
FA Cup Final
(Wembley Stadium)
Chelsea Flower Show
(Royal Chelsea Hospital)
end May/Jun

JUNE
Cricket Test Matches
(Lord's)
Lawn Tennis Championships
(Wimbledon) end Jun/Jul

JULY
Royal Tournament
(Earl's Court)
AAA Championships
(Crystal Palace)
Royal International Horse Show
(Wembley Arena)
Cricket – Benson & Hedges Cup Final
(Lord's)
First Night of the Proms
(Royal Albert Hall)
Open Air Theatre Season Starts
(Regent's Park)

AUGUST
Greater London Horse Show
(Clapham Common) Bank Holiday
Cricket – Test Matches**
(The Oval)
Outdoor Theatre Season Starts
(Holland Park)
Cricket – NatWest Bank Trophy Final
(Lord's)

SEPTEMBER
Battle of Britain Thanksgiving Service
(Westminster Abbey) around 15th
Druid Observance of Autumn Equinox
(Primrose Hill) around 23rd
Last Night of the Proms
(Royal Albert Hall)

OCTOBER
Costermongers' Harvest Festival
(St Martin's-in-the-Fields) 1st Sunday
Horse of the Year Show
(Wembley Arena)
Trafalgar Day Service and Parade
(Trafalgar Square)

NOVEMBER
RAC London to Brighton Veteran Car Run
(From Hyde Park)
Remembrance Day Service
(Whitehall – the Cenotaph)
Sunday nearest 11th

DECEMBER
Smithfield Show
(Earl's Court)
International Show Jumping
(Olympia)
Carol Singing and Lighting of the Christmas Tree
(Trafalgar Square) from 16th
Switching on the Decorations
(Regent's Street)
New Year's Eve Celebrations
(Trafalgar Square)

* Rugby Union: Of matches involving England versus Scotland, Wales, Ireland and France, two take place at Twickenham between January and March in any given year. Matches against other foreign touring teams may also be held.
** Subject to fixtures.

BOND STREET Where Oxford Street is famous for department stores Bond Street is traditionally known for jewellers, art dealers and expensive boutiques. Many of the best of the latter have now colonised South Moulton Street, an attractive pedestrian way which leads off Brook Street.

KNIGHTSBRIDGE Harrods, the largest department store in Europe, lords it over the many expensive shops in Knightsbridge. Its magnificent foodhalls are a study in themselves, but every department is worth a visit, for the legend is that Harrods sells everything. For those who are daunted by the sheer size of the place, the streets round about, such as Beauchamp Place and Sloane Street, are full of interesting smaller shops and boutiques.

OUTLINED *in lights, Harrods is a world of luxury.*

OXFORD STREET Selfridges is the doyen of Oxford Street, with John Lewis, C & A, Marks and Spencer and a number of others also competing to attract the millions of shoppers who descend on the West End at weekends and, above all, at sales time.

PICCADILLY Not many shops have held their own against the tourist and airline offices that now dominate Piccadilly, but Fortnum and Mason stands firm, still supplying the finest in food and drink and a select range of fashion, from its original elegant premises. Swaine, Ardeney, Brigg & Sons specialise in riding equipment, leather goods and umbrellas. Richoux sells tempting pastries and confectionery and Hatchards, books. Facing these establishments, Burlington Arcade has many luxuries for sale, as has Jermyn Street, with its famous cheese shop, Paxton and Whitfield. Well-dressed gentlemen might order hand-

Shops and Markets

Oxford Street, Bond Street, Regent Street and Knightsbridge are the traditional heart of London's shopping area, and many of the long-established department stores are found here. Charing Cross Road has its bookshops; Savile Row its high-class tailors; Soho its delicatessens; Tottenham Court Road its furniture. Street traders flourished before the days of shops, and their 'cries' are an evocative echo of Old London. Cheapside was once the centre of the City's trading ('ceap') being the Saxon word for barter or sale) but today there are markets all over the capital – large central wholesale markets and local 'village' and specialist markets.

MISSIONARY ZEAL *urges this 'man with a message' to mingle with the Oxford-Street crowds in hopes of converts.*

made shirts in Jermyn Street, or perfume as a gift from J. Floris, established here in 1739, on their way to wile away a peaceful afternoon at one or other of the many exclusive gentlemen's clubs that dominate Pall Mall and St James's. At the west end of Jermyn Street, in St James's Street, it is still possible to have a bowler hat made to measure at James Lock, or to have fine leather shoes made at John Lobb, a few doors away.

REGENT STREET Most of the shops are to be found near Oxford Circus, where easily the most famous are Liberty and Jaeger. Liberty, housed in a distinctive, Tudor-style building, has always

been a by-word for its beautiful fabrics. Nearby is Hamley's toyshop, a three-storey wonderland for children.

TOTTENHAM COURT AND CHARING CROSS ROADS High fashion in clothes is not to be found in either of these streets, but the best of modern furniture is displayed at Heal & Son and Habitat in Tottenham Court Road, and the whole range of bookshops, from paperback to antiquarian can be found in Charing Cross Road, where Foyles, occupying two buildings, sells not only these but very nearly all other categories of books. Music and musical instruments are also sold here.

TRADE MARKETS

NEW COVENT GARDEN This famous flower, fruit and vegetable market is now sited at Nine Elms, Battersea, but for hundreds of years it was held in the square in front of St Paul's Church, north of the Strand. It was originally the *Convent* Garden – a walled enclosure used by the monks of Westminster Abbey. After the Dissolution the land was eventually granted to the Earls of Bedford; the fourth Earl obtained permission from Charles I to build on the site, and an Italian-style piazza surrounded by gentlemen's residences was designed by Inigo Jones. Traders were soon attracted by the central square and its covered walks, and the market was well-known by the end of the 17th century. The 19th century saw the erection of special market buildings, and the second half of the 20th century the traffic problems that brought about its removal to the Nine Elms site. The old market has become the lively centre of a revitalised area; craft goods of high quality are sold at many of the stalls in the central market area, and a host of shops and restaurants have opened in the surrounding streets.

BILLINGSGATE Billingsgate Fish Market has also been moved from its original site because of traffic congestion in the City streets. It grew up round a medieval quay just below London Bridge, probably as early as the 9th century, although it did not receive its charter until 400 years later. In 1875 an arcaded building (which still stands) was erected to bring together the sale of all kinds of fish, 'wet, dry and shell', but in 1981 the market was transferred to a new site at the less-busy West India Docks. The name of Billingsgate has long been synonymous with bad language – its tradition of colourful expletive dating back to the original fishwives who squabbled round

SMITHFIELD *(left) is the last of the famous produce markets still operating in its original premises. Covent Garden (right) has turned to new crafts.*

OLD STREET CRIES

Street pedlars were, even until the beginning of this century, a familiar and colourful part of London life. The Rabbit Seller (top) and the Orange Girl (above), with her barrow of fine, ripe fruit, are woodcuts from a series by Bewick and his pupils.

the quay, but ably maintained by today's hard-pressed porter, carrying anything up to a hundredweight of fish balanced on his flat-topped 'bobbing' hat.

BOROUGH MARKET This Southwark market, a direct descendant of one held on old London Bridge, occupies buildings beneath the arches on a viaduct serving London Bridge station.

SMITHFIELD Smithfield, now one of the world's largest meat markets and famous for the quality of its beef, pork and lamb, dealt originally in hay, horses, cattle and sheep; its name recalls the 'smooth field' just outside the city walls to which the animals were driven through the streets of London until the practice was restricted by statute in the middle of the 19th century. At about the same time the market was modernised, when Sir Horace Jones built the Renaissance-style Central Meat Market Arcade, capable of holding up to 400 truckloads of meat at a time.

SPITALFIELDS The name of Spitalfields Market, in the East End, like that of Covent Garden recalls earlier Church ownership of the site: in the 12th century a priory dedicated to St Mary Spital was founded here. The surrounding land was fertile, and by the time of Charles II the volume of local produce for sale was such that he granted a market charter. During the 18th and 19th centuries the area was built up with close-packed houses that subsequently deteriorated into slums, but the market continued to deal in flowers, fruit and vegetables, though no longer locally produced.

STREET MARKETS

BERWICK STREET MARKET, *Berwick St, W1* One of the few survivors of the old Soho, Berwick Street Market (Monday to Saturday) offers excellent value in fruit and vegetables, and there are also shellfish, clothing and household goods stalls.

BRIXTON MARKET, *Electric Avenue, SW9* Brixton (Monday to Saturday) is a general market which reflects colourfully the local community it serves. Because of the largely West Indian population, many stalls are piled with exotic fruit and vegetables, and the compelling rhythms of Caribbean music throb in the background.

CAMDEN PASSAGE MARKET, *Camden Passage, N1* This market which has grown up near the Angel, Islington, is devoted to antiques, curios and bric-à-brac of all kinds. Some of its shops and stalls open all week, but Saturday is the liveliest day.

COLUMBIA ROAD MARKET, *Shoreditch, E2* Well-known to keen gardeners, Columbia Road Market (Sunday mornings) offers a wide variety of flowers, plants and shrubs.

CAMDEN LOCK MARKET, *Camden Lock Place, NW1* Antiques, bric-à-brac, period clothes, and crafts are on sale (weekends) in this lively market which has grown up around Camden Lock in Chalk Farm.

LEADENHALL MARKET, *Gracechurch St, EC3* Specialising in meat and poultry, this City market (Monday to Friday) also offers fish, fruit and vegetables and plants. Its origins go back to the 14th century.

NEW CALEDONIAN MARKET, *Bermondsey Sq, SE1* The New Caledonian is primarily a dealers' market in antiques, though members of the public are not excluded. Much of the serious trading, however, takes place before the official opening time of 7 am on a Friday.

PETTICOAT LANE, *Middlesex St, E1* This is probably the most famous of London's street markets, typically Cockney in character and very popular with tourists. It is actually sited in Middlesex Street but was dubbed Petticoat Lane in the 17th century, when it was the place where the local poor could buy cast-off clothing of their richer neighbours. Today's market (Sunday mornings) still sells clothing of all sorts, but it also deals in most household items.

PORTOBELLO ROAD, *Notting Hill, W11* A general market during the week, with a West Indian flavour, Portobello Road assumes its distinctive character on a Saturday, when a multitude of antique stalls, arcades and shops are opened up. The items offered for sale range from expensive antiques through Victoriana to pure junk. The scene is enlivened by buskers and street entertainers.

PORTOBELLO ROAD *Bric-à-brac stalls line the street.*

A London Directory

EXPERIENCE MUSEUMS

London Dungeon, *Tooley St, SE1:* Recreation of scenes of medieval torture in realistic settings.

London Experience, *Coventry St, W1:* London life and times displayed through different media.

Madame Tussaud's, *Marylebone Rd, NW1:* The famous collection of waxworks, including the fearful Chamber of Horrors.

The Planetarium, *Marylebone Rd, NW1:* Representations of planetary motions are projected on to the inside of the building's huge dome.

MARITIME MUSEUMS

HMS Belfast, *Symons Wharf, Vine Lane, SE1:* The largest cruiser ever built for the Royal Navy (11,000 tons).

Historic Ships Collection, *St Katherine's Dock, E1:* A collection of 18th- and 19th-century sail and steam vessels owned by the Maritime Trust.

Cutty Sark and Gypsy Moth IV, *Greenwich Pier, SE10:* The last of the clipper ships and Sir Francis Chichester's 'round-the-world' yacht lie side by side at Greenwich.

National Maritime Museum, *Romney Rd, SE10:* The magnificent collection includes exhibitions on Nelson and Captain Cook. *See* Old Royal Observatory (below).

Royal Naval College, *London SE10:* Wren, Hawksmoor and Vanbrugh were among the architects of these elegant buildings. The chapel and the Painted Hall only are open.

MILITARY MUSEUMS

Imperial War Museum, *Lambeth Rd, SE1:* Exhibits cover both world wars and other British and Commonwealth operations.

National Army Museum, *Royal Hospital Rd, SW3:* History of the British, Indian and Colonial forces since 1485.

Royal Air Force Museum, *Aerodrome Rd, NW9:* A display of 40 historic aircraft.

MUSIC MUSEUMS

Horniman Museum, see 'General Interest'.

National Musical Museum, *368 High St, Brentford:* Far-reaching collection of old instruments, including automatic pianos.

Royal College of Music, Museum of Instruments, *Prince Consort Rd, SW7:* Includes rare instruments, some dating back to the 15th century.

Fenton House, *Hampstead Grove, NW3:* Early keyboard instruments.

'PERSONALITY MUSEUMS'

Carlyle's House, *24 Cheyne Row, SW3:* Manuscripts and personal possessions of the writer known as the 'Sage of Chelsea'.

Dickens' House, *48 Doughty St, WC1:* Many of the author's personal belongings are preserved here.

HMS BELFAST *(above) The Royal Navy's World War II cruiser is now a museum.*

LONDON TRANSPORT MUSEUM *(below) This horse-drawn bus is one of many fascinating old vehicles on display.*

SCIENCE MUSEUM *The Apollo 10 Command Module which carried astronauts round the moon in 1969 in the final rehearsal for Apollo 11's landing.*

POLLOCK'S TOY MUSEUM *(right) The famous makers of toy theatres run a superb museum devoted to old toys.*

THE QUEEN'S HOUSE *(below) designed for Anne of Denmark, by Inigo Jones, is part of the National Maritime Museum.*

Dr Johnson's House

Dr Johnson's House, *17 Gough Sq, EC4:* Dr Johnson lived here from 1748–58 and compiled his famous dictionary in the attic.

Keats House, (Wentworth Place), *Keats Grove, NW3:* The two Regency Houses where Keats and Fanny Brawne lived from 1818–20 while Keats wrote some of his best work.

Leighton House, *Holland Park Rd, W14:* Contains paintings and sculpture by Lord Leighton, also a fabulous Arab Hall.

Sir John Soane's Museum, *13 Lincoln's Inn Fields, WC2:* Antiquities, curiosities and pictures in the setting of the house where he lived from 1812–1837.

Wellington Museum, *Apsley House, Hyde Park Corner, Piccadilly W1:* The home of the Duke of Wellington, once known as No. 1 London.

MUSEUMS OF GENERAL INTEREST (see also 'National Collections'.)

Bear Gardens Museum, *Bear Gardens, SE1:* On the site of the last bear-baiting ring on Bankside, the museum's exhibits relate to Elizabethan theatre, with scale models.

Bethnal Green Museum of Childhood, *Cambridge Heath Rd, E2:* Dolls' houses and model soldiers are among the toys exhibited.

Geffrye Museum, *Kingland Rd, E2:* Furniture and woodwork from the 16th century to 1939.

Horniman Museum, *London Rd, SE23:* Ethnographical and large natural history collections; also musical instruments.

London Transport Museum, *39 Wellington St, WC2:* Tells the story of the development of London transport, with old trams, trolleybuses, etc.

Museum of London, *London Wall, EC2:* Sited in the Barbican, the museum is devoted to the story of London and its people, from pre-historic times to the present.

Museum of Mankind, *Burlington Gdns, W1:* Houses the ethnography department of the British Museum. Special exhibitions of the culture of tribal and village societies outside western Europe. Small permanent display.

Old Royal Observatory, *Greenwich Park, SE10:* Exhibitions of astronomical, horological and navigational interest. It is now a part of the National Maritime Museum (see above).

Passmore Edwards Museum, *Romford Rd, E15:* Porcelain and exhibits relating to Essex history.

Pollock's Toy Museum, *1 Scala St W1:* Old theatres, toys and children's games are on display in two charming old houses.

Public Record Office Museum, *Chancery Lane, WC2:* The national archives on show include the Domesday Book.

Wallace Collection, see 'Art Galleries'.

THE NATIONAL COLLECTIONS

British Museum, *Gt Russell St, WC1:* Contains a wealth of archaeological treasures, books and manuscripts, and much else besides.

Geological Museum, *Exhibition Rd, SW7:* A piece of the moon is among the exhibits relating to geology and mineralogy: the world's largest exhibition on basic earth science is here.

National Gallery, *Trafalgar Sq, WC2:* Contains one of the world's most important collections of European Old Master paintings.

National Portrait Gallery, *St Martin's Pl, WC2:* Paintings, miniatures, engravings, photos and sculpture representing famous national figures.

Natural History Museum, *Cromwell Rd, SW7:* Five departments relate to botany, zoology, entomology, mineralogy and palaeontology.

Science Museum, *Exhibition Rd, SW7* Exhibits demonstrate the sciences and the development of technology – often with the help of working models.

Tate Gallery, *Millbank, SW1:* Contains the national collection of the work of British artists from the 16th to early 20th centuries and collections of modern art generally.

Victoria and Albert Museum, *Cromwell Rd, SW7:* Covers both fine and applied art, exhibiting work from all parts of the world and all periods. Includes sculpture, ceramics, furniture and costume.

ART GALLERIES (see also 'National Collections')

Courtauld Institute Gallery, *Woburn Sq, WC1:* Impressionist and post-Impressionist paintings, Old Master drawings and Italian primitives.

Dulwich College Picture Gallery, *College Rd, SE21:* The oldest public picture gallery in England, with works by Gainsborough, Reynolds, Rembrandt and Rubens.

Hayward Gallery, *The South Bank, SE1:* Used by the Arts Council for exhibitions.

Institute of Contemporary Arts, *Nash House, 12 Carlton House Terrace, SW1:* Displays, often controversial, of modern art.

Iveagh Bequest, *Kenwood, Hampstead Lane, NW3:* Old Master paintings.

Queen's Gallery, *Buckingham Palace, SW1:* Constantly changing display of art treasures from the royal collection.

Ranger's House, *Chesterfield Wk, SE3:* Jacobean and Stuart period Old Master paintings.

Royal Academy of Arts, *Burlington House, W1:* In summer, exhibition of works of living artists. Important special exhibitions on occasion.

Serpentine Gallery, *Kensington Gdns, W2:* Monthly exhibitions of the work of contemporary artists.

Wallace Collection, *Hertford House, Manchester Sq, W1:* British and European paintings, including some by Rubens, Titian, Holbein and Frans Hals. Also sculpture, ceramics, and furniture.

Theatres, Concert Halls and Cinemas
A Guide to Entertainments in the Centre of London

THEATRES AND CONCERT HALLS

1 **Adelphi**, The Strand, WC2. Tel: 836 7611
2 **Albery**, St Martin's Lane, WC2. Tel: 836 3878
3 **Aldwych**, Aldwych, WC2. Tel: 836 6404
4 **Ambassadors**, West Street, WC2. Tel: 836 1171
5 **Apollo**, Shaftesbury Avenue, W1. Tel: 437 2663
6 **Apollo** (Victoria), Wilton Road, SW1. Tel: 828 8665 (Not on plan)
7 **Arts** (Theatre Club), Gt Newport Street, WC2. Tel: 836 3334
8 **Astoria**, Charing Cross Road, WC2. Tel: 734 4291
9 **Barbican Centre**, Silk Street, EC2. Tel: 628 8795 (Not on plan)
10 **Cambridge**, Earlham Street, WC2. Tel: 836 6056
11 **Coliseum**, St Martin's Lane, WC2. Tel: 836 3161
12 **Comedy**, Panton Street, SW1. Tel: 930 2578
13 **Criterion**, Piccadilly, W1. Tel: 9303216
14 **Drury Lane**, Theatre Royal, Catherine Street, WC2. Tel: 836 8108
15 **Duchess**, Catherine Street, WC2. Tel: 836 8243
16 **Duke of York's**, St Martin's Lane, WC2. Tel: 836 5122
17 **Fortune**, Russell Street, WC2. Tel: 836 2238
18 **Garrick**, Charing Cross Road, WC2. Tel: 836 4601
19 **Globe**, Shaftesbury Avenue, W1. Tel: 437 1592
20 **Haymarket**, Theatre Royal, Haymarket, SW1. Tel: 930 9832
21 **Her Majesty's**, Haymarket, SW1. Tel: 930 6606
22 **Jeanetta Cochrane**, Theobalds Road, WC1. Tel: 242 7040.
23 **Lyric**, Shaftesbury Avenue, W1. Tel: 437 3686
24 **Mayfair**, Berkeley Street, W1. Tel: 629 3036

25 **Mermaid**, Puddle Dock, EC4. Tel: 236 5568 (Not on plan)
26 **National Theatre**, South Bank, SE1. Tel. 928 2252
27 **New London**, Parker Street, WC2. Tel: 405 0072
28 **Old Vic**, Waterloo Road, SE1. Tel: 928 7616
29 **Palace**, Shaftesbury Avenue, W1. Tel: 437 6834
30 **Palladium**, Argyll Street, W1. Tel: 437 7373
31 **Phoenix**, Charing Cross Road, WC2. Tel: 836 2294
32 **Piccadilly**, Denman Street, W1. Tel: 437 4506
33 **Prince Edward**, Old Compton Street, W1. Tel: 930 6877
34 **Prince of Wales**, Coventry Street, W1. Tel: 930 8681
35 **Queen Elizabeth Hall**, South Bank, SE1. Tel: 928 3191
36 **Queen's**, Shaftesbury Avenue, W1. Tel: 734 1166
37 **Royal Court**, Sloane Square, SW1. Tel: 730 1745 (Not on plan)
38 **Royal Festival Hall**, South Bank, SE1. Tel: 928 3191
39 **Royal Opera House**, Covent Garden, WC2. Tel: 240 1066
40 **Royalty**, Portugal Street, WC2. Tel: 405 8004
41 **St Martin's**, West Street, WC2. Tel: 836 1443
42 **Sadler's Wells**, Roseberry Avenue, EC1. Tel: 278 8916 (Not on plan)
43 **Savoy**, Strand, WC2. Tel: 836 8888
44 **Shaftesbury**, Shaftesbury Avenue, WC2. Tel: 836 6596
45 **Strand**, Aldwych, WC2. Tel: 836 2660
46 **Vanbrugh**, Malet Street, WC1. Tel: 580 7982 (Not on plan)
47 **Vaudeville**, Strand, WC2. Tel: 836 9988
48 **Victoria Palace**, Victoria Street, SW1. Tel: 834 1317 (Not on plan)

49 **Warehouse**, (Donmar), Earlham Street, WC2. Tel: 836 1071
50 **Westminster**, Palace Street, SW1. Tel: 834 0283 (Not on plan)
51 **Whitehall**, Whitehall, SW1. Tel: 930 7765
52 **Wigmore Hall**, Wigmore Street, W1. Tel: 935 2141
53 **Wyndhams**, Charing Cross Road, WC2. Tel: 836 3028
54 **Young Vic**, The Cut, SE1. Tel: 928 6363

CINEMAS

1 ABC 1 & 2, Shaftesbury Avenue, WC2. Tel: 836 8861
2 Academy 1, 2 & 3, Oxford Street, W1. Tel: 437 7881
3 Biograph, Wilton Road, SW1. Tel: 834 6574 (Not on plan)
4 Cinecenta, Panton Street, SW1. Tel: 930 0631
5 Cinecenta, Piccadilly, W1. Tel: 437 3561
6 Classic, Charing Cross Road, WC2. Tel: 930 6915
7 Classic Complex, Haymarket, SW1. Tel: 839 1527
8 Classic, 1, 2, 3, 4 & 5, Oxford Street, W1. Tel: 636 0310
9 Classic, Shaftesbury Avenue, W1. Tel: 734 5414
10 Classic Complex, Tottenham Court Road, W1. Tel: 636 6148
11 Curzon, Curzon Street, W1. Tel: 499 3737
12 Dominion, Tottenham Court Road, W1. Tel: 580 9562
13 Empire, Leicester Square, WC2. Tel: 437 1234
14 Eros, Piccadilly Circus, W1. Tel: 437 3839
15 Filmcenta, Charing Cross Road, WC2. Tel: 437 4815
16 Gate 2, Brunswick Square, WC1. Tel: 837 8402 (Not on plan)
17 Gate, Mayfair, Mayfair Hotel, Stratton Street, W1. Tel: 493 2031

18 Institution of Contemporary Arts, Carlton House Terrace, SW1. Tel: 930 6393
19 Leicester Square Theatre, Leicester Square, WC2. Tel: 930 5252
20 Lumiere, St Martin's Lane, WC2. Tel: 836 0691
21 Minema, Knightsbridge, SW1. Tel: 235 6225 (Not on plan)
22 Moulin Cinema Complex, Gt Windmill Street, W1. Tel: 437 1653
23 National Film Theatre, South Bank, SE1. Tel: 928 3232
24 Odeon, Haymarket, SW1. Tel: 930 2738
25 Odeon, Leicester Square, WC2. Tel: 930 6111
26 Odeon, Marble Arch, W2. Tel: 723 2011 (Not on plan)
27 Plaza, 1, 2, 3 & 4, Regent Street, W1. Tel: 437 1234
28 Prince Charles, Leicester Place, WC2. Tel: 437 8181
29 Scene, 1, 2, 3 & 4, Swiss Centre, Leicester Square, WC2. Tel: 439 4470
30 Sherlock Holmes Centa, Baker Street, W1. Tel: 935 2772
31 Studio 1, 2, 3 & 4, Oxford Street, W1. Tel: 437 3300
32 Times Centa 1 & 2, Chiltern Court, Baker Street, NW1. Tel: 935 9772
33 Warner West End, 1, 2, 3 & 4, Cranbourn Street, WC2. Tel: 439 0791

Key

Parking ⓟ
One Way Street
Cinema ●
Theatre ●
Underground ⊕

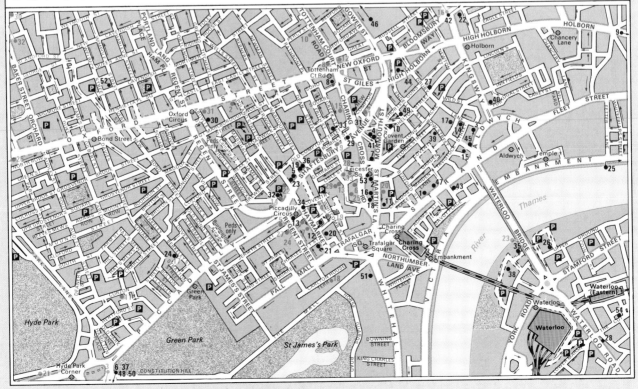

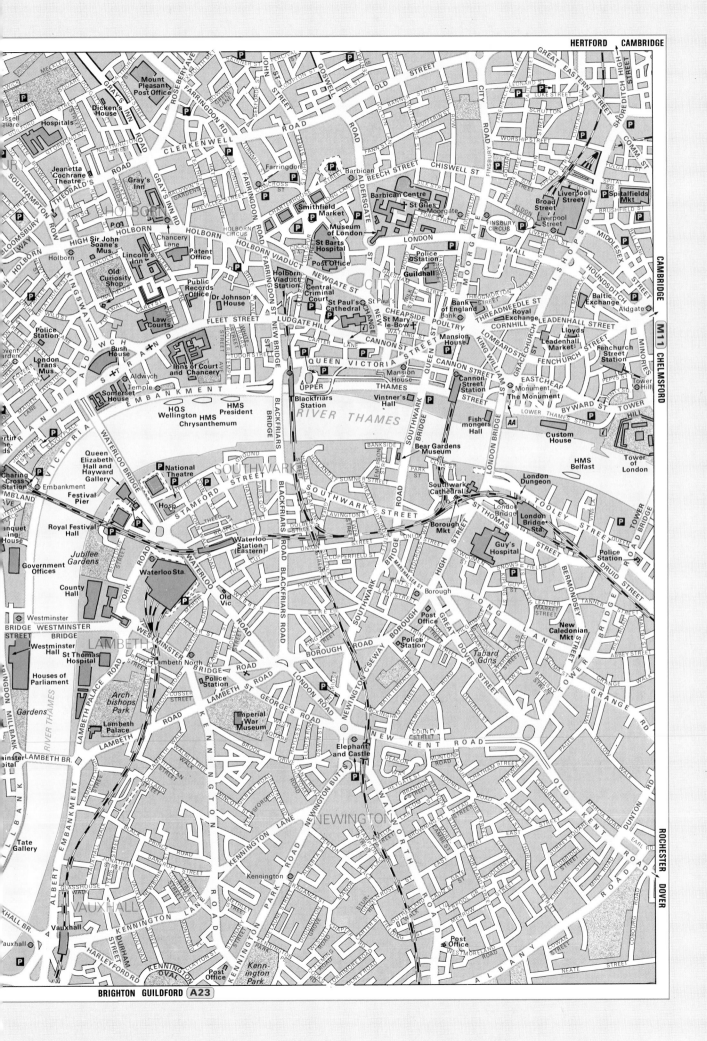

CAMBRIDGE

M11

CHELMSFORD

ROCHESTER
DOVER

MABLETHORPE, Lincolnshire
16 TF58
For the holidaymaker, Mablethorpe offers a wonderful sandy beach, the 11-acre Queen's Park – where there are facilities for bowling, tennis, and a boating lake, etc – and caravans galore. Down on the shore, at very low tide, the stumps of long-dead trees are uncovered. They mark the grave of a village and its surrounding forest, which were engulfed by a gale in 1289. Mablethorpe, like most east-coast towns, has been at war with the sea ever since.

MACCLESFIELD, Cheshire *14 SJ97*
According to the Domesday Book, Macclesfield used to belong to the Saxon Edwin, Earl of Chester. Edward I and his queen, Eleanor, founded the hilltop church of St Michael and All Angels, which can either be entered from the Market Place or from the valley below by a steep climb up 108 cobbled steps: locals say that if you can run up in one breath your wish will be granted. Macclesfield was, until about the middle of this century, a silk-manufacturing town, as several fine 18th-century mills by the River Bollin testify, but many of them have either been demolished or converted to other trades. It is planned, however, to establish a Silk Heritage Centre in the imposing three-storey Sunday School in Roe Street, which is itself a heritage of the industrial age. The town's museum and art gallery stands in West Park, and nearby is an enormous boulder, said to have been brought down by glacial action during the Ice Age.

MACHYNLLETH, Powys *8 SH70*
This modest and quietly elegant Welsh town, with a population of about 2000, does not thrust its greatness upon you. You must look for it. Dating back to the Iron Age, it was originally three villages, which shared a common market cross (in 1873 replaced by a clock tower). In 1404, having liberated his fellow countrymen from the thrall of Henry IV, Owen Glendower declared it the capital of Wales. His Parliament House, to which extensions have been made over the years, is now the Owen Glendower Institute. There is also the pioneering Centre for Alternative Technology, a working demonstration of ways of living by using only a minimum of the earth's dwindling resources.

MADRON, Cornwall *1 SW43*
The Church of Saint Maddern used to be the parish church of Penzance. Situated on high ground above Mount's Bay, this village – with its granite cottages – overlooks **St Michael's Mount**, that fairy-tale island castle that so closely resembles its namesake, Mont St Michel, in Brittany. A three-mile walk will take you to the ancient Men-an-Tol Stone, reputed to have healing powers: sufferers used to crawl through the 'porthole' aperture to be cured of their ailments.

MAENTWROG, Gwynedd *13 SH64*
The village of Maentwrog was built in the 19th century by a landowner named William Oakley, who also had an interest in the neighbouring slate quarries. Oakley created a single street flanked by stone cottages, climbing steeply up the hillside and framed by trees and rhododendrons.

MAIDEN CASTLE, Dorset *3 SJ55*
This Iron Age fort (AM), set on a hilltop to the south-west of **Dorchester** has been described as 'the largest and most perfectly designed earthworks in the world'. Just over 40 years ago, an ammunition store containing 20,000 sling-stones was excavated – and nearby, a mass grave. Some of the skeletons had axes embedded in their skulls. The site, which dates back to before 2000 BC, finally fell to the Romans in AD 43–44.

COURAGE SHIRE HORSES

Dray horses were once the pride of the brewery. About 12 are now kept at the centre near Maidenhead.

MAIDENHEAD, Berkshire *4 SU88*
Many years ago Maidenhead was associated with that famous waterside restaurant, Skindles, and with bright young things disporting themselves on the Thames – their gramophones playing ragtime fortissimo. The image owes something to the era of Edward VII and something to Evelyn Waugh. The town used to be an important stage post on the London–Bath road. Its splendid 19th-century railway bridge is a feature of Turner's painting *Rain, Steam and Speed*. Just outside the town at Littlewick Green is the Courage Shire Horse Centre (OACT).

MAIDSTONE, Kent *6 TQ75*
Maidstone is a town where business and administration are more important than tourist attractions. It has been an administrative centre ever since Saxon times: indeed, the first trial to be recorded in England took place on Penenden Heath. Maidstone's geographical position made it a natural collecting point for the fruit, the vegetables, and the hops, grown round about in the Vale of Kent. The more notorious inhabitants of days gone by included Wat Tyler, leader of the Peasants' Revolt, and Sir Thomas Wyatt, who headed the men of Kent during their rebellion against Mary I. Chillington

Manor houses the town's museum and art gallery, where exhibits range from Japanese *objets d'art* to Anglo-Saxon jewellery. The Archbishop's stables, near the former country palace of the archbishops of Canterbury, now contain the Tyrwhitt Drake Museum of horse-drawn carriages.

MALDON, Essex *6 TL80*
Maldon, a delightful old town on the River Blackwater, is noted for the quality of its salt. All Saints Church is unique in at least one respect: it has the only triangular tower in the country. All that survives of St Peter's Church, however, is the tower, which now serves as a vestibule to the public library. The 15th-century Moot Hall is not without interest – especially its slightly eccentric bellcage. The wide reaches of the river exert a stronger attraction even than the town.

MALHAM, N Yorkshire *15 SD96*
Malham, really, is more a landscape than a village, though there is a pleasant cluster of houses, an inn, a hump-backed bridge and Tarn House (NT), now the Field Studies Centre, where Charles Kingsley wrote a part of *The Water Babies*. Three of Yorkshire's most celebrated natural features lie within relatively easy walking distance: Malham Cove, the 240ft high limestone cliff created by the Craven Fault; the dramatically impressive rock bowl of Gordale Scar, where the water hurls itself down a 250ft ravine up which you can climb when the water is not in full spate; and finally, Malham Tarn, a 150-acre moorland lake. Near Malham passes the 250-mile long-distance pathway, the Pennine Way. The Yorkshire Dales National Park Centre is situated in the village.

MALLAIG, Highland *25 NM69*
The Road to the Isles comes to an end at Mallaig; and so, as any railway buff will tell you, does the West Highland railway line. Beyond lies Skye, and a car ferry plies regularly between this small but nonetheless important herring port and Armadale across the water. There is some excellent mountaineering for those that have the necessary skills; for less adventurous souls pleasure boats are a more satisfactory way of reaching otherwise unreachable places.

MALMESBURY, Wiltshire *3 ST98*
Malmesbury, not without reason on its side, claims to be the oldest borough in England. Certainly its position on top of a hill had a great deal to commend it in terms of defence. An abbey was founded here in the 7th century, and King Athelstan, grandfather of Alfred the Great, was buried in its grounds. The Abbey is, literally since it stands above the town, Malmesbury's crowning achievement. The present building, which serves as the parish church, dates from the 12th century and the gateway is remarkable for its superb Romanesque carvings. Its survival after the Dissolution was largely due to a local businessman named Stumpe who, instead of taking it to pieces for building materials, installed looms. All of which seems to show that the sacred can sometimes benefit from the profane. A colourful legend tells of one of the monks, a man named Egelmer, who tried to fly, with the aid of a pair of home-made wings, some time in the 11th century. Predictably, he fell and broke his legs.

GREAT MALVERN *The view from the Malvern Hills encompasses the town, where the tower of the magnificent priory church dominates the houses, and the wide green plain of the River Severn.*

MALPAS, Cheshire   *14 SJ44*

The name Malpas is derived from the Norman, meaning 'bad walk'. The badness was created by marauding Welshmen who, despite the building of a castle by the Normans, constantly harassed travellers along the road that marked the border between England and Wales. Indeed, in the 14th century, the chances of being attacked were so great that many inhabitants were afraid even to go to church. Nowadays, of course, things are very much quieter. The mixture of timbered and Georgian houses makes Malpas wholly delightful, and the red sandstone church stands proud at the top of a flight of steps, beneath which is the village cross.

MALVERNS, THE, Hereford & Worcester   *9 SO74*

The Malvern Hills cover 40 square miles and are designated an Area of Outstanding Natural Beauty. The highest point is the Worcestershire Beacon – 1394ft above sea level – but the flatness of the surrounding land makes them appear higher. Nestling at their foot are no fewer than six places each with the name of Malvern: Great Malvern, Little Malvern, North Malvern, West Malvern, Malvern Wells and Malvern Link. The hills are rich not only in beauty but also in mineral water. More than a million bottles are sold each year, some of them to HM Yacht *Britannia*: the Queen drinks it on her overseas tours as a precaution against ill-health. Great Malvern is also famous for its public school, its drama festivals, which have associations with George Bernard Shaw, a frequent visitor, and with the music of Elgar. In a churchyard on the road to Malvern Wells, is Elgar's modest gravestone. Elgar used to enjoy flying kites on the hills – and during his walks found inspiration for his music.

MANCHESTER, Gtr Manchester   *14 SJ89*

Coal and the cotton trade caused Manchester to grow into the vast industrial centre it became in the 18th and 19th centuries and the construction of the Manchester Ship Canal gave easy access to the flourishing port of Liverpool, and trade with the New World. With the growth of industry came appalling social conditions, which ultimately led to riots, and the notorious Massacre of Peterloo in 1819. Manchester was also, however, a centre for Radical thought, and the campaigning *Manchester Guardian* newspaper was founded in 1821 to give expression to new political ideas.

The old city centre was a monument to Victorian pride and prosperity, and the majestic Gothic Town Hall (OACT) stood at the centre of street upon street of solid Victorian commercial buildings, most of which have been swept away in an orgy of redevelopment. The past survives, however, in enclaves such as King Street, and St Anne's Square, the most elegant part of the shopping centre, and in an old half-timbered pub, which used to stand in the Shambles, and is now marooned incongruously behind the new Piccadilly shopping arcades.

Manchester has three great libraries, the oldest being the 17th-century Chetham Library (open by arrangement), the first free public library in Europe. The John Rylands Library (OACT) has a superb collection of jewelled medieval bindings, and the Central Reference Library has one of the most extensive collections of books in the country, and there is a lively theatre in its basement. The Free Trade Hall, although suffering bomb damage in 1940, has been restored, and is known as the birthplace of one of Manchester's great prides, the Hallé Orchestra. Among the many museums and art galleries are the Whitworth Art Gallery, run by the university, which has a distinguished collection of pre-Raphaelite and European paintings; the City Art Gallery, which contains many treasures, including a collection of the decorative arts, furniture and sculpture; the Manchester Museum, concentrating on archaeology and natural history; the Museum of Transport, and the North-western Museum of Science and Industry.

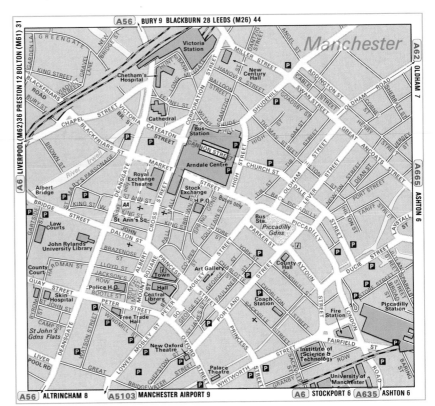

MANIFOLD VALLEY, Staffordshire
15 SK15
This lovely valley, which begins near Ilam
in Staffordshire and winds its way
northwards by way of the dramatic Beeston
Tor, begins in a low key – with gentle
slopes clad with fields. Half way along,
however, it changes dramatically: the
pastoral landscape becomes transformed
into a world of caves, and precipices. The
River Manifold itself has a strange habit of
vanishing underground in periods of dry
weather in stretches where the river bed is
porous, then reappearing later on, in the
grounds of Ilam Hall (*see* Ilam).

MANORBIER, Dyfed *7 SS09*
Manorbier Castle (OACT) overlooks the
village, which looks as if it still depends
upon it for protection. The work of
building this impressively well preserved
red sandstone masterpiece was begun in
1275 but not completed until 50 years later.
The great 12th-century historian Giraldus
Cambrensis was born here. He wrote *The
Itinerary through Wales* – an account of his
journey with Archbishop Baldwin to raise
support for the Third Crusade.

MANSFIELD, Nottinghamshire
15 SK56
Mansfield today is an important industrial
centre and the home of miners who work in
the surrounding coalfields. It used to be a
small town in the middle of Sherwood
Forest. Indeed, a plaque in Westgate marks
the site of the so-called 'centre oak' which
had to be chopped down in 1940. Evidence
of Mansfield's antiquity can be found in the
'Rock Houses', or cliff dwellings cut in the
sandstone beside the Southwell road, which
were still inhabited at the end of the 19th
century. The town is dominated by a vast
railway viaduct and in the market place
stands the Moot Hall, erected in 1752.

MAPLEDURHAM, Oxfordshire
4 SU67
Mapledurham is an idyllic little village on
the banks of the Thames, its pretty cottages
lying in the shadow of its imposing Tudor
manor house (OACT), home of the Blount
family. During the season when the house
is open, there are river trips from
Caversham (Reading) to Mapledurham.
Beside the river is a watermill, the last
working corn and grist mill on the Thames.

MARAZION, Cornwall *1 SW53*
Marazion itself is a little collection of
cottages on the south coast of Cornwall. A
causeway, useable at low tide, joins it to St
Michael's Mount (OACT).

JACK THE GIANT KILLER

Traditional tales of Jack the Giant
Killer include one in which he kills
Cormoran, the terrible giant of St
Michael's Mount, who terrorised the
surrounding farms. Jack dug a pit
down which the giant fell, and, so
they say, a well on St Michael's
Mount still marks the spot.

MARCH, Cambridgeshire *11 TL49*
March, which is a communications centre
for the Fen district, stood beside the River
Nene, until engineers decided that it might
help drainage and prevent floods if it was
diverted to run in a straight line between
Wisbech and Peterborough. The 15th-
century church of St Wendreda is justly
famous for its hammerbeam roof –
decorated with myriads of angels.

MARGAM, W Glamorgan *8 SS78*
Margam Abbey stands high above the
seashore, with some prehistoric burial
mounds and camp sites as neighbours. The
name may mean 'sea-margin', or it may be
derived from Prince Morgan, who was
killed in 800 BC. The Abbey was founded
in 1157 and a chapter house was added in
the 13th century – a beautiful twelve-sided
building with a circular interior. The 840-
acre country park has a herd of fallow deer
and several interesting buildings.

MARGATE, Kent *6 TR37*
In the 18th century the English discovered
that sea bathing was good for the health.
The problem for ladies was how to get into
the water without being watched by prying
eyes. Margate's answer was the bathing-
machine, invented by a Margate Quaker
named Benjamin Beale. Twentieth-century
Margate is often called the Blackpool of the
South, and has, in Dreamland, a full-scale
funfair. Amidst all the modern
entertainments, Margate preserves two
historic buildings: Salmestone Grange
(OACT), a restored medieval grange, and
the Tudor House (OACT) which contains
the town's museum.

ST MICHAEL'S MOUNT *The causeway joining the
island to the mainland at Marazion can just be
seen. When it is impassable visitors cross by boat
– in parties of 12, as the notice briskly orders.*

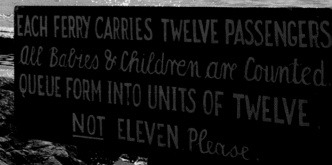

MARKET DRAYTON, Shropshire
14 SJ63
Robert Clive (of India) was born here; and attended the local grammar school, founded in 1558, where the desk on which he carved his initials is preserved. The market, still held every Wednesday, dates from the reign of Edward I. There are several fine black and white timbered buildings around the old town centre.

MARKET HARBOROUGH,
Leicestershire   *10 SP78*
Deep in the heart of hunting country – in this case, the Fernie Hunt – Market Harborough was the creation of Henry II. Some say that the church of St Dionysius, was founded by John of Gaunt – though the decorations and the Perpendicular style of architecture suggest that this is unlikely. Every November, the bells are rung to celebrate the rescue of a merchant who lost his way on the Welland marshes in 1500. The ringers receive the modest reward of 'one shilling for beer'. At West Langton, four and a half miles away, Langton House (OACT) dates from the 15th and 16th centuries and contains a fine collection of furniture.

MARLBOROUGH, Wiltshire   *3 SU16*
Marlborough College, the famous public school attended by Sir John Betjeman and William Morris, to name but two ex-pupils, is said to be the burial place of King Arthur's magician, Merlin. The wide High Street of the town is particularly attractive, with its handsome colonnades and a church at either end. In the 17th century, Marlborough suffered a series of disastrous fires, which caused the local authorities to ban the use of thatch.

MARLOW, Buckinghamshire   *4 SU88*
There are all sorts of attractive aspects to this little Thames-side town, notably the suspension bridge across the river, which was built in 1829, the 14th-century hall of the Old Vicarage; a mummified hand in St Peter's Church, long believed to be that of St James the Apostle. At Albion House in West Street, Shelley wrote *The Revolt of Islam* and his wife wrote *Frankenstein*. The Crown Hotel is said to have numbered Dick Turpin among its regulars, and the Compleat Angler Inn, on the Berkshire side of the river, is named after the famous angler, Izaak Walton.

MARSTON MOOR, N Yorkshire
15 SE45
On 2nd July 1644, a battle was fought here that marked a turning point in the Civil War. Sir Thomas Fairfax had learned that 20,000 Royalists under Prince Rupert were on their way from Lancashire to join the king. His object was to prevent these reinforcements from linking up with the main army. He failed, and the Royalists appeared to have won. Later in the day, however, Cromwell led a cavalry charge, which took the opposition's commanders, who were at supper, by surprise. By 10 pm in the evening 4000 Royalist troops lay dead, as against 300 Roundheads.

MARTIN MERE, Merseyside   *14 SD31*
Martin Mere (OACT), near Southport, is owned by the Wildfowl Trust. Among its residents are swans, ducks and water fowl of all species, habitats and dimensions.

Hunting Country
78 miles
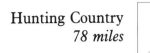

The coverts and spinneys of Old Rutland and Leicestershire are filled in autumn with the sounds of the hunt. The fox was not the only prey hunted over these peaceful acres, however, for this was the site of the Battle of Naseby and the crushing defeat of the Royalist cause in the Civil War.

From **Market Harborough** take A427 Corby road and in 7 miles turn left on to B670 (SP Rockingham). Turn left, then bear right through Middleton, turn right at Cottingham and drive to the edge of **Rockingham**. For the castle turn right, but the main route turns left on to A6003 (SP Oakham). At **Caldecott** turn right on to B672 (SP Morcott). In 1½ miles, following Morcott signs, keep left then turn right, and in another 2½ miles keep left again to pass under the viaduct before ascending out of the valley. Later keep left, then at the main road turn right then left to join A6121 Stamford road. Drive to **Stamford** and from there follow signs for Grantham then Oakham to leave on A606. Continue through Empingham and Whitwell, then 1 mile further turn right (unclassified), SP Exton, Cottesmore. At **Cottesmore** turn left on to B668 and drive through Burley to **Oakham**. Follow

Melton Mowbray signs and go over a level crossing, then turn left and left again (SP Leicester, Braunston) on to an unclassified road leading to Braunston and Tilton. Turn left on to the Market Harborough road, B6047. Cross the main road, A47, then in 3 miles, at the Three Gates crossroads, take the second turning right (unclassified, SP Kibworth) and proceed to **Kibworth Harcourt**. Here turn right (SP Leicester), then at the end of the main street, left on to A6 Market Harborough road. Shortly, at the Coach & Horses PH turn right into Church Road for **Kibworth Beauchamp**. At the roundabout turn right and take 1st left to leave on the Smeeton Westerby road. Pass through the village and proceed to Saddington. Leave by the Mowsley road and at Mowsley turn right (SP Theddingworth), then on leaving Mowsley keep left, then bear right and carry on to **Theddingworth**. Here cross the main road turning left then right, following signs to Sibbertoft and Naseby. From Sibbertoft, follow Naseby signs, in ¾ mile branching right to pass the battlefield. Continue to the T-junction and turn left into **Naseby** village. Leave on the Market Harborough road, B4036 and return to Market Harborough.

PLACES TO SEE

Market Harborough An attractive old market town with a magnificent parish church, old timbered grammar school, and several interesting old inns.

Rockingham Castle (OACT) was founded in the 11th century but the present building is mainly Elizabethan.

Stamford One of the most beautiful towns in the country, Stamford has five ancient churches and its old houses are stone-built. Its fine old hotel, the George, is nationally famous. The Stamford Museum and the Brewery Museum, Brown's Hospital and,

on the outskirts, Burghley House (OACT) are all worth visiting.

Oakham Former capital of the county of Rutland, this pleasant market town is the centre of the Cottesmore hunting country. The hall of the castle (OACT) has a unique collection of presentation horseshoes and the Rutland County Museum is of interest, as is Rutland Farm Park.

Naseby The story of the battle is told at Naseby Battle and Farm Museum, where there is a miniature layout of the battlefield as well as relics.

The Lammermuir Hills
83 miles

Between the Lammermuir and Moorfoot Hills run the valleys of the Gala Water and Lauderdale, the Tweed and the Yarrow. This wild country of the Scottish Borders, where Sir Walter Scott made his home, at Abbotsford, is the setting of many of his most popular novels.

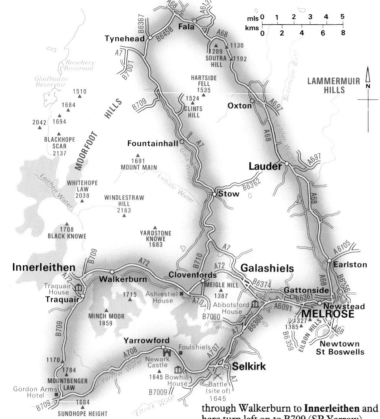

From **Melrose**, take B6361 to Newstead. Continue on this road for one mile then at the junction with A68 turn left, following Edinburgh signs and drive to **Lauder**. Continue along Lauderdale, then climb to Soutra Hill viewpoint. In 3¾ miles, turn left on to B6458 (SP Tynehead). At **Tynehead** go forward on to B6367 and in 1¼ miles turn left on to A7 Galashiels road. Drive through the Valley of the Gala Water to Stow, then 4 miles further on turn right on to B710 to Clovenfords. At **Clovenfords** crossroads turn right on to A72 (SP Peebles). On reaching the Tweed Valley, turn right but stay on A72. Drive through Walkerburn to **Innerleithen** and here turn left on to B709 (SP Yarrow). Cross the River Tweed, pass Traquair House, continue through Traquair and begin to ascend, passing to the right of the summit of Mountbenger Law at the start of the descent to the Gordon Arms Hotel. At the crossroads turn left on to A708 (SP Selkirk) and follow the Yarrow Water Valley to Yarrowford. Continue for a further 3 miles, then bear right and presently turn right to **Selkirk**. Leave Selkirk on A7 Galashiels road, then in 2¾ miles turn right on to B6360 for Abbotsford House. Continue past the house to the roundabout with A6091 and turn right to return to Melrose.

PLACES TO SEE

Melrose A popular touring centre for the Border country. Ruined Melrose Abbey (AM) is a magnificent 15th-century survival. Priorwood Gardens (NTS) are nearby.

Lauder Royal burgh of the old county of Berwickshire, Lauder, on the Leader Water, is an excellent angling centre.

Walkerburn In this old weaving village is the Scottish Museum of Wool Textiles, which illustrates the history of weaving.

Innerleithen On the outskirts, Traquair House (OACT) is Scotland's oldest inhabited house, standing in fine grounds.

Newark Castle Ruined Newark Castle, a 15th-century Border stronghold, overlooks the Yarrow Water.

Selkirk Museum occupies the first floor of the old town gaol. In the marketplace stands a statue of a standard bearer, representing the sole survivor of the Battle of Flodden.

Abbotsford House This historic house (OACT) was built by Sir Walter Scott in 1822, in the style that is now called Scottish Baronial. It contains many mementoes of the writer whose novels so well describe the Border country.

MARWELL, Hampshire *4 SU42*
Marwell Zoological Park was founded in 1972 and contains one of the most impressive collections of wild animals in the country. Within the 100 acres of spacious enclosures are to be found Siberian tigers, snow-leopards, Asian lions, Przewalski wild horses, and all manner of other creatures.

MARYPARK, Grampian *27 NJ13*
Glenfarclas Distillery (OACT), one mile west of the village, is a place of pilgrimage for all who appreciate the finer points of a really good malt whisky. An exhibition, a museum, a craft centre and a visitor centre explain the distilling and maturing processes.

MARYPORT, Cumbria *18 NY03*
In former times they used to ship iron and coal from Maryport. Now the harbour has become closed to trade. However, as a resort, the town has a fine stretch of sandy beach, and a Maritime Museum recalls the past.

MATLOCK, Derbyshire *15 SK36*
There are, in fact, several Matlocks – each adjoining the other and following the line of the beautifully wooded Derwent Valley. Matlock Bath (the capital, so to speak) became famous as a spa in the 19th century. The Grand Pavilion is the scene of an annual festival, and between the Pavilion and the river, the Derwent Gardens display their finery and contain some splendid grottoes. On the far bank, the 'Lovers' Walks' are suitably romantic. The town is dominated by the Heights of Abraham, which rise to 1000ft. They were so named by an officer who had fought with Wolfe at Quebec, and who likened them to the plateau on which the General fought his last battle. The Victoria Prospect Tower, perched on the highest point, affords impressive views, and Nestus Mine and Great Masson Cavern are exciting to explore, as is the Peak District Mining Museum. Near Matlock, Riber Castle (OACT) has a wildlife reserve and a collection of rare breeds of farm animals.

MAUCHLINE, Strathclyde *22 NS42*
In 1788, Robert Burns began his married life in the building now named Burns House. Gavin Hamilton, his friend and at whose house the ceremony took place, is buried in the churchyard – and so, too, are some of the poet's children. Mauchline crops up in several of the works, and thankfully you can still find evidence of it – for example, you can take a drink at the Jolly Beggars Inn. The Memorial Tower contains a Burns Museum. Apart from its associations with the bard, Mauchline is famous for its particularly fine curling stones.

MAYBOLE, Strathclyde *22 NS30*
Maybole used to be the capital of Carrick – the southern division of Ayrshire. It was also the stronghold of the redoubtable Earls of Cassillis, heads of the Kennedys. At one time or another, there were no fewer than 28 baronial mansions within the area. The only survivor is the restored 17th-century 'castle' in the High Street, which was originally the Earl's town house. Two miles south-west of the town are the ruins of 13th-century Crossraguel Abbey (AM).

THE MENAI STRAIT *The view from the Marquess of Anglesey's Column ranges across the strait, with its famous bridges, to the mountains of North Wales.*

MEDMENHAM, Buckinghamshire
4 SU88

Medmenham, with its handsome church and its no less picturesque Dog and Badger Inn stands innocently beside the Thames. However, the ruined Abbey – now part of a private house – was the scene of unholy goings-on in the mid-18th century, when Sir Francis Dashwood and his fellow members of the notorious Hell Fire Club met there.

MEIKLEOUR, Tayside   *27 NO13*

Not the least impressive feature of Meikleour is a beech hedge a third of a mile long, which was planted in 1746 and is now 90ft high. Its occasional pruning is a major undertaking. Opposite the Mercat (or 'market') Cross in the village centre stand the old jougs – to which wrongdoers were attached for punishment.

MELBOURNE, Derbyshire   *10 SK32*

Lord Melbourne, Queen Victoria's first Prime Minister, was born at the Hall (OACT). Years later, Melbourne in Australia, still no more than a small settlement, was named after him. Melbourne Hall, is, indeed, one of Derbyshire's most delightful stately homes. The formal gardens (especially the wrought iron 'Birdcage', as the summerhouse is called), are certainly something to see. Thomas Cook, who created popular 'package' travel, was Melbourne's other famous son.

MELROSE, Borders   *24 NT53*

The best description of Melrose Abbey (AM) is by Sir Walter Scott in the *Lay of the Last Minstrel*. Founded in 1136 by David I for Cistercian monks from Rievaulx in Yorkshire, it is undoubtedly the finest ruined abbey in Scotland. Sir Walter Scott made his home at Abbotsford House (OACT), two miles west of Melrose. A fine example of the Scottish Baronial style, the house contains many mementoes of the man who wrote so vividly of the Borders and Scotland's history.

MELTON MOWBRAY, Leicestershire
10 SK71

Pork pies, Stilton cheese, and the Quorn hunt are the more earthly contributions of Melton Mowbray to English life. Indeed, and largely due to the hunt, anyone said to be a 'Tip Top Meltonian' could feel well pleased with himself. On a more spiritual level St Mary's Church, with its 100ft tower, is one of the finest parish churches in Leicestershire. Next door to it is a house given by Henry VIII to Anne of Cleves 'so long as she remained in England'. But the 'Flanders Mare' bolted, and there is nothing to suggest she ever lived in it. At Thorpe End is the Melton Carnegie Museum of local history.

MENABILLY, Cornwall   *1 SX05*

At Menabilly, near Fowey, was the home for 26 years of the writer Daphne du Maurier. It is a very secret place, concealed by trees from even the most prying eyes. She featured it in *The King's General* and it can be identified without much difficulty as Manderley – the setting of *Rebecca*, (though, for the recent television serial, they used a nice example of Victorian Gothic named Caerhays, a few miles along the coast). Nearby a field provides parking space: after that, you can walk down to the beach at Polridmouth. The boathouse in which Rebecca died in the novel still stands: indeed, it has been restored and overlooks a lake separated from the shore by a stone wall.

MENAI BRIDGE, Gwynedd   *13 SH57*

Although, to the casual observer, there may seem to be two Menai Bridges, there are, in fact, three: the third (a road bridge built comparatively recently) is perched on top of the second (Robert Stephenson's tubular Britannia Bridge, which carries the railway). The first bridge to link Anglesey with Gwynedd was designed by Thomas Telford in 1826. Not only is it 1000ft long, 28ft wide, and 100ft above the highest level of the tide: it was also the first major suspension bridge to be built – a triumph of 19th-century engineering. In Water Street is a fascinating Museum of Childhood.

MENSTRIE, Central   *22 NS89*

Lying in the shadow of 1375ft Dumyat, Menstrie is notable for its large distillery, and its castle (NTS). The latter, built in the 16th century, was the birthplace of Sir William Alexander, who founded Nova Scotia. One of the rooms contains 107 coats of arms of existing baronets belonging to an order created in 1625 to finance the Nova Scotia project. Other rooms have been furnished as Nova Scotia Commemoration Rooms.

MENTMORE, Buckinghamshire
11 SP91

Sir Joseph Paxton, creator of the Crystal Palace for the 1851 Great Exhibition, designed Mentmore Towers (OACT) – a massive Victorian monument to wealth set in 80 acres of grounds. Once the home of Baron Meyer Amschel de Rothschild, it is now the seat of Maharishi Mahesh Yogi's World Government of the Age of Enlightenment movement. The interiors contain superb examples of ornate gilt work, and there are beautiful views of the Chilterns.

MERIDEN, W Midlands *10 SP28*
In the centre of the village, a medieval cross
marks another centre – that of England. It
is, of course, a matter of opinion, but most
Meriden inhabitants support the theory.
Meriden also has one of the oldest archery
societies in the country, the Woodmen of
Arden, which was formed in 1785. In 1788,
it established its headquarters in Forest
Hall – just to the west of centre.

MERTHYR MAWR, Mid-Glamorgan
8 SS87
Nearby, the River Ogmore makes its
leisurely way through woodlands to its
mouth a mile or so away. Merthyr Mawr
itself is a lovely collection of mostly
thatched cottages. From a motorist's point
of view, this is literally the end of the road,
which reaches an attractive conclusion in a
world of sand dunes. As the gales rage in
from the Atlantic, the dunes are frequently
being enlarged by fresh deposits: some of
them, indeed, are reckoned to be the tallest
in the country. However, this natural
violence has uncovered some interesting
relics of the Beaker (Bronze Age) Folk.
Some can be seen in the Museum of the
Royal Institute at **Swansea**.

MERTHYR TYDFIL, Mid-Glamorgan
8 SO00
Iron and coal created Merthyr Tydfil and, it
might be argued, destroyed it. In 1804, the
first steam locomotive – the invention of
that Cornish genius Richard Trevethick –
was built here. By 1831, it was the largest
iron-and-steel-manufacturing centre in the
world – and the largest town in Wales. Its
population exceeded the sum of inhabitants
of **Swansea**, **Newport** and **Cardiff**. But
coal and iron are capricious commodities. A
century later saw Merthyr Tydfil sadly
reduced. One in five of its people was
unemployed: many had moved on to seek,
if not fortunes, livelihoods elsewhere. The
gates of the ironworks were closed: the
great days were over – perhaps for ever.
Cyfarthfa Castle (OACT), built by the
ironmaster William Crawshay, is now used
as a museum and art gallery. Train rides
into the **Brecon Beacons** can be taken from
Pant Station (off A465) on the Brecon
Mountain Railway.

METHLICK, Grampian *27 NJ83*
For over 500 years, Haddo house (NTS),
two miles south-east of Methlick, was the
seat of the Gordons of Haddo, Earls of
Aberdeen. The present building is a
handsome Georgian mansion built by
William Adam in 1732. Amenities include a
theatre in which operas are staged and
concerts performed. Also in the vicinity are
the ruins of Gight Castle. Situated in a
delightfully wooded setting, it has never
recovered from the events of 1639, when it
was besieged by the Duke of Montrose.

MEVAGISSEY, Cornwall *1 SX04*
In summer, Mevagissey is so crowded with
tourists that it is hard to appreciate the
beauties of this delightful little fishing
village. As well as pilchard fishing,
smuggling was once an important local
industry: Mevagissey-built boats were so
fast they could out-sail the Revenue cutters.
A former boat-builder's workshop now
contains an interesting folk museum. A
model railway adds to the attractions for
tourists.

MEY, Highland *30 ND27*
The Castle of Mey is the Queen Mother's
personal residence in Scotland, purchased
in 1953. Overlooking the Pentland Firth,
and not far from John o'Groats, the setting
is bleak. Nevertheless, the gardens (OACT)
are magnificent and the Queen Mother has
carried out a great deal of renovation.

MICKLETON, Gloucestershire
10 SP14
Hidcote Manor Gardens, (NT), lie just
outside the attractive village and adjoining
them is Kiftsgate Court Garden (OACT),
famous for its display of old-fashioned
roses, among them the R Filipes Kiftsgate,
heralded as the largest rose in England.

MIDDLEHAM, N Yorkshire *20 SE18*
Before Newmarket came on to the map as a
horse breeding and training centre, the
monks of **Jervaulx Abbey** at Middleham
were in the business. It used, indeed, to be
the capital of Wensleydale. Now, it is a
small but pretty village. The castle (AM),
now in ruins, was once known as 'the
Windsor of the North', when the great
Neville family owned it. Richard III
acquired it in 1471, and his eldest son was
born here. The 13th-century chapel and the
14th-century gatehouse survive.

MIDDLESBROUGH, Cleveland
20 NZ41
In 1831 work began on an extension of the
Stockton and Darlington Railway – with
dramatic effects on Middlesbrough. What
had been a village community of about 40
people became transformed during the next
four decades into a town with 40,000
inhabitants. Its importance came partly
from its docks, from which coal mined in
South Durham was exported – and partly

from the discovery of iron ore in the
Cleveland Hills (the first iron works was
opened in 1841). The Dorman Museum
tells the history of Cleveland, and at nearby
Marton is the Captain Cook Birthplace
Museum: the great explorer was born here
in 1728. Middlesbrough is not only known
for industry but also for its parks and in
1982 it was declared Britain's Floral City.

MIDDLETON-IN-TEESDALE,
Co Durham *19 NY92*
Between the mid 18th and early 20th
centuries, Teesdale prospered from its lead
mines, which were run by a Quaker-owned
organization named the London Lead
Company. The firm's preoccupation with
the welfare of its employees is evident in the
fine stone buildings. The former head
office, Middleton House, now provides
accommodation for private shooting
parties. The village church has a detached
bell tower – rare in this part of the country.
One of its three bells can be traced back to
1558. Not far away are the famous
waterfalls: Cauldron Snout and High
Force.

MIDDLE WOODFORD, Wiltshire
3 SU13
Some time in the 13th century, Heale
House at Middle Woodford was built.
Charles II took shelter there five days after
the Battle of Worcester in 1651. But many
years later, in 1835, a fire broke out. Parts
of the building survived; others have since
been restored. Nowadays, it is much as
Charles II found it. The gardens, covering
five acres (OACT), are attractive –
especially the water garden with its
magnolias and acers, which surrounds a
Japanese teahouse and is spanned by a
nicely designed bridge.

MILTON ABBAS *The 'model' cottages of this attractive little village were built by the Earl of Dorchester, who had razed to the ground the old market town because it spoiled his view.*

MILTON KEYNES *Plastic cows in the fields do not seem inappropriate in this man-made town.*

MIDHURST, W Sussex   4 SU82
Midhurst has associations with H G Wells, who worked in a chemist's shop and studied (later, taught) at the grammar school. There are some fine 16th- and 17th-century houses – and, on the Petworth side, Cowdray Park (OACT). Now in ruins, it was originally the home of Sir Anthony Browne, Master of Horse to Henry VIII. Early in the 20th century, it was bought by Viscount Cowdray of Midhurst. Lord Cowdray carried out a rescue operation and thus prevented it falling into total decay. Within the park, there is a famous polo ground on which the Duke of Edinburgh used frequently to play. Matches are played at weekends during the season, which lasts from April to August.

MILDENHALL, Suffolk   12 TL77
Do not make the mistake of being put off by the huge American Air Force base and dismissing Mildenhall as just another dot on the map. It is, in fact, a rather lovely village situated beside the River Lark. Of particular interest is the Church of St Mary, with its 110ft tower and its elaborately carved roof. Biblical scenes, a host of angels, and fantastic beasts are depicted. The Puritan zealots did their best to destroy it in the 17th century, but only managed to fire off a few shots in its direction. In 1946, the Mildenhall Treasure – which consisted of a rich hoard of 4th-century Roman silver dishes, some of them probably manufactured in Rome itself – was discovered at nearby Thistley Green. It is now in the British Museum.

MILFORD HAVEN, Dyfed   7 SM80
Milford Haven (the haven) is an inlet 20 miles long, cutting into the south-west corner of Wales. Nelson described it as one of the world's finest natural harbours. A century or so earlier, Defoe had listed 16 creeks, 5 bays and 13 anchorages for shipping. He suggested that a thousand vessels could moor there 'and not the top mast of one be seen from another'. Henry II used it as a base for his invasion of Ireland in 1171. In 1487, Henry Tudor landed on its shore before proceeding to Bosworth Field and winning the crown of England. Milford Haven (the town) was founded in 1793 on land belonging to Sir William Hamilton, husband of Nelson's mistress. Originally, it was used as a port for whalers; nowadays, it is a major oil terminal.

MILTON, Highland   30 NH77
Milton, which is sometimes called Milntown, is a picturesque, rather old world, village on the northern shore of Cromarty Firth. On the far side of the firth, at **Nigg**, the world's largest dock has been constructed. It is used for the assembly of oil production platforms assigned to service in the North Sea.

MILTON, Oxfordshire   4 SU49
Milton is a pleasant starting point for walks in either direction along the banks of the small but none the less pretty River Ginge. Milton Manor (OACT) a 17th-century house with 18th-century wings is attributed to Inigo Jones. The evidence, admittedly, is vague, but appearances suggest it.

MILTON ABBAS, Dorset   3 ST80
The abbey founded by Athelstan in 938 was eventually converted into a mansion in the 18th century by Joseph Damer, subsequently Earl of Dorchester. The mansion (OACT) is now a public school, and the magnificent abbey church now serves as a school chapel. Milton Abbas was at the time of the conversion a market town, which Damer had razed, and created instead a model village of thatched cottages.

MILTON KEYNES, Buckinghamshire
10 SP83
In the late 1960s, the wind of change blew hard on Milton Keynes, when this formerly rather picturesque little village hard by the M1 was designated a New Town. The overwhelming impression nowadays is of ring-roads, concrete, walls of glass, and the very modern architecture of the vast shopping centre. Among the new enterprises is the Open University, which was established in 1971.

MINARD, Strathclyde   21 NR99
Minard Castle, which overlooks Minard Bay – an inlet of Loch Fyne – is one of those pleasant 19th-century conceits that are castles in name only. Where, indeed, was the enemy and where lay the need for defence? Crarae Gardens contain an interesting collection of rare trees, and it is good to see eucalyptus flourishing in a Highland glen.

MINCHINHAMPTON,
   Gloucestershire   3 SO80
Minchinhampton, crowning a high ridge of the Cotswolds, has ancient links with Normandy: William I's wife, Matilda, persuaded the king to give the Manor of Hampton to the Abbaye-aux-Dames at Caen. The restored cruciform church, with its curious tower, is interesting, as is the 17th-century market hall, raised on a forest of pillars. Anyone concerned with a child's health may care to consult the perforated Long Stone. It displays a legendary (though, perhaps, not infallible) cure for infantile rickets. For golfers, the Minchinhampton course is famous – and rightly so.

MINEHEAD, Somerset   2 SS94
Until the late 18th century, Minehead used to be quite an important port – for herring fishing and for the shipping of wool, hides, cattle and coal. But then the harbour began to silt up, and the herring shoals vanished. Minehead fell upon hard times until, in 1854, the railway came to the rescue and the town opened its hospitable doors to tourists. Traces of its former role can be seen in the 1630 Fishermen's Chapel. Holiday-making (20th-century version) is personified by the holiday camp – though it is discreetly hidden from the town and does not intrude. Every May Day, a Hobby Horse festival takes place, similar to, but not as famous as, the one at **Padstow**. The railway, abandoned by British Rail, is kept alive by enthusiasts of the West Somerset Railway, who run some steam trains in summer.

MINIONS, Cornwall   1 SX27
This area of Bodmin Moor is rich in ancient monuments, few more impressive than the line of three neighbouring circles of standing stones known as The Hurlers. A centuries-old legend, reported by the 16th-century historian Camden, explains the stones as 'men sometime transformed into stones, for profaning the Lord's Day with hurling the ball.' Camden did not believe the tale, and the stones are, of course, far more ancient than the coming of Christianity to these shores. The nearby Round Barrow, on the summit of the hill, once yielded an early Bronze-Age treasure of considerable importance, now in the British Museum.

MINSTEAD, Hampshire   *4 SU21*

Minstead is the kind of village one expects to come across in the New Forest; but, alas, seldom does. The original main street is now a cul-de-sac leading to the church, which is notable for its 'parlour pews' – each one private, and belonging to the occupants of the big houses in the neighbourhood. Sir Arthur Conan Doyle is buried in the graveyard. The cottages are thatched; the lawns and holly hedges smartly groomed; and the Trusty Servant Inn has a jokey sign. Furzey Gardens (OACT) covers eight acres of woodland glades, in the midst of which is an Art and Craft Gallery.

THE TRUSTY SERVANT

'A Trusty Servant's Portrait would you see', runs the verse on this inn sign at Minstead, 'this emblematic figure well survey.' The pig's snout means he will eat any scraps; the padlock, that he tells no tales; the stag's feet, that he is swift; and so on. The figure is a copy of the famous one in Winchester College.

MINSTER LOVELL, Oxfordshire
10 SP31

Situated beside the River Windrush, which ambles companionably by, Minster Lovell is an entirely delightful village. It is, then, strange to find its ruined 15th-century hall (AM) so haunted by tragedy. Francis Lovell (or 'Lovell the Dog' as his critics called him) was a follower of Richard III. After the disaster at Bosworth, he escaped to the Continent. Two years later, he unwisely returned to England to carry out a plot against Henry VII. Hounded by the authorities, he found sanctuary in the Hall, where he went to earth in a small room. And there, by all accounts, he starved to death when the only servant who knew his whereabouts died. Certainly a skeleton sitting at a table, with the skeleton of his faithful dog, was discovered in 1718 in the course of repair work. Another tale, that of the Mistletoe Bough, concerns the bride of one of the Lovells who, during a game of hide-and-seek hid in an old chest, the lid of which she could not then raise. She was never found . . . but many years later a skeleton was indeed found in that chest.

MISTLEY, Essex   *12 TM13*

Mistley stands beside the River Stour estuary, and is famous for the large number of swans that patrol its banks. In the 18th century, an entrepreneur named Richard

THE GREY MARE'S TAIL *waterfall in Annandale near Moffat plunges 200ft down a rocky gorge.*

Rigby had the idea of transforming the village into a spa. The original scheme – of building a bathing station beside the river – failed. The only relic of the venture nowadays is a fountain decorated with a swan. Mistley turned its attention to malting – and, conceivably, better times.

MOFFAT, Dumfries & Galloway
23 NT10

If anyone were unaware that Moffat is in the centre of sheep farming country, the question would soon be set to rights by the large bronze ram, a tribute to the prosperity of the wool trade, that tops the Colvin Fountain (1875) in the High Street. This small town lies encircled by the magnificent hill scenery of Annandale. The river Annan provides excellent fishing: as for walking, the 200ft Grey Mare's Tail waterfall and the sheer-sided Devil's Beef Tub (mentioned in Scott's *Red Gauntlet* and thought to have been a cattle raiders' cache) are two among many objectives. Among the sons of the town were John Macadam – the engineer who removed much of the discomfort of

travel by road – and Air Chief Marshall Lord Dowding, whose airmen won the Battle of Britain. Lord Dowding's father founded St Ninian's preparatory school.

MOLD, Clwyd   *23 SJ26*

Mold, the administrative centre of Clwyd, is a busy market town and has been since the days of its early history. After the Norman conquest, Lord Robert de Monte Alto built a castle on a mound north of the town. Nothing remains of it, though the name Mold may be a contraction of Monte Alto. The 15th-century church contains some remarkable animal frescoes.

MONIAIVE, Dumfries & Galloway
22 NX79

The village has a monument to James Renwick – the last of the Covenanters to die for the cause – who was executed at Edinburgh, in 1688 aged 26. It also has Maxwelton House (OACT), the home of 'bonnie' Annie Laurie who lived from 1682 to 1764. The poem that celebrated her was set in music in 1855.

MONNOW BRIDGE *The old Norman bridge spanning the river is a rare survival. Its 13th-century tower is one of four medieval gateways to Monmouth.*

MONMOUTH, Gwent   *9 SO51*
At the place which is now called
Monmouth, the Romans established a
military base named Blestium. Several
centuries later, the Normans built a castle,
which was eventually destroyed during the
Civil War, and Monnow Bridge, is a
fascinating survival, the only Norman
fortified bridge remaining in Britain. Its
13th-century tower formed one of the four
medieval gates to the town. The castle was
the birthplace of the future Henry V: a
statue on the 18th-century Shire Hall serves
as a reminder. Monmouth's second most
famous son was born in 1877, C S Rolls,
who is one half of the famous partnership of
Rolls-Royce. Places to see include the
Naval Temple on Kymin Hill, a pantheon
to a galaxy of admirals and naval heroes.

MONTACUTE, Somerset   *3 ST41*
Montacute (the name comes from the Latin
mons acutus, meaning 'steep hill') is an
ancient and lovely village of golden Ham
stone, the showpiece of which is the
magnificent Tudor mansion, Montacute
House (NT). Its superb Long Gallery
contains a collection of Tudor and Stuart
portraits from the National Portrait
Gallery. Wooded St Michael's Hill, once
the site of a Norman castle, is topped by an
18th-century folly. In the 11th century a
miracle-working cross was apparently
unearthed from the hill and taken to
Waltham Abbey.

MONTGOMERY, Powys   *8 SO29*
Elizabethan, Jacobean and Georgian houses
characterise the streets of this handsome
old town, formerly the county capital of
Montgomeryshire. The town's name comes
from its first Norman overlord, Roger de
Montgomery. The castle he built was
rebuilt in the reign of Henry III but is now
a ruin. A curiosity in the churchyard is the
grave of John Davies, hanged in 1821 for
highway robbery. He died protesting his
innocence and swore that no grass would
grow on his grave for 100 years: there is
reported still to be a bald patch. The
church itself has interesting monuments to
the Herbert family who owned the castle.

MONTROSE, Tayside   *27 NO75*
Montrose, with its four-square-mile basin
on the River Esk, is one of several Scottish
ports that have gained a new lease of life
from servicing North-Sea oil rigs. The town
was the birthplace in 1612 of James
Graham, Marquess of Montrose, who was
one of Scotland's greatest soldiers. A
curfew is rung every night at 10pm from St
Peter's Church. Montrose Museum tells the
long and interesting history of this old royal
burgh.

MORECAMBE, Lancashire   *18 SD46*
Morecambe is a large and rightly popular
seaside resort, with all the amenities anyone
could wish – from performing dolphins in
the Marineland Oceanarium and Aquarium
to illuminations, piers (and beauty
contests), go-kart racing and amusement
arcades. As a resort, it dates back to the
start of the 20th century, when holidaymakers from industrial towns in the North
of England discovered it: before that, there
had only been the village of Poulton le
Sands, now engulfed by the resort. At low
tide, you can walk for eight miles across the
sands of Morecombe Bay. But there are
traps – such as fast-flowing channels – that
have to be crossed. Anyone setting off must
be accompanied by an official guide.

MORETON-IN-MARSH,
   Gloucestershire   *10 SP23*
The word 'marsh' in this instance is a
corruption of 'march', meaning a
boundary. In fact four of them used to meet
in this attractive village on the edge of the
Cotswolds. The main street was part of the
Roman highway known as the Fosse Way.
Overlooking it, the Curfew Tower includes
a lock-up in its amenities. Two miles to the
north-west of Moreton-in-Marsh is the
extensive Batsford Arboretum and three
miles to the south-west is Sezincote
(OACT), an interesting house, said to have
been the inspiration for Brighton Pavilion,
with an attractive water garden.

MORPETH, Northumberland   *20 NZ28*
Morpeth is an attractive town, built on a
bend of the River Wansbeck and a good

starting point from which to explore the
Northumberland hills and coast. The
gatehouse is all that remains of the castle,
though a footpath near the site affords good
views of the town. Morpeth's clock tower
used to serve also as a prison and still
diligently sounds the curfew each evening.
St Mary's Church preserves a 14th-century
'Tree of Jesse' window, and in the
churchyard stands a 19th-century
watchtower, built to protect the graves
from body snatchers.

MORVAH, Cornwall   *1 SW43*
Beside an unclassified road, about midway
between Morvah (to the north) and
Penzance (to the south) stands Lanyon
Quoit (NT): an impressive Neolithic
sepulchral monument.

MORWELLHAM, Devon   *2 SX46*
Somewhat grandiosely, Morwellham used
to describe itself as 'the Greatest Copper
Port in Queen Victoria's Empire'. This
history is re-created in the Morwellham
Open-air Museum where quay workers and
coachmen, blacksmiths and coopers,
dressed in period costume re-enact scenes
from the past.

MOSELEY, Staffordshire   *9 SJ90*
Moseley Old Hall (NT) was originally a
half-timbered Elizabethan house. The
Victorians, seldom content to leave well
alone, encased it with bricks. Among the
interesting panelled rooms is one in which
Charles II rested after the Battle of
Worcester in 1651.

MOTHERWELL, Strathclyde   *22 NS75*
Motherwell is in the centre of a coal-mining
area – and, where there was coal, there was
usually an ironworks, in this case, the
Dalzell Works was founded by David
Colville in 1871. When it was converted to
the production of steel in 1914, it became
the largest plant of its kind in the country.
Metal for the hulls of the liners *Queen Mary*
and *Queen Elizabeth* was forged here.

MOTTISFONT, Hampshire   *4 SU32*
Mottisfont Abbey (NT), near the River
Test, is a lovely sight – with elegant lawns,
some enormous old trees, and with water
meadows beyond. Founded by the Austin
Canons at the beginning of the 13th
century, Henry VIII gave the priory to his
Lord Chamberlain – William, Lord Sandys
– at the Dissolution. Sandys pulled down
much of it, and converted the nave of the
abbey church into a house.

MOUSEHOLE, Cornwall   *1 SW42*
This is a pretty, unembellished, little
village that used to thrive off its harvest of
pilchards. In 1595, four Spanish galleys
eluded the Elizabethan warships, and
landed 200 Spaniards – who burned
Mousehole to the ground. Only the 15th-
century Keigwin Arms (no longer a pub)
survived.

MUCHELNEY, Somerset   *3 ST42*
In Anglo-Saxon times, Muchelney was an
island surround by marshes. In about 697,
a monastery was founded here, the second-
oldest (Glastonbury is the oldest) in
Somerset. After the Dissolution, the
buildings (AM) fell into disrepair. The
Abbot's House, the reredorter (wash-
room), and a stone staircase, survive.

MUCH HADHAM, Hertfordshire
11 TL41

There are those who hold that Much Hadham is the prettiest village in Hertfordshire, and they may very well be right. The long main street is rich with Georgian and other period houses – nearly all of them worth a second glance. For nearly 900 years, Much Hadham was a manor of the Bishop of London, who used the Palace as his out-of-town retreat. It was also the birthplace of Edmund Tudor, father of Henry VII. The sculptor Henry Moore has made his home here, and two heads sculpted by him are in the church.

MUCH MARCLE, Hereford & Worcester
9 SO63

The 13th-century church with its sensitive 14th-century effigy of Blanche, Lady Grandison, and the alabaster tomb of Sir John Kyrle is one of the delights of this charming village, in the heart of the cider-making country.

MUCH WENLOCK, Shropshire
9 SJ60

Time has been gentle with Much Wenlock and it still preserves the atmosphere of a small medieval market town. The stocks still stand outside the Guildhall (OACT), which rests on wooden pillars, and the old Market Hall is now a museum. A lane leads to the ruins of St Mildburga's Priory, founded in the 11th century. Much Wenlock lies at the northern end of Wenlock Edge, the landscape celebrated in the poetry of A E Housman.

MULLION, Cornwall
1 SW61

Mullion is a small village on the Lizard peninsula, not, perhaps, the most beautiful in the county – though the church has a magnificent set of 16th-century bench ends, and parts of the tower are built from serpentine – that strange, multi-coloured stone peculiar to the Lizard.

MUMBLES, THE, W Glamorgan
7 SS68

The Mumbles are two islands, on the outer of which there is a lighthouse that was established in 1794 and now relies on an automatic light. The islands, and Oystermouth, are now a popular resort with a pier (1898), Winter Gardens, and vestiges of the Mumbles railway – which ran from Oystermouth to Mumbles Head (but was alas, axed in 1960). Oystermouth Castle ruins date from the 13th and 14th centuries.

MUNCASTER, Cumbria *18 SD19*

Muncaster Castle (OACT) stands on land that has been owned by the Pennington family since the 13th century. It was reconstructed in the 19th century but one of the original towers survives. It contains among many other things, a bowl presented by Henry VI, who found sanctuary there after his defeat at the Battle of Towton in 1464. This, known as the 'luck' of Muncaster, is said to ensure the unbroken succession of the Pennington family who have lived here since the 13th century. The grounds contain a bird garden, a bear garden (the inhabitants come from the Himalayas), and a flamingo pool. At Muncaster Mill (OACT), one mile away, you can buy stone-ground flour.

MUTHILL, Tayside *22 NN81*

Muthill was burned down by the Highlanders when they were retreating after their defeat at the Battle of Sheriffmuir in 1715. Later that century, the Earl of Perth rebuilt it. Nearby Drummond Castle (gardens OACT) was even less fortunate. In 1745, it was razed to the ground on the orders of the Jacobite Duchess of Perth. She was afraid that the Hanoverian troops might requisition it. The 70ft tower of the old church at Muthill (now abandoned) may have been erected on foundations laid in the 9th century.

MUCH MARCLE *The countryside around this little village is filled with apple orchards.*

NAILSWORTH, Gloucestershire
3 ST89

Nailsworth is an ancient wool town. The streets are steep and narrow with several nice examples of Georgian architecture. The former cloth mills are fascinating to anyone remotely interested in industrial archaeology, and the 1680 Friends' Meeting House deserves to be seen. The 'super-tramp' poet, W H Davies ('What is this life if, full of care, We have no time to stand and stare?') died here in 1940. Nailsworth Ladder, a hill with a 1 in 3 gradient, is used for car-testing.

NAIRN, Highland *26 NH85*

Nairn has sometimes been called 'the Brighton of the North'. As this suggests, it is a popular seaside resort – with three golf courses, and a climate that shows a surprising disposition to be sunny. The harbour, originally made to a plan by Thomas Telford, has since been enlarged. About three miles to the south, Rait Castle, a 14th-century ruin was the scene of a massacre of the Comyns by the Mackintoshes.

NASEBY, Northamptonshire *10 SP67*

Naseby is famous for its Civil War battle, which was fought in 1645. The Royalists might have fared better if Prince Rupert of the Rhine had resisted the temptation to ride off into the town and attack the Roundheads' baggage train – thus exposing a flank. But even the Royalist defeat was eclipsed by the capture of letters written by King Charles seeking help from foreign powers. The discovery caused many who hitherto had been indifferent to the outcome of the war to take Parliament's side. A memorial marks the scene of the affray and there is a Battle and Farm Museum nearby.

NAYLAND, Suffolk *12 TL93*

Nayland is a pretty village on the River Stour. It is mentioned in the Domesday Book as the Lordship of Eilanda: Eilanda, as the sound suggests, meaning 'island'. Set in lovely countryside, the village was a former centre of the cloth trade. The original wooden bridge over the river was maintained from the bequest of a wealthy clothier, John Able, who died in 1523, and was also a benefactor of the church. The altarpiece of the church is an early work of John Constable. It depicts the Last Supper.

NEATH, W Glamorgan *8 SS79*

Neath is a town with a split personality. The western part has become submerged beneath the pall of industry, which may have made economic sense, but does little to please the tourist. Eastwards, however, there are some green and pleasant valleys. The Romans, who established a base here and named it Nidum, have left no traces. But there are ruins of a castle, an abbey and a church – all of them 12th century – which are worth looking for.

PENDLE HILL *Near Nelson looms the bulk of Pendle Hill, once the haunt of the notorious Lancashire witches, sentenced to death in the 17th century.*

NEEDHAM MARKET, Suffolk
12 TM05
Joseph Priestley, a minister of the
Congregational Church at Needham
Market, was also a gifted scientist. In 1774,
he isolated a gas which he called
'dephlogisticated air'. Put another way
(which is the way most people have since
put it), he 'discovered' oxygen. Needham
Market, the village, is worth seeing – if only
for the wooden hammerbeam roof of its
15th-century church.

NELSON, Lancashire   *14 SD83*
Once there was just a public house – named
Nelson's Inn after the famous admiral. As
the 19th century progressed, a town grew
up around it, and was named Nelson. It
developed into an important cotton centre
and is usually linked with its neighbour,
Colne. To the north-west is Pendle Hill,
associated with the Lancashire witches.

NETHER ALDERLEY, Cheshire
14 SJ87
Alderley Old Mill (NT) was constructed in
the 15th century and was last operated
commercially in 1939. However, the
wooden waterwheels have been preserved
and so, too, has the machinery. It offers an
interesting glimpse of milling as it was.

NETHER STOWEY, Somerset   *2 ST13*
Samuel Taylor Coleridge wrote *The Ancient
Mariner* in this attractive village, and you
can visit his cottage (NT). The surrounding
Quantock Hills provide fine country for
excursions.

NETHER WALLOP, Hampshire
4 SU33
The name Wallop is derived from the
Anglo-Saxon, meaning 'valley of the
stream'. It is a lovely place with thatched
cottages, willow trees, trailing their
reflections in the water, and a winding lane
along which cars cannot go. The 15th-
century church utters a stern reminder with
a mural entitled 'A Warning to Sabbath

WITCHES

The popular image of the witch, with
cat and broomstick, never changes,
but the Lancashire witches were
quite ordinary women.

Breakers'. Bats made by Nether Wallop
craftsmen used to be the *sine qua non* of all
top cricketers – including W G Grace.

NETHER WINCHENDON,
Buckinghamshire   *4 SP70*
Nether Winchendon House (OACT) six
miles south-west of Aylesbury, is a Tudor
manor to which additions were made in the
18th century. Originally the home of
monks who served in the churches and
worked the land, it later became the
property of Sir Francis Bernard who, in
1758, was appointed governor of New
Jersey – and then of Massachusetts Bay
(1760). The house contains his maps and
several portraits.

NEVERN, Dyfed   *7 SN04*
Nevern gives the impression of being a shy
place, tucked away in a picturesque valley
300ft beneath the road. It is, perhaps, hard
to think of it as the capital of a kingdom –
albeit a small one. But such it was in about
1087 after Robert Fitzmartin of Tours had
landed at what is now Fishguard.

NEW ABBEY, Dumfries & Galloway
18 NX96
New Abbey is not, of course, new, nor is it
the name of the abbey. Sweetheart Abbey
(AM), called 'new' to avoid confusion with
nearby Dundrennan Abbey was founded in
1273 by Devorgilla, wife of John Balliol –
who created the Oxford college of that
name in her husband's memory and, after
his death, had his heart embalmed in a
silver and ivory casket and buried with her.
The red sandstone ruins are remarkably
beautiful. Just outside the village is
Shambellie House Museum of Costume,
which is run by the Royal Scottish
Museum.

NEWARK-ON-TRENT,
Nottinghamshire   *16 SK85*
The first recorded owner of Newark is that
celebrated lady, Godiva, wife of Mercia's
Earl Leofric. Remains of the 12th-century
castle notably the impressive main gateway
and chapel and the west wall, overlook this
attractive old town. During King John's
struggle with the barons, which concluded
with the signing of Magna Carta the barons
captured it, held it for a year, and lost it to
King John. It was here, in 1216, that he
died from overeating. The centre of
Newark is the cobblestoned market place
with its many interesting old inns. Lord
Byron lodged at the Clinton Arms
(formerly Kingston Arms) while
supervising publication of his first book of
poems. Gladstone, as an ambitious young
orator, uttered his first political speech
from one of the windows. There are two
museums – the District Council Museum
and the fascinating Millgate Museum of
Social and Folk Life. An interesting piece
of Victorian social history is the flamboyant
Ossington Coffee Palace, built to advance
the cause of temperance.

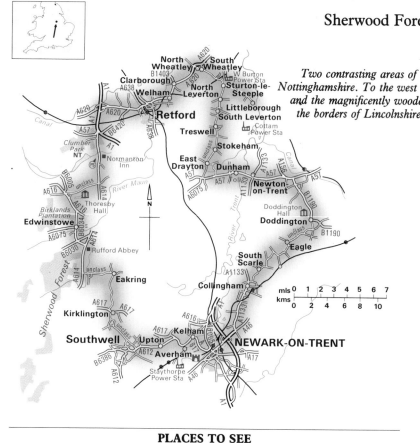

Sherwood Forest and the Trent Valley
73 miles

Two contrasting areas of countryside lend interest to this tour of Nottinghamshire. To the west is Robin Hood's country, Sherwood Forest and the magnificently wooded parks of the Dukeries: to the west, on the borders of Lincolnshire, the open country of the Trent Valley.

Leave **Newark** on the Lincoln road, A46, then at the roundabout follow Gainsborough signs to join A1133, and drive to **Collingham**. At the end of the village turn right (unclassified) for South Scarle then after ¼ mile, left. Reach a T-junction and turn right into the village of South Scarle. Follow Swinderby signs, then turn left, (SP Eagle). In ½ mile bear right, and at the T-junction turn right. In another ½ mile turn left (SP Lincoln), and in ¾ mile turn left again. From **Eagle** follow Lincoln signs, and in 1½ miles turn left (SP Doddington), then in ¾ mile left again. At **Doddington** continue on B1190, passing the Hall, and in 3 miles turn left on to A57. Drive past **Newton-on-Trent** and pass over a toll bridge to **Dunham**. 1¾ miles beyond the village turn right (unclassified) for East Drayton, then after a mile, left. At **East Drayton** church turn right and drive to **Stokeham**. Turn right (no sign), then left SP Leverton. Go on for 1¼ miles, and turn left into **Treswell**. Turn right for South Leverton, then continue through North Leverton to **Sturton-le-Steeple**. A detour, right, leads to Littleborough. From Sturton follow Gainsborough, then Wheatley signs and drive to South Wheatley. Here turn left to North Wheatley and at the junction with A620 turn left to **Retford**. Follow Worksop signs through the town and at the roundabout take the second exit. In 3¾ miles turn left (SP Newark) on to A1, and at the next roundabout follow Nottingham signs, A614, to enter Sherwood Forest. Pass the Normanton Inn and in 1½ miles at the crossroads turn right (unclassified) for **Thoresby Hall**. Carry on for 2 miles, then turn left on to A616, and in 1½ miles, right on to B6034 (SP Edwinstowe). Drive through **Edwinstowe**, and in 1 mile go over the crossroads, then turn right on to A614, pass Rufford Abbey and in 1¾ miles turn left (unclassified) to **Eakring**. From here follow Kirklington signs and on reaching the junction with A617 turn left, and before entering Kirklington, turn right (unclassified) for Southwell. Here turn right (unsigned) for the town centre. Leave on the Newark road, A612 for the return to Newark-on-Trent.

PLACES TO SEE

Newark-on-Trent Imposing remains of the castle (AM). There is a fascinating Museum of Social and Folk Life. The remarkable Ossington Coffee palace, a Victorian extravaganza, was built to advance the cause of Temperance.

Doddington Hall (OACT) is an Elizabethan Mansion with many Old Master portraits and fine furniture.

Littleborough King Harold and his Saxon Army crossed the Trent here on their way to the Battle of Hastings.

The Dukeries This is the name given to the northern part of Sherwood Forest, where 4 dukes bought estates in the 18th and 19th centuries.

Clumber Park The estate (NT) was created by the Duke of Newcastle in the 18th century. Trees he planted, especially the famous lime avenue can still be seen, but the house was demolished.

Thoresby Hall (OACT) is reputedly the largest Victorian house in England, standing in beautiful grounds. The interior is lavishly decorated.

Edwinstowe Birklands Plantation, the oldest part of Sherwood Forest, lies just outside the colliery village. In the Sherwood Country Park stands the famous Major oak, reputedly Robin Hood's hideout.

Rufford Abbey The grounds (OACT) of the ruined mansion built by Bess of Hardwick are now a country park.

Eakring One of Britain's oldest oilwells was first bored here in the 1920s. The village's rector was for a time William Mompesson, who had been the courageous vicar of Eyam during the Great Plague.

Southwell The great Minster Church is famous for the carvings in its chapter house.

NEWBURY, Berkshire 4 SU46
Now a pleasant market town and shopping centre, Newbury was formerly an important centre of the cloth trade. Its most famous citizen was Jack of Newbury who distinguished himself in peace and war. As a prosperous clothier, he financed the rebuilding of the church; as a warrior, he led 150 men at Flodden in 1513. The Jacobean Cloth Hall has been restored and is now a museum. The River Kennet, spanned by an 18th-century bridge, and the Kennet and Avon Canal add to the attractions, and Newbury racecourse is suitably frequented by characters that appear to have wandered out of the pages of a novel by Dick Francis.

NEWBY HALL, N Yorkshire 15 SE36
Robert Adam, architect to George III, MP for Kinross, and designer extraordinary of projects that included the streets of London and country mansions for the nobility and gentry, achieved one of his finest works at Newby Hall (OACT) in the early 18th century for coal magnate Sir Edward Blackett. Later that century, the house passed to William Weddle who, when making the Grand Tour of Europe, as almost every wealthy young gentleman did in those days, acquired the collection of sculpture now on display and a rare complete set of Gobelin tapestries. The gardens cover some 25 acres and contain a miniature railway.

NEWCASTLE EMLYN, Dyfed 7 SN34
Newcastle Emlyn, is a long street of pleasant houses leading down to the Teifi. The first printing press in Wales was installed here in 1718 by Isaac Carter and the first printed Welsh book produced in 1719 – an achievement recalled by a plaque mounted on the side of a house near the river. The castle, founded in the 13th century and extensively rebuilt in the 15th, was ruined in the Civil War. Felin Geri Mill, (OACT), two miles away is one of the last commercially operated watermills in the country producing stone-ground flour regularly. Visitors can see all stages of production and there is also a mill museum.

Northumbria's Capital

'Newcastle is a spacious, extended, infinitely populous place; 'tis seated upon the river Tyne, which is here a noble, large and deep river and ships . . . may come safely up to the very town.'
DANIEL DEFOE, *A Tour through the Whole Island*

Geordies, as Tynesiders call themselves, are a tough, resilient breed of people, with a taste for Newcastle Brown Ale, who speak an incomprehensible but lively dialect and traditionally work as miners, shipbuilders, or in heavy engineering. Their city, Newcastle, is a true regional capital, clinging to the north bank of the river and linked to the rest of England by seven bridges across the Tyne. The most famous is the great, arched suspension bridge that carried the A1, and the oldest is Robert Stephenson's high-level, combined road and rail bridge, erected in 1849. Between the two is the elegant swing bridge, turning on a central pivot, built in 1876. The other three bridges are 20th-century, one carrying the metro, Newcastle's most recent achievement, an over- and underground railway system which opened in 1980.

Newcastle began life as a Roman fort on Hadrian's Wall; later, a community of monks made a settlement here called Monkchester, and finally the Normans came and built their 'new' castle on the site of an old Roman fort. The castle keep and gatehouse remain today as museums, not far from the riverside. For centuries, the town lived on its river, confined within walls for protection against the Scots. All its finest pre-19th-century buildings are to be found in this area, notably the handsome 18th-century Guildhall; a group of tall, 17th-century merchants' houses on Sandhill; the beautiful elliptical Church of All Saints, now an urban studies centre; and St Nicholas' Cathedral, originally the parish church, built in the 14th century at a period when Newcastle was reckoned to be the third most prosperous town in

NEWCASTLE BROWN Geordies have made their local brew world-famous.

England. In Tudor times, the surrounding coalfields began to be exploited on a large scale – hence the expression 'coals to Newcastle' and the word 'Geordie', which originally meant 'pitman'. But the real boom came in the 19th century, with the development of heavy engineering and shipbuilding, and from this period, between 1825 and 1840, dates Newcastle's second phase of fine building, in a style that came to be known as 'Tyneside Classical'. This century has brought a third phase of building, and though some of the high-rise office blocks seem soulless, the new Civic Centre is impressive, as is the architecture of the nearby university and museum buildings.

THE TYNE BRIDGES *Seven bridges span the Tyne at Newcastle – the best known being the 'coathanger' suspension bridge.*

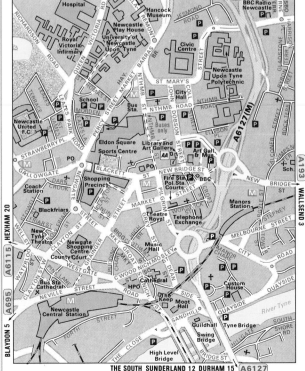

PLACES TO SEE

Black Gate Museum The 13th-century castle gatehouse houses Britain's only bagpipe museum – which of course lays special emphasis on Northumbrian pipes – though there are exhibits from all over the world.

Blackfriars This old Dominican priory used to be the temporary 'palace' of visiting royalty and Edward I received the King of Scotland here in 1334. It now houses a tourist and exhibition centre.

Castle Keep Begun in the reign of Henry II, the keep which, with the gatehouse, is the only part of the castle to survive, was restored in the 19th century; Great Hall, Garrison Room and Chapel can be visited.

John George Joicey Museum Housed in Holy Jesus Hospital, a 17th-century almshouse, the museum is devoted to city history and to the work of the engraver Thomas Bewick, who worked in Newcastle.

Hancock Museum This superb natural-history museum is named after John Hancock and houses his famous collection of birds.

Museum of Antiquities Part of the university complex, the museum has a fine collection of Roman relics.

Museum of Science and Engineering As befits a city of heavy engineering, the museum has more than 80 full-size engines on display.

LOST VILLAGES
Ghosts of the Past

Most people are surprised to learn that Britain contains the remains of thousands of lost villages, since the village is usually regarded as one of the most timeless and stable features in the countryside. However, ever since villages began to multiply, during the closing centuries of the Dark Ages, members of the village flock have fallen victims to the poverty of their lands, greedy landlords or the unfortunate accidents of fate. Only recently has it been realised that the deserted village is a very common feature of the landscape, and in recent decades the science of aerial photography has revealed thousands of unsuspected village relics, while new discoveries continue to be made.

THE NEW MONASTIC HOUSES which proliferated during the 12th and 13th centuries caused a number of villages to perish in their youth because they were too close to the religious communities. Most guilty were the Cistercians, whose rules required that their monks should avoid contacts with lay settlements. A few villages were removed in the course of building a monastery, but it was in the course of the creation of monastic agricultural empires that many more villages were demolished and superseded by monastic farms or 'granges'. A small flock of settlements perished in the course of monastic empire-building at Fountains and Rievaulx in Yorkshire and it is clear that the Cistercian perception of Christian charity was different from that of today, for the displaced villagers do not seem to have been given alternative homes.

CHANGING CONDITIONS account for the next and much more damaging wave of village destruction. During the early centuries of the Middle Ages, the population of Britain seems to have grown rapidly; farmland was in short supply and so new villages were established on the poorer, less rewarding lands. For a while the climate tended to encourage the colonisation of such lands, for it seems to have become progressively warmer during the years leading up to about 1200. Then, however, the climate began to deteriorate – and the brunt of these changes was borne by communities settled on exposed uplands and plateaux, or in clay vales where the soil became waterlogged and was slow to warm in spring. Peat spread across former pastures while crops stood unripened at the end of summer. Hundreds, perhaps thousands of villages were gradually abandoned in the face of unequal struggle; one such victim of the worsening climate was on Dartmoor, where the excavated and restored walls of peasant farmsteads lie a short walk beyond the bizarre rock formations of Hound Tor.

wherever they were of a reasonable quality. Cublington in Buckinghamshire is one village which was repopulated. Plague returned many times in the course of the Middle Ages and remained a terrifying scourge until the 17th century. Its indirect effects proved fatal for thousands of villages. Before 1348, the countryside was over-populated and labour was cheap. After the first onslaughts however, labour was suddenly in short supply and survivors responded by demanding higher wages and better terms of tenancy. In reply, many landowners chose to tear down the homes of their village tenants and labourers and convert the old croplands into sheep pastures. Wool fetched a very good price and a large flock could be managed by a handful of shepherds.

DELIBERATE CLEARANCE POLICIES in the Tudor and later periods resulted in the destruction of more English villages than any other single cause. During the 18th century, following the English victory at Culloden in 1746, many Scottish chiefs and lairds discovered that sheep paid better dividends than tenants, and so the grim saga of torn-down houses and homeless peasants was repeated. During the reign of Elizabeth I, the relative rise in grain prices and a long history of government attempts to end the destruction of villages gradually stemmed the tide of clearances, but further threats to the security and survival of the village were in store. During the Tudor period, the private castle had slipped into redundancy and the landowning aristocrats gradually began to discover the comforts associated with life in a prestigious and well-appointed mansion. As the fashion for great-house life developed in the 18th century, it became the norm for the mansion to be set at the heart of a vast expanse of landscaped parklands. Villages had no place in the designs of the fashion-conscious, and scores were removed in the quest for splendid isolation. This fashion continued into the early years of the 19th century, when it became increasingly normal for a replacement village to be provided outside the park for the dislodged tenants – though many communities had simply been turned out onto the roads. The now-attractive village of Milton Abbas results from the emparking of the small town of Milton; Castle Howard in Yorkshire is built almost upon the corpse of the village of Hinderskelfe, while New Houghton in Norfolk is a replacement for the original village of Houghton. Isolated churches can often be seen stranded in great parks, as at Holkham and Ickworth in Norfolk and these churches

usually mark the sites of the village victims of emparking. With the rise of democratic values during the 19th century, the destruction of villages became increasingly unacceptable, although in Scotland and Ireland, evictions continued into the early years of the 20th century. In modern times some villages have perished as the victims of unfortunate situations and circumstances. A number of narrowly-based coal mining and industrial villages have been abandoned as a result of changing economic conditions; a few villages, like West End in Yorkshire, have been destroyed in the course of reservoir construction, while several villages on the Salisbury Plain and the Brecklands of Norfolk were destroyed in the creation of military training areas.

VILLAGERS *abandon their homes in the 18th century (above). At Wharram Percy (below) in Yorkshire, detailed excavation is gradually revealing the history of village England.*

EXPLORERS OF LOST VILLAGE SITES can sometimes rediscover the lay-out of a deserted village by studying the patterns of bumps and hollows which cause undulations in the pasture. The hollow ways which mark former village streets often survive as U-shaped troughs, and so by noting their patterns one can often reconstruct the skeleton of roads and lanes. Where their remains have survived, overgrown peasant dwellings are usually represented by small rectangular platforms or depressions which lie beside the hollow ways, while fishponds are marked by low rectangular embankments, and the main pond was often flanked by two or three lesser ponds in which young fish were kept. Sometimes the margins of a medieval village were marked by embankments and other low banks often marked the divisions between different properties, while the appearance of the parallel corrugations of 'ridge and furrow' often marks the end of the former village and the start of its ploughland. Some deserted village sites lie far from the beaten track and farmers may discourage visitors. There are other accessible deserted medieval village sites that can be included among the most interesting and informative of antiquities. They include Hound Tor on Dartmoor, Egmere in Norfolk and Wharram Percy in Yorkshire, while of the recent village victims, the former quarrying village of Porth-y-Nant on the coast of the Lleyn peninsula in Wales is outstandingly attractive and well-preserved. The deserted villages also contain a wealth of information about medieval peasant life. Although the peasants owned nothing that would be of interest to modern treasure hunters, they entomb invaluable archaeological information.

LOST VILLAGES *include Knowlton in Dorset, whose ruined church stands inside the earthworks of a Neolithic henge, and West End in Yorkshire, drowned by the reservoir.*

THE BLACK DEATH, which arrived in 1348, solved the problem of over-population and land-shortage in the most terrible manner possible. In the years that followed, perhaps one-third to one-half of the British population fell victim to the plague. Surprisingly, however, the number of villages which can definitely be shown to be victims of the Black Death is relatively small. Where village remains are known to exist, local folklore almost invariably tends to present them as victims of the Black Death. As with most aspects of the distant past however, local mythology tends to be very unreliable, and the true story is much more interesting and complicated. It seems that although many villages did lose a large proportion or even all of their inhabitants, sooner or later settlers would move in and re-colonise the village lands

NEW FOREST PONIES *grazing with cattle on one of the broad New Forest heaths. Although not wild animals, they usually range freely in the forest.*

TROPICAL GIANTS *with wingspans up to 8 inches at the New Forest Butterfly Farm near Ashurst.*

NEWCASTLE-UNDER-LYME, Staffordshire   14 SJ84
A busy industrial centre, like those other towns of the north Midlands, Stoke-on-Trent and Crewe, Newcastle is very much a creation of the 19th century, and the nearby university at Keele has brought it a new vitality. The castle has all but vanished – only a wall remains, in Queen Elizabeth Park – and the 'Lyme' is of more obscure derivation, but probably refers to the Lyme Brook. The Borough Museum in Brampton Park contains an interesting display of Royal Charters and the Hobbergate Art Gallery a good collection of English watercolours.

NEWCASTLE UPON TYNE see p. 187

NEWENT, Gloucestershire   9 SO72
On the Cliffords Mesne road from Newent, and about a mile from this peaceful little market town in the heart of rural Gloucestershire, lies the unique Birds of Prey Conservation and Falconry Centre. Here will be found one of the largest collections of birds of prey in the world, with aviaries and a brooder room to visit. Visitors can study the ancient art of falconry and, weather permitting, see these graceful and fascinating birds of prey in flight.

NEW FOREST, THE, Hampshire   4
The New Forest covers approximately 145 square miles between the River Avon and Southampton Water. Partly owned by the Crown, it is a mixture of wood and heathland. William I appropriated it in 1079 and designated it a royal hunting preserve, imposing fierce penalties on local villagers – death for killing deer, blinding merely for disturbing them. Five common rights survived and in many cases still survive for the inhabitants of the Forest: pannage, the right to let pigs forage; turbage, the right to cut peat or turves; estover, the right to cut firewood; marl, the right to improve the soil, and pasturage, the right to graze stock. The most famous event associated with the Forest is the shooting of William Rufus (described as 'loathsome to well nigh all his people') by Walter Tirel, an obelisk marks the spot where he is thought to have fallen. Eventually, in the Tudor period, deer ceased to be protected because of the importance of New Forest timber for building warships. Herds of red, roe and fallow deer roam freely, as do the famous ponies. Verderers' Courts, which administer Forest laws, are held at **Lyndhurst**, one of the prettiest towns.

NEWHAVEN, E Sussex   5 TQ40
Newhaven owes its role as a Channel port to a freak of nature: until 1570, the River Ouse had entered the sea at Seaford, but one night, a tempest suddenly changed the geography, diverting the river three miles to a point near its present mouth. Thus Newhaven was born – though, to begin with, its trade was confined to barges making their way up the Ouse to Lewes. However, by the end of the 19th century, the London, Brighton and South Coast railway was running a regular steamer service to Dieppe. Fort Newhaven Museum is housed in a Victorian fort.

NEW LANARK, Strathclyde   22 NS84
New Lanark was the creation of a Glasgow merchant, David Dale, who acquired what was then swampland in the 18th century as a site for textile mills, which he built in partnership with Richard Arkwright. He also began to build cottages for his workforce, who were mostly dispossessed crofters, forced to abandon their homes in the notorious Clearances. Some years after, Robert Owen, the Lancashire cotton master married Dale's daughter and came

to live at New Lanark. An enlightened man, years in advance of his time, Owen abolished child labour at New Lanark, built schools, operated company shops on principles later adopted by the co-operative movement, and improved housing, making New Lanark a 'model' community. Owen's partners were not the same sort of men as he, and in 1825 he was forced to resign, and his great social experiment was abandoned. The New Lanark Association now owns village and mills and is restoring them.

NEWLYN, Cornwall   1 SW42
Newlyn has virtually been absorbed by Penzance, though it remains Cornwall's premier fish landing port. There used to be a colony of artists in residence during the 19th and early 20th centuries: the Passmore Edwards gallery recalls their work. The artists now prefer St Ives.

NEWMARKET, Suffolk   12 TL66
James I discovered Newmarket: he built a palace there as a base for his hunting and hawking expeditions and when, in 1619, the first horse race took place on Newmarket Heath, His Majesty was a delighted spectator. Charles II did rather better: he actually rode in events. In 1752, the Jockey Club (the ruling body of the Turf) took note of Newmarket's importance and moved its headquarters from the Star and Garter Inn in London. Nowadays, the statistics that proclaim this town on the Suffolk/Cambridgeshire border as the capital of the racing world are impressive. There are more than 40 training stables, 1500 race horses in residence, two race courses, more than 4000 race horses sold each year for a sum adding up to several million pounds, and 35 stud farms. The National Stud and the Equine Research Station are situated here. Newmarket's most famous races are the One Thousand and Two Thousand Guineas (both held in the spring), the Cesarewich and Cambridgeshire (in October). Newmarket's elegant Regency Assembly Rooms are the home of the National Racing Museum, recently opened. Exhibits include famous racing silks, paintings, and equine equipment and memorabilia of all sorts.

NEWMARKET
One of many historic prints at the National Racing Museum, this one shows Persimmon, the 1896 Derby winner, with the future Edward VII.

NEWPORT, Dyfed   7 SN03
The Welsh name for Newport (Dyfed) is
Trefdraeth, meaning 'town on the sands',
which is an appropriate name, as Newport
stand on the Nevern estuary beside the
well-known Newport Sands. Its importance
as a port is now a matter of history, but it is
a very pleasant resort. The castle, as so
often in Wales, is the most interesting
feature of the town.

NEWPORT, Essex   11 TL53
Lying peacefully beside the River Cam,
this village is one of the more sightly
adornments of the Essex landscape. There
are several timbered houses that deserve
attention – notably Crown House and
Monks Barn. The Links, which is
Georgian, used to be the House of
Correction or Workhouse. The 13th-
century church contains an old chest of the
same date with some interesting early
paintings. The delightfully named Mole
Hole Wildlife Park (OACT) occupies the
grounds of an Elizabethan manor.

NEWPORT, Gwent   8 ST38
A fast-growing, modern town, Newport
was originally called Gwynllyw after the
Christian warrior who governed the town
and was eventually canonised. The Norman
cathedral is dedicated to Gwynllyw –
though they now refer to him as St Woolos.
The 15th-century castle, now ruined,
controls the river crossing. The poet W H
Davies, author of *Autobiography of a Super-
Tramp*, was born here and is
commemorated by a bust in the town's
museum. Tredegar House (OACT) is
accounted the finest Restoration house in
Wales. Parts date back to the 16th century
and it is set in lovely grounds.

NEWPORT, Shropshire   9 SJ71
A small market town of handsome red brick
houses, set back from a spacious High
Street, Newport dates from the 17th
century and later, most of the medieval
town having been swept away by fire in
1665. The Royal Victoria Hotel opened in
1830 as the Union Hotel, but only two years
later changed its name by permission of the
then Princess, later Queen Victoria, who
had stayed there for a night on her visit to
the town.

NEWQUAY, Cornwall   1 SW86
Good bathing, excellent surfing and a
favourable climate combine to make
Newquay one of the most popular resorts in
Cornwall. Its sandy beach is backed by tall
cliffs, pierced with enticing caves. Evidence
of Newquay's past as a fishing port when
pilchards were plentiful is provided by the
Old Huer's Hut on the cliffs. The Huer was
the man who kept watch for the appearance
of the shoals and warned the fishermen to
make ready. Trenance Park, in a valley to
the east of the town, is the setting for
Newquay Zoo.

NEW QUAY, Dyfed   7 SN35
New Quay is a small seaside town that has
been described as 'rather Cornish looking' –
doubtless on account of the curving stone
pier that gives its protection to the snug
little harbour. The houses, many of them
Georgian and 19th-century, parade in well-
drilled ranks on the lower slopes of 300ft
Pencraig Hill. The sands are good; the
prospect, on the whole, is pleasing.

Cornwall's Atlantic Coast
40 miles

*From Newquay southwards to the promontory of St Agnes Head, the beaches of the
North Cornish coast, where the long Atlantic rollers race in towards the shore, offer
ideal conditions for surfing. Inland, the hills are dotted with the evocative ruins of the
engine houses of worked-out tin mines.*

Leave **Newquay** on A392 Bodmin road to
Quintrel Downs roundabout, and continue
on A3058 (SP St Austell). In ¾ mile turn
right (SP Newlyn East) and in 1 mile keep
left, pass Trerice Manor, then in a mile at
the crossroads turn left, and in ¾ mile
turn right at the T-junction (for a detour to
the Lappa Valley Railway turn left, SP
Benny Mill, here). Enter **St Newlyn East**
and bear right, then go over the crossroads
(SP Truro) to Fiddler's Green and turn
left. In 1¼ miles go over the crossroads
(SP Zelah) then turn right on to A30 to
reach **Zelah**. Continue for ½ mile, then at
the crossroads turn left (unclassified, SP
Shortlanesend), and at the Shortlanesend
Inn join B3284 and continue into **Truro**.
Leave the city on A390 following Redruth
signs, and continue for 3 miles to the
roundabout. Go forward here,
then at the next roundabout
take the 2nd main exit, B3277
(SP St Agnes). At **St Agnes**,

follow the Perranporth road, B3285
through Trevellas to **Perranporth**, then
continue on the Newquay road to
Goonhavern, where turn left on to A3075.
Continue for 2½ miles, then turn left
(unclassified) to **Cubert**. Holywell Bay
lies straight ahead, but the main drive
turns right for Crantock, and follows the
Newquay road again. In ¾ mile turn
left, then in 1 mile further left
again on to A3075 for the
return journey to
Newquay.

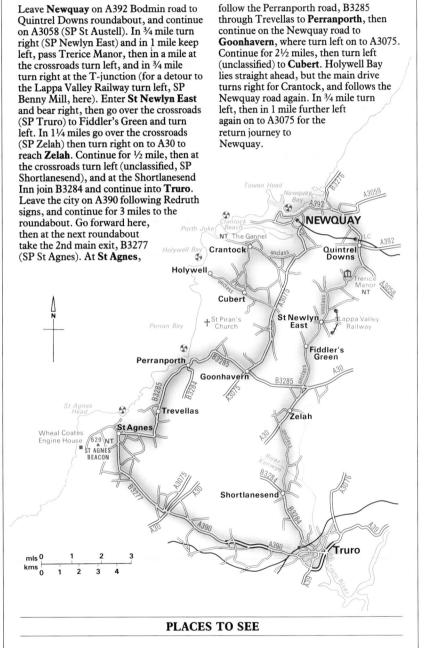

PLACES TO SEE

Newquay A popular resort with fine
beaches and cliff scenery. At Trenance
Gardens is an amusement park and zoo.

Trerice Manor (NT) Surrounded by terraced gardens, dates from 1573 and has
fine moulded ceilings.

Lappa Valley Railway Old steam trains
travel through lovely countryside.

Truro Cornwall's unofficial capital and
cathedral city. The cathedral was built in
1880 of local granite. The County Museum
has a superb collection of minerals.

St Agnes To the west of this charming
village is St Agnes Beacon (NT) on the
promontory of St Agnes Head. On the
cliffs is the ruined Wheal Coates Engine
House (NT). To the north is lovely Tre-
vaunance Cove.

Perranporth The 3-mile stretch of sandy
beach, ideal for surfing, is what attracts
visitors to Perranporth.

Crantock Crantock Beach, on the Gannel
estuary, is becoming a popular resort. The
countryside on the south of the estuary
belongs to the National Trust.

NEW ROMNEY, Kent *6 TR02*
New Romney was one of the original Cinq Ports; but nature interfered in 1287, changing the coastline and leaving the town high and dry one mile from the sea. However, the upheaval indirectly produced Romney Marsh (important sheep farming country) of which New Romney is, so to speak, the capital. There were once five churches in the town. Now there is only one: the parish church of St Nicholas, in which the mayor is still elected. The station is an important feature of that delightful mini-railway, the Romney, Hythe and Dymchurch.

NEWSTEAD, Nottinghamshire
15 SK55
Newstead Abbey (OACT), set in a wooded park nine miles from Nottingham, was founded in 1170 by Henry II for Augustinian canons. After the Dissolution, it was given to Sir John Byron, an ancestor of the famous poet, who could not afford to live in the ancestral home until 1808, and even then, he was heavily in debt. Some years later, when he left England for good, Byron sold the property to an old school friend but the house has much Byroniana, including the table on which *Childe Harold* was written and an elaborate grave in the grounds to his Newfoundland dog, Boatswain. The famous 19th-century missionary David Livingstone wrote his journals here.

NEWTON ABBOT, Devon *1 SX87*
When the railway came to Newton Abbot, the town was transformed from a sleepy little place into an important junction and a lively market town. It also served as a centre for the clay mines between Kingsteignton and Bovey Tracey. Forde House, in the centre, provided Charles I with overnight accommodation (in 1625) and, later, William of Orange, who was on his way to London. The town's name, incidentally, orginated in the 13th century. It was the 'new town' of the abbot of Torre Abbey. Nowadays, it is a gathering point for tourists, either bound for the coast or for Dartmoor. Bradley Manor (NT), a 15th-century house with an interesting Great Hall, lies in the valley of the River Lemon.

NEWTONMORE, Highland *26 NN79*
Newtonmore is the most southerly of the Speyside resorts: a base for skiing and pony-trekking. It was, indeed, here that in 1952, the latter activity was introduced to Britain. There are some good rides into the black Monadhliath Mountains and some fine views of the Cairngorms. The exhibits in the Clan Macpherson Museum include a gift from a fairy to the clan, known as the Black Charter.

NEWTON STEWART, Dumfries & Galloway *17 NX46*
At Newton Stewart you can visit a mill and watch mohair rugs and scarves being made; you can admire the 57ft edifice erected in 1875 to honour the 5th Earl of Galloway (Stewart is the family name: one of his ancestors persuaded Charles II to grant the town a charter), and the bridge spanning the River Cree designed by John Rennie. Newton Stewart is a most attractive little market town, a good centre from which to walk and explore.

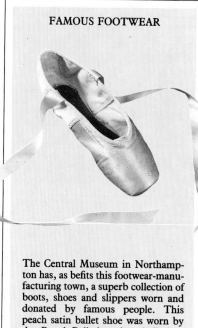

FAMOUS FOOTWEAR

The Central Museum in Northampton has, as befits this footwear-manufacturing town, a superb collection of boots, shoes and slippers worn and donated by famous people. This peach satin ballet shoe was worn by the Royal Ballet's prima ballerina, Dame Margot Fonteyn, and is autographed by her.

NEWTOWN, Powys, *8 SO19*
Newtown is the second largest town in north Powys. It used to be an important flannel and tweed manufacturing centre; nowadays, much of its wealth is accounted for by its role as market place to the surrounding sheep farming and agricultural community. Edward I granted it a charter – largely because he saw it as a good point from which to control a ford across the Severn. In those days, it was known as Llanfair until, in the 16th century, it was referred to as Nova Villa. This, perhaps, was harping too much on any Roman origins it may have had, and it soon became translated into Newtown. Robert Owen, the reformer who brought humanity to the employment of textile workers was born and died here and is commemorated in the Robert Owen Museum.

NIGG, Highland *30 NH87*
Overlooking Nigg bay on the Cromarty Forth, the 7th-century church is reputed to commemorate one of three sons of a Danish king, drowned not far away. Nowadays, North Sea Oil has made its mark on Nigg – in the shape of the world's largest dock, used for the construction of offshore production platforms.

NORFOLK WILDLIFE PARK (Great Witchingham), Norfolk *12 TG12*
Covering 50 acres, this contains a fine collection of British and European mammals, which are allowed to live in natural surroundings. There is also a great variety of birds, including peacocks and ornamental pheasants.

NORHAM, Northumberland *24 NT94*
The castle (AM) stands proud upon a rocky outcrop, lording it over the River Tweed (the impressive view was painted by Turner). Built in 1160 by the Bishop of Durham, it is now in ruins – but they are very fine ruins and, in 1900, an attempt was made at restoration.

NORTHAMPTON, Northamptonshire
10 SP76
Northampton's long connection with the now beleaguered boot and shoe trade can be said to have started in the Civil War when the town made footwear for Cromwell's army. The trade flourished, and during the Napoleonic Wars Northampton again made army boots. Fittingly, both the town's museums have large collections: footwear at the Central Museum, with such famous items as Nijinsky's ballet shoes and Queen Victoria's wedding shoes on display; other sorts of leather at the Leathercraft Museum. Northampton is an ancient town with many handsome buildings, mostly dating from the 17th century and later. It has several imposing churches including All Saints, rebuilt after a devastating fire in 1675, and Holy Sepulchre, one of the few surviving round churches in England, founded in the 12th century on the model of the Holy Sepulchre at Jerusalem. Delapre Abbey (OACT) a mainly 17th-century house, is now the County Records Office. The vast market square is thought to be the largest in the country and dates from the days of the cattle drovers when Northampton was an important market. Abington Park Museum, set in landscaped grounds, is an old manor house with interesting collections of porcelain, lace and toys.

NORTH BERWICK, Lothian *24 NT58*
North Berwick is an ancient royal burgh 23 miles from Edinburgh. It is a popular seaside resort and a residential area for commuters to the city. Among its attractions are two particularly good golf courses. One mile south, a volcanic hill named North Berwick Law (613ft) has the ruins of a watch tower on its summit (used during the Napoleonic Wars) and an archway constructed from the jawbone of a whale. Bass Rock, 3 miles out to sea is one mile in circumference and has a famous lighthouse. For a while after 1671, the rock was used as a place of imprisonment for Covenanters. Bass Rock and the other Firth of Forth islands, Fidra and Eyebroughty, are now a nature reserve. Tantallon Castle (AM), ruined by General Monk in 1651, commands a wild headland three miles east of the town.

NORTH DOWNS, THE, Kent and Surrey *5, 6*
This range of rolling chalk hills was the northern edge of a great dome that, 140 million years ago, covered all south-east England and joined it to France. It, and the **South Downs**, are all that remains, the highest point is near Woldingham (900ft) and has a large chalk pit at its base. Box Hill (nearly 600ft) is particularly beautiful. The Pilgrim's Way, along which the devout travelled from Winchester to Canterbury, follows the Downs for part of its route. The North Downs reach an abrupt but impressive conclusion in the white cliffs of Dover.

NORTH ELMHAM, Norfolk *12 TF92*
North Elmham used to be the site of an Anglo-Saxon cathedral (AM) indeed, it was the headquarters of the See of Norfolk before the Normans moved it to Norwich in 1095. In 1307, a bishop converted the building into a moated house. Now only the ruins remain, dating from the early 11th century and of great architectural interest.

THE ANDERTON BOAT LIFT *just outside Northwich lifts boats from the River Weaver Navigation to the Trent and Mersey Canal. A unique piece of engineering, it was built in 1875.*

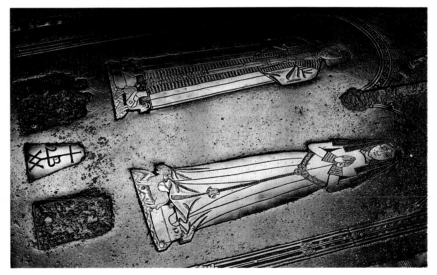

NORTHLEACH CHURCH *This brass of Thomas and Joan Bushe dates from the heyday of the wool trade.*

NORTHIAM, E Sussex 6 TQ82

A pretty little village in the Rother Valley, Northiam's old houses cluster round the traditional village green, shaded by an ancient oak tree under whose branches Elizabeth I is reputed to have breakfasted. Great Dixter (OACT) a 15th-century timbered manor house with a unique great hall, was restored by Sir Edwin Lutyens, who consulted the famous Gertrude Jekyll about the planting of the lovely gardens. Brickwall (OACT), now a school, is a 17th-century Jacobean house with 18th-century gardens.

NORTHLEACH, Gloucestershire 10 SP11

Northleach used to one of the most prosperous Cotswold wool towns: and this wealth is reflected in the permanence of its attractive old buildings. The great 15th-century church, with its clerestory, its vaulted roof, its brasses remembering bygone woolstaplers, and the touches of humour in its carvings is almost the definitive wool church. The Cotswold Countryside Collection, a fascinating series of exhibits, is housed in the former House of Correction.

NORTHUMBERLAND NATIONAL PARK 19, 24

Covering 398 square miles, the National Park boundaries are the Cheviot Hills in the north and Hadrian's Wall in the south. This is magnificent, sparsely populated hill country, where the remains of ancient hill forts and cup-and-ring-marked stones, testify to the presence of early settlers. The long-distance footpath, the Pennine Way passes through the park, and there are Information Centres at Byreness, Ingram and Rothbury.

NORTHWICH, Cheshire 14 SJ67

Northwich's motto is *Sal est Vita*, which means to say 'salt is life'. And so it is for this Cheshire town which sits on top of huge rock-salt beds. Salt-mining has been a major industry since Roman times, and much of it is bought by the chemical industry. Not far away is the remarkable Anderton boat-lift. This remarkable piece of engineering was assembled in 1875 to raise (and lower) barges of up to 100 tons (and pleasure craft) a height of 50ft from the River Weaver to the Trent and Mersey Canal at the top of the hill above Anderton. Arley Hall (OACT) is an impressive Victorian house, set in lovely gardens five miles north of the town, and Vale Royal Abbey (OACT), is a 16th-century house built on the site of a Cistercian Abbey.

NORTH WOOTTON, Somerset 3 ST54

Here, at North Town House three miles from Wells, a vineyard flourishes in the Mendips. The 9000 vines were imported from the Rhine and Alsace. The old farm buildings house a winery in which a dry white wine is produced – and one that does credit to its Continental origins. You can stroll through the vineyards and buy wine direct from the cellar.

NORTH YORK MOORS NATIONAL PARK 16, 20

This area, designated a National Park in 1952, covers 550 square miles extending from the Cleveland and Hambleton Hills, the highest ground, to the coast north of Scarborough and to the Vale of Pickering in the south. The colours on the predominantly high ground range from the purple of heather in August to the bronze of dying bracken in autumn. Attractive, steep-sided valleys break up the mass: moorland villages, early Christian crosses and the ruins of abbeys are scattered sparsely across the landscape. The Cleveland Way circles the northern edges of the Park, and the 40-mile Lyke Wake Walk crosses the moors from Osmotherley to Ravenscar. The North Yorkshire Moors Railway travels from **Pickering**.

NORTON ST PHILIP, Somerset 3 ST75

At Norton St Philip The George Inn is one of the most interesting medieval inns in Britain. The building began its life in 1230 as guest house run by the monks of Hinton Priory, two miles away, and assumed its present role after the Dissolution in 1539. The ill-fated Duke of Monmouth stayed here in 1685. In 1688, Pepys and his wife stayed here and on a tour of the village, the diarist noticed an unusual plaque in the church – commemorating unfortunate twin ladies who shared a common stomach.

Norfolk's Capital and Holiday Resorts
79 mile

Between Norwich, East Anglia's lovely regional capital, and Gt Yarmouth, most popular of all the resorts of the north-east coast, lie the watery channels and man-made lakes of the Norfolk Broads; within the triangle completed by Cromer, in the north, lies a holidaymaker's paradise where yachtsmen, anglers, sunbathers and swimmers find all they need.

Leave **Norwich** on A47, the Yarmouth road, and drive through Thorpe St Andrew and Blofield to **Acle**. Continue through Acle, still on the Yarmouth road, to reach **Gt Yarmouth**. Leave the town on the Caister road (A149), and go forward at the roundabout to enter **Caister-on-Sea**. Here turn left on to the Acle road. Take the 2nd exit (A1064) at the roundabout and drive past the entrance to Caister Castle, then take the next right (unclassified, SP Gt Ormesby). In 1 mile turn left to enter **Ormesby St Margaret**, and at the War Memorial turn right (SP Scratby), drive beside the green, then turn left. At the next T-junction turn right for **Hemsby**, at the far side of which turn left on to B1159 (SP Mundesley). Follow a winding road through Winterton, and West Somerton, then continue with Cromer signs to Sea Palling. Drive on for 1¾ miles, then turn right and pass through Lessingham to Happisburgh. After 1½ miles at the crossroads turn right for Walcott. Continue to **Bacton**, passing the remains of a priory then in ¼ mile turn right, and continue with B1159 through **Mundesley**, Trimingham and Overstrand to **Cromer**. Leave Cromer on A149, the Norwich road, and in 2¼ miles bear left. (SP North Walsham). Drive through Thorpe Market to **North Walsham** town centre and follow Norwich signs, B1150. Continue through Coltishall and Horstead back to Norwich.

PLACES TO SEE

Norwich One of the most lovely of England's regional capitals, Norwich's magnificent cathedral dates from the Norman period, as does the Castle (OACT), now a museum with a fine collection of paintings by Crome, Cotman and others. There are also interesting museums: local crafts and trades in the Bridewell and period rooms in Strangers Hall. At the University of East Anglia is the modernistic Sainsbury Centre for the Visual Arts.

Gt Yarmouth Five miles of sea front and many amusements cater for holidaymakers. In the Rows, the 300-year-old Merchant's House (AM) has been restored; the Elizabethan House contains a museum of local interest; the Tollhouse Museum has old dungeons, the Maritime Museum for East Anglia traces the history of herring fishery etc. Anna Sewell, author of *Black Beauty* was born in a house (OACT) near the parish church in 1820.

Caister Castle (OACT) was the home of Sir John Fastolf, model for Shakespeare's Falstaff. In the grounds is a motor museum.

Ormesby Broad There are 30 or so 'Broads' as these sheets of water created by ancient man in his excavation of peat, are called, and Ormesby Broad is one of the most attractive.

Happisburgh Pronounced 'Hazeboro', this little resort has a sandy beach, backed by extensive dunes, and a lighthouse.

Bacton The village is dominated by the huge North Sea gas terminal that stands high on the coast.

Cromer Famous for its excellent crabs, Cromer has fine Victorian hotels, a pier and a small zoo. The parish church has one of the tallest towers in Norfolk.

NOSTELL, W Yorkshire   *15 SE41*
Nostell Priory (NT) was built as a house in 1733 on the site of an Augustinian Priory, and about 30 years later Robert Adam remodelled a large part of it. There are many good paintings and some excellent Chippendale furniture, as well as murals executed by Angelica Kauffmann.

NOTTINGHAM, Nottinghamshire
10 SK54
Boots, Players and Raleigh are among some of the firms that have made Nottingham into a modern city, proudly proclaiming itself as 'Queen of the Midlands'. A more traditional industry is lace-making, and the old Lace Market still survives in the centre of the town. Nottingham Castle (OACT), which used to feature on Players' cigarette packets, crowns a high sandstone ridge overlooking the city. King John commanded it while Richard the Lionheart was occupied with the Crusades, and in this period the legends of Robin Hood and the Sheriff of Nottingham gained popularity. The Trip to Jerusalem Inn, built into the sides of the cliff, claims to be England's oldest inn, but there are several other contenders for the title. The great domed Council House stands on the site of Nottingham's famous Goose Fair, which is still held annually in October. St Mary's Church, in the Lace Market is a noble 15th-century edifice and contains a painting of the Madonna and Child by Fra Bartolomeo. The Brewhouse Yard Museum depicts life in bygone times, with 'period' rooms and cottage gardens; the Canal Museum depicts the history of the River Trent; the Industrial Museum and the Museum of Costume and Textiles portray the history of trade and industry in the city, and the Natural History Museum is housed in 16th-century Wollaton Hall. Four miles east of Nottingham is the Holme Pierrepont Hall (OACT) a Tudor manor house with a fine collection of English oak furniture.

NUNEATON, Warwickshire   *10 SP39*
Nuneaton today is largely dedicated to the manufacture of bricks, woollen goods and hats. There are some pleasing oddities in the town centre, such as the Leeds Permanent Building Society office which, unaccountably, has a spire, and the National Westminster Bank that, in 1909 demonstrated that Queen Anne architecture didn't die with Queen Anne. George Eliot was born in 1819 at one of the farms on Arbury Hall (OACT) estate. The Hall is an outstanding example of 18th-century Gothick architecture and interior design.

NUNNEY, Somerset   *3 ST74*
The village is delightful; the castle, before it was pounded by Roundhead cannon in the Civil War, must have been a little on the grim side. Built as a fortified house in 1373, it is said to have been modelled on the Bastille in Paris. Although there is no yardstick against which to measure it, the moat is thought to be the deepest in England.

NUNNINGTON, N Yorkshire   *16 SE67*
Nunnington Hall (NT) is a 16th- and 17th-century house with a fine panelled hall and an impressive staircase. The Carlisle Collection of Miniature Rooms should be seen. The nearest town is Helmsley.

Cathedral City on the Wensum

'On the Castle hill you see the whole City at once, . . . a rich, thriveing industrous place; Satturday is their great market day; . . . there is also a fine large Cathedrall and very lofty . . .'

CELIA FIENNES, *Journeys*

One of England's most attractive provincial capitals, Norwich lies on the River Wensum, a compact cathedral city which bears the marks, in many fine and ancient buildings, of 1000 years of history. If a city can be said to have a colour, then that of Norwich is yellow – from the mustard milled by Messrs Colman, whose quaint Old Mustard Shop in Bridewell Alley is a major tourist attraction – and from the Norwich canary, a breed which the locals developed from the cage birds originally imported by the 'strangers', as the Flemish weavers who settled in the city were known: 'Canaries' is now the nickname of the Norwich football team, who wear a yellow and green strip.

The city centre is the wide, sloping market place, overlooked at one end by the stern keep of the Norman castle, raised high on a mound; at the other by the neo-Egyptian City Hall. Norwich has a large and colourful produce market (daily except Sundays), where the choice of fruit and vegetables must be the best on offer anywhere outside London. Around the market place is a network of charming old streets, alleys and arcades, partly closed to traffic, that make shopping a pleasure. Most picturesque of all, and featured on many a calendar, Elm Hill, a steep, narrow, cobbled street, lined with pretty cottages, leads down to Tombland. This wide street was the old market place, and two imposing medieval gateways give access to the Cathedral Close. The Cathedral, crowned by a 315ft spire, added in the 15th century, is surrounded by a large and beautiful Close, whose green lawns run down to the Wensum at Pull's Ferry, a 15th-century watergate, often painted by the artists of the Norwich School, whose leading figures were John Sell Cotman and John Crome.

The city has rightly made great efforts to preserve its past and has won several Heritage Awards, but some of the new buildings are adventurous in design – particularly those at the University of East Anglia, by Sir Denys Lasdun, and the gleaming aluminium-clad Sainsbury Centre for the Visual Arts an art gallery and study centre designed by Norman Foster.

PLACES TO SEE

Norwich Castle The 12th-century keep contains a museum of local and natural history, and an outstanding collection of paintings by Crome, Cotman and others of the Norwich School.

The Guildhall Built by forced labour in the 15th century, in a distinctive chequered flint pattern, this is now used as a Magistrates' Court, but is open when the court is not sitting.

The Assembly Rooms This gracious 17th- and 18th-century building is used for exhibitions, and the spacious Music Room is a restaurant.

Strangers' Hall This rambling, 14th- and 15th-century building, named after the immigrant Flemish weavers who settled in the area, houses a folk museum with many period rooms, displays of toys and costumes and old shop signs.

Bridewell Museum A flint-face medieval merchant's house, used as a bridewell from 1583 to 1828, the building now contains a fascinating museum of crafts.

St Peter Hungate Church A museum of church art is housed in this fine, 15th-century, now redundant, church.

Norwich Cathedral Built of stone specially imported from Caen in Normandy by the first Bishop of Norwich, Herbert de Losinga, the cathedral is a masterpiece of Gothic architecture. Its cloisters, the largest in Europe, and its lofty, vaulted nave and chancel are ornamented with 600 finely carved roof bosses.

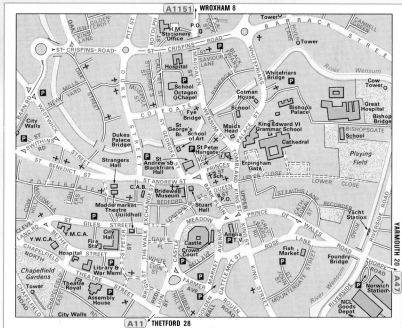

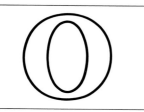

OAKHAM, Leicestershire 10 SK80

Oakham is now in Leicestershire, but locals do not forget that they belong to the vanished county of Rutland, and that Oakham is their county town. It is a most attractive old place, preserving its ancient stocks under the equally ancient buttercross in the cobbled market square. There has been a castle here since before the Conquest, but all that now remains is the 12th-century aisled hall, where there is a unique collection of horseshoes, dating perhaps from the 11th century when William I's farrier lived here, collecting a horseshoe from every noble or royal person who passed through the town. Rutland County Museum used to be housed in the old 16th-century schoolroom of Oakham Grammar School, but is now in a former indoor riding school. Rutland Farm Park on Uppingham Road is a working farm with many rare breeds of animals. Britain's largest man-made lake, Rutland Water, lies between Oakham and Stamford, and is a favourite local beauty spot.

OLD SARUM *Remains of the Norman keep on its fortified mound and of the cathedral abandoned by Bishop Poore in 1220 show up clearly on aerial photographs after more than 700 years.*

OAKHAM'S HORSESHOES

Horseshoes of many centuries and from many donors decorate the walls of the castle. Among them is one given by Elizabeth I; another by her namesake, Queen Elizabeth II.

OAKHILL, Somerset 3 ST64

The Mendip Hills near Bath are the setting for this pleasant country estate. Oakhill Manor (OACT) is a delightful house, and the gardens feature an extensive collection of model transport.

OARE, Somerset 2 SS84

Set in the heart of 'Lorna Doone' country, Oare's tiny church was, in the novel, the scene of Lorna's marriage to Jan Ridd. All around is some of the most beautiful countryside in Exmoor, and just west of the village a footpath leads up the valley of Badgworthy Water to Lank and Hoccombe Combes, which were R D Blackmore's models for Doone Valley.

OBAN, Strathclyde 25 NM83

Oban's most distinctive feature is McCaig's Folly – a mock Roman coliseum set high on a hill overlooking the town. A local banker conceived the idea as a memorial to his family and to give employment to local craftsmen during the slump of the 1890s. He intended it as a museum and art gallery, but unfortunately it was never finished. Oban is a popular Highland resort, with all the usual amenities, including golf, and is an ideal base for exploring the beautiful countryside of Lorne. Games Day, or the Argyllshire Gathering takes place at the end of August. At the Oban Glassworks (OACT) on Lochavullin Estate Caithness glass is made, and Macdonald's Mill (OACT) demonstrates spinning and weaving. Dunstaffnage Castle (AM) is a ruined Campbell stronghold where Flora MacDonald was once imprisoned. There are ferries from Oban to many of the islands of the Inner and Outer Hebrides: Mull, Iona, Coll, Tiree, Barra, South Uist, Colonsay and Lismore.

OFFA'S DYKE 8, 13

The dyke was an earthworks, built in the 8th century by Offa, King of Mercia, to mark the western boundary of his kingdom and to provide a defence against Welsh raiders. A long-distance footpath follows, as far as possible, the original line of the dyke for about 168 miles, from the River Severn near Chepstow to the sea near Prestatyn in North Wales.

OFFHAM, Kent 6 TQ65

Village greens are not usually associated with the martial arts but at Offham is preserved what is thought to be the only remaining quintain, or tilting pole, in England. The idea was to ride at the T-shaped pole and attempt to hit a revolving bar with a lance, as practice for jousting.

OKEHAMPTON, Devon 2 SX59

The high tors of Dartmoor, High Willhays and Yes Tor, brood over this busy market town on the edges of the National Park. Its castle (AM), overlooking the river, was once the seat of the Courtenay family, Earls of Devon, until they moved to Powderham Castle near Exeter.

OLD DAILLY, Strathclyde 22 NX29

Lovely Bargany Gardens (OACT) lie four miles north-east of this little Ayrshire town on the Water of Girvan. The woodland walks are noted for their displays of spring flowers and bluebells, and for displays of foliage when the leaves change their colour in autumn.

OLD DEER, Grampian 28 NJ94

Ruined Deer Abbey (AM) lies in a delightful setting in the grounds of Pitfour House. These buildings date from the 13th century, but the first monastery at Deer was a Celtic one, founded by St Columba in the 6th century. The famous *Book of Deer* now in Cambridge University Library, was compiled by Celtic monks: it contains the first known characters of Gaelic script.

OLDHAM, Gtr Manchester 14 SD90

One of the great cotton towns of the north-west, Oldham owes much to the Industrial Revolution and the mechanisation of spinning and weaving, although nowadays foreign competition has hit traditional industry hard. Like Manchester in the 19th century, Oldham was a centre of radical thought, and elected William Cobbett as its first MP in 1832. In 1900 it returned to Parliament Britain's greatest modern statesman, Sir Winston Churchill. His bust by Epstein is one of the many fine exhibits in the Central Art Gallery, which is also noted for its collection of English watercolours.

OLD MELDRUM, Grampian   *27 NJ82*
Whisky-drinkers will welcome the
opportunity to visit the Glengarioch
Distillery (OACT), while more serious
tourists take themselves to see Loanhead
stone circle (AM), a late Bronze-Age
monument four miles to the west.

OLD SARUM, Wiltshire   *3 SU13*
Remains of the castle, cathedral, and traces
of the surrounding wall are now all that
remains of Old Sarum, a site that was
inhabited in the Iron Age and became in
medieval times a flourishing town and an
important Episcopal See. A bitter feud,
however, eventually broke out between the
clergy and the military at the castle, and
there was a serious water shortage, so
Bishop Herbert Poore decided to move
himself and his cathedral some miles south.
He died before he could accomplish this
plan, but his brother and successor,
Richard, began to build the new cathedral
in 1220 and by 1258 it was finished. A new
town, **Salisbury**, grew up around the
cathedral and by the 19th century Sarum
had dwindled to a hamlet. It was one of the
most notorious of the 'Rotten Boroughs',
returning two MPs to parliament, although
there were only ten voters, until the Reform
Bill of 1832.

**OLD WARDEN, Shuttleworth
Collection,** *see* **Biggleswade.**

OLNEY, Buckinghamshire   *10 SP85*
Annually on Shrove Tuesday the ringing of
a handbell summons determined Olney
housewives wielding frying pans to the
famous pancake race. Competitors run
from the Market Place to the handsome
14th-century church, and must toss and
catch a pancake three times before
completing the course. This pleasant
custom is said to date back to the 15th
century.
   The poet William Cowper lived in Olney
for many years, and worked with his friend,
the curate John Newton, to write the
famous Olney hymns among them such old
favourites as 'Hark, my soul, it is the
Lord', and 'Glorious Things of Thee are
Spoken'. The cottage where he lived with
his companion, Mary Unwin, is now a
museum.

OMBERSLEY, Hereford & Worcester
9 SO86
This delightful little village has no less than
20 buildings listed as being of historical or
architectural interest, and its black and
white timber-framed houses are a
photographer's dream. A rare 'plague'
stone commemorates the ravages of the
Black Death in the 14th century. Afflicted
villagers left money for goods on such
stones, so that traders could leave their
wares in safety.

ORFORD, Suffolk   *12 TM44*
Further north on the Suffolk coast, at
Dunwich, the sea has eroded the shore and
drowned half the village, but at Orford the
same waves have deposited more and more
land and the village, though attractive and
well kept is no longer the thriving port it
was when Henry II built the massive castle,
whose complex and irregular fortifications
were designed to baffle attackers. The great
tower (AM) is all that survives, 90ft high,
with walls 10ft thick.

ORKNEY, Highland   *28*
Mainland, once more romantically called
Hrossey ('the horse island') when Orkney
was a Viking kingdom, is the largest of the
67 islands in the group which lies off the
northernmost tip of the Scottish mainland.
There are regular flights from the mainland
and ferries from Aberdeen and Scrabster.
   Unlike the Western Isles, Orkney is a
fertile place with low, rounded hills and a
surprisingly mild climate which favours
farming. The exception is Hoy – 'the high
island' – with its towering 1000ft cliffs and
the dramatic, wave-lashed rock stack
known as the 'Old Man of Hoy'.
   The early settlers of Orkney were Picts
and Celts, and from these times the islands
are rich in monuments and remains, an
archaeologist's paradise. The great
chambered tomb of Maes Howe (AM) near
Finstown on Mainland, is the finest
megalithic tomb in Britain, and still a place
of mystery. Nearby is the slightly later Ring
of Brogar (AM), another of the many relics
of Orkney's distant past. The Vikings
ousted the native Picts in the 9th century,
and Orkney remained a part of Norway and
Denmark, until 1468 when the islands were
given to Scotland as part of the dowry of
Margaret of Norway on her marriage to
James III of Scotland. Nordic traditions are
still evident in the speech and customs of
the Orcadians. The peaceful, timeless
quality of Orkney is now threatened by the
booming North Sea Oil industry: the little
island of Flotta, in the World War II
harbour of Scapa Flow, is now a terminal
for North Sea Oil.
   Kirkwall on Mainland is the capital of
Orkney, a charming old town of high,
gabled houses and narrow streets. The
beautiful St Magnus Cathedral, founded in
1137, commemorates an early Norse ruler

of Orkney, murdered by his cousin in 1115.
Nearby are the ruins of two palaces; the
13th-century Bishop's Palace (AM) and the
17th-century Earl Patrick's Palace (AM)
built for the tyrannical 2nd Earl of Orkney.
Tankerness House, a 16th-century town
house, is now a museum of Orkney life, and
at the little settlement of Harray in the
island's interior, is a restored Orkney
farmstead, the Corrigall Farm Museum.
Near Dounby are other historic relics:
Skara Brae, a remarkable survival of
incredibly well-preserved Stone-Age
houses; the Brough of Birsay, ruins of a
Romanesque Church and early Viking
dwellings, and Click Mill (AM), a rare
Orcadian horizontal watermill. Stromness
is also an attractive township, with distant
views of Hoy. It has an interesting maritime
museum, and a modern arts centre housed
in an 18th-century warehouse.
   South of Mainland and connected to it by
the Churchill Barriers, causeways built to
guard the approaches to Scapa Flow during
World War II, are the islands of South
Ronaldsay and Lamb Holm. Italian
prisoners of war built the causeways, and
also built themselves a chapel, elaborately
and beautifully painted, which still stands
as a memento. On the west side of Scapa
Flow is mountainous Hoy, legendary home
of many a troll and giant in Orcadian folk
tales. The composer Peter Maxwell Davies
has made his home here, and the crofters
are beginning to return to the long-
abandoned village of Rackwick.
   North of Mainland, Rousay is said to
have the loveliest scenery, and Sanday is
another popular holiday island. The other
major islands are Stronsay, Eday, Westray
and Papa Westray, and the most northerly
of all, North Ronaldsay, with its unique
flocks of sheep, who feed on seaweed.

ORKNEY *The ancient village settlement of Skara Brae has looked out over the Bay of Skaill on Mainland since about 2000BC. Amazingly, even stone beds, cupboards and fireplaces have survived.*

ORMESBY BROAD, Norfolk *12 TG41*
One of a group of five deep 'broads', as this unique system of inland waterways and meres are called, Ormesby Broad supports a rich variety of insect, plant and bird life.

ORMESBY, Cleveland *20 NZ51*
Ormesby Hall (NT) was built in the mid 18th century for the wealthy 6th Baronet, Sir James Pennyman. The architect is thought to have been John Carr of York, but the outstanding feature of the house is the decoration of the interior, carried out by a group of craftsmen from York.

OSMOTHERLEY, N Yorkshire
20 SE49
The Hambleton Hills form the setting for this attractive stone-built village on the edge of the **North York Moors National Park**. It is also the starting point for the Lyke Wake Walk, a 40-mile footpath which ends at **Ravenscar**, and the Cleveland Way also passes through the village. John Wesley once preached here, using as his pulpit a stone table which can still be seen. A mile to the north-west are the ruins (AM, NT) of Mount Grace Priory, founded in the 14th century by the Carthusians.

OSTERLEY, Gtr London *5 TQ17*
Osterley Park (NT), administered by the Victoria and Albert Museum in London, is a magnificent 18th-century mansion designed by Robert Adam for the wealthy Child banking family. Almost all of its exquisite interior decorations have remained intact.

OSWESTRY, Shropshire *13 SJ22*
A bone of contention between England and Wales for centuries, Oswestry nowadays makes an excellent centre for visiting both the Shropshire and the North Wales countryside. Few of its medieval buildings survived the years of conflict, but the old grammar school dating from 1407, is still there, now divided into cottages, and the interesting Llwyd Mansion, a black and white 17th-century timbered building bears the insignia of the Holy Roman Empire, a double-headed eagle, on its walls. The arms were granted to an ancestor of the family for service in the Crusades. To the north of the town is the Iron-Age hillfort known as Old Oswestry (AM).

OTTERTON, Devon *2 SY08*
Characteristic of Devon are the cob and thatched cottages of this charming village. Otterton Mill (OACT) has a history stretching back to the year of the Domesday Book. Corn is still ground here, and there are also craft workshops.

OTTERY ST MARY, Devon *2 SY19*
The magnificent 14th-century collegiate church is out of all proportion to the size of this small town on the River Otter. The church was originally a dependency of the Cathedral of Rouen in France, and was bought in 1335 by the Bishop of Exeter, who made it into a slightly smaller version of his own cathedral. It contains a rare Tudor clock which shows the phases of the moon. Celebrations in Ottery St Mary on 5th November include a carnival, and the ancient custom of rolling tar barrels.
    North-west of the town is Cadhay (OACT) one of the finest Tudor manor houses in the county.

PLACES TO SEE

The Colleges Most are open to visitors, and detailed information can be obtained from the Official Information Bureau in Carfax Tower. The following are among the best known, but there are many more worth visiting.

All Souls Founded in 1437 by Henry Chichele, it admits no undergraduates, only graduate fellows, elected for academic distinction.

Balliol Founded in the 13th century by John de Baliol, its most famous Master was Benjamin Jowett, the outstanding Greek scholar of the 19th century.

Christchurch Known as 'The House', has the largest and most famous quadrangle, Tom Quad, in Oxford, and a superb hall. It was founded by Cardinal Wolsey and its handsome chapel is the city's cathedral.

Magdalen Some say this is the most beautiful of the Oxford colleges. Its lovely Bell Tower is a noted landmark, and it is set in extensive grounds with a deer park.

Merton College Beautiful gardens and a 14th-century library are its outstanding features.

Queen's College Named after Philippa, Queen of Edward III, its classical buildings are by Wren and Hawksmoor.

University College One of three claimants to the title of Oxford's 'oldest college'.

Ashmolean Museum The basis of the museum was the collection of the 17th-century antiquary Elias Ashmole. It has a notable collection of Oriental treasures.

THE RADCLIFFE CAMERA *(above) is one of the reading rooms for the Bodleian Library.*

OXFORD *(below) The university in the 1830s.*

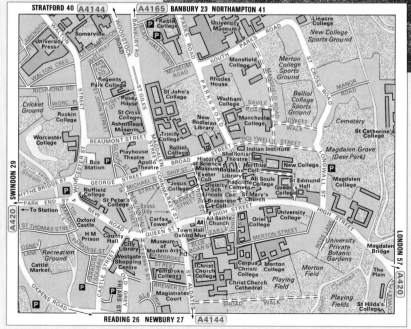

Although a flourishing industrial town has grown up at Cowley where Lord Nuffield founded his bicycle, and later his Morris car works, alongside Matthew Arnold's city of 'dreaming spires', Oxford remains a university town, *par excellence*, its streets dominated by the stone-built walls and quadrangles of its ancient colleges and in term-time by flocks of black-gowned undergraduates on foot or on bicycle. The Broad, where that famous Oxford institution Blackwell's Bookshop is to be found, the High, Cornmarket and the narrow lanes leading off them are the centre of university life, and where most of the old colleges, public houses frequented by the students, good restaurants and shops are to be found. In spring and summer the University Parks and the Rivers Cherwell and Isis, as the Thames is known here, from its old name of 'Tamesis', come into their own. On May Morning at 5am the Cherwell is packed with punts at Magdalen Bridge to hear the Choristers of Magdalen sing a Latin hymn to salute May Day from Magdalen Tower. Eights Week, on the Isis, also takes place in May, when the college crews compete for Head of the River', watched by crowds in Christ Church Meadows.

City of Dreaming Spires

'*Towery city and branchy between towers;*
Cuckoo-echoing, bell-swarmèd, lark-charmèd, rook-racked,
  river-rounded;
The dapple-eared lily below thee; . . .'

GERARD MANLEY HOPKINS, *Duns Scotus's Oxford*

MAGDALEN COLLEGE *is surrounded by lovely parkland.*

Academic life came to Oxford in a modest way in the 12th century, but really dates from the 13th century when foreign students expelled from the Sorbonne in Paris, came here and attached themselves to 'halls' belonging to religious orders. Learning was at that time in the hands of the church and all students were 'clerics' benefiting from the privileges of the clergy, and this gave rise to frequent troubles between 'town' and 'gown': until quite late in the 19th century, university dons were required to be celibate.

Among the oldest foundations are Merton College, founded in 1264, St Edmund's Hall, the only survivor of the medieval monastic halls that predated the college system and University College. Others followed thick and fast, throughout the medieval and Renaissance periods, and there are now quite a few 20th-century foundations. Women are comparative newcomers; the five 'women's' colleges were established, not without severe opposition, in the late 19th century. In the last 10 years however, again not without great debate, the trend has been for all colleges to admit undergraduates of both sexes, and only a few are holding fast to the old ways.

Oxford has at various times played its part in history. In Mary I's reign, the Protestant martyrs Latimer, Cranmer and Ridley were tried at St Mary's Church for heresy and burned to death: Martyrs' Memorial in St Giles commemorates them. During the Civil War, Oxford declared for the Royalist cause, and was Charles I's headquarters for three years. It has since led a quieter life, but is remembered in this century for the famous 1930s' 'King and Country' debate at the Oxford Union, that early training ground of many politicians.

Bodleian Library One of the oldest and most famous libraries in the world, the Bodleian has an unrivalled collection of rare books and manuscripts. Of interest to the visitor are Duke Humphrey's Library and the Old Divinity School.

Museum of the History of Science Housed in the original Ashmolean buildings, the museum concentrates on early astronomical, mathematical and official instruments.

Museum of Modern Art Exhibitions of 20th-century art are held here.

Sheldonian Theatre Degrees are conferred in this Wren building which is encircled by pillars bearing the busts of Roman emperors. From the cupola there are splendid views over the city.

Radcliffe Camera is a Classical domed building, used as a reading room for the Bodleian.

University Museums Set in the extensive grounds of the University Parks, the museums have geological and scientific collections.

University Private Botanic Garden This fascinating garden near Magdalen Bridge is the oldest in the country.

DREAMING SPIRES *The view from the Sheldonian Theatre.*

OULTON BROAD, Suffolk   *12 TM59*
The most southerly of the Broads, this
popular yachting centre lies to the west of
Lowestoft.

OUNDLE, Northamptonshire   *11 TL08*
Set in a loop of the River Nene, Oundle is a
busy sailing centre and a most picturesque
old market town, most of the houses in its
narrow streets and yards having been built
of the local limestone over the past four
centuries. The buildings of Oundle Public
School were founded by William Laxton, a
grocer who became Lord Mayor of London
in the 16th century.

OUTER HEBRIDES, THE, Highland
   29
From the windswept headland of the Butt
of Lewis in the north to Barra Head
Lighthouse on the tiny Island of Berneray
in the south, the 'Long Island' or the
'Western Isles' as they are also known,
stretch for 130 miles. The main islands are
Lewis and Harris, North Uist, Benbecula,
South Uist, Barra and Eriskay. Causeways
and bridges now link the Uists and
Benbecula. Ferry services run from the
mainland from Ullapool to Lewis; from Uig
to Harris; and from Oban to South Uist and
Barra.
   The Western Isles are one of the last
outposts of the Gaelic way of life, and the
crofters are resistant to change, as at least
two well-intentioned improvers, Sir James
Matheson and Lord Leverhulme
discovered. Matheson bought the islands in
the 19th century and spent a fortune on
building roads and bridges. He built
himself the Castle of Lews, now a technical
college, at Stornoway, importing tons of
soil from the mainland to establish the
lovely gardens (OACT) where he planted
the islands' only extensive woodlands.
After World War I Lord Leverhulme
bought Lewis and Harris, improved the
harbour at Stornoway and tried to set up
commercial fisheries, but the crofters did
not take kindly to working in factories and
his schemes came to nothing. The product
for which the islands are mainly known is
Harris tweed, and this traditional cottage
industry still thrives.
   The traditional home of the island
crofters was the 'Black House', a low,
thatched, windowless building with an

HARRIS TWEED

Throughout Harris and Lewis the
tweeds, 28½ inches wide and 80ft
long, are woven on handlooms from
'virgin wool spun, dyed and finished
in the Outer Hebrides, and hand-
woven by the islanders in their own
homes'. The various island tourist
offices give details of weaver's workshops which can be visited.

open central fire, and one room in which
both humans and animals sheltered. Two of
these, at Arrol on the north-west coast of
Lewis, and at Eochar on South Uist have
been restored as crofting museums.
   The islands, despite their inhospitable
climate and infertile soils, have been
inhabited since prehistoric times, as the
wealth of prehistoric monuments shows.
Most impressive of all is the great stone
circle and avenue of Standing Stones
occupying a bleak moorland site at
Callanish, overlooking a remote inlet of the
western coast. Not far away is another
impressive relic, Carloway Broch, a massive
Iron-Age stone tower, still standing 30ft
high.
   Harris is the most mountainous of the
Western Isles, and has some lovely beaches
in the south-west, although only the hardy
would bathe in the chilly Atlantic waters.
The main settlements are Tarbert in the
north, and Rodel in the south. The wild,
remote promontory of Toe Head is one of
the few British breeding grounds of the
Golden Eagle.
   North Uist and Benbecula are watery
islands, the land mass broken up by a
confusing maze of lochans, inlets and islets.
Army rocket ranges on Benbecula add a
touch of the surreal to this almost deserted
landscape. The island of Eriskay was the
setting for Sir Compton Mackenzie's novel,
later filmed, *Whisky Galore*, based on the
wreck of the SS *Politician* with its cargo of
20,000 cases of whisky in World War II.
Eriskay, where Bonnie Prince Charlie first
set foot on Scottish soil when he came from
France, and Barra, are noted for their
Gaelic folk songs.

OVERTON, Clwyd   *14 SJ34*
A well-kept, tidy village of 18th-century
houses in fact several times winner of 'best-
kept village' awards, Overton lies in the
region of Wales known as Maelor, once part
of Flintshire. The yews in its churchyard
feature in a traditional rhyme as one of the
Severn Wonders of Wales: 'Pystyll Rhaeadr
and Wrixham Steeple, Snowdon's
Mountain without its people; Overton
Yew-trees, St Winifred's Wells, Llangollen
Bridge and Gresford Bells'.

OXBOROUGH, Norfolk   *12 TF70*
Surrounded by a moat stocked with fat carp
who nibble away among the waterlilies,
15th-century Oxburgh Hall (NT) appears
as a romantic evocation of an idyllic past.
Even when it was built for Sir Edward
Bedingfield, the moat, drawbridge and
magnificent brick gatehouse can scarcely
have served a defensive purpose. Among
the many interesting relics of the
Bedingfield family are needlework wall
hangings worked by the imprisoned Mary
Queen of Scots and her gaoler, the
Countess of Shrewsbury.

OXWICH, W Glamorgan   *7 SS48*
Lovely countryside surrounds this
picturesque village, its cottages strung out
along a quiet lane leading down to a
sheltered sandy beach. Oxwich Marsh
provides a habitat for many birds and has
been designated a Nature Reserve. A short
distance away from the village stands the
Church of St Illtud. Medieval effigies are
thought to be those of the de la Mare family
who owned the now ruined castle on the hill
above the village.

*SOUTH HARRIS The most mountainous of the 'Western Isles', Harris has given its name to the famous
hand-woven tweed, and its rocky fastnesses are one of the last refuges of the Golden Eagle.*

PACKWOOD HOUSE, Warwickshire
10 SP17
Originally a Tudor farmhouse, Packwood (NT) has been sympathetically altered and extended over the years. Its most celebrated feature is the yew-garden, which is believed to represent symbolically the Sermon on the Mount, but the interior also has much of interest.

PADIHAM, Lancashire   *14 SD73*
Miss Rachel Kay-Shuttleworth's outstanding collection of textiles, embroideries, lace and the decorative arts is the centre of interest at Gawthorpe Hall (NT), a late Elizabethan mansion re-designed by Sir Charles Barry in the Victorian period. The rooms contain much handsome furniture, and the ceilings of the drawing room and long gallery are elaborately decorated.

PADSTOW, Cornwall   *1 SW97*
The great event in this picturesque old fishing village on the estuary of the Camel River is the May Day celebration, the focus of which is the extraordinary figure of the Hobby Horse. Draped in a great hooped skirt, the Horse frolics through the streets, led by another traditional figure, the Teaser, and a band of attendants. The custom is a very ancient one and the dance is believed to be among the oldest dance festivals in Europe. It celebrates the defeat of winter, and, from the amount of horseplay that goes on, it is clear that it was originally a fertility rite. In the prettily named Fentonluna Lane there is a Tropical Bird and Butterfly Garden.

PACKWOOD HOUSE *The gardens, with their ornamental ponds and well-stocked mixed borders, provide a typically English setting for the old Tudor manor house near Henley-in-Arden.*

PADSTOW HOBBY HORSE

Every May Day Padstow is decorated in honour of its bizarre festival which is believed to be the oldest in Europe. The horse, a boatshaped frame covered with black oilcloth, is trimmed with the colours that symbolise new life – red and white.

PAIGNTON, Devon   *2 SX86*
A popular resort on Tor Bay, Paignton's many attractions include a large and interesting zoo, and several historic homes. The most outstanding one is Oldway Mansion (OACT) built by the sewing-machine millionaire Isaac Merritt Singer in the last century. Kirkham House (OACT) has been restored to its original 16th-century appearance as a museum of domestic life. At Higher Blaydon is the Torbay Aircraft Museum with exhibits dating from 1924 to 1954. Steam trains run in summer along a stretch of the old Great Western line from Paignton to **Kingswear** where there is a ferry to **Dartmouth**.

PAINSWICK, Gloucestershire   *9 SO80*
Painswick's lovely old streets slope down a high Cotswold hillside, almost every one of its golden stone houses worth more than a passing glance. Although nowadays a quiet place, it was once a wool town of considerable importance, as the many handsomely decorated table tombs in the churchyard show. Ninety-nine yew trees stand sentinel around the churchyard, and by tradition the hundredth would never grow. A 'clipping' ceremony takes place here on Painswick Feast Sunday around 19th September. 'Clipping' comes from an old English word meaning 'to enclose', and the church is encircled by a ring of schoolchildren holding hands. Afterwards Painswickians eat 'puppy-dog pie'. What the origins of this delicacy may have been can only be imagined: nowadays it is a cake containing a china dog. Painswick House (OACT) has splendid 18th-century reception rooms.

PAISLEY, Strathclyde   *22 NS46*
The Museum and Art Gallery houses a priceless collection of the Paisley shawls for which the town has been famous for more than 200 years; their distinctive pattern was introduced from Kashmir in 1770. Paisley's most attractive building is the 17th-century Place of Paisley, a tall building with crow-stepped gables.

PARC, Gwynedd   *13 SH83*
Cyffdy Farm Park is the rare-breed centre of northern Wales. There is a museum of old farm implements, but the real attraction is the animals – among them llamas and goats as well as traditional old breeds of sheep, cattle and poultry.

PARSON DROVE, Cambridgeshire
11 TF30
When woad is mentioned, it conjures up a picture of wild Ancient Britons smeared with blue, and fighting against Roman legionaries. Woad, a dye extracted from the woad plant, continued in use however, until quite recent times. Parson Drove, lost in the Cambridgeshire fens, was a centre of this traditional industry until synthetic indigo was introduced at the end of the 19th century.

PASTON, Norfolk   *12 TG33*
Much of what we know of everyday life and business in the 15th century comes from the Paston letters, exchanged between members of this remarkable merchant family from 1422 to 1509. The mansion where they lived in the pleasant North Norfolk village is no more, but a great flint barn, 163ft long, stands as a reminder of their history. Memorials to some of the family can be seen in the attractive thatched church.

PATTERDALE, Cumbria   *18 NY31*
This small lakeland village stands at the head of Ullswater, one of the principal lakes of the Lake District, and is a popular touring centre, surrounded by superb mountain scenery. Helvellyn, High Street and Kirkstone Pass are all in the immediate area.

PEACEHAVEN, E Sussex   *5 TQ40*
This East Sussex resort lies on the Greenwich meridian, a fact that is marked by a monument. Peacehaven was founded specifically as a retreat for war veterans, hence the name, but this part of the coast is now very built-up.

PATTERNS OF BUILDING
COTTAGES
Housewrights and Masons

If fields, woodlands, villages and hills provide the broad patterns in the British countryside, cottages make up some of the most attractive details. The charm of the rural landscape is rooted in diversity, so that as one distinctive region yields to another, the local features change personality – and the identity of a region is nowhere more charmingly expressed than in its humbler or 'vernacular' buildings. Many Yorkshire dales would seem hopelessly incomplete without their complement of unadorned gritstone cottages, while flint-walled cottages are key components in the landscapes of the English chalklands.

GENUINE MEDIEVAL COTTAGES are rarely seen, these days, and the overwhelming majority of cottages that have survived were built in the 17th, 18th and 19th centuries. Traditionally, cottages were the homes of the poorer members of the rural community and most surviving medieval dwellings were the more substantial homes of yeomen, merchants or craftsmen who were higher up the social ladder. The mass of the peasantry occupied flimsy, insubstantial dwellings which swiftly perished. These came in various shapes and forms, but were invariably small and of just a single storey. The commonest type was the 'long'-house' which consisted only of a single domestic room and an adjoining byre for the family livestock. The foundations and lower wall courses of medieval stone long-houses can be seen at the excavated deserted medieval village of Hound Tor on Dartmoor.

'THE GREAT REBUILDING', as the process has been called, took place from the 17th century onwards, and members of the peasant classes began to obtain dwellings which were sufficiently robust to survive the passing centuries.

As the movement gradually spread northwards and westwards across Britain, local building traditions were embodied in thousands of new and more durable cottage homes. Until well into the 19th century, local transport conditions were usually extremely poor. This resulted in it being impracticable to transport bulky building materials over long distances. The uneven, muddy and rutted roads and the unsophisticated waggon designs that were available would not permit long hauls of timber and stone, for only the wealthy classes could afford to incur the high transport costs involved. In consequence, cottages were built of materials which were available close at hand and were constructed by local housewrights and rough masons who were well-versed in the building traditions of their

THATCH *was a traditional roofing material for cottages in areas where wheat, straw or reed was plentiful.*

regions. In areas where grain was grown, the straw-thatched cottage roofs blended with the surrounding wheat fields, while in Fenland areas they were capped in reed. In the Cotswolds and Yorkshire Dales, locally-quarried flagstone 'slates' were used in roofs which blended with the neighbouring rock outcrops while in the Lake District, walls of greenish, slatey rock echoed the hues of the overlooking crags. In areas where building stones of a good or moderate quality were easily available, the practice of building in stone tended gradually to supersede an older timber-based tradition, but in the English lowlands, reasonable stone was seldom available and the timber-framing method tended to survive into the 19th century.

TIMBER-FRAMED buildings followed two basic techniques: cruck-framing and box-framing. The 'cruck-framing' method seems to date back to Roman times and is still displayed in small dwellings in which the gable ends are formed of two massive curving timbers which are joined at the gable to

OTHER MATERIALS were used in certain parts of the country. In Devon and neighbouring areas, a daub-like material known as 'cob' was built up in stages to provide thick walls which were weatherproof so long as the protective skin of lime was maintained. In parts of Cornwall, slates from local quarries were attached to lathes to form slate-hung walls; tile-hung walls were popular in some eastern counties like Kent, while in Essex and adjoining regions, planks of elm were used in weatherboarding. Transport difficulties had determined the use of local building materials such as these and the vernacular styles survived until the revolutions caused by canal and railway developments allowed imported materials to undercut the local products. Brick-making gradually became concentrated in mass brick-producing works like those of Bedfordshire, while cheap slates from the Welsh quarries undermined the local thatching or flagstone-roofing crafts. The result was an increasing standardisation in rural housing. Many of the most attractive cottages had been built without any conscious effort to create local character and charm, with considerations of cost and convenience being paramount. However, around the time that the transport revolutions were beginning to extinguish the traditional designs and materials, the old vernacular styles had begun to capture the imaginations of the middle and upper classes. The *cottage ornée*, which parodied many of the more picturesque features of the vernacular dwellings appeared in many different British locations.

TIMBER-FRAME *techniques included cruck-frame (above) and box-frame (below).*

CLADDING *Tiles (above) and weatherboard (below) are much used in Sussex and Kent.*

DATING A COTTAGE, is seldom an easy task, since most dwellings pass through a long sequence of adaptations, enlargements and repairs. The older cottages were often not originally peasant dwellings, but small yeoman farmsteads and many a medieval timber frame lies hidden beneath a skin of plaster or a casing of brick. Similarly, many a thatched roof has been replaced by one of Welsh slate or clay or concrete tiles. Window designs are often the most obvious guide to the age of a house, but then the majority of old cottages have received new windows so that the tell-tale small panes of an 18th-century cottage may have been replaced by a large-paned sash window in the 19th century, while elsewhere, original 19th-century windows may have been replaced quite recently by mock Georgian windows.

While the older country cottage would mirror the local building materials and traditions of craftsmanship, it is also likely to mirror the changes in society. During the 17th, 18th and 19th centuries, cottagers were amongst the most deprived members of the population. Water was normally only obtained from the village pump or stream and there would be no bathroom or indoor lavatory. Large families and tiny dwellings were the norm and, even in the better times, the commoner and farm labourer barely managed to feed his family. And so, rather than being a symbol of former times, the rose-hung cottage of today, with its well-maintained thatch, manicured lawns and brilliant flower borders tells of changing times in the countryside.

form an 'A'-shaped frame. The 'cruck-framing' method was widely used in the construction of smaller homes in the northern and western parts of Britain although only a tiny proportion of dwellings built by this method survive today. In the eastern half of England, and for larger timber-framed houses, there and elsewhere, the 'box-framing' method was employed, with the main structural timbers being pegged and jointed together to produce box-like bays. There were many regional variations in this method; in East Anglia, 'close-studding' was common, with numerous slender uprights or 'studs' being displayed, while in the West Midlands, fewer but heavier timbers were employed in the building of square-framing patterns. With its great strength and weather-resistance, oak was almost invariably used in such constructions.

Various different wattle and daub techniques were used to fill the spaces between the framing timbers, but most commonly a latticework of hazel rods provided a supporting frame for a thick plastering of daub made from mud that was reinforced by fibrous materials such as cow hair or sometimes chopped straw.

PEAK DISTRICT, THE, Derbyshire/Staffordshire 15

Derbyshire and Staffordshire share the superb hill scenery of this lovely area of the Pennines between them, and dispute which of them has the finest countryside. The landscape, too, is divided; between the limestone hills of the 'White Peak' in the south and the harsh moorland of the millstone grit country to the north. The Peak District National Park covers about 540 square miles. Good touring centres are **Matlock**, **Buxton**, and **Ashbourne**. Kinderscout at 2088ft and Bleaklow Hill at 2060ft are the highest points, but the Peak District is more famous for its low ground than for its hills: Dovedale, Monsal Dale, Lathkill Dale, Edale and the valleys of the Rivers Manifold, Goyt and Dane are among the most popular beauty spots.

PEAKIRK, Cambridgeshire 11 TF10

Rare and unusual birds inhabit the water-fowl gardens of the Wildfowl Trust at Peakirk. Trumpeter, Black-necked and Coscoroba Swans are among the hundred or more different species of waterfowl that can be seen here. The village itself is stone-built, and set in unspoiled countryside on the edge of the Fens.

PEDDAR'S WAY, Norfolk 12

One of Britain's ancient trackways, believed to pre-date the medieval period, Peddar's Way runs from the Wash near **Hunstanton**, passing near **Swaffham** and across the Breckland to a point just east of **Thetford** near the Norfolk and Suffolk border.

PEEBLES, Borders 23 NT23

Three salmon feature on the town's coat of arms; aptly, as this dignified old county town of Peebleshire lies on the River Tweed and is a noted centre for salmon fishing. The wooded hills above the river are dominated by 15th-century Neidpath Castle (OACT); south-east of the town are pleasant, wooded Kailzie Gardens (OACT).

PEMBRIDGE, Hereford & Worcester 8 SO35

Like its neighbour, **Eardisland**, Pembridge is a charming village set in the peaceful meadows of the River Arrow. Black and white timbered houses overhang its pavements, and its tiny market place, behind the main street, boasts a fine market house standing on old oak pillars.

PEMBROKE, Dyfed 7 SM90

Pembroke Castle (OACT), on its rocky headland above the town is protected on three sides by the sea. The massive circular keep, dating from about 1200 stands within a curtain wall fortified by six towers and a forbidding gatehouse. Beneath it is a huge limestone cavern called the Wogan, which opens onto the river and was formerly linked to the castle by a winding staircase.

PEMBROKESHIRE COAST NATIONAL PARK 7

A 167-mile footpath follows the wild coastline of Pembrokeshire from Amroth to St Dogmaels. The wild coast and its outlying islands are part of the National Park, which stretches inland to encompass the Preseli Hills and Milford Haven.

PENDEEN, Cornwall 1 SW33

The Penwith peninsula is dotted with the gaunt ruins of engine-houses – the last visible remains of the once prosperous Cornish tin industry. Geevor tin mine near the hamlet of Pendeen is still worked however, and has a museum showing the history of tin-mining in Cornwall.

PENHOW, Gwent 9 ST49

The castle (OACT) at Penhow is the oldest inhabited castle in Wales. Originally a small border fortress, the buildings fell into disrepair and were used as part of a farmhouse. Now restored, Penhow presents a picture of life from medieval times through to the 19th century.

PENMACHNO, Gwynedd 13 SH75

A former quarryman's village, Penmachno lies in a little valley east of Betws-y-Coed. Its woollen mill (OACT) has an interesting history, having been set up in 1650 as a fulling mill. Cloth is still woven on 19th-century power looms. At Ty Mawr, two miles west, is the cottage (OACT) where Bishop William Morgan was born in 1545. He is revered for his translation; the first ever, of the Bible into Welsh.

PENMAENMAWR, Gwynedd 13 SH77

This pleasant North-Wales coastal resort benefits from a sheltered, sandy beach and from its breathtaking mountain scenery. The main road passes through, but away from the traffic the town is rewarding to explore. In years gone by, travellers did not have the same appreciation of the mountains as we have today and the forbidding slopes of Penmaenmawr, from which the town takes its name, could only be traversed with great danger by a narrow, precipitous road. Quarrying has carried off the top of the mountain, leaving only a single rocky crag to mark its original height, but it is nonetheless worth climbing up the steep hillside to the Druid's Circle, one of the best known groups of standing stones in Wales.

PENNINES, THE 14, 18, 19

Often called the backbone of England, this range of ancient hills, their weathered summits clothed in open heath and moorland, stretches from Derbyshire in the south to the Cheviot Hills on the Scottish border. The hills are sparsely populated, dotted with scattered sheep farms and stone-built villages; trees, except where the Forestry Commission has been active, are few. The Peak District National Park, the Yorkshire Dales National Park, the North York Moors National Park and the Northumberland National Park preserve much of its most unspoiled scenery. A 250-mile long-distance footpath, the Pennine Way, the longest in Britain, runs from **Edale** in Derbyshire to Kirk Yelholm on the Scottish border. It can be walked in 14 days, or even less by the exceptionally fit.

PENRHYN CASTLE, see Bangor

PENRITH, Cumbria 18 NY42

Literary associations – with Wordsworth, Scott and Coleridge – are strong in Penrith, a historic town, well situated as a touring centre both for the Lake District and for the Eden Valley. The parish church dates from the 12th century, though it was extensively remodelled in the 18th. In the churchyard is the so-called Giant's Grave, reputedly the tomb of Owen Caesarius, King of Cumbria in the 10th century. Nearby is the shaft of a contemporary cross, locally named the 'Giant's Thumb'.
The site of Penrith Beacon on the hill to the north-east of the town is now marked by a memorial built in 1719.

PEN-Y-GHENT *The sombre mass of one of Yorkshire's highest peaks dominates the moors near Stainforth. The 'three peaks race', over Pen-y-Ghent, Ingleborough and Whemside, is a famous event.*

Land's End and Penwith
43 miles

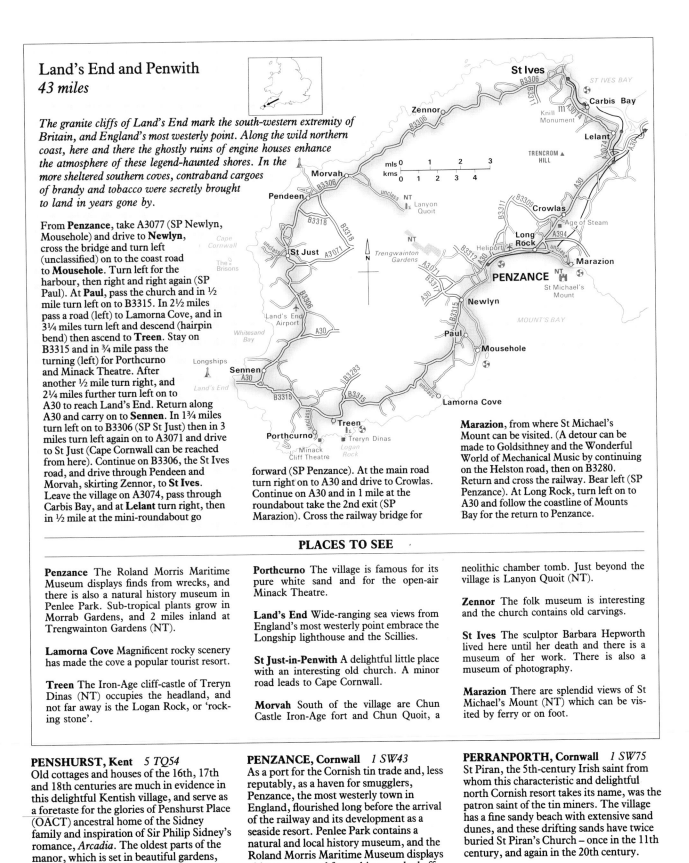

The granite cliffs of Land's End mark the south-western extremity of Britain, and England's most westerly point. Along the wild northern coast, here and there the ghostly ruins of engine houses enhance the atmosphere of these legend-haunted shores. In the more sheltered southern coves, contraband cargoes of brandy and tobacco were secretly brought to land in years gone by.

From **Penzance**, take A3077 (SP Newlyn, Mousehole) and drive to **Newlyn**, cross the bridge and turn left (unclassified) on to the coast road to **Mousehole**. Turn left for the harbour, then right and right again (SP Paul). At **Paul**, pass the church and in ½ mile turn left on to B3315. In 2½ miles pass a road (left) to Lamorna Cove, and in 3¼ miles turn left and descend (hairpin bend) then ascend to **Treen**. Stay on B3315 and in ¾ mile pass the turning (left) for Porthcurno and Minack Theatre. After another ½ mile turn right, and 2¼ miles further turn left on to A30 to reach Land's End. Return along A30 and carry on to **Sennen**. In 1¾ miles turn left on to B3306 (SP St Just) then in 3 miles turn left again on to A3071 and drive to St Just (Cape Cornwall can be reached from here). Continue on B3306, the St Ives road, and drive through Pendeen and Morvah, skirting Zennor, to **St Ives**. Leave the village on A3074, pass through Carbis Bay, and at **Lelant** turn right, then in ½ mile at the mini-roundabout go

forward (SP Penzance). At the main road turn right on to A30 and drive to Crowlas. Continue on A30 and in 1 mile at the roundabout take the 2nd exit (SP Marazion). Cross the railway bridge for

Marazion, from where St Michael's Mount can be visited. (A detour can be made to Goldsithney and the Wonderful World of Mechanical Music by continuing on the Helston road, then on B3280. Return and cross the railway. Bear left (SP Penzance). At Long Rock, turn left on to A30 and follow the coastline of Mounts Bay for the return to Penzance.

PLACES TO SEE

Penzance The Roland Morris Maritime Museum displays finds from wrecks, and there is also a natural history museum in Penlee Park. Sub-tropical plants grow in Morrab Gardens, and 2 miles inland at Trengwainton Gardens (NT).

Lamorna Cove Magnificent rocky scenery has made the cove a popular tourist resort.

Treen The Iron-Age cliff-castle of Treryn Dinas (NT) occupies the headland, and not far away is the Logan Rock, or 'rocking stone'.

Porthcurno The village is famous for its pure white sand and for the open-air Minack Theatre.

Land's End Wide-ranging sea views from England's most westerly point embrace the Longship lighthouse and the Scillies.

St Just-in-Penwith A delightful little place with an interesting old church. A minor road leads to Cape Cornwall.

Morvah South of the village are Chun Castle Iron-Age fort and Chun Quoit, a

neolithic chamber tomb. Just beyond the village is Lanyon Quoit (NT).

Zennor The folk museum is interesting and the church contains old carvings.

St Ives The sculptor Barbara Hepworth lived here until her death and there is a museum of her work. There is also a museum of photography.

Marazion There are splendid views of St Michael's Mount (NT) which can be visited by ferry or on foot.

PENSHURST, Kent   5 TQ54
Old cottages and houses of the 16th, 17th and 18th centuries are much in evidence in this delightful Kentish village, and serve as a foretaste for the glories of Penshurst Place (OACT) ancestral home of the Sidney family and inspiration of Sir Philip Sidney's romance, *Arcadia*. The oldest parts of the manor, which is set in beautiful gardens, date from the 14th century, and the superb Baron's Hall, roofed with chestnut beams, is also of this period. The state rooms are splendidly furnished and there is also a fascinating collection of old toys. The Sidney family became Earls of Leicester, and at the entrance to the churchyard is a small open-ended square of old, timbered cottages called Leicester Square. One of the houses has been built around the lychgate of the medieval church, which contains the Sidney family chapel.

PENZANCE, Cornwall   1 SW43
As a port for the Cornish tin trade and, less reputably, as a haven for smugglers, Penzance, the most westerly town in England, flourished long before the arrival of the railway and its development as a seaside resort. Penlee Park contains a natural and local history museum, and the Roland Morris Maritime Museum displays objects recovered from ships wrecked off the Scilly Isles. Exotic plants flourish in Morrab Gardens, and the exotic Egyptian House is a local curiosity, restored by the Landmark Trust and used as a holiday home. At Trengwainton Gardens (NT) two miles west, many exotic plants are grown in walled gardens and woodland glades. It was here that magnolias flowered for the first time in Britain. Ferry and helicopter services run between Penzance and the Scilly Isles.

PERRANPORTH, Cornwall   1 SW75
St Piran, the 5th-century Irish saint from whom this characteristic and delightful north Cornish resort takes its name, was the patron saint of the tin miners. The village has a fine sandy beach with extensive sand dunes, and these drifting sands have twice buried St Piran's Church – once in the 11th century, and again in the 20th century.

PERSHORE, Hereford & Worcester
9 SO94
Purple and yellow Pershore plums are the speciality of the abundant orchards round Pershore. The River Avon flows past one end of the High Street, and the gardens of many of the old houses run right down to the river banks, making an enchanting picture. The ruins of the great Benedictine Abbey include the transepts and a magnificent lantern tower.

J M W TURNER AND PETWORTH

J M W Turner (left), born the son of a London barber on St George's Day, 1775, became one of the most popular artists of the Romantic movement by the time he was 21. Later he became a friend of Lord Egremont, owner of Petworth House (above), and subsequently produced some of his best work while staying on the estate. Many of these paintings depict the house, grounds and guests.

PERTH, Tayside 23 NO12
Sir Walter Scott's 'Fair Maid of Perth' was Catherine Glover and the 14th-century house (OACT) where she lived is now a crafts centre. Perth was the capital of the Scottish Kingdom until 1437, and as such, the ancient royal burgh at the head of the Tay estuary is rich in historical associations. St John's Kirk, built in the 15th century, is famous for the fiery sermon preached by John Knox in 1559 against church idolatry, which was one of the events which inspired the Reformation. Balhousie Castle, (OACT) near North Inch golf course, houses the Black Watch Regimental Museum. Also of interest are the Perth Museum and Art Gallery, and a Caithness Glass factory, which is open to visitors. Branklyn Garden (NTS) on the road to Dundee, is famous for rhododendrons, shrubs and alpine plants, and has been called the finest garden of its size (two acres) in Britain.

PETERBOROUGH, Cambridgeshire
11 TL19
Pre-eminent among many historic buildings, Peterborough Cathedral dates from the 12th and early 13th centuries. It is a magnificent structure, built of local Barnack stone, and inside, the ceiling of the nave is decorated with figures of saints, kings, and many grotesques. Two queens were buried in front of the retrochoir: Catherine of Aragon and Mary Queen of Scots, both interred by the same gravedigger, Robert Scarlett, whose epitaph can also be seen: the body of Mary Queen of Scots was later removed to Westminster Abbey.
In recent years Peterborough has expanded at an enormous rate, and the modern roads and buildings tend to obscure the legacy of the past. The Longthorpe Tower (AM) is a nice example of a medieval fortified house.

PETERCULTER, Grampian 27 NJ80
Drum Castle (NTS), three miles west of the town, was the ancestral home of the de Irwin family for more than 600 years. The house stands in 400 acres of grounds.

PETERHEAD, Grampian 28 NK14
One of Scotland's biggest fishing ports, Peterhead is also involved in the North Sea oil industry, and has built a huge modern harbour to accommodate oil vessels. It was founded in 1593, and many of its houses are built of the attractive local red granite. The Arbuthnot Museum has many exhibits relating to the town's whaling and herring-fishing industries.

PETERLEE, Co Durham 20 NZ44
Founded in the 1950s in an effort to bring new employment to this part of the north-east, Peterlee is a flourishing industrial and attractive shopping centre. The town is named after Peter Lee, who started work down the mines at the age of ten, in 1874, and rose to become President of the Miners' Union. Castle Eden Dene (OACT) is a three-mile stretch of natural woodland, owned by the corporation and kept as a nature reserve.

PETERSFIELD, Hampshire 4 SU72
The equestrian statue of William II looks down on the market place – markets held every Wednesday – of this attractive country town on the River Rother. Eighteenth-century buildings predominate in the old streets of the centre.

PETWORTH, W Sussex 5 SU92
Though the Petworth estates have belonged to the earls of Northumberland since 1150, it was the 6th Duke of Somerset, husband of the Percy heiress, who was responsible for the re-modelling of this superb house in 1688. Petworth House (NT) stands in a park designed by Capability Brown in 1752. Turner painted it, an artist much admired by the then owner, the 3rd Earl of Egremont, a descendant of the Duke of Somerset. A number of Turner's paintings are among the masterpieces of European art, collected by various owners, that hang in Petworth's richly decorated and furnished rooms. The magnificence of the stately house should not cause the visitor to overlook the delights of the small town of Petworth with its old, narrow streets and timbered houses.

PEVENSEY, E Sussex 6 TQ06
To guard the southern coast, the Romans built their fort of Anderida on a spit of land then open to the sea. In AD 491 it was besieged by and fell to Aelle, King of the South Saxons, who massacred all the Romano-British defenders. When William the Conqueror landed in Pevensey Bay in 1066, he found the fort abandoned, and promptly had a castle (AM) built on the site. Over the centuries it has been fortified many times: in World War II, camouflaged pill boxes, still difficult to spot, were built into the ancient walls. In the village High Street stands the Old Mint House (OACT) built in 1342 as a mint. In 1542 Henry VIII's physician, Dr Andrew Borde, made alterations to it and used it as a residence.

PEWSEY, Wiltshire 3 SU15
An attractive little town on the banks of the River Avon, Pewsey has associations with King Alfred and a statue of him dominates the town centre. Thatched cottages and Georgian houses make an attractive contrast in the old streets, and all around is fertile countryside.

PICKERING *When these wall paintings were uncovered in 1851 the vicar whitewashed them over. His successor rediscovered them.*

PICKERING, N Yorkshire 16 SE78
Pickering is a lively market town with steep narrow streets climbing up the hillside. Looking down from a height over the market place stands Pickering's parish church, the walls of its nave decorated with a series of remarkably vivid wall paintings depicting legends of the saints, and believed to date from the 15th century. Pickering Castle, also high above the town, is very ruinous, but the North Yorkshire Moors Railway, closed by British Rail, has been restored. The Beck Isle Museum of Rural Life contains interesting folk and local history displays.

PIDDLETRENTHIDE, Dorset
3 SY79
Despite the unfortunate connotations of its name the village is exceptionally pretty and beautifully sited in the deep valley of the River Piddle.

PILGRIMS' WAY, Hampshire – Kent
4, 5, 6

This was a medieval route linking the two great cathedral cities of the south, Winchester and Canterbury, and their shrines of St Swithin and St Thomas Becket. It led across the slope of the North Downs, following for part of the way the line of a prehistoric track. Like the **Ridgeway**, it is now a long-distance footpath, (part of the North Downs Way).

PILTDOWN, E Sussex   *5 TQ42*

Piltdown is famous as the site of the discovery of the remains of Piltdown Man, one of the most notorious of all archaeological forgeries. The skull was 'discovered' in 1912 by Charles Dawson, and acclaimed by archaeologists as the 'missing link' between man and ape. The hoax lasted until 1953 when tests proved that an ape's jaw-bone and a tooth had been cleverly grafted on to genuine fragments of a prehistoric skull.

PITLOCHRY, Tayside   *26 NN95*

A popular touring centre for visitors to the Grampians, Pitlochry lies in a beautiful setting of hills and woods. There is a famous Festival Theatre, 'the theatre in the hills', where plays are performed in the summer months. To the west of the town Pitlochry Dam has created an artificial lake, Loch Faskally, where there is a permanent exhibition and salmon leap.

PITMEDDEN, Grampian   *27 NJ82*

Pitmedden Gardens (NTS) was originally laid out in 1675 by Sir Alexander Seton as a 'knot' garden, whose formal patterns are best appreciated from the raised terraces which surround it on three sides. When the garden became National Trust property in 1952, it was in a state of neglect, having been used as a vegetable garden, and the beds were redesigned, following authentic 17th-century plans. Two miles north-east of Pitmedden are the ruins (AM) of Tolquhon Castle.

PITSTONE, Buckinghamshire   *5 SP91*

Half a mile south of Ivinghoe, Pitstone windmill (NT) is one of the oldest post mills in Britain. Parts of it date from the original building, erected in 1627. It has been restored, after many years of neglect, to full working order.

PITTENWEEM, Fife   *24 NO50*

This part of the Fife coast has several picturesque resorts, among them the old royal burgh of Pittenweem, with its photogenic harbour surrounded by old houses. Near the harbour is the cave-shrine of St Fillan. The church has a notable 15th-century tower and incorporated in the parsonage are traces of a 12th-century priory. Kellie Castle (NTS) is three miles north-west of the town.

PLAS NEWYDD see Anglesey

PLOCKTON, Highland   *25 NG83*

Now safely in the care of the National Trust for Scotland, this delightful village on the shores of Loch Carron, set in beautiful mountain scenery, has had a chequered history. In 1801 most of the existing crofters were evicted to make way for a sheep-farming settlement planned by the new landlord, Hugh Innes. His plans did not get far, but his descendants tried to improve the fishing and the harbour. In 1850 Sir Alexander Matheson bought the area and built himself a castle, before moving on to grander projects on Lewis and Harris in the **Outer Hebrides**, and finally the estate was acquired by Sir Daniel Hamilton, who gave it to the Scottish National Trust. The village is sheltered by its surrounding hills, and the vagaries of the Gulf Stream make the climate so mild that palm trees flourish along the roadside.

PLYMPTON, Devon   *2 SX55*

The two villages of Plympton St Mary and Plympton St Maurice are nowadays almost part of **Plymouth**. The painter Sir Joshua Reynolds was born at Plympton St Maurice in 1723 and was educated at the local grammar school. Many of his paintings hang in Saltram House (NT), an 18th-century mansion, beautifully furnished, and built for the Parker family. Three miles north-east of Plympton is the Dartmoor Wildlife Park, occupying 25 acres of countryside.

Glen Lyon and Lochs Tay and Tummel
87 miles

From the attractive resort of Pitlochry the drive runs along the shore of Loch Tummel then through the Perthshire hills to enter Glen Lyon with its beautiful mountainous scenery. The magnificent Breadalbane Mountains, with mighty Ben Lawers at their centre, are the next feature of this rugged landscape, before the route drops down to Loch Tay and follows the valley on the return journey.

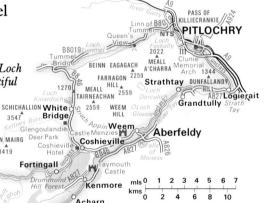

Leave **Pitlochry** on the Inverness road, A924 (A9). After 1 mile follow signs for Tummel Bridge and Kinloch Rannoch (B8019). One mile further, turn left and cross the River Garry. The road follows the River Tummel and then leads along the north shore of Loch Tummel. At **Tummel Bridge** turn left on to the Aberfeldy road (B846), and climb out of the valley before descending to the Coshieville Hotel. Here turn right on to an unclassified road to **Fortingall**. Half a mile beyond the village turn right (SP Glen Lyon, Bridge of Balgie) and follow the River Lyon into Glen Lyon. After 11 miles, pass Glen Lyon Post Office, turn left (unsigned) and cross the Bridge of Balgie (before joining a gated road) to begin the ascent into the Breadalbane Mountains. On the descent pass the Ben Lawers Mountain Visitor Centre and in 2 miles turn right to join A827 which follows the northern shore of Loch Tay to **Killin**. Cross the River Dochart and bear right, then take the next left turn (SP Ardeonaig, unclassified). Follow the southern shore of Loch Tay, passing through Ardeonaig and Acharn. Continue for 1½ miles, then turn right on to A827 (SP Aberfeldy). At **Aberfeldy** keep forward with A827 (SP Ballinluig) and in 5 miles pass through Grandtully. In a further ¾ mile turn left to

cross the River Tay. Later pass through Logierait, turn left (unclassified), and cross the River Tummel, turning right on to A9 to return to Pitlochry.

PLACES TO SEE

Pitlochry An attractive tourist resort on the River Tummel. Artificial Loch Faskally is surrounded by woodland with nature trails. The Power Station dam has exhibitions and a fish observation chamber.

Linn of Tummel (NTS), formerly known as the Falls of Tummel, is a lovely area of rushing water and woodland. Paths lead to Killiecrankie and the Queen's View.

Glengoulandie Deer Park Red deer, Highland cattle and many other interesting animals and birds can be seen here.

Glen Lyon Thirty-two miles long, Glen Lyon is one of the longest and most beautiful of all the Scottish glens.

Ben Lawers The Ben Lawers nature reserve is noted for its Alpine flowers and varied bird-life.

Killin In winter a ski-resort and in summer a centre for anglers and walkers, Killin is an attractive village on the western edge of Loch Tay.

Castle Menzies (OACT) A 16th-century, Z-plan tower, seat of the Chiefs of Clan Menzies.

FARMSTEADS

Houses, Byres and Barns

THE FARM HOUSE *has always been the focal point of a working farm (above) and its associated buildings – cowsheds, barns, dairy – were often ranged round a central courtyard (left).*

Farmsteads are an important part of the traditional rural scene, but like most other facets of the countryside, they have evolved and changed over the years. A farmstead is, of course, the home of a farmer, the organisational centre for the surrounding fields and it consists of the farm house and a number of associated buildings used for the storage of equipment, produce, fertilisers and foodstuffs and, sometimes, accommodation for livestock. Not all rural buildings are farms: the larger, older ones are likely to have been manor houses or the homes of medieval industrialists or traders, while the smaller cottages were the homes of farm labourers, commoners or small tradesmen.

DISPERSED FARMSTEADS in isolated locations are common features in most modern British landscapes, but in the Middle Ages, isolated farmsteads were rather uncommon in the English lowlands. When one finds a genuine medieval farm in an isolated lowland setting, then the existence of a deserted village should be suspected, for solitary farms often remained after the decay or destruction of a village, as at Muscott in Northamptonshire, and scores of other places. In other instances, the isolated lowland farm may be a legacy from an individual medieval exercise in 'assarting' or clearing a pocket of farmland from woodland or waste. A few more still developed from monastic farms or 'granges' or from medieval foresters' lodges.

In the lowland areas of England, medieval farmsteads tended to be grouped together in villages where the farmland was divided between scattered plough-strips, meadowland and common grazings. Many village-based farms still exist, while a good proportion of the older dwellings in a village will generally prove to be converted farmsteads. At Laxton in Nottinghamshire, where many features of the old open-field system of farming survive, working farmsteads still punctuate the village streets. It was only after the Parliamentary Enclosure of parish open fields in the 18th and 19th centuries that dispersed farmsteads became numerous in lowland England, for once the field-strips, meadows and commons had been partitioned into privately-owned, compact blocks of property it became practical for the owner to build new farm buildings outside the village and close to the centre of his recently allocated holding. Many scattered farmsteads therefore display the rather drab, symmetrical façades which were fashionable in the 18th and early 19th centuries.

In the rolling and hilly landscapes of Wales, Scotland and northern and western England, where population was always more thinly-spread and where livestock farming normally had precedence over grain-growing, dispersed farmsteads or farms grouped in hamlet-sized clusters were always the norm. Recent archaeological work in Cornwall suggests that some farm holdings may date right back to Romano-British times, while in Devon it has been shown that many of the dispersed farmsteads stand on the same sites as their Saxon predecessors.

and 19th centuries. In the course of the last two centuries, enormous changes have been wrought by the mechanisation of farming and the adoption of new techniques. Before mechanisation began to penetrate almost every aspect of farming in the latter part of the 19th century, a typical large farm might employ two or three score workers and support a dozen working horses. Substantial stabling and hay barns were needed, straw was stored in thatch-topped stacks, while the most imposing farm building was usually the threshing barn, with vast doors that were opened during the threshing of the grain by hand flails to allow the wind to blow away the chaff. The development of machines like the steam threshing engine, the reaper and binder and the tractor greatly reduced the need for both horses and men, while many of the old buildings became redundant. Stables and barns were often converted into machinery stores, while some of the buildings which harked back to the times when the farm was almost a self-sufficient unit were demolished.

TITHE BARNS were the most remarkable of all old agricultural buildings: gigantic timber-framed medieval structures which were mostly built to store produce that had been exacted as part of the parish tithe. A magnificent example can be seen at the rural-life museum at Stowmarket in Suffolk, while the Abbot's tithe barn at Glastonbury and the fine medieval example at Bradford-on-Avon in Wiltshire are equally impressive. A considerable number of dovecotes have escaped

GREAT COXWELL *The splendid stone tithe barn (above) was built in about 1250.*

WILLINGTON DOVECOT *This handsome building (above) houses 1500 nesting boxes, which indicates the importance of doves in the domestic economy of medieval times.*

destruction through being converted to other uses. A small number of large medieval examples survive, the most remarkable being preserved at Willington in Bedfordshire, but most dovecotes are round with conical roofs or square with pyramidal roofs and date from the 18th century. Granaries were usually box-like buildings which were raised above the ground on mushroom-like 'staddle stones' to protect the harvest from rats. A well preserved example stands on a green beside the ruins of the house in Cowdray Park at Midhurst in W Sussex.

PONDS are sometimes associated with farmsteads, and these have a variety of origins. Where the farm stands on a site which was occupied in medieval times, the pond may be all that remains of a rectangular surrounding moat, while other ponds were provided to water livestock, or for ducks. Medieval fishponds were not linked to particular farms but were created for the lord of the manor to provide a reliable and regular source of fresh protein. Most such fishponds have been dry and neglected for centuries, but their earthen banks often survive and one can frequently recognise the smaller ancillary ponds in which the young fish were reared. A good example lies amongst the deserted village remains on the outskirts of Cublington in Buckinghamshire.

THE TRADITIONAL FARM of popular perception – with its mixture of crop-growing and livestock-raising activities, free-range chickens, geese and ducks scratching in the yard and ranges of fine old buildings – is rarely seen today and may soon disappear completely. The buying-up and amalgamation of smaller farms and the abandonment of scores of unprofitable hill farms is gradually transforming the countryside and rural England is becoming increasingly dominated by large, highly mechanised and factory-like farm units. While a very small number of farm buildings are listed and enjoy a measure of protection, many others have been removed or are decaying. Some can be adapted to serve new uses but magnificent medieval timber-framed barns are vulnerable to fire and cannot withstand buffeting from large, modern farm machines. All but the largest and most obtrusive of modern farm buildings are immune from the planning restrictions which govern other rural developments and the surviving relics of the traditional farming scene are now facing a most uncertain future.

THE LONG-HOUSE was, during the Middle Ages, the most common design for the smaller farmstead, with the small, single-storey dwelling being sectioned to provide a living room for the people and a byre for the animals. More substantial, stone-walled long-houses were built in Scotland, Wales, northern and western England until well into the 18th century. Ruined long-houses are commonly seen in many areas of livestock farming from Orkney to Cornwall and many now serve as byres or storage buildings in the Yorkshire Dales. Here, 'laith-houses' in which the family and livestock were separated by an unbroken wall are also common.

'COURTYARD FARMS' were common for the larger medieval farmsteads: the farmhouse and the various barns, byres and other farm buildings were grouped around a rectangular yard which had an access way for carts. This was to prove a remarkably durable design and was employed in some of the improved and model farm designs of the 18th

THE GRANARY *was an important farm building in the past. It was often built only of wood, but many – such as the one preserved in Cowdray Park (below) – were more substantial.*

Plymouth, Devon 2 SY55

'The Marble-Streeted Town'

*'I reach the marble-streeted town, whose "Sound" outbreathes,
its air of sharp sea-salts.'*

THOMAS HARDY, *The Marble-Streeted Town.*

Its site at the head of Plymouth Sound, between the estuaries of the Rivers Plym and Tamar has made Plymouth a maritime city from its earliest days. The great Elizabethan sea captains, Drake, Raleigh, Hawkins and Frobisher, made it their base, and their exploits helped to bring fame and prosperity to Devon's principal city. Towards the end of the 17th century William III ordered the Devonport marshes to be drained, and the Royal Naval Dockyard to be built, thus giving the Navy an official presence in Plymouth. In World War II German bombs reduced the centre to rubble, but it has since risen again, its many new buildings dominated by the soaring 200ft tower of the Civic Centre, from the top of which there are magnificent views. Another excellent viewpoint is the Hoe (meaning 'High Place') where, as every schoolchild knows, Sir Francis Drake was enjoying a game of bowls in 1588 when the Armada was sighted, and insisted on finishing his game before setting sail to defeat the Spanish.

Other famous voyagers who embarked on historic journeys from Plymouth are commemorated by plaques on the Mayflower Steps in Sutton Pool, the ancient harbour which was the nucleus of the modern city. Most famous of all of them were the Pilgrim Fathers, who sailed for New England in the New World in their little ship *Mayflower* in

SIR FRANCIS DRAKE, *hero of the Armada, stands on the Hoe.*

1620. Just over 150 years later, in 1772, Captain James Cook set out on his round-the-world voyage of exploration, to be followed nearly 200 years later, in 1967, by Sir Francis Chichester, who landed here on his return from his solo voyage. Around Sutton Pool in the area known as the Barbican, is all that remains of Drake's Plymouth. Here, the narrow streets sloping down to the Quay preserve several Tudor houses.

Although this attractive and historic quarter has been sensitively preserved, Plymouth looks firmly to its future as a modern, commercial city.

PLACES TO SEE

Aquarium of the Marine Biological Association Fish and other kinds of marine life can be viewed in this fascinating aquarium.

Blackfriars Only the 16th-century refectory of this Dominican priory remains, on land belonging to a distillery where the famous 'Plymouth Gin' is made'.

City Museum and Art Gallery Paintings including some by Sir Joshua Reynolds; drawings, and finds from Dartmoor are among the collections displayed.

The Merchant's House One of the old houses in the Barbican district has been restored as a museum of Plymouth history.

Prysten House This is Plymouth's oldest house, built by a merchant in 1490 and used as a priests' house by monks of Plympton Priory. It has exhibits relating to the *Mayflower*.

Royal Citadel The barracks, beside the Hoe, date from the reign of Charles II, and feature a magnificent Baroque gateway designed by Sir Thomas Fitz.

St Andrew's Church This is the parish church of Plymouth, restored after bomb damage during World War II, and with magnificent modern windows designed by John Piper.

SMEATON'S TOWER *This old Eddystone lighthouse stood on the famous rock for 123 years (1759–1882). Then it was brought back to Plymouth to be erected on the Hoe.*

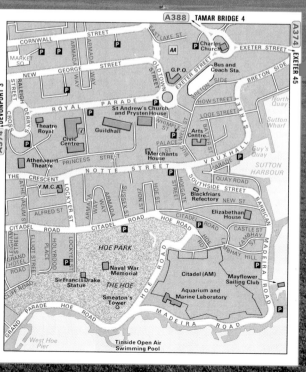

POCKLINGTON, Humberside
16 SE84
Magnificent water lilies can be seen at Burnby Hall Garden (OACT) where more than 50 different species bloom from May until October. The house once belonged to a Major Stewart, who gave it to the town, and his collection of sporting trophies and objects of interest from his travels is on display in the Hall. The town itself is pleasantly countrified and its church, All Saints, contains some remarkable carvings.

POLPERRO, Cornwall   *1 SX25*
One of the most enchanting of Cornwall's many picturesque fishing villages, Polperro acts as a magnet for tourists. It lies at the foot of a deep, wooded combe, its pretty cottages clustered round streets from which cars are banned in summer. One of the cottages houses a museum of smuggling; there is a miniature village, and an exhibition called The Land of Legend which portrays Cornwall's past history in miniature.

POLSTEAD, Suffolk   *12 TL93*
Notoriety came to this quiet little village in 1827 when Maria Marten was murdered at the Red Barn which stood near the church. The case was turned into a melodrama, *Maria Marten or The Murder at the Red Barn*, which became a 'smash hit' in Victorian times.

PONTEFRACT, W Yorkshire   *15 SE42*
The round black sweets known as Pontefract cakes were originally made of locally grown liquorice, but nowadays are made from imported roots. Where the liquorice field once was, stand the ruins of Pontefract Castle, where Richard II was imprisoned and eventually murdered. Many other notables were executed here in the Wars of the Roses and its reputation was so sinister that the townspeople petitioned Cromwell to pull it down. A painting of the castle before its destruction hangs in Pontefract Museum.

PONTYPOOL, Gwent   *8 SO20*
Tinplate was produced in this town in the heart of a coal-mining area for the first time in Britain in 1720, and it is believed that emigrants from Pontypool built the first forge in America in 1652. In Pontypool Park House, an exhibition called the Valley Inheritance relates the town's history.

PONTYPRIDD, Mid Glamorgan
8 ST09
Anchor chains for Nelson's Fleet, and, more recently for liners such as *Queen Elizabeth* and *Queen Mary* were made in this Rhondda Valley town whose main industries are coal and iron. The 18th-century bridge over the River Taff was designed by a self-taught engineer, William Edwards, and is considered a masterpiece. On a house in Mill Street is a plaque commemorating Evan and James James, clothmakers who wrote *Hen Wlad Fy Nhadau*, 'Land of My Fathers', the Welsh national anthem.

POOLE, Dorset   *3 SZ09*
Yachts and pleasure boats of all kinds throng Poole's enormous bay, a natural harbour, said to measure more than 100 miles round. Encroaching suburban development has now linked Poole to its

POLPERRO *Whitewashed, slate-roofed cottages cling to the hillside at the foot of a steep, wooded valley. The streets are so narrow that cars are forbidden to use them in summer.*

neighbour, **Bournemouth**, but Poole is much the older town of the two. The old Town House, Scalpen's Court, dating from the 15th century, is now a museum of local history, as is the former Guildhall, a nice example of Georgian civic architecture. At Poole Quay, some 15th-century cellars have been converted into a maritime museum, and the town also boasts an aquarium and a zoo. Poole Pottery, on the Quay was founded in 1875, and offers guided tours.

POOLEWE, Highland   *29 NG88*
Despite the fact that it lies on a more northerly latitude than Moscow, subtropical plants flourish in the remarkable gardens of Inverewe House (NTS), created by Osgood MacKenzie in 1862. He imported soil specially, planted extensive woodlands to shelter his more delicate plants, and the result is a maze of winding woodland walks where the flowers are at their best in spring and early summer.

PORLOCK, Somerset   *2 SS84*
Visitors have a choice of two routes into this attractive village: either the tortuous descent – 1 in 4 – of Porlock Hill, or more tamely, the toll road. It occupies a beautiful site, caught between Exmoor and the sea, but to get to the pebbly shore, visitors must first go to Porlock Weir, a tiny place clustered around a small harbour. From here, a footpath leads to Culbone Church – 'the smallest parish church in England', it is claimed – which occupies a lovely site in a deep, wooded combe beside a stream. Porlock holds a unique place in literature as the home of the anonymous 'person from Porlock' whose inconvenient visit interrupted Coleridge and caused him to abandon his unfinished poem, 'Kubla Khan'.

PORTHCURNO, Cornwall   *1 SW32*
Occupying a superb site 200ft up on the cliffs above the village, Minack Theatre, an open-air amphitheatre, modelled on the theatres of ancient Greece, was created in 1932 by Miss Rowena Cade. There is a

regular summer season of plays which attracts audiences from all over the world. Porthcurno has a fine beach of almost white sand.

PORTHMADOG, Gwynedd   *13 SH53*
A mile-long embankment along which a toll road runs, built in the early 1800s by William Madocks, created the safe harbour that made Porthmadog one of the best ports on the Welsh coast and ensured its prosperity. Extensive sandy beaches, such as Black Rock Sands have made it a popular tourist resort. It is also the start of the famous Festiniog narrow-gauge railway, which runs from the Harbour Station to the old slate quarries of **Blaenau-Ffestiniog**. There is a Railway Museum at the station. Porthmadog Pottery (OACT) offers visitors guided tours.

PORT ISAAC, Cornwall   *1 SW98*
The old village climbs up the hillsides from the picturesque harbour, a maze of lanes and alleys, called 'drangs', crowded with a jumble of attractive cottages. Fishing for shellfish is still almost as important as the tourist trade.

PORTLAND, ISLE OF, Dorset
3 SY67
An isthmus and the pebble spit of Chesil Bank are all that join Portland to the mainland. A community of scattered villages, Portlanders long claimed to be of different ancestry to their neighbours on the mainland, and jealously preserved their own customs, and traditions, including that of smuggling. Many famous buildings, such as St Paul's Cathedral, have been built of the stone from its vast quarries, and a large naval harbour was constructed by convict labour in the 19th century. On the southern tip, at Portland Bill, there is a lighthouse, and there are spectacular views out to sea, where the waves breaking on Pulpit Rock are an awesome sight. Portland Castle (AM) was erected in the reign of Henry VIII; Portland Museum is housed in a cottage associated with Thomas Hardy's novel, *The Well-Beloved*.

PORTMEIRION, Gwynedd *13 SH53*
The inspiration for this delightful fantasy, created by the architect Sir Clough Williams Ellis, who died in 1978, was the Italian fishing village of Portofino. On his return to Britain he searched for a suitable site, and finally found the ideal setting on a wooded, rocky promontory between **Porthmadog** and **Harlech**. Graceful, Italianate buildings, dominated by an elegant campanile, surround the main square, and all manner of exotic plants flourish in the picturesque streets. All the cottages are let as holiday homes, and there are also hotels, restaurants and shops. Visitors must pay an entrance fee.

PORT OF MENTEITH, Central
22 NN50
The resort lies on the shores of the beautiful Lake of Menteith, sheltered by the Menteith Hills. Ferries run to an island in the lake where the ruins of Inchmaholme Priory (AM) can be seen. It was founded as an Augustinian House in 1238. The four-year-old Mary Queen of Scots took refuge here in 1543 and the garden where she played, known as Queen Mary's Bower, still remains.

PORT SUNLIGHT, Merseyside
14 SJ38
The name of this Victorian 'model village' commemorates Sunlight soap, the product that helped to found the vast fortune of William Hesketh Lever, who became the 1st Viscount Leverhulme. The Lady Lever Art Gallery and Museum contains a magnificent collection of English painting and furniture.

PORT TALBOT, W Glamorgan
8 SS79
First copper-smelting, then the exporting of coal from the nearby Rhondda Valley, finally the vast Margam and Abbey steelworks and BP's chemical works have brought industry to Port Talbot, one of the larger towns of South Wales, and improvements to its docks, culminating in the huge tidal harbour constructed in 1970. The recession of the early 1980s has dealt Port Talbot's industries a hard blow.

POTTER HEIGHAM, Norfolk
12 TG42
In summer the vast numbers of visitors to this popular Broadland yachting centre make it difficult to appreciate the charm of the old village, with its thatched church and medieval bridge over the River Thurne. To the north lies Hickling Broad, to the south-east, Ormesby Broad.

POTTERIES, THE, Staffordshire
14 SJ84
This is the name given to the towns which were joined to Stoke to make the modern city of **Stoke on Trent**: Tunstall, Burslem, Hanley, Fenton and Longton.

POWDERHAM CASTLE, Devon
2 SX98
Cedars in the deer park make an appropriately lordly setting for Powderham Castle (OACT), seat of the Earls of Devon. Originally built in late 14th century, the castle was much altered in the 18th and 19th centuries, from which period most of the fine furnishings date. Family portraits include some by Kneller and Reynolds.

PORTMEIRION *was inspired by Italy, but some buildings, such as 'the Gloriette', above, are follies made up of architectural 'oddments'.*

POWERSTOCK, Dorset *3 SY59*
Ranks of stone-built houses climbing up the hillside to the square church qualify this Dorset village for the over-used epithet 'unspoiled', as does its idyllic setting at the foot of the Downs. Brooding over the village is the impressive Iron-Age fort of Eggardon Hill, and on another hilltop is the mound of the now vanished Powerstock Castle. St Mary's Church, although much restored, contains fine 15th-century carvings.

POWIS CASTLE, Powys *8 SJ20*
Set in an extensive park planted with ancient oak trees, the castle (NT) towers above beautiful terraced gardens, which drop 100ft in four dramatic stages. These were created in the 17th century by the Earl of Rochford, an interloper in the long line of the Herbert family who held the title of Earls of Powis. *See also* **Welshpool**.

PRESTATYN, Clwyd *13 SJ08*
Prestatyn is one of the most popular resorts on the North Wales coast, and caters for the holidaymakers' every need, with amusement grounds, boating lakes, two holiday camps and a miniature railway.

PRESTBURY, Cheshire *14 SJ97*
The charm of this ancient village, whose long main street winds over the River Bollin and past a noble church, has brought it almost as many critics as tourists. The critics find it the archetype of the Cheshire 'stockbroker belt', but while it is true that Prestbury is well placed for commuters, its centre has remained remarkably unaffected. The bank has taken over the old half-timbered priest's house, and looks across to St Peter's Church, which dates back to 1220 and has some fine old furnishings. In the churchyard are the remains of a Saxon cross and an unusually well preserved Norman chapel.

PRESTEIGNE, Powys *8 SO36*
Handsome Georgian houses line Broad Street, one of the most attractive thoroughfares in this old country town, once the capital of Radnorshire. In the half-timbered Radnorshire Arms a priest is said to have lived in hiding for two years, and the secret room still exists. The carillon mechanism in Presteigne church dates from the 17th century and is believed to be the only one of its kind in Britain.

PRESTON, Lancashire *14 SD52*
Preston was one of the most important centres of the cotton trade, and one of the cradles of the Industrial Revolution. The inventor of the spinning-frame, Richard Arkwright, was born at Preston, but had to take his invention to **Nottingham** to avoid riots. In the Harris Museum exhibits tell the history of the cotton trade, and there are interesting archaeological remains and collections of glass and ceramics.

PRESTONPANS, Lothian *24 NT37*
The famous battle took place in 1745 when Bonnie Prince Charlie's army won an astonishing and decisive victory in a mere ten minutes. The town was once a centre of salt-panning and was also famous for its oysters. Many of its attractive houses date from the 17th-century, as does the fine Mercat Cross.

PRESTWICH, Gtr Manchester
14 SD80
An industrial town, now inextricably part of **Manchester**, Prestwich boasts, in Heaton Hall (OACT), one of the finest late 18th-century houses in Lancashire, designed by James Wyatt for the Earl of Wilton. The interior is richly decorated.

PROBUS, Cornwall *1 SW84*
The village is famous for only one thing: the beautifully carved church tower, acclaimed as the finest in Cornwall. It dates from the 16th century and stands 125ft high. Not far away is the County Demonstration Garden and Arboretum (OACT) and at Trewitten, Trewitten House (OACT) stands in 20 acres of magnificent gardens.

PUDDLETOWN, Dorset *3 SY79*
As charming as its name suggests, Puddletown stands at the foot of the Piddle Valley, and only changed its old name of Piddletown in the 1950s. Hardy called it Weatherby in *Far from the Madding Crowd* and the open country between the village and Wareham features in several of his novels as Egdon Heath. A mile-long avenue of rhododendrons leads through Puddletown Forest.

PUFFIN ISLAND, Gwynedd *13 SH68*
Lying half a mile off **Anglesey**, Puffin Island is now deserted except for seabirds, especially puffins. There was once a monastic settlement here, founded by St Seiriol in the 5th or 6th century. Danish invaders destroyed it in 853, after which the island was used as a burial place by monks of Penmon Priory.

PULBOROUGH, W Sussex *5 TQ01*
Three miles south-east of this pleasant little market town is Parham House, an Elizabethan mansion set in beautiful gardens (OACT).

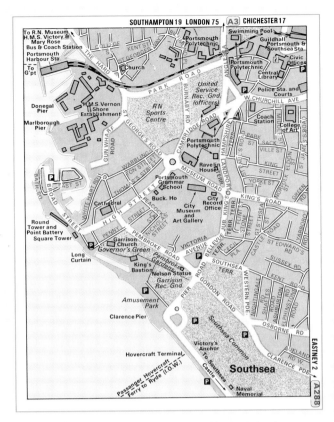

SOUTHAMPTON 19 LONDON 75 [A3] CHICHESTER 17

Southsea

Britain's Premier Naval Base

'A noble place, with pleasant waters.'

QUEEN VICTORIA

The first monarch to appreciate the strategic importance of Portsea Island in the defence of the English Channel was Richard the Lionheart, who ordered the first docks to be built in 1194: 'It pleased the Lord King Richard to build the town of Portsmouth', reads the entry in the Curia Regis rolls of that year. Over the centuries, succeeding monarchs have improved the defences and extended the docks to ensure that Portsmouth remained an impregnable fortress and secure base for the navy in times of war. The King's Bastion and the Long Cur-

HMS VICTORY *(above) and (below) the gun deck.*

tain Battery are all that remain of the medieval defensive ramparts, but the Round Tower, earliest of the fortifications, and the Square Tower, built by Henry VII, still remain, as do the sea and land forts built in the Victorian era.

The docks have grown steadily since the 12th century: in 1495 the world's first dry dock was constructed, and by the reign of Henry VIII, the docks had extended to cover about eight acres of land – they now cover about 300 acres. Henry not only built Southsea Castle to improve the defences, he also built ships, including the pride of his fleet, the *Mary Rose*, which tragically sank with all hands just off the coast. In 1982, in one of the most exciting marine salvage operations ever undertaken, she was raised from the seabed and will eventually be put on display. During the Napoleonic Wars the town played a key role as a base for the British fleet, and Nelson set out from here to take command at Trafalgar on 21st October 1805. The *Victory*, his flagship, was eventually brought to dry dock in Portsmouth Docks.

Portsmouth suffered much from bombing in World War II, and the centre has been largely rebuilt. The old town, clustered around the harbour mouth, has been restored, and is now an attractive and fashionable area. In these old streets stands the cathedral, raised from the status of parish church in the 1920s.

Southsea, Portsmouth's neighbour, grew up in the 19th century as an elegant seaside resort, with fine houses and terraces, an esplanade, and an extensive seafront common made by draining the marshes. Still a pleasant resort, Southsea is now part of the City of Portsmouth, as is Eastney, which grew up on its outskirts in the 19th century. Also 18th- and 19th-century developments are the 'villages' of Portsea, where many of the shipwrights and craftsmen employed in the docks had their homes, and Landport, now the commercial and administrative centre of the modern city. Charles Dickens was born in this area in 1812 in a house on Old Commerical Road.

PLACES TO SEE

Charles Dickens Birthplace Museum The modest family home is now a Dickens shrine.

HMS *Victory* and Royal Naval Museum Admiral Lord Nelson's flagship is the only surviving First Rate Ship of the Line of its period. The adjacent museum houses other relics of Trafalgar.

The Round Tower (OACT) is the earliest of Portsmouth's permanent defences.

City Museum and Art Gallery Housed in part of the old Pembroke Barracks.

Southsea Castle (OACT) Built in 1545, the castle houses a museum of historical and archaeological interest.

Cumberland House Museum Natural history exhibits, and an aquarium are housed here.

Royal Marine Museum, Eastney The museum is housed in the original Victorian Officers' Mess.

Eastney Pumping Station (OACT) Two Boulton and Watt engines can be seen working on most summer weekends.

Fort Widley (OACT) Built in the 1860s this fort and others like it were the last defensive structures to be built on the principles of a medieval castle.

PORTSMOUTH HARBOUR *in the days of sail, when the city was Britain's chief naval base.*

PURBECK, ISLE OF, Dorset *3 ST88, SZ09*
This is the name given to the stretch of land between Poole Bay and Lulworth Cove. Purbeck marble has been widely used as a building material.

PURSE CAUNDLE, Dorset *3 ST61*
In the centre of the village stands Purse Caundle Manor (OACT), a fascinating medieval house preserving its original great hall and upper chamber. It is well-known for its resident ghost.

PWLLHELI, Gwynedd *13 SH33*
One of the largest and oldest of the Butlin's holiday camps stands just outside this popular seaside resort. It is also the main town of the Lleyn Peninsula and has a long maritime history.

QUAINTON, Buckinghamshire *10 SP71*
The Quainton Railway Centre (OACT) has one of the country's most comprehensive collections of items relating to standard-gauge railways. The village itself is exceptionally attractive, with a large green and many thatched cottages. Many imposing monuments and medieval brasses embellish the interior of the church.

QUANTOCK HILLS, THE, Somerset *2 ST13*
The Visitor Centre for the Quantocks is at Fyne Court, Broomfield, and is worth visiting for information about this lovely range of hills. The slopes are heavily wooded, and the tops are clothed with attractive heathland. Red deer run wild, and there are regular hunts at the appropriate seasons. Crowcombe, East Quantoxhead, Spaxton and Enmore are among the most attractive villages, and there are some beautiful wooded valleys, particularly in the north-east.

QUEENSFERRY, SOUTH, Lothian *23 NT17*
The old ferry that used to ply across the Firth of Forth departed from Hawes Pier, where there is an old inn featured both by Sir Walter Scott, in *The Antiquary* and by Robert Louis Stevenson in *Kidnapped*. The ferry stopped in 1964 when the Forth Road Bridge was opened. This 2000yd-long bridge is as impressive a piece of engineering as the 2765yd-long railway bridge that was built at the end of the 19th century. Dalmeny House (OACT), home of the Earl of Rosebery, commands magnificent views of the Firth of Forth. The house contains the Rothschild Collection of 18th-century French furniture, porcelain and tapestries. Two miles west, Hopetown House (OACT) is Scotland's most distinguished Adam mansion, home of the Marquis of Linlithgow. Deer and St Kilda sheep co-exist peacefully in the grounds, and the house contains interesting furnishings.

RADNOR FOREST, Powys *8 SO16*
Main roads enclose this distinct, triangular, area of 2000ft-high hills, whose valleys are watered by many streams. The name 'Forest' is used here in the medieval sense, meaning a royal hunting ground, rather than dense woodland although in fact afforestation has taken place on the northern and eastern sides. In a wooded glen one and half miles west of New Radnor is the 70ft high waterfall picturesquely called 'Water-break-its-neck', best seen after heavy rainfall.

RAGLAN, Gwent *8 SO40*
On a knoll just outside the village are the impressive ruins of 15th-century Raglan Castle (AM). One of the latest examples of medieval fortification in Britain, it was a Royalist centre during the Civil War, holding out against Fairfax for 11 weeks in 1646. One side of the moated five-storey Great Tower was blown up and the rest of the castle slighted.

RAMSGATE, Kent *6 TR36*
A popular family resort with cliff-backed sands, Ramsgate has been a busy seafaring town since its harbour was built in the 18th century. It also has nowadays a busy yacht marina, and is a resort for sea-anglers. One mile south, at Pegwell Bay, where Vikings landed in the 5th century, there is a hovercraft terminal. A replica of a Viking ship crossed from Denmark in 1949 and now stands on the cliffs above the bay.

RANWORTH, Norfolk *12 TG31*
Particularly fine treasures in the parish church of this village between Ranworth and South Walsham Broads include a 14th- or 15th-century painted screen and an illuminated 15th-century choir book of great beauty, the Ranworth (or Sarum) Antiphoner. From the top of the church tower there are lovely views over Ranworth Broad. The Broadland Conservation Centre, on Ranworth Inner Broad, can be reached by a nature trail.

RAVENGLASS, Cumbria *18 SD09*
Once a port, this unspoilt fishing village stands on the estuary of the Rivers Esk, Mite and Irt. It is best known for the seven-mile long Ravenglass and Eskdale railway which runs to Dalegarth through the beautiful Eskdale Valley. Established in 1875 to carry iron ore, this 15-inch narrow gauge railway, affectionately known as 'L'aal Ratty', now carries passengers using both steam and diesel locomotives. There is a Railway Museum here. Also near Ravenglass, at Walls Castle, are some of the best-preserved Roman ruins in the north.

RAVENSCAR, N Yorkshire *20 NZ90*
For serious walkers this village is one end of the 40-mile Lyke Wake Walk which crosses the North York Moors from Osmotherley. The small rocky beach can only be reached by a steep descent down the cliff.

READING, Berkshire *4 SU77*
Situated on the Rivers Thames and Kennet, this large university town is a shopping and market centre for a large area, with varied industries and much redevelopment. The Romans settled in the area over 2000 years ago, and exhibits in the local Museum and Art Gallery include an exceptional collection of finds from the nearby Roman town of Silchester. There are scant remains of a once-important 12th-century abbey, where Henry I was buried. The Museum of English Rural Life, situated in the university, has an interesting collection of agricultural, domestic and crafts exhibits.

REAY, Highland *30 NC96*
Sand-dunes separate the village from the sandy beach of Sandside Bay: in the 18th century they engulfed an earlier settlement. Two miles north-east a farm contains the remains of Dounreay Castle, including a 16th-century tower. A 135ft sphere marks the site of the United Kingdom Atomic Energy Authority. There is an exhibition relating to fast reactors and nuclear energy.

POWER SOURCE OF THE FUTURE

Britain's first experimental nuclear fast-breeder reactor was built near Reay in the wilds of Caithness in the 1950s. Fast-breeders, like that pictured above, are controversial because of the amount of radioactive waste produced, but they generate more energy than other types of nuclear reactors.

RECULVER, Kent *6 TR26*
Two towers of a Norman church destroyed in 1809 are preserved to serve as a navigational guide for Thames shipping. They stand on the site of a 7th-century Saxon church, and walls also remain of a Roman fort (AM) built in about AD 200.

REDCAR, Cleveland *20 NZ62*
Miles of firm, sandy beaches stretch from here to the Tees estuary, where they are backed by sand dunes. Not surprisingly the town has become a lively resort, with a wide range of leisure and entertainment facilities, including Coatham Amusement Park, the largest indoor funfair in the north-east. There is also a well-known racecourse. The oldest lifeboat in the world, built in 1800, can be seen in the Zetland Museum on the Promenade, which also has displays relating to sea rescue, fishing and marine life.

RESTORMEL CASTLE *Once the stronghold of the Earls of Cornwall, Restormel saw little action and has been empty since the Roundheads used it in the 1600s.*

REDDITCH, Hereford & Worcester
9 SP06
Now being developed as a New Town,
Redditch has many new industries,
although it is still the centre of needle-
making, for which it is traditionally
famous. Two miles north, beside the
partially excavated ruins of a 12th-century
Cistercian abbey, is a forge mill. Open by
appointment only, it was converted to
needle-scouring between 1728 and 1730.

REDMIRE, N Yorkshire *20 SE09*
Pale stone cottages are scattered round the
large green of this peaceful, isolated
Wensleydale village. To the north are
limestone hills; to the south, the wooded
valley of the River Ure, with its waterfall,
Redmire Force, one mile south-west. Mary
Queen of Scots was imprisoned for a time in
14th-century Bolton Castle which stands
just over a mile to the north-east of the
village.

REDRUTH, Cornwall, see **Camborne &
Redruth**

REEDHAM, Norfolk *12 TG40*
The River Yare, on which the village is
situated, may be crossed by chain ferry,
which takes both cars and passengers.
Those interested in the art of taxidermy can
visit the museum at Pettitts Rural
Industries, where there are often craft
demonstrations too. The buildings are set
in gardens where pheasants, peacocks and
all sorts of waterfowl and game birds are on
show. There are several disused windmills
in the vicinity, but 19th-century Berney
Arms Windmill (AM), in a lonely part of
Havergate Marshes, three miles north-east,
is in full working order. It can be reached
by boat from Great Yarmouth, or there is a
train to Berney Arms station. The road to
the mill is not suitable for cars.

REEPHAM, Norfolk *12 TG02*
Centre of a barley-growing and brewing
region in the 18th century, the village has
an attractive market square, evidence of its
past prosperity. Many fine buildings
remain from this period, and there were
once three churches which shared one
churchyard although only two still stand. A
comprehensive collection of British and
European mammals, as well as birds of
prey, in natural surroundings, can be seen
in the 50-acre Norfolk Wildlife Park, two
miles south of the village.

REIGATE, Surrey *5 TQ25*
Pleasantly situated on the edge of the North
Downs, Reigate has good open spaces,
including the 130-acre Reigate Heath.
Church services are held in a converted
220-year-old windmill on the heath. The
town retains some interesting old buildings,
despite modern development. Founded in
1235, the priory was converted into a
Tudor mansion which now houses a school,
but part is used as a museum. Nothing
remains of the Norman castle except the
mound on which it stood, in Castle
Grounds. Beneath it is a cave and medieval
tunnels, used as air-raid shelters in World
War II.

RENFREW, Strathclyde *22 NS56*
Sprawling along the River Clyde west of
Glasgow, this heavily industrialised former
county town is an ancient Royal Burgh. Its
charter dates from 1396, and it is
considered to be the cradle of the Royal
House of Stuart. One of the Prince of
Wales' many titles is Baron Renfrew.

REPTON, Derbyshire *10 SK32*
This little village, whose broad main street
is lined by attractive timber-framed and
Georgian red-brick houses, was the 7th-
century capital of the Saxon kingdom of

Mercia. The tiny 10th-century crypt of the
medieval church is a treasured example of
Anglo-Saxon architecture. Ruins of a 12th-
century priory are incorporated into
Repton School, founded in 1557.

RESTORMEL, Cornwall *1 SX16*
One mile north of Lostwithiel,
commanding the Fowey Valley, stands
well-preserved Restormel Castle (AM). The
circular mound and gateway were built in
about 1100, the notable round keep about
1200. Nearby is a rectangular 13th-century
chapel.

RHAYADER, Powys *8 SN96*
A bustling but attractive market town on
the River Wye, Rhayader has become a
tourist centre for the Upper Wye Valley
and **Elan Valley**. One of the prettiest
stretches of the Wye can be seen between
here and Llangurig, eight miles upstream.
The Elan Valley, three miles west, is
popular for walking and pony-trekking.

RHONDDA, Mid Glamorgan *8 SS99*
A chain of towns in two valleys, Rhondda
Fawr ('large'), and Rhondda Fach ('small'),
make up the densely populated Rhondda
borough. The valleys are separated by the
Cefu Rhondda ridge, which reaches 2000ft
in places. In the 19th century these pleasant
rural valleys were transformed by
coalmines and miners' cottages, but only
three collieries are still working today.

RHOOSE, S Glamorgan *8 ST06*
A small village on the South Glamorgan
coast, four miles east of Barry, Rhoose has
recently begun to attract holidaymakers.
Just to the north is Cardiff Airport,
adjacent to which is the Wales Aircraft
Museum containing more than 20 aircraft,
as well as engines, photographs and
models.

RHUDDLAN, Clwyd *13 SJ07*
The majestic ruins of Rhuddlan Castle lie
on a mound above the banks of the River
Clwyd. Begun in 1277 by Edward I, the
castle (AM) was built on a diamond plan,
and the remains of towers, gatehouses and
9ft-thick curtain walls can be seen. A
Royalist stronghold in the Civil War, the
castle was slighted by the Roundheads after
it surrendered to them in 1648.
Bodryhddan Hall, one and a half miles east,
stands in fine grounds and contains armour,
furniture and notable pictures.

RHYL, Clwyd *13 SJ08*
With three miles of sandy beaches and a
good sunshine record, Rhyl has become the
most popular resort on the North Wales
coast. It offers the holidaymaker numerous
leisure facilities, with fun-fair, boating
lake, amusement park, roller-skating rink,
cycle track, bandstands and open-air
swimming pool. There are two theatres and
a golf links, and pleasant gardens include
the Botanical Gardens, and Royal Floral
Hall with sub-tropical plants.

RHYNIE, Grampian *27 NJ42*
The 1851ft Tap o' Noth, rising from the
Clashindarroch Forest, dominates this
village, set around an attractive green
which serves as a market square. There is
an ancient Crow Stone in a field near the
church, displaying various Pictish symbols.
Leith Hall (NTS) three and a half miles
north-east, dates in part from 1650. Built
round a courtyard, it contains Jacobean
relics and has a fine rock garden.

RIBCHESTER, Lancashire *14 SD63*
Green hills encircle this pleasant village
situated in a curve of the River Ribble,
crossed here by an 18th-century bridge. A
great Roman fort, built in about AD 80,

RHUDDLAN CASTLE *This was the second of the
eight massive fortresses Edward I built in Wales.*

covered six acres of ground. There are some
exposed remains of the granary, and a
museum contains many interesting finds,
including coins, pottery and jewellery and a
unique collection of celtic heads. Stones
and possibly even pillars from the fort were
used to build the 13th-century church.

RICHBOROUGH, Kent *6 TR36*
Some of the best-preserved Roman walls in
England, 12ft thick and up to 24ft high,
can be found here. They are part of the
ruins of a 3rd-century fort (AM) which
defended Rutupiae, the chief port of entry
for Roman legions. From here Watling
Street led to London and on to Chester. A
museum houses an interesting collection of
finds from the site.

RICHMOND, N Yorkshire *20 NZ10*
In the 11th century a splendid castle (AM)
was built on a hill here to guard the
entrance to Swaledale. Today one of the
best views of this lovely old country town, a
good centre for exploring the **Yorkshire
Dales National Park**, can be had from the
top of the 100ft tower. From here can be
seen the large cobbled market square, the
River Swale and the moors beyond.
Dominating the market square is a
medieval church, from the tower of which a
curfew bell is rung every evening. The
church now houses the regimental museum
of the Green Howards. The town has
several Georgian houses and a splendidly
restored Georgian theatre, built in 1788 and
reopened in 1962.

**RICHMOND-UPON-THAMES, Gtr
London** *5 TQ17*
Beautifully situated on the slopes of a hill,
with sweeping views of a wide curve of the
Thames below from the Terrace at the top,
Richmond is well known for the 2400-acre
Richmond Park, the largest of the royal
parks. Enclosed for hunting by Charles I in
1637, it has large stretches of unspoilt
pasture, heath and woodland, with herds of
red and fallow deer. Royalty from Queen
Victoria to the present Queen have stayed
in the 18th-century White Lodge, now part
of the Royal Ballet School. Little remains of
the old medieval royal palace, but Thatched
Cottage is the home of Princess Alexandra
and Mr Angus Ogilvy.

RICKMANSWORTH, Hertfordshire
5 TQ09
Situated at the meeting point of three
rivers, this former market town is set
among lakes and water-meadows. A lovely
old town, its long winding High Street
boasts several handsome Georgian
buildings, including an imposing seven-
bayed house, once the home of William
Penn, the Quaker leader and founder of
Pennsylvania.

RIDGEWAY, THE *11 SP91–3 SU06*
In 1973 an 85-mile long-distance footpath
was opened by the Countryside
Commission. Running between **Ivinghoe
Beacon** in Buckinghamshire and **Avebury**
in Wiltshire, part of it follows the route of
an ancient trackway along the Berkshire
Downs above the Kennet Valley, which
was in use as a trade route long before the
coming of the Romans.

RIEVAULX, N Yorkshire *15 SE58*
In a lovely, secluded, wooded site in the
Rye Valley, below the North York Moors,
are the majestic and extensive ruins of
Rievaulx Abbey (AM). The once-
prosperous abbey was founded in 1132 by
the Cistercians and at one time had 140
monks and more than 500 lay brothers.
Overlooking the abbey, with beautiful
views of Ryedale and the Hambleton Hills,
is the half-mile sweep of Rievaulx Terrace
(NT), landscaped in the 18th century by
the owner of nearby Duncombe Park.

ISABELLA PLANTATION *These lovely water-gardens situated in Richmond Park are famous for their
beautiful varieties of azaleas and the Plantation can be seen at its best in May and June.*

RINGWOOD, Hampshire *4 SU10*
To the west of the New Forest, this market town is situated on the trout-rich River Avon. Although divided by a fast dual carriageway, the town has attractive old houses, some thatched. Monmouth House is so called because in 1685 the Duke of Monmouth stayed here after his defeat in the Battle of Sedgemoor, before being taken to London for execution.

RIPLEY, N Yorkshire *15 SE26*
West of the village square is magnificent 16th- to late 18th-century Ripley Castle (OACT), with Cromwellian associations and grounds landscaped by Capability Brown. The Ingilby family have lived at a castle here since 1350, and in 1827 the lord of the manor attempted to remodel the village on the lines of a French village.

RIPON, N Yorkshire *15 SE37*
Narrow winding streets lead from the rectangular market-square of this small town on the River Ure. The town has a cathedral dating from the 12th century and later. It stands on the site of an Anglo-Saxon church, of which the crypt remains, now containing an exhibition of church treasures. At one corner of the Square is the medieval Wakeman's house, now a local museum. It was the home of the town's night-watchman, and a 1000 year tradition is still observed each night at 9pm, when the present Wakeman blows his horn. This once marked the start of his nightly vigil.
   The ruins of Cistercian Fountains Abbey can be seen three miles south-west, as well as the extensive 650-acre Studley Royal Country Park, with deer, lake and ornamental gardens.

ROBIN HOOD'S BAY, N Yorkshire *20 NZ20*
At the northern end of a three-mile long bay, sheltered by rocky cliffs, the little houses of this picturesque and colourful old fishing village cling precariously to the steep slopes of a ravine. Cars are best left at the top of the hill, as the narrow streets can only be satisfactorily explored on foot. Sand is exposed at low tide and the village has become a popular tourist resort. The **North Yorkshire Moors National Park** lies to the south-west, and there is a scenic coastal path to **Whitby**.

ROCHDALE, Gt Manchester *14 SD81*
This old mill town near the Pennine moors now has had to turn to new industries to supplement the traditional textile industry on which its wealth is based. Although a few of the old weavers' houses with top stories lined by long horizontal windows remain, large new blocks of flats are dominant. The town was the birthplace of the world-wide co-operative movement – the Rochdale Equitable Pioneers' Society – and the original shop, opened in 1844 at 31 Toad Lane, is now a museum. Two miles east, at Blackstone Edge, is one of the best preserved stretches of Roman road in Britain.

ROCHE ABBEY, S Yorkshire *15 SK59*
Although in ruins, the walls of the north and south transepts of this 12th-century Cistercian abbey (AM) still stand to their full height. The abbey has a particularly fine setting, in a grassy valley landscaped by Capability Brown in the 18th century.

Nidderdale and the Washburn Valley
55 miles

On the edge of the Yorkshire Dales is a region of rich farmland watered by pleasant rivers. The landscape is gentle, dotted with strangely weathered outcrops of rock, ancient ruins and little country towns and villages.

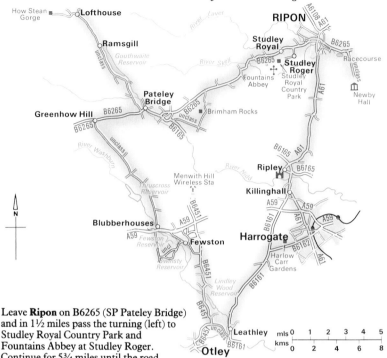

Leave **Ripon** on B6265 (SP Pateley Bridge) and in 1½ miles pass the turning (left) to Studley Royal Country Park and Fountains Abbey at Studley Roger. Continue for 5¾ miles until the road emerges on to Pateley Moor. Near the summit turn left (unclassified, SP Brimham Rocks). Two miles further, on the right, is Brimham Rocks carpark, and ½ mile further, at the crossroads, turn right (SP Pateley Bridge). Descend and in 1¾ miles turn right on to B6165 then join B6265 for **Pateley Bridge**. Cross the bridge and either detour right (unclassified) up the valley of the River Nidd to Lofthouse, a return journey of 13 miles, or continue with the main route, B6265 (SP Skipton), to **Greenhow Hill**. Beyond the hamlet turn left (unclassified, SP Blubberhouses) and drive for about 7 miles to **Blubberhouses** in the Washburn Valley. At the junction with A59 turn right, then shortly left at the church on to the unclassified Otley road. In just under 1½ miles turn left (SP Timble) and left

again (SP Fewston). Cross over a dam, then bear right with the Norwood road. At the junction with B6451 turn right (SP Otley) and later cross Lindley Wood Reservoir, then in 1¾ miles at the T-junction turn left (unclassified, SP Leathley, Pool). In another 1¼ miles cross the River Washburn and turn left on to B6161 (SP Killinghall) for Leathley. Continue on B6161 for 5 miles, then turn right on to B6162 (SP Harrogate) and pass the turning (left) for Harlow Car Gardens before entering **Harrogate**. Leave the town following Ripon signs on A61 and drive through Killinghall, cross the River Nidd, then at the roundabout turn left (unclassified) into **Ripley**. At the end of the village, at the roundabout, take the 2nd exit to rejoin A61 and drive back to Ripon.

PLACES TO SEE

Ripon The gateway to the Dales, Ripon has an impressive cathedral and many historic buildings. Every evening the 'Wakeman' blows the town's horn in the market square, a ceremony dating back to Saxon times.

Studley Royal Country Park Deer, a lavishly decorated 19th-century church and other buildings grace this attractive country park.

Fountains Abbey Ruins (AM) of the once-great Cistercian Abbey stand in a lovely setting in Studley Royal Country Park.

Brimham Rocks (NT) An outcrop of rocks sculpted by natural forces into strange shapes.

Pateley Bridge The Nidderdale Museum in this attractive little town contains many interesting exhibits of life in the Yorkshire Dales. Stump Cross Caverns, west of the town, are well worth a visit.

Lofthouse and How Stean Gorge The gorge, a dramatic 70ft cleft in Upper Nidderdale is accessible from Lofthouse.

Harrogate A former spa resort, Harrogate is famed for its beautiful Valley Gardens, leading into Harlow Car Trial Gardens, used for experimental horticulture. The Pump Room houses a costume museum.

Ripley The castle (OACT) dates from the 16th and 18th centuries and stands in a beautifully landscaped park.

ROCHESTER *An Anglo-Saxon church originally stood on the site of this imposing cathedral, which is largely Norman, despite suffering damage during the Civil War and undergoing restoration.*

ROCHESTER, Kent   6 TQ76
Strategically placed on the lower reaches of the River Medway, Rochester has been inhabited since pre-Roman times, and was developed to guard the important crossing over the river, on the route between London and Dover. The Romans built a walled city here, later re-fortified by the Saxons in about AD 600. The town's importance was recognised by William the Conqueror, who ordered a castle (AM) to be built to defend it: only the 113ft-high keep remains. Today the town is a busy port and industrial and commercial centre, whose older buildings are clustered round the cathedral and in the High Street. The cathedral, founded by St Augustine, was consecrated in AD 604, and became England's second bishopric. The present building is mainly Norman, dating from 1080, with a fine north-west door and impressive west front. The crypt is particularly fine, and the tombs of several medieval bishops can be seen. Ancient manuscripts in the cathedral library include a copy of Miles Coverdale's English version of the Bible, printed in 1535. The cathedral is set in peaceful open lawns, where the ruins of the chapter house, cloisters and gateways of a monastery destroyed during the Reformation can be seen.

Rochester has many associations with Charles Dickens, who lived at Gad's Hill for many years until his death in 1870. The Charles Dickens Centre at Eastgate House, a fine late Tudor house in the High Street, contains a display of Dickens' characters and makes clever use of sound and light to bring the displays to life. Many of the houses and inns in the town, including Eastgate House, feature in his novels, and a re-erected Swiss chalet from the garden of Gad's Hill can be seen in the grounds. Also of interest is the museum, housed in the red-brick Guildhall, built in 1687. It contains general collections of arms and armour, ship models, Victoriana, and toys.

ROCKBOURNE, Hampshire   3 SU11
A stream, dry in summer, runs beside the main street of this delightful village in a hollow of the Hampshire Downs. The 16th- to 18th-century houses and cottages are a blend of styles: cob wall and thatch; brick and tile; timber and stone. The 13th-century church lies on a grassy hillside. Half a mile south-east are a large Roman villa and a museum.

ROCKINGHAM, Northamptonshire   10 SP89
On a summit of a hill, overlooking the pleasant thatched and slated village on its slopes, is the magnificent castle (OACT), which dates mostly from Elizabethan times, although a keep was first built here on the orders of William the Conqueror, and used by King John as a hunting lodge for Rockingham Forest, which then covered a vast area. The gardens alone are well worth a visit, and the house has many associations with Charles Dickens, who was a frequent visitor of the Watsons, the then owners, to whom he dedicated *David Copperfield*. The house served him as a model for Chesney Wold in *Bleak House*.

RODE, Wiltshire   3 ST85
The Tropical Bird Gardens (OACT) in this pretty village cover 17 acres and contain 180 species of colourful tropical birds. In the summer a pets' corner is open and there are donkey rides for children.

RODINGS, THE, Essex   6, 12, TL61
Eight villages in the River Roding valley have Roding as a suffix, and are sometimes known as Roothings. They are Abbess, Aythorpe, Beauchamp, Berners, High, Leaden, Margaret and White.

ROLLRIGHTS, THE, Oxfordshire   10 SP22
Between the villages of Great and Little Rollright, on the edge of the Cotswolds, are the Rollright Stones. There is a Bronze Age stone circle known as the 'King's Men', a solitary standing stone, known as the 'King Stone', and at a distance, a group of stones called the 'Whispering Knights'. All date from before 1500 BC and were probably used in funeral ceremonies. The legend is more picturesque, however: a local king and his men were said to have met with a witch on this spot. She promised the king that if he could see the neighbouring village of Long Compton from the hill he would be king of all England. Of course, he was sure that he could, and went to look, but the witch had raised up a thick mist and he and his men were turned to stone. The Whispering Knights were supposed to be a group of malcontents already plotting to overthrow their leader.

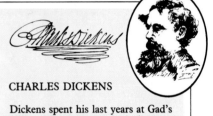

CHARLES DICKENS

Dickens spent his last years at Gad's Hill near Rochester, a city he knew as a boy when his father worked as a clerk in Chatham Dockyards. Rochester features in several of his novels; scenes from the books are re-created at the Dickens Centre – (*below*), Fagin in his prison cell.

ROMNEY MARSH, Kent   6 TR02
Protected by a sea wall, this expanse of flat, sheep-grazed land, 17 miles long by 12 miles wide, has been reclaimed from the sea over centuries and lies barely above sea level, drained by deep dikes. In the west and north it is bounded by the Royal Military Canal, and its seaward fringe is crossed by the Romney, Hythe and Dymchurch narrow-gauge steam railway. To the south are Walland and Denge marshes. A new industry in the area is tulip-growing, but Romney Marsh is historically associated with smuggling; historically, too, it was here that Russell Thorndyke set the exploits of his hero, *Dr Syn*.

ROMSEY, Hampshire *4 SU32*
This ancient market town stands on the
Test, a river noted for its trout and salmon.
Broadlands (OACT), originally the home of
Lord Palmerston, whose statue stands in
the town's market place, is better known as
the home of the late Lord Mountbatten of
Burma. It is an elegant 18th-century
country house surrounded by a 400-acre
park, landscaped by Capability Brown. It
contains an exhibition devoted to Lord
Mountbatten's eventful life. Only the 12th-
century abbey church remains of the great
abbey founded in the 10th-century.
However this Norman building is a
splendid sight and contains many treasures,
including an Anglo-Saxon rood and a
Crucifixion, the Romsey Psalter, an
illuminated manuscript of the 15th century,
and several interesting monuments.

ROS CASTLE, Northumberland
24 NU20
Outlines of an Iron-Age fort can be traced
on the summit of this 1000ft-high conical
hill. A ten-minute climb from a parked car
is rewarded by superb views: Chillingham
Park below; the Farne Islands, Bamburgh
and Dunstanburgh Castles to the east; and
the Cheviot Hills to the west.

ROSEDALE ABBEY, N Yorkshire
20 SE79
Some of the houses in this little hamlet in
the seven-mile-long moorland valley of
Rosedale contain stones from the Cistercian
nunnery which gave the village its name but
was demolished in 1322. Built round an
attractive green, it is reached by roads
which descend steeply to the valley bottom.

ROSEHEARTY, Grampian *27 NJ96*
To the west of this peaceful, pretty fishing
town is the Cave of Cowshaven, where
Lord Pitsligo hid after he had been
outlawed in 1745 for his part in the Jacobite
Rising. He was the Lord of the now-ruined
Castle of Pitsligo, and already an old man
when he took part in the rebellion, but he
spent the rest of his long life hiding from
his pursuers, in caves, under bridges, and
in friends' houses until his death in 1762.
To the east, the rocky beach, amid rugged
cliffs, has patches of sand, and there is an
open-air sea-water swimming pool.

ROSSLYN, Lothian *23 NT26*
A small mining village on the North Esk
river, Rosslyn has a particularly impressive
18th-century chapel, originally intended as
part of a collegiate church, and containing
much fine stone carving. Overlooking the
river and Rosslyn Glen from a cliff-top
setting is the 14th-century and later castle.

ROSS-ON-WYE, Hereford &
**   Worcester** *SO62*
Situated on a bend of the River Wye, with
views of the Welsh hills, this cliff-top
market town has become a tourist centre for
the Wye Valley. Dominating the market
place is the gabled Market Hall which dates
from the 17th century, and there are many
Georgian and earlier houses lining the steep
streets. John Kyrle (1637–1724) did much
for the town, including giving it a walled
public garden, the Prospect, and a water
supply. He also repaired the spire of St
Mary's Church, where he is buried. He is
praised by Alexander Pope in his *Moral
Essays* as the 'Man of Ross'.

EYE CATCHER *Aptly named, this exceptional folly
at Rousham House resembles a castle gateway.*

ROSTHERNE, Cheshire *14 SJ78*
Near this attractive and well-kept village,
built for the workers on **Tatton Park** estate,
which it adjoins, is 100-acre Rostherne
Mere, now a wildlife sanctuary.

ROTHBURY, Northumberland
24 NU00
A busy market town, Rothbury's stone
houses are grouped on a sloping green on
the north bank of the River Coquet. Backed
by the Simonside Hills, it is popular with
tourists, walkers and anglers. Two miles
north is Cragside, a Victorian house in a
900-acre Country Park, which has the
distinction of having been the first house in
the world to be lit by electricity generated
by water power.

ROTHERHAM, S Yorkshire *15 SK49*
An industrial town in the Don valley,
Rotherham has coal-mines, and iron, steel,
brass and glass works. Its fine church dates
from the 15th century as does a bridge with
an old chapel (AM) over the Don. The
town's museum is housed in a late 18th-
century mansion, and, in addition to the
period furniture, has collections of
Victoriana, china, and local history.

ROTHES, Grampian *28 NJ24*
The well-known Glen Grant Distillery was
established in the town in 1840. It produces
a fine malt whisky, and also whisky used for
many of the best blended whiskies.
Traditional methods are used and visitors
are welcome. On the opposite side of the
Spey Valley is the wooded viewpoint of
Conerock Hill, and there are two newly
planted forests nearby.

ROTTINGDEAN, Sussex *5 TQ30*
Only three and a half miles along the coast
from Brighton, Rottingdean maintains a
village atmosphere, with a little green and

pond, just off the High Street. Rudyard
Kipling lived here in a house overlooking
the green for several years, and a room in
the Grange Museum and Art Gallery, once
the home of the painter Sir William
Nicholson, is devoted to the author. The
museum also contains a delightful and
comprehensive toy collection. On the South
Downs nearby is a well-restored 18th-
century smock mill, used by Nicholson as
his design for the colophon of the
publishers William Heinemann.

ROUSHAM, Oxfordshire *10 SP42*
Near the greystone village of Steeple Aston,
the great Jacobean mansion of Rousham
House (OACT), built in 1635, has a fine
library with over 150 portraits and other
paintings. A Royalist stronghold during the
Civil War, the house was enlarged in the
18th century by William Kent, but it is in
the 30-acre landscaped garden, through
which the River Cherwell flows, that his
genius can still be seen. Of particular
interest, although, involving a brisk uphill
walk, is the folly he built known as the 'Eye
Catcher'.

ROXBURGH, Borders *24 NT73*
Now a small village on the west bank of the
River Teviot, Roxburgh was one of
Scotland's four Royal Burgh's in the 13th
century, but the original town has
disappeared completely. Only traces
remain of Roxburgh Castle, three miles
north-east, once a royal residence.

ROYSTON, Hertfordshire *11 TL34*
This small town developed round the
intersection of two important roads, the
Roman Ermine Street, and the ancient
Icknield Way. A cave with crude religious
carvings of uncertain date on the walls, was
discovered beneath the crossroads in 1742.
The town's attractive streets contain a
variety of interesting houses and inns
dating from the Georgian period and later,
and there is a local museum in the Old
Town Hall.

RUDDINGTON, Nottinghamshire
10 SK53
Two interesting museums can be found in
this village. A unique complex of early
19th-century frameshops and knitters'
cottages illustrate the working and
domestic conditions of handframe knitters'
families. The village's oldest building
displays archaeological and folk material.

RUDYARD, Staffordshire *14 SJ95*
Chief attraction of this pretty village is the
two-mile long Rudyard Reservoir,
surrounded by lovely woods and hills.
There are lakeside walks and boating and
fishing are permitted. Novelist and poet
Rudyard Kipling was named after the
village, where his parents became engaged.

RUFFORD, Lancashire *14 SD41*
Rufford Old Hall (NT), dates from the
15th century, though the wings were added
in 1662 and 1821. It is a particularly good
example of a late-medieval, timber-framed
hall. The great hall has remarkable
woodwork, with a notable hammer-beam
roof, and contains a rare 15th-century
movable screen. The hall contains 16th-
century arms and armour, 17th-century
furniture and tapestries, and in one wing is
the Philip Ashcroft folk museum.

RUGBY SCHOOL

The school buildings (*above*) were the setting for Thomas Hughes' famous novel of public-school life, *Tom Brown's Schooldays*. The headmaster in the book is modelled on the famous Victorian educationist Dr Thomas Arnold, father of the poet Matthew Arnold. The game of Rugby football (*below, in 1845*) originated in 1823 when William Webb Ellis picked up the ball and ran with it during a game of football.

RUGBY, Warwickshire   *10 SP57*
A manufacturing town, with important railway and engineering works, Rugby is the home of the famous public school, founded in 1567. The game of rugby football originated here in 1823, when one William Webb Ellis, according to school tradition, picked up the ball during an ordinary game of soccer and ran with it. The pattern of education established by headmaster Dr Thomas Arnold between 1828 and 1842 was followed by many other public schools, and served as the model for Thomas Hughes' immortal novel, *Tom Brown's Schooldays*, published in 1857.

RUNCORN, Cheshire   *14 SJ58*
On the River Mersey, with large chemical and alkali works, Runcorn is the site of a New Town, designated in 1964. The extensive excavation of Norton Priory won the 1978 National Archaeological Award. Seven acres of woodland surround the landscaped remains of the priory, which includes the 12th-century undercroft, notable for its beautifully carved passage. A museum contains displays of finds, and there is also a wildlife display.

RUSHTON, Northamptonshire
10 SP88
A picturesque humpback bridge spans the River Ise, at Rushton, a delightful country village. In a remote corner of the grounds of Rushton Hall, built about 1500 and now a school for blind children, is the unique Triangular Lodge (AM), built by Sir Thomas Tresham. Every part of the 16th-century building – sides, floors, windows, gables – is based on the number three, an emblem of the Trinity, and an ancient mystical symbol.

RYE *The River Rother is now this ancient port's only direct link with the sea, but views from the top of the town stretch out across the Channel.*

RUTHIN, Clwyd   *13 SJ15*
An unusual feature of this old market town on a hill in the fertile Clwyd valley is the curfew bell, which has been rung every night at 8pm since the 11th century. The town has some interesting old buildings, including ruins of a 13th-century castle round which a fortified town grew up. In the 19th century a Gothic castle was grafted on to the original building and has been turned into a hotel. A bank is now housed in the early 15th-century courthouse and prison in the square. Also here is the Maen Huail stone, on which King Arthur is said to have beheaded Huail, a rival in love.

RUTHWELL, Dumfries & Galloway
18 NY06
In a special apse of the parish church is the late 7th-century carved cross for which the town is famous: 18ft high, the cross is richly carved with scenes from the life of Christ and with Runic characters. These relate in parts the *Dream of the Rood*, an ancient poem probably by the first Anglo-Saxon poet, Caedmon. In 1810 the first savings bank was established in the town, commemorated in the Henry Duncan Museum.

RUYTON-THE-ELEVEN-TOWNS,
Shropshire   *9 SJ32*
Ruyton's long name originates from the amalgamation (by the Earl of Arundel) of eleven townships into one manor in 1301. He built a castle, but today there are only scanty remains of it in the churchyard, and Ruyton is a village straggling along the mile-long main street. This road runs along the side of a red sandstone hill above the River Perry. Many of the houses are built of the local red stone, as is an unusual 10ft war memorial which stands in an alcove carved out of the rock.

RYDAL, Cumbria   *18 NY30*
Situated in the Lake District National
Park, Rydal is at the east end of Rydal
Water, one of the most delightful of the
smaller lakes, sheltered by 2000ft Rydal
Fell on the north side. In 1813 William
Wordsworth moved to Rydal Mount
(OACT), a house incorporating an early
16th-century farmer's cottage, where he
died in 1850. Beautifully situated in a 4½-
acre fell garden, it overlooks Windermere
and Rydal Water. The house contains
family portraits, possessions and books.

RYE, E Sussex   *6 TQ92*
Once a flourishing coastal port, Rye was
one of the original Cinque Ports but in the
16th century the harbour silted up, and
today this hilly town is nearly two miles
inland. Best-known of Rye's picturesque
cobbled streets is Mermaid Street, lined by
15th- to 17th-century houses, including the
Mermaid Inn, dating from 1420, a
notorious smugglers' haunt in the 18th
century. The 13th-century Ypres Tower
contains an interesting local museum, and
18th-century Lamb House (OACT) was the
home of novelist Henry James from 1898
until his death in 1916.

RYHOPE, Tyne & Wear   *20 NZ45*
There is a splendid coastal cliff walk here,
although care should be taken. Ryhope
Engines Museum contains restored twin
beam engines built in 1868, under steam
power on certain weekends.

RYTON, Tyne & Wear   *20 NZ16*
Now an attractive village, many of whose
residents work in Newcastle upon Tyne,
Ryton was a colliery village for over 150
years. After its last pit closed, landscaping
was carried out, and the village won a
Britain in Bloom trophy in 1968.

ST ABBS, Borders   *24 NT96*
A picturesque fishing village, a fine sandy
beach, and a splendid coastline: these are
some of the features that explain why St
Abbs is such a popular holiday resort. On
St Abbs Head stands a lighthouse built in
1861. Three miles north, the ruins of Fast
Castle stand proud over land and sea –
perched 70ft up on the clifftop. This
fortress appears in Sir Walter Scott's *The
Bride of Lammermoor* as 'Wolf's Crag', the
tower of Edgar of Ravenswood.

ST AGNES, Cornwall   *1 SW75*
Until late in the 19th century, St Agnes was
a tin-mining centre, and the ruins of the old
workings now add to its charm. It is a
pleasant little resort with a sandy beach and
some fine coastal scenery. You can motor to
the top of 700ft St Agnes Beacon and enjoy
some of the most extensive views in
Cornwall. On the cliffs between St Agnes
and Chapel Porth is the ruined Wheal
Coates Engine House (NT).

ST ALBANS, Hertfordshire   *5 TL10*
The Roman city of Verulamium, from
which St Albans grew, was the only British
city important enough in Roman times to
be accorded the status of *municipium*, which
meant that its inhabitants had the right to
Roman citizenship. Although sacked by
Boudicca in AD 61, it was rebuilt and soon
regained its importance. After the Romans
left, however, Verulamium was abandoned
and eventually the remains were covered
over. The old site was not excavated until
the 20th century, and remains of a theatre,
a hypocaust and several mosaic pavements
were discovered. The Verulamium
Museum houses finds from the site. On the
opposite bank of the River Ver, the
medieval city of St Albans grew up around
the massive abbey church, now St Albans
Cathedral, which was built on the site
where Alban, the first British saint, was
martyred in 287. The abbey dates from the
11th century, though there have been many
later additions. St Alban's shrine of
Purbeck marble was destroyed, but the
fragments were found and pieced together
again in the 19th century. Around the town
centre are several attractive old streets,
centred on the 15th-century curfew tower.
Other places of interest include the City
Museum; St Albans Organ Museum; the
Kingsbury Watermill Museum in the
village of St Michael's; the Royal National
Rose Society's Gardens, and Gorhambury
House (OACT), a fine, late-Georgian
mansion.

ST ANDREWS, Fife   *24 NO51*
This lovely old Royal Burgh on the east
coast of Fife has a long and ancient history.
A mecca for the world's golfers, it is also a
distinguished university city – St Andrews
University was founded in 1411 – and was
for centuries the ecclesiastical centre of
Scotland. According to tradition it was here
that St Rule was shipwrecked, carrying the

WHEAL COATES ENGINE HOUSE *stands as a
striking memorial to Cornwall's industrial past.*

relics of St Andrew the Apostle, who was
adopted as Scotland's patron saint. Little
still stands of the small 12th-century church
built to house the relics but the massive bell
tower, and the sacred remains were soon
installed in St Andrew's Cathedral, in its
day the largest and finest of all Scotland's
churches, built in the 12th and 13th
centuries. In 1559 however, it fell victim to
the iconoclasm of John Knox. He preached
one of his most eloquent and fiery sermons
from the Cathedral pulpit and this inspired
the mob to destroy much of the rich
interior. Over the years, it gradually fell in
ruins and only fragments have survived. St
Andrew's Castle (AM), also in ruins, stands
in grim isolation on a rock overlooking the
North Sea. Golf, however, flourishes, and
the town boasts no less than four courses:
the Old, the New, the Eden and the
Jubilee. Written records of the Old Course
date back at least to the 15th century, and
the 'R & A', as the Royal and Ancient Golf
Club is familiarly known, had its origins in
the Society of St Andrews Golfers, founded
in 1764. King William IV gave his consent
to the use of the words 'Royal and Ancient'
in 1834, and by 1897 the game had become
so popular that a governing body was felt to
be desirable. All the other leading clubs
assented to the R & A taking on this role,
which it still fulfils. As the St Andrews golf
courses are not private club courses, anyone
can play on the Old Course in return for a
relatively modest fee.

ST ANTHONY-IN-MENEAGE,
   Cornwall   *1 SW72*
From a bleak plateau about 250ft above sea-
level, and exposed to the gales that storm
over the Lizard peninsula, the road drops
down to an inlet sheltered by tall pines. The
holy well – said to have been dug by
shipwrecked Norman sailors in
thanksgiving to St Anthony for their
survival – lies behind the church which
they had vowed also to build for the saint
on this spot.

GRAIN MILLS
Sources of Natural Energy

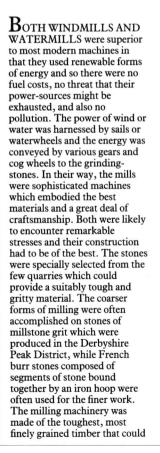

BOTH WINDMILLS AND WATERMILLS were superior to most modern machines in that they used renewable forms of energy and so there were no fuel costs, no threat that their power-sources might be exhausted, and also no pollution. The power of wind or water was harnessed by sails or waterwheels and the energy was conveyed by various gears and cog wheels to the grinding-stones. In their way, the mills were sophisticated machines which embodied the best materials and a great deal of craftsmanship. Both were likely to encounter remarkable stresses and their construction had to be of the best. The stones were specially selected from the few quarries which could provide a suitably tough and gritty material. The coarser forms of milling were often accomplished on stones of millstone grit which were produced in the Derbyshire Peak District, while French burr stones composed of segments of stone bound together by an iron hoop were often used for the finer work. The milling machinery was made of the toughest, most finely grained timber that could

PAST AND PRESENT *West Burton Power Station (above), now overshadows North Leverton's 19th-century tower mill. Picturesque Duddington watermill (left) was built in 1664.*

The sight of a well-restored windmill or watermill can be a show-stopper on any country drive, but antiquities such as these were formerly amongst the most commonplace features of the countryside, and every grain-growing community needed its mill.

In the prehistoric period, such complicated machines did not exist and grain was ground by hand, using stone 'querns'. Some involved two grinding-stones, the lower of which was saddle-shaped; on these the grain was milled with a to-and-fro motion; there were also 'rotary' querns, in which there were two circular stones, the upper revolved by a short handle. Querns of similar type were still in use – often furtively – during the Middle Ages, when peasants might be fined for grinding grain at home instead of giving their custom to the lord's mill.

be found, with the strongest oak providing the framework, and elm favoured for the construction of waterwheels, which were constantly wet. In the course of the 18th and 19th centuries, timber machinery and waterwheels were increasingly replaced by cast-iron components.

WATERMILLS SEEM to have been introduced to Britain during the Roman period, although not a great deal is known about the design of these early mills. One very old form is represented by the horizontal or 'click' mill, in which a small waterwheel was set horizontally in the water. Hundreds of these

simple mills were used by the small communities of upland areas, but only one example remains in working order. This is the Dounby mill on Orkney, and although it was built early in the 19th century, its basic concept is very old. A Saxon mill is recorded as having existed in AD 726, while Domesday Book shows that in 1086 England contained at least 5624 watermills.

Watermills were mainly either of the 'undershot' or 'overshot' types, according to whether the millstream flowed under or over the top of the wheel. At the typical smaller mill, the wheel would generate about the same power as a motor car. Watermills were not entirely reserved for the milling of grain and their power could be harnessed to drive the hammers of medieval fulling or ironworking mills, while the early stages of the Industrial Revolution were mainly accomplished at sites where there was water-power.

THE WINDMILL'S ANCESTRY is somewhat uncertain, but it is thought that they were introduced by returning Crusaders who had seen such mills on their travels to the Holy Land.

Medieval windmills were smaller and simpler than those which survive today. The oldest surviving windmills date from the 17th century, while many are only around 100 years old. The medieval ones were generally built on small artificial mounds, and these may survive long after the disintegration of the mill. The older windmills were of the 'post-mill' type, in which the body of the mill was supported by a massive post.

WINDMILLS *Post-mills, as at Saxtead Green (above), differ from smock-mills, as at Cranbrook (right), in that the whole body of the mill – rather than just the sails – revolves to catch the wind.*

This design remained in favour throughout the long lifespan of the windmill, and well-preserved examples can be seen at Stevington in Bedfordshire, Saxtead Green in Suffolk, or Outwood in Surrey, while an elaborate example with turning gear is maintained at Great Chishill in Cambridgeshire. Some of the later post-mills were built on low, cylindrical brick bases, but the weakness of the design, according to which the whole body of the mill had to be turned to catch the wind, was solved around 1600 by the introduction of the new 'tower' or 'smock' mills. In this design, the body of the mill remained rigid, while the sails were mounted on top of the mill on a revolving cap. Most tower-mills have tapering, cylindrical bodies of brick, but a few stone-built examples exist, as at New Bradwell in Buckinghamshire and High Ham in Somerset. Many of the surviving tower-mills were built during the Victorian era, like the famous

example at Billingford in Norfolk which dates to 1860. 'Smock-mills' resembled tower-mills, but had their stationary bodies built of timber rather than of brick or stone. The Union Mill at Cranbrook in Kent is a fine example and a recently-restored smock-mill can be seen at Turville in Buckinghamshire.

THE CHOICE between different windmill designs was governed by costs, local traditions and the preferences of mill-owners and of the available millwrights. That between wind power or waterpower was determined more by the nature of the local environment. In the flat, exposed and relatively dry lands of a region like East Anglia, windmills tended to be

RARE SURVIVALS *Pitstone windmill's timber machinery (above) and the tide-operated mill at Woodbridge (below).*

favoured. The gentle gradients and broad, shallow valleys did not favour waterpower and the middle phase in the draining of the flat, windswept Fens was accomplished by windmills; one Fenland mill survives intact and is conserved by the National Trust at Wicken Fen in Cambridgeshire. In the west, the heavier rainfall and the suitability of the many narrow valleys for damming to create millponds tended to favour the watermill. Even so, watermills were not uncommon in the east of England and a good example has been restored and is open to the public at the rural life museum at Stowmarket in Suffolk. A watermill which was powered by tides rather than a millstream was operational at Woodbridge on the estuary of the River Deben in the same county until 1952.

OTHER MILLS that are now regarded as antiquities were worked until relatively recently. At the end of the First World War it has been estimated that England still had around 350 operational windmills, but by 1970 the number had fallen to about 25. In the course of the last decade, local conservation societies have achieved the preservation of many threatened and decaying mills and a number are back in working order. The decline of the wind and water mills was caused by a conspiracy of factors. Improvements to the transport system allowed grain to be taken beyond the localities in which it was grown, to bulk-milling centres established in towns. The new mills tended to use electric power and consumers developed a taste for the whiter flour which resulted when grain was ground between iron rollers rather than millstones. Perhaps, however, the old wind and water mills should not simply be regarded as redundant antiquities, for in this energy-conscious age any machine which can be efficiently developed and requires only renewable energy-sources of wind or water should be valued.

ST ASAPH, Clwyd   *13 SJ07*
The attractive little village of St Asaph lies
at the head of the lovely Vale of Clwyd. It is
not only a village but also a cathedral city,
and its cathedral is the smallest in the
country and one of the oldest in Wales. The
present structure, rebuilt after being sacked
by Owain Glyndwr, dates from the 15th
century and numbers among its treasures a
first edition of William Morgan's Welsh
translation of the Bible.

ST AUSTELL, Cornwall   *1 SX05*
St Austell is the centre of the china-clay
industry – a raw material that is used not
only in porcelain but also in the
manufacture of paper, cosmetics,
medicines, paint and many other things.
Outside the town lies a fantastic moon
landscape of what appear to be white
mountains: they are, in fact, the spoil from
the diggings. St Austell was a tin-mining
village until, in 1755, William Cookworthy
discovered the clay and decided it might
have industrial possibilities. Now,
dispatched in ships from Fowey and Par
and Charlestown (where there is a Visitor
Centre incorporating an interesting
museum of shipwrecks), it is a major
export. Just outside the town, the Wheal
Martyn Museum tells the history of the
china-clay business.

ST BRIAVELS, Gloucestershire
3 SO50
St Briavels stands above a thickly wooded
valley, not far from a point at which the
ground falls sharply towards the River
Wye. The remains (the gatehouse and two
rounded towers) of a 13th-century fort
recall the days when defences were needed
to fend off the marauding Welshmen. The
castle was, indeed, the administrative
centre for the Forest of Dean, and St
Briavels is a very good point from which to
explore the Forest.

ST CLEER, Cornwall   *1 SX26*
St Cleer stands 700ft above sea level on the
edge of Bodmin Moor. It has a church with
a 15th-century tower, a holy well, and not
very much else. However, the views are
fantastic, and, if you walk a mile or two
from the village, you will find yourself in a
landscape rich in prehistoric monuments.
Most famous is Trevethy Quoit, an
imposing chambered tomb. The Hurlers,
three stone circles, said to be men turned to
stone for playing a game on Sunday, the
Cheesewring, a curiously shaped natural
phenomenon, and King Donert's Stone,
believed to commemorate a 9th-century
Christian king, are all within easy reach.

ST DAVID'S, Dyfed   *8 SN72*
Only 2000 people live in St David's, and yet
this tiny city might reasonably be described
as the Canterbury of Wales. It was here, in
the 6th century that St David – the
country's patron saint – established a
stronghold for Christianity in the west. The
cathedral that bears his name is the third to
be built on the spot – the original was
destroyed by raiders. Work on the present
building began in 1180 and was not
completed until 1572. The interior is as rich
as the exterior is plain, and there is much
fine carving. Nearby stand the ruins (AM)
of the medieval Bishop's Palace. Ramsey
Island, half-a-mile offshore, is a privately
owned bird sanctuary; Grassholm Island,
12 miles west of St David's Head, has one
of the world's largest gannetries.

ST FAGAN'S, S Glamorgan   *8 ST17*
When the second phase of the Civil War
swept across South Wales, many of the
people rose against Parliament, and a unit
of the New Model Army crushed the revolt
at St Fagan's, on the outskirts of Cardiff.
Nowadays, St Fagan's has more pleasant
associations – as the home of the Welsh
Folk Museum, which is accommodated in

the grounds of the 16th-century castle
(OACT). The exhibits include a woollen
mill, several old Welsh farmhouses, a
tannery, a tollgate, a chapel and a
quarryman's cottage. In addition to the
buildings, which have been brought here
from all parts of Wales and re-erected,
there are interesting galleries devoted to
Welsh life, and craftsmen regularly display
their skills.

ST FLORENCE, Dyfed   *7 SM10*
One hundred years ago, it was possible for
small boats to make the voyage to St
Florence, a village about four miles west of
Tenby, but nowadays, the only way of
getting there is by road. The village was
once inhabited by Flemish immigrants, and
their influence can still be seen in the
architecture of the attractive cottages. The
Manor House Wildlife and Leisure Park is
set in 12 acres of woodlands, and features a
model railway.

ST GERMANS, Cornwall   *2 SX35*
St Germans stands beside a river and is
enclosed by glorious woodland. In 1162, a
priory of Augustinian canons was
established, but only the church has
survived. The west face is Norman, with a
magnificent doorway; the east window, by
the Pre-Raphaelite painter Burne-Jones, is
evidence of Victorian restoration – but none
the worse for that.

ST HELENS, Merseyside   *14 SJ59*
St Helens has two famous names to its
credit: Pilkingtons, the glass
manufacturers, and the late Sir Thomas
Beecham – conductor extraordinary. The
latter was born here in 1897. The
Pilkington Glass Museum contains many
fascinating items. A former director of the
firm, Major W.N. Pilkington, had the
distinction of being the first fare-paying air
passenger in the UK.

CHINA CLAY *On the moors to the east of St Austell, waste heaps of sand and quartz from the works give the landscape a strange, unnatural appearance.*

ST HILARY, S Glamorgan *8 ST07*
Old Beaupré Castle (AM, the locals pronounce it 'Bewper') stands a mile south of the village down a very quiet lane. It is a manor house built in 1596: much of it, unfortunately, in ruins. However, the Italianate gatehouse and porches have survived. Once the home of the Bassetts, the family's arms are displayed on the wall of the outer porch.

ST IVES, Cambridgeshire *11 TL37*
An attractive town on the River Ouse, associated with Oliver Cromwell, who had farming interests in the vicinity. The Lord Protector, as he called himself, is remembered by a statue in the Market Place. The name is a corruption of St Ivo, a Persian bishop to whom the priory (of which only a ruined wall remains) was dedicated. The 15th-century six-arched bridge across the river has that rare thing, a bridge chapel. There are only two others in the country. The Norris Museum provides a sound guide to local history.

ST IVES, Cornwall *1 SW54*
During the 19th century St Ives was one of Cornwall's most prosperous pilchard ports. According to one account, no fewer than 75 million were caught during one day in 1864. It was also used for the shipping of tin and copper until these industries began to decline in the late 1800s. Thereupon the artists moved in, and it is greatly due to their efforts that this pleasing little town, with its narrow streets (one named Teetotal and another, Salubrious, recall that John Wesley received a good hearing when he preached at St Ives) and its old houses, has escaped total inundation by the tourist trade. The Barnes Museum of Cinematography should be seen, and the 15th-century church has a Madonna and Child, carved by Barbara Hepworth, in the Lady Chapel. Dame Barbara was one of St Ives' most famous artists and there is a museum of her works in the village.

ST JUST-IN-ROSELAND, Cornwall
1 SW83
Cornwall has a reputation, not necessarily deserved, for sub-tropical luxuriance. However, the churchyard at St Just-in-Roseland helps to give credence to the idea. The work was begun by a tree-loving vicar in the mid-19th century. Now you can see such rarities as an African strawberry tree, a Chilean myrtle, palms and camellias.

ST KEVERNE, Cornwall *1 SW72*
St Keverne is notable for its large square: something that is rare in Cornish villages. Its church contains a nicely crafted Jacobean pulpit, and in the churchyard are the graves of shipwreck victims: the Manacles – those dreaded rocks off the Lizard – have accounted for many ships. For Space-Age enthusiasts the Post Office Satellite Tracking Station at Goonhilly Downs makes an interesting excursion.

ST KEYNE, Cornwall *1 SX26*
Just east of the village is the remarkable Paul Corin Collection (OACT) of automatic (and, in many cases, very large) musical instruments such as the Mortier organ, which measures 27ft by 20ft, the Hoogluys fairground organ, and – an exquisite rarity – a 1929 German theatre organ. On no account should it be missed.

ST IVES *The narrow medieval bridge spanning the River Ouse forms an attractive centrepiece to this pleasant market town. In the 19th century the bridge chapel was heightened and converted into a house.*

ST KILDA, Highland
St Kilda is a group of islands – Hirta, Soay, Boresay and Dun – with spectacular scenery 50 miles out in the Atlantic to the west of Harris. Until 1930 they were inhabited, but nowadays, the only residents are puffins, fulmars and gannets. However, working parties from the National Trust visit St Kilda every summer. With help from a detachment from the Forces, they carry out research on Soay sheep, the St Kilda mouse, study nesting birds, and are restoring relics of the old community at Village Bay. Access is difficult because of mountainous seas, and restricted.

ST MAWES, Cornwall *1 SW83*
St Mawes has just about everything in its favour: its situation on the Roseland peninsula is magnificent; its houses suggest a comfortable affluence; the tourist industry has not cheapened it. Even the castle (AM), built by Henry VIII to defend the Fal estuary, escaped the depredations of the Roundheads in the Civil War and is well preserved. A ferry connects the town with **Falmouth**.

ST MAWGAN, Cornwall *1 SW86*
The full name is St Mawgan-in-Pydar, and this is one of those splendid surprises Cornwall has such a talent for providing: a sudden enclave of greenery and luxuriance that cuts into the harsh uplands. The 13th-century church has some fine bench-ends. One mile to the north, Lanherne used to be the home of the Arundell family. In 1794, the house was given to Carmelite nuns who had fled the French Revolution. The chapel contains a Rubens and a Van Dyck.

ST MICHAEL'S MOUNT, Cornwall
1 SW53
Seen from the land, St Michael's Mount looks rather like one of those dream castles associated with King Ludwig of Bavaria. It used to be joined to the mainland (tree stumps discovered under the sea prove it). In 1044, a Benedictine monastery was founded by monks of Mont St Michel in Brittany – hence the similarity of name and appearance. After the 12th century, it

assumed the role of a fort; and, in 1425, the crown acquired it. In 1657, during the Civil War, the St Aubyn family moved in and remained here until 1954, when the National Trust took over. The island can be reached by foot or by boat depending on the tides from **Marazion**.

ST MONAN'S, Fife *24 NO50*
St Monan's is a particularly attractive seaside town and fishing port. The shipyard used to build 'Fifie' fishing boats; now it concentrates on pleasure craft. The Old Kirk of St Monance (St Monan's original name) was built during the 14th century. Ruined Newark Castle, on the cliffs south-west of the town, was the home of Lord Newark, who defeated the Marquess of Montrose at Philiphaugh in 1645.

ST NEOT, Cornwall *1 SX16*
Bodmin Moor rises behind the charming village, which nestles in a river valley. The church has a remarkable collection of stained-glass windows – many of them 15th- and 16th-century. Legend, told in one of the windows, asserts that St Neot was only 15 inches high, and that he could make crows obey him. There is also a well dedicated to him in the village.

ST NEWLYN EAST, Cornwall
1 SW85
The nearby Lappa Valley Line is a 15-inch gauge steam railway that runs along part of the old GWR Newquay–Chacewater route. The train makes a round trip of two miles and stops at East Wheal Rose Halt – the site of a once famous silver and lead mine. There is also a five-acre pleasure area (boating lake etc.) accessible only by rail.

ST OSYTH, Essex *6 TM11*
St Osyth stands beside one of the many little creeks that stem from the River Colne. Proof of its presumed strategic importance during the Napoleonic Wars is provided by three Martello towers in the vicinity. The remains of a 12th-century priory were incorporated into a mansion in the 16th century. Mainly of flint construction, the building is superb.

SAFFRON WALDEN *Pargeting was a traditional skill in Essex and Suffolk and the decorative figures, animals and designs which adorn the medieval houses in Church Street are fine examples of the art.*

SAFFRON WALDEN, Essex *11 TL53*

Saffron Walden is, without argument, one of the most beautiful towns in Essex: a town in which several periods of architecture co-exist in perfect harmony. Two old inns – the Sun (now an antique shop) and the Cross Keys – are worthy of attention: the first is famous for its pargeted plasterwork, a decorative art, typical of East Anglia. The magnificent 15th–16th-century Perpendicular Church of St Mary should also be treated to more than a quick glance. The interior is richly carved and has several fine brasses. Among the tombs is that of Thomas, Lord Audley, founder of Magdalene College, Cambridge, and Lord Chancellor to Henry VIII (he sanctioned Henry's divorce from Catherine of Aragon). There is evidence of an Iron-Age settlement; the Romans certainly established themselves here; and, in the 12th century, a castle (now in ruins) was built. But the wealth of Saffron Walden came from the cloth trade – assisted by the growing of saffron crocuses. Not only did these versatile plants provide flavouring for cakes and other confections: they repaired the damage of illness and, much to the benefit of local industry, could be used as a dye. The common has a rare surviving maze and the Town Museum has many interesting items. One mile away, **Audley End** is a superb 17th-century mansion.

SALCOMBE, Devon *2 SX73*

There may be more beautifully situated towns in England, but it is hard to think of one. The broad and placid waters of Kingsbridge estuary are confined by steep, thickly wooded banks: there are many small and sandy bays – and, two miles away, imposing cliffs around Bolt Head. Salcombe clings to the hillsides, its streets gay with subtropical plants. Overbeck's Museum and Garden (NT) is an Edwardian house set in lovely gardens. The tower of a ruined Tudor castle, Fort Charles, is all that survived a battering by the Roundhead artillery in the Civil War. A passenger ferry connects Salcombe with East Portlemouth on the opposite bank.

THE CROCUS COAT OF ARMS
'Saffron' Walden is so called from the saffron crocuses once grown here.

SALFORD, Gtr Manchester *14 SJ79*

The boundary between Manchester and Salford is the River Irwell. Industry came to Salford in the form of cotton mills, and it has never departed. You can see what it used to be like in the reconstruction of Lark Hill Place, a 19th-century North-of-England industrial street in Salford Museum and Art Gallery in Peel Park. The town has associations with Sir Charles Hallé, founder of the world-renowned Hallé Orchestra. The ship canal and docks reflect another side of Salford's contribution to commerce – and, likewise, a replica coal mine in the Buile Hill Park Science Museum. Some historic buildings, like the partly 15th-century Ordsall Hall (OACT) and the old mansion of Kersal Cell recall a much older and rather quieter aspect of Salford. But contemporary Salford lies in the art gallery, where there is a lavish collection of Lowrys. L S Lowry knew his Salford and painted it with a sad relish.

SALLE, Norfolk *12 TG12*

Salle – sometimes spelt Sal and always pronounced 'Saul' – has a large and beautiful church out of all proportion to the size of this tiny Norfolk village. Its magnificence is due to the generosity of three local families: the Briggs, the Fountaynes and the Boleyns (the family of Anne Boleyn, wife of Henry VIII). The 15th-century pulpit was enlarged into a three-decker in 1611; and the chancel roof has a wonderfully carved 'Life of Christ'.

SALTASH, Cornwall *2 SX45*

In the northern part of Saltash, Brunel's Royal Albert Bridge across the Tamar dominates the scene. Built in 1859, it is a triumph of civil engineering, made the more impressive by the Admiralty's insistance that it should stand at least 100ft above the river at high tide. Nowadays, Saltash is really a suburb of **Plymouth**, though it is the older of the two towns.

SAMLESBURY, Lancashire *14 SD53*

Samlesbury is situated in the attractive Ribble Valley. The church was rebuilt in the 16th-century and has 17th- and 18th-century box pews and a two-decker pulpit. Samlesbury Hall (OACT) dates back to the 14th and 16th centuries. Among the objects on view are paintings and European and Oriental casks and cabinets.

SAMPFORD COURTENAY, Devon *2 SS60*

White-washed cob and thatched cottages, the imposing prospect of Cawsand Beacon (1799ft) on Dartmoor, and a 15th-century church – all these add up to one of Devonshire's many pretty villages. Trouble came to Sampford Courtenay in 1549, when Edward VI introduced his new prayer book – with the text in English. The villagers (Roman Catholics almost to a man) were so incensed, that they rioted and killed one of the local Protestant gentry. The villagers took part in the 'Prayer Book Rebellion', but they were defeated and many of them were hanged.

SANCREED, Cornwall *1 SW42*

The 14th-century church, with its richly carved screen and its nicely embellished crosses, should certainly be seen – also the Iron-Age settlement named Carn Euny (AM), complete with 'fogous', ancient subterranean hiding holes characteristic of Cornwall.

SANDBACH, Cheshire *14 SJ76*

Sandbach used to be a salt-mining town. Old black-and-white houses, winding streets and a cobbled market place suggest antiquity. Two tall Anglo-Saxon crosses in the square take one back even further in time. Thought to be more than 1300 years old, they were erected to celebrate the conversion to Christianity of the King of Mercia's son.

SANDFORD ORCAS, Dorset *3 ST62*

A most attractive village, its houses built of golden Ham stone, Sandford Orcas lies in a pretty, stream-fed valley. The manor house, though built on earlier foundations, is mostly Elizabethan and the impressive stone gatehouse is all Elizabethan. The owners were the Knoyle family and an impressive monument to William Knoyle can be found in the 13th-century church.

Salisbury, Wiltshire 4 SU12

Cathedral City of the Plain

'Let us in God's name descend into the Plain. There are rich champaign fields and ... a seat for the Virgin Patroness of our church, to which the world cannot produce a parallel.'

PETER OF BLOIS (1198), quoted in *Salisbury Town Guide*.

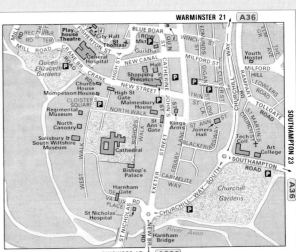

The 'new' city of Salisbury dates back to the 13th century when Bishop Poore decided to move his clergy and cathedral from **Old Sarum**, where lack of water and quarrels with the military governor of the castle were making life difficult. There is a story that the new site for the Cathedral was chosen by an arrow shot from a bow drawn at a venture, but all the evidence points to a decision taken after long and careful planning and the site, in the middle of the fertile plain and at the confluence of the rivers Avon and Nadder, was an obvious choice. The foundation stone of the Cathedral was laid on 28th April 1220, and the building, one of the finest expressions of Early English architecture in the country, was completed, apart from the spire, cloisters and chapter house, by 1258.

The city grew up around the Cathedral Close, its streets laid out on the usual medieval grid plan, intersecting to form square blocks or 'chequers' where the old houses were packed tightly together. This old plan can still be seen in the streets around the Close, where many historic timbered buildings have survived. The finest of them is probably the 17th-century Joiners' Hall, with its intricately carved woodwork;

and the most unusual is certainly the house of the wealthy 15th-century wool merchant, John Halle, which is now the foyer of a local cinema.

Salisbury was granted its first charter in 1227 and, thanks to its far-sighted bishops, who bridged the rivers and diverted the road to the west country to run through their new town, it became a thriving market and wool centre. There is still a twice-weekly market in the spacious market square, and the handsome stone Poultry Cross, dating from the 15th century when fowl were sold there, still stands.

Salisbury reached the height of its prosperity in the 18th century from which era many of the most elegant houses in the beautiful, walled Close survive. Although Salisbury owed much to its bishops, in the past, relations were not harmonious, and the clergy had to protect themselves by building a wall, and fortified gateways, still the northern and eastern entrances to the Close, for protection. By the 18th century, however, behaviour was more civilised, and the Close assumed the aspect it has today, of tranquil lawns shaded by trees and ringed by handsome mansions, many of which were formerly the town houses of the wealthiest citizens.

THE CATHEDRAL *(above)*. MOMPESSON HOUSE *(below)* is famous for its plasterwork.

ST ANNE'S GATE *(below) seen from North Walk in 1885.*

PLACES TO SEE

The Cathedral A masterpiece of the Early English style, Salisbury is one of the most beautiful cathedrals in the country, set in an equally lovely walled Close. The graceful spire, which is such a well-known landmark, was added at the end of the 13th century. The cloisters completed immediately after the cathedral itself, are the earliest cathedral cloisters in England. They lead to the chapter house, famous for its wealth of sculpture. The library houses many rare books and manuscripts, including one of the four contemporary copies of Magna Carta.

Mompesson House (NT) Built in the early 18th century for a wealthy merchant family, this gracious house is one of the most splendid in the Close and is noted for its plasterwork and woodwork.

Museum of the Duke of Edinburgh's Royal Regiment Militaria and regimental memorabilia are housed in one of the Close's most attractive buildings.

St Thomas's Church Built in the 15th century, this Perpendicular church contains a magnificent 'Doom' painting.

Salisbury and South Wiltshire Museum Relics from Stonehenge and Old Sarum, of the city's medieval and later history, and the Pitt Rivers collection of archaeology, are housed in the King's House in the Close.

THE NATURAL HABITAT
WOODLANDS
Trees in the Landscape

THE LAST ICE AGE closed around 12,000 years ago, and it was then that trees gradually returned to recolonise the British landscape. The first arrivals were the hardiest species like the birch and the pine. As the climate and environment continued to improve, so deciduous species like elm, oak, alder, lime and hazel displaced the pioneer trees from the more attractive lowland settings, but even as the woodland blanket was being established, human activities began the removal of forest to create the unnatural landscapes that became increasingly characteristic of the prehistoric environment. The first clearances were achieved by Middle Stone Age or 'Mesolithic' hunting communities who seem to have created clearings by burning in order to open-up hunting ranges or encourage the growth of grazings. They also seem to have achieved the domestication of animals like the red deer or reindeer.

Around 5000 BC, farming was introduced to Britain and the removal of the natural

Woodlands are a much-loved and traditional feature of the British landscape, but they are disappearing at an alarming rate. In previous centuries, deciduous woodlands were carefully-managed resources that yielded a wealth of valuable products. Every single old deciduous wood in England existed because of human decisions to create and maintain a forest or copse, for the last remnants of the primeval woodlands of Britain disappeared long ago.

wildwood began in earnest, so that by the end of this millennium most of the more inviting farmlands will have been stripped of forest. The farming communities, however, needed copious supplies of woodland products for their house-building, tool-making and fencing activities and so it was about this time that the deliberate management of woodlands probably began. The clearance of the native wildwood continued throughout the Bronze and Iron Ages, so that the landscape which awaited the Roman conquerors may have been even less wooded than that of today. Smelting; building houses, palisades and ramparts and enclosures all resulted in an enormous demand for timber, and so we must imagine that the surviving woodlands were carefully harvested in order to yield timber of many different sizes and qualities.

DEER PARKS *were often enclosed by bank and ditch – (left) in the New Forest.*

WOODLAND TRADES *included charcoal burning (below).*

WOODLAND MANAGEMENT was practised throughout the Middle Ages and there are plenty of surviving records to show that very sophisticated techniques were used. On most manors the peasants had rights to take timber for essential uses like house-, plough- and fence-making, while oak woodlands provided roots and acorns for the village swine. Woodlands also provided a setting for the bloodsports which were avidly pursued by the aristocrats. Vast areas of the country were designated as 'forests' or royal hunting reserves and shortly after the Norman Conquest the area of the New Forest was expanded at the expense of a number of uprooted village communities. The royal forests spanned not only wooded areas, but also enormous acreages of peasant farmland and common grazings, but throughout the designated areas the hated forest laws were enforced. In addition to the royal forests, other extensive areas were defined as 'chases', where other members of the aristocracy had hunting rights.

SCOTS PINE *seen here at West Stow were planted as windbreaks, for landscaping and in the earlier conifer plantations.*

As well as serving as hunting reserves, most medieval woodlands were exploited commercially. They were usually divided into a number of areas which were cleared according to different rotations in order to yield different types of timber. Coppices were cut on a short rotation to produce charcoal for smelting, poles for light constructional work and handles for tools. In other areas, longer rotations allowed trees to grow tall as 'standards' which provided the heavy constructional timber which was needed in enormous quantities for the building of timber-framed houses and ships. Where livestock grazed the woods, trees were often beheaded or 'pollarded' above the reach of the grazing animals so that a crop of poles could be grown from the crown of the trunk.

In addition to the open forests, many nobles created deer parks beside their homes. These were compact, often oval-shaped areas of woodland defined by elaborate earthworks and palings, with 'deer leaps' which allowed deer to enter the park but prevented their escape, ensuring that a supply of fresh venison was always to hand. Throughout this period most woods were healthy, productive and essential resources so that licences to clear land for farming were not granted without good cause.

FOREST CUSTOMS *The right of pannage (above) still exists in the New Forest, and in Hatfield Forest (top) hornbeams are still pollarded.*

THE RETREAT OF THE WOODLANDS resulted, it is often said, from the insatiable demands of the iron-smelting and ship-building industries. In certain localities the woodland resources were over-stretched, but so long as timber was a commercially valuable commodity the woods tended to remain intact and in production. During the 17th and 18th centuries some new woodlands were also created for purposes of landscaping and game cover, while trees like the Scots pine, sycamore and poplar were planted in parks, shelter belts or game reserves. Trees such as the oak, ash and elm produced timber which was essential for construction work, cart building and tool-making and they were often grown as

field or hedgerow timber. The decline and decay of the British woodlands was really a feature of the 19th and 20th centuries and resulted from commercial competition from cheaply imported softwood timber and the substitution for wood of other materials, which caused a deterioration in the skills and practices of woodland management.

A number of old woods still survive with their boundaries still marked by the banks and ditches which were characteristic features of medieval woods. The majority of woods however are untidy and ill-managed, with overgrown coppices that are no longer renewed by felling, old and diseased standards and tanglesome thickets of seedlings and undergrowth. The demand for coppice poles has virtually evaporated while few farmers are prepared to invest in a crop of hardwood timber which will take decades to mature. Increasingly, the old woodlands are being grubbed-out to provide new farmland or else yield to the stereotyped ranks of alien commercial conifers.

THE OLD WOODS do survive and where they are accessible to the public they offer enormous interest to nature lovers. Most comprise a number of different tree species, with one being dominant, while shorter species like the hazel, birch or holly provide a secondary tier below the canopy. Beech woods, many of them planted during the post-medieval period for landscaping and game cover, are common in the chalklands and their dense canopy allows little light to filter through so that there is usually very little undergrowth. Over much of England oak and elm woodland tended to be preserved on the heavier clay soils, while alder often claims a foothold in the damper corners of the wood. Less common but very attractive members of the woodland community are the lime, hornbeam and maple. As woodland management declined, the elm seems to have gradually encroached at the expense of other tree species in a number of woods but the recent onslaughts of Dutch elm disease have ravaged field and woodland elms, removing a much-loved keynote of the English landscape and opening new ecological niches. The many expressions of popular dismay associated with this disaster and the frequently voiced outrage at the bulldozing of old woodlands offer at least the hope of a planting revival and many authorities have tree-planting schemes which should favour native species like the oak, lime, ash, field maple, black poplar and holly.

SANDHURST, Berkshire 4 SU86
Sandhurst means only one thing: the Royal
Military Academy, built by French
prisoners of war during the Napoleonic
Wars. The first cadets arrived in 1812.

SANDRINGHAM, Norfolk 12 TF62
Sandringham House (OACT), built in the
19th century, is the Royal Family's country
residence. It was bought in 1861 by
Edward, Prince of Wales (later Edward
VII). The Norwich gates were, as their
name suggests, manufactured in Norwich
as a wedding present to the Prince from the
County of Norfolk when he married
Princess Alexandra in 1863. King George V
and King George VI both died at
Sandringham. In the Church of St Mary
Magdalene, the Royal Parish Church, are a
silver altar and memorials to Edward VII,
Queen Alexandra, George VI and Queen
Mary. The estate includes a country park
covering 300 acres. Vintage Royal Daimlers
are on show in the Royal Car Museum, and
there is also a Big Game Museum.

SANDTOFT, Humberside 16 SE70
Sandtoft Transport Centre, 15 miles east of
Doncaster, is primarily dedicated to the
preservation of the trolleybus – though
motorbuses and other vehicles are also on
display. Over 60 vehicles have been
lovingly restored.

SANDWICH *Players visiting the Royal St George
Golf Course often stay at the Bell Hotel, from
which this stained glass panel comes.*

SANDWICH, Kent 6 TR35
One of the original Cinque Ports, Sandwich
used to be an important naval base – to such
an extent that Henry VIII built a castle
(now gone) to safeguard his coastal
defences. Since those days, nature –
through storm and tempest – has reshaped
the landscape and it is now two miles from
the sea. Nevertheless, it is a beautiful little
town that displays ample evidence of its
former glory. The 16th-century Guildhall
in the Cattle Market has a museum that
recalls local history. The Barbican and
Fishergate were both gateways to the town:
the former is now used for collecting tolls
from travellers crossing a bridge over the
River Stour. St Bartholomew's Hospital
guesthouse is 15th century; Marwood
Court was built in 1564; and St Clement's
church has a Norman tower. Nearby, the
Royal St George is one of England's most
famous and exclusive golf clubs. Edward
VIII (as Prince of Wales) and the late Ian
Fleming (creator of James Bond) were both
members of the club.

SANDY, Bedfordshire 11 TL14
This small but growing town, framed by
undemanding countryside, was listed in the
Domesday Book. St Swithun's Church
(14th century) has a statue to Prime
Minister Sir Robert Peel's son, Captain
William Peel – one of the first men to be
awarded the VC. Sandy Lodge houses the
headquarters of the Royal Society for the
Protection of Birds. A nature trail leads to
the Bird Sanctuary (OACT).

SANQUHAR, Dumfries & Galloway
22 NS70
The Covenanters' fight to defend
Presbyterianism against the Stuarts is
commemorated in a granite monument on
the site of the old Town Cross where their
famous Declarations in 1680 and 1685 were
read out. A toll booth, erected in 1735, has
nicely withstood the erosion of time: a
castle owned by the Crichtons and, later, by
the Douglases, has fared less well and is
now in ruins. To the east of the town stand
the Lowther Hills where, in the late 17th
century, persecuted Covenanters hid out.

SAUNDERSFOOT, Dyfed 7 SN10
Saundersfoot used to be a port for
anthracite mined in Pembroke – much of it
a few miles inland at Kilgetty – but the
industry is long gone. The resort makes few
concessions to the tourist other than sands,
seascapes, and a glorious coastline.

SAVERNAKE FOREST, Wiltshire
3 SU26
This delightful area of woodland, covering
2300 acres, dates back to the days before
the Normans arrived. Beech and oak trees
form a magnificent canopy and there are
some splendid avenues – notably the Grand
Avenue, from the centre of which radiate
walks and rides.

SAWREY, Cumbria 18 SD39
Hill Top Farm (NT) at Near Sawrey, is a
17th-century house – still without electric
light – in which Beatrix Potter lived, and in
which she wrote and illustrated many of her
books (a picture of the Tower Bank Arms at
Sawrey appears in *The Tale of Jemima
Puddle-Duck*). Several of her drawings,
pieces of furniture, china, etc. are on
display. Owing to the smallness of the
house, it is necessary to restrict the number
of visitors at any one time.

SAXMUNDHAM, Suffolk 12 TM36
This long village stretches out along the
main road, and despite the traffic, many
fine buildings can be distinguished. The
Church of St John the Baptist has a
hammerbeam roof and contains interesting
monuments. Bruisyard Winery and
Vineyard (OACT) lies just outside the
village main street.

SCARBOROUGH, N Yorkshire
20 TA08
Scarborough is a resort with a wonderful
mixture of identities: it has a harbour, a
fishing village, stately hotels, towering cliffs
and, of course, the required amusements
that make a seaside place 'popular'. The
Romans built a signal station here, and
eventually the Normans built an imposing
castle, on the headland, of which the large
square keep (AM) survives; the rest
suffered the fate, so common to English
castles, of being reduced to rubble by

Roundhead artillery in the Civil War.
The town's career as a spa began in the
17th century. A Mrs Farrow noticed that
the water that ran over certain russet-
coloured rocks had an acid tang. She found
that it was good for her, and soon came to
the conclusion that it might be a cure for
scurvey, jaundice, depression – even
leprosy. Before very long, the sick and
those who believed themselves to be ill,
came flocking, especially when, nearly a
century later, sea bathing became so
popular a pastime.

DONKEY RIDES *are just one of the perennial
attractions that Scarborough has to offer.*

SCOLTON MANOR, Dyfed 7 SM92
Scolton Manor Museum and Country Park
consists of a late Georgian country mansion
set in 44 acres of grounds, which contain
many fine trees and ornamental shrubs.
Within the house and the stable block,
there is a worthwhile display of
Pembrokeshire's history and natural
history.

SEVEN SISTERS *Between Cuckmere Haven and Beachy Head seven dramatic cliffs at the edge of the South Downs swoop along the coast. Fine views of the Sisters can be obtained from Seaford Head.*

SCONE, Tayside   23 NO12

Scone (pronounced 'Skoon') was the capital of the Pictish kingdom. The Stone of Destiny, reputed to be Jacob's pillow, was brought here from Iona in AD843. In 1296 it was captured by Edward I of England and forms part of the Coronation Chair in Westminster Abbey. The abbey and palace at Scone were founded by Alexander I in about 1114. The early kings of Scotland – until the time of James I – were crowned here. But in 1559 an angry mob from Perth, drunk with the rhetoric of that religious pedagogue John Knox, destroyed them. The palace was rebuilt in the 16th century, and Charles II was the last king to be crowned in it. In 1950, the Stone of Destiny was stolen from Westminster, and later discovered beneath the high altar in the ruins of Arbroath Abbey. The present Scone Palace (OACT) was built in the early 19th century as the home of the Earl of Mansfield. The grounds contain a pinetum; the house, a fine collection of furniture, china, and ivory.

SCUNTHORPE, Humberside   16 SE91

Scunthorpe, now a large industrial town, evolved from the coming together of a group of villages after the discovery, in 1864, of large ironstone deposits. The Borough Museum and Art Gallery has interesting exhibits. Normanby Hall (OACT), is set in 350 acres of parkland, with a Countryside Interpretation Centre.

SEAFORD, Sussex   5 TV49

The beach is shingle – though, at low tide, the stones give way to sand. The Seven Sisters, those beautiful cliffs so popular with walkers, are nearby: Lullington Heath and the Cuckmere Valley (leading to Cuckmere Haven) are not far away.

SEASCALE, Cumbria   18 NY00

Seascale is a pleasant little resort with a sandy beach and a golf course. Entry to the Ravenglass Gullery Nature Reserve is by permit only. Its main feature of interest is the largest collection of black-headed gulls in Europe. About two miles north are the Windscale and Calder Hall atomic power stations.

SEATHWAITE, Cumbria   18 NY21

Seathwaite is very remote and none the worse for that. Tucked away in the Dunnerdale valley, it is overshadowed by Harter Fell (2140ft) – with precipitous Wrynose Pass away to the west at the head of the valley. In the village churchyard sleeps 'Wonderful Walker', born in 1709, and for 67 years vicar of the parish. He stars in Wordsworth's poem, *The Excursion*.

SEATOLLER, Cumbria   18 NY21

Seatoller is in the beautiful valley of Borrowdale. Having said this, it is necessary to declare the facts about high rainfall figures. At Sprinkling Tarn, the average rainfall is over 185 inches. Seathwaite Farm, two miles away, holds some sort of record for being one of the wettest inhabited places in England. In the 17th and 18th centuries, they used to mine plumbago (a kind of graphite) at Seatoller.

SEATON DELAVAL, Northumberland   20 NZ37

Sir John Vanbrugh designed this great 18th-century mansion (OACT) for Admiral George Delaval and it was constructed between 1718 and 1728. Built in the Palladian style and set in exquisite gardens, the Hall is considered to be Vanbrugh's masterpiece. Paintings, documents and statuary can be seen.

SEDBERGH, Cumbria   18 SD69

This is a hill-town. The boys' public school was founded in 1525 by a Canon of Windsor and Provost of Eton. A new school – built in 1716 – now serves as library and museum to the present establishment, which was erected in the late 19th century. Sedbergh itself is a busy market centre with a mainly 13th-century parish church. The Quaker meeting house, a mile to the south-west, dates back to 1675. George Fox once preached a sermon under a yew tree – part of which is preserved. There is a National Park Centre in the town.

SEDGEMOOR, Somerset   3 ST33

Sedgemoor is an expanse of fenland, much of which was once covered by the sea. Now it affords valuable grazing for cattle, and pollarded willow trees are to be found everywhere, their twigs used to provide canes for basket-making. Historically, Sedgemoor was the scene of the Duke of Monmouth's defeat in 1685.

SELBORNE, Hampshire   4 SU73

Gilbert White, born in 1720 and one-time curate of the parish, recorded the natural history of Selborne in a marvellously interesting book of that name which was published in 1788 and has remained in print ever since. Most of his observations were made in the steep beechwood 'hangers' that climb the slopes of the hills above the village, and he and his brother constructed a walk, called, appropriately, 'the Zig-Zag' that leads from what is now the carpark at the end of the village, up through the woods to Selborne Common (NT) a sheltered grassy space on top of the hill. Gilbert White's house and garden, The Wakes, is now a museum, devoted partly to his work and partly to an exhibition concerning Captain Oates (who died heroically on Scott's last expedition to the Antarctic), and also had connections with Selborne.

SELBY, N Yorkshire   15 SE63

The abbey was founded in 1069 by Benedict of Auxerre on the rather slender assumption that three swans landing on the River Ouse amounted to a 'sign from heaven'. Perhaps it was, though, for despite the fact that Benedict was trespassing on royal property, William I gave his consent, and some say his son, later Henry I, was delivered at Selby. The magnificent abbey church survives.

SELKIRK, Borders   24 NT42

Selkirk, once a royal burgh, stands on a hill overlooking Ettrick Water and is an admirable touring centre. A statue to Sir Walter Scott in the market place is a reminder that he was sheriff of the county from 1799 until 1832. His chair and some of his letters are preserved in the Sheriff Court House. At the other end of the High Street, there is a statue to Mungo Park, the African missionary and explorer, who was born at nearby Foulshiels in 1771. A third monument, erected in 1913, inspires uneasy thoughts of the burning of Selkirk by the English after their victory at Flodden in 1513. Bowhill (OACT) was the ancestral home of the Dukes of Buccleugh. It contains outstanding collections of paintings, porcelain and furniture, and relics of Montrose, Sir Walter Scott and Queen Victoria.

SHAP, Cumbria *18 NY51*
At 1300ft above sea level, Shap Fell is the highest point on the old A6, and the village stands at nearly 1000ft. One mile to the west you will find the ruins of a 14th-century abbey (AM) and a sulphur well. The surroundings are bleak but rather magnificent.

SHARDLOW, Derbyshire *10 SK43*
Shardlow stands beside the Trent and Mersey Canal. It used to be an inland port; now the narrow boats have been replaced by pleasure craft. The 200-year-old Clock Warehouse contains an exhibition showing – in words, pictures, models, and artefacts – how England's waterway system was created.

SHEBBEAR, Devon *2 SS40*
The Alscott Farm Agricultural Museum contains a collection of vintage tractors, ploughs, and dairy and household implements – plus photographs. It adds up to a fascinating picture of north Devon's agricultural past. A traction engine and a scale model of an Edwardian travelling fairground add to the interest. Shebbear itself is remote, peaceful, and beautiful. The name comes from the Old English *sceaftbearu*, meaning 'the grove where poles were got'. The Devil's Stone, outside the churchyard, is identical to those brought from South Wales for the building of Stonehenge: suggesting that (despite its name) this has always been a sacred place.

SHEEPWASH, Devon *2 SS40*
A charming village set on top of a hill, and still set out in a small square – just as the Saxons must have planned it. The Half Moon Inn is low and rambling. There are some picturesque thatched cottages and, not far away, where the parish borders on Highhampton, a packhorse bridge with five arches spans the River Torridge.

SHEERNESS, Kent *6 TQ97*
Sheerness stands on the north-western tip of the Isle of Sheppey at the point where the Medway joins the Thames. The dockyard was founded by Charles II, who also built a fort; with the coming of steam, Sheerness became a base at which naval vessels could take on coal without having to make the trip up river to Chatham. Nowadays, the town is a developing commercial port. The air is said to be particularly salubrious.

SHEFFIELD, S Yorkshire *15 SK38*
Nature provided Sheffield with all the requirements of a steel-manufacturing centre: the hills upon which it stands contained iron ore; there were trees to provide charcoal and the River Don to generate power; finally, there was coal in the vicinity. There had, in fact, been a settlement here back in the Iron Age (in a Sheffield context, one might say 'the *other* Iron Age').

The city's cutlery business is almost as old as the Norman castle, of which only fragments remain. Chaucer mentions a Sheffield knife in *The Canterbury Tales* – the miller carries one in the Reeve's Tale. By the accession of Elizabeth I, scissors, scythes, and shears had been added to the output. During the reign of James I, the Company of Cutlers in Hallamshire was established. The Master Cutler yields only to the Lord Mayor in precedence.

SELSEY, W Sussex *4 SZ89*
Selsey Bill used to be an island. Now it is a peninsula abounding in wild life and with an unusually good record for sunshine. Selsey's parish church of St Peter was moved to its present site in 1870. It was originally built in the 12th century at Church Norton on Pagham Harbour.

SELWORTHY, Somerset *2 SS94*
Selworthy is probably the prettiest village in the lovely Vale of Porlock. There are old cottages, a 15th-century tithe-barn, and thatched almshouses. The mainly 16th-century church has, unusually, a white exterior. Selworthy Beacon (1013ft) provides some fine views.

SETTLE, N Yorkshire *15 SD86*
Settle is a good – and, indeed, picturesque – centre from which to tour the surrounding countryside of the Yorkshire Dales. The Elizabethan-style Town Hall (1832, actually) deserves more than a passing glance, and so does the 17th-century Shambles. Pig Yard Club Museum contains prehistoric finds from nearby Victoria Cave.

SEVENOAKS, Kent *5 TQ55*
Sevenoaks nowadays is a residential town largely populated by commuters to London. Tradition says that its name was derived from a clump of seven oak trees. Sevenoaks School for boys was established in the 15th century by Sir William Sevenoke – a foundling who assumed the

name of the town and rose to become Lord Mayor of London. Cricket was played on The Vine in the 18th century – and still is. Knole Park (NT) on the outskirts dates back to 1456. It is said to have 365 rooms, 52 staircases, and 7 courtyards. Home of the Sackville family for more than 400 years, Knole is a treasurehouse of 17th-century furniture.

SHAFTESBURY, Dorset *3 ST82*
Shaftesbury, the only hilltop town in the county, is where Knut died in 1035. It is situated on top of a 700ft-high plateau overlooking Blackmoor Vale. Its old name was Shaston and that is how Thomas Hardy refers to it in his Wessex novels. The Abbey (AM), of which only fragments remain, was founded in AD981, and it was here that King Edward the Martyr was brought after being murdered by his step-mother at **Corfe Castle**. The town has an excellent museum which stands at the top of the picturesque, cobbled Gold Hill and contains a fascinating collection of locally made buttons, needlework toys, agricultural and domestic items, fans, pottery and finds from local excavations.

SHALLOWFORD, Staffordshire
9 SJ82
Izaak Walton, author of the 'fisherman's Bible', *The Compleat Angler*, lived in a cottage here which has been restored and a small museum and a period garden established. Before he took up writing and fishing, Walton was a London ironmonger.

Mary Queen of Scots spent a year in Sheffield Castle as a prisoner and 13 more in a Tudor house which has long been demolished. The site of the castle is now occupied by the Castle Market, which was opened in 1959. This roofed shopping centre, like the Crucible Theatre, is a nice example of modern city planning and design. This, indeed, is one of the more pleasant aspects of Sheffield: industry and the environment seem to have reached an accommodation. Dark satanic mills there may be, but the centre is neither dark nor satanic, and the modern buildings of the university are architecturally interesting.

As one might expect, the City Museum houses a remarkable collection of cutlery dating back to the 16th century. The Bishop's Palace, a 15th-century, timbered house, is also a museum – portraying life as it was lived when it was built. The city boasts two art galleries: the Mappin and the Graves. Also of interest are Sheffield Industrial Museum and Sheffield Manor; and the Abbeydale Industrial hamlet, on the outskirts, should certainly be seen. Using waterwheels turned by the River Sheaf, it produced scythes and other agricultural tools from 1712 until 1933. On certain days the furnaces are lit, and visitors can see how it was done. The Shepherd Wheel, in nearby Whitely Woods, is an even earlier water-powered grindery.

THE BLUEBELL LINE

The Bluebell steam railway line, run by enthusiasts, travels through the countryside between Sheffield Park and Horsted Keynes. This old signal box near Sheffield Park has been restored to its original state.

SHEFFIELD PARK, E Sussex   *5 TQ42*
Sheffield Park station was built in 1882 and retains its Victorian atmosphere. The line – part of British Rail's Lewes to East Grinstead track – was closed in 1960. Almost immediately, a group of enthusiasts set about resurrecting the section between Sheffield Park and Horsted Keynes, and called it the Bluebell Line; vintage steam

SHEPPEY *comes from the Anglo-Saxon word for sheep – still a familiar sight on the island.*

trains run most weekends and daily in the summer season. There is a railway museum at the station. Sheffield Park (NT) was laid out between 1769 and 1794 by the 1st Earl of Sheffield. It is always beautiful, but never quite so much as in spring, when the rhododendrons and azaleas are in bloom. The house (OACT) dates back to the Tudor period, but was remodelled in the 18th century.

SHEPPEY, ISLE OF, Kent   *6 TW07*
Sheppey is an island ten miles long by five miles wide to the east of the River Medway, where it joins the Thames. A bridge, built over the River Swale, connects it to the mainland. The soil is very fertile; sheep – the Isle of Sheppey means 'the island of sheep' – grazed on pastures reclaimed from the Swale. The main town is **Sheerness**.

SHEPTON MALLET, Somerset   *3 ST62*
Shepton Mallet is an agricultural town and the permanent site of the Bath and West Show. Cider and brewing, glove- and shoe-making, the manufacture of agricultural machinery are its industries and it originally derived its prosperity from the wool trade. The church, with its beautifully carved barrel ceiling and fine stone pulpit dates from this era. Shepton Mallet Museum contains discoveries from the Mendip caves.

SHERBORNE, Dorset   *3 ST61*
Sherborne Abbey (15th-century) is a magnificent church and the focus of this ancient town. The church bell, Great Tom, was a gift from Cardinal Wolsey, and, in the Lady Chapel there is a fine glass reredos engraved by Lawrence Whistler in 1958. The feature that excites most admiration, however, is the roof of golden Ham stone. Sherborne School occupies part of the original abbey buildings and the abbey gatehouse now houses the town's museum. Sherborne has two castles: the Old and the New. The Old (AM) was built in the 12th century by Bishop Roger, Chancellor to Henry I, and stood until the Civil War. Sir Walter Raleigh built the New Castle (OACT) and it was here, so the story goes, that his servant, seeing the smoke rising from his master's new-fangled pipe of

tobacco, drenched Sir Walter in ale to put out the fire. Two and a half miles west of the town, at Compton House, is the Lullingstone Silk Farm and Worldwide Butterfly Farm (OACT).

SHERBORNE ST JOHN, Hampshire
4 SU65
Near the village of Sherborne St John stands the Vyne (NT), a fine Tudor house built by Henry VIII's Lord Chamberlain, William Sandys. Of a later date are the elegant Rococo plaster ceilings and beautiful furnishings. Especially interesting are the Gothic chapel and tomb chamber of Chaloner Chute, Speaker of the House of Commons in the Cromwellian era, who had bought the house from Lord Sandys.

Sherborne St John's old church contains several interesting features – notably the 15th-century brasses in the Brocas Chapel.

SHERINGHAM, Norfolk   *12 TG14*
There are really two Sheringhams: Lower Sheringham, which is an attractive resort that was largely developed at the end of the last century, and Upper Sheringham – the village. The beach is shingle, though sand emerges at low tide. Sheringham Hall, a Regency house built between 1812 and 1817, stands in beautiful parkland: the gardens are occasionally open, the house by arrangement only. The ruins of 13th-century Beeston Abbey are nearby. The North Norfolk Railway Company has a display of steam locomotives and rolling stock at what used to be Sheringham station and trains are actually in operation at certain times in the summer season.

SHERWOOD FOREST,
Nottinghamshire   *15 SK57*
Centuries ago, at the time when Robin Hood was said to have led his outlaws through the glades, Sherwood Forest covered 100,000 very densely wooded acres. The oaks, so characteristic of ancient woodland were needed for shipbuilding and, as time went by, the forest was stripped of its assets. Nowadays, little of its grandeur remains. However, the Major (or Queen) Oak the meeting place, according to legend, of the outlaw band, has survived at Bilhagh. It measures 30ft around the trunk and has an overall circumference of nearly 270 yds.

SHETLAND ISLANDS, THE,
Highland *28*

The Shetlands comprise more than 100 islands, some little more than isolated rocks, but only 17 are inhabited. Muckle Flugga, an islet off Unst, is the most northerly point in the British Isles and lies 170 miles north of John o'Groats and only 300 miles from the Arctic Circle. Mainland, the largest of the Shetlands, has the islands' capital, Lerwick, a bustling little place of distinctly Scandinavian character. Ferries run from Aberdeen on the mainland, and there is an airport at Sumburgh, in the south of Mainland. The most powerful presence on the island nowadays is the gigantic North Sea oil terminal at Sullom Voe, although now, having radically changed the islanders' traditional crofting and fishing way of life, North-Sea oil is offering less and less employment.

The first settlers were probably Picts – followed in the 9th century by the Norsemen. The Shetlands remained part of Scandinavia until the marriage of the king's daughter Margaret to James III of Scotland in 1469 when Christian I ceded them as part of her dowry. Norse influence remained strong and the old Norn dialect survived for centuries. Remains of medieval, Viking, and earlier Pictish settlements can be seen at Jarlshof (AM) near Sumburgh. Near Scalloway are the Tingwall Agricultural Museum, and ruined Scalloway Castle (AM). Remains of Pictish brochs are common, but the best example is on Mousa, an attractive little island off the south-east coast of Mainland. Other islands to visit are Bressay, not far from Lerwick; East and West Burra, and Trodra, linked by bridges to each other and to Mainland; Muckle Roe, also linked by bridge to Mainland; Unst, the northernmost of the inhabited islands; Whalsay, and Yell. Fetlar and Foula are noted for their birdlife; Papa Stour is honeycombed with spectacular caves. Remote from the main group of islands are the Out Skerries. Fair Isle, half-way between the Orkneys and the Shetlands, is famous not only for its knitwear but also for the richness of the birdlife: the island is run by the National Trust for Scotland. Wild life also abounds on the Shetlands; seals and otters are a familiar sight, in some parts almost as familiar as the small, sturdy Shetland ponies, once the mainstay of the crofters, which are now so highly prized as pets.

SHIELDAIG, Highland *25 NG85*

The joy of Shieldaig, pleasant though this crofting and fishing village on an inlet of Loch Torridon is, is not so much the destination as the journey. The road linking it with Torridon provides some fantastic views of 3456ft Liathach; 3232ft Ben Alligin, and 2995ft Beinn Dearg. A newly built road west of the village to Applecross has opened up a panorama over the Inner Sound to the islands of Raasay and Skye. Many of the rocks in the vicinity have characterisitc horizontal red bands of Torridon sandstone.

SHOTTERY, Warwickshire *10 SP15*

Shottery is famous for Anne Hathaway's Cottage (OACT) the childhood home of Shakespeare's future wife. It is a long, timber-framed, farmhouse set at a right-angle to the road. The oldest part dates back to the 15th century.

Wenlock Edge and Ironbridge Gorge
73 miles

The tranquil landscapes of Wenlock Edge and the Long Mynd inspired the poetry of A E Housman, Shropshire's native poet, but hidden in this rural countryside is Ironbridge Gorge, cradle of the Industrial Revolution.

Leave **Shrewsbury** on the Leominster road, A49, skirt Baystonhill, then in ½ mile turn left (unclassified) to **Condover**, where the drive again turns left (SP Pitchford). After ¼ mile bear right, then in ½ mile bear left and continue for 1½ miles to the crossroads where the drive turns right for **Pitchford**. Continue from here to **Acton Burnell**, and at the crossroads turn right (SP Church Stretton). After 2 miles bear right and on reaching A49 turn left and drive for 5 miles to the crossroads, where turn right on to B4371 (SP Town Centre) into **Church Stretton**. The main drive turns left at the Midland Bank on to B4370 (but a detour up on to the Long Mynd can be made by driving up Burway Hill). Pass through Little Stretton, then turn right to rejoin A49. Pass the turning (left) to Acton Scott

Farm Museum and continue to Craven Arms. (To visit Stokesay Castle, continue on A49 for ¾ mile, then turn right, unclassified.) The main drive turns left on B4368, the Bridgnorth road. Pass through Munstow and continue for 3½ miles, then branch left on to B4378 for Shipton and **Much Wenlock**. Leave on A458 for Bridgnorth. From the Upper Town at **Bridgnorth** follow the High St through the North Gate to leave on the Broseley road, B4373. Continue for 6 miles, then bear right with the Wellington/Telford road and descend into the Seven Gorge, crossing the river bridge (here a detour can be made, right, to Blists Hill and the Coalport China Works). The main drive turns left into **Ironbridge** and joins the Wellington road (A4169). In ½ mile A4169 turns right to Coalbrookdale, but the main drive continues on B4380, the Shrewsbury road, passing Buildwas Abbey (on the opposite side of the river). Drive through Buildwas and Leighton, then after 4½ miles, at the junction with A5, turn left and return to Shrewsbury.

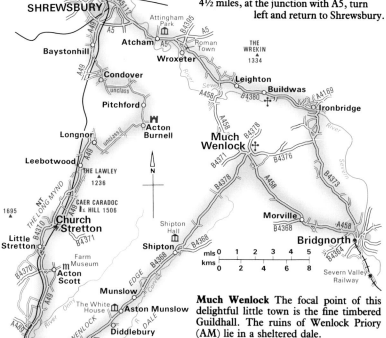

PLACES TO SEE

Shrewsbury The castle (OACT) dominates the historic town. Bear Steps (OACT) is a well-restored 14th-century cottage-complex. Clive House and Rowley's Museum are both of interest, and there are famous public gardens.

Stokesay Castle (AM) This picturesque fortified manor house, surrounded by a moat, dates from 1280.

Much Wenlock The focal point of this delightful little town is the fine timbered Guildhall. The ruins of Wenlock Priory (AM) lie in a sheltered dale.

Bridgnorth Upper and lower halves of this attractive Severn Valley town are joined by a cliff railway. Bridgnorth is the terminus of the Severn Valley Railway.

Ironbridge Gorge The famous Iron Bridge, Blist's Hill Open-air Museum, Coalport China Works, and Coalbrookdale Museum are fascinating monuments of the Industrial Revolution, all operated by the Ironbridge Gorge Museum Trust.

Buildwas Abbey Ruins of Buildwas Abbey (AM) stand beside the River Severn.

Atcham A charming village, near which stands Attingham Hall (NT), a magnificent 18th-century mansion.

SHREWSBURY, Shropshire 9 SJ41

Shrewsbury, which is situated on a bend of the River Severn, has ten bridges spanning the river; even the railway station is built over it. The town may have been founded by Britons who fled from the Roman city of Viroconium (now Wroxeter) five miles to the south-east, and there are relics of the Roman occupation to be found in Rowley's House Museum, one of the half-timbered buildings in which Shrewsbury abounds. In the old part of the city, Bear Steps (OACT), a restored 14th-century cottage, with old shops and a meeting hall, is well worth a visit, and there are winding old streets and alleys to explore – such as Wyle Cop, Grope Lane and Gullet Passage. The Norman castle (OACT), built high above the river, was much enlarged by Edward I, and in the 18th century was converted into a house by the architect and engineer Thomas Telford for Sir William Pulteney. St Mary's Church, with its lofty spire, dates from the 12th century. The nave has a 15th-century carved roof and some fine stained glass, particularly in the Jesse Window. St Chad's Church is notable for its circular nave.

Among the many fine things to be seen in Shrewsbury are the monuments to its famous sons: Charles Darwin attended Shrewsbury School and is commemorated by a bronze statue. Clive (of India), who was MP for the town from 1761 until his death in 1774, is similarly commemorated and his house is now a museum. Lord Hill, who commanded a brigade at Waterloo, tops them all – with a column 134ft high, just shorter than Nelson's Column in Trafalgar Square. Shrewsbury's largest park, the Quarry, is the work of the famous gardener, Percy Thrower. At its centre he has planted the lovely formal gardens known as the Dingle.

SHUGBOROUGH, Staffordshire 9 SJ92

Shugborough Hall, (OACT) home of the Earls of Lichfield, and Staffordshire County Museum lies five miles to the east of Stafford. The mansion, which dates back to 1693, contains a fine collection of French furniture and some interesting relics of Admiral George Anson – the intrepid navigator who inherited the property in 1720 and lived there until his death in 1762. Among the features of the garden, are the 'Chinese House', the Cat's Monument and the Tower of the Winds. The stable block houses the County Museum which contains exhibitions of costume, domestic life and crafts. Park Farm is an agricultural museum and raises rare breeds of animals.

SIBLE HEDINGHAM, Essex 12 TL73

Sible Hedingham was the birthplace of Sir John Hawkwood – a 14th-century mercenary of more than common interest. He fought in the Black Prince's forces at Poitiers, then moved on to Italy, where he and his band of hand-picked mercenaries became so much in demand by warring states that they were almost continually in action. Sir John is one of the figures in a frieze painted by Paolo Uccello in Florence, and he died there in 1394. There is a monument to him in the south aisle of St Peter's Church. Not far from the church stand two handsome buildings, the 15th-century White Horse Inn, and the rectory, which dates from the 18th century.

BAYLEAF HOUSE *is one of several interesting old buildings that have been saved from demolition and reassembled and restored, piece by piece, at the Weald and Downland Open Air Museum near Singleton.*

SIBSON CUM STIBBINGTON, Cambridgeshire 11 TL09

This double village has a quietly elegant air of prosperity, its 17th-century stone buildings inter-mingled with thatched cottages. Just outside the village, on the A1 as it heads for Stamford, is the Haycock Inn – built as a posting house in the mid-17th century with its bedrooms centring on the courtyard.

SIDMOUTH, Devon 2 SY18

Steep wooded hills guard the landward approaches to Sidmouth, a select resort, its centre still preserving the tall Regency houses, with their wrought-iron balconies, that recall Sidmouth's standing in the early 19th century. The pleasant beach is flanked by spectacular red cliffs and the town began life as a fishing village. During the Napoleonic Wars, the well-to-do, unable to visit Europe, came to Sidmouth instead. The Old Manor in Church Street houses the museum – and rightly so – it is one of the town's oldest houses.

SILCHESTER, Hampshire 4 SU66

The Romans called Silchester 'Calleva Atrebatum' and it was a considerable town, with a dyeing industry, a poulterer, a butcher and doubtless other tradesmen. The inhabitants worshipped in three temples, and eventually, in the 4th century, a small Christian church was built within the town walls. It is, so far as anyone can tell, the *only* one built in Britain during the years of occupation. But the Romans departed and Calleva Atrebatum fell into total decay, except for the walls and a gateway, which are still substantial. The remains of an amphitheatre can be seen outside the walls and there is a site museum, though the best finds are in Reading Museum.

SILSOE, Bedfordshire 11 TL03

Wrest Park Gardens (AM) are a fine example of 18th-century design, with formal canals and some nice touches added by Capability Brown. The Baroque 18th-century Banqueting House and the Bowling Green House also merit attention.

SIMONBURN, Northumberland 19 NY87

Simonburn is a beautiful exercise in simplicity: a village green, surrounded by cottages and trees. The castle has all but gone: finally demolished, they say, by the villagers themselves – searching for hidden treasure (it remained hidden). On the nearby crags, four standing stones known as the Goat Stones stand sentinel. St Mungo's Church dates from the 13th century.

SINGLETON, W Sussex 4 SU81

Linch Down rises 818ft to the north-west of this lovely little Sussex village and offers some splendid views. It is the perfect setting for the Weald and Downland Open Air Museum, an outstanding collection of historic buildings from all over the South Country which have been re-erected on the slopes of the Downs. From time to time there are demonstrations of rural crafts.

SISSINGHURST, Kent 6 TQ73

Sissinghurst Castle (NT) was built during the reign of Mary Tudor. During the Seven Years War (1756–1763), by then in a delapidated condition, it was used as a prison for captured French seamen. Afterwards, the buildings served as a workhouse, then as a farmhouse; eventually they fell into complete decay. In 1930, the estate was bought by the writer Victoria Sackville-West and her husband, Harold Nicolson. They restored the gatehouse, parts of two wings, and created what must surely be one of the most beautiful gardens in Britain.

SITTINGBOURNE, Kent 6 TG96

Sittingbourne, on an inlet of the River Swale, used to be important to Britain's paper making industry. A four-mile length of railway track, which connected the mills with the dock at Kemsley, survives – with locomotives and rolling-stock: many of the mills do not. The New Dolphin Sailing Barge Museum on Milton Creek has an original sail-loft and forge, and collections of riggers' tools, etc. There are often barges in the process of being restored.

SIXPENNY HANDLEY, Dorset
3 ST91
Isaac Gulliver, Dorset's most famous
smuggler, lived here. In 1768, having
married the landlord's daughter, he made
the local pub the headquarters of his
widespread operations. Poaching in
Cranbourne Chase was another occupation
of the less law-abiding folk, but Nemesis
struck in 1892 when a fire destroyed many
of the buildings. The name is derived from
Saxpena and *Hanlega* – both ancient sub-
divisions of the county, but one signpost in
the vicinity takes it more literally. It reads:
'To 6d Handley'.

SIZERGH, Cumbria *18 SD48*
For 700 years the home of the Strickland
family, Sizergh Castle (NT) has a pele
tower built in 1370 as a defence against
border raiders. Later additions include a
Tudor great hall. The house contains much
fine panelling and early Elizabethan
carving.

SKEGNESS, Lincolnshire *16 TF56*
The reputedly bracing air of Skegness was
enjoyed by Lord Tennyson; nowadays, it
braces thousands of holiday-makers, mostly
from the Midlands. The sands are splendid;
the resort wants for nothing in the way of
popular entertainment and its Promenade
boasts the Natureland Marine Zoo.
Gibraltar Point, to the south, is a well-
populated nature reserve. Church Farm
Museum demonstrates 19th-century
farming techniques.

SKENFRITH, Gwent *9 SO42*
Skenfrith grew up around its Norman
castle, built on an artificial mound 50ft in
diameter and 15ft high. The river provided
a natural defence on the east side; an
artificial moat, 40ft wide, served a similar
purpose on the others. As so often, the
dominating feature is the keep (AM, NT), a
three-storey, very solid, building with a
turret on the top.

SKIPTON, N Yorkshire *14 SD95*
Skipton, set in a valley that slices through
the Airedale moors, stands at the farthest
northerly point of the Leeds and Liverpool
Canal (opened in 1816, it runs for nearly
130 miles). Despite connections with the
textile industry, the town has plenty of
greenery and a countrified look about it,
which makes it a pleasant point of
departure for trips into the Dales. The
14th-century castle (OACT) was the home
of the Clifford family. After it had been
partially demolished in 1649, Lady Anne
Clifford rebuilt it, and added the family
motto 'Desormais' (henceforth) to the
gatehouse. A yew tree planted by Lady
Anne stands in the grounds. The Craven
Museum concentrates on local geology for
its exhibits; the fascinating George Leatt
Industrial and Folk Museum is
accommodated in the 1750 High Corn Mill.

SKOMER ISLAND, Dyfed *7 SM70*
Skomer is littered with the relics of ancient
hutments – which suggest that, at one time,
it was heavily populated. It may, indeed,
have been a haven when man first set forth
to sail the seas. The present inhabitants are
all of them navigators by nature: kittiwake,
cormorant, petrel, puffin, razorbill,
guillemot, and shearwater. There are even
some normally land-based birds such as
buzzard and peregrines.

SLAUGHTERS, THE,
Gloucestershire 10 SP12
There are two Slaughters: Lower and
Upper. Both have streams ambling through
them – both are places of very considerable
charm with everything built from that
honey-coloured local stone peculiar to the
Cotswolds. Lower Slaughter has one or two
newish houses, but nothing unsightly.
Nothing has been built in Upper Slaughter
since 1904. Lower Slaughter was once the
seat of a court that met at three-weekly
intervals from the Middle Ages until the
17th century.

SLEAFORD, Lincolnshire *16 TF04*
Sleaford is a small market town with
associations with the Bishops of Lincoln.
The Church of St Denis in the market place
is on a scale that would not discredit a
cathedral and is remarkable for the
beautiful stone tracery of its windows.
Other buildings of distinction are the 16th-
century vicarage, the Black Bull Inn (once
the scene of that horrendous and now,
thankfully, defunct sport of bull-baiting),
the Corn Exchange, the former workhouse,
and the Sessions – all of them early 19th-
century. Sir Robert Carre was a generous
local benefactor, who gave the town its
almshouses and Sleaford Grammar School.

SLEDMERE, Humberside *16 SE96*
Sledmere village and the surrounding
Yorkshire Wolds owe a great deal to the
Sykes family's foresight. In Tudor times,
they were Leeds merchants; and then, in
1751, Richard Sykes began work on
Sledmere House (OACT) – the site of
which had once been that of a medieval
manor. His nephew, Sir Christopher,
carried on the work in the 1780s. The house
is beautifully decorated and contains many
handsome pieces of furniture. Sir
Christopher's most important achievement
was the introduction of agriculture to the
Wolds – an achievement celebrated by a
Classical temple beside the main gate. On
top of Gaston Hill, a 120ft Gothic tower was
erected in memory of Sir Tatton Sykes after
his death in 1863. Sir Tatton, it seems, was
renowned for his skill as a bare-knuckle
fighter. Indeed, there seem to be
monuments great and small to Sykes
wherever you look in Sledmere. They are
well deserved. Before this industrious
family took the village under its protection,
the inhabitants used to live in fear of raids
by packs of wolves from the wilderness that
surrounded them.

SLIMBRIDGE, Gloucestershire
3 SO70
Slimbridge, four miles east of Sharpness, is
the home of the Severn Wildfowl Trust
founded by Sir Peter Scott in 1946. It
contains the largest and most
comprehensive collection of wildfowl in the
world: some resident, and some arriving
and departing according to the seasons.
Well-sited observation towers are available
to the public, with whom the Trust is justly
very popular.

SLOUGH, Berkshire *5 SU97*
'Come, friendly bombs, and fall on Slough/
It isn't fit for humans now. . .' wrote Sir
John Betjeman. Many Slough people would
doubtless disagree with his sentiments, for
the town has many open spaces, and
facilities for sports and leisure are good. A
few miles away, at **Stoke Poges**, Thomas
Gray was inspired to compose his *Elegy
Written in a Country Churchyard*.

SMALLHYTHE, Kent *6 TQ83*
Nowadays, taking a direct line, Smallhythe
is seven and a half miles from the sea. In
medieval times, when the River Rother was
wider and deeper, it was a prosperous port
and shipbuilding centre. The one-time
harbour master's house, now named
Smallhythe Place (NT), was the actress
Ellen Terry's home from 1901 until her
death in 1928. A theatrical museum has
now been set up in the house.

LOWER SLAUGHTER *Pretty stone-roofed cottages overlook the shallow waters of the River Eye in this charming Cotswold village that derives its name from the Saxon word 'sloghtre', meaning 'muddy place'.*

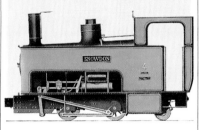

SNOWDON

None of North Wales' narrow-gauge railways is quite so famous or so popular as the one that climbs up Snowdon (above) – the highest summit in England and Wales. The line, which covers 4⅝ miles and has the distinction of being the only rack and pinion railway in Britain, was completed within two years and opened in 1896. All the steam locomotives are powered solely by coal and provide memorable trips, affording spectacular views of Snowdonia.

SMARDEN, Kent *6 TQ83*
In the days of Edward III, Smarden was a busy market town. Now, with its black-and-white timbered houses, it must settle for being one of the prettiest villages in the country. Reminders of its days of prosperity occur in the Dragon House (decorated with a frieze of dragons) near the village pump, and Chesenden – a Wealden hall-house. The church has often been called 'the barn of Kent' due to the height (36ft) of its wooden roof.

SMOO CAVE, Highland *30 NC46*
Smoo Cave, which lies a mile or so to the east of Durness, is a huge cavern cut into the base of the limestone cliff. The first of the three chambers is the largest – 200ft long by 120ft high, and is entered through a 53ft-high arch. The name probably comes from *smjuga* ('a rock').

SNAPE, Suffolk *12 TM35*
In the 19th century, Newson Garrett, father of Britain's first woman doctor, Elizabeth Garrett Anderson, established a maltings on the edge of the village. It was served by sailing barges travelling up and down the River Alde to the Maltings Quay. As a result of the Aldeburgh Music Festival inaugurated in 1948 by Benjamin Britten, part of the premises was transformed into a concert hall.

SNOWDONIA NATIONAL PARK,
  Gwynedd *13 SH73*
The Welsh name for Snowdonia is *Eryi* – 'the haunt of the eagle'. Alas, the eagles have gone, but the grandeur remains. Snowdon itself dominates the scene, at 3560ft it is the highest mountain in Wales. The Park covers 845 square miles of mountainous countryside stretching as far as the coast of Cardigan Bay. This is superb country for the walker and rock-climber. The mixture of mountain, lake and deep valley creates some of the loveliest scenery in north Wales, and noted beauty spots such as **Betws-y-Coed** attract visitors in their thousands.

SOLVA, Dyfed *7 SM82*
The creek, sheltered by steep green slopes, is not unlike a fjord, and the village of small white cottages clinging to the hillside enhances this impression. There were lime-kilns in business during the 19th century, and the quay was built in 1861 to handle stone used in the construction of Small Rocks lighthouse 15 miles offshore. Solva is now a haven for pleasure craft.

SOMERLEYTON, Suffolk *12 TM49*
In 1844, Somerleyton Hall (OACT) of Elizabethan foundation, was rebuilt in the Italianate style by Sir Samuel Peto – who also created a village to go with it. Carvings in the Oak Parlour show Grinling Gibbons at his best. Within the 12 acres of grounds, there are a maze, a nature trail, and a miniature railway.

SOMERTON, Somerset *3 ST42*
In the days of the West Saxons Somerton was the capital of Somerset. An attractive country town, there is a most pleasing uniformity about its grey stone buildings grouped round the square. The church tower is particularly interesting: it was built in stages from the 12th century to the 15th, and has a notable tie-beam roof.

SONNING, Berkshire *4 SU77*
Sonning is one of the prettiest of the Thames-side villages, despite the fact that it is only a stone's throw from Reading. The arched bridge spanning the river is one of the oldest across the Thames, and the lock is by no means the least of the many attractive features, which include thatched cottages, old houses and a mill.

SOTTERLEY, Suffolk *12 TM48*
Sotterley Agricultural Museum, which is housed in Alexander Wood Farm, presents a splendid collection of hardware – mechanical and non-mechanical. The blacksmith's shop, the farmhouse kitchen, and agricultural implements splendidly evoke the past. There is also a collection of cars and motorbikes.

SOUTHAMPTON, Hampshire 4 SU41

For many years the main port of departure
for the USA was Liverpool, but in 1911 the
White Star Line moved its base to
Southampton and the others followed. Not
only was it closer to London, and had a
sheltered anchorage, it also enjoyed that
unique phenonenon – two high tides in
every 24 hours. For the better part of half a
century, the docks were enlivened by the
massive and beautiful shapes of great ocean
liners – some plying between England and
New York, others (the Union Castle ships)
running a service to South Africa. When air
travel came into its own, however, the
liners disappeared, apart from occasional
appearances by the QEII and the Canberra.

Southampton had been in business as a
port long before the luxury ships came to it.
It was a place of embarkation for the
crusades, for the Napoleonic Wars, and,
indeed, during both World Wars when
more than ten million troops set off for
France. In 1620, the Mayflower set sail from
here – an event that is celebrated by a tall
stone column near the spot where the
Pilgrim Fathers walked up the gangplank.
Later, bad weather forced them into

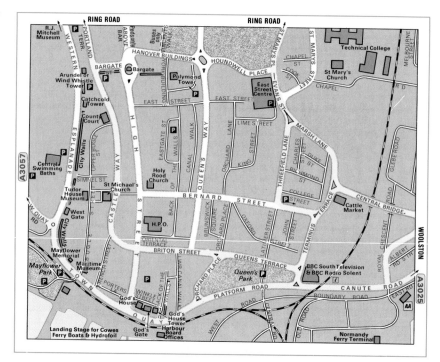

OCEAN LINERS

Q.S.T.S. "QUEEN MARY"

Queen Mary, immortalised here on an
old cigarette card, was one of the
greatest of the stately ocean liners
that regularly set sail from Southampton for the continents of Africa
and America during the first half of
this century. This was the heyday of
luxury sea travel and the great ships
epitomised a more leisured and gracious era.

Plymouth for repair. A sadder memorial,
carved in white marble, stands in East
Park. It is dedicated to the engineers of the
Titanic – that ill-starred if magnificent
shipbuilding folly that foundered at sea.

Marlands Hall is a museum devoted to
the achievements of R J Mitchell, designer
of the Spitfire – the first of which was built
in Southampton. Among the exhibits is
Mitchell's Supermarine S6B, which won
the Schneider Trophy race in 1931 with a
speed of 340mph. Neither Spitfires nor
Hurricanes could save Southampton from
bombardment by the Luftwaffe in World
War II. The damage was awesome and
much of the past was smashed to rubble. As
a result a good deal of the town is new.
However, among the historic buildings
which survived is the Bargate, which once
served as guildhall and courthouse and is
now a museum; the 14th-century Wool
House (now the Maritime Museum); and
God's House Tower, the remains of a
Norman hospital originally founded in
1185. The fine 16th-century Tudor House,

set in a charming Elizabethan garden, now
houses a museum of local history. Also of
interest are the City Art Gallery,
Southampton Zoo, and HMS *Cavalier*, the
only surviving destroyer to have seen active
service in World War II. She has been
restored and is now a museum ship.

SOUTHEND-ON-SEA, Essex 6 TQ88

Southend was – and still is, really – the
seaside resort of London. The feature for
which it is best known is the pier, which
stretches out one and a quarter miles over
the rather muddy foreshore: it is the longest
in the world. Among the better examples of
seaside kitsch are the floral clock with a dial
20ft in diameter, and the Kursaal.
Although partly demolished now, and built
over, the Kursaal was, in its heyday, the
epitome of Bank Holiday amusements.
Places of interest include Prittlewell Priory
Museum and Southchurch Hall (OACT), a
restored 14th-century manor.

SOUTH DOWNS, W and E Sussex 5, 6

The chalky uplands of the South Downs
extend from a point near **Petersfield** in
Hampshire to **Beachy Head** in Sussex,
forming the southern rampart of the Weald
as the **North Downs** form the northern.
Woodlands clothe the western end, but in
the east the Downs offer great expanses of
windswept turf. A long-distance footpath,
the South Downs Way, crosses the length.
The highest points are Butser Hill (889ft),
Duncton Down (837ft) and Ditchling
Beacon (813ft). Almost without exception,
the views are tremendous, and there are
pleasing interludes – such as the intrusion
of the Cuckmere river to form a valley in
which nestles that most charming of small
towns, **Alfriston**. Birling Gap is within easy
walking distance of that relic of early
lighthouses, Belle Tout (built in 1831); and
then, over to the west and due north of
Worthing, there is Chanctonbury Ring: a
triumphant copse, a kind of arboreal
crown. It is not officially haunted, though
many who have been there claim to have
experienced a strange sensation of awe.

SOUTH HARTING, W Sussex 3 SU71

High on the South Downs, near the village
of South Harting, stands Uppark (NT), a
late 17th-century mansion, much improved
in the 18th century by the fabulously
wealthy Sir Matthew Fetherstonhaugh,
whose collections of paintings, porcelain
and furniture can still be admired.

SOUTH MOLTON, Devon 2 SS72

From the Middle Ages until the mid 19th
century South Molton enjoyed a long
period of prosperity: the coach between
Barnstaple and Bideford used to stop here;
it was the nearest town to the surrounding
iron and copper mines; the wool trade
contributed handsomely to its fortunes.
One by one these trades died off and South
Molton settled down to a peaceful existence
as a country town. Part of its 18th-century
Guildhall is now a museum. Three and a
half miles west, Castle Hill is a
handsome Palladian mansion set in
attractive gardens.

SOUTHPORT, Merseyside 14 SD31

Southport is a thoroughly nice resort, with
elegant shops in Lord Street, beautiful
gardens, some good golf courses, a pier,
and six miles of sandy beach (once used for
motor racing). The Atkinson Art Gallery
has interesting collections of 19th- and
20th-century painting and sculpture; the
Botanic Gardens Museum is devoted to
natural and local history; all manner of
historic locomotives, buses, trams and
other old vehicles can be seen at the
Steamport Transport Museum; on the
Promenade there is a model village and
model railway, and a zoo.

SOUTH SHIELDS, Tyne & Wear 20 NZ36

The port at South Shields was established
by the Romans as a kind of preliminary
before they moved on to found Newcastle.
Finds from the Roman period are displayed
in the museum on the site of Arbeia, the
excavated Roman fort. Although less
important than Newcastle, industry did not
pass South Shields by.

SOUTHWELL, Nottinghamshire
16 SK65
Charles I gave himself up to the Scottish army at the Saracen's Head in Southwell in 1647 and they promptly sold him to Parliament. Happier memories are recalled by Burgage Manor, where Byron used to spend his holidays, and by the Bramley seedling apple, which was developed in the garden of Bramley Tree Cottage. But the most imposing feature of this Nottinghamshire town is the great Norman minster, famous for the exquisite carvings in the Chapter House.

SOUTHWOLD, Suffolk   *12 TM57*
Southwold is an altogether delightful little resort at the mouth of the River Blythe. Among its many pleasant features are numerous greens, which came about at the result of a fire that laid waste most of the town in 1659. The parish church of St Edmund is a beauty – with a fine tower (100ft), a medieval painted pulpit, and a Seven Sacraments font. Next to neighbouring **Blythburgh** and **Long Melford** it is indisputably the finest church in Suffolk. The beach is a mixture of sand and shingle. Unusual but by no means unattractive features of Southwold are the lighthouse, which stands within the town, and the famous Adnams brewery.

SPALDING, Lincolnshire   *11 TF22*
More than half the bulbs grown in Britain come from the area around Spalding, which suggests that the best time to visit it is late spring. The River Welland flows through the centre of the town, spanned by seven bridges. Ayscoughfee Hall (early 15th-century) is now a museum of ornithology. Springfield Gardens contain more than a million bulbs and thousands of roses.

SPEKE, Merseyside   *14 SJ48*
Speke is the home of Liverpool's airport. It also has Speke Hall (NT), a beautiful half-timbered house set in 35 acres and nicely sheltered by trees. Completed by Sir Edward Norreys in 1598, one of the wainscots is said to have come from Holyrood Palace in Edinburgh (Sir Edward's ancestor, Sir William, fought at Flodden, so anything is possible). Among the treasures are rare Mortlake tapestries.

SPETCHLEY, Hereford & Worcester
9 SO85
Spetchley Park, built in 1810, is an imposing mansion set in extensive grounds (OACT). The partly 14th-century church contains interesting monuments. Isolated three miles away to the north-east, the small church at Warndon has a picturesque timbered tower and a 15th-century font.

SPILSBY, Lincolnshire   *16 TF46*
Spilsby is an attractive market town beyond which the flatlands of the Fens stretch out towards the North Sea. Sir William de Willoughby gave the town its charter in the 14th century, and it is not surprising to find memorials to the family, and to the d'Eresbys with whom they inter-married, in the church. One of them, 2nd Baron Willoughby d'Eresby, fought at Crécy. Sir John Franklin, the explorer, is also remembered by a tablet. Born in Spilsby, he died in the Arctic while leading the expedition which discovered the North-West Passage in 1847.

SOUTHWOLD *The lighthouse soars up from the heart of the town to guard the North Sea.*

SPROATLEY, Humberside   *16 TA13*
Sproatley is a straggling village, mostly surrounded by flat, green and obviously very arable countryside – though, to the north there are woods and avenues of trees. Approaching from this direction, you come to Burton Constable Hall (OACT) a Tudor house standing in 200 acres of parkland landscaped by Capability Brown.

STAFFA, ISLE OF, Strathclyde
25 NM33
Staffa is uninhabited and ships from Oban can land visitors only when the weather is calm. The island is famous for its caves – notably Fingal's, celebrated by Mendelssohn. Fingal (or Finn McCoul to be correct) was a giant who was credited with the creation of Staffa.

STAFFORD, Staffordshire   *9 SO92*
Stafford comes as a surprise to many people: rather than an industrial centre of the North Midlands, it has more the air of a country town, with several historic houses, notably High House, a four-storey timbered building where Charles I and Prince Rupert once stayed. Izaac Walton, (*see* **Shallowford**) the ultimate authority on angling, was born in Stafford and baptised at the Norman font in the Church of St Mary. Richard Brinsley Sheridan, playwright and onetime owner of Drury Lane Theatre in London, was Stafford's MP from 1790 until 1806. He lived at Chetwynd House (1745), which now, rather quaintly, serves as the post office. Stafford used to have two castles: the one built by William I has vanished without trace; the other (Robert de Stafford's) was rebuilt in the 19th century, and is now virtually a ruin once more.

STAGSDEN, Bedfordshire   *11 SP94*
The village is a place of thatched cottages and a church, St Leonards, that has a 13th-century tower. Stagsden Bird Gardens (OACT) contain more than 1500 specimens of rare wild life and a fine collection of shrub roses.

STAINDROP, Co Durham   *20 NZ12*
Staindrop's church, St Mary's, is understandably rich with monuments to the Nevill family, who owned Raby Castle (OACT) for three centuries. The castle passed from the Nevills to the Vanes in the early 17th century. Its historical associations are numerous and its octagonal drawing-room is probably the best example of a Victorian drawing-room in the country.

STAITHES, N Yorkshire   *20 NZ77*
Staithes is an uncommonly picturesque village at the foot of a steep hill. It is rich with associations with its neighbour, the sea. Time was, in the 18th century, when 400 fishing boats sailed from here, and returned laden with mackerel and cod but the trade moved to **Whitby**. Captain Cook, the supreme navigator, was bound apprentice to a local grocer before running away to Whitby to join his first ship.

STAMFORD, Lincolnshire   *11 TF00*
Many people hold that Stamford is England's most beautiful, small, stone-built town, and it would be hard to argue with them. History pours through the town quietly, moving unobtrusively from one style of architecture to another, from cottage, to town house, to church; it was the first town in England to be designated a conservation area. Originally the capital of the Fens, it was the scene of great destruction during the Wars of the Roses in the 15th century, but quickly recovered; most of the buildings we see today date from after this period, but Stamford's oldest building, the ruined chapel of St Leonard's Priory, is much more ancient. Of the town's five churches, St Mary's, dating largely from the 15th century, contains the lovely 'Chapel of the Golden Choir', which takes its name from the gold stars of the beautifully painted roof. All Saints Church has a magnificent angel roof in the chancel. In the churchyard of St Martin's Church, Daniel Lambert is buried; the fattest Englishman who ever lived, he weighed over 52 stone and his waist measured 92 inches. Thanks to the wealth of its wool merchants, Stamford has many fine almhouses, notably Browne's Hospital founded in the 16th century. Its chapel contains an exquisite Tudor screen and fine stained glass. The ancient grammar school has an even more ancient pointed-arched-gateway in its wall, a relic of a breakaway movement by Oxford students from Brazenose and other colleges who fled to Stamford and Northampton for a period, having quarrelled with the authorities at Oxford. Just outside the town and in the neighbouring county of Cambridgeshire stands Burghley House (OACT), ancestral home of the Cecils. It was built by William Cecil, Chief Secretary of State and Lord High Treasurer to Queen Elizabeth I. The house is vast, and there are many sumptuously furnished apartments, particularly the 'Heaven Room' whose walls and ceiling were painted by Verrio.

Stirling and the Trossachs
88 miles

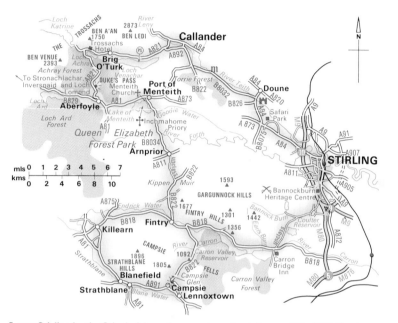

The ancient Royal Burgh of Stirling, historic seat of the Scottish kings, is aptly named the Gateway to the Highlands; to the north-west rise the dramatic peaks of the Trossachs; to the south-west, the heights of the Campsie Fells.

Leave **Stirling** by the Crianlarich road, A84, and at the M9 roundabouts take the 2nd and then 3rd exits. Cross the River Forth, and after 3 miles pass the road (right) to Blair Drummond Safari Park. In 2½ miles, turn left on to B8032 (SP Deanston), then bear left (SP Callander). After 6¼ miles turn right on to B822 and right again (no signs) on to A81 and proceed to **Callander**. From here follow Crianlarich signs, A84, pass through the hamlet of **Kilmahog**, then turn left on to A821 (SP Aberfoyle, the Trossachs). Drive alongside Loch Venachar to **Brig o' Turk** and then continue into the Queen Elizabeth Forest Park. Pass the Trossachs Hotel (in ¼ mile a detour can be made by keeping forward to the pier on the eastern end of Loch Katrine where pleasure-steamer trips run during summer). The main drive turns left on the Aberfoyle road through the forest to **Aberfoyle** (where a detour can be taken along B829 to Inversnaid on Loch Lomond – 28 miles round trip). The main drive continues on the Stirling road, A821, then after a mile

branches left on to A81, SP Callander. Pass the Lake of Menteith and in 1 mile turn right, SP Arnprior, on B8034. (By Menteith Church there is a passenger ferry to Inchmaholme Priory on an island in the lake.) At **Arnprior** turn right on to A811, then left on to an unclassified road, SP Fintry. At **Fintry** turn right (no sign) on to B818, then in 5½ miles join the Glasgow road, A875, and pass through Killearn. Two miles further turn left on to A81 and drive through Blanefield to the edge of **Strathblane**, then turn left on to A891 (SP Lennoxtown). At **Lennoxtown** turn left (SP Fintry) on to B822, and start the ascent on to the Campsie Fells. The road crosses the moors, then descends to the valley of Endrick Water, where the drive turns right on to B818 (SP Denny). Continue along the valley, then in 7¾ miles at the Carron Bridge Inn turn left (unclassified, SP Stirling), and after about 4 miles turn left and later cross the M9. In ¾ mile turn right and left on to A872 at Bannockburn, then join A9 for the return to Stirling.

PLACES TO SEE

Stirling An ancient Royal Burgh, this attractive old town has a magnificent castle (AM) housing the Museum of the Argyll and Sutherland Highlanders. Also of interest are the ruins of Cambuskenneth Abbey (AM), and Mar's Wark (AM), built by the Earl of Mar in 1570. Stirling's story is told through film-shows and exhibits at the Landmark Centre (OACT).

Blair Drummond Safari Park (OACT) Many species of wild animal, including Siberian Tigers, are kept in conditions which approximate as nearly as possible to their natural habitats.

Callander An attractive touring centre for the Trossachs. Kilmahog Woollen Mill (OACT) is nearby.

Queen Elizabeth Forest Park The Park covers more than 41,000 acres of mountains and lakeland scenery, and there are many marked forest trails.

Inchmaholme Priory (AM) The ruins stand on an island in the Lake of Menteith.

Bannockburn Battlefield (NTS) South of Stirling is the site of the battle of which Robert Bruce defeated Edward II in 1314.

STAMFORD BRIDGE, Humberside
15 SE75
In 1066 at the Battle of Stamford Bridge, King Harald of Norway, who had sailed up the Humber and the Ouse and sacked York, was decisively beaten by King Harold of England. The battle took place on the flats above which now stands a fine 18th-century bridge. As everyone knows, immediately after the battle, Harold and the English army had to race south to meet William of Normandy at Hastings, where they were defeated.

STANHOPE, Co Durham   *19 NY93*
High on the moors, this peaceful little town used to be the administrative centre of Weardale and not unimportant as a lead-mining centre. Nowadays it is used by holidaymakers as a base from which to explore the adjacent countryside. St Thomas's Church dates from the beginning of the 13th century and has in the sanctuary two interesting old painted tablets.

STANHOPE *Found in a nearby quarry, this tree stump is thought to be over 250 million years old.*

STAPLEFORD, Leicestershire
10 SK81
Stapleford Park (OACT) is a Tudor mansion with a hall that dates back to 1500. Among the wealth of interesting items is a collection of 400 statuettes of famous men and women. In the grounds, there are a lake, a safari park, and a miniature railway.

STEVENAGE, Hertfordshire   *11 TL22*
Anyone planning a new town could hardly do better than inspect Stevenage. The new has been accomplished at no sacrifice to the old. Now Stevenage is spaciously planned, and contains several examples of good modern architecture. Old Stevenage centres on the High Street, which is attractively shaded by trees. Old cottages line the narrow streets, leading off the High Street. The undercroft of St George's Church contains a museum.

STEVENTON, Hampshire   *4 SU54*
For more than 40 years, Jane Austen's father was rector of the 13th-century church, which contains several monuments to the family. Miss Austen was born in the village in 1775. While living at Steventon, and in her early twenties, she wrote the first versions of *Sense and Sensibility*, *Pride and Prejudice*, and *Northanger Abbey*.

STICKLEPATH, Devon   *2 SX69*
When in Sticklepath, make a point of visiting the Museum of Rural Industry at the old Finch Brothers Foundry. The foundry was in business from 1814 until 1960, taking its power from water-wheels.

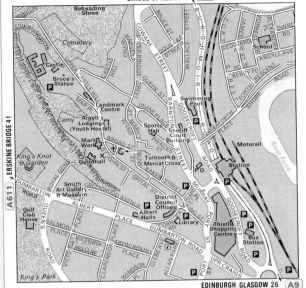

Capital of the Stuart Kings

'Land of the mountain and the flood,
Land of my sires! What mortal hand
Can e'er untie the filial band,
That knits me to thy rugged Strand.'

SIR WALTER SCOTT, *O Caledonia*

Stirling occupies a strategic site on the River Forth, and its great castle stands high on a rocky crag commanding the approaches by sea and by land. Until the opening of the bridge at Kincardine-on-Forth in 1936, Stirling was the lowest bridging point over the river before the Firth of Forth estuary.

The castle visitors see today dates from the Renaissance period, the 15th and 16th centuries, but the rock is known to have been fortified in the 11th century, and in the 12th century the small settlement that had grown up round the castle was granted its royal charter, enabling it to hold markets and form trade guilds. Since the infant royal burgh was well placed on the only route between the Highlands and Lowlands, it became a thriving market centre, and remained so despite the turbulent wars that were fought around this area

during the Middle Ages. Two of them were decisive in the history of Scotland: at the Battle of Stirling Bridge in 1297 William Wallace defeated the English armies; and at the more famous Battle of Bannockburn in 1314 Robert the Bruce inflicted such a savage defeat on Edward II of England that he not only won himself the throne but also assured Scotland's independence. After the Stuarts gained the ascendancy in 1370, the castle became a royal residence. James II and James V were born here; Mary Queen of Scots lived here for several years and also celebrated her secret marriage to Lord Darnley at the castle. The last Scottish king to live here was James VI, who on the death of Elizabeth I also became king of England, thus uniting the two crowns. After the departure of James VI, the castle became a military garrison, but has now been restored.

STIRLING CASTLE *(above) seen from the gardens, and (below), in an old engraving which shows the Renaissance detail of the Royal Palace.*

PLACES TO SEE

Argyll's Lodging The fine 17th-century mansion was built by the 1st Earl of Stirling in 1630 but takes its name from a later owner, the 1st Marquis of Argyll. It is now a youth hostel.

Bannockburn Two miles south of Stirling is the battlefield where Robert the Bruce defeated the English armies.

Cambuskenneth Abbey The ruins of the 13th-century abbey stand beside the River Forth, north-east of the town.

Castle The oldest parts of the castle date from the 11th century, but most of the buildings are Renaissance. The Royal Palace was built by James V in the 16th century, and the ornate stonework was carved by French masons. There is a fascinating collection of carved oak medallions from the ceiling of the king's presence chamber, known as the Stirling Heads. The upper rooms of the palace house the Museum of the Argyll and Sutherland Highlanders. Within the castle precincts there is a Landmark Centre which tells the history of the castle.

The Guildhall Built in 1639, the Guildhall was originally Cowane's Hospital, an almshouse for members of the Merchant Guildry of Stirling. It became the Guildhall in the 18th century.

Holy Rude Church When James VI was crowned here in 1567, John Knox preached the sermon. The nave has a fine, timbered roof. The church was restored in the 1930s and a wall which had partitioned the kirk into two separate churches, east and west, as a result of a theological dispute in 1656, was removed.

Mar's Wark Partly ruined, the mansion was begun in the 1570s for the Earl of Mar, Keeper of Stirling Castle and Regent of Scotland during the minority of James VI.

King's Knot This elaborate knot garden was laid out in the 1620s. It is thought that the octagonal centrepiece featured in tournaments held here.

Smith Art Gallery Temporary exhibitions and local museum displays are held in this Victorian art gallery endowed by Thomas Stuart Smith.

The Tolbooth Dating from 1704, the tolbooth was formerly both town hall and jail.

STOBO, Borders *23 NT13*

Stobo lies in the valley of the Tweed, which is testimony enough to beauty of its surroundings. The Norman church received additions in the 16th and 17th centuries, though the 13th-century doorway escaped unhurt. Stobo Castle was restored in the 19th century. Across the river, Dawyck Arboretum (OACT) is among the best known in Scotland. It contains some fine specimens of trees – including larch – that were imported from Sweden in the 18th century.

STOCKBRIDGE, Hampshire *4 SU33*

Situated in the Test Valley, Stockbridge is a famous angling centre, and the Grosvenor Hotel is the place to go if you like listening to fishing stories. There are some fine buildings in the main street (Stockbridge is virtually all main street and little else). The surrounding countryside is beautiful.

STOCKPORT, Gtr Manchester *14 SJ89*

Stockport has not been completely swamped by industry; there are still houses around the market place built by the landed gentry of Cheshire in the Middle Ages. It came into greater prominence in the 19th century, when soft water from the Peak District turned out to be ideal for the textile industry. Silk hats were among the local specialities. The railway viaduct, built in 1839–40 (22 arches and more than 100ft high) is a masterpiece – and so is a more recently constructed shopping precinct that spans the River Mersey. Stockport Grammar School, founded in 1487, is famous as one of the most ancient schools in the country.

STOCKTON, Wiltshire *3 ST93*

Stockton – at any rate in terms of the land it covers – has not changed very much since the Domesday Book was compiled. Its thatched cottages and Elizabethan farmhouse lie in the beautiful surroundings of the Wylye Valley.

STOCKTON-ON-TEES, Cleveland *20 NZ41*

On 27th September 1825, the first ever passenger-carrying train steamed into Stockton. Thereafter, the shipbuilding and engineering industries multiplied and this town on the Tees was never the same again. Nonetheless, the open-air market, established in 1310, is still held in the High Street, reputed to be the widest in England. In 1827 a local chemist invented the friction match, and Thomas Sheraton, creator of great furniture, was born here in 1731.

STOKE-ON-TRENT, Staffordshire *14 SJ84*

Stoke-on-Trent *is* 'The Potteries' – or has been since 1910, when the original six towns (Tunstall, Burslem, Hanley, Stoke-on-Trent, Fenton and Longton) were brought together under one administration. Admittedly, Arnold Bennett, who was born in the Potteries, wrote of *five* towns, but he had his reasons. Many people were responsible for creating the industry, though Josiah Wedgwood (1730–95) was the great pioneer – technically, artistically, and as the initiator of improvements and extensions to the canal network. The smoothness of this form of transport made it the ideal form of conveyance for his fragile products. Another distinguished son of the Potteries was Reginald Mitchell (1895–1937), who designed the Spitfire aircraft. He is commemorated in the Spitfire Museum. The rebuilt Church of St Peter ad Vincula contains memorials to Wedgwood, Spode and Minton. The Spode factory can be toured and the Spode Copeland Museum has a splendid, collection of ceramics but it is surpassed by that of the City Museum in Hanley, in which there are examples of the potter's art from Roman times to the present day. At Longton, the Gladstone Pottery Museum is a restored Victorian Pottery, with the traditional bottle ovens. There is also the fascinating Chatterley Whitfield Mining Museum at Tunstall.

STOKESAY CASTLE *is the oldest fortified manor in England, dating back to the 12th century. This gatehouse dates from the 16th century.*

STOKE POGES, Buckinghamshire *5 SU98*

The poet Thomas Gray has made this little village eternally famous through his poem, *Elegy in a Country Churchyard*, and he himself is buried in the church. The churchyard is a tranquil spot, surrounded by trees; alongside it are beautiful memorial gardens, established in the 1920s, leading down to a lake with a fountain and rose garden. It is easy to forget that one is only a few miles away from Slough.

STOKESAY, Shropshire *9 SO48*

Stokesay Castle (OACT), is one of the earliest fortified manor houses in England – the oldest parts date from the 12th century and the great hall from the 13th. It is an extraordinary structure – its massive stone towers topped with a timber-framed house – and of outstanding interest.

STOKE-SUB-HAMDON, Somerset *3 ST41*

The key to Stoke-sub-Hamdon is Hamdon Hill (426ft) to the south of the village. The Britons fortified it; the Romans, very sensibly, saw it as a source of building materials and began quarrying it. From it comes the yellow Ham stone – from which the village has been built, and which has done so much to adorn the rest of the area. The church is Norman; the Priory (NT) dates back to the 15th century and was once a chantry (endowed for priests) house. Behind the Fleur-de-Lys Inn is a fives court built about 1756. The idea was to provide an alternative to the church wall for games.

STOKESLEY N Yorkshire *20 NZ50*

This is a charming market town in the Cleveland Hills, with many old houses, cobbled alleyways, and the well-bridged River Leven running along one side. The Manor House, facing the Town Hall, now serves as library and various offices. Jane Pace of Stokesley was the first white woman to settle in Victoria, Australia. A row of trees was planted in her honour along the river bank just over a century ago.

POTTERY *was first produced in the Stoke-on-Trent area during the Bronze Age and the slipware at Hanley's City Museum is just one example of the collection there that spans the centuries.*

STONE, Staffordshire   *14 SJ93*
Among the famous sons of Stone was
Admiral John Jervis – or Earl St Vincent as
he became after his victory off Cape St
Vincent in 1797 (greatly helped by Nelson's
initiative). The Admiral lies in a suitably
elaborate mausoleum in the parish
churchyard. The name of the town, some
say, is derived from a cairn of stones that
marked the graves of two Christian Mercian
princes murdered by their pagan father. On
the other hand, it could have been inspired
by a stream that petrifies plant life.

STONEHAVEN, Grampian   *27 NO88*
Lovely scenery, good fishing (fresh water
and saltwater), and enough history to
intrigue the curious – these are the delights
of Stonehaven. The 16th-century Tolbooth
on the quay has variously been used as a
storehouse, a court and as a prison. More
recently, it has been modernised and is now
a museum. At the south end of Market
Square, Robert William Thomson (1822–
73) was born. The inventive Mr Thomson
produced the first ever pneumatic tyre, the
first fountain-pen, and the first dry dock.
Near the harbour stand the Mercat cross
and an 18th-century steeple beside which,
in 1715, the Old Pretender was proclaimed
king.

STONEHENGE, Wiltshire   *3 SU14*
Stonehenge (AM) is one of the world's great
mysteries. We know that it was built in
three phases; that its construction covered a
period between 2200 BC to 1300 BC – from
the Neolithic to the Bronze Age; that its
axis is aligned with sunrise on the longest
day of the year – 21st June. What we do not
know is precisely why it was built. It
certainly had nothing to do with Druids:
they hadn't yet arrived in Britain when
work was in progress; it may have served as
a sort of calendar, as well as for religious
purpose, but there is no evidence that
Stonehenge was ever a place of human
sacrifice. The most intriguing problem of
all is how those enormous stones were
transported to Salisbury Plain from their
points of origin on the Marlborough Downs
and even further away in the Prescelly
Mountains of Pembrokeshire.

STONELEIGH, Warwickshire
10 SP37
Stoneleigh is an interesting mixture of
ancient and modern. The present day
appears in the form of the Royal Show, that
annual event to which farmers travel from
all over the country. Its permanent site is in
the grounds of Stoneleigh Abbey, a
magnificent 18th-century house that was
badly damaged by fire in 1960. However,
parts of the original 14th-century abbey –
the gatehouse and the hospice – survive.
Other manifestations of the past can be seen
in the nine-arched bridge across the river,
the Norman features of St Mary's Church,
and several charming timbered houses.

STONOR, Oxfordshire   *4 SU78*
Stonor Park (OACT), a substantially Tudor
house with 18th-century modifications – is
set in beautifully wooded parkland on the
outskirts of Henley-on-Thames. Among
those who worshipped in its Roman
Catholic chapel was St Edmund Campion,
16th-century priest and martyr to 16th-
century religious intolerance. Campion also
operated a secret printing press.

STOURHEAD GARDENS *Henry Hoare laid out these exceptional gardens in the 18th century. His designs were inspired by his travels through Europe and the result was a masterpiece.*

STOURBRIDGE, W Midlands   *9 SO88*
Stourbridge is an industrial town mostly
concerned with iron and, since the 17th
century, glass-making. The church is 18th
century; the canal is popular with inland-
waterway enthusiasts and the surrounding
countryside is beautiful. Nearby Hagley
Hall (OACT), the family home of the
Lytteltons, contains lovely Rococo work.

STOURHEAD, Wiltshire   *3 ST73*
Stourhead (NT) is a beautiful 18th-century
Palladian mansion situated in what must
surely be one of the most imaginatively
embellished parks in the country. Near the
gates stands a 13th-century stone cross that
was removed from Bristol, where it used to
mark an intersection of two roads. In its
niches are small statues of eight kings of
England. The circumference of the lake is
about a mile. Walking round it, the visitor
comes across a grotto and three little
temples – one of them copied from the
Pantheon in Rome. But, wherever one
walks, there are pleasant new vistas.

**STOURPORT-ON-SEVERN, Hereford
& Worcester**   *9 SO87*
Stourport has several industries – the
manufacture of carpets and chains, for
example – but its real interest is as an inland
port. It was the creation of James Brindley,
a Derbyshire farmer's son, who, in 1756,
determined to build a waterway linking the
Rivers Trent and Severn. The original
warehouses survive, complete with a little
wooden clocktower, and so does the
Tontine Inn, opened to thirsty customers in
1788. The basin, carefully and
sympathetically restored, is nowadays
populated by pleasure craft.

STOWE, Buckinghamshire   *10 SP63*
Now a famous public school, Stowe used to
be the seat of the Dukes of Buckingham
and Chandos. Robert Adam, Vanbrugh,
William Kent and Grinling Gibbons all had
a hand in the building of the house and the
far from foolish follies that decorate its
grounds (by Capability Brown inevitably).
Among them are the Temple of Worthies

(the 'worthies' are busts of Sir Francis
Drake, King Alfred, Inigo Jones and
Shakespeare); two other temples and the
remains of 19th-century Stowe Castle. The
lakes are a delight – and so, too, is the
unpretentious medieval church. The
obelisk is in memory of General Wolfe.

STOWMARKET, Suffolk   *12 TM05*
John Milton used to visit his tutor in this
small market town. George Crabbe is
another poet associated with it: he spent
some of his schooldays here. An unusual
feature of its Perpendicular church is a
wigstand. The Victorian mock-Elizabethan
railway station is not without interest. For a
graphic review of East Anglian rural life,
there is the Abbots Hall Museum. Stow
Lodge Hospital (late 18th century) used to
be a workhouse, or 'House of Industry' as
they liked to call it.

**STOW-ON-THE-WOLD,
  Gloucestershire**   *10 SP12*
Situated 800ft above sea level, Stow-on-the-
Wold is the highest town in the Cotswolds.
Since it stands at the junction of eight
roads, it is not surprising to learn that it was
once the most prosperous wool town in
England. During the 18th century, in one
year alone, no fewer than 20,000 sheep
were sold at Stow Fair. The market place
has a fine cross and some scarcely less fine
gabled houses grouped around it. Within
the church – begun in Norman times and
developed spasmodically over the next few
centuries – Cromwell imprisoned 1000
Royalist captives during the Civil War. The
Town Hall contains a collection of
paintings depicting the Civil War and a
statue of that saintly monarch, King
Edward the Confessor.

STRANRAER, Dumfries & Galloway
17 NX06
Stranraer is only 36 miles from Northern
Ireland – a crossing that takes just over two
hours. Consequently, the town's greatest
importance is as a terminal for the short sea
route. It is, however, becoming
increasingly popular as a resort.

Shakespeare Country
47 miles

Many of the little country lanes and the charming old villages around Stratford-upon-Avon would still be familiar to Shakespeare, were he to return to the scenes of his boyhood. This tranquil corner of the Midlands is aptly called the 'Heart of England'.

Leave **Stratford** on A439 (SP Evesham); presently cross over a level-crossing and pass Shottery Road, right, to Anne Hathaway's cottage. Continue on A439 and later skirt Bidford-on-Avon. Pass through Salford Priors, then in 1¼ miles turn right (unclassified) to **Harvington**. Here turn right (SP The Lenches), then cross the main road and drive through part of the Vale of Evesham to **Church Lench**. Here turn right to reach Rous Lench, and continue towards Inkberrow for 1 mile then at the T-junction turn right (SP Alcester) and after 1½ miles left for Abbots Morton. Bear right through **Abbots Morton**, then in ¾ mile at the T-junction, turn left and in 1½ miles, right, on to A441 for ½ mile, then left (SP

Birmingham) on to A435. Pass (left) the entrance to Ragley Hall and continue to **Alcester**. Leave by the Birmingham road (shortly, a detour along the Droitwich road, B4090, can be made to Pleck Gardens). Remain on A435 through Coughton and **Studley**. Here, at the end of the town, go forward at the roundabout then in 2 miles at the next roundabout turn right on to B4095 for **Henley-in-Arden**. At Henley turn right on to A34, the Stratford road, and drive to **Wootton Wawen**. Here take the Alcester road, B4089 (right), then in 2 miles branch left (SP Aston Cantlow), cross the river and turn right for **Aston Cantlow**. Drive through the village, then turn left (SP Wilmcote) and a mile further, again left and continue into **Wilmcote**. Here turn left (SP Stratford) and on reaching the junction with A34 turn right for the return to Stratford-upon-Avon.

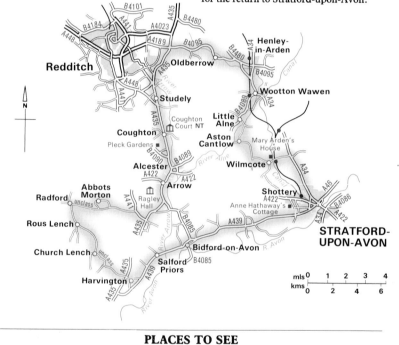

PLACES TO SEE

Stratford-upon-Avon Shakespeariana is everywhere in this attractive little town: his birthplace; the ruins of New Place, where he lived after he was married; Hall's Croft, where his daughter lived, are all (OACT) preserved by the Birthplace Trust. Also of interest is Harvard House (OACT) and the 1920s Motor Museum.

Ann Hathaway's Cottage The childhood home of Shakespeare's wife is an idyllic half-timbered and thatched cottage in the hamlet of Shottery.

Abbots Morton A showplace village of black-and-white timbered cottages surrounding a green.

Ragley Hall (OACT) Magnificent 17th-century house with superb interior decoration and Old Master paintings.

Alcester A charming little town at the confluence of the rivers Alne and Arrow.

Pleck Gardens Three acres of roses, heathers and azaleas.

Coughton Court (NT) The family home of the Roman-Catholic Throckmorton family has relics of the Gunpowder Plot.

Henley-in-Arden This lovely village, consists of one long, broad, main street.

Aston Cantlow Shakespeare's parents are believed to have married in the church of this attractive village.

Wilmcote The handsome, timbered farmhouse (OACT) that was the home of Mary Arden, Shakespeare's mother, is the highlight of this peaceful village.

STRATA FLORIDA, Dyfed *8 SN76*
Strata Florida (AM) – its Welsh name is *Ystrad Fflur* – was a great Cistercian abbey built in the 12th century in an isolated valley not far from Aberystwyth. Such was its importance at one time that it was called 'the Westminster of Wales'. It did not escape the Dissolution, and only the church and a gatehouse remain.

STRATFIELD SAYE, Hampshire
4 SU66
Stratfield Saye House (OACT) was built in 1630, rebuilt in 1795, and, in 1817, presented by a grateful Parliament to the Duke of Wellington as a reward for his victory at Waterloo. During his long retirement from the army, the Duke divided his time between Stratfield Saye, his house in Piccadilly, and Walmer Castle – which he occupied as Lord Warden of the Cinq Ports. The Duchess, a talented water colourist despite her short sight, made several attractive paintings of the estate. Among the relics of the Iron Duke are a collection of leather-bound volumes collected during his service in India, Napoleon's Tricolour, and a brass statuette of Copenhagen – the charger he rode at Waterloo – who is buried in the grounds.

STRATHPEFFER, Highlands
26 NH45
In the days before World War I Strathpeffer was a famous spa. Even foreign royalties, tiring, perhaps, of the pleasures of Spa itself or Homburg, came here to take the waters. There are five springs in all: four sulphur and one chalybeate, discovered in the 18th century; the first pump room was built in 1820. The Station Visitor Centre has interesting craft workshops.

STRATH SPEY, Grampian &
Highland *26, 27 NJ13*
Strath Spey is the wide, lower valley of the River Spey. It begins as the Upper Spey emerges from the very much narrower route it takes between the Cairngorms and the Monadhliath mountains (where it originates). An important salmon river, it is also rich in brown trout and, funnily enough, or so the story goes, pearls: according to one estimate, one out of every hundred mussels fished out of the river contains a pearl.

STRATHYRE, Central *22 NN51*
Strathyre is a pleasant little resort in the heart of country made famous by Sir Walter Scott in *Lady of the Lake* and *Legend of Montrose*. It is not too remote; the climbing is not too difficult; and the River Balvaig is full of brown trout. The Ben of the Fairies rises to the west.

STRATTON, Cornwall *1 SS20*
Stratton, only a mile or two from the resort of Bude, is an altogether charming small Cornish town built on the side of a hill. Its streets are steep; some of the houses are thatched; and the church has a window by Burne-Jones and a brass commemorating Henry VIII's Vice-Admiral, Sir John Arundell. The Tree Inn, once the manor-house home of the famous Grenville family, served as Royalist headquarters, during the Civil War, on the eve of the Battle of Stamford Hill (1643); the site is about half a mile north-west of the town.

Shakespeare's Birthplace

> *Good friend for Jesus sake forbeare*
> *To digg the dust enclosed heare;*
> *Bleste be ye man yt spares thes stones,*
> *And cursed be he yt moves my bones.*

WILLIAM SHAKESPEARE, *Epitaph on his tomb*

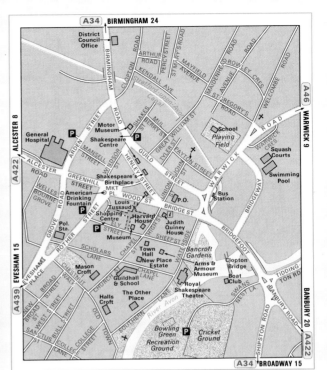

As the birthplace of England's greatest poet, Stratford is second only to London as a tourist attraction, but the throngs of visitors and the inevitable 'Shakespeare industries' have not quite managed to submerge the character of this thriving Midlands market town. There is no doubt that Stratford owes its state of preservation to the interest in Shakespeare and everything connected with him. His birthplace; the house where his daughter, Susanna, lived after her marriage to Dr Hall; the poet's tomb in the church, with its famous inscription; the Royal Shakespeare Theatre; are all places of pilgrim-

age for the enthusiast. American visitors also come to see Harvard House, the 16th-century timbered house owned by the grandparents of John Harvard, founder of Harvard University. Just outside the town, at Shottery and at Wilmcote, for those who are not already sated with Shakespeariana, there are the old thatched and timbered cottages where Shakespeare's wife, Anne Hathaway, and his mother, Mary Arden spent their childhoods.

William Shakespeare was born on 23rd April 1564 in the fine, timbered house on Henley Street that now, restored and furnished in period, has become a museum. His own house, New Place, was demolished in the 18th century, but a garden marks the site. Shakespeare's early life is not well documented, but he is known to have attended the Grammar School, an ancient foundation whose history goes back at least 200 years before his birth, and was first founded by the Guild of the Holy Cross; their chapel, rebuilt in the 15th century by Sir Hugh Clopton, a wealthy merchant who became Lord Mayor of London, contains an impressive 'Doom' painting of the Last Judgement. Clopton was a famous benefactor of the town

TWIN ATTRACTIONS *Harvard House (top) and mementoes of Shakespeare, such as his statue and that of Prince Hal (above), or Anne Hathaway's cottage (below, right) at Shottery draw thousands of visitors to the town.*

and built, among other things, the old 14-arched bridge that spans the River Avon. Modern buildings are not prominent in the centre of Stratford, where half-timbered and Georgian brick buildings are the keynote, but the Royal Shakespeare Theatre, erected in 1932 to replace its burnt-out Victorian predecessor, dominates the river bank. The drama festival takes place every summer and the outstanding new productions usually go on to London. This is one of the oldest of Britain's drama festivals – inaugurated some 200 years ago by the actor David Garrick.

Stratford has a life, however, apart from its Shakespearian connections. It stands at the meeting point of many routes and has been a market centre for centuries. The building of the Stratford-upon-Avon canal in the early 19th century also increased trade with other Midlands centres and the town now supports a number of light industries.

PLACES TO SEE

Hall's Croft A Tudor house, the former home of Shakespeare's daughter, Susanna, and her husband Dr John Hall. Relics of the medicine of their day make an interesting display.

Harvard House A fine timbered building, lived in by the grandparents of John Harvard, founder of Harvard University.

Louis Tussaud's Waxworks Tableaux from Shakespeare's plays are displayed here.

Model Car Museum More than 2400 miniature and scale-model cars are on display.

Motor Museum Sports cars, touring cars and other Vintage cars and motor-cycles are displayed in 1920s' settings.

New Place Only foundations of Shakespeare's house remain, but there is a well-maintained knot garden and in adjacent Nash House are many items belonging to his day.

Shakespeare's Birthplace and Shakespeare Centre The old family home of Shakespeare's parents has been restored, furnished in period and opened as a museum. Adjacent to it is the new Shakespeare Centre, designed for study and as the headquarters of the Shakespeare Birthplace Trust.

STREATLEY, Berkshire *4 SU58*
Goring and Streatley are villages – linked by a bridge over the Thames. Streatley with its handsome Georgian houses, and 19th-century malthouse, is the more attractive of the two. Both are set in lovely countryside, lying in a gap between the Chilterns and the Berkshire Downs.

STREET, Somerset *3 ST43*
In 1820, an apprentice to a Street sheepskin rug firm had the idea of putting sheepskin linings into slippers. As a result of his inspiration, a not unimportant footwear industry developed, and its history is traced in the Shoe Museum. In the neighbourhood of Street are Millfield School (famous and expensive), and a monument to Admiral Lord Hood (on top of Windmill Hill to the south-east).

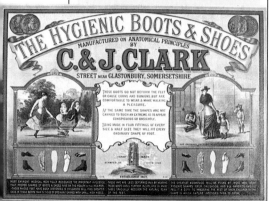

CLARK'S SHOE MUSEUM

In 1825 two brothers, Cyrus and James, founded the shoe firm of C & J Clark in Street. From then on the business mushroomed and eventually grew into the worldwide concern it is today. The museum in Street illustrates the firm's early history and has a collection of slippers, shoes and boots from Roman to modern times. Clark's have always been known for well-fitting children's shoes, as this poster of 1883 shows.

STROUD, Gloucestershire *3 SO80*
Cloth is the chief business of Stroud and especially the sort which is used in the manufacture of billiard tables. There is also an old-established dyeing industry, and more recently, the town has turned to the manufacture of pianos. Stroud stands on the River Frome and the Stroudwater canal, closed in 1954, is now being restored. Some of the 18th-century woollen mills have survived, and there are some good examples of typical Cotswold cottages. The Stroud District Museum has an interesting emphasis on local crafts.

STURMINSTER NEWTON, Dorset
3 ST21
Sturminster Newton is a singularly pretty Dorset village, locally famous for its Monday livestock market. The six-arched bridge spanning the River Stour is one of the finest medieval examples of bridgecraft in Dorset. A plaque threatens deportation as the penalty for 'injury' – not necessarily by vandalism, but by driving an overloaded cart across.

DORSET'S COAST *These isolated chalk stacks standing off Handfast Point are known as Old Harry Rocks. A path to them leads northwards from Swanage past Whitecliffe Farm and over Ballard Down.*

STYAL, Cheshire *14 SJ88*
A beautiful little Cheshire village complete with an 18th-century mill (Quarry Bank, NT) situated where the River Bollin debouches from a wooded glen. The mill has been well restored and there is still much to see as well as frequent demonstrations of spinning and weaving.

SUDBURY, Suffolk *12 TL84*
This is an attractive and very ancient borough. Readers of *Pickwick Papers*, will, perhaps recognise it as 'Eatanswill' and find themselves at home in the 15th-century Salter's Hall. Art lovers will, of course, recall that it was the birthplace of Thomas Gainsborough (1727–88), one of the founders of the Royal Academy in London.

SULGRAVE MANOR,
Northamptonshire *10 SP54*
For a century the ancestors of George Washington lived in Sulgrave Manor (OACT) a 15th-century house with later additions. Among the relics of Washington are his black velvet coat and a fragment of Mrs Washington's wedding dress. The interior has been considerably restored, and it is now virtually a museum.

SUNDERLAND, Tyne & Wear
20 NZ45
Sunderland is a coal port on the River Wear, and is also renowned for its shipbuilding. Its name is derived from the fact that it was 'sundered' from a monastery founded on the far bank of the river in 674. The 18th-century Wearmouth Bridge (it was replaced in 1929) was one of the first cast-iron bridges in the country. The designer was Thomas Paine, better known as the author of the *Rights of Man*; it was originally intended for Philadelphia on the far side of the Atlantic. The new Civic Centre (1970) is evidence of the town's progressive attitude to planning. Other places of interest include the Grindon Close Museum, which specialises in the Edwardian period; Monkwearmouth Station Museum, and the Sunderland Museum and Art Gallery.

SUTTON COLDFIELD, W Midlands
10 SP19
Basically, Sutton Coldfield is a residential town for its neighbour, **Birmingham**. In the early 16th century, Bishop Veysey (he became Bishop of Exeter in 1519) created some fine buildings that time has not destroyed. The bishop lived in Moor Hall, which adjoins the golf course: he founded the grammar school, designed several houses – all of them with spiral stone staircases, altered the church, and also paved the town's streets. The original members of the Free Foresters cricket club came from the nearby Forest of Arden, and played their first match one day in 1856 in Rectory Park. Sutton Park, a gift from Henry VIII, covers 2400 acres. Well equipped with lakes, it is one of the largest and finest in the Midlands.

SWAFFHAM, Norfolk *12 TF80*
Swaffham's legend tells of Jack the pedlar who dreamed that if he went to London he would be told where to discover treasure. Off he went and met a stranger who said that he had had a dream of great wealth buried under a certain tree in Swaffham. Jack hurried home, discovered the hidden fortune, and used it to build the north aisle of the Church of SS Peter and Paul. His generosity is remembered in the village sign, by a monument in the market place, and by several carvings in the church. Swaffham is a most attractive market town, its wide main square graced by many mellow brick houses.

SWANAGE, Dorset *3 SZ07*
Swanage is a nice little resort: the only place between Poole and Weymouth where you can drive to the beach in your car. There are several old houses in the town and the oldest part is the area around the Mill Pond. The church, though rebuilt, has a 13th-century tower, and the façade of the Town Hall (erected in 1883) originally graced the Mercers' Hall in London – for which Wren designed it in 1670. Another import from London is the clock tower, which once stood near London Bridge.

SWANSEA, W Glamorgan *8 SS69*
Swansea docks were established as early as 1306. In the 17th century, they were developed for the shipping of Welsh coal, copper, and ion ore. In World War II, the city was severely bombed, though the damage has been more than sufficiently repaired by an admirable new centre – spacious and with abundant greenery. Places of interest include the Glynn Vivian Art Gallery and Museum; the Maritime and Industrial Museum and the University College Museum.

SWINDON, Wiltshire *3 SU18*
The coming of the Great Western Railway did a lot for Swindon, and Swindon did a good deal for the GWR. In 1835, it became the site of a station on the route from London to Bristol. Four years later, Isambard Kingdom Brunel and Daniel Gooch – the visionary and the mechanical engineer – chose it as the location for the company's main locomotive depot. Nowadays, the GWR museum is housed in a converted Methodist chapel. Engines,

signalling equipment, more or less everything to do with trains, are on show, and nearby is the Railway Village House.

SWINFORD, Leicestershire *10 SP57*
Stanford Hall, on the Leicestershire bank of the Avon, was built by Sir Roger Cave between 1697 and 1700. It is possibly the most handsome house of its period in the county. The contents include a fine collection of paintings, furniture, and old family costumes. In a nearby meadow, a pillar marks the spot where P. S. Pilcher crashed and was killed while trying to fly in 1899. He had reached an altitude of 50ft. A replica of his machine is in the vehicle museum attached to the house.

SYON HOUSE, Gtr London *5 TQ17*
This majestic house stands near the River Thames at Isleworth. Its splendid interior was designed by Robert Adam for the Duke of Northumberland in the 18th century. The park was laid out by Capability Brown. There are rose gardens, a car museum, a butterfly house, and a large garden centre.

The Marlborough Downs and Vale of the White Horse
63 miles

The relics of ancient man have survived for thousands of years and remain an enigma to scholars. The White Horse, Wayland's Smithy, and Uffington Castle stand as mute sentinels of our mysterious past.

Leave **Swindon** from the County Roundabout and follow signs for Oxford, A420. In 1¼ miles at the next roundabout, turn left on to A361 (SP Stow) and continue to the traffic lights where turn left and right to reach Highworth. Drive through the village and continue to **Lechlade**, where the route turns right on to the Faringdon road, A417. At **Faringdon**, follow signs for Swindon then Highworth to leave by B4019. After 1¼ miles turn left (unclassified) for **Gt Coxwell**. Here turn left (no sign) and on reaching the roundabout turn right and left on to the Oxford road, A420. Take the next right turn (unclassified, SP Fernham) and at Fernham turn left on to B4508 and shortly branch right (unclassified) to Uffington. On the edge of **Uffington** turn right, then take the 2nd right turn to White Horse Hill. Cross the main road and drive up the hill to Uffington Castle, an Iron-Age hillfort. Follow exit signs and descend to the main road, B4507, where turn right. After 2 miles, at the crossroads, turn right (unclassified) to Lambourn. Continue for 4¼ miles, then turn right on to B4001 to enter **Lambourn**. At the crossroads here turn right on to B4000, then take the next left (unclassified) to **Baydon** (for a detour to Ashdown House, continue on B4000 for 3½ miles). The main drive continues for 2¼ miles to a T-junction and turns right for Baydon. At the Red Lion PH turn left and continue to Aldbourne. Here turn left (SP Hungerford) on to B4192, and in 1¾ miles turn right to Ramsbury. Turn right and continue to **Marlborough**. Leave (SP Chippenham on A4 and drive through Fyfield, passing (left) West Kennet Long Barrow and (right) Silbury Hill, to the Beckhampton roundabout. Here take the 3rd exit (SP Swindon) on to A361 and in 1 mile keep left for Avebury and the stone circle. Continue on A361 back to Swindon.

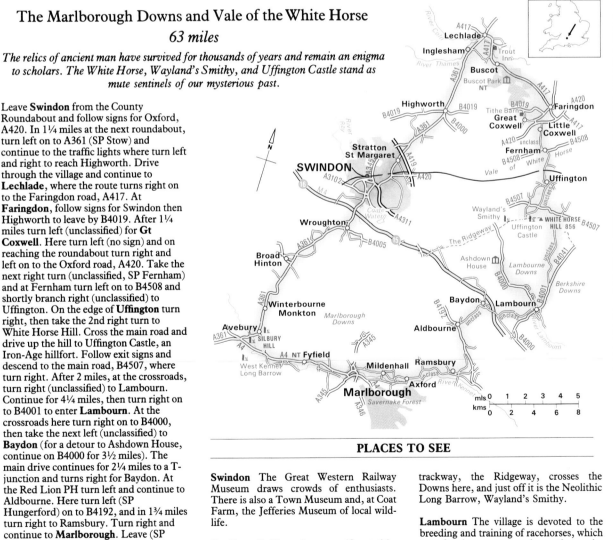

PLACES TO SEE

Swindon The Great Western Railway Museum draws crowds of enthusiasts. There is also a Town Museum and, at Coat Farm, the Jefferies Museum of local wildlife.

Gt Coxwell There is a magnificent tithe barn (NT) in this quiet little village.

Vale of the White Horse The prehistoric turf-cut figure of a white horse gives the valley its name. Above it stands Uffington Castle, an Iron-Age hillfort. A prehistoric

trackway, the Ridgeway, crosses the Downs here, and just off it is the Neolithic Long Barrow, Wayland's Smithy.

Lambourn The village is devoted to the breeding and training of racehorses, which can often be seen at exercise on the nearby Downs. Nearby Ashdown House (NT) dates from the 17th century.

Marlborough The famous public school stands just outside this attractive and historic town.

FIELDS & HEDGES

Ploughland and Meadowland

The typical lowland landscape in Britain is a patchwork of fields, but when looked at more closely, it becomes plain that many distinctive shapes of fields combine in the patchwork patterns. Also, with a little practice, one can learn to recognise different types of fields and make informed guesses about the ages and origins of different examples.

FIELD BOUNDARIES were used by farmers for thousands of years to divide the landscape into practical, workable packages. Hedges, walls, banks or fences were needed to mark out properties, separate livestock and deer from the growing crops and divide holdings into land units for the operation of crop rotations. We do not know when fields first appeared in Britain, but farming was introduced around 7000 years ago and as the isolated pioneer clearings began to merge with one another, so the cleared areas may have been partitioned into fields. The oldest fields discovered so far in Britain or Ireland are in County Mayo, where a network of stone field walls dating to about 3300 BC are emerging as the covering blanket of peat is stripped away.

During the Bronze Age considerable expanses of countryside were covered by networks of smallish, roughly rectangular fields. Usually, these ancient patterns can only be recognised in aerial photographs, but there are a number of fascinating places where the outlines of the walls or banks bounding Iron-Age or Romano-British fields can still quite clearly be seen amongst the different patterns of walls or hedgerows which define existing fields. One particularly fine set of such 'Celtic' fields can be seen above Grassington in Yorkshire, where the hollows which mark old droveways which were used in Roman times run between the rubble-strewn banks of small, irregular fields and the fainter traces of circular native huts can also be recognised. Much older, and dating to the Bronze Age, are the low stone walls or 'reaves' which survive on many parts of Dartmoor and preserve an ancient division of the landscape in days before the spread of the peaty-moorland.

FIELD PATTERNS *At the shrunken village of Cold Newton (above) in Leicestershire traces of 'closes' or house, garden or paddock plots can be seen. Medieval ridge and furrow patterns near Southam in Warwickshire are enclosed by curving hedgerows of the pre-Parliamentary Enclosure period.*

Roman field patterns are less evident, and it seems that over the greater part of England and Wales, the natives continued farming according to the traditional methods. Various types of fields for different purposes will have existed at all times, but the typical prehistoric and Romano-British field tended to be rather small and squarish. Such shapes may have facilitated ploughing by the light 'crook ard', a curved and sharpened tree bough pulled by a pair of oxen and depicted in some prehistoric Scandinavian rock carvings. Probably it was necessary to plough with the ard in two directions in order to produce a tilth, and hence the preference for compact field units.

Throughout most of the Dark Ages, the older methods of farming probably persisted. It is quite possible that in parts of western England and Wales which have escaped the worst of the modern blight of hedgerow removal there are small hedged fields which date back to the time of King Alfred, for the hedgerow-dating method seems to show that some hedges may be more than 1000 years old. Well-tended old hedges tend to be robust and packed with trees and shrubs of different types; particularly where they marked estate and parish boundaries, they often stand on banks. It seems that the age of a hedge can very roughly be guessed by counting the number of different species growing in a series of 30-metre sections: each section tends to have one species for every 100 years of the hedgerow's age – but why this should be so, is rather mysterious.

THE OPEN-FIELD SYSTEM

was introduced perhaps around a couple of centuries or so before the Norman Conquest, and this revolution in the organisation of farming affected many parts of the countryside. The working of the land seems to have been recast so that the area surrounding each (perhaps equally new) village was divided into two, three, or more, vast 'open fields'. These fields were in turn blocked off into broad, oblong units or 'furlongs' and the furlongs were divided into strips or 'selions'. The selions were allocated in scattered packages to peasant farmers and each selion was ploughed in such a way as to produce a series of long parallel plough ridges. In this way, the ploughland gained a corrugated, corduroy-like appearance which will have helped drainage. Although the ridge-and-furrow method of ploughing has long since been abandoned, one can often still recognise the ridges in old ploughland which has been converted into pasture and preserved from the levelling caused by modern ploughing.

ENCLOSURES, passed by Acts of Parliament from about 1750 to 1850, brought an end to open-field farming, which had evolved through many stages, but in some places had survived for 1000 years. Parishes now were forced to surrender piecemeal to the Acts. The old common grazing and other common lands – including some village greens – were carved up into private holdings, while the selion-striped ploughlands were divided into compact rectangular fields. The owners of these new holdings were obliged to hedge or wall their fields and so areas of Parliamentary Enclosure can often still be recognised by the gridwork of straight hedgerows.

HEDGES (right) were the most common field boundaries in the lowlands. This, at Lomer in Hampshire is 1000 years old. STRIP LYNCHETS at Winspit near Worth Matravers in Dorset. DAMP HAY meadows (below) are seen at Mangersta in the Hebrides.

In other places, the enclosure of former open-field land had been achieved long before by agreement between local farming interests. Such 'early enclosure' countryside is usually particularly attractive, with rich old hedges, many of medieval age, that tend to sweep and curve, tracing the slightly 's'-shaped sides of former field strips.

IN NORTHERN AND UPLAND parts of Britain the cooler, damper climates did not encourage crop-growing and this activity was confined to the favoured pockets of lowland in each parish. Various types of 'in-field, out-field' farming were practised, with the in-field being heavily manured and farmed almost continuously, while sections of out-field were occasionally and briefly farmed but usually existed as pasture. Distinctive medieval features which can often be recognised in hilly or undulating landscapes like those of the Yorkshire Dales or the Wiltshire and Dorset Downs are 'strip lynchets'. These are elongated terrace-like features which are often arranged in steps biting deeply into the hillsides and they result from ploughing across slopes in order to win a little extra ploughland.

In lowland areas, hawthorn hedges were usually chosen as the most economical and effective means of defining fields, but in upland areas, drystone walls were convenient depositories for rocks from the fields and they could be built in exposed settings where hedges were reluctant to grow. Like the hedges, walls can be of many different ages. Some of the field walls in Cornwall have been shown to date back to Romano-British times, some large walls trace the bounds of medieval monastic estates, other lower ones, the divisions of early or Parliamentary enclosures. Around the villages of Castleton and Chelmorton in Derbyshire the walls trace out the shapes of elongated medieval field strips. Each locality tended to have its own stone-walling tradition which was strongly based on the local geological resources. Thus, the neat limestone walls of the Cotswolds contrast with the lumpy granite boulder piles seen in parts of Cornwall, while in some parts of Orkney, vertical sandstone sheets provide unusual walls.

MUCH OF THE CHARM of the countryside is produced by the network of hedgerows, but if the removal of hedges continues at its present rate, then few will remain by the end of the century. Over many parts of England, a third or more of the hedgerows have been removed since the war to create the vast prairie-like fields that mechanised farming demands. Not only do the hedgerows add detail and variety to the countryside, but they have also provided refuges for wild plants, shelter for nesting birds and havens for a rich variety of insects and small animals. Farming landscapes have always evolved, but many country-lovers are alarmed by the present practices.

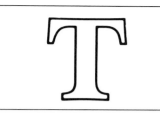

TADCASTER, N Yorkshire 15 SE44

A beer-making town since the 18th century, Tadcaster is still the home of John and Samuel Smith's rival breweries: real-ale addicts prefer the latter's product. St Mary's Church, with its Perpendicular work and embattled tower, dates from the 15th century. It was moved stone by stone between 1875 and 1877 to a position 5ft higher than its original site to afford greater protection from the flood-prone River Wharfe. The river itself is spanned by an 18th-century, seven-arched bridge and, more forlornly, by the 'virgin Viaduct' – built in 1849 in the rather optimistic anticipation of the railway that never did come.

TAIN, Highland 30 NH78

Tain, on the Dornoch Firth, is an ancient royal burgh; a trading centre for the prosperous agricultural district and a holiday resort for golfers, fishermen and bathers, affording fine views of Sutherland and Caithness. The birthplace of St Duthac in AD 1000, Tain became a place of pilgrimage and sanctuary when his remains were brought home from Ireland. An Earl of Ross wore St Duthac's shirt, believed to confer immunity, at the Battle of Halidon Hill in 1333, but was fatally wounded. In 1371 the Earl and Bishop of Ross built the Collegiate Church of St Duthac. It is in Decorated style, with fine windows. James IV made regular pilgrimages to Tain along the King's Causeway – the road across Glen Aldie to Logie Easter. James V, too, came this way. Near Tain you can visit Loch Eye and the ruins of Lochslin Castle.

TALGARTH, Powys 8 SO13

This small market town in the valley of the Nant Lynfi lies inside the **Brecon Beacons National Park**, with the Black Mountains to the west. Talgarth has a fortified tower, dating from the 11th to 13th centuries, now a shop. The church, too, has a striking tower, 14th-century, solid and defensive. Hywel Harris, the Methodist revivalist, is buried here. Harris founded, at nearby Trefecca House, 'The Connection', a religious and trading community commemorated in the museum. Llangorse Lake to the south, four miles around, is the second biggest natural lake in Wales. It attracts water-sportsmen, but also crested grebes and coots, and many species of duck. On an island in the lake is the only evidence in Wales of prehistoric lake dwellings.

TALLEY, Dyfed 7 SN63

This village, whose ancient name means 'End of the Lakes', is prettily positioned by one small lake and another lies just north. Talley is sheltered by the steep, 1000ft slope, clad in beeches and conifers, of Mynydd Cynros. It has a main street of attractive cottages, their view towards the eastern hills dominated by the ruined tower of Talley Abbey (AM), founded by Rhys ap Gruffydd, Prince of South Wales, at the end of the 12th century for the White Canons.

TAL-Y-CAFN, Gwynedd 13 SH77

Here, among the woods and moors of the Vale of Conwy, on the boundary of the **Snowdonia National Park**, is one of Britain's most beautiful gardens. Bodnant Garden (NT) slopes down over seven acres to the Conwy, with the Snowdonian peaks in the background. It was planned in 1875 by Henry Pochin, a Lancashire industrialist; and extended by his daughter, Lady Aberconwy, then by his grandson.

TAL Y LLYN, Gwynedd 13 SH71

The oldest narrow-gauge railway in the world runs the twisting seven and a half miles up the Fathew Valley from **Tywyn** to Abergynolwyn. Built in 1865 to serve Bryneglwys slate quarry the line was closed in 1947 but happily rescued from oblivion by the first British Railway Preservation Society in 1951.

The line affords fine views of the long and beautiful Tal y Llyn Lake and **Cader Idris**. The wayside halt at Dolgoch gives access to the spectacular 125ft waterfalls nearby.

TARBERT, Strathclyde 21 NR86

At the head of East Loch Tarbert, the village's near-perfect harbour is encompassed by fishermen's cottages, small hotels, pubs, holiday homes and craft shops. It is the surviving centre of the Loch Fyne herring industry and still builds boats. Tarbert is strategically sited on the isthmus linking the Knapsdale and Kintyre peninsulas, and dividing two sea lochs: Loch Fyne and its branch, East Loch Tarbert, from the beautiful West Loch Tarbert. From here ferries sail to Islay. The highest of the high hills on either side of Tarbert is 1840ft Sliabh Gasil in the Knapsdale range.

The name Tarbert derives from the Gaelic word for portage: its isthmus is an ancient nucleus of conflict between Scots' factions and a short-cut on the route between the Clyde and the Western Isles.

As government stabilised, so Tarbert Castle decayed. Only two ivy-clad storeys of the castle's 15th-century keep still stand, overlooking the harbour.

TARBOLTON, Strathclyde 22 NS42

A rural and mining village, it has strong connections with Robert Burns. The poet's family lived at nearby Lochlea Farm and his father died here. Burns was a co-founder of The Bachelors' Club in the 17th-century house (NTS) which is now a Burns museum.

TATTERSHALL, Lincolnshire
16 TF25

Tattershall Castle (AM, NT) and its church were both built in the mid 15th century by Ralph Cromwell, Lord Treasurer to Henry VI. The splendid, moated, brick keep is all that survives of the castellated house. It was finely restored by Lord Curzon, Marquess of Kedleston, former Viceroy of India. Over 100ft high, its walls over 20ft thick, it affords from its battlements a lovely view over the fenlands, as far as Lincoln Cathedral and the Boston Stump. Holy Trinity Church is Perpendicular, plainly furnished, and lit by more than 60 plain-glass windows. Ralph Cromwell is buried here. The gatehouse between castle and church is a museum and a National Trust shop.

BODNANT GARDEN *The 18th-century garden house known as Pin Mill was brought to Tal-y-Cafn from Gloucestershire in 1938. It stands at one end of the lovely canal terrace.*

TATTON PARK, Cheshire   *14 SJ78*
This exceptional late 18th-century mansion
(NT) was built by Samuel and Lewis Wyatt
for the Egerton family. It is beautifully
proportioned, maintained and furnished,
with Canalettos in its picture collection.
The old kitchens and servants' quarters
have been restored and are exceptionally
interesting. Its extensive park includes two
large meres, one part of Humphry Repton's
original plan for the grounds, one caused by
subsidence from the mining activities of a
neighbour of the Egertons. The gardens at
Tatton are magnificent, and particularly
appealing is the Japanese Garden, complete
with a teahouse and Shinto Temple. There
are also extensive glasshouses and a unique
fernery (*see* Knutsford).

TAUNTON, Somerset   *3 ST22*
The hub of Somerset, surrounded by the
rolling, wooded Quantocks and Blackdown
Hills, Taunton lies on the River Tone in the
Vale of Taunton Deane, and was a major
centre of the wool trade for 500 years.
Today it is a lively commercial and
agricultural centre whose livestock market
rivals Exeter's as the most important in the
West Country. Apple orchards thrive in the
mild climate and fertile soil of the Vale, and
cider-making is an important local
industry.
    As befits a county town, it is the
headquarters of Somerset's cricket team,
one of the country's most consistently
successful and entertaining sides. It also
offers National Hunt racing, no less than
three public schools and, somewhat
improbably, the British Telecom Museum.
Notable buildings include the Castle (AM)
which dates from Norman times and now
houses the Somerset County and Military
Museums.
    Hestercombe Gardens (OACT) three
miles north, were laid out in 1905 by Sir
Edwin Lutyens and Gertrude Jekyll.

TAVISTOCK, Devon   *2 SX47*
The town grew up around its great
Benedictine Abbey, founded in the 10th
century and largely destroyed at the
Dissolution. Sadly, few traces remain of
what must have been an imposing building.
Traditionally, the 'capital' of the western
side of Dartmoor, it has always been a
market town but one also with an industrial
past. Its Victorian buildings are a legacy
from the days when it was an important
centre of the then thriving copper-mining
industry. In the mid-19th century, the
nearby Great Consols mine was one of the
biggest in the world. Tavistock is now a
popular touring centre offering easy access
to the Dartmoor National Park.

TEALBY, Lincolnshire   *16 TF19*
On the slopes of the Wolds, this is a well-
tended ironstone village, with gardeners'
gardens. From the 12th- to 16th-century
church at the top of the slope, the main
street descends steeply to ford the River
Rase. The King's Head has a fine Norfolk-
reed thatch.
    Tealby has a mock Norman Castle –
Bayons Manor – built in 1840 by
Tennyson's uncle. You can admire the
countryside, despite the RAF presence,
from wooded Bully Hill, a 480ft vantage
post. The late 18th-century Thorpe Mill
(OACT – occasionally) is in the hamlet of
Tealby Thorpe.

TEIGNMOUTH *is one of Devon's oldest resorts
and has a long history as a fishing and ship-building
centre. The sheltered harbour and safe beach
(above) are among its chief attractions, but curious
details such as the boat door at Salt Cottage (right)
give the town an individual charm.*

TEFFONT, Wiltshire   *3 ST93*
In the pretty, wooded Nadder Valley, the
twin villages of Teffont Evias and Teffont
Magna stand by the waters of the Teff,
crossed by many small stone bridges.
Teffont Evias' turreted manor, Tudor and
early 17th-century and St Michael's Church
(rebuilt in the early 19th century), with its
graceful spire, together make a lovely sight.
The cream Chilmark stone from the local
quarry, now closed, also built Salisbury
Cathedral. Teffont Magna, is a little more
modest, with thatched cottages and a
medieval church.

TEIGNMOUTH, Devon   *2 SX97*
Writers have long been attracted here: Jane
Austen, Keats and Fanny Burney have all
stayed at this elegant and largely unspoilt
Regency and Victorian town situated where
the River Teign drifts placidly down from
the Devon hills to the sea. Its situation and
temperate climate made it a popular holiday
resort as early as the 18th century, and it
remains so today, spared the developments
which have disfigured so many English
seaside towns. Its sandy beach, handsome
esplanade, beautifully kept public gardens
and golf course 800ft above sea level are
complemented by the cheerful pier,
Aqualand (OACT) and model railway
exhibition. A 1700ft-long bridge across the
Teign Estuary links the town with the
village of Shaldon, a charming holiday and
yachting centre lying below the wooded
headland of The Ness, through which a
romantically named 'smugglers' tunnel
leads to the beach.

TELFORD, Shropshire   *9 SJ61*
Stand on the wooded slopes of the Wrekin
(1334ft) and behold Britain's newest New
Town, named after the famous 18th-
century engineer and former county
surveyor of Shropshire, Thomas Telford.
    The planners, ever optimistic, believe
they can successfully weld this arbitrary

conglomeration of a number of established
industrialised towns and villages into a
'Forest City'. Over a million trees and
shrubs are to be planted to justify that
description and a new city centre is planned
to arise at Randley Lake. **Ironbridge** and
Coalbrookdale form part of the
conurbation and are safeguarded by being
designated areas of special architectural and
historical interest.

TEMPLE SOWERBY, Cumbria
18 NY62
Once called the 'Queen of Westmoreland
Villages' it boasts two village greens and lies
under a high Pennine ridge in the lovely
Eden Valley. Its Manor – Acorn Bank – is
now a Sue Ryder home with splendid
gardens (NT).

**TENBURY WELLS, Hereford &
    Worcester**   *9 SO56*
The pretty River Teme, on which the old
market town stands, winds through apple
orchards and hop fields, meadows, woods
and hills. A medieval, arched bridge crosses
the river into Shropshire. Tenbury Wells
has some half-timbered black-and-white
buildings, such as the King's Head and the
Royal Oak inns; some Georgian houses,
and a church with a 12th-century tower.

TENBY, Dyfed 7 SN10

Tenby is finely situated on a rocky headland segmenting two big, sandy-beached bays. Tenby Castle occupies the green tip of the headland, projecting onto the beach above the old harbour. Its 13th-century ruins, including a gatehouse and double tower, inherited the site of an ancient Welsh fort cited in a 9th-century poem: *Dinbych-y-Pysgod*, 'Little fort of the Fish'. The town clusters closely inside its medieval walls, its surviving old buildings almost touching across narrow crooked streets. St Mary's Church is the accretion of centuries. Its oldest work – the tower, for example, is 13th-century, itself the rebuilding of an even older church, but the main structure is 15th-century. Tenby was a flourishing port in the 14th to 16th centuries. From these high days dates the gabled Tudor Merchant's House (NT), with a Flemish chimney, and fine extant frescoes.

Tenby Museum, on Castle Hill, specializes in finds from Hoyle's Mouth; the cave where archaeologists have found palaeolithic flints, a human jaw and teeth, and bones of extinct animals such as the cavebear and reindeer. St Catherine's Rock, just offshore, has a Victorian fort, now a house, and a small zoo. On **Caldy Island**, two and a half miles away, men have lived for thousands of years, monks for hundreds. St Margaret's Island, a bird sanctuary, can only be visited with a permit.

TENBY used to be a busy local port but now its little harbour, set in the bay known as Tenby Roads, caters mainly for tourists. Popular diversions include sailing, sea-fishing and boat trips to Caldy Island.

TENTERDEN, Kent 6 TQ83

A snug market town on the edge of the Weald, which enjoyed Cinque Port privileges, although not on the coast, through its little port at **Smallhythe** on the River Rother two miles south. Originally founded in the 7th century by monks from Minster Abbey in Thanet, it grew into a significant local wool-trading centre. The attractive main street contains a happy blend of Elizabethan, Georgian and white weather-boarded houses with bow windows and porticoed doorways, set off well by wide grass verges and trees. St Mildred's Church has a particularly fine carved and panelled nave roof. William Caxton, of printing fame, was reputedly born here. The Tenterden and District Museum is devoted to local history; the Town Station (OACT) is the principal station of Britain's first Light Railway. Eighteen or so steam locomotives are being restored, and trains run regularly.

TETBURY, Gloucestershire 3 ST89

Visitors disappointed in their quest for a glimpse of Tetbury's most famous royal inhabitants from nearby Highgrove House (not open) will find ample consolation by exploring this unassuming and, until now, unspoilt Cotswold town.

Lying on the Avon and near the Wiltshire border it has a pillared Elizabethan market hall and quietly dignified grey, stone-built houses, many of 18th-century origin. The aisled parish church, with its 19th-century tower and spire, was a victim of the Gothic revival, but has very fine box pews.

Three miles south-west is Westonbirt, a 19th-century, Italianate house set in a beautiful park. The Aboretum (OACT), one of the finest in the world, was started in 1829 and is now managed by the Forestry Commission. Chavenage (OACT), two miles north-west, is an interesting Elizabethan house containing fine furniture and tapestries.

TEWKESBURY, Gloucestershire 9 SO83

The fine abbey church of St Mary in this attractive town on the River Avon owes its survival to the public-spiritedness of the Tewkesbury townspeople. To avoid its probable destruction in the Dissolution of the Monasteries they somehow found the money to buy it from Henry VIII and so it remains intact today. Its massive Norman tower dominates both town and the surrounding countryside and is the largest surviving one of its type in Britain, as is the six-fold Norman arch in the west front. From the top of the tower are views of the Malvern Hills and the Welsh Mountains. Inside the Abbey is more Norman work and a particularly handsome vaulted ceiling in Decorated style. There are impressive tombs and monuments to the old local ruling families and a Chantry Chapel endowed by the Beauchamps – family of Warwick the Kingmaker.

The buildings in the town itself do not fail by comparison with the Abbey. There is a wealth of timberwork here, much of it medieval. Many of the attractive houses bear unusual names – 'The House of the Nodding Gables'; 'The House of the Golden Key' and, most eccentric of all, 'The Ancient Grudge'. Old inns abound also: the Black Bear claims to date from 1308 and the Royal Hop Pole is yet another hostelry to feature in the works of Dickens – in *The Pickwick Papers*.

The Coast of South Pembrokeshire
48 miles

The drive follows the borders of the Pembrokeshire Coast National Park, travelling through splendid natural scenery from the lovely old town of Tenby to Pembroke, with its magnificent castle, and returning via the inland route.

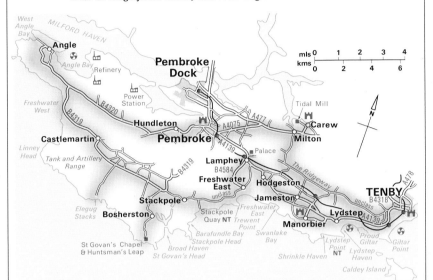

From **Tenby**, take the Pembroke road, A4139 passing through Lydstep. Half a mile further, turn left (SP Manorbier) on to B4585. At **Manorbier** keep left (one-way), then turn right following Pembroke signs. (Alternatively, keep forward for beach and castle.) In ½ mile, at the T-junction, turn left to rejoin A4139, and drive through Jameston and Hodgeston to the edge of **Lamphey**. Either keep forward to visit the Bishop's Palace, or, on the main drive, turn sharp left on to B4584 (SP Freshwater East). At **Freshwater**, turn right on to the Stackpole road (unclassified). Descend, and in 2¼ miles a detour can be made (left) to Stackpole Quay. The main drive continues to Stackpole, then descends through woodland before turning left (SP Bosherton) on to B4319. In ½ mile, the main drive bears right, SP Castlemartin. Alternatively, for a detour to Bosherton, turn left (unclassified). At Bosherton church, a path leads to the fish ponds.

Beyond the village, bear right for St Govan's Chapel. Return to the Castlemartin road and continue into **Castlemartin**. Here turn left (SP Angle, Freshwater West). After 3¼ miles turn left on to B4320, then in 1½ miles, right (unclassified), descend, then turn left into **Angle**. At the end of the village turn left to leave on the Pembroke road, B4320 (or keep straight on for West Angle Bay) then in ½ mile, on the ascent, turn sharp left and continue to **Pembroke**. Follow the one-way system into the town, keep forward (SP Tenby) along the main street, then turn left (SP Carmarthen) on to A4075. After 2¼ miles, at the T-junction turn right on to A477 to reach the edge of Milton. (For Carew, keep forward for ½ mile, then turn left on to A4075.) The main drive turns right (unclassified SP Lamphey, Manorbier), ascends, and at the T-junction turns left. Follow Tenby signs and drive past Penally to the main road. Turn left (A4319) to return to Tenby.

PLACES TO SEE

Tenby An attractive, old-world resort with a Norman keep, housing the town museum. The Merchant's House (NT) dates from Tudor times. St Catherine's Island, not far from the shore, is accessible on foot at low tide and launches run to Caldy Island where Cistercian monks farm and produce perfume.

Lydslep A tiny village with the ruins of Bishop Gower's hunting lodge. Lydslep Point (NT) lies to the east.

Manorbier The castle (OACT) overlooks an attractive, sandy beach. Giraldus Cambrensis, the 12th-century historian, was born here.

Lamphey Nearby are the ruins of the 13th-century Bishop's Palace (AM).

Stackpole Quay (NT) A charming spot on a beautiful stretch of coastline.

Bosherton The village is famous for its lily ponds. St Govan's Chapel is a tiny building wedged into the cliffs.

Pembroke Dominating the town is the great 12th-century castle. Beneath it is a huge limestone cavern, the Wogan.

Pembroke Dock Vintage and veteran cars and motorcycles can be seen at the Pembrokeshire Motor Museum in the Garrison Theatre.

Carew The ruined castle stands on the banks of the Cleddau river. Nearby is an 18th-century cornmill (OACT). Carew Cross (AM) dates from the 11th century.

THAME, Oxfordshire *10 SP70*
The imposing sign of the Spread Eagle – immortalised between the wars by John Fothergill in his minor classic *An Innkeeper's Diary* – dominates the wide main street of this Thames-side market town. St Mary's Church displays well the development of English architectural styles from Early English to Perpendicular. This variety is repeated in the town buildings – a happy mixture of medieval cottages and elegant Georgian houses. The Birdcage Inn dates from the 15th century and the grammar school from 1575.

THANET, ISLE OF, Kent *6 TR36*
This flat coastal segment of north-east Kent, edged with chalk cliffs, is now an island in name only. Traditionally where the Saxons first landed, Thanet was then divided from the mainland by the Rivers Stour and Wantsum, which gave safe anchorage and access to the Thames Estuary. Thanet has three popular resorts – **Broadstairs**, **Margate** and **Ramsgate**. Minster-in-Thanet, once its leading town and trading centre, now secluded among its fruit farms, has one of Kent's best parish churches: St Mary's preserves Roman bricks, Norman work, and exemplary 15th-century choir stalls.

THAXTED, Essex *11 TL63*
Thaxted's plastered, half-timbered, overhanging buildings represent the old Essex. The fine, early 15th-century Guildhall derives from the village's dominance of the cutlery industry. So too does the austere magnificence of St John's Church, its endowment shared by the great Essex family of Clare. One chapel commemorates the priest John Ball, a leader of the Peasants' Revolt. The tower, with its high spire, was rebuilt in the early 19th century by Peter Platt: 'Where Peter lies, 'tis fit this tower should show, but for his skill, itself had lain as low'. Thaxted's windmill (1804) houses a small museum.

THETFORD, Norfolk *12 TL88*
This Breckland town stands at the meeting of the River Thet and the Little Ouse, spanned by a three-way bridge and bordered by riverside walks. Thetford Heath is a National Nature Reserve and Thetford Chase, planted in 1919, is Britain's second largest forest.
    Thetford is an ancient settlement, standing on the Icknield Way, England's oldest trade route. After the Danes conquered East Anglia in the 9th-century, they made Thetford their capital. Later it became the See of the Bishops of East Anglia, and the seat of its first kings.
    Thetford Castle is one of our biggest original motte and bailey castles, and of Thetford's ecclesiastical eminence, the principal relic is the Priory (AM) of which the 14th-century gatehouse remains intact. Among the town's many interesting medieval, Tudor and Georgian buildings are the early 16th-century Bell Inn and the brick and flint Dolphin Inn (1694). The Ancient House Museum, in an early Tudor timbered house, illustrates the life of the early Breckland farmers.
    Warren Lodge (AM), just north-west, is a 15th-century hunting lodge in flint and stone. The old pump-room (1818) marks Thetford's unsuccessful attempt to become popular as a spa.

THIRSK, N Yorkshire 15 SE48

The 'Darrowby' of James Herriot's evocative books, this thriving old market town nestles at the foot of the Hambleton Hills in the Vale of Mowbray. The Golden Fleece, a large, handsome, Georgian inn, bears witness to the town's former importance as a stagecoach posting station in the 18th and 19th centuries.

Disconsolate punters from the popular local racecourse can also drown their sorrows in the 18th-century Three Tuns or the Crown, reputedly dating from 1682. The cluster of old buildings round the cobbled square represent a complementary range of small commercial and domestic buildings. Appropriately perhaps for such a cricket-conscious county Thomas Lord, founder of Lords Cricket Ground, was born here in 1755.

KILBURN WHITE HORSE *Cut into the chalk of the Hambleton Hills near Thirsk in 1857 by a local schoolmaster and his pupils, the horse stands 228ft high and is 314ft long.*

THORESBY HALL *One of the features of the house is the magnificent library fireplace with its detailed wood carving depicting Sherwood Forest, and statues of Robin Hood and Little John.*

THORESBY, Nottinghamshire 15 SK67

Thoresby Hall (OACT), built 1864–75 in the heart of Sherwood Forest, is one of the great ducal mansions that gave the name 'Dukeries' to this part of the countryside. Descendants of its original owners, the Earls of Manvers, still live there. It was the Duke of Kingston who built the first house on the site, in the late 17th century. His daughter, Lady Mary Wortley Montague, the famous letter-writer, lived here. The Duke established Thoresby Park, with its splendid chestnut avenues and lovely lake, made by damming the River Meden. At one end of the lake there is a model village dating from 1807 and a castellated folly named Budby Castle.

THORNEY, Cambridgeshire 11 TF20

Thorney was once an island village where Hereward the Wake made his stand against William the Conqueror. Then the fens were drained, much being done by the Dukes of Bedford. It was the Duke of Bedford who in the 17th century gave asylum to the French Protestants whose names you can read in the churchyard. The ochre-coloured, mid 19th-century model village was built by the contemporary Duke.

The 12th-century ruins of Thorney Abbey are part of the Abbey Church, restored by Inigo Jones. They stand on the site of a 7th-century Saxon monastery, plundered by the Danes, rebuilt by the Normans. Beside the church, built on abbey foundations and from abbey stone, are 17th- and 18th-century houses.

THORNTON, Humberside 16 TA11

The principal representative of the old magnificence of Thornton Abbey (AM) is its 14th-century castellated, stone-and-brick gatehouse. The approach to the ruined abbey, founded in the 12th century, lies across a 120ft bridge with arcaded walls and two circular towers.

THORNTON DALE, N Yorkshire 16 SE88

Thornton Beck threads through this pretty village on the edge of the North York Moors, and footbridges give access to many of the stone-built cottages and their well kept gardens. All Saints Church, re-built in the 14th century, has been heavily 'restored' but the 17th-century almshouses and grammar school remain unspoiled, as does a thatched cruck-built Tudor cottage. To the north lies Newtondale, a remote and beautiful valley up which the preserved North Yorkshire Moors Railway snakes, en route from **Pickering** to Grosmont.

THURNHAM, Lancashire 14 SD45

Thurnham has a splendid hall (OACT) principally 16th-century but originally 13th-century. Inside it has a notable Great Hall with Elizabethan plasterwork, Jacobean panelling and staircase.

THURSFORD GREEN, Norfolk 12 TF93

Here you can see the result of one man's lifetime enthusiasm in the Thursford Collection of steam locomotives, traction and fairground engines, and Wurlitzer and barrel organs. The musical instruments, from all over Europe, are almost all in working order, and are played at intervals. Musical evenings, with concerts on the Wurlitzer organs, are also held.

THURSO, Highland 30 ND16

Thurso is splendidly situated: on a broad, sandy bay in the Pentland Firth, between the towering cliffs of Holborn Head and Clairdon Head. Its hinterland is the fertile Caithness plain. Scotland's northernmost mainland town affords grand views of its northernmost point, Dunnet Head, and across to the cliffs of Hoy in the Orkneys. The Vikings named this rivermouth settlement, *Thorse*, and Old St Peter's Kirk, by the once-important harbour, occupies the site of a Viking church. Gilbert Murray, Bishop of Caithness, established his church here in the 13th century: the present ruins are 16th- to 17th-century. The medieval Bishop's Palace stands on Thurso Bay. The old fishermen's houses by the harbour have been carefully restored. From nearby Scrabster, the Orkney ferries sail; and, in both world wars, convoys sailed for Scapa Flow. Dounreay atomic reactor station, ten miles west (*see* **Reay**), has meant much expansion around Thurso.

TICHBORNE, Hampshire 4 SU53

This is a pretty village in the Itchen Valley, made up of 16th- and 17th-century houses, many thatched, a part-Saxon, part-Norman church on a hillock, and Tichborne Park, the Tichborne family mansion since Anglo-Saxon times, rebuilt early in the 19th century. Tichborne has two claims to celebrity. First is the Tichborne Dole, an annual ceremony originated in the 12th century by Lady Mabella de Tichborne. The story is that her husband Roger charmingly consented to grant the poor the produce of as much land as the dying Mabella could walk around – she managed to crawl round 20 acres before expiring. Second is the celebrated Tichborne Claimant case: in 1871 an Australian butcher represented himself as Sir Roger Tichborne, the long-lost heir. Many people believed him, but after a long-drawn-out trial, his claim was disproved and he ended in gaol.

TIDESWELL, Derbyshire 15 SK17

This small, stone-built town is finely set among the limestone hills of the **Peak District**. Miller's Dale and Chee Dale (both NT) lie within easy visiting distance. Fourteenth-century St John's Church is impressive enough to be known as the 'Cathedral of the Peak'.

Tideswell is one of several Peak District villages that hold an annual 'well-dressing' ceremony.

TILBURY, Essex 6 TQ67

This ancient port in the suburbanised and industrialised Thames Estuary marshlands is the first outpost of the Port of London. Its great passenger days are over, it is now a key container port. There is a ferry service to Gravesend; and, from Purfleet, the Dartford Tunnel. Its nautical past is illustrated in the Thurrock Riverside Museum. Tilbury Fort (AM) was one of Henry VIII's creations.

The Cleveland and Hambleton Hills
66 miles

Seeking tranquillity and a retreat from worldly life, Benedictine and Carthusian monks came to these remote, North Yorkshire dales and built the abbeys and priories whose ruins stand as an eloquent testimony to the ideals of the contemplative life.

From **Thirsk** follow Scarborough signs to leave on A170. Drive through Sutton-under-Whitestonecliffe and ascend Sutton Bank (1 in 4 with hairpin bends). Continue along a ridge of the Hambleton Hills for 3¾ miles before turning right and right again (unclassified, SP Wass, Coxwold). Later descend to **Wass** (here keep forward to visit Byland Abbey, Coxwold Hall and Newburgh Priory). The main drive turns left for **Ampleforth**, and at the end of the village bears right (SP Oswaldkirk). At **Oswaldkirk** keep forward to join B1363 (SP Helmsley), then in ¼ mile turn left on to B1257. At **Sproxton** turn right on to A170 (SP Scarborough) and drive to **Helmsley**. Rejoin B1257 (SP Stokesley) through the village, and in 1½ miles, turn left (SP Scawton). Descend steeply, then before the river bridge turn right for Rievaulx Abbey. Ascend to the junction with B1257. Here, on the right, is the entrance to Rievaulx Terrace. Turn left

(SP Stokesley). Later enter Blisdale and after Chop Gate drive over the Cleveland Hills to Great Broughton. Two miles further, at the roundabout, take the 2nd exit for **Stokesley**. Leave the town following Thirsk signs and in ¾ mile turn right on to A172. After 8 miles branch left on to A19. In ½ mile, a detour can be made (left) to Mount Grace Priory, but the main drive continues on A19 for ½ mile then branches left on to A684 (SP Northallerton). From **Northallerton** follow signs Thirsk to leave on A168. Drive on for 7 miles then turn right on B1448 to return to Thirsk.

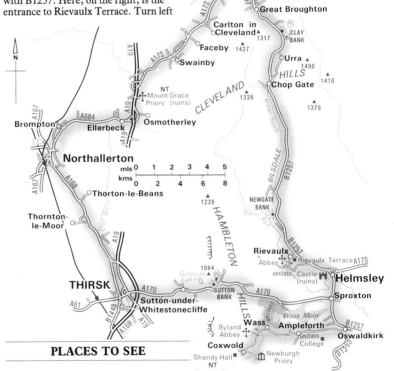

PLACES TO SEE

Thirsk An attractive market town with an outstanding Perpendicular church and vast, cobbled market square.

Sutton Bank A dramatic scarp of the Hambleton Hills, with a white horse carved in 1857.

Byland Abbey Ruins of the Cistercian abbey stand near the village of Wass.

Coxwold Thomas Sterne, author of *Tristram Shandy* was rector in this pleasant village for 7 years. His home, Shandy Hall (OACT) is a medieval farmhouse.

Newburgh Priory An 18th-century house (OACT) built on the site of a Norman priory.

Helmsley Ruins of the castle stand in the grounds of Duncombe Park School.

Rievaulx Abbey and Terrace (AM) Magnificent ruins of the Cistercian abbey stand beside the River Rye. Rievaulx Terrace was built by the owner of Duncombe Park to provide views of the ruins.

Stokesley An old market town whose many trees were planted to commemorate Jane Page, the first white woman to settle in Victoria, Australia, in 1846.

Mount Grace Priory One of the cells of this 14th-century Carthusian monastery has been restored to show the austere and solitary life of the original inhabitants.

THE OLD POST OFFICE *at Tintagel was built in the 14th century to the plan of a medieval manor house. It was used as a post office between 1844 and 1892 and the National Trust bought it in 1903.*

TILFORD, Surrey *4 SU84*
King John's Oak, by the village green, is about 900 years old, 26ft round, and described by Cobbett in his *Rural Rides*. The two bridges across the River Wey are medieval; the Institute was designed by Sir Edwin Lutyens. Tilford also has an attractive common, a Bach festival, and the interesting Old Kiln Agricultural Museum, set in ten acres of woodland and gardens.

TINTAGEL, Cornwall *1 SX08*
Legend has it that King Arthur was born here, although the castle (AM) on Tintagel Head which bears his name is Norman in origin. It was originally built in 1145 for the then Earl of Cornwall. The surviving ruins date mainly from the 13th century. Augmenting the Arthurian legend are 'Merlin's Cave' below the castle, and King Arthur's Hall, built in 1933 as the headquarters of the Fellowship of the Round Table. It has no less then 73 stained-glass windows showing Arthur's Knights.
   The nearby coastline has been designated an Area of Outstanding Natural Beauty, it is rocky, wild and romantic with stark cliffs and slate caves. Much of it is secure in the ownership of the National Trust.

TINTERN ABBEY, Gwent *9 SO50*
A beautiful ruin (AM) in an equally beautiful setting, Tintern Abbey lies in a bend on the Wye in a meadow overlooked by the wooded hills which form the boundary between England and Wales. A victim of the Dissolution, the Abbey is one of the finest reminders of monasticism. It was founded in 1131, although most of the ruins date from the 13th and 14th centuries. The Abbey Church itself survives almost intact.

TISBURY, Wiltshire *3 ST92*
Tisbury, an ancient settlement traversed by an Anglo-Saxon track, is divided into East and West, and more a town than a village. It is poised on a steep slope by the River Nadder, in the rich valley farmlands of

Wiltshire. The church has a lovely panelled and carved roof, and memorials to Lady Blanche Arundel, who defended nearby Wardour Castle in the Civil War, and to Catherine Howard's sister. Rudyard Kipling and his parents are buried in the churchyard. The yew tree, 36ft in circumference, is believed to be 1000 years old. There are two Wardour Castles: the Old, a 14th-century ruin (AM), with 16th-century additions; and the New, an 18th-century house (OACT) designed by James Paine, restored for Cranbourne Chase School in 1960. Pythouse (OACT), is a fine Palladian mansion.

TISSINGTON, Derbyshire *15 SK15*
A handsome village in the Peak District National Park, east of Dovedale, Tissington is distinguished by its limestone buildings, a good example being the 18th-century vicarage; triangular green; broad, grassy verges, and fine trees. In an 1830s' improvement programme, the Fitzherberts of Tissington Hall contributed many new buildings and restored the church, originally Norman and Early English in style, retaining a curiously-carved Norman font. Tissington 'dresses' its five wells with an elaborate floral tapestry in an ancient annual ceremony which has survived in a number of Derbyshire Peak District villages.

TITCHFIELD, Hampshire *4 SU50*
Titchfield is two miles from the mouth of the River Meon, which winds across Titchfield Haven to the Solent. This small town used to be a seaport until Dutch engineers drained the marshes in the 18th century. Titchfield has a bridge across the river built in 1625; and many 17th- and 18th-century buildings, such as the Queen's Head. Titchfield Abbey (AM), or Place House, is the splendid ruined survivor of a great 13th-century building. After the Dissolution it was converted into a house by the Earl of Southampton. The pride of the ruins is the Tudor gatehouse.

TIVERTON, Devon *2 SS91*
Textiles and wool brought prosperity to this thriving market town, set in the rounded hills and wooded valleys of mid Devon. The textile industry here dates from the 13th century and is evidenced today by mills and factories around the fringes of the town. Wool merchants' money paid for the 15th- and 16th-century enlargement and alteration of the imposing St Peter's Church, with its richly carved and decorated Greenway Chapel and south porch. Tiverton Castle, former house of the Courtenay family, Earls of Devon, dates from the 12th century. Built of local pink sandstone its ruins include two towers and a 14th-century gateway, now part of a private house. Tiverton Museum, one of the best folk museums in the West Country has a large railway gallery complete with restored GWR tank locomotive and the restored Grand Western Canal, 11 miles long, offers trips by horse-drawn barges.

WELL DRESSING

Tissington is one of the many Derbyshire villages that annually 'dresses' its wells. Every Ascension Day flowers, feathers, moss and other natural materials are worked into a variety of biblical scenes.

TOLLARD ROYAL, Wiltshire *3 ST91*
Tollard's right to call itself Royal was granted by King John, who stayed here to hunt in Cranborne Chase. Despite disafforestation, some attractive woodlands survive, that can be surveyed from 911ft Win Green Hill (NT). Gardiner Forest, 1800 acres, was endowed by Balfour Gardiner, the composer.
   King John's House, originally 13th-century, was restored by the archaeologist General Pitt-Rivers. He lived in Rushmoor House, now a school, and worked on several sites in its grounds. Pitt-Rivers was responsible for the restoration of Larmer Gardens, named after the larmer tree – wych-elm – under which King John would supposedly meet his huntsmen. Here too the Court Leets were held. The old tree blew down in 1894 and was replaced by an oak tree.

TOLLESBURY, Essex 6 TL91

Among the creeks and marshes of the Blackwater Estuary, this sizeable fishing village is the pivot of the oyster trade. In about 1900 Tollesbury had over 100 sprat-catching boats. Tollesbury's square is framed by plaster-and-brick houses. St Mary's Church, built of pebble, stone, brick and tiles, has a Norman tower and nave. The 18th-century font is inscribed: 'Good people all pray take care, that in ye church you do not sware. As this man did.' 'This man' atoned by paying for the font.

TOLPUDDLE, Dorset 3 SY79

Tolpuddle is remembered for its martyrs, agricultural workers sentenced to transportation in 1834 for uniting to resist a wage reduction. A hundred years later, the TUC built a museum of six cottages named after 'The Martyrs'. Among the village's other memorials is the Martyr's Tree (NT), the old sycamore under which it is thought that they met.

TOMINTOUL, Grampian 27 NJ11

Between the River Avon and the Conglass Water, 1160ft up on the remote moors of old Banffshire, Tomintoul is the highest village in the Highlands, a centre for tourists, anglers, skiers. It is a whisky village, near the Glenlivet country, with four inns. Its limestone houses and slate cottages are centred round the village green and main street. The Avon rises amid the high tops of the Cairngorms to the south-west, flowing into Loch Avon, through Glen Avon, past 3843ft Ben Avon, and so north-east to Tomintoul. One of the river's many tributaries is the Water of Ailnack, which cuts through a series of spectacular, inaccessible gorges, beneath 2692ft Geal Charn. Alongside the Conglass Water to the south-east runs the famous Lecht road, built by the army in 1745, that made Tomintoul possible.

TONBRIDGE, Kent 6 TQ54

This prosperous market town at the navigable extremity of the River Medway, where it diverges into fordable streams, has been strategically important since Anglo-Saxon and perhaps Roman times. The River Walk along the Medway, through willow-lined meadows, affords a fine view of Tonbridge Castle (AM). Its Norman to 13th-century ruins, on a site defended since 1088, are substantial: the shell of the keep, curtain walls, round-towered gatehouse. Some of Tonbridge's 18th-century houses are built of castle stone.

TONGUE, Highland 30 NC55

The very remoteness of this village on the east side of the Kyle of Tongue enhances its popularity as a holiday centre for climbers, anglers and walkers. Approaching from the south the road from Lairg runs along the west shore of Loch Loyal, with spectacular views of the multi-peaked granite mass of Ben Loyal (2504ft). To the north of the village a modern bridge crosses the Kyle, with its sandy shores, and leads to the coastal village of Durness and Cape Wrath. The little road south round the Kyle, past Loch Hacoin, is no longer the main route westwards but is nevertheless worth the detour. The ruins of Castle Varrick overlook the village. It was the home of an 11th-century Norse king and later became a Mackay stronghold.

TOLPUDDLE MARTYRS

In 1834 six Dorsetshire farm workers were sentenced to be transported to Tasmania for trying to form an agricultural union to press for higher wages. After public outcry and massive demonstrations of sympathy, they were reprieved and five of them (below) returned to England. In 1934 the TUC built these cottages (right), near to where the men used to meet, as a permanent memorial.

TOPPESFIELD, Essex 12 TL73

The Museum of The Working Horse includes blacksmith's and wheelwright's shops, a sawpit, harness-maker's shop, horse-drawn vehicles and agricultural implements among many exhibits from the days when horsepower was all that farmers had.

TOPSHAM, Devon 2 SX98

Any owner of a thriving main road business who loses his trade on the opening of a nearby motorway will appreciate how Topsham once felt. From 1282 this handsome town on the Exe estuary had thrived as a port, largely by courtesy of a bad-tempered gesture by an early Countess of Devon who built a weir across the Exe to deny boats passage to up-river **Exeter**. The good times ended in 1567, when the city responded by opening the first English ship canal, by-passing the Exe and allowing the big ships into the cathedral city's centre. Topsham, unable to offer the same deep-water facilities, began to decline as a port although continuing as a boat-building and trading centre. Now more of a genteel residential suburb of Exeter than an identifiable town in its own right, reminders of its commercial past remain in its riverside warehouses, dignified 'Dutch' merchants' houses in the Strand, and some fine old pubs.

TORPHICHEN, Lothian 23 NS97

Torphichen is a quiet village near the Bathgate Hills; with a good view from The Knock (1017ft). Cocklerue, a local hill originally called Cuckold le Roi, is cited in an RL Stevenson poem. Cairnpapple Hill (AM) is one of Scotland's principal prehistoric sites. Originally a Neolithic sanctuary, it was enlarged in the Bronze Age, when a circular temple was built. Torphichen Preceptory (AM) was the chief seat of the Knights of St John, a church that looked like a castle. Of the original Norman Church, only the chancel arch survives. The transepts are 13th-century the tower 15th-century. Over the ancient nave, the 16th-century parish church stands.

TORPOINT, Cornwall 2 SX45

Antony House (NT) is a fine, unspoilt 18th-century building in brick and stone, with a notable 19th-century *porte-cochère*. From Torpoint, on the Hamoaze, a car ferry runs to Devonport.

TORQUAY, Devon 2 SX96

Famous for its panoramic setting on the wooded hill above Tor Bay, Torquay is a superior and expansive resort, with a continental air. This has been Devon's most popular coastline since the Napoleonic Wars drew first the naval establishment and then tourists. The Devon Riviera is distinguished by its brilliant blue sea, kind climate, and colourful and luxuriant sub-tropical vegetation, notably its palm trees. Torquay's focal point is its yachting harbour, protected by huge break-waters. Above it rise luxury hotels and high-rise flats, fine 19th-century terraces and crescents, such as Hesketh Crescent (1846) and – the price of popularity – guest houses, caravan sites and holiday camps.

Torre Abbey (AM) was originally built in the 12th century. Its surviving ruins are a gateway, the abbot's tower, and two crypts. It was the monks who built the first quay on the bay. The site is shared by the 18th-century Torre Abbey Mansion, incorporating an art gallery, and the 12th-century Spanish Barn, made a prison for captured sailors from the Armada.

Torquay has all kinds of attractions: Aqualand, the largest aquarium in the West Country; the Torbay Steam Railway; the Natural History Museum. Ilsham Marine Drive affords fine views, as do the weathered cliffs – along which you can walk to Anstey's Cove and Babbcombe. The model village here is a show-piece; and a rack-and-pinion railway runs down to the beach. Kent's Cavern (AM), on the edge of the town, was inhabited during the Ice Age, putting it among the oldest known sites in Britain. The bones of sabre-toothed tigers and bears are preserved, amid red, green and white stalagmites and stalactites, by the limestone in the water that drips through the rocks.

TORRIDON, Highland   25 NG85

This village, on Loch Torridon, at Glen Torridon's west end, is set amid splendid Highland scenery. The National Trust for Scotland has a Visitor Centre here to guide you, and a Deer Museum. Loch Torridon is a magnificent sea loch, opposite the north-eastern tip of Skye. It extends into Loch Shieldaig to the south, and into Upper Loch Torridon through the narrow straits to the east. On the Ploc of Torridon, a promontory in the Upper Loch, are the prehistoric stones of the Church of Ploc. The wild and beautiful Glen Torridon, with its Corrie of a Hundred Hills, cuts through the Torridon mountains where the peaks of Ben Eighe (3309ft), form a National Nature Reserve: Liathach, the highest peak in the Torridons, is one of Scotland's finest mountains: 3456ft high, its terraces extend for three miles, towering above the spectacular Coire na Caime. The mountains, of stratified red sandstone, some topped in white quartzite, attract geologists and climbers and afford views stretching from Cape Wrath to Ardnamurchan and the Outer Hebrides.

TOTNES, Devon   2 SX86

The old town of Totnes stands on a steep hill above the River Dart, at its highest navigational point. The British Council of Archaeology made it one of its 40 towns of outstanding architectural and historic interest, despite its spreading suburbs. The rich and sheltered farming country, and now retirement country, of the South Hams enfolds it. From Totnes you can take a boat downriver to Dartmouth; or a private train to Buckfastleigh. Totnes still builds boats and imports timber, but is not a port on its medieval scale. On the Quay is now a motor museum of vintage sports and racing cars.

In the great days of the medieval cloth trade, Totnes was a walled town, and the lines are still detectable; the 15th-century East Gate has been restored and there are remains of the castle (AM). St Mary's Church is a remarkable relic of the 15th century, with a 120ft tower and a famous stone screen. The Elizabethan and Georgian eras contributed some fine architecture to Totnes, particularly along its steep main street. The four-storey Elizabethan House is now a museum; with a section on computers, which were pioneered by Charles Babbage (1792–1871), a one-time pupil at the King Edward VI Grammar School. The Guildhall, gabled and colonnaded, standing on the site of the medieval Totnes Priory, contains a smaller museum. The Seven Stars Inn is 17th-century, the Butterwalk prettily arcaded.

TOWCESTER, Northamptonshire   10 SP64

An unassuming place, but it is amongst the oldest towns in Britain. Originally a settlement on the Roman Watling Street, it later became an important coaching stop, as its surviving inns testify. The Saracen's Head features in *The Pickwick Papers* and the Talbot dates from 1440. The Post Office – one of a number of fine Georgian buildings – dates from 1797. St Laurence's Church, with its soaring, ironstone, Perpendicular tower, houses an interesting collection of chained books.

The peace of the neighbouring broad, pleasant, landscape is sometimes shattered by motor racing at the famous Silverstone circuit, four and a half miles south-west. The more appropriate rural pastime of National Hunt racing takes place at the attractive course in the grounds of Easton Neston House.

TRANENT, Lothian   24 NT47

Prestongrange Historical Site and Mining Museum accounts for the 800-year history of this mining district inland of the Firth of Forth. The centrepiece of the exhibition is the only Cornish beam engine which remains in Scotland. Tranent has a 16th-century dovecote; a 19th-century church on ancient foundations; a place in Scott's *Waverley* – Colonel Gardiner died here after the Battle of Prestonpans; and, nearby, the 15th- to 16th-century ruin of Falside Castle.

TRAQUAIR, Borders   23 NT33

A neat and ancient village in the sheep-farming Southern Uplands, Traquair stands on Quair Water, a tributary of the River Tweed. St Bryde's Church, on a knoll that has been an ecclesiastical site since before the 12th century is an 18th-century building and has a galleried outside staircase. Traquair House (OACT), seat of the Stuarts of Traquair, tall, turreted, elegant and austere, is a famous, château-style mansion inhabited for 1000 years, probably longer than any house in Scotland. Originally 10th-century, preserving its tower, the house was largely rebuilt in 1642, the wings added later. Among its special contents are 13th-century glass, tapestries, embroideries, and relics of Mary Queen of Scots. Since William the Lion held Court here in 1209, 26 English and Scottish monarchs have visited the house, among them, Mary Queen of Scots and Darnley, and Bonnie Prince Charlie. Montrose perhaps sheltered here after the Battle of Philliphaugh, travelling by the old drovers' road that climbs to 1856ft over Winchmuir between Selkirk and Peebles. Traquair House ale is still made in the 18th-century brewery.

THE TORRIDONS *Ben Eighe, one of the highest peaks of these spectacular mountains, forms part of the 10,000 acre Ben Eighe National Nature Reserve.*

TRECASTLE, Powys *8 SN82*
In the **Brecon Beacons National Park**, the village stands on the site of the Park's biggest motte-and-bailey castle.

From Trecastle you can explore the Black Mountain, at 2630ft the second highest in South Wales (except for the Beacons themselves) its north face scarred with precipices, and the great, wooded Usk Reservoir, near the shores of which rises a massive standing stone.

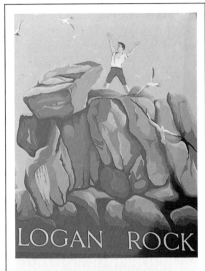

THE LOGAN ROCK

The inn sign at Treen depicts a curious local landmark – the Logan Rock. Weighing about 65 tons, it is balanced so precariously on the edge of the cliff that it can be rocked by hand. Its name is derived from the Cornish word 'log' which means 'to move'.

TREEN, Cornwall *1 SW32*
Treen Castle (NT) is a fortified headland, shared by the ancient fort of Treryn Dinas and the Logan Rock, a rocking stone overturned by Oliver Goldsmith's nephew in 1824. It was promptly replaced and he was made to pay for it. Boscawen-un, Cornwall's most famous prehistoric stone circle, and the ancient ruined settlement of Carn Euny are also near Treen.

TREFRIW, Gwynedd *13 SH76*
Trefriw is on the wooded west slope of the Conwy Valley, by the River Crafnant. Llewelyn the Great had a house here and would take the steep path to the plain, 13th- to 16th-century church at Llanrhychwyn, until reputedly he built one in Trefriw. At Trefriw Woollen Mill (OACT), built in 1859 on the River Crafnant, all stages of woollen manufacture can be seen.

TREGARON, Dyfed *8 SN65*
Tregaron is a relatively big town for its situation in the remote heartland of Wales, by the River Teifi. It is a centre for the sheep-farms in the surrounding hills and for visitors, especially pony-trekkers. The Bog of Tregaron, a raised bog, four miles long and still spreading, on either side of the River Teifi, is a National Nature Reserve: the habitat of rare plants such as sundew, bog rosemary, bladderwort and sedges, and a refuge for pole-cats.

TRENTHAM GARDENS *Little remains of the Italianate mansion belonging to the estate but the gardens, including an elaborate parterre and a lake, form part of Staffordshire's chief pleasure park.*

TRELISSICK, Cornwall *1 SW71*
In Trelissick Gardens (NT), a woodland park at the head of Falmouth Harbour, grow the kind of sub-tropical shrubs that in England are unique to south Cornwall, where the sheltered climate allows them to flourish.

TREMADOG, Gwynedd *13 SH54*
Tremadog and its twin town **Porthmadog** guard the entrance to the River Glarlyn and so to the Lleyn Peninsula. William Maddocks the rich MP for Boston, Lincolnshire, built Tremadog in the early 19th century on reclaimed land behind the Cob, an embankment across the river. He intended it to be a key point on the route to Ireland but Parliament voted for **Holyhead** instead. Tremadog was designed as a model town in classical style, with neat stone buildings, a broad main street and a square headed by the former Market Hall. The sheer cliffs behind the Hall include the *Coed Tremadog* National Nature Reserve, rich in oak trees and in plants profiting from the exclusion of sheep.

TRENT, Dorset *3 ST51*
Elegant stone houses and lovely gardens give this pastoral village its character. In its manor house Charles II hid after the Battle of Worcester, to the sound of the villagers cheering rumours of his capture. Trent's 13th- to 15th-century church has a fine 14th-century tower and spire, and an interior that escaped the worst attentions of the Puritans.

TRENTHAM, Staffordshire *14 SJ84*
Trentham Hall, property of the Dukes of Sutherland, was built in the 14th century, enlarged into a palatial mansion in the 19th century and has since been almost demolished. It appears in Arnold Bennett's *The Card*. Trentham Gardens (OACT), landscaped principally by Sir Joseph Paxton, are Staffordshire's largest pleasure ground. They have been open to the public since the early 1900s, half a century earlier than most. The village of Trentham is an ancient settlement, whose history goes back to early Saxon times when Wulfhere, the first Christian King of Mercia, built a palace in the neighbourhood in AD 660.

His daughter founded a nunnery on the site of the 19th-century church which preserves the Norman pillars of the priory that inherited the site from the 12th to 16th centuries.

TREORCHY, Mid Glamorgan *7 SS99*
The town is famous for its Royal Male Voice Choir, the oldest in Wales, given its title by Queen Victoria after its Command performance at Windsor in 1885. Treorchy contributed to the history of Rhondda's diversification, by the establishment of the clothing factory here in 1939.

TRE'R-DDOL, Dyfed *7 SN69*
Yr Hen Gapel, a branch of the National Museum of Wales, run by the Welsh Folk Museum, specializes in religious life in 19th-century Wales. From Tre'r-ddol you can explore (with a permit for the first two areas) the Dyfi National Nature Reserve; the Dyfi Estuary, haunt of wildfowl and migrant waders – but keep an eye on tides and mud; Borth Bog, fascinating to botanists; and the Ynyslas Dunes.

TRERICE, Cornwall *1 SW71*
The stone Elizabethan House (NT) is exemplary, especially the aspect of its south and east façades with their unusual curly gables. Elaborate plaster ceilings are a feature of the interior and the immense latticed window of the main hall has 576 panes. A curious museum of old lawn-mowers is housed in the outbuildings.

TRETOWER, Powys *8 SO12*
Tretower, on the eastern edge of the **Brecon Beacons National Park**, is distinguished by its Court and Castle (AM). Tretower Court is a good and unusually intact example of a 14th- to 15th-century fortified manor, seat of the Vaughan family. Next to it stand the ruins of a Norman 13th-century castle, remarkable for its round keep and tower.

TREWINT, Cornwall *1 SX28*
Wesley's Cottage (OACT) is a small 18th-century building visited by the Methodist leader on his missions to Cornwall between 1744 and 1762. Wesley Day celebrations are held on 24th May.

TRING, Hertfordshire *10 SP91*
This Chiltern town boasts the largest
collection of fleas in the world. Luckily,
they are deceased specimens and, together
with an impressive selection of preserved
birds, mammals and other insects, are
housed in the town's Zoological Museum,
founded by Lionel Rothschild in the late
19th century and now part of the British
Museum.

TROON, Strathclyde *22 NS33*
Golfers say that you can play on a different
course here each day of the week: five of
them are of championship standard. Troon
is on the narrow strip of rocky coast
dividing Ayr Bay from Irvine Bay; with
views across the Firth of Clyde to the Arran
mountains, miles of turf-bordered sands,
and a train service to Glasgow. Lady Isle,
just offshore, is a bird sanctuary.

TROSSACHS, THE, Central *22 NN50*
'The Highlands in miniature', as this
famous landscape area north of Glasgow is
known, has been popular with tourists
since the early 19th century. The
combination of mountains, lochs, rivers
and woods rich in hazel, oak, birch and
mountain ash, proved irresistible to Sir
Walter Scott. His poems *Lady of the Lake*
and *Rob Roy* were both inspired by the
region and were an early cause of its
popularity. Ellen Douglas was the 'Lady'
and Loch Katrine – along with Lochs
Achray and Venacher one of three in the
area – was 'her' Lake. Steamers still ply
Loch Katrine in the summer and call at
Stronachlacher from where Rob Roy's
birthplace at Glengyle can be reached. Part
of the area now lies in the 45,000 acre
Queen Elizabeth Forest Park and all of it is
dominated by Ben Venue (2393ft), to the
east of Loch Katrine.

TROUTBECK, Cumbria *18 NY40*
This Lake District village, delightfully
situated in the wild and beautiful
Troutbeck Valley, extends along the
hillside from Town Head to Town End. To
the north is the high Kirkstone Pass; to the
west is Lake Windermere, into which the
beck flows. Most of Troutbeck's older
houses were built by its 'statesmen' –
yeomen farmers making a subsistence
living from the hillsides. The east window
of the church, rebuilt in the 18th century is
the joint work of Burne-Jones, William
Morris and Ford Madox Brown. Park Farm
(NT) shows visitors how a 2000-acre sheep
station is run. Townend Farm (NT),
previously owned by the same family for
300 years, is a characteristic yeoman's
house built in about 1626. It is whitewashed, with the tall, tapering chimneys
that are a feature of Lake District
architecture, stone-mullioned windows,
carved woodwork, and much of its original
oak furniture.

TROWBRIDGE, Wiltshire *3 ST85*
Trowbridge is the administrative centre of
Wiltshire; a touring centre for the Wiltshire
Downs and the Cotswolds; and a centre of
the weaving trade since the 14th century.
West-of-England broadcloth is still made
here. Among the legacies of Trowbridge's
cloth-based prosperity is the clothiers'
group of stone houses in the Parade, and it
was a clothier who in 1483 endowed the
Perpendicular Church of St James.

THE PANTILES *This charming Regency arcade was originally built for the pleasure of the fashionable set
that came to Tunbridge Wells to take the mineral waters in the 18th century.*

TRURO, Cornwall *1 SW84*
In the Middle Ages this former Stannary
town, lying on Truro River, an arm of the
Fal Estuary, was an important port
exporting mineral ore. It still has a small
port, but is now better known as Cornwall's
administrative centre.
    The cathedral which dominates the town
is comparatively modern. Designed by JL
Pearson, building began in 1879 and it was
the first English Protestant cathedral to be
built since St Paul's in London. Lemon
Street is one of the best preserved examples
in Britain of a Georgian street, and the
Assembly Rooms (1770) were an important
rendezvous for Cornish high society. The
County Museum – arguably the best in
Cornwall – houses a world-famous
collection of minerals. At Lake's Pottery –
one of the county's oldest – modern-day
potters can be seen in action. Wheal Jane
Gold Fields suggests something different,
but is in fact a tin mine opened in 1971 –
the first to do so in Europe for over 50
years.

TUNBRIDGE WELLS, ROYAL, Kent
6 TQ53
This distinguished spa had its heyday
among persons of fashion in the 18th
century, though the waters can still be
drunk. Beau Nash left Bath to be master of
Tunbridge Wells' ceremonies in 1735. Its
waters were first popularised over a
hundred years earlier, by Lord North.
Charles I's wife, Henrietta Maria, came
here after the birth of the future Charles II
in 1630. This was when the building of the
town began: until then, society had camped
out, or lodged in neighbouring towns. The
Church of St Charles the Martyr was built
between 1678 and 1696 in the Baroque
style, with fine ceilings and a wooden
cupola. Tunbridge Wells' oldest street is
the Pantiles, started in 1700, an elegant

ROYAL TUNBRIDGE WELLS *Beautifully
ornamented plasterwork decorates the ceiling of
the 17th-century Church of St Charles the Martyr,
which is dedicated to Charles I.*

arcade enhanced by lime trees; its Italianate
pillars support diverse frontages and a
music balcony. The tiles were laid because
Princess (later Queen) Anne threatened not
to return after her son slipped on the
original walk. Flagstones have replaced all
but a few of the tiles. The town's life has
many facets: the Museum and Art Gallery,
orchestra, theatre, county cricket ground.
Tunbridge Ware, mosaics of all kinds of
local wood, such as holly, yew and plum,
was worked here from the end of the 17th
century until the 1920s.
    Royal Tunbridge Wells has plenty of
parks and gardens; and a fine common,
with outcrops of weathered sandstone
rocks. Such rocks are typical of the area,
the source of its mineral waters, and an
attraction for climbers: the nearby High
Rocks; the Toad Rocks on Rustall
Common; Bowles Rocks, Eridge;
Harrison's Rocks, Groombridge; the
Happy Valley are all outcrops.

TURRIFF, Grampian 27 NJ85

This ancient and thriving market town's present church is 18th-century; its ruined church, originally 11th-century, belonged to the Knights Templar, and has a double belfry and a bell dated from 1559. Turriff retains few other old buildings, but is encircled by castles and tower houses. Craigston Castle (OACT – with written permission), perpetual seat of the Urquhart family, was built from 1604–1607 in the grand Renaissance manner and little altered since Delgaty Castle (OACT – by arrangement) is the 13th-century seat of the Clan Hay.

TUTBURY, Staffordshire 10 SK22

The castle (OACT), perched impressively on a rock, dates from the 11th century and originally belonged to Henry de Ferrers, one of William the Conqueror's barons. One of its three towers was built by John of Gaunt in the 14th century, and from it are fine views over the oak-filled former royal forest of Needwood. Mary Queen of Scots was twice imprisoned here. The village itself, large and old, spreads down the hillside. Its wide main street offers a pleasant variety of Tudor, Georgian and Regency houses. The 'Dog and Partridge', an attractive black-and-white, timbered inn, dates from the 15th century and was once the home of the Curzons of Kedleston Hall. St Mary's Church, originally an 11th-century priory, is one of the finest Norman churches in the Midlands and has a particularly imposing west front.

TWEEDSMUIR, Borders 23 NT02

This pretty village is in pastoral countryside encircled by the Lowland hills, such as the flat-topped 2754ft Broad Law and 2680ft Dollar Law. John Buchan, who took the title of Lord Tweedsmuir, lived here as a boy and made the countryside the background of many of his books. The rivers Annan, Tweed and Clyde all rise about eight miles south-west. Near

Tweed's Well, 1500ft up, a cairn on the lonely Moffat road commemorates the death, in a snowstorm in 1831, of the driver and guard of the Edinburgh mailcoach. The Talla and Fruid Reservoirs hold Edinburgh's water; and from the former, the Gameslope Burn flows down from Molls Cleuch Dod (2571ft), forming on the way the waterfalls of Talla Linfoot. Here the Covenanters held the secret meetings described in *The Heart of Midlothian*.

TWICKENHAM, Greater London 5 TQ17

More of an 'area' than a town or village; undeniably part of Greater London but with a clear identity of its own, Thames-side Twickenham has long been a haunt of the Royal and famous. George II's mistress, Henrietta Howard, Countess of Suffolk, lived in Marble Hill House (OACT) built for her in 1728 by her royal lover. Horace Walpole had built for him Strawberry Hill, a Gothic revival villa and now a Roman Catholic teachers' training college. Walter De La Mare died in 1956 in South End House, part of Montpelier Row which, with Sion Row, forms an unspoilt early 18th-century terrace. Alexander Pope lies buried in the churchyard of St Mary's, built between 1713 and 1714 by John James. Another Twickenham church – All Hallows – is unusual in that, although modern, it has had a tower transplant from one of Wren's 17th-century City churches. The only surviving part of the 18th-century Orleans House – the fine Octagonal room designed by James Gibbs in 1736 – is now in use as an art gallery. York House, mainly dating from the 17th century, is now the Town Hall. The famous rugby ground has been the headquarters of the Rugby Union since 1907.

TWYCROSS, Leicestershire 10 SK30

Twycross Zoo Park houses a collection of large animals, particularly primates – gorillas, orang-utans and chimpanzees. You can also see reptile and butterfly houses, and all kinds of exotic birds.

TYNDRUM, Central 26 NN33

Anglers and climbers alike are drawn to this isolated village in Strath Fillan, near its junction with Glen Lochy. The climbers, spoilt for choice, make for the imposing nearby peaks – Beinn Chaluim (3354ft), Creag Mhor (3305ft) and, further south-west Ben Lui (3708ft) well known for its north corrie.

TYNEMOUTH, Tyne & Wear 20 NZ36

A rather unusual animal, Tynemouth is an industrial seaside resort. It lies on the north side of the Tyne Estuary, a home of shipbuilding and other heavy coal and steel-based industries. Yet it has another side to its character: for years north-easterners have holidayed and day-tripped here, attracted by some of the finest but least known beaches in England, such as Long Sands and Prior's Haven. The sheer cliffs and high river banks offer fine views of the busy River Tyne and the North Pier offers a three-quarter-mile long trip out to sea without getting into a boat. The ruins of the moated castle-towers, gatehouse and keep, dating mainly from the 11th and 14th centuries – stand on the cliffs overlooking the pier. Alongside are the remnants of the

TUTBURY *Castle ruins include the tower where Mary Queen of Scots was imprisoned.*

nave and chancel of the former Priory, itself built to replace the original Anglo-Saxon foundation destroyed by the Danes. The main street contains some fine 18th-century houses, and the town also boasts an imposing monument to Admiral Lord Collingwood, who led the British Fleet at Trafalgar.

TYSOE, Warwickshire 10 SP34

Tysoe is divided into three parts: Upper Tysoe, which has a 16th-century manor house; Middle Tysoe, distinguished by the splendid, late-11th-century Church of the Assumption, and cottages with Venetian-style windows and doors; and the small hamlet of Lower Tysoe.

Tysoe has two claims to fame. The first is the Great Red Horse of Tysoe, alas scarcely visible now, cut into Sun Rising Hill. This is the source of the ancient tradition of festivals of the Red Horse; of local legends of a giant horse; and of the name Red Horse Vale. The Institute of Archaeology's investigation of the Great Red Horse, and aerial photographs, concluded that Tysoe has had five horses at various times: three cut into the hill called Hangings, between Lower and Middle Tysoe.

TYWYN, Gwynedd 7 SH50

This seaside town, with miles of sand, is on the edge of the **Snowdonia National Park**, at the foot of the Cader Idris range. The head of the Talyllyn Railway (see **Talyllyn**) is Wharf Station, adjoining the Railway Museum.

The Church of St Cadfan – founder of the Bardsey Island monastery – originally 6th-century, but rebuilt in the 19th century, preserves its early Norman nave. Inside, St Cadfan's stone is inscribed with perhaps the earliest example of written Welsh. Tywyn's church, vicarage and school are the distinctive work of the Victorian architect GE Street.

UCKFIELD, E Sussex 5 TQ42

Two houses in this small Ouse Valley town open their gardens to the public at certain times. The Beeches, a 16th-century farmhouse, has a sunken garden and fine yews, whilst Horsted Place, a Victorian Gothic mansion, gives special emphasis to herbs and fragrant flowers. Neither house is normally open to the public.

UDDINGSTON, Strathclyde 22 NS66

Calderpark Zoo has a wide range of mammals, reptiles and birds, housed in spacious new enclosures and buildings. There are special displays for children, and the grounds also include picnic sites.

UFFINGTON, Oxfordshire 4 SU38

From Uffington the most famous of the white horses is clearly visible – the semi-abstract quality of its 374ft-long figure suggesting that it may have been cut by Iron-Age Celts, though the theory that it commemorates King Alfred's 9th-century victory over the Danes remains popular. White Horse Hill, a well-known viewpoint overlooking five counties, retains traces of an Iron-Age camp. Nearby are the earthworks of Uffington Castle (AM), standing on the line of the ancient Ridgeway. One-and-a-half miles south-west of the village lies the so-called Wayland's Smithy (AM), a Stone-Age barrow within a larger, later one; how the legend of Wayland the Smith, a mythical Scandinavian figure, the maker of invincible weapons, came to be associated with the much earlier barrow, is unknown. Uffington's church has some fine Early English work, with an octagonal tower, a set of 11 consecrated crosses and many lancet windows.

ULLAPOOL, Highland 29 NH19

Ullapool was founded in 1788 to expand the herring industry and it is still a traditional fishing town, though today it also attracts deep sea anglers, especially those in pursuit of shark. Its lovely setting near the mouth of Loch Broom has has made it a popular resort and touring centre; the attractive Outer Loch islands – only one of which is now occupied – can be reached by motor launch, and to the north the Inverpolly National Nature Reserve offers sanctuary to wildcat, pine-marten and golden eagle in a 27,000-acre expanse of unspoiled Highland countryside. One of the original buildings of Ullapool houses the Lochbroom Highland Museum.

ULVA, ISLE OF, Highland 25 NM43

The caves and basalt cliffs of Ulva, the island traditionally associated with the popular ballad *Lord Ullin's Daughter*, have attracted some famous visitors – Dr Johnson, Boswell, Sir Walter Scott and Livingstone among them. It is separated from Mull (see **Inner Hebrides**) only by the tiny Sound of Ulva, and a passenger ferry links the two.

UNAPOOL, Highland 29 NC23

At Unapool the waters of Loch Glencoul and Loch Glendhu come together, and a ferry operates just to the north, at Kylesku, on the narrows which divide these two stretches of water from Cairnbawm. The road to the south passes the seven peaks of Quinag, and Eas Coul Aulin, Britain's highest waterfall, plunges from 2541ft Glas Bheinn, its sheer drop of well over 600ft exceeding that of Niagara Falls.

UPNOR, Kent 6 TQ77

The ruins of a 16th-century castle (AM), probably built with stone taken from Rochester's medieval walls, face the River Medway; Queen Elizabeth I reviewed the fleet here in 1581, and the castle saw action (though ineffectively) when the Dutch sailed up the river in 1667. The training ship, *Arethusa*, is now moored in the Medway. The Whittington Stone, named after the one-time Lord Mayor of London, marks the boundary rights of local fisherman.

UPTON CRESSETT, Shropshire 9 SO69

Upton Cressett Hall (OACT), set in beautiful Shropshire countryside and surrounded by attractive gardens, is an Elizabethan manor house with a Great Hall dating back to the 14th century.

UPTON HOUSE, Warwickshire 10 SP34

About seven miles north-west of Banbury stands Upton House (NT), a William-and-Mary mansion set in terraced gardens that rise gently to the woodland behind. The house contains interesting tapestries and furniture, fine Sèvres porcelain and a collection of pictures which includes work by Stubbs and Breughel.

UPTON-ON-SEVERN, Hereford & Worcester 9 SP84

This little market town of old-fashioned shops and inns is remarkably unspoiled; many of its houses are Georgian or older, and the 14th-century tower of the demolished church (surmounted by an 18th-century octagonal dome and cupola) looks out over the meadows of the River Severn. Two of Upton's inns are of particular interest – the Bell, which has a real bell as its sign, and the White Lion, which features in Fielding's novel, *Tom Jones*.

USK, Gwent 8 SO30

The old market town of Usk is an established touring centre, set as it is between the **Brecon Beacons National Park** and the Wye Valley; its situation on the River Usk also makes it popular with those seeking a fishing holiday. The town itself is built above the remains of Burrium, a Roman settlement eight miles north of that at **Caerleon**. It is overlooked by the ruins of a Marcher lord's stronghold dating back to the 12th century and dismantled after its support of the Royalist cause in the Civil War. St Mary's Church, parts of which are 700 years old, was once attached to a Benedictine priory of nuns. It has a fine Tudor screen and a 17th-century pulpit.

UTTOXETER, Staffordshire 10 SK03

Locally pronounced Utchettor, this market town on the River Tean, has held its charter, granted by Henry III, since 1251. A sculpture on the market place conduit recalls how Samuel Johnson, in his 70s, did 'penance' for his boyhood refusal to look after his father's bookstall, standing bareheaded in the market place in the rain, and a ceremony recalling the incident is held here each September.

THE FLEECE INN *at Bretforton in the Vale of Evesham dates from the 13th century and is now in the care of the National Trust. It houses valuable collections of Stuart pewterware and antique furniture.*

V

VALE OF EVESHAM. Hereford & Worcester   9, 10 SP04

Much of the fertile land south and east of **Evesham** is given over to fruit growing and market gardening; the massed blossoms of orchards and flower fields are famous for their beauty in spring and early summer, and the area is particularly well-known for its fine asparagus. Evesham itself is a town of historic significance; the Avon is navigable to small craft here, and a regatta takes place each May. Many of the surrounding villages are of interest: Offenham is one of the few places still to have a maypole; the mainly modern development of Badsey contains a timber-framed manor house which was once an infirmary for the monks of Evesham; Middle Littleton has the biggest tithe barn in the county and a perfect little village church, and Bretforton the famous 600-year-old Fleece Inn and several interesting dovecotes; Cleeve Prior is a prosperous village of broad streets and stone cottages set round a village green.

VALLE CRUCIS ABBEY, Clwyd   14 SJ24

The existing buildings of Valle Crucis Abbey (AM), set below the famous 1500ft Horseshoe Pass two miles north-west of **Llangollen**, date mainly from the 13th century. It was founded in 1201 by Madog ap Gruffydd, Prince of Powys, for Cistercian monks. A good deal of the church survives, including the west front, restored by Sir George Gilbert Scott; four

VIRGINIA WATER

An unexpected sight here is the genuine totem pole from British Columbia which stands by the lake.

windows – one rose and three Early English in style – surmount an elaborately carved doorway. The remains of the monastic buildings, lying to the south and at one time used as a farmhouse, include a Chapter House with fine vaulting. The Abbey's name means 'Vale of the Cross', referring to Eliseg's pillar (AM), which was erected in 603.

VERYAN, Cornwall   1 SW93

The delightful village of Veryan lies in a sheltered position in a wooded valley and produces a wealth of sub-tropical trees and plants. It is famous for its five curious round houses – whitewashed, thatched and surmounted by a cross – standing two at each end of the village and one in the middle. Legend has it that they were built by a vicar for his five daughters; they were made round so that the devil could find no corners in which to lurk. The Church of St Symphorian, named after a third-century French martyr, contains a Norman font. Two miles south-west of the village is Gerrans Bay, overlooked by Nare Head. Nearby Caerhays Castle (not open) was used in the television production of Daphne du Maurier's *Rebecca*.

VIRGINIA WATER, Surrey   5 SU96

This 160-acre artificial lake at the south-eastern corner of Windsor Great Park, laid out by the Duke of Cumberland in 1746, offers good boating and is surrounded by pleasant picnic spots; the Valley and Heather Gardens are attractive, and Kurume Punch Bowl is a mass of different coloured azaleas. The Totem Pole is genuine and was raised in 1958 to commemorate the centenary of British Columbia. The colonnade of pillars on the south shore was brought from Leptis Magna and set up here on the instructions of George IV.

VOWCHURCH, Hereford & Worcester   8 SO33

Vowchurch stands at the heart of the Golden Valley – whose picturesque name probably stems from a misunderstanding by the Normans, who translated *Dwr* (the Welsh word for 'water') as *d'or* ('of gold').

W

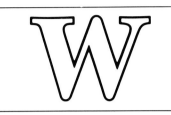

WADDESDON, Buckinghamshire   10 SP71

The Manor (NT) of this picturesque village is a mock-Renaissance château, built in the 19th century for Baron Ferdinand de Rothschild. As well as personal mementoes of the family, it contains paintings by Gainsborough, Reynolds, Romney and Rubens, whilst the fine collection of furniture includes writing tables that belonged to Marie Antoinette and Louis XVI; there is also a museum of small arms. The gardens are formal, with sculptures brought from France, Italy and the Netherlands grouped about fountains, but the grounds also include two deer enclosures and a well-stocked aviary.

WADEBRIDGE, Cornwall   1 SW97

Wadebridge is connected with Egloshayle, on the other side of the Camel Estuary, by one of the finest medieval bridges in Britain; it is 320ft long, and originally had 17 arches, though only 14 remain today. Its building was instigated by the Vicar of Egloshayle, who worried about his Wadebridge parishioners making the dangerous ferry-crossing to church. On an arm of the estuary two miles north is the Walmsley Bird Sanctuary, noted for its geese and waders. The Cornish Motor Museum contains displays of vintage cars and old traction engines.

WADENHOE, Northamptonshire   11 TL08

Wadenhoe's Norman church, St Michael and All Angels, stands on an escarpment above the banks of the River Nene and has an unusual saddleback tower and a font roughly carved with a medieval head. Farmhouses and thatched stone cottages line the main street and there is an old mill beside the ford. A Rural Implements Museum is housed in outhouses belonging to deserted Lifford Hall, about two miles to the east.

WALBERSWICK, Suffolk   12 TM47

No longer a busy port, Walberswick has mellowed into a pleasant residential village, its substantial houses set round an attractive green. A passenger ferry links the village with **Southwold**. The shore is more sandy than many in the area, and the dunes are interspersed with holiday homes; these dunes, which proved an inadequate barrier against the floods of 1953, have been planted with marram grass in the hope of providing a more substantial sea defence. The National Nature Reserve which overlooks the Blythe Estuary provides sanctuary for waders and rare birds.

BROOKLANDS IN ITS HEY-DAY

Between 1907 and 1939 Brooklands racing circuit, near Weybridge, was an essential proving ground for the blossoming British motor industry. The Members' Banking, round which Sir Henry Birkin stormed in his 4½-litre 'blown' Bentley in 1930 (below) is, sadly, now derelict and overgrown.

WALKERBURN, Borders   24 NT33
This textile village on the River Tweed was founded in 1854 by Henry Ballentyne, when he and his sons built the first woollen mill to incorporate all the processes of cloth production under one roof. Tweedvale Mill Museum, the Scottish Museum of Wool Textiles, is sited here and illustrates the history of the industry from its earliest days, including demonstrations of hand spinning and weaving.

WALLASEY, Merseyside   14 SJ29
Though connected by wharves and docks to the busy industrial and shipbuilding centre of Birkenhead, Wallasey is the 'playground' of this Merseyside area. Set on the south-eastern tip of the Wirral peninsula, if offers safe bathing from good beaches, together with piers, promenades and parks. The country's first Hovercraft service operated from Wallasey to **Rhyl** in 1962.

MAURETANIA

For 22 years this great liner held the Atlantic Blue Riband – a unique distinction. When she was 20 years old she steamed at a remarkable 29 knots to rescue a disabled cargo ship, and during World War I she was used as a hospital ship.

WALLSEND, Tyne & Wear   20 NZ36
This River Tyne town, standing at the eastern end of **Hadrian's Wall**, is traditionally involved in engineering and shipbuilding: *Mauretania*, the Cunard liner that held the Atlantic crossing record for 22 years, was launched here in 1907. In 1967 the new Tyne Road Tunnel was opened east of the town.

WALPOLE ST PETER, Norfolk
11 TF51
This marshland village is dominated by the impressive church of St Peter, the 'Queen of the Marshes'. The interior is noted for a 17th-century screen which extends its full width and for the 15th-century carving on its stalls and benches. An unusual feature is the 'hudd' (or 'hood') – a movable shelter once used at funerals which took place in bad weather.

WALSALL, W Midlands   9 SP09
The nickname of the town's football team – the Saddlers – recalls Walsall's traditional role as a leather-working centre specialising in fine saddlery; now this typical Black-Country town embraces 100 industries. Its oldest building is St Matthew's Church, whose crypt dates from the early 13th century and whose high altar is built above a vaulted archway that once spanned a road. Modern Rushall Church adjoins the remains of a 14th-century castle which was dismantled after the Civil War. A statue in the town centre commemorates Sister Dora (Dorothy Pattison), who spent the last 12 years of her life nursing the sick and the poor of the area in the late 19th century. A plaque in Bradford Street marks the birthplace of Jerome K. Jerome, author of *Three Men in a Boat*. The Museum and Art Gallery in the Central Library contains works by Blake, Degas, Van Gogh and Epstein.

WALSINGHAMS, THE, Norfolk
12 TF93
In 1061 a shrine was built at Little Walsingham by Lady Richeld, commanded to do so in a vision. It remained a centre for pilgrimage – numbering kings among its visitors – until the Reformation; the cult was revived in the late 19th century and the building of the New Shrine was completed in 1937. The ruins of the old priory, including a 15th-century gateway, can be seen in the grounds of the modern abbey. Of the original shrine, which probably stood to the north of the north aisle of the priory church, nothing remains. The restored 15th-century Church of St Mary houses a Seven-Sacraments font and an Epstein sculpture, 'The Risen Christ'. Picturesque old houses surround the village square, and a nearby 18th-century Court Room contains the Shirehall Museum. Great Walsingham's church contains magnificently carved bench ends.

WALTHAM ABBEY, Essex   5 TL30
Waltham Abbey (AM) was founded on the edge of Epping Forest by King Harold, and his body is believed to have been buried here after his death at the Battle of Hastings. The cloister entrance and the nave of the church date from the 12th century, displaying some of the oldest Norman workmanship in the country. A second phase of building took place in the 14th century, and Harold's Bridge and the gatehouse date from this period. Much of the abbey was destroyed at the Reformation, but the remains are magnificent, and the restored church contains fine monuments and stained glass and has an undercroft museum.

WALTON & WEYBRIDGE, Surrey
5 TQ06
Walton appears in the Domesday Book as 'Waletona', listed as having a church, two mills and a fishery; the same church still stands, though altered and restored over the centuries. The town has now merged with Weybridge – a similarly ancient settlement with a Norman church – which was the site of two royal residences in the Tudor period and the setting for Henry VIII's marriage to Catherine Howard. Weybridge is a town of 'firsts', having been the home of the world's first racing track, Brooklands, the world's first air-travel booking office and Britain's first aerodrome.

WALTON-ON-THE-NAZE, Essex
12 TM22
On the Naze, which juts into the North Sea just south of Harwich, stands the great Naze Tower, set there to warn shipping of the treacherous West Rocks offshore. The resort of Walton on the Naze, with its 800ft-long pier, offers fine sands, good bathing and facilities for golf.

WANLOCKHEAD, Dumfries & Galloway   22 NS81
Wanlockhead, situated at 1380ft above sea level, is Scotland's second highest village. It is surrounded by the Lowther Hills, Green Lowther rising to 2403 feet – and this remote area provided refuge from persecution to Covenanters in the 17th century. Gold, silver and lead have been mined here since Roman times, and the remains of old mine workings can be seen around Wanlockhead and the neighbouring village of Leadhills; the Museum of Scottish Lead Mining, with its one-and-a-half-mile Visitor Walkway, stands at the north end of Mennock Pass.

WANSFORD, Cambridgeshire
11 TL09

Two bridges span the River Nene at Wansford – the modern one, and a 16th-century one with ten fine arches. The Haycock Inn, which dates from the 17th century, has a quaint sign recalling the story of drunken Barnaby and records that Queen Victoria slept in one of the bedrooms set around its courtyard. The Nene Valley Railway (OACT) passes through Nene Park on its journey from Wansford to Olton Mere; various British and Continental steam locomotives and rolling stock operate on five miles of standard-gauge track.

WANTAGE, Oxfordshire   *4 SU48*

A quiet town with cobbled streets and 17th- and 18th-century houses, Wantage lies at the foot of the Berkshire Downs in the Vale of the White Horse. King Alfred the Great was born here in 849 and his statue stands in the market place. Parts of the Church of Sts Peter and Paul date back to the 13th century; it has a fifteenth-century hammerbeam roof, some fine woodcarvings and the tombs of members of the Fitzwaryn family, into which Dick Whittington married. In 1873 the first steam tramway in the country began operation here, the line remaining open until 1948.

WARDOUR CASTLE, Wiltshire
3 ST92

Wardour Castle (OACT), a magnificent Palladian mansion near Shaftesbury which was once the home of the Arundel family, now houses a girls' school; the beautifully decorated Baroque chapel adjoining it contains some fine art treasures. The existing 18th-century building is a replacement for a 14th-century hexagonal castle which fell into decay after being badly damaged in the Civil War and whose ruins (AM) stand in landscaped gardens about a mile away.

WARE, Hertfordshire   *5 TL31*

The Great Bed of Ware – 10ft wide by 11ft long, and mentioned in Shakespeare's Twelfth Night – originally stood in the Saracen's Head Inn here, but it is now on display in the Victoria and Albert Museum. It was in Ware that Lady Jane Grey was proclaimed Queen in 1553, and William Cowper immortalised the town as John Gilpin's destination in his famous poem. The River Lea once carried heavy traffic connected with the local malting industry but it is now used only by pleasure boats and anglers. The town has several notable old buildings, including Bluecoat House with its 15th-century timbering and the early 17th-century Canons Maltings.

WAREHAM, Dorset   *3 SY98*

Wareham, still encircled by ancient earthworks, was a market town in Saxon times; its centre is Georgian, however, rebuilt after an extensive fire. Set on the River Frome, just above the Frome Marshes, it is popular with fishermen and small boat enthusiasts. Extensive heathland between Wareham and Puddletown, now partly wooded as the result of an afforestation scheme, is the basis of Hardy's fictional Egdon Heath, and there are several nature reserves in the area. Lawrence of Arabia had connections with the town and St Martin's Church contains a fine sculpture of him in Arab dress by Eric Kennington, whilst a small museum on St John's Hill has numerous Lawrence relics.

WARKWORTH, Northumberland
24 NU20

Overlooking Alnmouth Bay stand the impressive ruins of Warkworth Castle (AM), probably built by the 1st Earl of Northumberland in the 12th century, and used by Shakespeare as the setting for part of *Henry IV*. The curious 14th-century Hermitage (OACT), with its small chapel hewn from solid rock, can be reached by rowing boat. An old bridge with a rare bridge tower at one end spans the River Coquet, and the stone spire of the Norman church is one of only two ancient examples in the county. In 1715, during the Jacobite Rising, the Old Pretender was proclaimed King James III at the old cross in the market place. The village itself has many attractive old terraces.

WARMINSTER, Wiltshire   *3 ST84*

The beautiful houses and attractive cottages of Warminster, together with two fine inns, are a legacy of the prosperity it gained in the 18th century as a wool town and corn market. The church, though much rebuilt, retains a 14th-century nave, and the Grammar School (founded in 1707) numbers Dr Arnold of Rugby and Dean Stanley among its former pupils. Two miles to the west, 800ft Cley Hill (NT) rises on the Ridgeway, the prehistoric route which ran from South Devon to the Wash.

WARRINGTON, Cheshire   *14 SJ68*

The industrial town of Warrington, situated on the Manchester Ship Canal, has been designated a New Town and is developing rapidly. Its traditional involvement is in clockmaking, but ironworks and soap factories are the modern employers of labour. Bank Hall, originally the home of the Patten family but serving as the Town Hall since 1872, was designed in 1750 by James Gibbs, who was also probably the architect of Holy Trinity Church. A few old houses remain, and the Barley Mow is a fine half-timbered inn. In 1848 Warrington became the first town to have a public library supported by the rates; it has two museums – the Municipal Museum and Art Gallery in Bond Street and the Military Museum of the South Lancashire Regiment. Near the bridge stands a statue of Cromwell, who entered the town in 1648 after his victory at Preston.

WARMINSTER *Several military camps in the area and the Army's School of Infantry at Warminster use Salisbury Plain for practising manoeuvres.*

Warwick, Warwickshire 10 SP26

County Town on the River Avon

❛That shire which wee the hart of England well may call,

....

Brave Warwick; that abroad so long advanc't her beare,
By her illustrious Earles renowned every where;❜

MICHAEL DRAYTON, *Poly Olbion, (1612)*

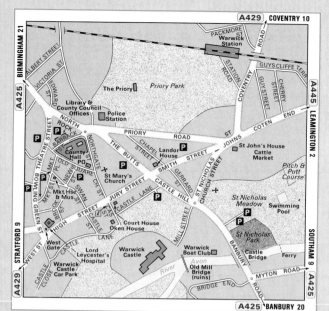

The county of which Warwick is the county town is called by many, and has been since at least Tudor times, the 'heart of England'. It is a splendid town, standing on a rise above the River Avon at the meeting point of many roads. Originally founded by Ethelfleda, a daughter of Alfred the Great, in about 914, Warwick became an important borough under the Normans. It is dominated by its great medieval castle, built by the Beauchamps, who were the first Earls of Warwick, and enlarged and beautified by the Dudleys, descendants of Ambrose Dudley for whom Elizabeth I had revived the then defunct title, and later by the Grevilles, who were granted it in 1759 and have held it ever since.

In 1694 the centre of Warwick was almost completely destroyed by fire; the few medieval buildings that escaped lie round the edges of the 18th-century buildings that constitute much of the present-day centre, in streets such as Castle Street, Bridge End, and Mill Street. The finest of all the medieval buildings are Lord Leycester's Hospital and Oken House. The hospital was established in 1571 as a home for military veterans (a function it still fulfils today); the buildings incorporate Westgate, one of the two remaining medieval gateways. The other, Eastgate, stands at the opposite end of the High Street. Of the many fine buildings erected after the fire, the Court House, containing the Tourist Information Centre, and Shire Hall,

home of the County Court, are the most outstanding public buildings. Beneath the octagonal courtrooms of the Shire Hall is the old town dungeon, where as many as 50 prisoners were sometimes confined, shackled, in a single small room. Northgate House and Abbotsford, now the Registrar's house, are the best of the post-fire town houses. A landmark for miles around is the 174ft tower of St Mary's Church. This, and the nave and aisles were rebuilt after the fire, but the crypt, chancel, chapter house and the magnificent Beauchamp Chapel, containing the tombs of the Earls of Warwick and their families, display Norman and 14th-century architecture.

BRIDGE END *This group of brick and timber cottages is one of the few that survived the devastating fire of 1694. Behind the cottages can be seen the massive medieval towers of Warwick Castle.*

PLACES TO SEE

The Castle Most of the buildings of this great fortress date from the 14th century and later. The massive gatehouse is flanked by two forbidding towers: Guy's Tower and Caesar's Tower. There is an extensive collection of weaponry in the Armoury, and there are many famous paintings by European masters in the State Apartments. The spacious park was landscaped by Capability Brown in the 18th century.

Lord Leycester's Hospital This fine range of medieval buildings, some dating from the 14th century when they formed the Guild House of St George, was converted by Robert Dudley, a favourite of Elizabeth I, into a hospital for old soldiers.

Oken House An outstanding example of a timbered merchant's house, now containing a fascinating collection of old dolls.

St John's House Standing just east of the town, this 17th-century mansion houses a branch of the County Museum, displaying crafts, costume and musical instruments. On the first floor is the Museum of the Royal Warwickshire Regiment.

Warwickshire Museum The Sheldon Tapestry Map of the county is the pride of the collection of local history housed in the 17th-century Market Hall.

Warwickshire Yeomanry Museum Housed in the Court House, the museum has military exhibits and paintings dating back to 1794.

WARWICK CASTLE *The engraving shows its massive size. Most of it was built by the Beauchamp family, the first Earls of Warwick.*

WASHFORD, Somerset *2 ST04*
Cleeve Abbey (AM) is a ruined Cistercian
monastery dating from the 13th century
and preserving some interesting wall-
paintings. Bardon Manor (OACT) was
built in the 14th century and is said to be
haunted; it houses an exhibition of
paintings and craftwork by West Country
artists.

WASHINGTON, Tyne & Wear
20 NZ35
A New Town, intended eventually to have
a population of 80,000, is developing in the
expanding colliery area around
Washington. In the original village stands
17th-century Washington Old Hall (NT),
the home of George Washington's ancestors
before they moved to **Sulgrave**, in
Northamptonshire, where their manor has
been restored as a museum. Three miles to
the south-east rises the lofty Penshaw
Monument (NT), built in 1844 to
commemorate the 1st Duke of Durham.
On the north bank of the Wear the
Wildfowl Trust maintains a 103-acre park
(OACT) where visitors can see a
comprehensive collection of the world's
waterfowl against a background of
attractively landscaped surroundings.

WATFORD, Hertfordshire *5 TQ19*
Watford is a busy modern town, the largest
in Hertfordshire and involved in a
multitude of industries (the chief being
printing and brewing). The old town is still
in evidence, however – notably in the group
of ancient buildings round the flint-built
Church of St Mary. The Bedford
Almshouses were founded in 1580 and the
Elizabeth Fuller Free School in 1704. The
church itself is restored Perpendicular, the
Essex Chapel dating from 1595.
Cassiobury, to the west of the town centre,
is now merely an attractive public park
through which the River Gade and the
Grand Union Canal flow, but the mansion
that once stood within it was the home of
the Earls of Essex.

WEALD, THE, Kent *6 TQ53*
This area of broken country between the
North and South Downs, Kipling's
'wooded, dim blue goodness of the Weald',
was once part of the Forest of Anderida;
today there are still wooded areas in which
wild deer roam, notably the forests of St
Leonards and Ashdown. Much of the
British navy was built of oak from these
woodlands, and the wood was also used to
smelt Sussex iron, many of the hammer
ponds that turned the waterwheels of the
forges still existing. Much of the cleared
land has been given over to orchards and to
the hop fields, with their oast houses.

WEDNESBURY, W Midlands *9 SP09*
The Black Country town of Wednesbury
has large iron and steel works and is well-
known for the manufacture of railway
rolling stock, metal pressings for the motor
industry and steel tubes. The Church of St
Bartholomew has an unusual 15th-century
lectern which depicts a fighting cock.

WEEM, Tayside *26 NN84*
Castle Menzies (OACT), one of the 12 most
important castles in the country, is a fine
example of a Z-plan fortified tower dating
from the 16th century. It now houses a
small museum.

THE WEALD *Hammer-ponds such as this one near Lower Beeding are a distinctive feature of the
Wealden countryside. They were created in the 17th century to provide power for the iron industry.*

WEETING, Norfolk *12 TL78*
Weeting Castle (AM) is a ruined fortified
manor house dating from the 11th century;
sections of flint walling standing in a
rectangular enclosure are the only remnants
of its three-storeyed cross-wing. Weeting
Heath is a 338-acre nature reserve.

WELBECK ABBEY, Nottinghamshire
15 SK57
This interesting old house (not open) in its
magnificent park stands on the site of a
12th-century monastery which was granted
to the Whalley family after the Dissolution.
They eventually sold it to Bess of
Hardwick, and one of her descendants, the
1st Duke of Newcastle, built the south
wing in about 1630. The house
subsequently passed to the Dukes of
Portland and remained their property until
the 20th century when it was taken over as
an Army College. The most fascinating
feature of the building is the labyrinth of
passages and suites of rooms that
undermines it – the brainchild of the
eccentric 5th Duke of Portland who became
a recluse with a phobia about being seen by
strangers.

WELFORD-ON-AVON, Warwickshire
10 SP15
The Avon loops round to enclose this
picturesque village on three sides. The
green, amid thatched and timbered houses,
bears a fine chestnut tree and a tall red,
white and blue striped maypole. The
churchyard lych-gate is a replica of one that
stood there from the late 14th century.

WELLAND, Hereford & Worcester
9 SP74
Little Malvern Court (parts, OACT) was
originally part of monastic buildings,
probably reconstructed in the 15th century
when the adjacent Priory Church
underwent extensive restoration. The
original foundations were laid in 1171 and
the north wing dates from the 15th century.
The Priory has a carved rood-screen,
interesting misericords and 14th-century
stained glass.

WELLINGBOROUGH,
   Northamptonshire *10 SP86*
Wellingborough stands in the valley of the
River Nene; there are large ironworks in
the area, and the manufacture of footwear is
also a well-established industry. The two
churches of the town form an interesting
contrast: All Hallows retains traces of
medieval workmanship and has a 17th-
century house as well as a church hall,
whilst St Mary's is a modern building,
designed by Sir Ninian Comper. Cromwell
is said to have stayed at the Hind Hotel,
then an inn, on his way to the Battle of
Naseby in 1645.

WELLINGTON, Somerset *2 ST12*
Three miles south-west of the town, on the
highest point of the Blackdown Hills,
stands the Wellington Monument (NT), an
obelisk erected in 1817 to commemorate
the famous Duke who took his title from
here. The woollen industry has long
flourished in Wellington, and cloths are still
exported to all parts of the world. Some fine
Georgian houses survive, as do two ancient
inns – the 400-year-old Squirrel (now being
converted into a house) and the Three
Cups, first recorded in 1694. The
Perpendicular church has a mid-side stair
turret, a stylistic feature more typical of
Devon.

WELLOW, Avon *3 ST75*
On Wellow's sloping village street stand
cottages of gold-coloured stone, ancient
farm buildings and a fine manor house that
was once the home of the Hungerford
family. It was Sir Thomas Hungerford, the
first recorded Speaker of the House of
Commons, who rebuilt St Julian's Church
in about 1372; a statue over the south porch
shows St Julian – the patron saint of
ferrymen – holding an oar, and fine
wallpaintings in the north chapel date from
the early 16th century. Dr John Bull –
reputed to be the composer of the national
Anthem – was born in Wellow in 1562.
Two miles south-west of the village lies
Stoney Littleton Long Barrow, a neolithic
burial chamber.

MEDIEVAL STRONGHOLDS
CASTLES
The Defence of the Kingdom

Keeps and castles are, with churches, the most prominent of the surviving monuments to the Middle Ages. Whereas the majority of medieval churches are still living monuments which have been restored and adapted to meet the needs of passing generations, castles tend to be fossils which have lost all their original military credibility. A proportion of medieval castles were royal fortresses and the Tower of London, Dover, and Harlech Castles are examples. The majority, however, were private strongholds and were built partly because of the warlike and insecure nature of life in the Middle Ages, but also because society expected that anyone of an aristocratic background would occupy a castle.

THE HISTORY OF FORTIFICATIONS in Britain seems to go right back to the New Stone Age, and a river-flanked promontory at Meldon Bridge near Peebles, which was protected by a palisade of massive timber posts, dates from this period. However, it was in the later Bronze and Iron Ages that defence became a major preoccupation, and hundreds of hillforts and smaller defence works were built during the unsettled centuries between about 1000 BC and the Roman invasion in AD 43. Roman fortifications, in the form of earth-banked camps, forts of timber, earth or stone, long earthworks like the Antonine Wall, Hadrian's Wall and the Saxon shore forts are well known. Unlike the earlier hillforts and most private medieval strongholds, these military works were built according to a coherent vision of broad strategic needs.

THE FIRST MEDIEVAL CASTLES appeared in the form of 'mottes', of which a few were built in the years just before the Norman Conquest in 1066, while a spate of motte-building followed the Conquest as the new lords sought to secure their estates. During the remaining centuries of the medieval period, the design of castles passed through many stages as military architecture was perpetually improved in order to meet the challenges of new developments in siege warfare. In its simplest form, the Norman motte was a ditched, conical earth-mound with a flat summit that was ringed by a timber palisade. Some

mottes, like those at York, Cambridge, or Clun in Shropshire, were massive and imposing, but many others were small and likely to impress only the local peasants. Often the motte was regarded as a last refuge and was linked to a banked and ditched 'bailey' enclosure in which the lord had his main domestic buildings, while a second, outer bailey might provide an extra defensive line. The stone keep or 'donjon' was another important component in Norman military architecture. It was normally built as a simple, massive, rectangular tower, although a rather different and more elaborate design is

beautifully preserved at Castle Rising in Norfolk. Sometimes rectangular stone keeps superseded the wooden palisades on mottes; some keeps were freestanding, while others were built on natural cliffs or knolls. Contrasting designs can be seen at Castle Hedingham in Essex, above Castleton in Derbyshire and at Castle Acre in Norfolk, where the bailey earthworks are still imposing and the motte was crowned by a circular wall or 'shell keep'. While the stone keeps were less vulnerable to fire than the motte palisades, they were susceptible to sapping, particularly when tunnels were driven under their corners.

BRAMBER CASTLE *The Alan Sorrell painting (inset) shows a 12th-century motte and bailey.*
BALLONE CASTLE *(above) on the Dornoch Firth shows a late 15th-century Z-plan design.*

Sometimes attempts were made to counter this threat by providing the towers with broad, splayed bases, as at Hedingham and at Conisbrough near Doncaster. Other responses included the building of rounded corner towers and the surrounding of the keep by an outer curtain wall. A curtain wall with towers in the older rectangular mode which dates from around 1200 is well-preserved at Framlingham in Suffolk, although evolution progressed increasingly in the direction of curtain walls with rounded wall or 'mural' towers which were carefully placed in order to protect every section of the curtain against attack.

THE SUBJUGATION OF WALES by Edward I at the end of the 13th century has given us several of the most impressive and formidable castles in Britain – like Caernarfon, Conwy, Harlech and Beaumaris. In most cases, the military architecture was influenced by the dictates of the local terrain, but at Beaumaris on Anglesey a fairly level site was chosen and the concept of the 'concentric' castle found its fullest expression. A heavily-fortified rectangular stronghold was enclosed by a strong but less formidable barrel-shaped curtain wall that was studded with round towers and moated. The castle still remains a fine example of medieval military architecture.

MILITARY FORTRESSES *Burgh Castle (above) was built by the Romans as part of a chain to defend the East Coast and Bodiam (below), dating from 1385, guarded the River Rother.*

MOST MEDIEVAL ARMIES consisted largely of mercenaries whose loyalty could often be bought. As a result, castle owners tended to distrust their own troops and in later medieval castles an increasing emphasis was placed on massively fortified gatehouses which could serve as a last refuge for the family and some loyal retainers. Such a gatehouse survives at Donnington in Berkshire, although the remainder of the castle is ruined. During the 15th century, the improvements in cannon design led to a strengthening of some castles, while many had gunports inserted in their walls.

DURING THE WARS OF THE ROSES many members of the castle-owning aristocracy perished and in the closing decades of the Middle Ages the Tudor monarchs succeeded in centralising power and imposing their will upon the provincial potentates. As a result, the private fortress passed gradually into redundancy and the emphasis shifted towards the castle built for the purpose of national defence. The culmination of medieval castle design is represented by the Tudor fortresses like Deal in Kent and St Mawes in Cornwall which were strong links in a chain of defenceworks guarding the southern invasion coast. With its cylindrical central tower tightly embraced by two tiers of semi-circular 'lunettes' on which cannon were mounted and its encircling dry moat, Deal Castle, dating from 1540, was more formidable than older castles several times its size. During the

following centuries, the emphasis in England remained on the armouring of the southern coast, with the number and sophistication of the blockhouses and batteries increasing with each new invasion scare. The eruption of the Civil War took the military strategists by surprise, and some venerable castles were hastily pressed into service. Time did not permit the construction of new stone castles, but the hostilities have left a legacy of earthen forts and gun positions, the larger being moated and equipped with projecting triangular corner bastions. A good example survives on the outskirts of Earith in Cambridgeshire.

LESSER STRONGHOLDS are found in many parts of Britain, as well as the formidable royal and private castles of the nobility. The medieval moated manors of the smaller lords are often regarded as being defensive, but often it seems that the moats were really status symbols, mimicking the castle moats of the greater aristocrats. In the North of England however, small but sturdy pele towers reflect a genuine fear of Scottish raiders and they were built as refuges by both landowners and clergy. A good example can be seen in the churchyard at Corbridge in Northumberland. In Scotland and Ireland, many districts remained unstable until well after the close of the Middle Ages and feuds between the local landowning dynasties were common. Small castles, fortified manors and tower houses remained in use and often held garrisons until the 18th century.

WELLS, Somerset   3 ST54

This lovely cathedral city lies at the foot of the Mendip Hills. The Cathedral, with the buildings associated with it, forms England's largest medieval ecclesiastical precinct and the Cathedral itself has a superbly adorned west front. A favourite with visitors is the 14th-century clock, with its moving figures that strike the hours. The moated Bishop's Palace (OACT) has interesting state rooms, and the remains of a 13th-century undercroft and banqueting hall. A medieval gateway, the Bishop's Eye, marks the entrance to the grounds. On the moat are swans that have been trained to ring a bell for food. Wells Museum illustrates the natural history of the Mendips.

WELLS-NEXT-THE-SEA, Norfolk   12 TF94

This small town, in an area of salt marshes, is well-known for its sprats and whelks. It is traditionally a port, and its old houses cluster near the quayside, but it has also developed as a resort, offering good sands at low tide and safe bathing in the creek.

WELNEY, Norfolk   11 TL59

At Welney the Wildfowl Trust maintains a sanctuary for native and migratory birds which covers over 800 acres of the Ouse Washes. As well as a winter refuge for thousands of Bewick's swans and several species of duck, it provides a spring nesting place for ruff, redshank, snipe and black-tailed godwit. Visitors can watch the birds from the observatory or from hides.

WELSHPOOL, Powys   14 SJ20

The Welsh name of this low-lying Severnside town, Y Trallwng, literally means 'the marshy or sinking land'; it became known first as Pool and then as Welshpool to distinguish it from **Poole** in Dorset. Many fine Georgian buildings still stand in today's busy market town, and **Powis Castle** (NT), originally medieval, with late 16th-century plasterwork and panelling, lies one mile to the south. The history of the area is traced in the Powysland Museum, its most notable exhibit being an Iron-Age shield.

The Land of Arthurian Legend
72 miles

Beyond Glastonbury, repository of the Holy Grail and legendary cradle of Christianity in these islands, rises the low range of the Polden Hills, sheltering Sedgemoor where the hapless Duke of Monmouth was defeated by the troops of James II. In the east lies Cadbury Castle, claimed by many to be the Camelot of the Arthurian romance.

Leave **Wells** on A39, the Glastonbury road, and drive through Coxley to **Glastonbury**, turning right for the town centre. At the market cross turn right on to B3151 (SP Meare). From Meare continue for 1¼ miles to the edge of Westhay and turn left (unclassified, SP Shapwick, Bridgwater), then at the T-junction turn left again. At Shapwick church tower turn right on to the Bridgwater road. Make the gradual ascent of the Polden Hills, cross the main road, then turn right on to A39. Continue along the ridge for 5 miles, then descend and bear sharp left over the King's Sedgemoor Drain. Continue, crossing M5, into **Bridgwater**. At the roundabout take the 1st exit, A38, then at the traffic lights turn left on to the Langport road, A372 (for the town centre turn right here). Re-cross M5 and cross

Sedgemoor to **Westonzoyland**. Here turn left, and continue for 2¼ miles to the edge of Middlezoy. Skirt the village, and 1 mile further turn right on to A361 and follow Taunton signs through Othery. In 1¾ miles at Burrow Bridge cross the River Parrett, and immediately turn left (no sign) and follow the river to Stathe. Here follow Curry Rivel signs, and in ¾ mile branch right to cross a railway bridge. Ascend Red Hill, then bear right and in ¾ mile turn left on to A378 to reach **Curry Rivel**. Pass the Bell Hotel and in ¼ mile turn right (unclassified, SP Drayton, Muchelney). Drive through Drayton and at **Muchelney** bear left (SP Langport). In 1 mile at the T-junction turn right, pass Huish Episcopi church, then turn right on to A372, (SP Wincanton). Skirt Long Sutton and in ½ mile turn left on to B3165 (SP Somerton). In 2¼ miles turn right (SP Ilchester) to enter **Somerton**. By the church turn right (SP Ilchester, Yeovil)

and at the end right again on to B3151. In 2¾ miles turn right then left to cross A372, and continue to the edge of Ilchester. At the roundabout turn left (SP Yeovilton, Wincanton). Pass the Fleet Air Arm Museum and in ¼ mile turn right on to the unclassified Queen Camel road. In 2¼ miles, go forward on to A359 (SP Sparkford, Frome) to enter **Queen Camel**. Continue for ¾ mile, then turn right on to A303 to enter **Sparkford**. Bear right, cross the railway bridge, then immediately turn left on to the Frome road, A359. Drive on for 3¼ miles, then branch left on B3152 to reach Castle Cary. Turn left and left again following signs Bath, Bristol, and in 1 mile turn left on to A371 (SP Shepton Mallet). Shortly bear right across a railway bridge and in ½ mile, at Brook House Inn, turn left (unclassified, SP Alhampton). At **Alhampton** bear right and continue to Ditcheat. Entering **Ditcheat** turn left at the T-junction, then right at the Manor House Inn. Beyond the church bear left (SP East Pennard) and drive to Wraxall. At the crossroads turn right on to A37. Ascend and at the top turn left, unclassified (SP East Pennard), then in ½ mile turn right (SP Pilton). Entering Pilton pass a tithe barn, then at the crossroads turn left. At the church, turn left again (SP Shepton Mallet) and continue to the T-junction where turn right on to A361. In 1 mile turn left on to B3136 and drive to Shepton Mallet. From here follow signs for Wells, and take A371 for the return journey to Wells.

PLACES TO SEE

Wells The cathedral, with its elaborate clock, is magnificent. The Bishop's Palace is famous for its swans and gardens.

Glastonbury The tor and the abbey ruins are associated with King Arthur. Legend has it that Joseph of Arimathea first came here, with a part of the Crown of Thorns, from which the famous thorn tree is said to have sprung.

Sedgemoor The battlefield where Charles II's natural son, the Duke of Monmouth, was defeated by James II.

Muchelney Extensive remains of a Benedictine Abbey (AM) can be seen here. Also a 14th-century Priest's House (NT).

Yeovilton The Fleet Air Arm Museum displays the history of marine aviation.

Cadbury Castle Stone-age and Bronze-age man occupied this site.

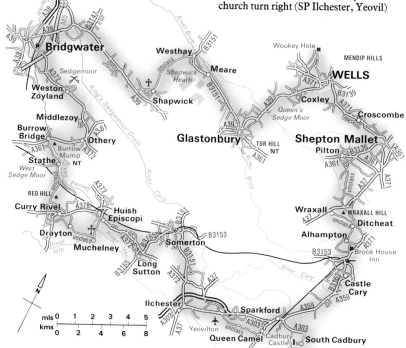

WEMBWORTHY, Devon *2 SS60*
The Ashley Countryside Collection
(OACT), at Ashley House, incorporates a
unique collection of 48 breeds of British
sheep, including rare species. Displays also
include the tools and workshops of
wheelwrights, coopers, blacksmiths and
other country craftsmen.

WENDENS AMBO, Essex *11 TL53*
The name of this attractive small village
commemorates the amalgamation of the
parishes of Great and Little Wenden
('ambo' meaning 'both') in 1662. The
Church of St Mary the Virgin contains a
fascinating cycle of 14th-century wall
paintings, a 15th-century carved pulpit and
a 16th-century domed font cover; the lane
leading to it has delightful cottages on one
side and the Hall Barn on the other.

WENDOVER, Buckinghamshire
10 SP80
The old Chiltern town of Wendover stands
on the edge of the ancient Icknield Way; to
its west rises Coombe Hill (NT), at 852ft
the highest point of the Chiltern range, said
to afford a view of St Paul's Cathedral on a
fine day and surmounted by a monument to
Buckinghamshire men who died in the
South African War. Though a busy road
now runs through the town, many quaint
old buildings survive, including the half-
timbered Lion Hotel where Cromwell slept
in 1643 and a windmill and watermill which
have been turned into houses. Bosworth
House – now divided into cottage, house
and Post Office – revealed 16th- and 17th-
century wall paintings when alterations
were being made. Two remain in the house,
though the others were taken to the
Victoria and Albert Museum. The church
is mainly 14th-century, though much
restored, and contains some interesting
carvings and a curious brass to William
Bradshawe.

WENDRON, Cornwall *1 SW63*
A 17th-century lych-gate gives access
to the 14th- to 15th-century church of
Wendron, and the churchyard contains a
very early cross-slab with an incised cross.
This was a tin-mining area, and the Poldark
Mine and Wendron Forge complex is open
to the public, with museums and the West
Country's largest collection of working
antiques, including a 40ft-high beam
engine.

WESSEX
Wessex, the old West Saxon kingdom,
embraced Hampshire, Wiltshire, Dorset,
Somerset and Berkshire; later it also
included Devon and Cornwall. The works
of Thomas Hardy revived interest in
Wessex, for his fictional place-names barely
conceal the vividly-painted communities
and natural features in his books,
Sturminster Newton showing clearly
through the 'Stowcastle' of *Tess of the
d'Urbervilles* and the great heath of *The
Return of the Native* unmistakably
Bockhampton. Wessex also figures
prominently in the legends about the
Round Table, for the earthwork of
Cadbury Castle traditionally marks the site
of Camelot, whilst **Glastonbury** was the
resting-place of the Holy Grail, Dozemary
Pool, the lake from which Excalibur rose,
and **Tintagel** the setting for another
Arthurian castle.

THE WESTBURY WHITE HORSE *carved into the chalk hillside dates from 1778, but a white horse is
believed to have adorned the landscape here since about AD878.*

WEST BROMWICH, W Midlands
9 SP09
'Bromwich' means 'broom village' – a
reference to the fact that this area was once
broom-covered heathland. In the late 18th
century, however, coal-mining led to
industrialisation, and heavy industry is still
much in evidence today. The town's oldest
building is a 14th-century partly-timbered
manor house which has been restored for
use as an inn, whilst Tudor Oak House,
which dates back to the 15th century, has a
curious lantern tower and is used as a
museum.

WESTBURY, Wiltshire *3 ST85*
Moated Palace Green is believed at one time
to have been the site of the residence of the
Kings of Wessex. Georgian houses set
round the market place reflect a later period
of prosperity, when the town was involved
in the weaving industry and was famous for
its glove-making. The restored
Perpendicular church has a central tower
and contains a chained New Testament,
17th- and 18th-century monuments and an
interesting modern screen. Above the town
stands the oldest White Horse in Wiltshire,
probably cut originally in the 9th century
but remodelled to a more 'elegant' shape in
the eighteenth century. Chalcot House
(OACT) is a charming Palladian villa just
over two miles away near the village of
Dilton Marsh.

**WESTBURY-UPON-SEVERN,
Gloucestershire** *9 SO71*
Westbury Court Garden (NT) is the only
surviving example of a Dutch-style water
garden, most having been destroyed by the
craze for landscaping in the 18th century.
This one was derelict for years, its canals
silted and its vegetation wild, but
meticulous restoration has brought it back
to its original appearance – the colonnaded
pavilion rebuilt and the flowers and shrubs
mentioned in the old records replanted.

WESTBURY-ON-TRYM, Avon
3 ST57
Westbury-on-Trym is divided from Bristol
by the 442 acres of the Clifton and
Durdham Downs. The restored 13th- to
15th-century church was once attached to
Westbury College (NT), the 15th-century
tower of which survives from the ancient
College of Priests. A Wildlife Park has been
developed in a nearby secluded valley.
Picturesque Blaise Hamlet, about a mile to
the north of Westbury, has a group of Nash
cottages (NT), a folk museum housed in
Blaise Castle and a three-storey 18th-
century mill (OACT).

WEST CLANDON, *See* **East Clandon**

WEST DEAN, W Sussex *4 SU81*
The Weald and Downland Museum,
England's first organised open-air crafts
display which will eventually include some
40 re-erected old buildings, is sited at
Singleton, near West Dean. West Dean
itself is a charming downland village of flint
and half-timbered houses standing in the
valley of the River Lavant. At West Dean
Gardens (OACT) old tools and implements
– including antique lawnmowers – are on
show in the Museum of the Garden, and the
wild garden is of ecological interest.

WESTERHAM, Kent *5 TQ45*
Quebec House (NT) is a 16th- to 17th-
century house which was once the home of
General Wolfe, of whom it contains relics.
Squerryes Court (OACT) is also connected
with General Wolfe and a cenotaph to him
stands in the grounds. The house contains
fine pictures, china, tapestries and period
furniture, whilst the park is particularly
attractive, with a lake and azaleas and
rhododendrons. Two miles to the south of
the town stands Sir Winston Churchill's old
home, **Chartwell** (NT), now housing a
Churchill Museum and noted for the
beauty of its gardens.

WEST HOATHLY, E Sussex   *5 TQ33*

This village in the heart of the Weald dates back to Saxon times and was once the centre of the iron industry. Its church stands on a ridge with fine views to the south, and smugglers used to signal down the valley from the church tower before meeting at the Cat Inn. They used nearby Gravetye Manor – a fine gabled Elizabethan house which was once the home of the famous garden designer William Robinson and is now a hotel – as a store for contraband goods. The 15th-century Priest's House contains an interesting folk museum. Great-upon-Little, in the grounds of Rockhurst, is a rock formation where a large piece of sandstone is balanced on a smaller one.

WEST MALLING, Kent   *6 TQ65*

Norman influence is evident in West Malling, as it is in its twin village of East Malling also. St Leonard's Tower (AM) is all that remains of a Norman castle built of Kentish ragstone by Bishop Gundulf of Rochester in about 1090. Remains of the Abbey include an 11th-century tower and a Perpendicular gateway. The church – again, with a Norman tower – displays the Royal Arms of James II. The half-timbered Priest's House dates from the 14th-century, and some fine 18th-century houses exist in the area.

WESTONBIRT, Gloucestershire   *3 ST88*

Westonbirt Arboretum (OACT) was founded in 1829 by a local squire, Robert Stainer Holford, and is now part of a 600-acre Forestry Commision development; the Arboretum itself covers 117 acres and extends into Wiltshire. This collection of trees is one of the finest in the country and is particularly beautiful in autumn, though the large banks of rhododendrons also provide a mass of colour in the late spring.

WESTON RHYN, Shropshire   *SJ23*

Tyn-y-Rhos Hall Museum of Victoriana, two miles west of the village near Bron-y-Garth, is a small manor house (OACT), preserved and furnished down to the last detail in the style of the late Victorian period. There is a fascinating family chapel and among the many items of interest on display is a portrait of Charles I.

WESTON-SUPER-MARE, Avon   *3 ST36*

A hundred years ago Weston-Super-Mare was a little fishing village on the Bristol Channel, now it is a popular resort. Holiday-makers are attracted by its splendid sands and good bathing, piers, attractive parks and gardens, two-mile marine parade and golf-course. Worlebury Hill, a mile to the north-east, is topped by an Iron Age Camp (AM) and looks over the islands of Steep Holme and Flat Holme to the Welsh coast. Woodspring Museum, set in the old workshops of the Edwardian Gaslight Company, has displays on transport and the wildlife and minerals of the area; it also portrays scenes from Victorian life – the seaside holiday being particularly appropriate. There is a nature reserve at nearby Brean Down.

WESTON-UNDER-LIZARD, Staffordshire   *9 SJ81*

Seventeenth-century Weston Park (OACT), the seat of the Earls of Bradford, displays a fine collection of pictures and a selection of letters by Disraeli; the huge park – once landscaped by Capability Brown – now contains a miniature railway, an aquarium and a woodland adventure playground in addition to its three original lakes. Just outside the village the Hilton Valley Railway operates five steam and three diesel locomotives on narrow gauge track. The 'Lizard' suffix of the placename refers to a nearby hill.

WEST TARRING, W Sussex see Worthing

WEST WEMYSS, Fife   *23 NT39*

In 1565 the first meeting between Mary Queen of Scots and Darnley took place at West Wemyss, a small Firth of Forth town with a castle dating from the 15th century and a curiously inscribed tollbooth with an outside staircase. The caves in the rocky coastline to the north-east are famous for their Bronze-Age, Iron-Age and early Christian carvings.

WESTWOOD MANOR, Wiltshire   *3 ST85*

Parts of stone-built Westwood Manor (NT) date back to the 15th century, and there are fine Jacobean plaster ceilings. The topiary gardens are interesting, though modern, and an old tithe barn stands nearby.

WEYMOUTH

George III was a familiar figure in Weymouth and this cartoon of the period can be seen in the town's museum. He was the first monarch to bathe in the sea, and by doing so at Weymouth ensured its future as a holiday resort.

After the railway reached the town in 1857 it became an important cross-Channel ferry port (below).

WEST WYCOMBE PARK *Humphry Repton landscaped the grounds around the mansion.*

WEST WYCOMBE, Buckinghamshire
4 SU89

West Wycombe, much of which is under the protection of the National Trust, is a picturesque village. Its old buildings, many of which date back to the 15th century, include a fine inn. West Wycombe Park (NT), partly designed by Robert Adam, was built for Sir Francis Dashwood of Hell-Fire-Club fame in the 18th century, and he also instigated the rebuilding of the church, the large ball on the tower of which is a well-known local landmark and used to be a meeting place for the club. West Wycombe Caves (OACT) are also associated with Dashwood and the Hell Fire Club. West Wycombe Motor Museum is at Cockshoot Farm.

WETHERINGSETT, Suffolk   *12 TM16*

Richard Hakluyt, the author of the famous 16th-century book on English voyages and discoveries, spent the last 26 years of his life as rector here; the 14th-century church, with its carved nave roof, is surrounded by thatched cottages.

WEYHILL, Hampshire   *4 SU34*

Weyhill is an old-established settlement, dating from the 16th century and granted its charter by Queen Elizabeth I. The Hawk Conservancy Park (OACT) contains a specialist collection of birds of prey – including falcons, hawks, vultures, eagles and owls – which are flown daily (weather permitting). Motor racing takes place at Thruxton, to the west.

WEYMOUTH, Dorset   *3 SY67*

Weymouth, a dignified town of fine Georgian houses, was favoured by King George III who once lived at Gloucester House (now a hotel); a statue has been raised to him. Author Thomas Hardy was also well-acquainted with the resort, which appears in his novels under the pseudonym of Budmouth. Weymouth is still popular with holiday-makers, offering good sands, bathing and fishing, together with facilities for golf. There are picturesque alleys to explore in the Melcombe Regis quarter, and a 17th-century house in Trinity Street has been restored and refurnished in contemporary style (OACT). Weymouth is also a port, however, and a terminus for Channel Island ferries.

In the Heart of Hardy's Wessex
60 miles

The Dorset countryside, with its exposed, windswept heaths and rolling downs, stone-built villages and bustling market towns, forms the background to Thomas Hardy's Wessex novels. The Isle of Portland, with its vast stone quarries was for him the 'Isle of Singers'; Dorchester, the county town, was Casterbridge.

From **Weymouth** centre or sea-front follow signs Portland, A354 into the one-way system. Cross the harbour area, and turn right along North Quay, then left to ascend through Rodwell. Later turn left and descend through Wyke Regis, then drive down part of Chesil Bank on to the **Isle of Portland**. At Fortuneswell roundabout take the 2nd exit and follow signs Portland Bill into the one-way system, passing (left) the road to Portland Castle. Continue the ascent through Fortuneswell, up the steep slope of Portland Hill and into **Easton**. At the village centre bear left (SP Southwell, Portland Bill). At **Southwell** turn left (SP Portland Bill) and drive to Portland Bill. Return to Southwell and turn left for Weston and Fortuneswell. Drive through Weston and at St George's Church turn left. At the summit of Portland Hill turn left on to A354 (SP Fortuneswell, Weymouth) and descend to Fortuneswell. Here turn left (one-way) and return to Wyke Regis. At the right-hand bend, on

the ascent, turn left on to B3157 (SP Bridport). Keep following Bridport signs through Charlestown and Chickerell and drive to the edge of Portesham. Here bear left and continue to **Abbotsbury**. At the end of the village, bear right (the unclassified road ahead leads to Abbotsbury Gardens), ascend on to the downs and continue to Burton Bradstock. After a mile pass the turning to West Bay (on left), then in another mile at the roundabout take the 2nd exit for **Bridport**. Leave on the Dorchester road, A35, and drive to **Winterbourne Abbas**. At the end of the village, branch right, B3159 (SP Weymouth) and shortly right again (SP Hardy's Monument, Abbotsbury). Ascend on to downland and in 2½ miles at the crossroads turn left to reach the monument. Descend and in 2 miles turn right onto B3159 to enter **Martinstown**. At the end of the village branch left (unclassified) and in 1¼ miles at the T-junction, turn right on to A35 for **Dorchester**. Leave Dorchester on A354 Weymouth road (on leaving the town, an unclassified road to the right leads to Maiden Castle), and return through Broadwey to Weymouth.

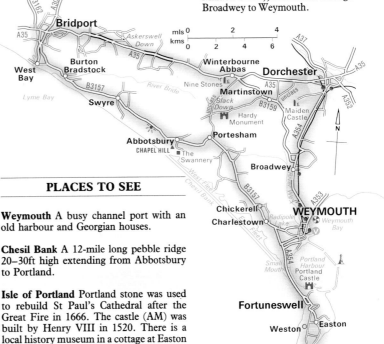

PLACES TO SEE

Weymouth A busy channel port with an old harbour and Georgian houses.

Chesil Bank A 12-mile long pebble ridge 20–30ft high extending from Abbotsbury to Portland.

Isle of Portland Portland stone was used to rebuild St Paul's Cathedral after the Great Fire in 1666. The castle (AM) was built by Henry VIII in 1520. There is a local history museum in a cottage at Easton associated with Thomas Hardy.

Abbotsbury The famous swannery (OACT), originally founded by monks, lies about half a mile south of the village. The gardens (OACT) lie 1½ miles west.

Nine Stones A prehistoric stone circle (AM) half a mile west of Winterbourne Abbas.

The Hardy Monument Not the novelist, but the Hardy who was Nelson's contemporary, is commemorated by an obelisk.

Dorchester Hardy's birthplace (OACT) is at Lower Bockhampton, 2 miles north-east of the county town. The museum, has many items of interest. The old Shire Hall (OACT) is now a memorial to the Tolpuddle Martyrs who were tried here.

Maiden Castle (AM) One of the best-known Iron-Age hillforts in the country.

WHERWELL *Picturesque thatched cottages, a stream and a bridge all contribute to the delightful character of this tiny Hampshire village.*

WHALTON, Northumberland
20 NZ18
At the east end of this pretty village stands the Manor, converted from four village houses by Sir Edwin Lutyens in 1909. Its grounds are occasionally open to the public, and the Whalton Gallery (inside the house entrance) specialises in 18th- to 20th-century watercolours and drawings. St Magdalene's Church, though much restored, dates back to the early 13th century, traces of the original workmanship still being visible in the chancel. The ancient ritual of the baal fire is still observed on the fourth of July, the old Midsummer Eve: cattle used to be driven through the fire to purify them, and at one time the villagers themselves leapt through the flames. Until quite recently, burning branches were carried round the village to defend the fields from blight and the houses from witchcraft.

WHERWELL, Hampshire *4 SU34*
The thatched and timbered cottages of the beautiful village of Wherwell (traditionally pronounced 'Orrell') stand beside a tributary of the River Test. The 19th-century church near the bridge contains part of an Anglo-Saxon cross and two small 14th-century reliefs. The once-famous abbey, founded by King Ethelred's mother, Queen Elfrida in expiation of the murder of her stepson, was destroyed at the Dissolution; fragmentary remains can be seen in the grounds of the 19th-century house known as The Priory.

WHICHFORD, Warwickshire *10 SP33*
The village pumps and wide green of Whichford are surrounded by mullioned stone houses, some with thatched roofs. The castle, of which little remains, and the church are Norman in origin. Mainly 18th-century Whichford House, next to the church, was once the rectory; its gardens are sometimes opened to the public. Two miles to the south of the village are the Rollright Stones, Bronze-Age monolithic circles thought to have been connected with burial ceremonies.

WHIPSNADE, Bedfordshire *11 TL01*
Set in 500 acres of beautiful Chiltern countryside, Whipsnade Park Zoo was originally intended more or less as a convalescent home for sick animals from London Zoo. When it opened in 1931 the provision of large, open enclosures rather than heated cages was a revolutionary step; the experiment was successful, however, and the Zoo's breeding record is so good that about 80 per cent of its 2000 occupants were born there. The conservation of endangered species is high on Whipsnade's list of priorities, rare breeds on display including Black, White and Great Indian Rhinos, North American Bison and Przewalski's Horses. The 'traditional' animals have not been forgotten, however; the Children's Zoo and the dolphins are particularly popular. A novel way of seeing the African Section is via the Whipsnade and Umfolozi Railway – a narrow-gauge, steam-operated line.

WHITBY, N Yorkshire *20 NZ91*
The resort and harbour of Whitby stands in a picturesque situation at the mouth of the River Esk, with the **North Yorkshire Moors National Park** rising behind the town. It has been a fishing town for hundreds of years and was once a whaling port. Terraces of fishermen's cottages rise beneath East Cliff, and a fishing fleet still plies from the harbour. Its name has a place in history, for it was at the Synod of Whitby in 663 that the divided church in England accepted the authority of the Roman Catholic church. The remains of Whitby Abbey (AM) on East Cliff are those of the 13th-century building; the first abbey was founded in 657 by St Hilda, and it was here that the 7th-century monk Caedmon wrote the Song which is considered to mark the beginning of English literature. A cross commemorating him stands nearby in the churchyard of St Mary's, a Norman-towered edifice approached by the 199 Church stairs. On West Cliff stands a statue of Captain Cook, who lived in Whitby as a young man, and his house in Grape Street is marked with a plaque. There is a museum of local history in Pannett Park.

WHITE CASTLE, Gwent *8 SO31*
The ruins of White Castle (AM), a Marcher stronghold built in the 12th and 13th centuries, stand on a hill near Llantilio Crossenny. It was the finest of the three 'trilateral' castles of Gwent, the others being Skenfrith and Grosmont.

WHITEHAVEN, Cumbria *18 NX91*
Whitehaven was a small village until the end of the 17th century; the development of the collieries and the coming of industry, however, have turned it into a busy coal and seaport town. Sir James Lowther, the son of the man who instigated the town's industrial development, built Whitehaven Castle (now a hospital) during the 18th century, and St James's Church also dates from this period. George Washington's grandmother was buried in St Nicholas's Church in 1701 and this is commemorated by an inscribed tablet, although the church has since been rebuilt.

WHITHORN, Dumfries & Galloway
17 NX44
Whithorn Priory (AM) stands on the site of the first Christian church in Scotland – St Ninian's 'Candida Casa' or White House, part of the 4th-century monastery he founded here. The Priory was built in the 12th century by Fergus, Lord of Galloway, and excavations of its ruins have revealed traces of the earlier church. Little remains of the 12th-century building, but there is a fine Norman doorway to the nave, and the ancient crosses and tombstones contained in the town museum include the 5th-century Latinus Stone.

WHITLEY BAY, Tyne & Wear
20 NZ37
Whitley Bay, two miles to the north of Tynemouth, is Tyneside's most popular seaside resort. As well as fine sandy beaches, good swimming and sea fishing, it has a large amusement park and facilities for golf, whilst accommodation is available in a wide range of hotels. St Mary's Island, at the north end of the bay, can be reached by causeway at low tide; on it stand a lighthouse and some picturesque cottages.

WHITSTABLE, Kent *6 TR16*
Long renowned for its oysters, the resort of Whitstable also offers fishing and bathing from a shingle beach and good yachting facilities. A spit of land known as 'the Street' juts about a mile and half into the sea, providing a pleasant promenade at low tide. 'The Castle', a crenellated building dating mainly from the 19th century, has a 15th-century brick tower originally used as a look-out post, and its parkland is open to the public. Stevenson's *Invicta* (now preserved at **Canterbury**) pulled a train on the Whitstable to Canterbury line – the first passenger line to be opened – in 1830. The tunnel through Tyler Hill was the first railway tunnel to be built in Britain and the line was finally closed in 1953.

WHITTINGHAM, Northumberland
24 NU01

Two bridges span the River Aln at
Whittingham, an arched stone one for
motorists and an attractive footbridge for
pedestrians. The interior of St
Bartholomew's Church still shows signs of
Saxon workmanship, though its original
tower was replaced in the 19th century. On
the other side of the village the
battlemented top of a restored 15th-century
pele tower overlooks a new housing
development. Parts of Callaly Castle
(OACT), two miles away, date back to the
14th century.

WICK, Highland   *30 ND35*

The ancient settlement of Wick is an
important sea-fishing centre, its large
harbour designed originally by Telford.
The 'Old Man of Wick', a windowless 14th-
century tower (AM), crowns a rock which
juts into the sea about a mile south of the
town. Nearby are the curious rock stacks
known as Brig o'Tram and the Brough.
The coastal scenery of the area is dramatic,
with enormous rocks topping the rugged
cliffs. To the east stands Noss Head
Lighthouse, looking across Sinclair's Bay to
the ruins of Castle Sinclair and Castle
Girnigoe, both destroyed in 17th-century
clan wars. The Wick Heritage Centre near
the harbour is devoted to local history, and
the Caithness Factory on Harrow Hill can
be visited. All aspects of glass blowing can
be observed here and there is also a shop.

WICKEN FEN, Cambridgeshire
11 TL57

The nature reserve of Wicken Fen (NT)
consists of three main areas – Sedge Fen,
Adventurers Fen and St Edmund's Fen – of
which the first is open to the public. Here
bird and insect life can be observed in
conditions little changed from those of
primeval fenland. The 'lodes', ancient
canals which acted both as highways and as
irrigation channels, remain, and a derelict
windmill has been restored to pump water
into the dykes.

WIDECOMBE-IN-THE-MOOR,
Devon   *2 SX77*

Widecombe is famed for its fair, held on the
second Tuesday in September; a sign
commemorating the well-known song
stands on the village green. The large 14th-
century Church of St Pancras – 'the
Cathedral of Dartmoor' – had its tower
struck by lightning in 1638, and it is
recorded that several people were killed in
the incident. Nearby Church House (NT)
is a picturesque building. The village
stands at 800ft, surrounded by the
Dartmoor National Park and with
Hameldown Beacon rising to 1697ft in the
north-west. A well-preserved group of
Bronze-Age barrows lie to the west.

WIDNES, Cheshire   *14 SJ58*

Chemical and alkali works began to develop
in Widnes after 1845, when the Runcorn
Gap and St Helen's Railway Company
replaced the ferry across the Mersey with
the world's first railway, canal and dock
complex, welding the scattered villages
into a whole and bringing coal from Lancashire and salt from Cheshire into the area.

WIGAN, Gtr Manchester   *14 SD50*

Though it is one of the great industrial
towns of the north, Wigan did not spring
into life in the 19th century; the Romans
had a fort here, and by the 13th century the
settlement had developed sufficiently to
merit a royal charter. The Industrial
Revolution reached the town with the
construction of the Leeds and Liverpool
Canal, and it gradually developed
ironworking, engineering and textile
industries, whilst coal – discovered here
centuries earlier – continued to be mined
until 1967, when the last big colliery closed.

WILLIAM MORRIS

A variety of original fabrics and wall-
papers designed by William Morris
have been preserved at Wightwick
Manor. Morris, a man of many ta-
lents, was also an architect sculptor,
author and musician.

WIGHTWICK MANOR, W Midlands
9 SO89

Wightwick Manor (NT), though Jacobean
in style, was not built until 1887. Set in
terraced gardens remarkable for their Irish
yews and golden holly trees, it houses a fine
collection of pre-Raphaelite art, including
work by Rossetti, Burne Jones, Ford
Madox Brown, Watts, Ruskin and **Millais**.
Much of the beautiful stained glass is by
C E Kempe.

*WIDECOMBE-IN-THE-MOOR is one of Dartmoor's best-known villages. It owes its fame to the song
about Uncle Tom Cobley – a local landowner – riding to Widecombe Fair. He was buried in the village.*

WIMBORNE MINSTER *lies in the shadow of its great twin-towered minster dedicated to Cuthberga. Sister of the Wessex King Ine, she founded a nunnery here in the 8th century.*

WIGMORE, Hereford & Worcester
9 SO46
Wigmore lies at the heart of the Mortimer Forest, an area which the Forestry Commission has been replanting since the 1920s. The hall has a two-storey gabled porch, and the church incorporates some fine Norman herring-bone masonry and the Royal Arms of Queen Elizabeth I; between the two buildings runs the village street, with its delightful groups of half-timbered cottages. Nearby stand the mound of a moated 14th-century castle, the seat of the powerful Mortimer family, and the remains of a 12th-century Augustinian abbey.

WIGTOWN, Dumfries & Galloway
17 NX45
Wigtown's harbour is now silted up, but the town is still one of the main centres of the Machars Peninsula, an area noted for its fishing and wild-fowling. In the town square stand two crosses – one dating from the 18th century and topped with a sundial, the other from the 19th century. A post at the mouth of the River Bladnoch commemorates the death in 1685 of two women Covenanters, tied to stakes until they were drowned by the rising tide as a punishment for supposedly attending meetings of their sect. A mile to the south-west of the town lie the remains of Baldoon Castle, the setting of Scott's *Bride of Lammermoor*, and a Bronze-Age circle of 19 stones stands three miles north-west.

WILLOUGHBRIDGE, Staffordshire
14 SJ74
The Clive Memorial Garden (OACT) is set in a 200-year-old gravel quarry at the top of a small hill. Within the existing woodland framework a mass of azaleas and rhododendrons have been planted, and in the spring the banks are yellow with daffodils. The character of the setting has been enhanced by rock and water gardens.

WILMCOTE, Warwickshire   *10 SP15*
Wilmcote is best known for Mary Arden's Cottage (OACT), the lovely old timbered farmhouse in which Shakespeare's mother was born. It is simply furnished in the style of the period and has a huge fireplace with one of the largest ovens in England. The old-fashioned garden contains a dovecote and a cider-mill, and the stone barns house a collection of agricultural implements.

WILMINGTON, E Sussex   *5 TQ50*
The village of Wilmington lies in agricultural country at the foot of the South Downs, near the point where the famous Long Man is carved into the chalk. The origin of the figure – about 230ft in height and carrying a staff in each hand – is obscure; though first recorded in 1779 it may date back to the 6th century, and it has been variously attributed to Romans, Saxons and medieval pilgrims. The church is part Norman and part Gothic, with stone ledges where the monks used to sit and a canopied Jacobean pulpit; in the churchyard stands an ancient yew tree, believed to be the oldest in the country, with a trunk 23ft in girth. A cloister once joined the church to a 12th-century Benedictine priory, the remains of which now house the Sussex Archaeological Society's Agricultural Museum.

WILTON, Wiltshire   *3 SU03*
Wilton is famous for the fine carpets that have been made there since the 17th century. Even before that time, however, it was a town of note, the capital of Wessex, set at the point where the Rivers Wylye and Nadder meet. Wilton House (OACT), with its well-known double cube room, was originally Elizabethan; Holbein, Inigo Jones and his son-in-law, John Webb, all contributed to it and the collection of paintings is magnificent. The grounds are noted for their cedars.

WIMBORNE MINSTER, Dorset
3 SZ09
One interesting way of appreciating Wimborne's famous minster is to visit that faithfully-reproduced scale model, over 12ft high and built of authentic materials, in the model town just off the Cornmarket. The minster embraces almost every known architectural style, from Norman to Gothic; the west tower carries an attractive quarter-jack clock, the quarter-hour bells struck by a grenadier bearing a hammer in each hand. The Priest's House Museum has an interesting display of agricultural implements and a fine collection of horse-brasses among its exhibits. A wide variety of birds, including many tropical species, can be seen at Merley Bird Gardens, to the south of the town.

WIMPOLE HALL, Cambridgeshire
11 TL35
Wimpole Hall (NT) is a large country mansion begun in 1632 by Sir Thomas Chichele but considerably altered in the 18th century; it eventually became the property of Rudyard Kipling's daughter. Of interest are Lord Harley's library and the yellow drawing-room designed by Sir John Soane. The chapel has frescoes by Sir James Thornhill. It was approached, until the advent of Dutch elm disease, by a fine double avenue of elms some two-and-a-half miles long and 100 yards wide, and stands in a park landscaped at different times by Capability Brown, Humphry Repton and Sanderson Miller.

WINCHCOMBE, Gloucestershire
9 SP02
This small Cotswold town is rich in interesting buildings – notably the George Inn, with its gallery, and the strangely-named Corner Cupboard. The church is adorned with curious gargoyles and contains an embroidered altar cloth on which much of the work was done by Catherine of Aragon. Sudeley Castle (OACT) stands to the south-east, rebuilt in the 15th century and restored in the 19th. It houses fine pictures and furniture alongside collections of toys and Victoriana; Katherine Parr, who married the owner of the castle when Henry VIII died, is buried in the chapel. The grounds contain an extensive waterfowl collection. Two miles north-east is Hailes Abbey Museum, the remains of a 13th-century Cistercian abbey. The museum contains relics found on the site.

WINCHELSEA, E Sussex   *6 TQ91*
A new town was built on high land above the River Brede marshes in the 13th century after the old one had been submerged, and it became an Ancient Port, attached to the original Cinque Ports. Winchelsea Museum, located in the restored 14th-century Court Hall, traces the history of these ports. Three of the gates of the original walled town still exist, the Strand Gate being of most interest. Fine workmanship from the Decorated period can be seen in the church, the nave of which was at one time the chancel; 13th-century monuments in the Farnecombe Chantry and the famous Alard tombs are noteworthy. Winchelsea's attractive houses are laid out in a regular pattern – perhaps providing the earliest example of medieval town planning.

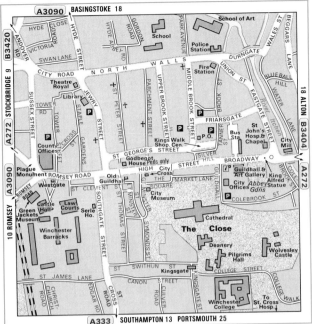

Winchester, Hampshire 4 SU42

King Alfred's Capital

' From the Hill at the Eastern extremity you see a prospect of Streets, and old Buildings mixed up with trees. Then there are the most beautiful streams about I ever saw – full of Trout. '

JOHN KEATS, *Letters.*

Already a sizeable town in the Roman period, Winchester became, under the Anglo-Saxons, the capital of their kingdom of Wessex, and the place of coronation and burial of their kings. In Alfred the Great's reign its influence grew and it became the capital of England, a status it retained until after the Norman Conquest. Although gradually eclipsed by London, Winchester retained its importance as a regional capital and maintained close links with the Crown until the reign of Charles II. At the centre of the city stands the magnificent cathedral, built by the Normans to replace the one erected by King Alfred. The crypt, transepts and part of the cloisters date from the 11th century; the choir and Lady Chapel from the 12th century; the nave and west front were rebuilt in Perpendicular style in the 14th century. The bishop at this time was William of Wykeham, founder of Winchester College, one of the most famous public schools in the country, and also founder of New College at Oxford. Some of the college buildings can be visited. They lie just outside the peaceful Close, which itself contains several buildings of outstanding interest. Nearby are the Bishop's Palace and remains of Wolvesley Castle, one of Winchester's two Norman castles. Of the other castle, only the Great Hall survives, just outside the Westgate, one of two of the original five city gates still standing. Above the other, Kingsgate, is St Swithun's Chapel. St Swithun, associated in the traditional rhyme with rain, was a Saxon bishop of Winchester, who at his death humbly asked to be buried outside the door of the cathedral. His wishes were not at first carried out, and the result was a protracted storm which caused his monks hurriedly to inter him where he had wished. His shrine in the Norman cathedral was unfortunately destroyed at the Reformation, but its site is marked.

As a city Winchester has remained compact, the small streets around the cathedral still containing many charming old houses. In one of these, near Winchester College, Jane Austen spent the last months of her life: her gravestone can be seen in the cathedral. The main streets, Westgate and High Street, are spacious and attractive, lined with buildings of different periods, and partly colonnaded. A magnificent 17th-century clock projects over the street from the former Guildhall, now a bank. A curfew bell is still rung from the turret at 8pm. In Broadway stands a statue of King Alfred, near the River Itchen. The river banks are laid out with gardens and a pleasant walk leads alongside the remnants of the city walls. Here can be seen fragments of the wall built by the Romans to defend their settlement of Venta Belgarum, from which the modern city sprang.

PLACES TO SEE

Winchester Cathedral Norman, and all the later Gothic styles can be seen in this magnificent building which contains the tombs of many Saxon kings and queens. Its treasures include the 12th-century Winchester Bible, the graves of Jane Austen and Isaak Walton and much fine carving.

Pilgrims' Hall One of several fine buildings in the Close, the hall has a superb hammer-beam roof.

The City Museum Items of local historical interest are displayed here.

Westgate Museum Above the medieval gate, in a room formerly used as a prison, is a collection of weaponry and weights and measures of the Tudor period.

Serle's House This elegant 18th-century mansion houses the Museum of the Royal Hampshire Regiment.

The Royal Greenjackets Museum is housed in their barracks just outside the city centre.

The Great Hall (OACT) The only surviving part of the Norman castle is this austere, aisled hall. On the wall hangs a massive circle of oak, held to be King Arthur's legendary Round Table. It was re-painted in Tudor times by order of Henry VIII to impress his guest, the Emperor Charles V.

Winchester College Several of the old buildings of this famous school can be visited.

St Cross Hospital The hospital was founded in 1136 by Bishop Henry of Blois, and the adjoining Almshouses of the Noble Poverty in 1445 by Cardinal Beaufort. The buildings stand beside the River Itchen and the old tradition of the Wayfarer's Dole of bread and beer is still preserved.

THE CITY CROSS *(above)* stands in the High St.

THE FONT *(right)* in the cathedral is Norman and made of black marble.

ST CROSS HOSPITAL *(below)* the high Norman buildings date from the 12th century.

Windsor, Berkshire 5 *SU97*

Royal Stronghold on the Thames

'... and proudly doth pursue
His wood-nymph Windsors seate, her lovely site to view.
Whose most delightful face when once the river sees,
Which shewes her selfe attir'd in tall and stately trees.'

MICHAEL DRAYTON, Poly Olbion, (15th song)

The castle, built by the Normans on a high chalk ridge overlooking the River Thames and thus guarding the approaches to London dominates the small town whose centre is squeezed into the low ground between the castle walls and the river. The old streets, although attractive in themselves and graced with a number of fine buildings, only serve in summer to funnel the tens of thousands of visitors into the castle precinct. The original Norman round tower now stands at the centre of a multitude of towers, walls, courtyards, and apartments added at different times by various kings. In the medieval period, Henry III, and later Edward III did most to extend and strengthen the fortifications and give the castle its present shape. Edward III is particularly remembered as the instigator of the Order of the Garter, the most prestigious order of knighthood in the country, which he founded at Windsor in 1348. The best-known story about the founding is that the king, while dancing with the Countess of Salisbury at Windsor, picked up the garter she had dropped, then quelled his sniggering courtiers with the words that are the motto of the Order: '*Honi soit qui mal y pense*', – (evil be to him who evil of it thinks). The Tudor monarchs took over the Plantagenet links with Windsor, and Henry VIII built the impressive gateway now used as the main entrance. Elizabeth I built the North Terrace, which has magnificent views over the Thames valley, as a promenade, and also commanded Shakespeare to write a play for the court at Windsor: the result was *The Merry Wives of Windsor*, in which not only Sir John Falstaff fea-

WINDSOR GREAT PARK *The view from the statue of George III shows the Long Walk.*

tures, but several local personages of that time, such as Master Ford and Mistress Page whose names are recorded in the parish registers. The Garter Inn stands on the site of the Harte and Garter Inn, where, in the play, Falstaff and his companions met to drink.

During the whole of the Civil War Cromwell's forces kept firm control of the castle, which therefore escaped being slighted, the fate of so many British strongholds, and it was to Windsor that his friends secretly brought the body of Charles I for burial in the vaults of St George's Chapel. Charles II often lived at Windsor,

and his contribution to the castle was the Long Walk in Windsor Great Park. George IV and Queen Victoria spent much time at Windsor, and Queen Victoria and Prince Albert used the castle both as a family house, and for social occasions and State visits. Her grandson, George V, took Windsor as his family name in 1917, and this decision was ratified by Queen Elizabeth II.

PLACES TO SEE

The Castle Second only to Buckingham Palace as a royal residence, Windsor Castle dates back to Norman times. The State Apartments are magnificent, as is St George's Chapel, the resting place of eight kings, with its superb fan-vaulted ceiling. Queen Mary's Doll's House is an exquisite model house of the 1920s, complete down to the last detail. Works of art and Old Master drawings from the Royal Library are also exhibited in the castle.

The Guildhall A fine 17th-century colonnaded building by Sir Christopher Wren, which contains a small museum of local interest.

The Household Cavalry Museum is housed in Combermere Barracks. It tells the history of the regiment from 1685 to the present day.

Madame Tussaud's Royalty and Railways Exhibition is housed in the Victorian station buildings.

Savill Garden These beautiful woodland gardens occupy a part of Windsor Great Park.

Valley Gardens, famous for rhododendrons and azaleas, link Windsor Great Park to Virginia Water.

Windsor Safari Park and Sea-world A drive-in zoo where animals are kept in conditions as near to a natural habitat as it is possible to achieve.

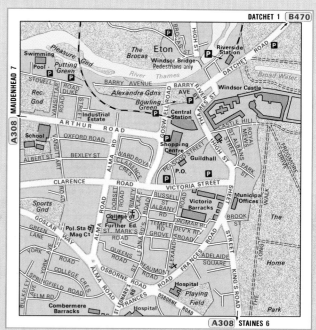

WINDERMERE, Cumbria *18 SD49*
Windermere, the centre of the Lake
District National Park, stands to the east of
Lake Windermere, which is the largest
expanse of fresh water in England. At
Brockhole, south-west of the town, is the
National Park Information Centre. The
town is one of England's busiest tourist
centres. (See also **Bowness**).

WING, Buckinghamshire *10 SP82*
Among the modern buildings of this fast-
growing village stand many 17th- and 18th-
century cottages, and the Dormer Hospital
dates from 1569. All Saints Church is
noteworthy for its Anglo-Saxon crypt, one
of only eight remaining in England; of
interest, too, is the rare Anglo-Saxon apse,
set on pilasters. Ascott (NT), on the eastern
outskirts of the village, is a mansion dating
mainly from the 19th century but
incorporating medieval timbers and some
Jacobean work. It contains the Anthony de
Rothschild collection of pictures, together
with fine examples of furniture and oriental
porcelain, and is set in fine parkland.

LAKE WINDERMERE *Rising beyond the wooded shores of England's largest lake is the mountain known as Coniston Old Man. One of the best ways of appreciating the scenery is from the lake steamers.*

TURF MAZES

Turf mazes are one of the mysterious
relics of bygone cultures that are to
be found all over Britain. Their origins and meaning are unknown, but
experts believe that they must have
played a significant part in the ancient ceremonies that influenced the
earth's natural powers. At one time
there were probably hundreds of
mazes throughout the country, but
considering that they need continual
maintenance, in order to survive, it is
remarkable that any exist at all. One
of the very few survivors is to be
found at the east end of the village of
Wing, Leicestershire (above). This
has a medieval Christian design.

WIRKSWORTH, Derbyshire *15 SK25*
An ancient town, with its steep terraces of
stone houses, Wirksworth was once an
important lead-mining centre, and a unique
16th-century bronze dish which was used as
the standard lead measure is preserved in
the Moot Hall. Parts of St Mary's Church
date back to the 13th century, and it has a
wealth of early carving; an inscribed Anglo-
Saxon coffin lid is thought to be 9th-
century. Each May the centuries-old
ceremony of well-dressing is still observed
in the area. The town of Snowfield in
George Eliot's *Adam Bede* is probably based
on Wirksworth.

WIRRAL, THE, Cheshire *14 SJ38*
The fine stretches of sandy coast on the
Wirral, a narrow peninsula separating the
estuary of the River Dee from that of the
Mersey, have encouraged the development
of holiday towns. These resorts stand
cheek-by-jowl with busy ports such as
Birkenhead, whose impedimenta of grain
elevators, oil-refinery tanks and cranes
contrast starkly with the trappings of
enjoyment sported by their neighbours.

WISBECH, Cambridgeshire *11 TF40*
Wisbech is situated in an area renowned for
bulb growing and fruit cultivation, and
fruit canning is an important local industry.
The town stands on the River Nene, 12
miles from the sea – though at one time,
before changes in river patterns altered its
relation to the Wash, it was only four miles
away. From the North and South Brinks an
impressive array of Georgian houses,
several with Dutch characteristics, looks
across the quays and the river; the most
notable is Peckover House (NT), built in
the 1720s and displaying some fine rococo
plasterwork. Near the bridge is Sir George
Gilbert Scott's memorial to Thomas
Clarkson, a campaigner for the abolition of
slavery whose father was schoolmaster
here. The church of Sts Peter and Paul is
mainly Norman and Perpendicular, with a
fine 16th-century tower. The Museum
contains Clarkson relics and illustrates
Fenland life.

WISLEY, Surrey *5 TQ05*
The 300-acre grounds and gardens of the
Royal Horticultural Society (OACT) are
particularly striking when the azaleas and
rhododendrons are in bloom, but at all
times of the year there are pleasant walks
among trees or beside rock gardens of
heath and alpine plants; new varieties of
fruit and vegetables are tried out here, and
student gardeners are trained. Wisley
Pond, surrounded by fir trees, is a well-
known beauty spot. A Norman church with
a 17th-century timbered porch stands
between the River Wey and the Wey
Navigation Canal (NT).

WITHAM, Essex *6 TL81*
The history of Witham begins when
Edward, son of King Alfred, built a great
mound here as defence against the Danes.
Near the site of this mound stands the
Church of St Nicholas, rebuilt in the 14th
century and noteworthy for its Norman
south doorway and a fine screen. Houses
from the Georgian period – and a few even
older ones – still stand in the town.

WITNEY, Oxfordshire *10 SP31*
This pleasant little town, standing on the
River Windrush at the edge of rich
Cotswold sheep-farming land, has long
been associated with the weaving industry;
the Domesday Book records that there were
two mills here in 1085, and the traditional
blanket-making began in the 17th century.
Today's modern blanket factories have
been designed to blend unobtrusively with
the warm-coloured Cotswold stone
buildings that surround them, buildings
that reflect the prosperity brought to the
area by weaving from an early date. Among
the most impressive are the 18th-century
Old Blanket Hall, with its curious one-
handed clock, the substantial merchants'
houses round the square and the old
grammar school. Manor Farm Museum at
Cogges shows Edwardian methods of
farming.

WOBURN, Bedfordshire *11 SP93*
Eighteenth-century Woburn Abbey, the
seat of the Dukes of Bedford, is one of
Britain's most famous stately homes. The
palatial house contains superb state
apartments (where the newly-married
Victoria and Albert once slept in the four-
poster state bed) and a magnificent art
collection which includes works by
Gainsborough, Rembrandt, Reynolds and
Van Dyck. Perhaps the greater attraction,
however, is the Wild Animal Kingdom in
the woodland surrounding the Abbey.
Visitors can drive through the monkey
jungle and the lion and tiger reserves, take a
Boat Safari round the chimpanzees' island,
or be entertained by the antics of the
dolphins in the Dolphinarium.

Epping Forest and the Roding Valley
89 miles

The woodland glades around Epping and Hatfield are the last remnants of a great Norman hunting preserve; the former woodland settlements are now prosperous villages set in rich farmland.

From **Woodford Green** take the Epping Road, A104 and in ¾ mile turn left on to A110 (SP N. Chingford). In ¾ mile turn right into Forest Side (no sign). At the end right again into Rangers Road (A1069) and pass Queen Elizabeth's Hunting Lodge. After ¾ mile turn left on to A104. In 1¼ miles at the roundabout turn left, (SP High Beach), then bear right (SP King's Oak) for High Beach. Here turn right, and in 1 mile cross a main road and M11; later turning right (SP Epping) for Upshire. On reaching B1393 turn left, and in 1 mile turn left again on to B182 (SP Roydon). In 1¼ miles turn left on to B181, then in ¾ mile left again to Epping Green and **Roydon**. Here turn left (SP Hertford) and on reaching A414 turn right (SP Chelmsford). In 3 miles keep forward for High Wych. Later turn left, A1184, and enter **Sawbridgeworth** where, turn right for **Hatfield Heath**. Here turn right on to A1060, and shortly left (SP Takeley) on to B183. At **Hatfield Broad**

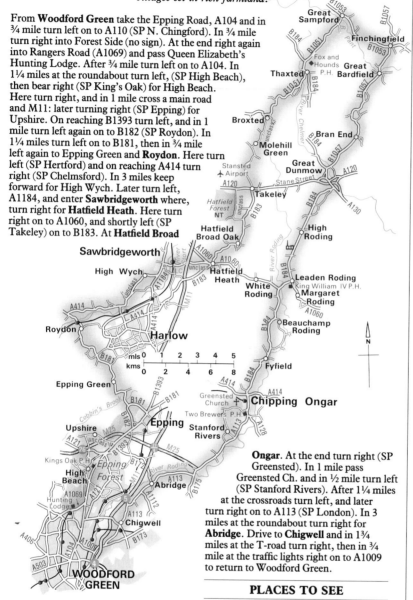

Oak keep left, then in 1¼ miles turn left (SP Hatfield Forest). Drive past the country park, then turn right on A120 for **Takeley**. At the traffic lights turn left (SP Broxted); in 1½ miles turn right, and in 1¼ miles right again into Molehill Green. Drive to Broxted, then join B1051 and continue to Thaxted. Here turn left on to B184 and at the end turn right to rejoin B1051 for **Great Sampford**. Turn right on to B1053 and drive to **Finchingfield** where, turn right on to B1057 for **Great Bardfield**. Here turn right (SP Dunmow). After 6¾ miles turn left on to B184 for **Great Dunmow**. Follow Chelmsford signs and in ¾ mile turn right on to B184 (SP Ongar), through High Roding to **Leaden Roding**. Here turn right on to A1060 then in 1 mile left to rejoin B184 and continue to **Fyfield**. In 2½ miles at the roundabout go forward on to A128 for **Chipping**

Ongar. At the end turn right (SP Greensted). In 1 mile pass Greensted Ch. and in ½ mile turn left (SP Stanford Rivers). After 1¼ miles at the crossroads turn left, and later turn right on to A113 (SP London). In 3 miles at the roundabout turn right for **Abridge**. Drive to **Chigwell** and in 1¾ miles at the T-road turn right, then in ¾ mile at the traffic lights right on to A1009 to return to Woodford Green.

PLACES TO SEE

Queen Elizabeth's Hunting Lodge The timber-framed building houses the Epping Forest Museum.

Thaxted A prosperous town once famous for its cutlery. It has a magnificent church and a beautiful old Guildhall.

Finchingfield Thought by many to be the loveliest village in Essex.

Great Bardfield An old market town with a restored windmill and a museum.

Great Dunmow A peaceful town, famous for the centuries-old tradition of the Dunmow Flitch.

Greensted Church A unique example of a Saxon log church, where the body of the martyred King Edmund lay in 1013.

WOKING, Surrey *5 TQ05*
A residential and commuter town on the disused Basingstoke Canal, Woking developed as a direct result of the coming of the railway in the 1830s. Its most distinctive feature is its large Mosque, built in 1889 and still the centre of Islamic observance in this country, though the Oriental Institute to which it was originally attached has ceased to function. Nearby is Brookwood Cemetery – one of the most extensive in the world, incorporating burial grounds for several London parishes.

WOKINGHAM, Berkshire *4 SU86*
Much of Wokingham is the product of fairly recent expansion, but it has been a market town – known also for its silk industry and its bell-foundry – for centuries. Half-timbered houses with overhanging gables can still be seen, particularly in Rose Street, where John Gay is said to have been inspired to verse by the landlord's daughter when he passed a wet afternoon at the Rose Inn (now demolished) in company with Pope and Swift. All Saints Church is much restored, but five medieval bays with carved capitals are preserved in the nave and the font is finely carved.

WOLDS, THE, Humberside *16 SE96*
The Yorkshire Wolds are part of a line chalk hills which includes the Chilterns, the Gog Magog Hills of Cambridgeshire and the Lincolnshire Wolds. Situated just north of Beverley, the hill group rises to 800ft at its highest point.

WOLVERHAMPTON, W Midlands *9 SO99*
The name 'Wolverhampton' comes from 'Wulfrunishamtun', the town of Wulfrun, but it was earlier known as 'Heantun' and is referred to thus in a royal charter of the 10th century. Its coat of arms includes a cross, ascribed to the Anglo-Saxon King Edgar, and a woolpack – but more obviously relevant to the 'Queen of the Black Country' are the flaming brazier and padlock which are also incorporated. Today, not only locks and keys but many kinds of iron and brass components and aircraft parts are manufactured here. The Church of St Peter is basically 15th-century, with a panelled tower and a fine stone pulpit; in the churchyard an ancient carved cross shaft stands near a holed Bargain Stone. Nineteenth-century Bantock House contains a museum of items made by Midland craftsmen. Bilston Museum and Art Gallery also has many examples of craftsmanship and English enamels. *See also* **Wightwick Manor**.

WOODBRIDGE, Suffolk *12 TM24*
Woodbridge, a market town on the River Deben, was once a busy seaport; it has a Shire Hall that dates back to the 16th century and several interesting old houses, including a half-timbered one with an old weighing machine attached in New Street. Edward Fitzgerald, translator of *The Rubaiyat of Omar Khayyam*, once lived at Little Grange. The building of the Abbey in Church Street began in 1564, and the Perpendicular church contains a seven-sacraments font and part of a 15th-century screen, whilst the Friends' Meeting House dates from 1678. The famous 18th-century Tide Mill on the estuary has now been restored and is open to the public.

WOODSTOCK, Oxfordshire   *10 SP41*

Blenheim Palace (OACT), richly furnished and containing many art treasures, stands adjacent to Woodstock, in a large park which is always open to pedestrians. Vanbrugh designed the building in 1707 for John Churchill, 1st Duke of Marlborough – and part of the cost was defrayed by Parliament in recognition of his victory over the French at Blenheim. The park was landscaped by Capability Brown, who planted trees in groups to represent the Battle of Blenheim and formed a lake from the waters of the River Glyn; a column was erected in honour of the great Duke. In 1847 another famous member of the family, Sir Winston Churchill, was born here.

WOOKEY HOLE

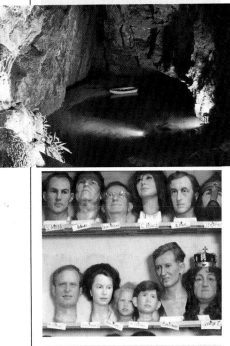

The Great Cave (top) is one of three floodlit caverns accessible to the public, but cave explorers have discovered nearly 20 others.

One of the oldest papermills in Britain stands by Wookey Hole and visitors can see waxwork heads belonging to Madam Tussaud's here.

WOOKEY HOLE, Somerset   *3 ST54*

The River Axe, flowing through the heart of the Mendips, has hollowed out the great caves of Wookey Hole (OACT), inhabited more than 2000 years ago; the higher caverns are crossed by steel bridges which look down on the rushing torrent below. A small museum displays pottery and coins from the Celtic and Roman British periods. The Mill (OACT), which made fine paper by hand in the 17th century, has now been restored and visitors can see the old machinery used for its original purpose. The building also houses the store room of Madame Tussaud's Waxworks, and the disembodied heads of the famous (together with the moulds from which they were made) are on display. Lady Bangor's Fairground Collection includes some beautifully carved and painted figures from the era of steam-driven fairground rides.

WOOLACOMBE, Devon   *2 SS44*

Surfers and swimmers, in particular, are attracted to Woolacombe's three miles of firm sands. Barricane Bay is noted for its shells, and two prominent headlands – Morte Point and Baggy Point (both NT) – flank Morte Bay, affording fine views of the surrounding slate-rock scenery and of distant **Lundy Island**.

WOOLPIT, Suffolk   *12 TL96*

Woolpit's name derives from 'wolf-pit', a pit into which captured wolves were flung before they were killed in Saxon times. The church has a magnificent south porch, reminiscent of a castle gateway, and a fine hammerbeam roof carved with angels; the 16th-century brass eagle lectern is said to have been a gift from Queen Elizabeth I. The waters of nearby Lady's Well were reputed in the 14th century to cure any ailment. Beside the green is an 18th-century coaching inn, and attractive timber-framed Tudor and Georgian houses are scattered throughout the village.

WOOLSTHORPE, Lincolnshire   *11 SK92*

In 1642 Sir Isaac Newton was born within the grey stone walls of Woolsthorpe Manor (NT). The orchard in front of the house is a reminder of the falling apple reputed to have prompted Newton's realisation of the theory of gravitational pull – a theory that revolutionised man's understanding of astronomy.

WORCESTER, Hereford & Worcester   *9 SO75*

This county town and cathedral city stands on the banks of the Severn in an area of rich agricultural land. The cathedral, which overlooks the river and the city's county cricket ground, is mostly Early English in style although the oldest part – the crypt – was built in the 11th century. In the lofty chancel are the tombs of King John, and the elder brother of Henry VIII, Prince Arthur, who died at the age of 15.

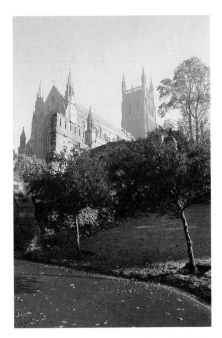

WORCESTER CATHEDRAL *was begun in 1084 by Bishop Wulfstan but it was not completed until the tower was added in the 14th century.*

Unfortunately much of Worcester has been rebuilt over the years but there are still several buildings to note in the old city centre. These include The Commandery and Tudor House which also both house museums, Greyfriars – a 15th-century Franciscan house, and the Guildhall. The latter, with its elaborate façade, is one of the finest examples of early Georgian architecture in the country. Worcester has become famous for its porcelain industry which was founded in 1751 as an alternative to the ailing cloth trade. The present factory in Severn Street is open by appointment and the Dyson Perrins Museum next door has the best collection of Worcester porcelain in the world, with pieces dating from 1751 to the present.

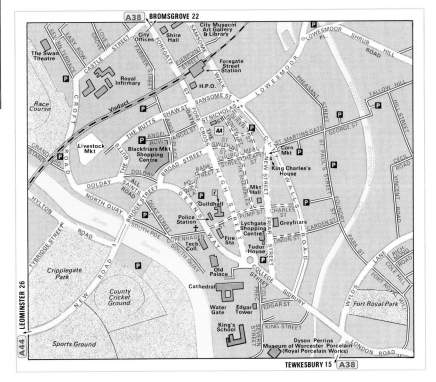

HAMPTON COURT PALACE *was begun during Henry VIII's reign but Christopher Wren made many improvements after William III's accession. The gatehouse (above) is Tudor brickwork.*

ARISTOCRATIC DWELLINGS

COUNTRY HOUSES

The Rise of the Great Estate

THE DECAY OF FEUDAL VALUES helped bring about the birth of the great house. The more powerful medieval lords did not live in mansions, but in castles. These medieval strongholds were seldom particularly comfortable places, but they were built and occupied not simply because of the needs for defence and security, but because society and particularly the nobility, expected that a person of

The great country mansion, which was once a symbol of aristocratic wealth and privilege, is today, as often as not, a public monument attracting scores of visitors and a testimony to the rise of democratic values. The great houses can be enjoyed for their gardens and architectural splendour, but any visit will be even more fascinating if one understands how such buildings evolved.

power, wealth and breeding would own a castle. Some quite difficult changes in attitudes were involved in the transfer of the aristocratic lifestyle from castle to mansion. Towards the end of the 15th century, it became apparent that the private fortress was militarily redundant and nobles began to be tempted by the comforts and opulence which less severely functional, yet less expensive types of residences might offer.

However, the castle was not only a stronghold, but also a potent status symbol and so the first generations of great houses attempted to mimic many of the castle's hallmarks, while at the same time providing much more agreeable and impressive living conditions.

THE DECLINE OF THE CASTLE

and the rise of the great house occurred at a time when brick was beginning to be accepted as an as yet quite expensive and prestigious alternative to building in wood or stone. There were a few attempts to employ brick in military architecture, as at Caister Castle in Norfolk (1432), but the new material really made its impact in the late-medieval palaces and fortified mansions, like Cardinal Wolsey's Hampton Court, begun in 1514, Compton Wynyates, begun in 1480 and Herstmonceux Castle in E Sussex, built in 1440. At Herstmonceux and other great Tudor brick mansions like Oxburgh Hall in Norfolk, begun in 1482, the military trappings of the castle were retained in the form of the encircling moat and imposing gatehouse, but such features were mainly for show and the true nature of such places was evident in their large window spaces and relatively thin walls. As the norms concerning status and aristocratic living evolved, so the military pretensions were abandoned and wealth and prestige were flaunted in other ways – but certain traditional values sill exerted an important influence on architectural fashions. Of these, the concept of the 'hall' was the most important.

THE HALL

was a multi-purpose room used for feasting and other social gatherings, administration and the reception of guests. It was at least as old as the Saxon period and the Dark Age epics and sagas are packed with colourful tales about the feasting, boasting and story-telling performed in such places. Halls tended completely to dominate the dwellings of the lesser Dark Age and medieval lords and were the main chambers in all residential castles. They continued to be an important social and architectural feature of the greater houses until centuries after the passing of the Middle Ages, even if today they have shrunken and degenerated into the little entrance halls of modern houses.

Some features of the great houses were related to the norms of day-to-day living, while others were embraced because of the dictates of fashion. The merging of these two important strands of

KIRBY HALL *the elaborate early Renaissance facade (above) conceals an almost medieval set of rooms within.*

RUFFORD OLD HALL *During the 17th century additions, often in brick, were made to much older, timbered buildings.*

GOTHIC REVIVAL *can be seen at its most extravagant in Knebworth House (left) which was rebuilt in the 19th century. Many different styles are seen in the interior.*

influence are excellently demonstrated at Kirby Hall near Deene in Northamptonshire. The house dates from 1570–5 and was embellished with the latest ornate motifs borrowed from French architecture, with a range of two-storey rooms enclosing an inner courtyard. Yet inside the main building a very traditional layout was preserved, with a massive hall and a range of kitchen buildings to one end and at the other, a parlour with bedrooms above. No 13th-century lord would have felt lost in such a house. Gradually however, changing values had an effect and halls

became imposing vestibules surrounded by the separate newly-fashionable suites of private apartments, reception rooms and guests' quarters and servants' accommodation.

AS THE RENAISSANCE

extended its influences to the western seaboards of Europe, so ideas distantly inspired by the Classical architecture of ancient Greece and Rome became paramount. Until the 16th century, the external appearance of a house simply tended to mirror its internal layout and rambling mansions with uneven roof-lines and jumbles of spiky gables were quite acceptable. To meet the dictates of the new fashion, a house was obliged to have symmetrical elevations. In a few older and lesser houses this was achieved by masking the old arrangements with a new façade, but in the building of new mansions it was necessary to plan the rooms to meet the demand for external symmetry. In many attractive Elizabethan and Jacobean houses the use of decorative motifs in the stonework or brickwork and chimneys relieved the severity of the symmetrical style.

Until the end of the 16th century, houses had tended to be just one room in width and were increased by adding new bays, either lengthways or to produce 'E' or 'H'-shaped plans, or by planning the building range around a rectangular courtyard. Slowly during the 17th century, the idea of the more box-like house which was two or more rooms in depth was accepted, with Coleshill, in Berkshire, dating from 1650, as an early example. In the grander mansions which developed during the 18th century, balancing wings or linked pavilions enhanced these 'double-pile' boxes, while every effort was made to maintain symmetry in the elevations. Throughout this century and into the next, the aristocratic home became increasingly the social focus for polite society and was expected to be as commodious and imposing as wealth would allow and to offer splendid hospitality.

THE GOTHIC REVIVAL

began some time towards the end of the 18th century, when some people began to express their boredom with the continuing fashion for symmetrical elevations, and during the 19th century the uninhibited and rambling appearance of medieval or Gothic architecture was imitated. The great houses of the Victorian era borrowed motifs and styles from medieval, Elizabethan, French, Italian and many other sources and this 'Gothic Revival' involved much more than the parodying of just the Gothic designs. Knebworth House in Hertfordshire is one of the most interesting and extravagant exercises in Gothic Revival building and was built between 1843 and 1870.

MAINTAINING A HOUSE

and the necessary retinue of servants gradually became too great a financial burden for many aristocratic families during the 19th century. Most of the mansions built in the earlier part of the 20th century were built to smaller, more economical designs, and by the 1939-45 war, the era of the great house had really ended and no more vast and magnificent examples were built. Today, the burden of supporting these costly and aging relics is often eased by the revenues earned from public visits. Hardly any of the houses that are open to the public are supported by entrance fees alone; some still control profitable estates, some are in state care, while the National Trust plays an invaluable role in preserving a remarkable spectrum of historically interesting but otherwise insolvent properties.

WORKINGTON, Cumbria 18 NX92

Workington occupies an important site at the mouth of the River Derwent – a site first developed by the Romans, who built a fort and then a town there. Today Workington is involved in the production of coal and the making of railway lines, the deep-water port being used for the freight of these commodities. Little remains of the old town except the elegant Georgian houses around cobbled Portland Square, the ruins of 14th-century Workington Hall (not open) and the restored Church of St Michael. Workington's history can be traced through to 1948 in the Helena Thompson Museum, which also has collections of costumes, glass and ceramics.

WORKSOP, Nottinghamshire 15 SK57

Set on the edge of the Midlands coalfield, Worksop is a good base for exploring Sherwood Forest and the Dukeries – the group of neighbouring estates owned by the Dukes of Kingston, Newcastle and Portland. The twin-towered Church of St Mary and St Cuthbert is part of a 12th-century priory and has a fine 13th-century Lady Chapel. The 14th-century gatehouse once housed an elementary school, founded in 1623. The town museum numbers among its exhibits two Bronze-Age beakers, found in nearby **Clumber Park** (NT), once the estate of the Duke of Newcastle.

WORSTEAD, Norfolk 12 TG32

Flemish weavers settled in East Anglia in the 12th century, and one of the techniques they introduced to the wool trade was the production of a tightly-twisted yarn for the manufacture of a firm, hardwearing cloth – worsted, which took its name from this village at the heart of the industry. Until the coming of the Industrial Revolution weaving was carried out in the worker's own home, and several weavers' houses still exist in and around Worstead. St Mary's Church dates from the 14th century, and its tower, rising over 100ft, reflects the prosperity of the weaving era.

WORTHING, W Sussex 5 TQ10

Worthing, the largest town in West Sussex, was a small fishing village until Princess Amelia, the youngest daughter of George III, holidayed there in 1798. When society followed her lead the resort expanded to accommodate the influx, and it has continued to grow as the extensive pebble-and-sand beach and attractive South Downs scenery have proved popular with successive generations. In addition to safe bathing, a pier and four miles of promenades, the town today offers concert halls and two good theatres. Unusual travelling stocks can be seen in the town museum, and at **West Tarring**, to the north-west, a half-timbered house contains a collection of bygones. Cissbury Ring marks the site of an Iron-Age camp dating from about 800 BC. At West Tarring, the Museum of Sussex Folklore is housed in three 15th-century cottages belonging to the Sussex Archaeological Trust.

WORTH MATRAVERS, Dorset 3 SY97

Worth Matravers was for centuries an important centre for the quarrying of Purbeck marble (used, notably, in the tower-supports of Salisbury Cathedral), and there are still signs of the workings in the hills around the village. In St Nicholas' churchyard is buried Benjamin Jesty, who inoculated his wife and sons against smallpox in 1774 – four years before Edward Jenner's famous report. Two miles south-west of the village is St Adhelm's Head, affording wide views over a coastal area of outstanding natural beauty. The small, square 12th-century chapel of St Adhelm was possibly built on the headland as a marker for sailors.

WRAGBY, W Yorkshire 15 SE41

Nostell Priory (NT) is a magnificent mansion on the site of a 12th-century Augustinian priory; it was built by James Paine in 1733 and extended by Robert Adam some 30 years later. The village church stands within its beautiful park.

WORTH MATRAVERS *Whinspit Cliff Quarry is one of several old marble workings to be found in the Isle of Purbeck. The village of Worth Matravers was one of the major centres of this industry.*

WREKIN, THE, Shropshire 9 SJ60

The Wrekin, probably the country's oldest hill, lies two miles south of the town of Wellington. Its summit, at 1334 feet, is not the highest point in Shropshire, but it offers incomparable views that take in several counties. A beacon fire on this hilltop warned of the coming of the Spanish Armada – and traces of an Iron-Age camp indicate that it was recognised as a good defensive site almost 2000 years ago.

WREXHAM, Clwyd 14 SJ35

Wrexham lies just across the Welsh border; it actually stood in Mercia when the boundaries between the Saxons were defined by Offa's Dyke in the 8th century. The town became a prosperous industrial centre in the 19th century through its involvement in brickmaking, brewing, steel and coal. Only one coal-mine is now being worked in the area, but industries such as the manufacture of textiles and chemicals have been introduced to take the place of mining. The town's weekly cattle market continues to be held, however, providing the raw material for the town's oldest industry – tanning – which is still active. The 15th-century Church of St Giles has a pinnacle tower 136ft high, accounted one of the 'Seven Wonders of Wales'. Another such 'Wonder' is the peal of twelve bells at the church of Gresford, three miles to the north. Erddig Hall (NT) illustrates life on a country squire's estate 700 years ago.

WROXETER, Shropshire 9 SJ50

Wroxeter, on the ancient highway of Watling Street, contains the remains of the Roman settlement of Viroconium (AM). Viroconium was established as an army camp about the middle of the first century, and when the garrison moved north a new town grew up, probably remaining inhabited until the eighth. The site was excavated in the 1920s, and finds are exhibited in the local museum and in Rowley's House in Shrewsbury. Some Roman material can be seen in the church – though the workmanship is Saxon – and the columns flanking the entrance to the churchyard are Roman.

THE WREKIN *According to local folklore, this wooded hump of volcanic rock was created when a giant mistakenly put down a load of earth with which he was going to dam the Severn and drown Shrewsbury.*

WROXHAM, Norfolk   *12 TG21*

The village of Wroxham overlooks Wroxham Broad (formed by the River Bure) and is an established centre for sailing; the headquarters of the Norfolk Broads Yachting Club stands on the western bank of the Broad. The bridge which spans the river here dates from 1614, though it has been widened. Beeston Hall (OACT), a Gothic mansion, two and a half miles north-east, with a neo-Classic interior, has been inhabited by the Preston family since 1640.

WYE, Kent   *6 TR04*

This quaint town, rich in interesting old buildings, was the birthplace in 1640 of the restoration dramatist Aphra Benn. Wye College is part of the University of London and specialises in research to improve the standards of British farming; some of its buildings date back to the 15th century, and an old barn houses an agricultural museum. To the north stands Olantigh Towers – built in the 18th century, then rebuilt in the same style after being almost totally destroyed by fire in 1903, and now a summer venue for music festivals. A crown cut into the chalk of the Downs to the east commemorates the coronation of King Edward VII.

WYLYE, Wiltshire   *3 SU03*

This delightful village is set in the valley of the River Wylye, with a wooded hill rising behind it. Attractive flint-and-stone chequerwork distinguishes its 17th-century houses.

WYMONDHAM, Leicestershire   *10 SK81*

Wymondham has an Early English church displaying some fine carving in the nave and containing a 14th-century effigy of a knight. The 17th-century grammar school is now used as a parish room. It is said that Stilton cheeses were originally made here and then taken to Stilton to be sold to travellers using the Great North Road.

WYMONDHAM, Norfolk   *12 TG10*

The parish church of this delightful country town (pronounced 'Windham') was originally part of a Benedictine abbey; it has a tower at each end and contains a fine hammerbeam roof and terra-cotta sedilia. Nearby stands Sir Thomas Becket's Well, once a shrine frequented by pilgrims. The 14th-century Green Dragon in Church Street was one of the few medieval buildings to survive the great fire that swept through Wymondham in 1615 and is among the oldest inns in the country. The timbered 17th-century market cross, raised on wooden pillars, stands at the centre of the town, and in the streets round about are many old and picturesque buildings.

WYMONDHAM *(Norfolk) A fire devastated the town in 1615 and among the many fine buildings to arise as a result was the charming octagonal market cross in the market place.*

Y

YARM, Cleveland   *20 NZ41*

Until it was superseded by Stockton in the 18th century, Yarm was the main port of Teesside, much involved in the shipment of corn and lead. It is now a small, old-world market town – the eight public houses in its High Street standing as a reminder of its 19th-century prominence as a coaching stop, when it had 16 inns.

YAXLEY, Cambridgeshire   *11 TL19*

One must turn off the main road of this large and busy village to find the interesting buildings – a thatched inn, black-and-white thatched cottages, 17th- and 18th-century houses – and the green with its old pump. St Peter's Church dates back to the 13th century and has a beautiful steeple supported by flying buttresses; the font is original, and a fine oak chancel screen is 15th-century. To the south-east lies Holme Fen Nature Reserve, in what is believed to be the lowest land in England – eight to ten feet below sea level in some places.

YEALAND CONYERS, Lancashire   *14 SD57*

An attractive village of traditional stone houses, Yealand Conyers is separated from Morecombe Bay by a Limestone ridge. Its Quaker Meeting House dates from 1692, the year that George Fox, the founder of the movement, first preached in this part of the country. Neo-Gothic Leighton Hall (OACT) has an interesting collection of early Gillow furniture.

YEALMPTON, Devon   *2 SX55*

The Devon Shire Horse Farm (OACT) at Dunstone recaptures the atmosphere of a bygone era, the work on its sixty acres – devoted mainly to cattle and sheep – being done by these great horses. Kitley Caves (OACT), on the banks of the Yealm, offer the chance to explore floodlit caves and lime kilns.

YELVERTON, Devon   *2 SX56*

Yelverton stands south of **Dartmoor National Park**, between the Rivers Walkham and Meavy. The Paperweight Centre exhibits some 800 examples, both antique and modern, many of which are for sale. Buckland Abbey (NT) lies two miles to the south-west; once a Cistercian house, it was converted into a private dwelling and purchased in the 16th century by Sir Francis Drake. Today it contains a Drake Museum (including the legendary Drake's Drum) and is famous for its great yew avenue and the 180ft-long tithe barn.

YEOVIL, Somerset   *3 ST51*

Traditionally a market town serving a prosperous agricultural area, Yeovil is now a busy industrial centre, still engaged in the 300-year-old craft of glove-making but also known as home of one of the world's foremost helicopter constructors. Much of the town is built of the honey-coloured Ham limestone which is quarried locally.

York, N Yorkshire 15 SE65

Minster City of the Vale

'The antiquity of York . . . showed itself so visibly at a distance that we could not but observe it before we came quite up to the city . . .'

DANIEL DEFOE, *A Tour through the Whole Island*

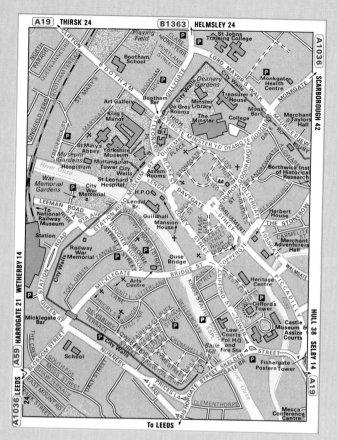

Capital of the Roman province of Lower Britain, the Roman settlement of Eboracum, the fore-runner of present-day York, became one of the most important cities in the Roman empire. Both Hadrian and Constantine stayed at York, and when the latter died there in AD306, his son – who became known as Constantine the Great – was proclaimed emperor from York, the only Roman emperor to be proclaimed in Britain. After the Romans departed the city suffered a decline in its fortunes, although the Saxons made it the capital of their kingdom of Deira, but when the Danes invaded and settled in the north-east of England, they built it up into an important centre: from their name, Jorvic, is derived the modern name of York. The Danish influence has also survived in many of the old street names, such as Goodramgate, Micklegate and Walmgate, while from the Roman period only some parts of the walls, and the multangular tower still stand.

When the Normans came, they sacked York, but it rose again as a great medieval city, encircled by massive walls, the greater part of which still stand, pierced by the medieval gateways of Micklegate Bar, Bootham Bar, Monk Bar and Walmgate. The circuit of the walls is about three miles, and a walk around them takes about two hours, but offers magnificent views of the old town and the Minster. Within the old walls, the medieval street pattern was a maze of lanes and alleys, some of them so narrow that the over-hanging upper storeys of the buildings almost touched across the streets. A well-preserved example of such a street is the Shambles, formerly the butchers' quarter, but now colonised by antique and tourist shops.

York Minster, built between about 1220 and 1470 is one of the greatest cathedral churches in the country and, as an archbishopric, ranks second to Canterbury. The south transept is the oldest part, then came the octagonal chapter house, the nave, the choir, and the west towers. The massive crossing tower was the last part to be completed, in 1480, and was a replacement for an earlier tower that had collapsed. More than half of England's surviving medieval stained glass is contained in the windows of the Minster.

YORK MINSTER *Some of the best views of the minster are those that can be obtained from the heights of the old city walls.*

Eighty of them were removed for safety during World War II, and this enabled them to be cleaned and properly repaired. The great east window is almost the size of a tennis court, and the lovely west window is known as the 'Heart of Yorkshire'. Although the Minster is magnificently preserved, thanks to extensive restoration work in recent times, little remains of the castle that was built in the 13th century.

Throughout Tudor, Stewart and Georgian times, York continued to flourish and handsome buildings of all these periods can be seen in its streets. With the coming of the railway age, York became a busy railway centre, and its fine Victorian railway station is a monument to the age of prosperity. In the 1960s, York became a university city; the university buildings, grouped around a lake, are attractively modern.

THE MINSTER *and the city walls a century or more ago.*

THE RIVER OUSE *This engraving shows the fine arches of the Old Ouse Bridge.*

YORK'S HERITAGE *(above) Stonegate, one of the old streets. (Below) 'Columbine', an early locomotive in the National Railway Museum.*

PLACES TO SEE

Borthwick Institute of Historical Research This late 15th-century Guildhall houses part of York University's collection of documents and archives.

Castle Museum An outstanding folk museum, with reconstructed streets of shops.

City Art Gallery European Old Master paintings are the nucleus of an interesting collection.

Guildhall This 15th-century building has a fine timbered roof and an underground passage.

King's Manor Once the home of the Abbot of St Mary's Abbey, this largely 17th-century building is now part of the university.

Merchant Adventurers' Hall One of the most important of York's medieval, timber-framed houses, this once belonged to the Company of Merchant Adventurers.

National Railway Museum Displays and historic locomotives tell the history of railway engineering.

Treasurer's House Fine paintings and furniture decorate this 17th- to 18th-century house.

York Castle Clifford's Tower is all that remains of castle built by the Normans.

York Story An exceptionally interesting Heritage Centre, with audio-visual displays and exhibitions of crafts.

Yorkshire Museum and Gardens Roman, medieval and natural history collections are housed here. In the grounds are the ruins of St Mary's Abbey, some remains of the Roman wall and multangular tower, and St Leonard's Hospital.

YEOVILTON, Somerset *3 ST52*
The Fleet Air Arm Museum illustrates the development of aviation at sea from 1903, containing over 40 restored planes and numerous engines, models and photographs. A new exhibition hall, Concorde 002, follows the progress of passenger supersonic flight.

YORKSHIRE DALES, N Yorkshire
15 SK88
The greater part of the Yorkshire Dales, which cover a 700-square-mile stretch from the industrial area around Leeds to the River Tees, has been formed into a National Park. Teesdale, famous for its High Force waterfall, is the most northerly of the Dales. Swaledale and Wensleydale – known for its cheese – are linked by Buttertubs Pass. Wharfedale, wild and bare in its upper reaches, becomes exceptionally beautiful between Kilnsey Crag and Bolton Abbey. Nidderdale takes in several reservoirs and How Stean Gorge, whilst the spectacular scenery of Airedale includes 300-foot Malham Cove and Gordale Scar.

YOXFORD, Suffolk *12 TM36*
Yoxford, surrounded by the parklands of Cockfield hall, Rookery Park and Grove Park, is known locally as 'the garden of Suffolk'. Cockfield Hall (not open) was built during the reign of Henry VIII; the central block was rebuilt early in the 17th century and the Great Hall added in the 19th. The main street of the village contains attractively timbered, balconied and bow-windowed houses, whilst St Peter's Church has a large number of brasses. Four miles to the north-east lies the National Nature Reserve of Westleton Heath.

ZEAL MONACHORUM, Devon
2 SS70
The unusual name of this River Yeo village was originally Sele Monacor – 'the place among the sallow (willow) trees belonging to the monks' (of Buckfast). It stands in a lonely spot 400ft above sea level and to the north of the **Dartmoor National Park**. The twisting main street is lined with thatch-and-cob cottages, and the churchyard contains two interesting crosses.

ZENNOR, Cornwall *1 SW43*
The village, named after St Senara, stands below rocky uplands; the sea is less than a mile away and there is fine coastal scenery with bathing from sandy coves. On a bench-end in the 15th-century church is the famous carving of a mermaid reputed to have lured the squire's son into the sea after hearing him sing. The Wayside Cottage Folk Museum illustrates Cornish life and archaeology, displaying household, farming and mining equipment, together with a cottage kitchen and open hearth. A rare Iron Age beehive hut exists south of the village at Bosporthennis, and a Neolithic dolmen known as the Zennor Quoit lies two miles to the south-east.

ROAD ATLAS

The road atlas pages are numbered 1–30 (see the key map opposite).
Placenames printed in red on the key map indicate towns that are either
specially featured in the book (see the list on p. 4) or for which town
plans are given. For an explanation of the National Grid system, see p. 5.

CROMER *The resorts of Norfolk's northern coast have retained something of
the atmosphere of the Victorian era when they became popular for quiet
family holidays.*

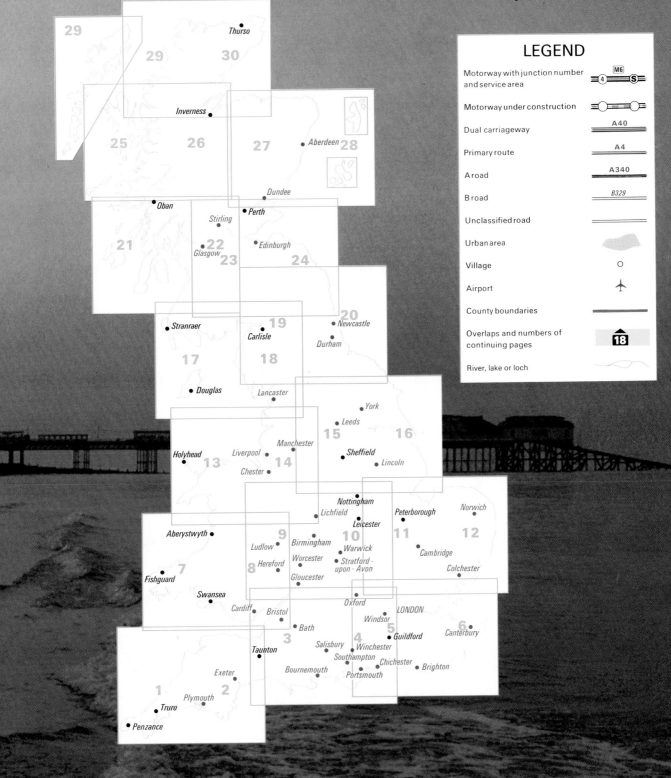

LEGEND

Motorway with junction number and service area	
Motorway under construction	
Dual carriageway	A40
Primary route	A4
A road	A340
B road	B329
Unclassified road	
Urban area	
Village	O
Airport	✈
County boundaries	
Overlaps and numbers of continuing pages	18
River, lake or loch	

29   29   30   Thurso

Inverness

25   26   27   Aberdeen   28

Dundee

Oban   Perth

Stirling

21   22   Edinburgh

Glasgow   23   24

Stranraer   19   Newcastle

Carlisle   Durham

17   18

Douglas   Lancaster

York

Leeds

15   16

Holyhead   Liverpool   Manchester   Sheffield

13   14   Lincoln

Chester

Nottingham

Lichfield   Peterborough   Norwich

Aberystwyth   9   Leicester   11   12

Birmingham   10   Warwick

Ludlow   Cambridge

8   Hereford   Worcester   Stratford-upon-Avon   Colchester

7   Gloucester

Fishguard

Swansea   Oxford   LONDON

Cardiff   Bristol   Windsor   5   Canterbury

3   Bath   4   Guildford   6

Taunton   Salisbury   Winchester

Southampton   Chichester   Brighton

Exeter   Bournemouth   Portsmouth

1   2

Plymouth

Truro

Penzance

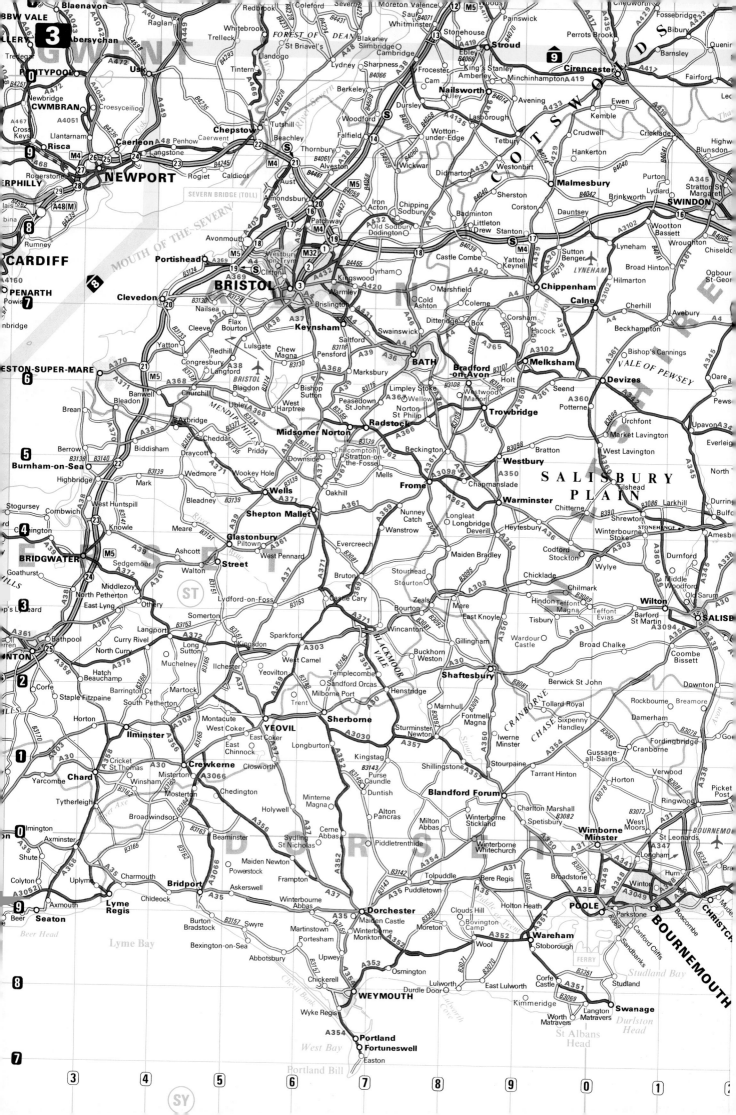

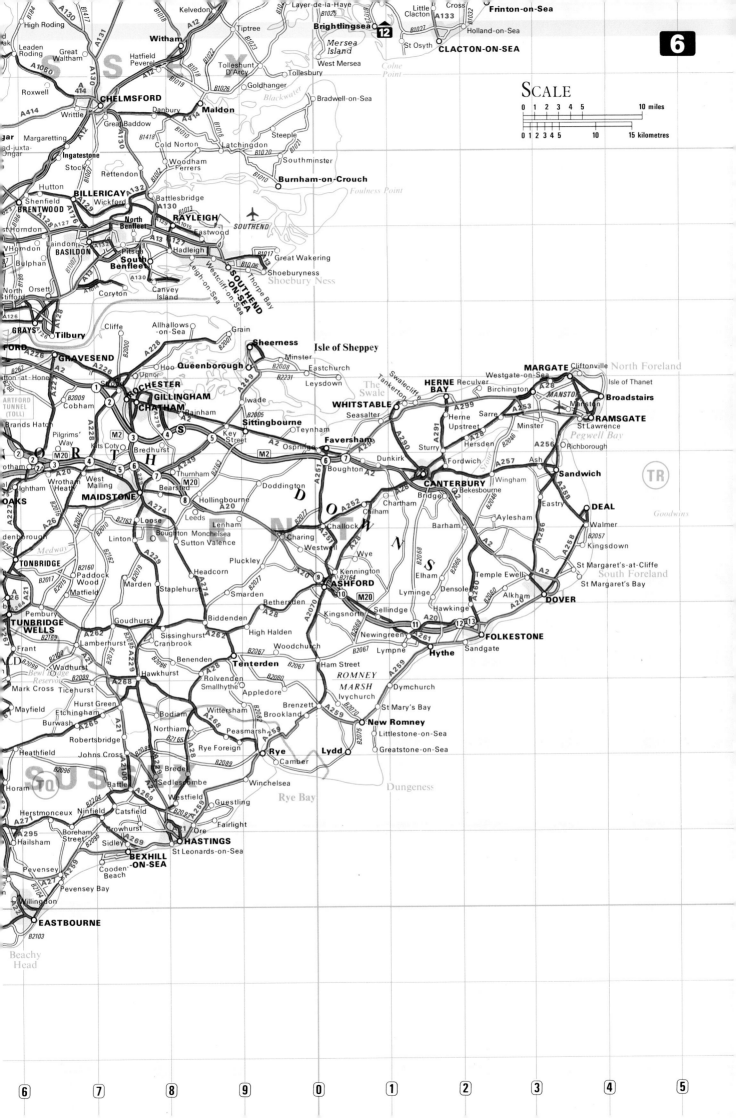

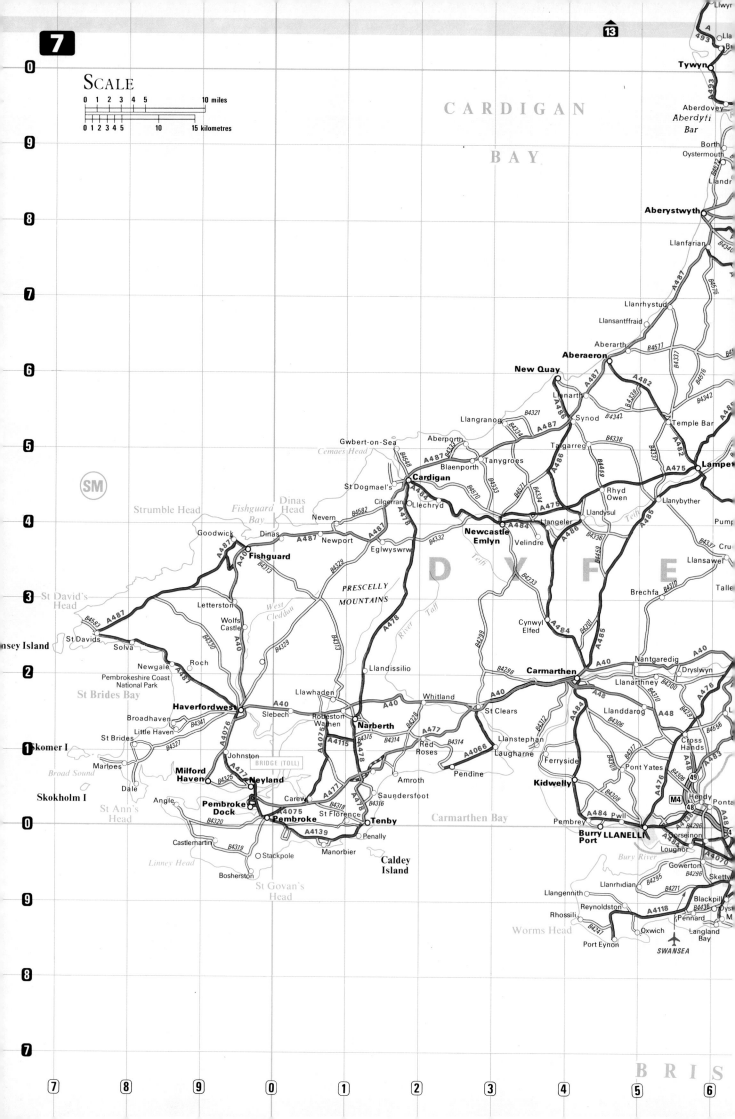

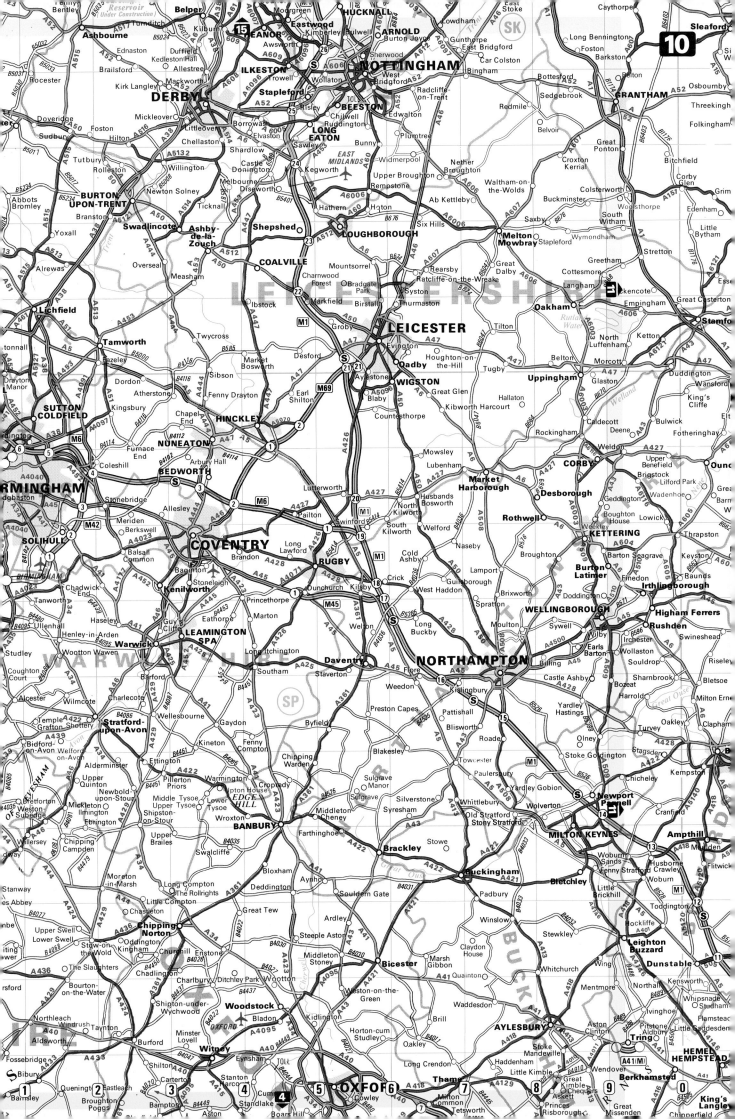

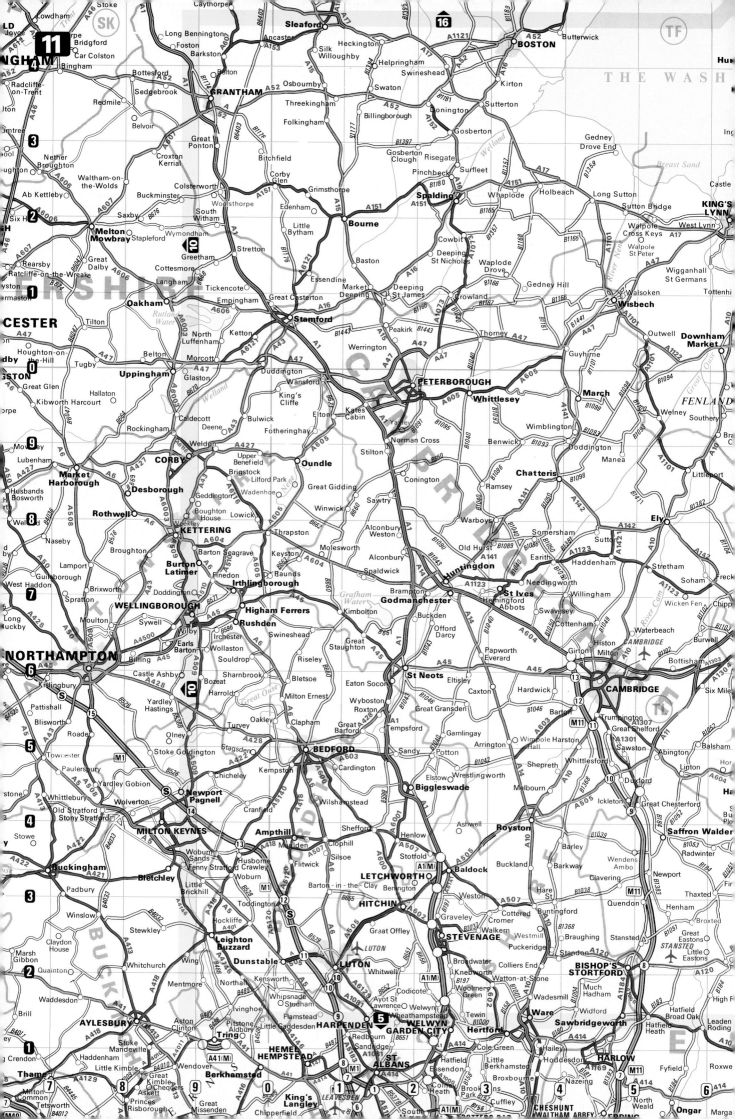

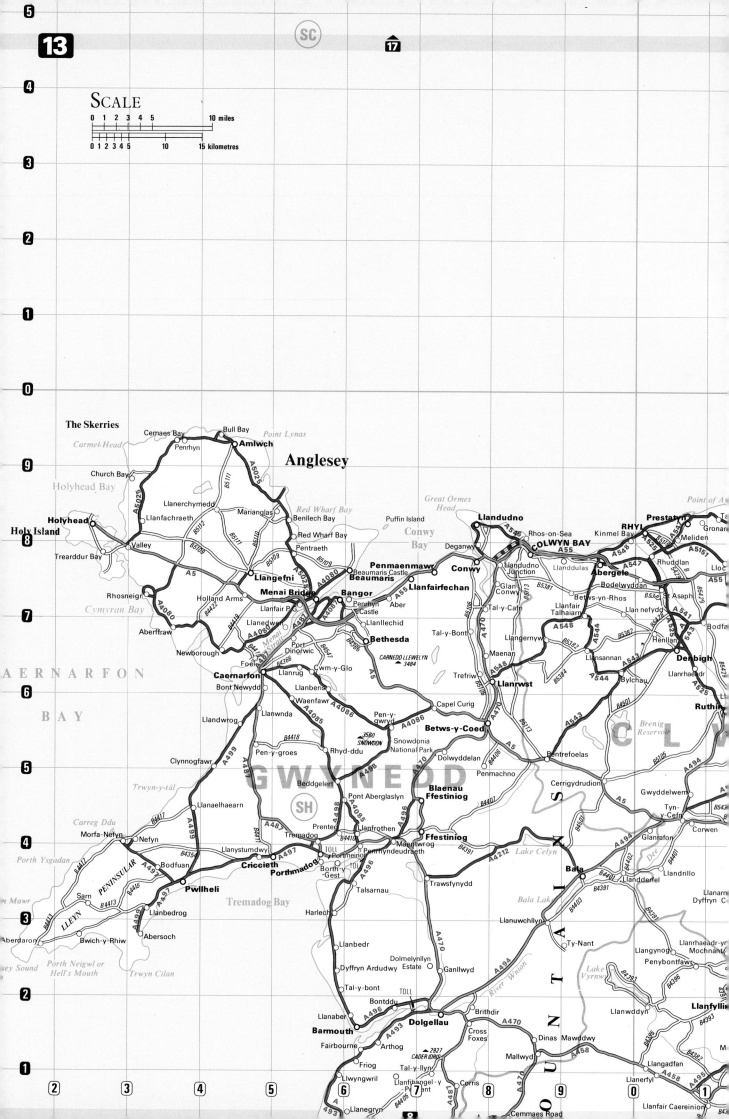

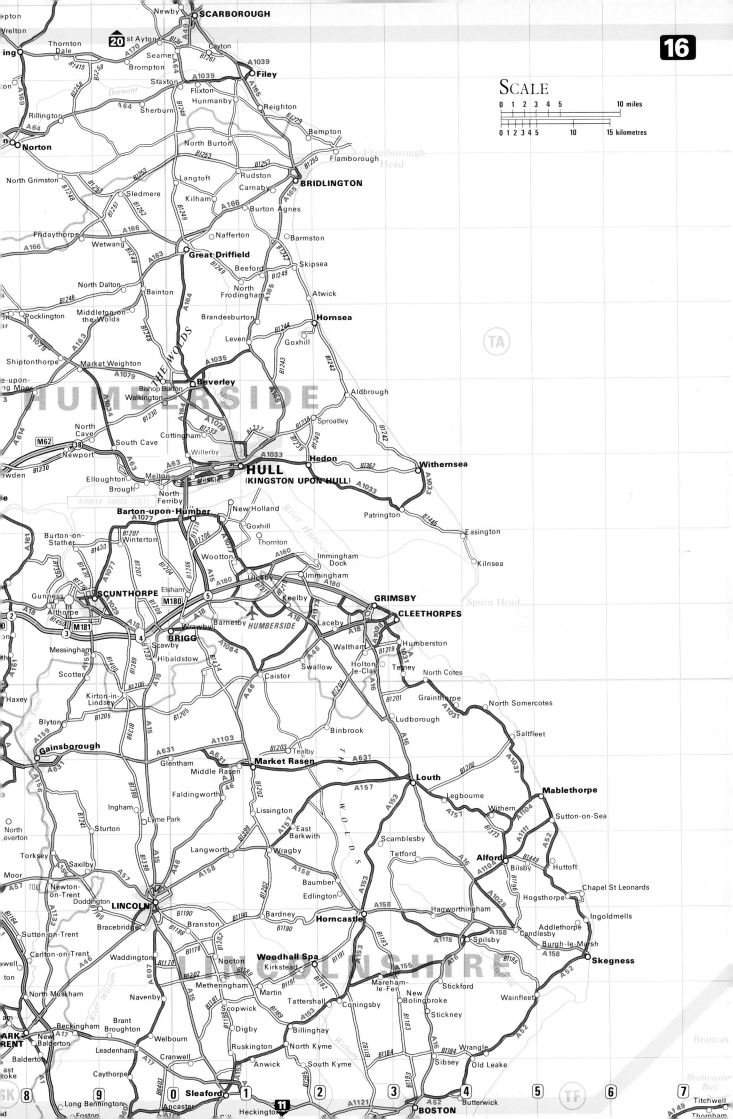

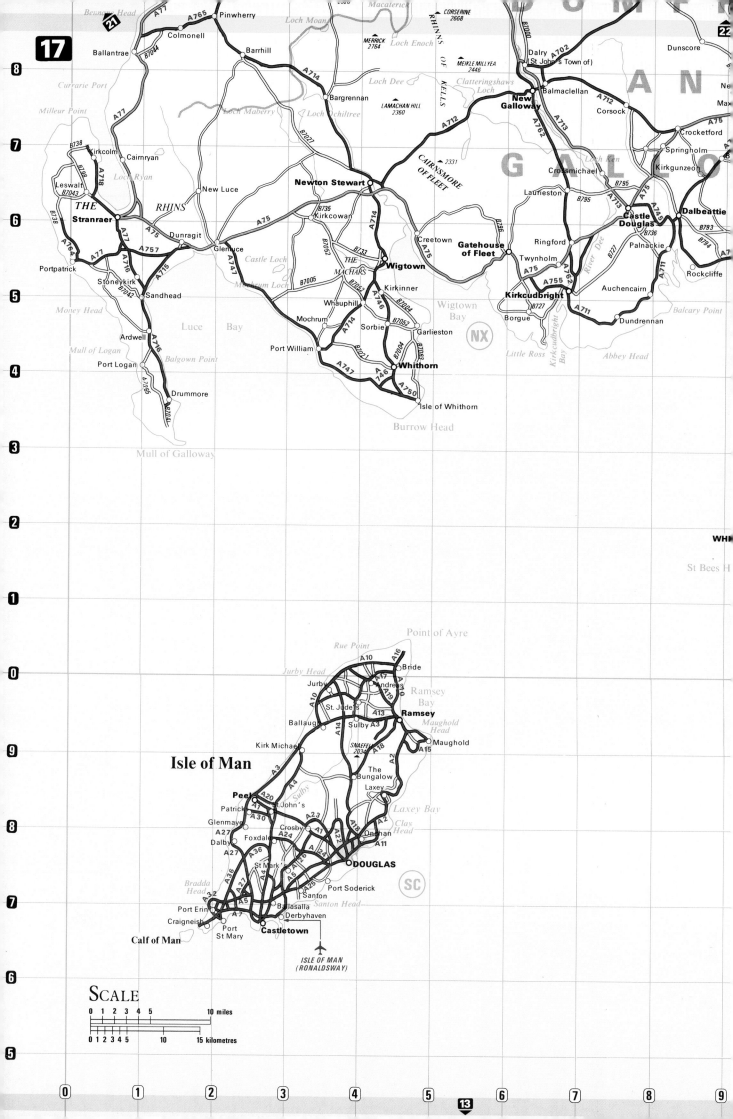

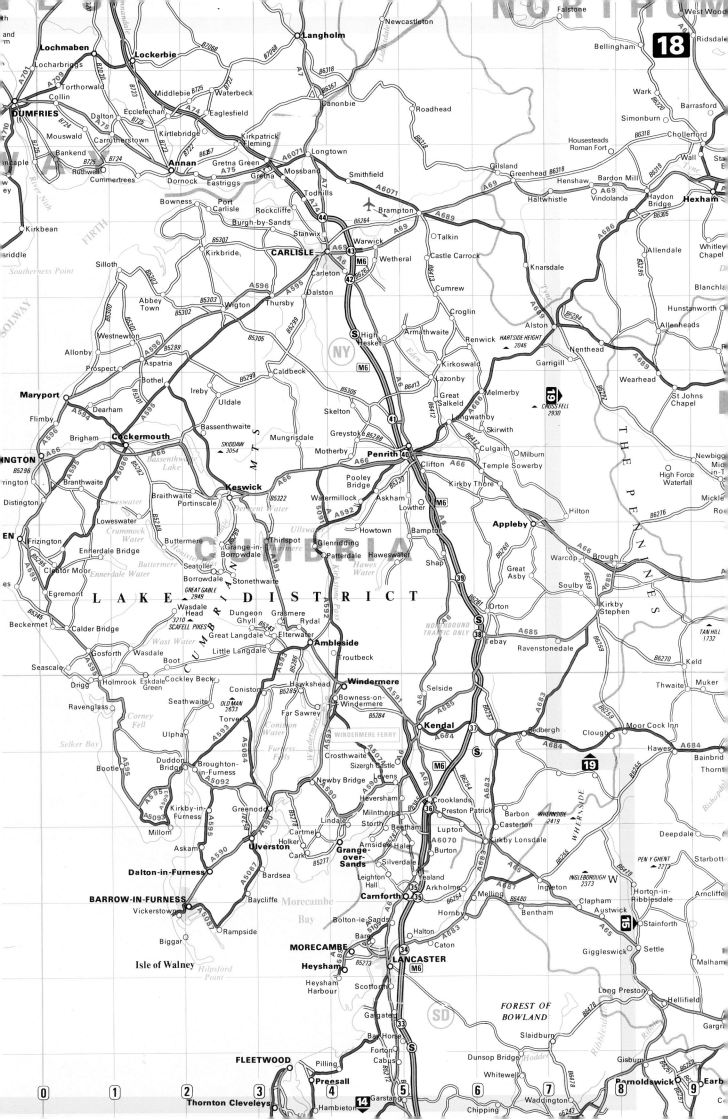

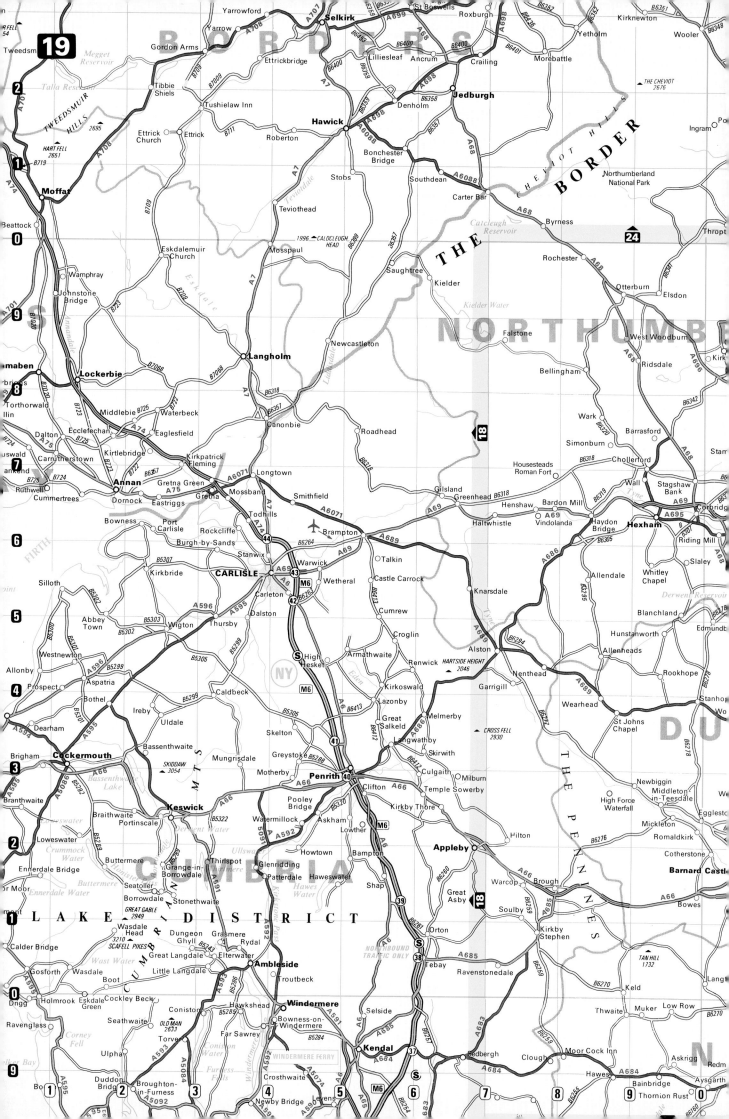

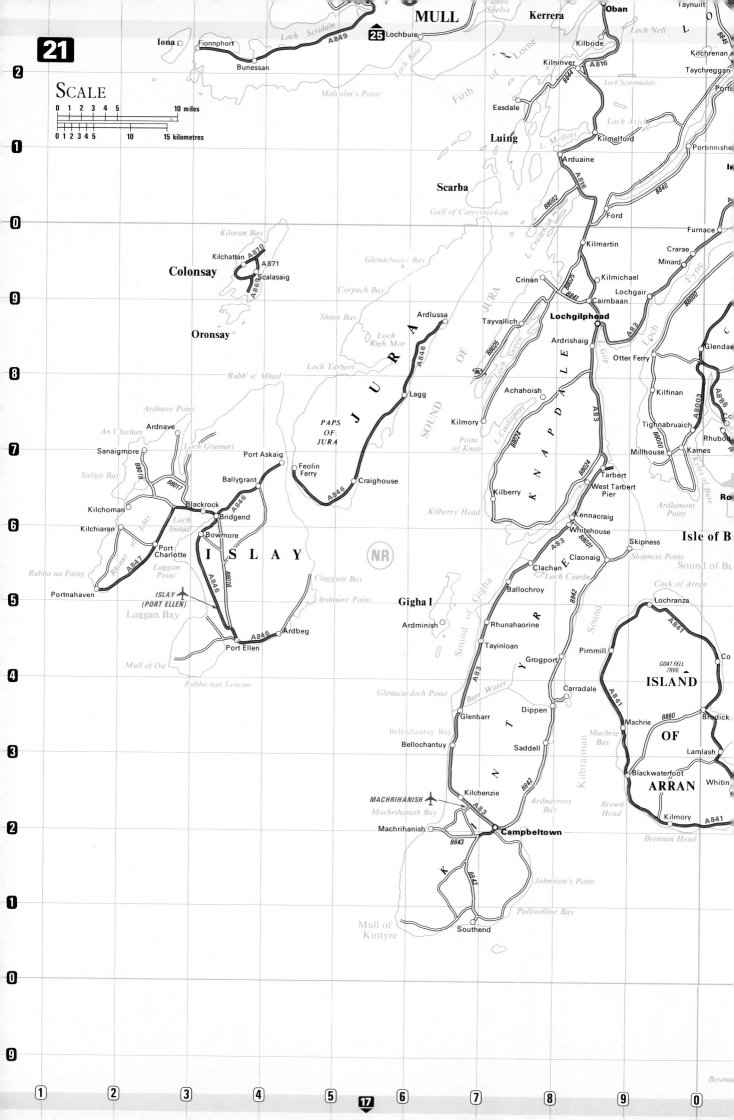

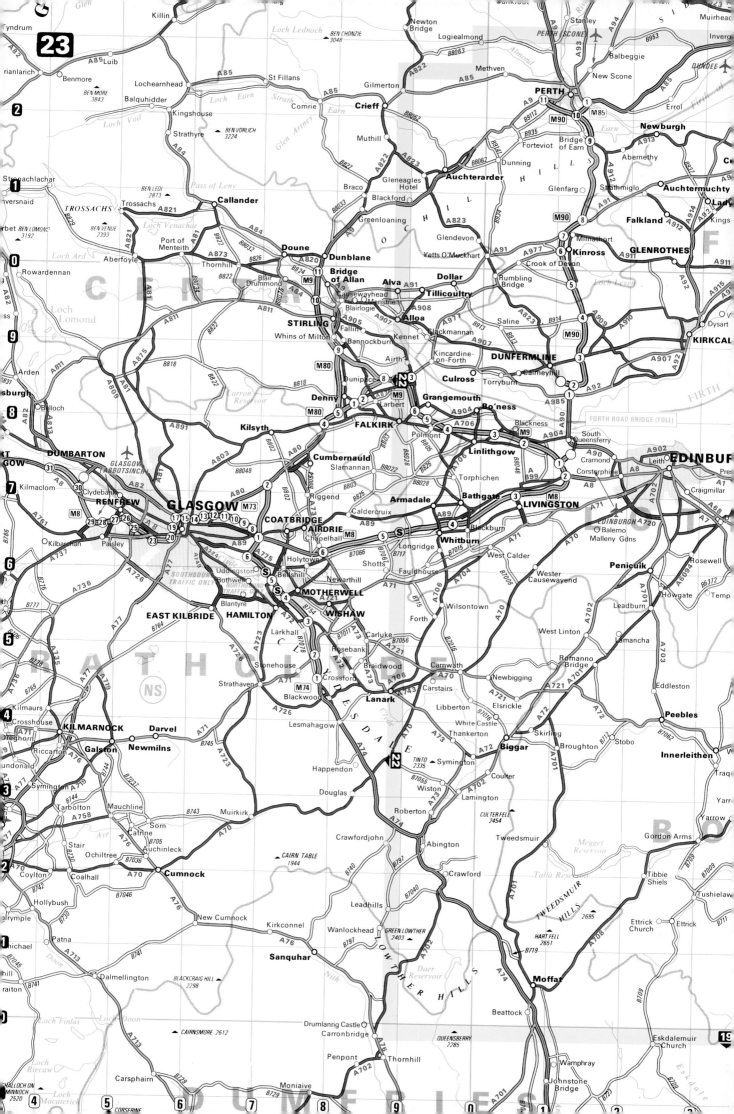

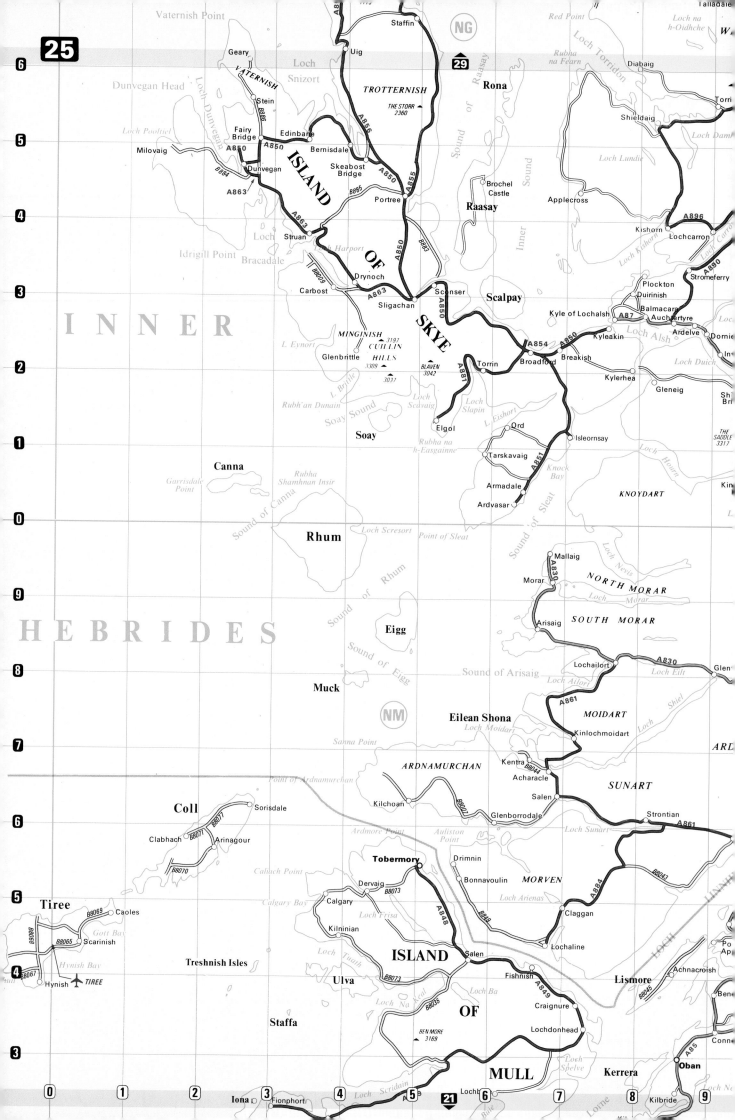

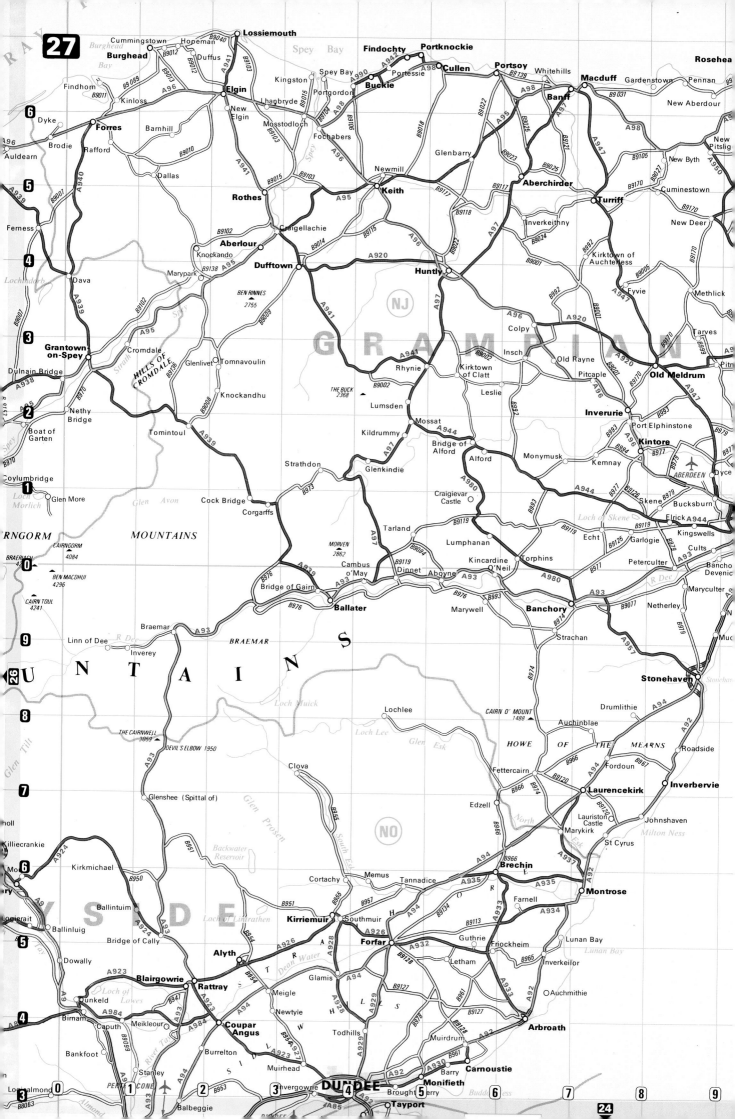

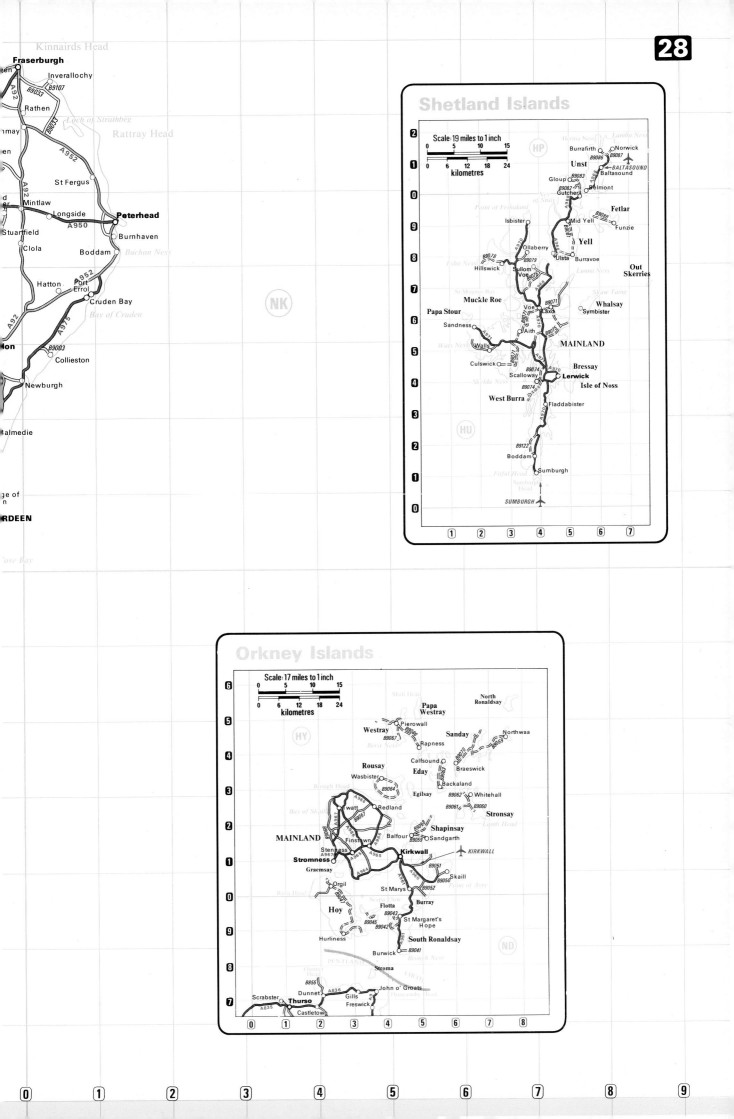

Shetland Islands

Scale: 19 miles to 1 inch

0   5   10   15

0   6   12   18   24
kilometres

Herma Ness   Lamba Ness

HP

Burrafirth   Norwick
B9086   B9087
Unst
B9083   BALTASOUND
Gloup   Baltasound
B9082   Belmont
Gutcherl
Fetlar
B9088
Mid Yell   Funzie
Isbister   **Yell**
Point of Fethaland
Ollaberry   Ulsta   Burravoe
Out
Esha Ness   B9078   Sullom   **Skerries**
B9079   Voe
Hillswick   Lunna Ness
St Magnus Bay
Skaw Taing
Muckle Roe   B9071   **Whalsay**
Papa Stour   Voe   Symbister
Laxo
Sandness   Aith
MAINLAND
Walls   B9074   **Bressay**
Wats Ness   Culswick   Scalloway   **Lerwick**
B9074   **Isle of Noss**
Skelda Ness   **West Burra**
HU   Fladdabister

B9122
Boddam
Sumburgh
Fitful Head
Sumburgh Head
SUMBURGH ✈

① ② ③ ④ ⑤ ⑥ ⑦

Kinnairds Head

Fraserburgh
Inverallochy
B9107
Rathen
A952
Loch of Strathbeg
Rattray Head
may
B9033
St Fergus
A92
Mintlaw
Longside   **Peterhead**
A950   Burnhaven
Stuartfield
Clola   Boddam
Buchan Ness
Hatton   A952
Port
Errol
Cruden Bay
A975   Bay of Cruden
B9003
Collieston
Newburgh

NK

almedie

ge of

RDEEN

ove Bay

Orkney Islands

Scale: 17 miles to 1 inch

0   5   10   15

0   6   12   18   24
kilometres

Mull Head
North
Papa   **Ronaldsay**
Westray
Pierowall
HY   **Westray**   B9066
B9067   **Sanday**   Northwaa
Berst Ness   Rapness   B9069
Calfsound   B9070
Rousay   **Eday**   Braeswick
Wasbister   Backaland
B9064   Egilsay   B9062   Whitehall
Brough Head   B9061   B9060
watt   Redland   **Stronsay**
Bay of Skaill   B9058   Lamb Head
B9057   **Shapinsay**
B9066   Balfour   Sandgarth
MAINLAND   Finstown   B9059
Stenness   **Kirkwall**   ✈ **KIRKWALL**
Stromness   A965
Graemsay   A964   B9051
Orgil   A960   Skaill
St Marys   B9050
Rora Head   B9052
Scapa Flow   Point of Ayre
Flotta   Burray
Hoy   B9043   St Margaret's
B9045   Hope
B9042   **South Ronaldsay**
Hurliness
ND
Burwick   B9041
Brough Ness

PENTLAND
Stroma

Dunnet   FIRTH
Head
B855
Scrabster   Dunnet   A836   John o' Groats
A835   Gills   Freswick
Thurso
Castletown

⓪ ① ② ③ ④ ⑤ ⑥ ⑦ ⑧

⓪ ① ② ③ ④ ⑤ ⑥ ⑦ ⑧ ⑨

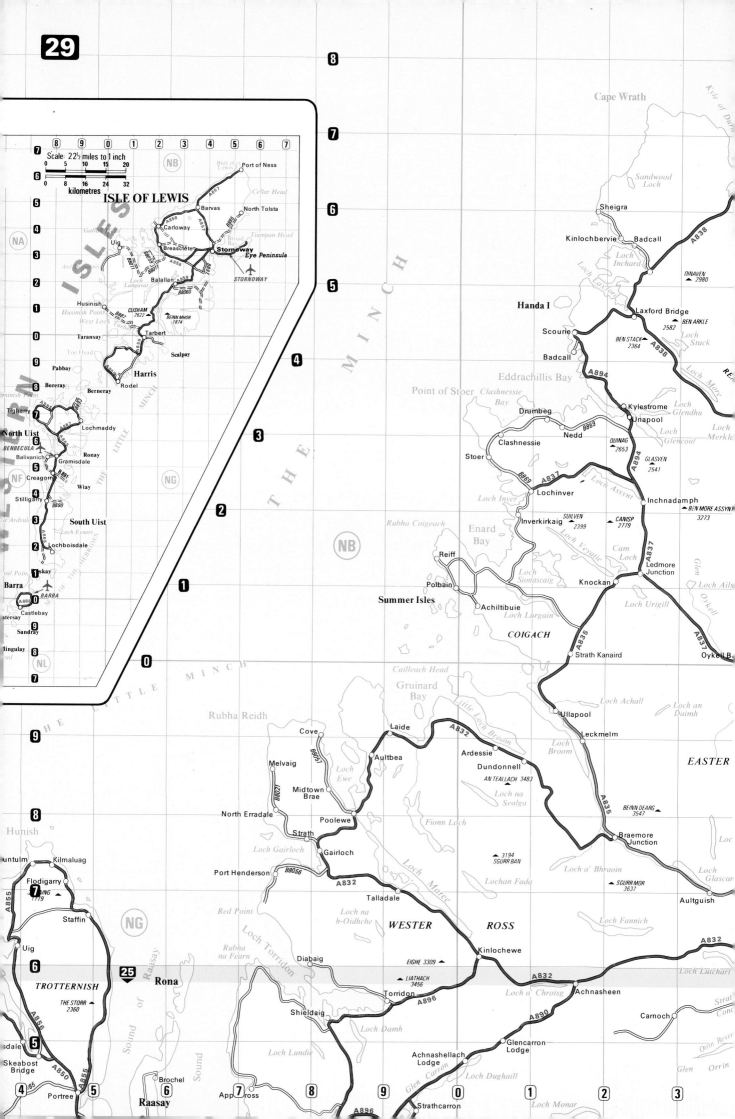

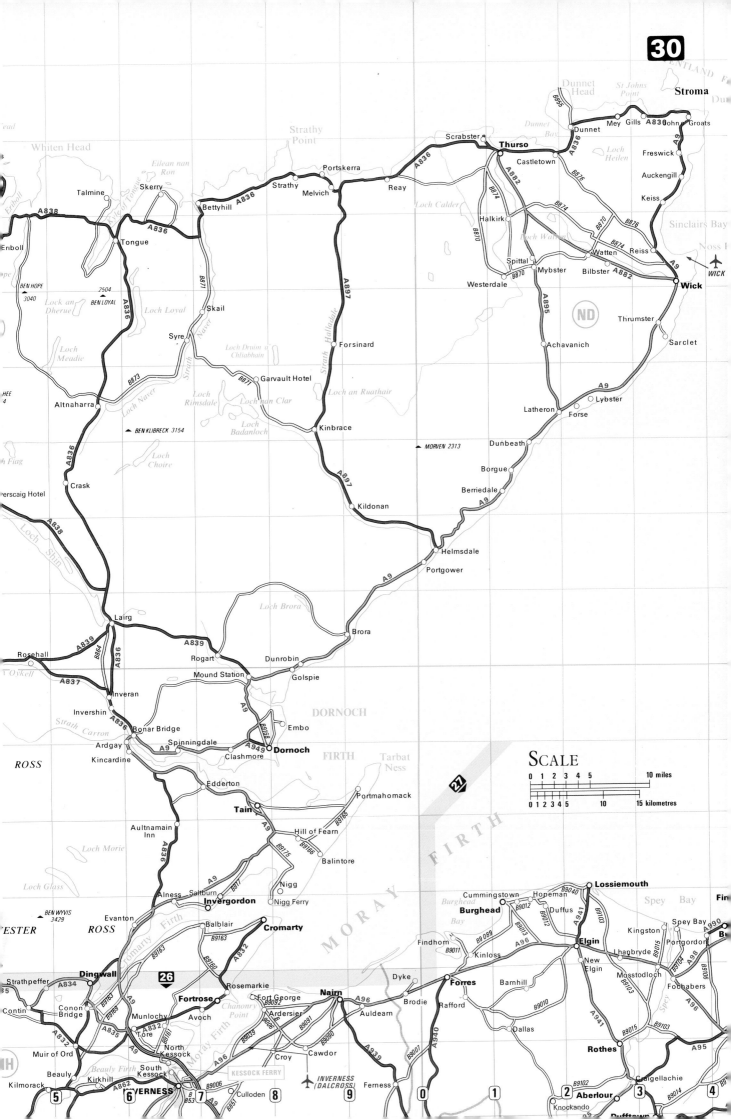

Acknowledgments

Many of the photographs used in *The Touring Book of Britain* are the
copyright of the Automobile Association Picture Library. The
Automobile Association also wishes to thank the following
photographers, organisations and libraries for the use of their material.

MARTYN ADELMAN: Aldworth 11; Rollright Stones, Devil's Arrows, Callan-ish 22–3; Bibury 26; Boston 33; Pentre Ifan 38; Wayland's Smithy 39; Sandham Chapel 42; Cardington 48; Cliveden 63; Crich 70; Dundee 81; Pen y Garreg 89; Finchingfield 94; St Fagan's 98; Templeton factory 102; Glencoe 103; Greensted Church 106; Hatfield House 111; Patrington Church 117; Ardvreck Castle 120; Skye 121; Inverness Museum exhibits 122; Duncansby stacks 127; Knebworth 132; Chysauster 150; Urquhart Castle 152; Lynmouth 158; London – River Thames police launch 163, St James's Park 164, football fans 167, sandwich-board man 168; Pollock's Museum 170; Milton Keynes 181; Harris 200; Tenterden 203; Pen-y-Ghent 204; Rye 220; St Agnes Mine 225; Saffron Walden 226; Stanhope 240; Mangersta 247; Tissington 256; Beinn Eighe 258; Weymouth 272; Widecombe 275; Windsor 278; Wookey Hole 281; Ballone Castle 282–3; Knebworth House 283; Greensted Church, Skye (back cover). AEROFILMS LTD: Avebury 22–3; Buckingham Palace 165; Southam ploughland 248. ASSOCIATED PRESS: St Paul's Cathedral 160. VIC BATES: Isle of Man TT 124. BIOFOTOS: Scottish wild cat 44. P & G BOWATER: Aberdeen 8; Durham – Castle staircase, Cathedral sanctuary ring 82; Preston Mill 87; Falkland 93; Edinburgh – Greyfriars Bobby, Holyrood House 88; J.M. Barrie's House 131; Lancaster Shire Hall 136; Newcastle upon Tyne bridges 187; Stirling Castle 241; York – Minster, Stonegate, Railway Museum 286–7. BRITISH MUSEUM: Mold golden collar 39. BRITISH TOURIST AUTH-ORITY: Cairngorms 44; Scara Brae 197. JULIA BRITTAIN: Exeter Mari-time Museum 91; Hereford 114; Ludlow – Feathers Inn 155. J. ALLAN CASH PHOTOLIBRARY: Packwood House 201. CAVERN MECCA: The Beatles 145. CLARKS LTD: Poster 246. RICK CZAJA: Oughtershaw 113. IAN DAWSON: Cardiff Castle (inset) 50; Chester street scene 57; Monnow Bridge 183; Worcester Cathedral 281. DEPARTMENT OF THE ENVIRON-MENT: (Crown copyright. Reproduced with the permission of the Controller of Her Majesty's Stationery Office) Maiden Castle 73, the Fosse Way 98. ROBERT EAMES: Puffin Island 13; Bala 16; Bardsey 19; Blaenau Ffestiniog 28; Borth-y-Gest 31; Chirk – Castle gates 61; Llanberis quarries 145; Llangollen – Plas Newydd, Horseshoe Falls 148; Menai bridges 179; Styal – cruck cottage 203; Portmeirion 212; Rhuddlan Castle 216; Snowdon and railway 237; Bodnant Gardens 250. MARY EVANS PICTURE LIBRARY: engravings of the following: Botallack 45; Cambridge 47; Cardiff 50; Colches-ter 65; Fish smoking 69; Gold-mining 78; Dundee 81; Durham 82; Edinburgh 88; Gloucester 104; Hereford 114; Lancaster 136; Lincoln 143; Witches 185; Agricultural clearances 189; Turner portrait 207; Salisbury 227; Queen Mary 238; Stirling 241; SS Mauretania 264; Warwick 266; Winchester 277; Windsor 278; York 286. ROBIN FLETCHER: Stonehenge 22–3; Buckler's Hard 41; Cerne Abbas 54; Corfe Castle 67; Isle of Wight – Cowes, the Needles 124; Kimmeridge Nodding Donkey 129; Lulworth Cove 154; Lyme Regis 156; Milton Abbas 180; Minstead inn sign 182; Knowlton 188; New Forest – Stoney Cross, Butterfly farm 190; Portsmouth – HMS Victory 213; Lyndhurst – forest boundary 228; New Forest pigs 229; Worth Matravers – strip lynchets 248; Tolpuddle cottages 257; Warminster 265; Wimborne Minster 276; Worth Matravers quarry 284. FOTOBANK INTERNATIONAL COLOUR LIB-RARY: Scilly Isles 126. V.K. GUY: Crail 68; Grassington 106; Rievaulx 134; Windermere 179. MICHAEL HOLFORD: Visscher Map of London 159. IRONBRIDGE GORGE MUSEUM: Ironbridge Gorge kilns 123. JARROLD & SONS LTD: Kimmeridge Bay 129. BOB JOHNSON: Gairloch 100; Bryndriniog, Cwm Farm 208; Lomer – hedge boundary 248; Winchester – St Cross Hospital 277. GEOFFREY KICHENSIDE: Isle of Wight pier railway 125. BARBARA LITTLEWOOD: Lichfield – Dr Johnson's statue 141. MANSELL COLLECTION: Engravings and photographs of the following: Grace Darling 17; Brighton Pier 36; Early scout camp 40; Bournemouth 32; Chester 57; Chichester 58–9; Jack the Giant-killer 176; Oxford 199; Hand weaving tweed 200; Portsmouth 213; Rugby 220; Tolpuddle Martyrs 257. S & O MATTHEWS: Castle Combe – front cover; Charlwood Church screen 2–3; Cirencester – Corinium Museum mosaic 4–5; Peacock 7; Acton Scott 10–11; Ashby de la Zouche, Arundel – Curiosities Museum 14; Avebury 15; Barlaston – Wedgwood 18; Bath – Royal Crescent 20; Beconscott 21; Bedruthan Steps 24; Blickling Hall 29; SS Gt Britain 36; Bromsgrove – blacksmith 40; Buckfast – Bee-keeper, Burton-on-Trent – Bass Museum 42; Camborne engine-house 45; Canterbury (two) 49; Castle Acre 52; Chatham Docks 54; Chester – clock 57; Cheviots – strip lynchets 58–9; Chichester – altar, St Richard's Walk 58–9; Chiddingstone – oasthouses 60; Chilterns – chairmaking 61; Cirencester – park and mosaic 62; Colchester oysterman 65; Cree estuary 68; Cricket St Thomas 70; Cromer 71; Dartmoor – Hound's Tor 74; Didcot 77; Inn sign 78; Dover Castle 79; Durdle Door 83; Lullingstone

mosaic 84; Eastnor Castle 87; Exeter – Moll's Coffee House 91; Exmouth 92; Fairford 93; Girvan 100; Gloucester Cathedral Cloisters – Beatrix Potter sign 104; Polesden Lacey 106; Guildford 108; Michelham Priory, Happisburgh 109; Farleigh Church, Kilpeck Church, Cheltenham stained glass 116–17; Hunstanton, Ightham 119; Kersey 128; Scotney Castle 133; Fountains Abbey 135; Lanhydrock House 137; Lavenham 138; Lewes 142; Llandudno – Punch & Judy 146; Llanfair Caereinion 147; Long Melford 153; Lulworth (inset) 154; Lydford – ammonite 156; Watersmeet 157; Valley of the Rocks 158; London – Eros, the Monument, Royal Albert Hall, 161; Houses of Parliament 162; the Tower 163, Greenwich, Hampton Court, Victoria Memorial 165, Pearly King, Hampton Court Clock 167, Harrods, Smithfield, Jubilee Market, Portobello Road 168–9; HMS Belfast, Science Museum 170; Courage horses 174; St Michael's Mount 176; Waterfall 182; Much Marcle orchard 184; Pendle Hill 185; Northleach Church 193; Norwich 195; Oxford – Radcliffe Camera 198, Magdalen College, Rooftops 199; Powerstock 202; Lewes 203; Pickering Church 206; Petworth House 207; Gt Coxwell, Wilmington 209; Plymouth – Smeaton Tower, Drake statue 210; Polperro 211; Portsmouth, HMS Victory 213; Restormel Castle 215; Richmond Park 216; Rochester Cathedral 218; Pitstone, Woodbridge 223; Claypits 224; Salisbury – cathedral, Mompesson House 227; Hatfield Forest – hornbeams 229; Sandwich – Bell Hotel, Seven Sisters 230; Sheffield Park – railway, Sheppey 232; Singleton 235; Lower Slaughter 236; Southwold 239; Old Harry Rocks 246; Teignmouth (two) 251; Tintagel 256; Tunbridge Wells (two) 260; Tutbury 261; Fleece Inn 262; Furnace pond 267; Hampton Court, Rufford Old Hall 268–9; Weymouth – George III 272; West Wycombe House 273; Winchester font 277; Bodiam Castle 269; the Wrekin 284; Wymondham 285; Cromer 288–9; Kit's Coty, Nymans Dovecot, Polesden Lacey (back cover). COLIN MOLYNEUX: Belvoir Castle 24; Pen-y-Fan 35; Grantham Church 105; Barton-on-Humber Church 116; Lincoln – Cathedral, old streets 143; Llandudno Bay 146; Ludlow – Broad St 154; Tenby 252. DR RICHARD MUIR: Stoney Littleton 38; Lavenham Church 117; Lower Slaughter 150; West End 188; Wharram Percy 189; Avebury Truscoe cottage 202; Cowdray Park granary 209; Saxtead Mill 223; West Stow 229; Kirby Hall 283; Burgh Castle 269. NATION-AL HORSERACING MUSEUM: Derby winner 190; NATIONAL MOTOR MUSEUM, BEAULIEU: Brand's Hatch 34; Brooklands (two) 264. NATION-AL MUSEUM OF WALES: Llanmelian (Alan Sorrell) 72; Llantwit Major (Alan Sorrell) 85. NATIONAL PORTRAIT GALLERY: Lloyd George portrait 149. NORTHAMPTON BOROUGH COUNCIL: Ballet shoes 192. RICHARD NEWTON: Alton Towers 12; Blue John 53; Chatsworth House 55; Empingham Church 90; Hodnet Hall 115; Ingestre Church 121; Iron Bridge 123; The Roaches 139; Oakham Castle 196; Rugby School 220; Stoke-on-Trent – slipware, Stokesay Castle 242; Thoresby Hall 254; Trenton House 259; Wightwick Manor 275; Wing maze 279. ROCHESTER UPON MEDWAY CITY COUNCIL; Fagin, Charles Dickens 218; ROLLS-ROYCE LTD: Rolls-Royce car 76. DOC ROWE: Haxey Hood Game 113; Padstow Hobby Horse 201. ROYAL COMMISSION ON HISTORICAL MONUMENTS: Old Sarum 196. SAFFRON WALDEN TOWN COUNCIL: Coat of Arms 226. SCOTTISH & ALLIED BREWERIES: Beer bottles 187. SPECTRUM: Ben Nevis 25. SPENCER SMITH: Stourhead 242. L.P. SPORTS: Castle Howard 53; Coniston 64; Dumbarton 80; Dunnet Fort 84; Fylingdales 97; Bolton Abbey 134; Liverpool Docks 145; Scarborough 231. RICHARD SURMAN: Birmingham – Gas Street Basin 27; Cambridge – market, college backs 47; Colchester – St Botolph's 65; Gt Malvern – British Camp 72; Harrogate Pump Room 111; Hadrian's Wall 118; King's Lynn Custom House 130; Leeds – Ivanhoe Clock 139; Lichfield Cathedral 141; Lindisfarne 144; Cutty Sark 163; National Maritime Museum 170; Gt Malvern 175; Stratford upon Avon – Harvard House, Shakespeare statue 245. TOPHAM: Glasgow street scene 102; River Thames scene 162. UKAEA: Dounreay 214. UNIVERSITY OF CAMBRIDGE COMMITTEE FOR AERIAL PHOTOGRAPHY: Llanmelian, 72; Middleton 151; Cold Newton 247–8. UNIVERSITY OF READING: Institute of Agricultural History and Museum of English Rural Life: Cotswold sheep 67, Charcoal burners, 223. VICTORIA AND ALBERT MUSEUM: endpapers. WALES TOURIST BOARD: Carew Castle 51. DEREK WID-DECOMBE: Hambleton Hills 255. ANDY WILLIAMS: Ross-on-Wye (title page); Warwick cottages 266. HARRY WILLIAMS: Selworthy 232; Logan Rock inn sign 259. WOODMANSTERNE: London – Westminster Abbey 160, Changing the Guard, Trooping the Colour, Lord Mayor's Coach 166. WORTH-ING BOROUGH COUNCIL: Bramber Castle (Alan Sorrell) 268. JON WYAND: Bournemouth – bandstand 32; Grimspound 74; Devizes locks 76; Romsey Abbey psalter 134; Abbots Morton – cottage 203; Virginia Water – totem pole 262; Westbury White Horse 271; Wherwell 274; Wookey Hole – Tussaud waxworks 281.